THE NEW CAMBRIDGE SHAKESPEARE

GENERAL EDITOR
Brian Gibbons

ASSOCIATE GENERAL EDITOR
A. R. Braunmuller, *University of California, Los Angeles*

From the publication of the first volumes in 1984 the General Editor of the New Cambridge Shakespeare was Philip Brockbank and the Associate General Editors were Brian Gibbons and Robin Hood. From 1990 to 1994 the General Editor was Brian Gibbons and the Associate General Editors were A. R. Braunmuller and Robin Hood.

CORIOLANUS

This generously annotated updated edition of *Coriolanus* provides a thorough reconsideration of Shakespeare's remarkable, and probably his last, tragedy. A substantial introduction situates the play within its contemporary social and political contexts – dearth, riots, the struggle over authority between James I and his first parliament, the travails of Essex and Ralegh – and pays particular attention to Shakespeare's shaping of his primary source in Plutarch's *Lives*. It presents a fresh account of how the protagonist's personal tragedy evolves within Shakespeare's most searching exploration of the political life of a community. The edition is alert throughout to the play's theatrical potential, while the stage history also attends to the politics of performance from the 1680s onwards, including European productions following the Second World War. A new introductory section by Bridget Escolme covers recent productions of *Coriolanus*, and criticism of the last ten years, with particular focus on identity, gender and the politics of the play.

D1550540

THE NEW CAMBRIDGE SHAKESPEARE

All's Well That Ends Well, edited by Russell Fraser
Antony and Cleopatra, edited by David Bevington
As You Like It, edited by Michael Hattaway
The Comedy of Errors, edited by T. S. Dorsch
Coriolanus, edited by Lee Bliss
Cymbeline, edited by Martin Butler
Hamlet, edited by Philip Edwards
Julius Caesar, edited by Marvin Spevack
King Edward III, edited by Giorgio Melchiori
The First Part of King Henry IV, edited by Herbert Weil and Judith Weil
The Second Part of King Henry IV, edited by Giorgio Melchiori
King Henry V, edited by Andrew Gurr
The First Part of King Henry VI, edited by Michael Hattaway
The Second Part of King Henry VI, edited by Michael Hattaway
The Third Part of King Henry VI, edited by Michael Hattaway
King Henry VIII, edited by John Margeson
King John, edited by L. A. Beaurline
The Tragedy of King Lear, edited by Jay L. Halio
King Richard II, edited by Andrew Gurr
King Richard III, edited by Janis Lull
Love's Labour's Lost, edited by William C. Carroll
Macbeth, edited by A. R. Braunmuller
Measure for Measure, edited by Brian Gibbons
The Merchant of Venice, edited by M. M. Mahood
The Merry Wives of Windsor, edited by David Crane
A Midsummer Night's Dream, edited by R. A. Foakes
Much Ado About Nothing, edited by F. H. Mares
Othello, edited by Norman Sanders
Pericles, edited by Doreen DelVecchio and Antony Hammond
The Poems, edited by John Roe
Romeo and Juliet, edited by G. Blakemore Evans
The Sonnets, edited by G. Blakemore Evans
The Taming of the Shrew, edited by Ann Thompson
The Tempest, edited by David Lindley
Timon of Athens, edited by Karl Klein
Titus Andronicus, edited by Alan Hughes
Troilus and Cressida, edited by Anthony B. Dawson
Twelfth Night, edited by Elizabeth Story Donno
The Two Gentlemen of Verona, edited by Kurt Schlueter
The Two Noble Kinsmen, edited by Robert Kean Turner and Patricia Tatspaugh
The Winter's Tale, edited by Susan Snyder and Deborah T. Curren-Aquino

THE EARLY QUARTOS
The First Quarto of Hamlet, edited by Kathleen O. Irace
The First Quarto of King Henry V, edited by Andrew Gurr
The First Quarto of King Lear, edited by Jay L. Halio
The First Quarto of King Richard III, edited by Peter Davison
The First Quarto of Othello, edited by Scott McMillin
The First Quarto of Romeo and Juliet, edited by Lukas Erne
The Taming of a Shrew: The 1594 Quarto, edited by Stephen Roy Miller

CORIOLANUS

Updated edition

Edited by
LEE BLISS

CAMBRIDGE
UNIVERSITY PRESS

CAMBRIDGE
UNIVERSITY PRESS

University Printing House, Cambridge CB2 8BS, United Kingdom

Cambridge University Press is part of the University of Cambridge.

It furthers the University's mission by disseminating knowledge in the pursuit of education, learning and research at the highest international levels of excellence.

www.cambridge.org
Information on this title: www.cambridge.org/9780521728744

© Cambridge University Press 2000, 2010

First published 2000
Updated edition 2010
11th printing 2017

Printed in the United Kingdom by Clays, St Ives plc

A catalogue record for this publication is available from the British Library

Library of Congress Cataloguing in Publication data
Shakespeare, William, 1564–1616.
Coriolanus / edited by Lee Bliss ; [new introduction by Bridget Escolme]. – Updated ed.
    p.   cm. – (The new Cambridge Shakespeare)
Includes bibliographical references.
ISBN 978-0-521-42960-3 (hardback)
1. Coriolanus, Cnaeus Marcius – Drama.   2. Generals – Drama.   3. Rome – Drama.   4. Shakespeare, William, 1564–1616. Coriolanus.   I. Bliss, Lee, 1943–   II. Title.
PR2805.A2B58   2010
822.3'3 – dc22   2009046281

ISBN 978-0-521-42960-3 Hardback
ISBN 978-0-521-72874-4 Paperback

CONTENTS

ILLUSTRATIONS

Illustration 1 is reproduced by courtesy of the Guildhall Library, Corporation of London; illustration 2 is from the Samuel H. Kress collection, © 1997 Board of Trustees, National Gallery of Art, Washington, DC; illustration 6 is reproduced by courtesy of the Guildhall Gallery, Corporation of London; illustrations 3, 4, 5, 7 and 8 are reproduced by permission of the Folger Shakespeare Library, Washington, D.C.; illustration 10 by courtesy of the estate of Angus McBean; illustrations 9, 11 and 12 by courtesy of the Shakespeare Centre Library, Stratford-upon-Avon; illustration 13 by courtesy of Shakespeare's Globe. Photograph by John Haynes; illustration 14 copyright Shakespeare Birthplace Trust.

ACKNOWLEDGEMENTS

Editors of Shakespeare owe debts stretching back to those hard-working souls who produced the First Folio, despite the fact that we also revile them for the problems they bequeathed us. At the other end of the time-line, recent editors have offered a fresh scholarly look at the text, which forced me to wrestle with my own choices, and have contributed substantially to the Commentary in this edition: Philip Brockbank (Arden Shakespeare, 1976), the editors of the Oxford *Complete Works* (1986) and *Textual Companion* (1987), and Brian Parker (Oxford Shakespeare, 1994). An editor also owes a great debt to those associated with her publisher. A. R. Braunmuller, Associate General Editor, painstakingly read drafts of this edition and offered invaluable advice on matters of style as well as content. At Cambridge University Press Sarah Stanton was unfailingly supportive (and patient), and Paul Chipchase and Judith Harte were meticulous in catching lapses in consistency and accuracy of transcription.

F. J. Levy kindly read and commented on the historical sections of the Introduction. I am also grateful to the editors of the forthcoming New Variorum *Coriolanus*. Thomas Clayton read an earlier, longer version of the Textual Analysis, although that should not imply his endorsement of all its conclusions; David George generously shared his typescript of the Variorum's stage history and offered a few corrections to the collation. *Studies in Bibliography* has kindly granted permission to present in the Textual Analysis a condensed version of arguments that appeared in 'Scribes, compositors, and annotators: the nature of the copy for the First Folio text of *Coriolanus*', *SB* 50 (1997), 224–61. More general thanks for informative conversation and reference suggestions are extended to Bertrand Goldgar, Charlotte Morse, Linda Levy Peck and G. R. Proudfoot. In financial matters, the Committee on Research of the Academic Senate at the University of California, Santa Barbara, has supported work on this project over a number of years. A National Endowment for the Humanities–Folger Shakespeare Library fellowship in 1992–3 was crucial in allowing me to complete the collation, and the Folger's wealth of early printed books, theatrical promptbooks and art collections has enriched the Commentary and provided several of the illustrations. Barbara Mowat and the Folger staff proved most generous and helpful. I would also like to thank the librarians and staff at the British Library, the Guildhall Library and Gallery, the London Theatre Museum, the Victoria and Albert Museum, the Royal National Theatre, the National Youth Theatre, the Shakespeare Centre at Stratford-upon-Avon and the Birmingham Public Library's Shakespeare Library. Although the failings of this edition are my own, many good and knowledgeable people tried to make it better.

Santa Barbara, California   L.B.

ABBREVIATIONS AND CONVENTIONS

1. Shakespeare's plays

Shakespeare's plays, when cited in this edition, are abbreviated in a style modified slightly from that used in the *Harvard Concordance to Shakespeare*. Other editions of Shakespeare are abbreviated under the editor's surname (Rowe, Bevington) unless they are the work of more than one editor. In such cases, an abbreviated series title is used (Cam., Oxford). When more than one edition by the same editor is cited, later editions are discriminated with a raised figure (Collier²). All quotations from Shakespeare, except those from *Coriolanus*, use the text and lineation of *The Riverside Shakespeare*, under the general editorship of G. Blakemore Evans.

Ado	*Much Ado about Nothing*
Ant.	*Antony and Cleopatra*
AWW	*All's Well That Ends Well*
AYLI	*As You Like It*
Cor.	*Coriolanus*
Cym.	*Cymbeline*
Err.	*The Comedy of Errors*
Ham.	*Hamlet*
1H4	*The First Part of King Henry the Fourth*
2H4	*The Second Part of King Henry the Fourth*
H5	*King Henry the Fifth*
1H6	*The First Part of King Henry the Sixth*
2H6	*The Second Part of King Henry the Sixth*
3H6	*The Third Part of King Henry the Sixth*
H8	*King Henry the Eighth*
JC	*Julius Caesar*
John	*King John*
LLL	*Love's Labour's Lost*
Lear	*King Lear*
Mac.	*Macbeth*
MM	*Measure for Measure*
MND	*A Midsummer Night's Dream*
MV	*The Merchant of Venice*
Oth.	*Othello*
Per.	*Pericles*
R2	*King Richard the Second*
R3	*King Richard the Third*
Rom.	*Romeo and Juliet*
Shr.	*The Taming of the Shrew*
STM	*Sir Thomas More*
Temp.	*The Tempest*
TGV	*Two Gentlemen of Verona*
Tim.	*Timon of Athens*

Tit.	*Titus Andronicus*
TN	*Twelfth Night*
TNK	*The Two Noble Kinsmen*
Tro.	*Troilus and Cressida*
Wiv.	*The Merry Wives of Windsor*
WT	*The Winter's Tale*

2. Editions, adaptations, other works of reference and periodicals

Works mentioned once in the Commentary appear there with full bibliographical information; all others are cited by the shortened titles below.

Abbott	E. A. Abbott, *A Shakespearian Grammar*, 1869 (references are to numbered sections)
AEB	*Analytical and Enumerative Bibliography*
Averell	William Averell, *A Mervailous Combat of Contrarieties*, 1588
Badham, *Crit.*	Charles Badham, *Criticism applied to Shakspere*, 1846
Badham, 'Text'	Charles Badham, 'The text of Shakspere', *Cambridge Essays*, 1856, pp. 261–91
Becket	Andrew Becket, *Shakspeare's Himself Again*, 2 vols., 1815, II
Bevington	*The Complete Works of Shakespeare*, ed. David Bevington, 3rd edn, 1980
Bevington²	William Shakespeare, *Three Classical Tragedies*, ed. David Bevington, 1988 (Bantam Shakespeare)
Boswell	*The Plays and Poems of William Shakspeare*, ed. James Boswell, 21 vols., 1821, XIV
Brockbank	*Coriolanus*, ed. Philip Brockbank, 1976 (revised Arden Shakespeare)
Brooke	*Coriolanus*, ed. C. F. Tucker Brooke, 1924 (Yale Shakespeare)
Brower	*Coriolanus*, ed. Reuben Brower, 1966 (Signet Classic Shakespeare)
Bullough, *Sources*	*Narrative and Dramatic Sources of Shakespeare*, ed. Geoffrey Bullough, 8 vols., 1957–75, V and VI
Cam.	*The Works of Shakespeare*, ed. W. G. Clark and W. A. Wright, 9 vols., 1863–6 (Cambridge Shakespeare), VI (1865)
Cam.²	*The Works of Shakespeare*, rev. W. A. Wright, 9 vols., 1891–3, VI
Camden	William Camden, *Remaines of a Greater Worke, Concerning Britaine*, 1605
Capell	*The Works of Shakespeare*, ed. Edward Capell, 10 vols., 1767–8, VII
Capell, *Notes*	Edward Capell, *Notes and Various Readings to Shakespeare*, 3 vols., 1779–80, I
Case	*Coriolanus*, ed. R. H. Case and W. J. Craig, 1922 (Arden Shakespeare)
Chambers	*Coriolanus*, ed. E. K. Chambers, 1898 (Warwick Shakespeare)
Clarendon	*Coriolanus*, ed. William Aldis Wright, 1878 (Clarendon Press Series)
Coleridge	*The Literary Remains of Samuel Taylor Coleridge*, ed. Henry Nelson Coleridge, 4 vols., 1836–9, II
Collier	*The Works of William Shakespeare*, ed. J. P. Collier, 8 vols., 1842–4, VI
Collier²	*The Plays of William Shakespeare*, ed. J. P. Collier, 1853

Collier³	*Shakespeare's Comedies, Histories, Tragedies, and Poems*, ed. J. P. Collier, 6 vols., 1858, IV
conj.	conjecture, conjectured by
Cornwall	*The Works of Shakspeare*, ed. Barry Cornwall, 3 vols., 1843, II
Cotgrave	Randle Cotgrave, *A Dictionarie of the French and English Tongues*, 1611
Craig	*The Complete Works of William Shakespeare*, ed. W. J. Craig, 1891 (Oxford Shakespeare)
Daniel	Peter A. Daniel, *Notes and Conjectural Emendations of certain Doubtful Passages in Shakespeare's Plays*, 1870
Deighton	*Coriolanus*, ed. Kenneth Deighton, 1891
Delius	*The Complete Works of William Shakespeare*, ed. Nicolaus Delius, 1854
Dent	Robert Dent, *Shakespeare's Proverbial Language: An Index*, 1981
Dyce	*The Works of William Shakespeare*, ed. Alexander Dyce, 6 vols., 1857, IV
Dyce²	*The Works of William Shakespeare*, ed. Alexander Dyce, 9 vols., 1864–7, VI
Edwards	Thomas Edwards, *A Supplement to Mr. Warburton's Edition of Shakespear. Being the Canons of Criticism and Glossary*, 1748
ELH	*English Literary History*
ELN	*English Language Notes*
ELR	*English Literary Renaissance*
F	*Mr. William Shakespeares Comedies, Histories, & Tragedies*, 1623 (First Folio)
F2	*Mr. William Shakespeares Comedies, Histories, and Tragedies*, 1632 (Second Folio)
F3	*Mr. William Shakespear's Comedies, Histories, and Tragedies*, 1663 (Third Folio)
F4	*Mr. William Shakespear's Comedies, Histories, Tragedies*, 1685 (Fourth Folio)
Fletcher	John Fletcher, *The Captain*, ed. L. A. Beaurline, in *The Dramatic Works in the Beaumont and Fletcher Canon*, gen. ed. Fredson Bowers, 10 vols., 1966–96, I
Furness	*Coriolanus*, ed. A. H. Furness Jr, 1928 (New Variorum)
Globe	*The Works of William Shakespeare*, ed. W. G. Clark and W. A. Wright, 1864 (Globe Edition)
Gomme	*Coriolanus*, ed. H. H. Gomme, 1968 (Shakespeare Workshop)
Gordon	*Coriolanus*, ed. George S. Gordon, 1912
Hanmer	*The Works of Mr William Shakespear*, ed. Thomas Hanmer, 6 vols., 1743–4, V
Heath	Benjamin Heath, *A Revisal of Shakespear's Text*, 1765
Hibbard	*Coriolanus*, ed. G. R. Hibbard, 1967 (New Penguin Shakespeare)
Hudson	*The Works of Shakespeare*, ed. H. N. Hudson, 11 vols., 1851–9, VIII
Hudson²	*The Complete Works of William Shakespeare*, ed. H. N. Hudson, 20 vols., 1880–1, XVIII (Harvard Edition)
Jervis	Swynfen Jervis, *Proposed Emendations of the Text of Shakespeare's Plays*, 1860
Johnson	*The Plays of Shakespeare*, ed. Samuel Johnson, 8 vols., 1765, VI

Keightley   *The Plays of William Shakespeare*, ed. Thomas Keightley, 6 vols.,
                     1864, VI
Keightley, *SE*   Thomas Keightley, *The Shakespeare-Expositor*, 1867
Kellner   Leon Kellner, *Restoring Shakespeare*, 1925
King   A. H. King, 'Notes on *Coriolanus*', *English Studies* 19–20 (1937–8),
                     13–20, 18–25
Kittredge   *The Complete Works of Shakespeare*, ed. George Lyman Kittredge,
                     1936
Knight   *The Pictorial Edition of the Works of Shakspere*, ed. Charles Knight,
                     8 vols., 1838–43, VI
Leo   *Coriolanus*, ed. F. A. Leo, 1864
Lettsom, *NQ*   William Nanson Lettsom, 'Note on *Coriolanus*', *N & Q* 7, 16 April
                     1853, 378–9
Lettsom, *BM*   William Nanson Lettsom, 'New readings in Shakespeare – no. 2',
                     Blackwood's Edinburgh Magazine, 74 (Sept., Oct., 1853), 302–25,
                     451–75
Livy   Titus Livius, *The Romane Historie*, trans. Philemon Holland, 1600
Malone   *The Plays and Poems of William Shakspeare*, ed. Edmond Malone,
                     10 vols., 1790, VII
Malone, *Supp.*   Edmond Malone, *Supplement to the Edition of Shakspeare's Plays
                     Published in 1778*, 2 vols., 1780, I
Mason   John Monck Mason, *Comments on the Last Edition of Shakespeare's
                     Plays*, 1785
MLR   *Modern Language Review*
MP   *Modern Philology*
N & Q   *Notes and Queries*
Neilson   *The Complete Dramatic and Poetic Works of Shakespeare*, ed. W. A.
                     Neilson, 1906; rev. edn with C. J. Hill, 1942
NS   *Coriolanus*, ed. John Dover Wilson, 1960 (New Shakespeare)
OED   *Oxford English Dictionary*, 2nd edn
Onions   C. T. Onions, *A Shakespeare Glossary*, 1911 (revised Robert D.
                     Eagleson, 1986)
Oxford   William Shakespeare, *The Complete Works*, gen. eds. Stanley Wells
                     and Gary Taylor, 1986 (Oxford Shakespeare), *Coriolanus* ed. John
                     Jowett; collations and apparatus for this edition appear in *Textual
                     Companion*
P & P   *Past and Present*
Parker   *Coriolanus*, ed. R. B. Parker, 1994 (Oxford Shakespeare)
Perring   Philip Perring, *Hard Knots in Shakespeare*, 2nd edn, 1886
PMLA   *Publications of the Modern Language Association*
Pope   *The Works of Shakespear*, ed. Alexander Pope, 6 vols., 1723–5, V
Pope²   *The Works of Shakespear*, ed. Alexander Pope, 9 vols., 1728, VI
Proudfoot   Richard Proudfoot, 'Textual studies', *S.Sur.* 30 (1977), 203–5
Q   quarto
Rann   *The Dramatic Works of Shakspeare*, ed. Joseph Rann, 6 vols., 1786, V
RenD   *Renaissance Drama*
Riverside   *The Riverside Shakespeare*, gen. ed. G. Blakemore Evans, 1974
Rowe   *The Works of Mr. William Shakespear*, ed. Nicholas Rowe, 6 vols.,
                     1709, IV

Rowe²	*The Works of Mr. William Shakespear*, ed. Nicholas Rowe, 6 vols., 1709 [1710], IV
Rowe³	*The Works of Mr. William Shakespear*, ed. Nicholas Rowe, 9 vols., 1714, V
RSC	Royal Shakespeare Company
SB	*Studies in Bibliography*
Schmidt	*Coriolanus*, ed. Alexander Schmidt, 1878
SD	stage direction
SEL	*Studies in English Literature, 1500–1900*
Seymour	E. H. Seymour, *Remarks Critical, Conjectural, and Explanatory Upon the Plays of Shakspeare*, 2 vols., 1805, I
SH	speech heading
Shaheen	Naseeb Shaheen, *Biblical References in Shakespeare's Tragedies*, 1987
Singer	*The Dramatic Works of William Shakespeare*, ed. S. W. Singer, 10 vols., 1826, VIII
Singer²	*The Dramatic Works of William Shakespeare*, ed. S. W. Singer, 10 vols., 1856, VII
Singer, *SV*	Samuel Weller Singer, *The Text of Shakespeare Vindicated*, 1853
Sisson	*William Shakespeare: The Complete Works*, ed. C. J. Sisson, 1954
Sisson, *NR*	C. J. Sisson, *New Readings in Shakespeare*, 2 vols., 1956, II
SP	*Studies in Philology*
SQ	*Shakespeare Quarterly*
S.St.	*Shakespeare Studies*
S.Sur.	*Shakespeare Survey*
Staunton	*The Plays of Shakespeare*, ed. Howard Staunton, 3 vols., 1858–60, III
Steevens	*The Plays of William Shakespeare*, ed. George Steevens and Samuel Johnson, 10 vols., 1773, VII (Variorum Shakespeare)
Steevens²	*The Plays of William Shakespeare*, ed. George Steevens and Samuel Johnson, 10 vols., 1778, VII
Steevens³	*The Plays of William Shakespeare*, ed. George Steevens and Isaac Reed, 15 vols., 1793, XII
Steevens⁴	*The Plays of William Shakespeare*, 'revised and augmented' by Isaac Reed, 21 vols., 1803, XVI
subst.	substantively
Textual Companion	Stanley Wells *et al.*, *William Shakespeare: A Textual Companion*, 1987
Theobald	*The Works of Shakespeare*, ed. Lewis Theobald, 7 vols., 1733, VI
Theobald²	*The Works of Shakespeare*, ed. Lewis Theobald. 7 vols., 1739, VI
Theobald, *SR*	Lewis Theobald, *Shakespeare Restored*, 1726
Tilley	M. P. Tilley, *A Dictionary of Proverbs in England in the Sixteenth and Seventeenth Centuries*, 1950
TLS	*Times Literary Supplement*
Tyrwhitt	Thomas Tyrwhitt, *Observations and Conjectures upon some Passages of Shakespeare*, 1766
Walker	William Sidney Walker, *A Critical Examination of the Text of Shakespeare*, ed. W. N. Lettsom, 3 vols., 1860, III
Warburton	*The Works of Shakespear*, ed. William Warburton, 8 vols., 1747, VI
White	*The Works of William Shakespeare*, ed. R. Grant White, 12 vols., 1857–66, IX

White²   *Mr. William Shakespeare's Comedies, Histories, Tragedies, and Poems,*
         ed. R. Grant White, 3 vols., 1883 (Riverside Shakespeare), III
White, *SS*   R. Grant White, *Shakespeare's Scholar,* 1854
Williams   W. W. Williams, 'Notes on Coriolanus', *The Parthenon* 1 (3 May
         1862), 19

Unless otherwise noted, biblical quotations are taken from the Geneva Bible (1560).

INTRODUCTION

Date, theatre, chronology

While there is no early quarto or Stationers' Register entry before that of 1623 for the First Folio and no record of performance to assist in dating *Coriolanus*, it is generally agreed to have been written late in Shakespeare's sequence of Jacobean tragedies. Although their evidence is not decisive, stylistic tests place *Coriolanus* after *King Lear*, *Macbeth* and *Antony and Cleopatra* (that is, later than 1606),[1] and contemporary allusions suggest it was known, at least to some, by late 1609.

The 1605 publication of William Camden's *Remaines of a Greater Worke, Concerning Britaine*, sets one firm limit, for Menenius's phrasing in the belly fable (1.1.79–129) is closer to Camden's version than to that in North's Plutarch.[2] Edmond Malone, who pointed out the Camden parallels in 1790, also noted Ben Jonson's recollection in *Epicoene* of a distinctive phrase in Cominius's speech to the senate.[3] *Epicoene* was possibly performed in late 1609, for after 7 December the plague death-rate seems to have been low enough to have permitted reopening the playhouses, though the authorities might have delayed out of caution;[4] certainly it was played in early 1610, when Lady Arabella Stuart complained of a personally offensive allusion, and the Venetian ambassador reports the play's suppression in a letter dated 8 February 1610.[5]

Two other apparent references suggest that *Coriolanus* was well enough known by this date to be worth alluding to. Coriolanus tells Menenius that when the citizens heard their petition for tribunes had been granted, 'they threw their caps / As they would hang them on the horns o'th'moon' (1.1.195–6), and this phrasing seems echoed in Robert Armin's preface to his verse translation of an Italian novella, *The Italian Tailor and his Boy* (1609): 'A strange time of taxation, wherein every Pen & inck-horne Boy, will throw up his Cap at the hornes of the Moone in censure' (A4ʳ).[6] Finally,

---

[1] Philip Brockbank (ed.), *Coriolanus*, 1976, p. 28; Stanley Wells *et al.*, *Textual Companion*, 1987, p. 131; and see p. 2 n. 2 below.

[2] Brockbank notes the chance that Shakespeare might have seen a pre-publication manuscript copy of *Remaines*, since Camden's dedicatory epistle is dated June 1603, and they may have known each other (p. 24). For North's Plutarch, see pp. 10–11 below.

[3] Cominius describes Coriolanus's deeds of valour as having 'lurched all swords of the garland' (2.2.95). In *Epicoene* Truewit remonstrates that Dauphine has 'lurch'd your friends of the better half of the garland, by concealing this part of the plot' (5.4.203–4); quotation taken from L. A. Beaurline (ed.), *Epicoene*, 1966.

[4] In *Politics, Plague, and Shakespeare's Theater*, 1991, Leeds Barroll assumes that, after more than a year of severe plague, the authorities would not have acted hastily, on the basis of one week's promising death-toll (p. 182).

[5] Beaurline (ed.), *Epicoene*, p. xix.

[6] T. W. Baldwin, *The Organization and Personnel of the Shakespearean Company*, 1927, suggests that Heminges played Menenius and Armin First Citizen (p. 241). Martin Holmes (*Shakespeare and Burbage*, 1978, p. 194), R. B. Parker (ed.), *Coriolanus*, 1994, and I believe Menenius was Armin's part; in either case, Armin was on stage in 1.1. While he cites the parallel, Parker is not convinced that Armin's phrasing can be traced to *Coriolanus* (p. 3).

John Fletcher's topsy-turvy version of *The Taming of the Shrew* in *The Woman's Prize, or, The Tamer Tam'd* (*c.* 1611[1]) appears to make comic capital out of alluding to Coriolanus's heroic valour. Both Beaumont and Fletcher were prodigious borrowers and parodists, and they had shown a particular fondness for Shakespeare even before they began writing for the King's Men as well as the boy companies in 1609.[2] In *The Woman's Prize*, after twenty-one lines describing the ways she has tormented her foolish wooer Moroso, which might themselves be a parodic version of Cominius's account of Coriolanus's 'deeds', Livia sums up her accomplishments with a boast that seems meant to play off Coriolanus's final self-assertion to Aufidius: 'All this villany / Did I: I *Livia*, I alone, untaught' (5.1.96–7).[3]

Within this period – 1605 to late 1609 – some non-literary events are pertinent to narrowing the parameters. In condensing Plutarch's narrative Shakespeare had immediate reasons to skip the Roman citizens' first protest, over usurers, to concentrate on the second, over grain: the anti-enclosure riots of late spring 1607 and the fact that the dearth they anticipated lasted throughout 1608 (see pp. 17–20 below). Helping to pinpoint the date of composition a bit more closely, the River Thames froze solid in December 1607 and January 1608 (the first time since the winter of 1564–5), and one of Coriolanus's analogies for the citizens' untrustworthiness probably alludes to this event: they are 'no surer, no, / Than is the coal of fire upon the ice' (1.1.155–6). The title page of the Thomas Dekker [?] 1608 pamphlet *The Great Frost* (see illustration 1) shows children at play on the ice and adults conducting trade, and his citizen interlocutor says to the countryman, 'Are you colde with going over? you shall ere you come to the midst of the River, spie some ready with pannes of coales to warme your fingers' (B1ᵛ).[4] The freezing of the Thames is not crucial to the analogy, but it is more unusual than its companion phrase, 'Or hailstone in the sun', and memories of a recent severe winter would have given it sharper point.

[1] Although not recorded in the Stationers' Register until 4 September 1646, for the Beaumont and Fletcher First Folio, topical allusions and possible reminiscences of Jonson's *Epicoene* (1609) and, less certainly, *The Alchemist* (1610) suggest a first performance in early 1611. The most persuasive attempt at dating *The Woman's Prize* is Baldwin Maxwell, *Studies in Beaumont, Fletcher, and Massinger*, 1939 (rpt 1966), ch. 4. See also Fredson Bowers's introduction in *The Dramatic Works in the Beaumont and Fletcher Canon*, gen. ed. Fredson Bowers, 10 vols., 1966–96, IV, 3; the quotation is taken from this edition.

[2] In *The Woman Hater* the comic parasite Lazarello parodies not only Hamlet with his ghostly father but also Antony's speech on joining Cleopatra: in a mock-heroic lament for the loss of his umbrana fish, he cries out, 'I will not sure outlive it, no I will die bravely, and like a Roman; and after death, amidst the Elizian shades, Ile meete my love againe' (3.2.112–14); see the edition by George Walton Williams, in *The Dramatic Works in the Beaumont and Fletcher Canon*, I. *The Woman Hater* was entered in the Stationers' Register on 20 May 1607 but acted sometime before the Paul's boys stopped playing; their last recorded performance was in July 1606.

[3] In '*Coriolanus' on Stage in England and America, 1609–1994*, 1998, pp. 51–2, John Ripley suggests that the mother–son vignette in Beaumont and Fletcher's *A King and No King* (1611), 3.1.47–52, owes a good deal to *Coriolanus* 5.3.53–62. He also hypothesises continued popularity or a recent revival to explain the echo of Coriolanus's lines to Virgilia (5.3.46–8) in the Fletcher/Massinger/Field collaboration *The Queen of Corinth* (1616–17), 1.2.58–62. (Fletcher references are to the editions in *The Dramatic Works in the Beaumont and Fletcher Canon* (see above, n. 1): *A King and No King*, ed. George Walton Williams, in vol. II, and *The Queen of Corinth*, ed. Robert Kean Turner, in vol. VIII.)

[4] See also Chamberlain's letter to Dudley Carleton of 8 January 1608, in *The Letters of John Chamberlain*, ed. Norman McClure, 2 vols., 1939, I, 253, and Edmund Howes's continuation of Stow's *Annales* (1631), quoted in Bullough, *Sources* V, 559–60.

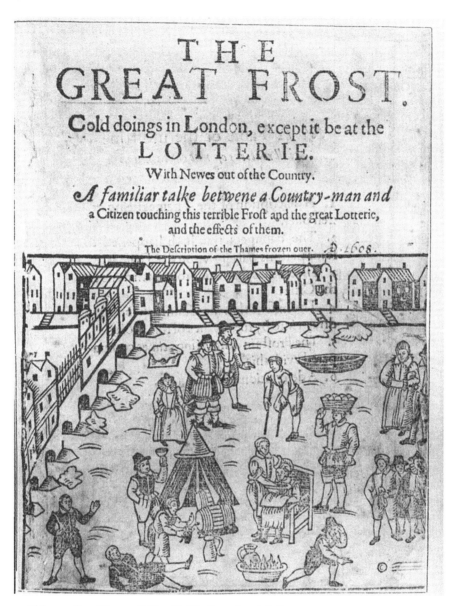

1   Title page from Thomas Dekker [?], *The Great Frost* (1608)

Some have seen another topical allusion in Coriolanus's warning to the patricians that the power-hungry Sicinius will 'turn your current in a ditch / And make your channel his' (3.1.97–8). On 20 February 1609 work began on the goldsmith Hugh Myddelton's project to bring fresh water to London by channels from Hertfordshire, a project that according to Stow met with 'many causeless hindrances and complaints of sundry persons through whose ground he was to cut his water passage'.[1] A contemporary reference does not seem necessary here, since the idea of disputed water-rights is sufficient and seems equally applicable to farming. It is worth noting, however, that the plan for transporting water was being discussed as early as March 1608.[2] Finally, Malone's suggestion that Volumnia's advice to her son to act 'humble as the ripest mulberry' (3.2.80) alludes to a royal proclamation of 19 January 1609 encouraging mulberry cultivation is unpersuasive, since references to mulberries appear in two much earlier Shakespearean works, *Venus and Adonis* (line 1103) and *A Midsummer Night's Dream* (3.1.159).

Such topical allusions cannot be decisive, but they do coincide with stylistic evidence for composition later rather than earlier in the period bounded by Camden's *Remaines* and Jonson's *Epicoene*. If the 'coal upon the ice' does derive from the experience of the Great Frost of 1607–8, the earliest date of composition would be that winter and the earliest date of performance would be spring 1608, between March and late July, the only months that year when the theatres were not closed because of plague.[3] This is the period favoured by Brockbank, John Dover Wilson and David George, although George specifies performance 'in early June or before' at the indoor Blackfriars Theatre rather than the Globe.[4] I am less confident of an early 1608 performance, though composition may have begun as early as March, when the theatres were temporarily closed as punishment for the production by the Children of Blackfriars of George Chapman's two-part *The Conspiracy and Tragedy of Charles Duke of Byron*. The king vowed that the children 'should never play more, but should first begg their bred' and ordered their troupe dissolved.[5]

At this point the King's Men might fairly have expected soon to come into possession of the fashionable private theatre across the river which Burbage owned but had leased to the children. *Coriolanus* appears to be Shakespeare's first play written with the Blackfriars in mind as a possible venue. It is divided into acts; more importantly, and unlike the scenic construction of its predecessor *Antony and Cleopatra*, it is composed in terms of the five-act structure common at the indoor private theatres, where there were intervals between acts. Act 1 is concerned with exposition and Coriolanus's military success; it ends with Aufidius announcing his envy and his intention to defeat Coriolanus by 'wrath or craft'. Coriolanus's triumphal return to Rome, nomination to the consulship and initial confirmation occupy Act 2, which

[1] Quoted in G. B. Harrison, 'A note on *Coriolanus*', in *John Quincy Adams Memorial Studies*, ed. J. G. McManaway *et al.*, 1948, p. 240.

[2] David George, '*Coriolanus* at the Blackfriars?', *N&Q* 236 (December 1991), 490.

[3] See Barroll's chart on plague closings, *Politics, Plague, and Shakespeare's Theater*, p. 173.

[4] Brockbank, p. 29; Wilson (ed.), *Coriolanus*, 1960, p. x; George, '*Coriolanus* at the Blackfriars?', p. 492. E. K. Chambers, *William Shakespeare*, 2 vols., 1930, I, 480, also, though more tentatively, dates performance in early 1608. It seems doubtful, however, that the King's Men would have begun playing at the Blackfriars before the new leases were executed on 9 August 1608, by which time all theatres were closed.

[5] There were actually two offending plays; the other, possibly by Marston, has not survived. The French ambassador, in a letter dated 29 March 1608, reported that all the theatres were closed, though the other owners were petitioning to reopen (E. K. Chambers, *The Elizabethan Stage*, 4 vols., 1923, II, 53); the quotation is from an 11 March letter from Sir Thomas Lake to Robert Cecil (II, 54).

also concludes on an ominous note as the tribunes persuade the citizens to rescind their vote. Act 3 works out the first consequences of that decision, descending into near civil war and, on the tribunes' urging, Coriolanus's banishment. Act 4 builds to Coriolanus's gaining the means to take his revenge on Rome, switches to Rome's reception of the news of imminent attack, and concludes with Aufidius again contemplating his enemy and vowing to destroy him. Finally, a series of pleas for mercy culminate in Coriolanus's confrontation with his mother and decision to spare Rome, followed by Aufidius's long-predicted revenge.[1] Two of what I suspect to be scenes added or at least expanded in the process of revision (the final scene of Act 1 and, especially, the final scene of Act 4) accentuate the formal breaks by returning to Aufidius; they strengthen the contrast between him and Coriolanus and focus our attention on questions of character rather than physical prowess.[2] These unPlutarchan scenes also counterpoise the protagonist's apparent progression toward acknowledged superiority and public acclaim, first in Rome and then among the Volscians. Acts 2 and 3 are virtually continuous in action but so structured that Act 3 replays in a more desperate key Act 2's movement: apparent civic success cut short not only by Coriolanus's own behaviour but by the tribunes' stratagems. Whether or not the actual act notations were first entered in the hand of the author, Shakespeare composed *Coriolanus* to be playable with intervals that reinforce its structure. Stage directions also repeatedly call for cornets, instruments with a mellower tone than trumpets and associated with the indoor private theatres.[3]

Coriolanus would also have been an appropriate opener for the Blackfriars Theatre's more affluent and educated clientele. Chapman was Shakespeare's most serious rival as a tragedian, and he specialised in heroic tragedy. His *Bussy D'Ambois* (performed 1603; Q 1607) had been an earlier Blackfriars success, and the Byron plays were now notorious (they were printed later in 1608 in a truncated version, presumably in part to take advantage of the public's curiosity). Both Byron and Coriolanus were military heroes turned renegade, willing to destroy their country rather than submit to it. Shakespeare's own interest in heroic individualism would have nicely coincided with an opportunity to take on Chapman on his home ground while also providing the Blackfriars audience with a play in a genre for which it had a known taste.[4] *Coriolanus*'s intense political debates and prominent use of legal terminology would also have appealed to the law students of the nearby Inns of Court, who frequented the Blackfriars and often themselves entered politics, and these features would have

---

[1] Parker argues that the F division between Acts 3 and 4 'seems a mistake' and is perhaps therefore unShakespearean; yet since in his designation of three main movements in the play's action the first also overlaps an act division (between 1 and 2), he concludes that 'the asymmetry may be intentional' and retains F's notation of Acts 3 and 4 (p. 28).

[2] The theatrically effective pause and ironic foreshadowing created by the conversation between Roman and Volscian spies in 4.3 might be another scene added in revision to heighten effects already sketched out in the first draft; it is of a length to fit on one sheet of paper, easily inserted into what had already been composed.

[3] See John H. Long, *Shakespeare's Use of Music: The Histories and the Tragedies*, 1971, p. 222, and W. J. Lawrence, *Shakespeare's Workshop*, 1966, pp. 52–3.

[4] In *Possessed with Greatness*, 1980, Richard Ide goes further: 'Shakespeare, I suspect, designed *Coriolanus* to respond not only to the *Byron* plays but to Chapman's theory of titanic heroism as well' (p. 170).

benefited from 'the more intense audience concentration which the smaller theatre allowed'.[1]

Composition could have begun in March 1608, but it is also possible that it was delayed by other company responsibilities until after plague closed the theatres again in late July. In August Shakespeare brought suit in Stratford against John Addenbrook; his mother died on 2 September and was buried on the 9th. Shakespeare may have attended the christening in Stratford of his nephew, Michael Hart, two weeks later, and on 16 October he stood as godfather to the son of an old friend.[2] Some or all of these events could have been handled by proxy, but possibly he resided in Stratford more or less continuously, avoiding the plague in London and writing *Coriolanus* while also attending to family business. He may even have consciously begun his gradual withdrawal from playwriting for the King's Men, although he certainly chose to invest in the Blackfriars venture by becoming a sharer in the new leases signed in August.[3] As it turned out, plague closed the theatres not only for the remainder of 1608 but for nearly all of 1609 as well. Such a disaster for the theatrical troupes could not be predicted, however; it seems reasonable to suppose that there were hopes that cooler weather would bring an abatement in plague deaths and that Shakespeare's target was an autumn 1608 Blackfriars opening.

A probable literary borrowing from Chapman's translation of the first twelve books of the *Iliad* would suggest that Shakespeare was (still?) writing after the Stationers' Register entry for Chapman's book (14 November 1608) and its subsequent publication. Yet we do not know the rate at which Shakespeare composed *Coriolanus*, and the line might have been added later, or Shakespeare could have had access to a manuscript.[4] That he would be interested seems likely: he had already used the earlier *Seaven Bookes of the Iliads* (1598) when writing *Troilus and Cressida*, and since he was still writing about epic heroes, there was likely to be pertinent material in the newly translated Books III–VI and XII. Chapman's version of Zeus's paradoxical words to Hera when he consents to the destruction of Troy – 'I grant thee willingly, although against my will' (*Iliad* IV, 43) – becomes in *Coriolanus* a comic expression of the citizens' confused

[1] Martin Wiggins, 'The King's Men and after', in *Shakespeare: An Illustrated Stage History*, ed. Jonathan Bate and Russell Jackson, 1996, p. 29. On the pervasive use of legal terminology, see G. Thomas Tanselle and Florence W. Dunbar, 'Legal language in *Coriolanus*', *SQ* 13 (1962), 231–8.
[2] Mark Eccles, *Shakespeare in Warwickshire*, 1961, p. 110. Parker assumes Shakespeare's personal attendance at all of these events (pp. 6–7); Eccles is more cautious.
[3] *Coriolanus*'s often unusually full, narrative stage directions may indicate semi-retirement and an author who knew that he might not be present at rehearsals. In March 1613 Shakespeare purchased a house in London near the Blackfriars Theatre, but this may have been simply a real-estate investment; see S. Schoenbaum, *William Shakespeare: A Compact Documentary Life*, 1987, pp. 272–3, and for the document itself, Chambers, *William Shakespeare*, II, 154–7. In contrast, E. A. J. Honigmann takes the Blackfriars investments as a sign that Shakespeare 'intended . . . to resume his career in London' ('"There is a world elsewhere": William Shakespeare, businessman', in *Images of Shakespeare*, ed. Werner Habicht et al., 1988, p. 43).
[4] Among the rather tightly-knit group of playwrights for the Children of Blackfriars – Jonson, Chapman, Marston, Beaumont, Fletcher – an assumption of manuscript exchange would be reasonable. To what extent Shakespeare was a part of this group we cannot know; yet Jonson also wrote for the King's Men and knew Shakespeare, and negotiations to add Beaumont and Fletcher to their roster may have been already under way.

attempt to evade responsibility: 'though we willingly consented to his banishment, yet it was against our will' (4.6.148–9).[1]

Nothing decisively excludes composition in spring 1608 and first performance before late July at the Globe. But if the paradox was borrowed from Chapman, and not inserted later, it points to composition, or completion, in late 1608.[2] The Stationers' Register entry for Armin's *The Italian Tailor and his Boy* (6 February 1609) suggests that the company had at least rehearsed the play by then. Prefaces tend to be written last, and Armin presumably worked on his translation while the theatres were closed. Thus *Coriolanus* may have had its premiere in late 1608 at Blackfriars, though perhaps before only a few friends: in April 1609 the King's Men were reimbursed an extra £40, beyond the payment for their performances during the 1608–9 Christmas holiday season, for 'private practise in the time of infeccion' to prepare their plays for court.[3] *Coriolanus*'s official opening is likely to have been at court, as one of the twelve unnamed plays performed by the King's Men for the 1608–9 Christmas season.[4] Given plague restrictions, unless it was played illegally *Coriolanus* was first available to the general London public in late December 1609 or February 1610, in which case it would have been competing, briefly, with Jonson's *Epicoene* put on by the regrouped Blackfriars boys (now the Children of Her Majesty's Revels) at the Whitefriars Theatre.

Chronology

Shakespeare knew the Coriolanus story, at least in rough outline, as early as *Titus Andronicus*, for Titus's exiled son Lucius, having joined the enemy Goths to lead them against Rome, is said to threaten 'in course of this revenge, to do / As much as ever Coriolanus did' (4.4.66–7).[5] He could have known the basic narrative from general reading, or in the abbreviated version taken from Livy in William Painter's *Palace*

---

[1] John A. Scott, 'An unnoticed Homeric phrase in Shakespeare', *Classical Philology* 33 (1938), 414. Parker suggests that Martius's prayer for his son (5.3.70–5) might have been inspired by that of Hector for Astyanax in Book VI of the *Iliad*, though he notes there are no parallels in thought or phrasing (p. 4). If the prayer's central image has a classical source, I expect it is Virgil, either directly or *via* Montaigne (see p. 15 below).

[2] It is possible that in translating the 'Homeric phrase' Chapman employed a common coinage and that no borrowing is involved (see 4.6.148–9 n.), but other evidence suggests late 1608. This is also Parker's estimate, although he allows more weight than I to the possible reference to Myddelton's irrigation project and so is willing to extend the date of composition to early 1609 (p. 7).

[3] Chambers, *Elizabethan Stage*, IV, 175. The 'private practise' might, of course, have taken place elsewhere. Still calling themselves the Children of Blackfriars, the offending boys themselves presented three plays at the Christmas revels. It is possible, given plague conditions, that the King's Men had not rushed to take over their new theatre.

[4] I am unpersuaded by arguments that would push composition to 1609 and first performance to spring 1610, but see Barroll, *Politics, Plague, and Shakespeare's Theater*, Appendix 5, and Annabel Patterson, *Shakespeare and the Popular Voice*, 1989, pp. 138–46.

[5] The first recorded performance of *Titus* was in 1594, possibly in a revised version since Henslowe noted it as 'ne' (new); there is good reason to think it was composed and performed earlier and that it preceded *The Rape of Lucrece* (1593); see Eugene M. Waith (ed.), *Titus Andronicus*, 1984, pp. 4–11. Jonathan Bate, however, thinks *Lucrece* preceded *Titus* (Bate (ed.), *Titus Andronicus*, 1995, pp. 69–79).

of Pleasure, which he also employed for *The Rape of Lucrece* (1593).[1] Yet it is likely that he was already reading Plutarch and that he there found Coriolanus's march on Rome at the head of an enemy army to use as the basis for Lucius's threatened attack.[2] Several characters' names were taken from Plutarch's 'Life of Scipio Africanus';[3] in the comparison of Hannibal with Scipio, Shakespeare would have found that Scipio 'would not come against his contry with ensignes displaied, nether would be solicite straunge nations . . . to come with force, and their ayde, to destroy the citie . . . as Martius Coriolanus, Alcibiades, and divers others did'.[4] This mention would have been sufficient for the brief analogy in *Titus*, though it might have led him to further reading in *The Lives of the Noble Grecians and Romanes* where, in Plutarch's format of parallel Greek and Roman 'lives', Coriolanus and Alcibiades are paired.

Whether he read their stories this early or was sent to them at some point after *Julius Caesar* (1599), Shakespeare developed them further in two later plays, *Timon of Athens* and *Coriolanus*. Unfortunately, chronology at this point becomes uncertain. The dating of *Timon* is highly conjectural, the only consensus being that it is later than *Othello* (*c.* 1604). While *Timon*'s primary source is an anecdote in Plutarch's 'Life of Marcus Antonius', this fact does not help in pinning down a late date for *Timon* (that is, after *Antony*), since Shakespeare had consulted that life for *Julius Caesar* and material from it appears in *Macbeth*.[5] The Alcibiades material in *Timon* is largely unPlutarchan, patterned instead on the career of Coriolanus, but since he had used Coriolanus's story as early as *Titus*, this does not mean that *Coriolanus* preceded *Timon*. A plausible chronology would see *Julius Caesar* as the beginning of Shakespeare's substantial engagement with Plutarch, though he had at least dipped into the *Lives* for earlier plays.[6] Using the life of Antony for some details, especially *Julius Caesar* 4.1, he was struck with material for a very different kind of tragedy, *Antony and Cleopatra*. A good deal of other work intervened before he returned to Plutarch for that play, though when he did, the 'Life of Marcus Antonius' led him to consider a play on Timon and to use the Alcibiades and Coriolanus stories to eke out Timon's.[7] Characterisation in *Timon* is flat and schematic, and in formal terms it is as odd an experiment in tragedy, if indeed it can be called that, as *Troilus and*

---

[1] Both appear in the First Tome (1566; 2nd edn, including both books, 1575). In *The Sources of Shakespeare's Plays*, 1977, Kenneth Muir suggests that Shakespeare first knew Coriolanus's story from Livy, read in grammar school (p. 238).

[2] Bullough thinks a few other details were transferred from Coriolanus's career in Plutarch to Titus's in Shakespeare's play (*Sources*, VI, 23–4).

[3] Robert Adger Law, 'The Roman background of *Titus Andronicus*', *SP* 40 (1943), 147. Rome showed ingratitude not only to Scipio but to his brother Lucius, one of the names borrowed for *Titus*.

[4] Bullough, *Sources*, VI, 78.

[5] Both *Textual Companion*, pp. 129–30, and Nicholas Brooke (ed.), *Macbeth*, 1990, pp. 63–4, date composition in 1606; Brooke, who favours the second half of 1606, allows the possibility that the usually assumed chronology, in which *Macbeth* precedes *Antony*, may be incorrect. See also A. R. Braunmuller (ed.), *Macbeth*, 1997, p. 6.

[6] See p. 10 below. C. M. Eccles has also argued that Amyot's foreword, 'Englished' and included by North in his *Lives*, influenced Shakespeare in Sonnet 55 ('Shakespeare and Jacques Amyot: Sonnet LV and "Coriolanus"', *N&Q* 210 (March 1965), 100–2).

[7] Although Thomas Middleton may have collaborated on the script of *Timon*, I take the choice of subject matter to be Shakespeare's.

Cressida.[1] One feature of its publication history may lend some support for the theory that, if not 'unfinished', *Timon* had not received its final polish: in the printing of the First Folio it was a last-minute substitution for *Troilus and Cressida*, and Heminges and Condell may not originally have intended to include it.[2] The 'Life of Coriolanus' offered a richer social and political canvas and, though its hero is as unself-analytical as Timon or Alcibiades, it sketched a central character who could be made more psychologically compelling. Yet while it seems 'logical' that the simpler character would precede the more complex, with *Timon* therefore the earlier play, the critic's resort to Occam's razor may not come even close to capturing the workings of the creative imagination.

If we cannot be certain of the chronology of *Timon* and *Coriolanus*, we can be of the strong connections between the two plays in structure, both culminating in an exiled soldier's march against his native city and a theatrical supplication scene; *via* the theme of ingratitude, both also reveal their kinship with *Lear*. And while in terms of its historical period *Coriolanus* drops back to pick up the early years of the Roman Republic initiated at the end of *The Rape of Lucrece*, many features link it to Shakespeare's more recent work. Michael Neill notes that while *Julius Caesar* and *Antony and Cleopatra* together chronicle the final collapse of the Republic and the institution of the Empire, with *Coriolanus* they can also be 'read as a loose trilogy in which Shakespeare ponders certain great issues of classical historiography': questions about alternative forms of government (republic or monarchy), distributions of power (aristocratic or democratic), and the role of the 'great man' in shaping history.[3] Geoffrey Miles reads these three Roman tragedies as 'a triptych on the theme of constancy'.[4] They also in varying ways explore the nature of Roman 'virtue' (*virtus*), the idealisation of martial valour and of the public life, and the troubling relationship between name and identity.

Plutarch's story also offered Shakespeare another opportunity to explore the complexities of his own world by setting versions of it off against an earlier, apparently simpler, feudal or heroic one, a way of organising his material that had engaged him since the second tetralogy on English history in the late 1590s but took sharper outline in *Julius Caesar* and *Hamlet*. That the contrast can be established on the battlefield itself is clear in *Troilus and Cressida*, where the world of honour confronts the market-place in the persons of Troilus and Hector, who romanticise war as chivalry, and Ulysses and Achilles, who do not. More commonly the heroics of war give place to the complexities

---

[1] Maurice Charney favours the term 'dramatic fable' and notes that the form necessitates rejecting opportunities for developing 'psychological thickness' of character (Charney (ed.), *Timon of Athens*, 1965, p. xxviii). Charney thinks *Timon* finished 'in conception' and believes it to be Shakespeare's last tragedy; other critics speculate that 'Shakespeare abandoned *Timon* to write *Coriolanus*' (Bullough, *Sources*, v, 239).

[2] See Textual Analysis, p. 295 below. There is no evidence that *Timon* was ever publicly acted. Another sign of its awkward 'fit' is that, although printed with the Tragedies in 1623, its title page reads *The Life of Timon of Athens*, and the running title, unlike that of the other tragedies, is simply *Timon of Athens* on both recto and verso pages.

[3] Michael Neill (ed.), *Anthony and Cleopatra*, 1994, p. 7. See also Paul A. Cantor, *Shakespeare's Rome: Republic and Empire*, 1976, p. 16, and Robert S. Miola, *Shakespeare's Rome*, 1983, p. 17.

[4] Geoffrey Miles, *Shakespeare and the Constant Romans*, 1996, p. vii.

of peacetime politics.[1] *Macbeth* and *Antony and Cleopatra*, as well as *Coriolanus*, at least open in a world in which superlative warriors crucially matter, but where the bringer-home of victory might also pose the greatest danger. Macbeth, Antony and Coriolanus in different ways exemplify the soldier's failure to dominate the political arena. In a further connection, *Macbeth*, *Antony* and *Coriolanus* all examine their martial heroes' interaction with strong, ultimately destructive women. The problem lies deeper than the plays' particular women, however. For Macbeth and Coriolanus, and for Antony in his 'Roman mood', power and identity are understood in terms of a definition of masculinity that consciously excludes maternal values;[2] violence is self-validating, and through it they seek to author themselves, to become invulnerable and godlike. Each of these plays interrogates in its own way the hierarchic division between the sexes and the qualities assigned them, and they look forward to the late plays in suggesting a different definition of what 'manhood' means.

Sources

Shakespeare's primary source was 'The Life of Caius Martius Coriolanus' in *The Lives of the Noble Grecians and Romanes*, translated from Plutarch's Greek into French by Jacques Amyot and then from the French into English by Thomas North. Both Amyot and North added their own colouring,[3] but Shakespeare knew his Plutarch in North's version only and, of the available editions (1579, 1595, 1603), probably for this play he used the 1595 edition.[4] He follows his source narrative fairly closely, though he omits some details, alters others, and creates whole scenes that complicate Plutarch's central figure. The primary structural changes to Plutarch's narrative lie in the greatly expanded roles of Menenius, Volumnia, the tribunes and Aufidius, all of whom become not only actors in the drama but commentators on the protagonist. Plutarch's parallel-lives format paired Greek and Roman figures, and Shakespeare also borrowed from 'The Comparison of Alcibiades with Martius Coriolanus', primarily for the Officers' analysis of Coriolanus that opens Act 2, Scene 2.[5]

The evidence is less certain that he turned elsewhere in Plutarch for some local details, although it would not be surprising if he had. The course of Shakespeare's career shows a fairly wide perusal of this congenial historian, with certain use of the lives of Scipio Africanus (for *Titus Andronicus*),[6] Theseus (*A Midsummer Night's*

---

[1] The contemporary context in which these issues resonated is discussed below, pp. 33–40.
[2] For remarks on Macbeth's 'equation of masculinity with violence as a denial or defense against femininity', see Madeline Gohlke, '"I woo'd thee with my sword": Shakespeare's tragic paradigms', in *Representing Shakespeare*, ed. Murray M. Schwartz and Coppélia Kahn, 1980, pp. 176–7. See also Eugene M. Waith, 'Manhood and valor in two Shakespearean tragedies', *ELH* 17 (1950), 262–73, and D. W. Harding, 'Women's fantasy of manhood: a Shakespearian theme', *SQ* 20 (1969), 245–53.
[3] For a comparison of the translations with each other and with the original, see Hermann Heuer, 'From Plutarch to Shakespeare: a study of *Coriolanus*', *S.Sur.* 10 (1957), 50–8.
[4] Brockbank notes (p. 29) that 1595 'conduits' corresponds with the Folio's 'Conduits' (*Cor.* 2.3.228) and that only the 1595 edition contains the two spellings 'Latius'/'Lartius' which appear in the Folio text.
[5] See Commentary notes to 2.2.0 SD and 2.2.18. For ease of reference, quotations from North's Plutarch will be taken from Bullough, if available there, rather than from the 1595 edition.
[6] See p. 8 above, n. 3.

Dream), Caesar, Brutus, Antonius, Coriolanus and Alcibiades, as well as the comparisons attached to these lives. Others have proposed acquaintance with the lives of Pompeius, Cicero, Cato, and possibly Romulus, Lycurgus and Numa.[1] In picking Roman names for three minor characters who do not appear in the Coriolanus narrative, Shakespeare may have at least skimmed the lives of Agesilaus (whose King Cotys may lie behind Cotus, one of Aufidius's servingmen), Phocion (for Nicanor, the Roman turncoat in 4.3) and Lucullus (for Adrian, the Volscian spy in 4.3).[2] Two other elements of the play might have been prompted by Plutarch's life of Furius Camillus, to which it would have been natural to turn since authors commenting on Coriolanus frequently referred to Camillus as the contrasting example of a great soldier's response to unjust banishment. Camillus exiles himself before the tribunes and ungrateful plebeians can find a pretext to banish him, but he pauses at the gates of Rome to pray 'that the Romaines might quickly repent them, and in the face of the world might wish for him, and have neede of him' (1595 edn, p. 148). In 'The Life of Coriolanus' the protagonist refuses to come to the Forum to hear the sentence against him, and he departs in silence; in Shakespeare he is given a final harangue and wish for Rome's defeat in his absence (3.3.135–41). The other possible suggestion comes from later in Camillus's story, after he has agreed to return to save Rome from the besieging Gauls and when Rome nearly breaks into civil war over his being named consul by the senators. The tribunes send a 'sergeant' to arrest him, and his friends rally to beat back the officer (p. 165). This 'tumult' over the consulship is closer to Shakespeare's Act 3, Scene 1 than Plutarch's 'Life of Coriolanus', where Coriolanus nurses anger over being refused as consul but the attempted arrest and struggle come later, when he urges the senate to abolish the tribunate. However, the need to compress Plutarch's time-frame might have led Shakespeare to independent development of these theatrically effective scenes.

Whether Shakespeare in minor ways found inspiration in other Plutarchan passages, or in other authors (as will be discussed below), 'The Life of Coriolanus' provided him with the play's basic narrative outline and the foundation for three of its speeches: Coriolanus's denunciation of the corn dole (3.1.69–75, 114–40), his appeal to Aufidius in Antium (4.5.62–98) and Volumnia's plea for mercy (5.3.94–125, 132–71). The major exception to his reliance on Plutarch and his own dramatic abilities is Menenius's fable of the belly (1.1.79–129). It is recounted as a single, uninterrupted speech in Plutarch, and after it Menenius disappears from the story; because it was to be central to his thematic development, Shakespeare moves the occasion to the beginning of the play and greatly expands North's version with the help of several other texts. As a social and political trope, the parable of the body and its members had become a commonplace. Shakespeare may have known Sir Philip Sidney's brief retelling in *An Apologie for Poetrie* (1595), although the identical opening phrase ('There was a time', 1.1.79) is

---

[1] E. A. J. Honigmann, 'Shakespeare's Plutarch', *SQ* 10 (1959), 25–33; Fred Chappell, 'Shakespeare's *Coriolanus* and Plutarch's Life of Cato', *Renaissance Papers*, ed. G. W. Williams, 1963, pp. 9–16. See Brockbank, 2.1.54 n. for Lycurgus and 2.1.74 n. for Numa.

[2] Brockbank (p. 30 n. 4) notes, however, that all three names also appear in Holland's translation of Plutarch's *Moralia* (1603) and in his Livy (1600). They also appear in Montaigne's *Essays* (see p. 15 below).

a common formula.[1] He consulted Livy's version of the Coriolanus story in Book II of *The Romane Historie*, translated by Philemon Holland (1600), and although where Livy's narrative diverged from Plutarch Shakespeare followed Plutarch, he borrowed and expanded some of Holland's phrasing of the fable (see 1.1.118–23 n.). William Camden's *Remaines* (1605) offered a translation of the Latin version, attributed to Pope Adrian IV in John of Salisbury's *Policraticus*, that included a description of the function of the body's 'instruments' (see 1.1.84 n.). The heaviest verbal borrowing is from William Averell's *A Mervailous Combat of Contrarieties* (1588), from whose title page Shakespeare probably took 'contrariety' and 'malignantly' and from the allegory itself, in which Back's and Belly's tyranny is resisted by the rest of the body's members, more than a dozen words.[2] In addition, the repeated complaints about Belly's gluttony and excessive drinking may have influenced the characterisation of Menenius, who in Plutarch is no *bon vivant*.

While Shakespeare preferred to follow Plutarch's version of the events of Coriolanus's life, verbal borrowings indicate that he read all of Livy's version in Book II, where he would also have found the suggestion that Martius entered Corioles alone rather than with Plutarch's few brave soldiers.[3] In more general terms, the warrior heroes of classical epic lie behind Shakespeare's development of his historical material, as they do in his other Greek and Roman tragedies. He had made some use of Chapman's translation of the early books of the *Iliad* in *Troilus and Cressida* and appears to have consulted the later translation of the first twelve books for *Coriolanus*.[4] The descriptions of battles in the *Iliad* and Chapman's own use of an epic report of a duel in *Bussy D'Ambois* may have suggested Shakespeare's addition of a formal account of Coriolanus's 'deeds' (2.2.76–116). Achilles has been suggested as a model for Coriolanus, as has Turnus in Book IX of the *Aeneid*.[5] Seneca, as both moralist and dramatist, lies somewhere in the background, for Shakespeare shapes Plutarch's

[1] Sidney notes that 'the tale is notorious, and as notorious that it was tale'; see *Sir Philip Sidney*, ed. Katherine Duncan-Jones, 1989, pp. 227–8.
[2] See Kenneth Muir, 'Menenius's fable', *N&Q* 198 (1953), 240–2, who lists probable borrowings, some rare or even unique in Shakespeare: 'superfluity, crammed, malicious, viand, instruments, mutually, participate, cormorant, sink, rivers, offices, dissentious'. Muir adds that Averell's 'Pantry' may also have suggested Shakespeare's 'cupboarding' and 'storehouse'.
[3] See also Commentary notes to 3.3.27–8, 102; for a possible recollection from Livy's account of the career of Furius Camillus in Book V, see 3.1.208 n. In 'Livy, Machiavelli, and Shakespeare's *Coriolanus*', *S.Sur.* 38 (1985), 115–29, Anne Barton goes further and argues that Livy's work as a whole, his account of the evolving republic, and probably also Machiavelli's commentary upon Livy in his *Discourses* helped shape the play's political debates (p. 128).
[4] See pp. 6–7 above.
[5] Reuben A. Brower, *Hero and Saint: Shakespeare and the Graeco-Roman Heroic Tradition*, 1971, chs. 1 and 9; Miola, *Shakespeare's Rome*, ch. 6. Howard Felperin suggests Turnus (*Shakespearean Representation*, 1977, pp. 113–14), and in 'Cracking strong curbs asunder: Roman destiny and the Roman hero in *Coriolanus*', *ELR* 13 (1983), 58–69, John W. Veltz argues that Shakespeare understood the careers of both Turnus and Coriolanus in terms of the ages in the history of Rome he would have found in Lucius Annaeus Florus's *Epitome Bellorum Omnium Annorum*, which he may have read in grammer school. In *The Herculean Hero in Marlowe, Chapman, Shakespeare and Dryden*, 1962, Eugene M. Waith reads Shakespeare's protagonist in terms of the tradition derived from the Hercules myths (pp. 39–45, 121–43).

merely uncivil Coriolanus into a Senecan figure seeking the kind of 'radical, unpredi-
cated independence' beyond class or family bonds exemplified in Medea's attempt to
establish 'personal integrity as a force that transcends its origin and context'.[1]

   Other Renaissance authors have been suggested as possible influences.[2] While Cori-
olanus was a lesser-known classical figure than the protagonists of *Julius Caesar* or
Antony and Cleopatra, there was interest in his story in the early seventeenth century,
and it was alluded to by Thomas and Dudley Digges in *Foure Paradoxes, or politique
Discourses* (1604), Jean Bodin in *Six Bookes of a Commonwealth* (translated by Thomas
Knolles, 1606), and William Fulbecke in *The Pandectes of the Law of Nations* (1602);
Menenius's fable opens Edward Forset's defence of monarchy in *A Comparative Discourse of the Bodies Natural and Politique* (1606).[3] Of the four, Shakespeare is most
likely to have known the *Foure Paradoxes*, where the first two, written years before
by Thomas Digges, treat military discipline both ancient and modern, and the second
two, by his son Dudley, praise war and warriors. In 1600 Dudley Digges and his
brother became step-sons to Shakespeare's friend and testamentary overseer, Thomas
Russell,[4] so there may have been a personal reason for the dramatist to at least glance
at it, especially when he was turning to dramatise the stories of Roman warriors, Mark
Antony and Coriolanus. There are parallels in thought and even phrasing, although
they are generally commonplaces and so not decisive.[5] In the fourth paradox, however,
Dudley Digges uses the 'dissention' and 'contentious factions' in Rome 'in Coriolanus
time' to promote war as a sharp but necessary 'Physicke' since, 'like quick-silver and
mercurie, that may endanger life', correctly applied they can be 'sovereign medicines
to purge and clense' (O1^r). Foreign war as a solution to domestic strife is hardly a new
idea, and Shakespeare had used it in Henry IV's advice to his son (*2H4* 4.5.213–14), but
Digges's extended praise of war may have influenced the Volscian servingmen's comic
preference for war over peace (4.5.210–16), and his metaphor prompted Coriolanus's
unPlutarchan urging that the patricians risk civic violence and 'jump a body with a
dangerous physic / That's sure of death without it' (3.1.155–6).

[1] Gordon Braden, *Renaissance Tragedy and the Senecan Tradition: Anger's Privilege*, 1985, pp. 67, 34. *Medea*
was among the Senecan plays Shakespeare knew, and its influence had been felt as recently as *Macbeth* and
Antony and Cleopatra. On *Macbeth*, see Inga-Stina Ewbank, 'The fiend-like queen: a note on "Macbeth"
and Seneca's "Medea"', *S.Sur.* 19 (1966), 82–94, and James C. Bulman, *The Heroic Idiom of Shakespearean
Tragedy*, 1985, pp. 175–7, and on *Antony*, Bulman, *Heroic Idiom*, p. 202.
[2] Further possible sources for minor details, as in Shakespeare's account in 2.1 of Coriolanus's triumphal
return to Rome, are noted in the Commentary. In 'Shakespeare and *The Orator*', *Bulletin de la Faculté
des Lettres de Strasbourg* 43 (1965), 813–33, Winifred Nowottny argues for the influence of this collection
of Alexandre Sylvain's declamations (trans. 1596) on *Cor.* 3.1.155–6 and 3.3.135–41, but the passages
could as easily have been prompted by Digges (see below) and the story of Camillus, or generated by the
Coriolanus material itself.
[3] Kenneth Muir, 'The background of *Coriolanus*', *SQ* 10 (1959), 137–46; see also Muir, *Sources*, ch. 32.
[4] Both step-sons had ties to the literary life of London. Dudley contributed commendatory verses to Jonson's
Volpone (1607), acted by the King's Men in 1605, and his brother Leonard Digges, an Oxford scholar and
translator, did the same for the Shakespeare First Folio; see Leslie Hotson, *I, William Shakespeare*, 1937,
pp. 203, 214, 217, and Schoenbaum, *Documentary Life*, pp. 181, 300, 313.
[5] On the extensive contemporary literature dealing with war and the professional soldier, see Paul A.
Jorgensen, *Shakespeare's Military World*, 1956, chs. 5, 6.

Montaigne's *Essays* was published in John Florio's translation in 1603, though perhaps available to Shakespeare earlier.[1] The significance of similarities of thought and phrasing has been much debated. While it is possible that they result from the independent response of like minds to Seneca, Cicero and Plutarch and that apparent parallels derive from classical commonplaces reproduced in Renaissance anthologies and handbooks,[2] there is good reason to think Shakespeare was reading Montaigne well before he wrote *The Tempest*, where borrowings from 'Of the Canniballes' (for 2.1.141 ff.) and 'Of Crueltie' (5.1.25–8) have been generally accepted.[3] However fortuitous in individual cases, parallels in phrasing and the first appearance in Shakespeare of vocabulary used in Florio's translation have a cumulative weight and, for *Hamlet* and *King Lear*, suggest a fairly wide-ranging acquaintance.[4]

Geoffrey Miles argues that, at a deeper level, Montaigne helped focus and shape Shakespeare's interest in the Stoic theme of constancy and that Montaigne's critique of the Stoic ideal is particularly helpful in understanding *Coriolanus* and *Antony and Cleopatra*.[5] Miles traces in the *Essays* a shift from early admiration to, especially in Book III, an increasing scepticism about the Stoic insistence that man can raise himself above humanity, a presumption that looks foolishly arrogant when one recognises that life is 'an action imperfect and disordered by its owne essence'.[6] Throughout, Montaigne wrestles with the conflicting claims of the public and private lives. His deep distrust of public performance as a threat to personal integrity is tempered by his recognition that as social beings we must adopt roles; the difficult task lies in negotiating these claims to learn what is appropriate to the role of human being – or, as he finally puts it in 'Of Experience', learning 'to play the man well and duely' (III, 13, 379).[7] The Shakespeare who wrote the intensely paradoxical late Roman tragedies would have found this Montaigne congenial, useful for more than pithy commonplaces, and Miles persuasively argues that Montaigne helped Shakespeare understand, and explore through the figure of Coriolanus, the dangerous contradictions within the Roman Stoic ideal of constancy, constructed as it was of both Senecan aspiration and insistence on

[1] Florio may have been personally known to Shakespeare, either through common ties to the Earl of Southampton or as members of ovelapping literary circles. Florio's translation was completed at least by 4 June 1600, when it was entered in the Stationers' Register. In 1600 Sir William Cornwallis states in his own *Essayes* that he has read 'divers of his [Montaigne's] peeces' in English (II4^r), although he does not name the translator, so it is possible that another 'Englished' Montaigne was circulating in manuscript.

[2] Alice Harmon, 'How great was Shakespeare's debt to Montaigne?', *PMLA* 57 (1942), 988–1008.

[3] The first was noted by Capell in 1781, the second by Eleanor Prosser in 'Shakespeare, Montaigne, and the rarer action', *S.St.* 1 (1965), 261–4.

[4] For *Hamlet*, see Harold Jenkins's judicious discussion in his Arden edn, 1982, pp. 108–10; Kenneth Muir summarises the evidence for *Lear* in Appendix 6 of his Arden edn, 1952, pp. 249–53. In *Mighty Opposites: Shakespeare and Renaissance Contrariety*, 1979, Robert Grudin argues for a possible influence of Montaigne's final essay, 'Of Experience', on *Ant.* (pp. 173–6), and Miles suggests a wider reading of the *Essays* for the same play (*Shakespeare and the Constant Romans*, pp. 88–91, 169). See also Robert Ellrodt, 'Self-consciousness in Montaigne and Shakespeare', *S.Sur.* 28 (1975), 37–50.

[5] Miles, *Shakespeare and the Constant Romans*, pp. 84–5 (ch. 5 is devoted to Montaigne).

[6] *Montaigne's Essays*, trans. John Florio, Everyman edn, 1965, III, 9, 237 ('Of Vanitie'); further citations by book, chapter and page number will be to this edn.

[7] Without arguing for a necessarily direct influence of Montaigne on Shakespeare, Joan Lord Hall discusses theatrical explorations of man's histrionic abilities in '"To play the man well and duely": role-playing in Montaigne and Jacobean drama', *Comparative Literature Studies* 22 (1985), 173–86.

being true to oneself, against all if necessary, and Cicero's idea of constancy as a decorous consistency found within a necessary conformity to universal nature and to what is socially possible.[1]

Beyond Montaigne's general contribution to Shakespeare's response to Plutarch (also one of Montaigne's favourite authors), I would suggest that at the time of writing *Coriolanus* Shakespeare read, or returned to, 'How One Ought to Governe His Will' III, 10).[2] In it Montaigne's own effort to maintain tranquillity by withholding himself from full engagement with the perturbations of public life is frequently illustrated by descriptions of the opposite behaviour of those who 'are without life, if without tumultuary agitation . . . They are busie that they may not be idle, or else in action for actions sake. They seeke worke but to be working' (p. 254). Such men 'cannot stand still' because to them public action is the only means of self-validation. In contrast, the need to conserve the self, to preserve the distinction between public role and private integrity, lies behind Montaigne's ambivalent attitude toward the necessarily theatrical nature of our lives. Since 'Most of our vacations [vocations] are like playes', and 'All the world doth practise stage-playing', he cautions, 'Wee must play our parts duly, but as the part of a borrowed personage. Of a visard and apparance [appearance], wee should not make a real essence' (p. 262). At times Coriolanus seems the man devoted to 'tumultuary agitation', lost in his public warrior role. But he also struggles with the problem of 'visard' and 'essence' for, unlike Plutarch's Coriolanus, Shakespeare's is endowed with an inchoate but intense private sense of self and fear that he will be irreparably compromised by playing any role that would falsify 'mine own truth' (3.2.122).

Shakespeare here re-explores concerns evident in other plays, and Montaigne is no necessary source for developing Coriolanus in this direction, but other details not found in Plutarch suggest a familiarity with III, 10. Shakespeare could have taken the name Cotus from Montaigne's comic anecdote connecting a King Cotys with choler against servants (p. 266).[3] Montaigne in this essay also quotes the passage from *Aeneid*, x, 693, that may lie behind Coriolanus's prayer for his son (5.3.72–5).[4] In Montaigne, characteristically, the Virgilian heroic metaphor is offered as a negative illustration of those who falsely 'assure themselves of their own strength' in 'contrary events'. Such are not to be imitated: 'They opinionate themselves resolutely to behold, and without perturbation to be spectatours of their Countries ruine, which whilome possessed and commaunded their full will' (p. 267). Discussing men who seek revenge, he quotes

---

[1] Miles, *Shakespeare and the Constant Romans*, pp. 149–68; also Brower, *Hero and Saint*, p. 144.

[2] Montaigne's differentiation in this chapter (III, 10, 260–1) between the material nourishment the body requires ('how good cheape our life may be maintained') and the different needs of our sense of our identity ('the custome and condition' which he calls 'Nature') may have contributed some of the terms of Lear's 'O reason not the need' speech (*Lear* 2.4.264–7).

[3] The choice would have been apt, since Coriolanus loses his temper and plays the bully with Aufidius's servants. The other two names lacking in 'The Life of Coriolanus' but usually thought to have come from elsewhere in Plutarch, Adrian and Nicanor, could have been found in other of Montaigne's essays, where there are several Adrians, though only one Nicanor.

[4] Shakespeare had earlier used the sea-mark image (*Oth.* 5.2.268; Sonnet 116.5), but not, as in Virgil, for a warrior in the midst of battle.

2 *Soldiers attacking a gate.* Bronze plaquette, Italy *c.* 1500, by the Master of Coriolanus. Although later influenced by translations of Shakespeare's play, Europe also displayed an independent response to the Coriolanus story in the visual arts as well as drama and opera

Cicero's observation that 'they drive themselves headlong, when once they are parted and past reason, and weakness soothes it selfe, and unawares is carried into the deepe' and soon observes that 'Our greatest agitations, have strange springs and ridiculous causes' (pp. 269, 270), a suggestive combination that could have prompted Coriolanus's rationalising soliloquy on 'Some trick not worth an egg' turning enemies into fastest friends (4.4.18–22). Finally, contemplating the modern falsification of true honour and reputation leads Montaigne to analyse the larger problem of reputation as a goal: 'All publike actions are subject to uncertaine and divers interpretations' (pp. 272–3; compare Aufidius, 4.7.49–50). The observations are commonplaces, yet that they should all appear in III, 10, together with a name and a Virgilian metaphor that appear in *Coriolanus*, suggests that Montaigne's essay may have contributed to Shakespeare's shaping of his primary source, North's Plutarch.

Equally important as a 'source' for Shakespeare's version of the Coriolanus story is of course his own historical period, since author as well as audience brought recent events and current preoccupations to their responses to classical subject matter. These will be the subject of the three sections of 'Contemporary contexts'.

Contemporary contexts

DEARTH, RIOTS, REBELLIONS

A series of riots in Northamptonshire, Leicestershire and Warwickshire, now collectively known as the 1607 Midland Revolt, presumably lies behind Shakespeare's decision to collapse Plutarch's two citizen rebellions – the first over usurers, the second over dearth of corn (i.e. grain) – into the riot that opens the play.[1] The Midland insurrections of 1607 were agrarian protests against the enclosure of formerly open-field farming units into commercially profitable large tracts of hedged-off sheep pasture, a procedure that meant fewer jobs for agricultural labourers and fewer acres devoted to grain production.[2] As the largest, most wide-spread rebellion since 1549 and, unlike most of its sixteenth-century predecessors, one in which economic and social grievances were not overshadowed by religious or political issues, it was disturbing in its own terms;[3] it also invoked the spectre of recent hard times when subsistence problems created by long-term economic and demographic changes were exacerbated by more immediate fears of suffering and starvation.

The 1590s witnessed both an increase in the rate of enclosure and an increasingly critical shortage of grain following four successive bad harvests from 1594 to 1597. Dearth, higher than normal mortality rates and sporadic rioting marked the 'famine years' of 1596–7;[4] the early seventeenth century threatened a repetition. As early as 1604 Sir Edward Montague, MP for Northamptonshire, warned parliament of the high degree of unrest over depopulation and enclosure in his county and petitioned for a redress of grievances to prevent more serious trouble.[5] The severe winter of 1606–7 boded a poor harvest to come, and fear of dearth grew during the spring of 1607.

---

[1] The connection was first made by E. C. Pettet, '*Coriolanus* and the Midlands insurrection of 1607', *S.Sur.* 3 (1950), 34–42.

[2] On the various forms of enclosure and contemporary concern with the resulting depopulation of towns, see Eric Kerridge, *Agrarian Problems in the Sixteenth Century and After*, 1969, pp. 94–133, and C. G. A. Clay, *Economic Expansion and Social Change: England 1500–1700*, 2 vols., 1984, I, 67–77. In 'The belly politic: *Coriolanus* and the revolt of language', *ELH* 59 (1992), 53–75, Arthur Riss links this background conflict 'between a communal and private organization of property' with Shakespeare's dramatisation in *Coriolanus* of the 'conflict between communal and private notions of the body' (p. 55).

[3] Edwin F. Gay, 'The Midland revolt and the inquisitions of depopulation of 1607', *Transactions of the Royal Historical Society*, n.s. 18 (1904), 196.

[4] R. B. Outhwaite, 'Dearth, the English crown and the "crisis of the 1590s"', in *The European Crisis of the 1590s*, ed. Peter Clark, 1985, pp. 28, 35. In *Feudalism to Capitalism: Peasant and Landlord in English Agrarian Development*, 1983, John E. Martin notes that, despite later recovery elsewhere, the Midlands suffered chronic grain shortages from the 1590s to the 1620s, and grain prices were rising steeply from 1601 to 1607 (pp. 161–2).

[5] Gay, 'The Midland revolt', p. 212.

The Midland rebels were quite clear about the connection between enclosures and grain shortages, price rises and the depopulation of towns whose inhabitants could no longer find agricultural employment or grow their own food on the now hedged-off common lands. After asserting their loyalty to the king, their manifesto, 'The Diggers of Warwickshire to all other Diggers', condemns those landlords who, interested only in 'their private gain', have 'depopulated and overthrown whole townes, and made therof sheep pastures, nothing profitable for our Commonwealth, for the common fields being layd open, would yeeld us much commodity, besides the increase of Corne, on which standes our life'. It is feared that even one poor harvest, such as that in prospect, would bring famine to rival that of the early fourteenth century, 'in King Edward the seconds time, when people were forced to eat Catts and doggs flesh, and women to eate theyr owne children'.[1]

Shakespeare may have known the manifesto, for the First Citizen's bitter complaint about class pride as well as greed – that 'our misery, is as an inventory to particularise their abundance; our sufferance is a gain to them' (1.1.16–17) – certainly echoes the Diggers' accusation about the 'devouring' enclosers: 'there is none of them but do taste the sweetness of our wantes'. Yet the manifesto's imagery of famine and cannibalism, and its stated preference to 'manfully die' while levelling hedge-rows rather than slowly starve, belong to the common language of enclosure protest; they appear in depositions made before inquiry commissions after other riots, as well as in sermons and other literature concerned with the causes of resistance, stretching back over the length of the sixteenth century.[2] On the stage, Parson Ball in *The Life and Death of Jacke Straw* (Q 1953) deplored the fact that 'rich men triumph to see the poore beg at their gate'.[3] Like the mutinous citizens in *Coriolanus*, the Midland rebels had real and substantial complaints against a system that denied them the basic staff of life. As the Diggers' manifesto suggests, they felt justified in themselves enforcing the king's anti-enclosure laws. In the play, Menenius's claim for the patricians' paternalistic care of the plebeians, given the fact that only commoners are suffering a grain shortage, rings as hollow as the admonitions of the county JPs who had in fact not enforced the government's legislation against hoarding, engrossing and depopulating enclosures.[4] It is surely no accident that one of the charges against Coriolanus, who argues against distributing corn to the poor and for the patricians' right to ignore the commoners' pleas, is that he 'would depopulate the city and / Be every man himself' (3.1.266–7). This is the only occurrence of 'depopulate' in the canon.

---

[1] BL MS Harl. 787, art. 11, reprinted in J. O. Halliwell (ed.), *The Marriage of Wit and Wisdom*, 1846, pp. 140–1. Although undated, the document is commonly assigned to 1607 and the Midland disturbances.

[2] On similar remarks recorded from previous rebellions, see Gay, 'The Midland revolt' (pp. 196–212); for the mid-century response both before and after Kett's 1549 revolt, see Whitney R. D. Jones, *The Tudor Commonwealth, 1529–1559*, 1970, pp. 52–4. Jones also notes (p. 53) similar sentiments in More's *Utopia* (1514), and Parker (p. 36) quotes a passage in *Utopia*, Book II, that expresses both the First Citizen's and the Diggers' accusation that the impoverished many are a necessary measure of the prosperity of the few.

[3] *The Life and Death of Jacke Straw*, Malone Society Reprints, 1957, line 79. The play was reprinted in 1604.

[4] Rebellion in time of dearth provoked both violent suppression and attempts to redress the underlying causes, such as commissions to investigate depopulation, orders that the poor be provided with corn, and anti-enclosure legislation. The problem was lack of enforcement, since the local JPs were frequently themselves among the offending gentry (Martin, *Feudalism to Capitalism*, pp. 173, 175).

Despite the fact that the Midland Revolt was non-violent and aimed only at levelling hedges and restoring common lands to the people's use, it alarmed the authorities for a number of reasons. It was large and apparently well organised as well as well-disciplined. Rioting began in Northamptonshire in early May, but soon three counties were involved, more were feared at risk, and in several places the levellers numbered as many as 5,000.[1] It was feared that local authorities had been too timid and that such 'lenitie' had only encouraged the protesters 'to gather themselves in greater multitudes, as well in that Countie [Northamptonshire], as in some others adjoyning'; hence the proclamation of 30 May 1607 urges using 'force of Armes' if necessary, and the county gentry were ordered to mobilise.[2] In this spirit of fierce repression, worthy of Coriolanus seeking the patricians' armed support against the tribunes and the commons, the Earl of Shrewbury on 2 June 1607 wrote to his brother in Bedfordshire, the Earl of Kent, that if the insurrection spread there he should not 'temporise' with the rioters but rather must be militarily prepared 'to cutt them of [f] at fyrst' and 'neyther to use any perswation at all till you have some 40 or 50 horss well apoynted, which will run over and cutt in peeces a thousand of suche naked rog[u]es as thos are'.[3] Unlike the Roman patricians, the Midland gentry responded. At the crisis point on 8 June 1607, the gentry with their armed retainers and household servants confronted a thousand rebels at Newton, Northamptonshire, killing forty or fifty and capturing others. The ringleaders were hanged, drawn and quartered, and their remains displayed in local market towns.[4]

Shakespeare doubtless had at least some personal knowledge of the rioters and their demands. His family still lived in Stratford-upon-Avon, Warwickshire, and he had begun amassing property and local influence in 1597 by buying one of the town's finest houses. In 1602 he invested in a sizeable acreage of land, both arable and pasture, north of the town, and in 1605 one-half interest in a lease of tithes which brought him a yearly income of £60.[5] Increasingly, he had a practical interest in the town's affairs and in the local struggle over enclosure. When Sir Edward Greville had tried to enclose town common lands in 1601, Shakespeare's friend Richard Quiney was among those who levelled the hedges and was sued by Greville, some of whose servants seem to have been responsible for the death of Quiney, then town bailiff, in 1602.[6] Shakespeare was possibly in Stratford at the time of the Midland Revolt for his daughter Susanna's marriage to John Hall on 5 June 1607;[7] the Warwickshire riots, both to the north and south of Stratford, had just taken place.[8] Later, in 1614, Shakespeare's interests were

---

[1] Gay, 'The Midland revolt', p. 215.

[2] 'A Proclamation for suppressing of persons riotously assembled for the laying open of Inclosures', 30 May 1607, in *Stuart Royal Proclamations*, ed. James F. Larkin and Paul L. Hughes, 2 vols., 1973, I, 153. Coriolanus warns the patricians of the dire ramification of their 'dangerous lenity': 'rebellion, insolence, sedition' (3.1.100, 71).

[3] The letter is reprinted in full as Appendix II in Gay, 'The Midland revolt', pp. 240–1.

[4] Gay, 'The Midland revolt', pp. 216–17; see also Martin, *Feudalism to Capitalism*, p. 167, and Roger Manning, *Village Revolts: Social Protest and Popular Disturbances in England, 1509–1640*, 1988, p. 232.

[5] Eccles, *Shakespeare in Warwickshire*, pp. 86, 101, 104; see also Schoenbaum, *Documentary Life*, ch. 13.

[6] Eccles, *Shakespeare in Warwickshire*, pp. 97–9. One of Quiney's sons later married Shakespeare's daughter Judith, 10 February 1616.

[7] *Ibid.*, p. 100.

[8] See the map on p. 34 of *An Atlas of Rural Protest in Britain 1548–1900*, ed. Andrew Charlesworth, 1983.

directly involved in an acrimonious and ultimately unsuccessful enclosure attempt at
nearby Welcombe; the town council was again opposed and, in rallying support from
those whose lands or financial interests were threatened, invoked the 1607 troubles
over enclosures, 'at the last dyggynge'.[1]

The underlying problems that sparked the month of wide-spread rioting in 1607
did not evaporate with the Newton suppression or the king's promise to investigate
unlawful enclosures. Sporadic, small-scale rioting continued through the rest of 1607
and 1608, sometimes against enclosing rural gentry, but sometimes, as at Coventry
in 1608 and 1609, over the city corporation's diversion of communal lands to private
uses.[2] In a letter of 2 June 1608 to the Earl of Salisbury, William Combe warned
of dearth in Warwickshire and the threat of resistance to enclosure by the common
people.[3] A proclamation of the same date orders that 'all Owners and Farmers, (having
Corne to spare) to furnish the markets rateably and weekely'.[4] The proclamation of 12
December 1608 vows to enforce statutes limiting malters' and brewers' use of grain,
and as late as 4 January 1609 another mentions continued dearth and high prices. In
London, grain had to be imported to relieve the poor and forestall the possibility of
food riots there.[5]

The Midland Revolt holds more than the immediate significance that sporadic disturbances and the feared dearth persisted throughout 1608.[6] Its effect, on Shakespeare
and his audience, also needs to be seen in the light of its embeddedness in a context
of popular insurrections. After each rising had been put down, in denunciatory official
documents its leaders were compared with their infamous predecessors and so added
to a list stretching back through Kett's rebellion of 1549 to Jack Cade's of 1450, and
frequently as far back as Wat Tyler, Jack Straw and the Great Rebellion of 1381. There
was also a literary tradition, pertinent to *Coriolanus*, of parallel lists of biblical, English
and Roman popular rebellions.[7] And the commoners who swelled rebellion's ranks
had their own long memories. Bartholomew Steere chose Enslow Hill in Oxfordshire
as the site for his 1596 rebellion for the same reason Robert Kett's followers were said
to have selected Mousehold Heath in 1549: both were in local tradition the sites of

[1] Eccles, *Shakespeare in Warwickshire*, p. 137. Shakespeare's own attitude toward enclosure cannot be
deduced with any certainty from his actions or the two surviving remarks recorded by the town clerk; for a
fuller account of the 1614 controversy and the reproduction of such documents as remain, see Chambers,
William Shakespeare, II, 141–52, and Eccles, *Shakespeare in Warwickshire*, pp. 136–8.
[2] Buchanan Sharp, *In Contempt of All Authority: Rural Artisans and Riot in the West of England, 1586–1660*,
1980, pp. 22–3. For the conflict in Coventry between commoners and city aldermen (the urban equivalent
of the powerful rural gentry), see Derek Hirst, *The Representative of the People? Voters and Voting in
England Under the Early Stuarts*, 1975, p. 52, and Charlesworth, *An Atlas of Rural Protest*, p. 36.
[3] Cited in Gay, 'The Midland revolt', p. 213 n. 3; Gay also quotes a letter of 12 August 1608 indicating that
enclosures continued, as did the people's discontent (p. 219 n. 2).
[4] Larkin and Hughes, *Stuart Royal Proclamations*, I, 186.
[5] F. J. Fisher, 'The development of the London food market, 1540–1640', in *London and the English Economy,
1500–1700*, ed. P. J. Corfield and N. B. Harte, 1990, p. 67.
[6] Martin notes that 'throughout the next decade' the 1607 rising 'was engraved in the minds of peasant and
authorities alike . . . Moreover, the passage into common usage of the terms "Levellers" and "Diggers" . . .
indicates the long-term impact of the Midlands Revolt' (*Feudalism to Capitalism*, p. 168).
[7] See Brents Stirling, *The Populace in Shakespeare*, 1949, pp. 131–50, for examples of double and sometimes
triple comparisons, and also Patterson, *Shakespeare and the Popular Voice*, pp. 38–45.

previous commoner risings.[1] While keeping in mind that for both sides any contemporary insurrection had a long history, two of the more recent seem to be particularly relevant to the characterisation of the citizens' mutiny that opens *Coriolanus*: the Oxfordshire rebellion of 1596 and the London riots of 1595.

While the Oxfordshire rising was poorly organised and dispersed when only ten or twenty men answered Steere's summons to Enslow Hill, it seriously alarmed the authorities because its leaders threatened violence against the gentry and because it was intended as more than an anti-enclosure protest in time of dearth. After levelling hedges, the rebels had planned to sack gentry houses for weapons, horses and provisions and then march to London, where they assumed the city apprentices would willingly rise again to join their cause.[2] Protests motivated by fear of dearth and starvation were always condemned and the ringleaders punished, but they were understandable. Such protesters claimed they sought not to revolutionise the political or social order but rather, after petitions had failed, to push those in authority into fulfilling their traditional paternalistic obligations.[3] Steere's abortive revolt raised the possibility of a much more fundamental social breakdown. In contrast with most of the earlier sixteenth-century rebellions, there was no local gentry leadership in 1596; even more disturbing, among the fifteen implicated, eleven were artisans and labourers, not husbandmen, and they were charged by Attorney-General Coke with being in comfortable circumstances and therefore without plausible reasons for rebelling.[4] It appeared that general social grievances, not specific economic ones, were at issue, and the intended alliance of rural artisans, labourers and apprentices with their London counterparts boded class war and revolutionary intentions. Steere told his followers that the 'world would never be well untill some of the gentlemen were knockt downe', assured them that 'the Commons, long sithens in Spaine did rise and kill all the gentlemen . . . and sithens that time have lyved merrily there', and that 'it was but a monethes work to overrunne England'.[5]

Despite the failure of the Enslow Hill rebellion, to the authorities it was clear that exemplary punishment was needed. After two months of local interrogation, the ringleaders were sent to London for questioning under torture and, after some twisting of the treason laws to include conspiracy to level hedges, executed in June 1597.[6] Knowledge of the intended Oxfordshire rising in late November 1596 may have led Shakespeare to add to Plutarch's peaceful protest the play's armed rebels and First Citizen's claim that killing Martius will bring down the price of corn. Such knowledge was not necessary, of course: *Coriolanus*'s deep class antagonism was already in Plutarch, and Shakespeare could have drawn on his researches into Hall

---

[1] Manning, *Village Revolts*, p. 223; John Walter, 'A "rising of the people"? The Oxfordshire rising of 1596', *P&P* 107 (1985), 107.

[2] Manning, *Village Revolts*, p. 221.

[3] John Walter and Keith Wrightson, 'Dearth and the social order in early modern England', *P&P* 71 (1976), 32.

[4] Manning, *Village Revolts*, p. 228.

[5] Quoted in *ibid.*, p. 224; see also Sharp, *In Contempt of All Authority*, pp. 38–9. The last two assertions appear in a paper drawn up in connection with the trial at Westminster, reprinted as Appendix 1 in Gay, 'The Midland revolt', p. 238.

[6] Walter, 'A "rising of the people"?', pp. 129–30; Manning, *Village Revolts*, pp. 226–8.

and Holinshed for the earlier rebellions of Cade and Tyler for *2 Henry VI*.[1] Still, as we have seen, the following spring Shakespeare was buying property in Stratford, where the continued dearth and suffering would make talk of social unrest likely,[2] and the trial and executions were held in London. The 1596 'rising' has, moreover, been proposed as the historical background for *A Midsummer Night's Dream* and *As You Like It*.[3]

The 1607 riots probably stirred memories of 1596 for some in Shakespeare's audience;[4] they certainly coloured the official response. The fact that the 1607 protesters were non-violent, that their manifesto proclaimed their loyalty to the king and the limited nature of their goal (local enclosure reform), and that they exhibited discrimination in attacking the hedge-rows of only the most flagrant offenders, should perhaps not have reinvoked Attorney-General Coke's 1596 vision of an armed commoner rebellion against the *status quo*. But as the protest developed, certain features were particularly disturbing and, to authorities lacking either a police force or a standing army, any signs of organised discontent posed a significant threat. First, like the abortive Oxfordshire rising, it was an entirely popular movement. Second, the local militia and trained bands proved unreliable; by June some had joined their rioting neighbours and others refused to attend the muster.[5] Third, and perhaps most threatening, radical discontent seemed to have spread beyond those who, in the authorities' eyes, could be said to have a 'legitimate' reason to protest.[6] Grain shortages and high prices spelled extreme hardship in both town and country, and as the protest movement spread it evinced glimmerings of a political awareness that basic social conflict lay behind the immediate economic difficulties and that rural artisans and labourers might have common cause with urban artisans and apprentices.[7] Rioters, who sometimes travelled many miles from their homes to attack targeted enclosures, were fed, housed, given tools and transported to protest sites by sympathetic villagers in adjacent

---

[1] In the introduction to his edn of *2H6*, 1991, Michael Hattaway finds that details of the 1381 Great Rebellion were incorporated into Cade's of 1450 to intensify the sense of a general social challenge beyond its local grievances (p. 24).

[2] On the exceptional severity of the dearth in Warwickshire in 1596–7, see J. M. Martin, 'A Warwickshire market town in adversity: Stratford-upon-Avon in the sixteenth and seventeenth centuries', *Midland History* 7 (1982), 36.

[3] For *MND*, see Theodore Leinwand, '"I believe we must leave the killing out": deference and accommodation in *A Midsummer Night's Dream*', in *Renaissance Papers*, ed. Dale B. J. Randall and Joseph A. Porter, 1986, pp. 17–20, and Patterson, *Shakespeare and the Popular Voice*, pp. 55–6; for *AYLI*, Richard Wilson, *Will Power: Essays on Shakespearean Authority*, 1993, pp. 65–81.

[4] Between 1550 and 1600 London's population grew from around 120,000 to 200,000, an increase dependent on massive immigration; see Roger Finlay and Beatrice Shearer, 'Population growth and suburban expansion', in *London 1500–1700: The Making of the Metropolis*, ed. A. L. Beier and Roger Finlay, 1986, p. 48. The largest segment of the immigrant population, jobless because of bad harvests or enclosures, was from the Midlands and the North (Manning, *Village Revolts*, p. 189).

[5] Martin, *Feudalism to Capitalism*, p. 173.

[6] The Privy Council (falsely) assumed that townspeople's interests differed from rural husbandmen's: in a 12 June 1607 letter to the Earl of Huntingdon, lord-lieutenant and thus responsible for Leicestershire, it declared the townsmen to have offended 'more heynouslie' because 'they had lesse pretence of greevance, having little or nothing to do with Enclosures' (quoted in Martin, *Feudalism to Capitalism*, p. 192).

[7] Manning, *Village Revolts*, p. 246; Patterson relates this possibility to *Coriolanus* in *Shakespeare and the Popular Voice*, pp. 135–41.

communities, and townspeople issued forth from Leicester and elsewhere, despite attempts to keep them within the city gates, to join in the levelling; even some town officials seemed dangerously sympathetic.[1] The 1596 Oxfordshire rising failed, but for a few weeks in 1607 Steere's dream of a broad-based commoner rebellion seemed to be materialising.

Such a disturbing possibility colours the interpretation offered in the initially sympathetic assize sermon delivered on 21 June 1607 by Robert Wilkinson to the Northamptonshire officials dealing with the revolt's aftermath; it was printed in London the same year. In the dedicatory epistle and for much of the sermon Wilkinson's evenhanded approach translates into some surprisingly sharp rebukes to the local gentry enclosers, since it is 'the excessive covetousness of some [that] hath caused the extreame want to other, and that want not well disgested hath rioted to the hazard of all'; the 'Oppression of the mighty' is as much to blame as 'the Rebellion of the manie'.[2] Yet the spectres of 1549 and 1596 hang over Wilkinson's continuing treatment of the protesters. Not only are they guilty of failing in Christian patience; what began as no more than the reformation of one abuse is declared to have escalated, inevitably since Satan is 'evermore the maister of rebellion', into a threat to all order: 'First they professe nothing, but to throwe downe enclosures, though that were indeed no part of common powre; but afterward they will reckon for other matters . . . and counsell is given to kill up Gentlemen, and they will levell all states [estates, classes] as they levelled bankes and ditches' (F2ᵛ). The prospect is of chaos come again, where 'both civill and divine law and all goe downe' because 'so many men so many Kings' (F2ᵛ–3ʳ). Ironically, of course, in publishing this portrait of the authorities' worst fears, Wilkinson also offers the protesters' grievances and the possibility of violent social struggles to an audience beyond the Midland counties where it had already been largely contained.[3]

The nascent class consciousness that seemed to surface in the countryside in 1596 and 1607 was also a threatening potential in at least some of the outbursts of disorder in the capital, and London riots were larger than most rural enclosure protests as well as more difficult to control and more likely to threaten or enact personal violence. Here, too, both official and popular memories were long, stretching back to the Ill May-Day Riots of 1517.[4] The late-Elizabethan 'epidemic of disorder' dates from the Ludgate Prison riot of 1581; it peaked in 1595 in a period of prolonged disorder

---

[1] Gay, 'The Midland revolt', p. 214, and Martin, *Feudalism to Capitalism*, p. 176. Martin notes that for his seemingly half-hearted efforts to quell the rioting in its early stages, the mayor of Leicester was replaced, and the mayor, sheriff and JPs of Northampton were later prosecuted in Star Chamber (pp. 170–3).

[2] *A Sermon preached at North-hampton the 21. of June last past, before the Lord Lieutenant of the county and the Commissioners there assembled upon occasion of the late Rebellion and Riots in those parts committed* (1607), A3ʳ⁻ᵛ; further references will follow quotations in the text.

[3] Not only sermons but royal proclamations and pious tracts arguing against rebellion had to state the people's grievances if they were going either to pose solutions or refute the claims. For other instances, see Patterson, *Shakespeare and the Popular Voice*, pp. 41–3.

[4] The 1517 disturbance was the subject of the collaborative play *Sir Thomas More* to which Shakespeare may have contributed the scene in which More dissuades a crowd from rioting (see Textual Analysis, pp. 296–7, 297n. 3, 298 below).

unparalleled between the accession of the Tudors and 1641.[1] At least thirteen insurrections broke out in different parts of London and Southwark, most during the month of June. Two were food riots in which apprentices seized over-priced food-stuffs (butter in one, fish in the other); practising popular market regulation such as that desired by *Coriolanus*'s First Citizen when he hopes to have corn 'at our own price' (1.1.8), they sold the food at what they considered fair prices. The arrest and punishment of the butter-rioters sparked further violence and the voicing of more pervasive and proto-revolutionary discontent. On 29 June a large crowd assembled on Tower Hill intending, according to the crown prosecution, to seize the city armoury, rescue prisoners, and kill the lord mayor and burn his house. Martial law was proclaimed and a provost-marshal appointed, backed by thirty cavalry, with the power of summary execution. The leaders of the rebellion were tried for treason and five were executed on 24 July.[2]

The severity of the charge and punishment of the Tower Hill rebels set a precedent for the handling of the Enslow Hill conspirators the next year. Indeed, following the Oxfordshire scare, a conference of judges in 1597 decided that, in retrospect, the butter-rioters of 1595 should have been tried for treason, not misdemeanour charges of riot and sedition: as much as rescuing prisoners or threatening to kill the lord mayor, popular market regulation 'constituted an attempt to alter the laws of the realm by force' and was tantamount to levying war against the queen.[3] There was reason for continued concern: another disturbance occurred in October 1595; in July 1596 the popular writer Thomas Deloney was arrested for publishing a ballad containing a complaint of dearth of corn that might aggravate the commons' discontent, and in September there was another spate of seditious libelling. Two years later, in the summer of 1598, there was more apprentice agitation and calls for a rising against the lord mayor.[4] It is perhaps not surprising that, despite Essex's failure in 1601 to raise the city on behalf of his rebellion, the executed London apprentices of 1595 as well as the Enslow Hill conspirators of 1596 were brought up at his trial as examples of resistance to the crown's authority which had been declared treason.[5]

Shakespeare's citizens' belief that disturbing the peace brings results was not unfounded, however. As with enclosure riots, the use of force could only prevent a further breakdown of order when combined with official efforts to improve food

[1] Manning, *Village Revolts*, pp. 202, 208. Valerie Pearl, 'Change and stability in seventeenth-century London', *London Journal* 5 (1979), 3–34, and Steve Rappaport, *Worlds within Worlds: Structures of Life in Sixteenth-century London*, 1989, stress London's overall stability, yet both agree that 1593–6 proved a time of real tension and suffering, when the price of flour more than doubled and real wages had fallen by more than 23 per cent (Rappaport, *Worlds within Worlds*, p. 170).

[2] Details in this paragraph are taken from Manning, *Village Revolts*, pp. 208–10; see also M. J. Power, 'London and the control of the "crisis" of the 1590s', *History* 70 (1985), 379. Theodore B. Leinwand traces connections between the 1595 London riots and *Coriolanus* in 'Shakespeare and the middling sort', *SQ* 44 (1993), 297–9.

[3] Manning, *Village Revolts*, pp. 206–7.

[4] Peter Clark, 'A crisis contained? The condition of English towns in the 1590s', in *The European Crisis of the 1590s*, ed. Peter Clark, 1985, p. 54; Power, 'London and the "crisis" of the 1590s', p. 380.

[5] G. B. Harrison, *The Life and Death of Robert Devereux, Earl of Essex*, 1937, pp. 298–9; on the use of the Enslow Hill conspirators, see Walter, 'A rising of the people?', p. 130.

supplies and redress grievances. Soaring bread prices in 1596 produced increased poverty and vagrancy, but also a swifter official response than in 1595: in July 1596 the London aldermen ordered a collection of money for the poor, and in August weekly distributions of bread;[1] additional grain was imported, as it was again in 1608 after the bad harvest that provoked the Midland Revolt. The various measures adopted by the city authorities, in conjunction with the national Poor Laws enacted by the 1597–8 parliament, kept London from following the Midlands in 1607–8 when dearth threatened to recreate earlier crisis conditions. Disorder was contained, but the staging of a corn shortage and riots in fifth-century B.C. Rome would have seemed anything but 'ancient history' to *Coriolanus*'s first audiences, though their responses may well have differed depending on the play's venue: the poorer, more largely artisanal spectators at the Globe, or the wealthier Blackfriars audience, less immediately affected by food shortages but more threatened by the prospect of rebellion. All would have seen the effects on the poor in the streets and, for those not themselves suffering, in the increased amount they were taxed for relief of the poor; all would have experienced the high prices of bread in 1607–8 and of fuel from 1606 to 1608.[2]

Although *Coriolanus*'s citizens' militant response might have proved disquieting to some in the audience, their accusations against the patricians had, in this context, a kind of official sanction, and the protagonist's opposition to the distribution of imported corn would have sounded particularly harsh at a time when the London city fathers were doing the opposite and the philanthropic sharing of food was being urged on all from the pulpit. Shakespeare uses the language of the recent subsistence crisis to heighten the impact of the Plutarchan figure's refusal of traditional communal responsibilities.[3] Coriolanus becomes linked with the gentry whose enclosures produced depopulation, unemployment, poverty and, in years of bad harvests, extreme dearth; he even believes the common people deserve their suffering. His comment to Menenius that the citizens should 'wash their faces / And keep their teeth clean' (2.3.54–5) has a subtext beyond its contemptuous reference to personal hygiene, for Shakespeare gives him an apparently proverbial phrase denoting hunger and starvation: as argued by one speaker in the 1597–8 parliamentary debates that produced the Poor Laws and acts against engrossing and enclosure, 'no realm . . . can either long have joy in the streets or continuance in the State, where there groweth cleanness of teeth through scarcity of bread'.[4] Nor would Menenius's exculpatory appeal to a metaphysical explanation for dearth – 'The gods, not the patricians, make it' (1.1.59) – have seemed the necessarily proper response. While the government occasionally referred to dearth as God's punishment, 'in its

---

[1] Beier and Finlay, introduction to *London 1500–1700: The Making of the Metropolis*, p. 18; Rappaport, *Worlds within Worlds*, p. 158.

[2] Jeremy Boulton, *Neighbourhood and Society: A London Suburb in the Seventeenth Century*, 1987, p. 43.

[3] J. L. Simons discusses Coriolanus as a divisive figure for the real audience as well as its social and political counterparts on stage in '"Antony and Cleopatra" and "Coriolanus", Shakespeare's heroic tragedies: a Jacobean adjustment', *S.Sur.* 26 (1973), 100; see also Marion Trousdale, '*Coriolanus* and the playgoer in 1609', in *The Arts of Performance in Elizabethan and Early Stuart Drama*, ed. Murray Biggs *et al.*, 1991, pp. 126–7.

[4] Quoted in J. E. Neale, *Elizabeth I and her Parliaments 1584–1601*, 1957, p. 340.

public utterances it almost invariably chose to explain dearth as the result of the evil practices of the covetous and uncharitable'.[1]

How closely Shakespeare's language mirrors that of the 1607–8 crisis and its attendant heightening of class oppositions is also clear from contemporary pamphlets cranked out while the theatres were closed by plague and aimed at a popular audience. In *The Great Frost* (1608), probably by Thomas Dekker, a London citizen blames the high cost of fuel that endangers the poor on 'the unconscionable and unmercifull raising of prices' by those who 'meant to lay the poore on the Rack', and his interlocutor offers similar news from the country (B3ʳ). Dekker's *Worke for Armorours* (1609) – the rest of whose title page reads 'or, The Peace is Broken. Open warres likely to happen this yeare, 1609: God helpe the Poore, The rich can shift' – allegorically figures through two princesses and their followers a 'quarrel between money and poverty' set, its topographical references suggest, in London. Poverty and her 'army' are not sentimentalised – her counsellors include Discontent and Sloth as well as 'Beggery, Miserie' (C2ᵛ) – but Money is an even more vicious oppressor than that envisioned by the Diggers' manifesto or *Coriolanus*'s citizens. Her counsellors are 'Covetousnesse, Parsimony, Deceipt, Providence, Monopoly, Violence, Usury' (D3ʳ), and she charges her followers

to hoord up your corne till it be musty, and then bring it forth to infect these needy *Barbarians* . . . let mice and rats rather bee feasted by you, and fare well in your garners, then the least and weakest amongst *Poverties* starved infantry, should get but one mouthfull, let them leape at crusts, it shall be sport enough for us, and our wealthy subjects about us, to laugh at them. (F1ʳ)

Coriolanus's 'barbarians' (3.1.240), 'musty superfluity' (1.1.210) and 'rats' (1.1.233) are all here; elsewhere in *Worke for Armorours*, the poor are referred to as dogs and 'rascal deere' (compare Menenius at 1.1.142) and the rich as 'Cormorants'. And one of the proverbs Coriolanus attributes to the complaining plebeians – 'That hunger broke stone walls' (1.1.189) – is enacted by Dekker's allegorical character Hunger (C3ʳ).

The topicality of dearth and threatened rebellion is not the *raison d'être* for turning to the Coriolanus story in 1608, but by recasting Plutarch's introductory narrative in this way and deploying throughout language charged with contemporary significance, Shakespeare provides an effective dramatic hook with which to snag his audience's attention. The play's violent opening aims to enlist its audience members in its events and, more significantly, its debates on a personal, even visceral level. Roman history and politics are set firmly in an immediate, still-pressing context, enhanced by the fact that the entering 'company of mutinous citizens' were almost certainly dressed as Jacobean labourers and artisans.[2] When the patricians enter in togas, their words may be cued by Plutarch, but they continue to fit the non-theatrical context of official and aristocratic responses. As the number of sources suggests, Menenius's placatory belly fable had long been a staple of Elizabethan common-weal theory. Martius's contempt for the commons and insistence on violent suppression could have been lifted from

---

[1] Walter and Wrightson, 'Dearth and the social order', p. 31.
[2] See pp. 63–4 below for a discussion of costuming in the Roman plays.

the Earl of Shrewsbury's 1607 letter to his brother. Such an emphatically 'local' initial context meant that as Plutarch's Roman history unfolded, it would continually resonate with contemporary applications that lent immediacy to the story.

POLITICS AND THE FRANCHISE

Rebellion and questions of representation are naturally linked in *Coriolanus* when the citizens' mutiny gains them not only corn but five new, popularly elected officials to look out for their interests. More than this natural link makes the issue of the franchise of interest: at the centre of *Coriolanus* lies an election – indeed the dramatisation of a whole selection process – which goes so terribly wrong that it ends in the trial and banishment of the candidate and provokes a new rebellion of its own. In *Coriolanus* the struggle to command the people's 'voices' – indeed the struggle over whose voices should count – dominates Acts 2 and 3. Plutarch offers the basis for some of these eminently theatrical scenes, but Shakespeare shaped his material to capitalise on its contemporary reverberations, both in the process itself and in the issues raised when that process breaks down.

The modern idea of elections – as popular contests between candidates with differing ideological platforms that are decided by the counting of ballots cast by those entitled to vote – only slowly gained significance in this period. Nor was it a welcome development to either the crown or the ruling oligarchies of the boroughs and counties. Popular elections potentially bred disquiet and 'factious humours'; hence, to avoid even the appearance of division between factions and classes any contest at all was, if possible, forestalled.[1] In many towns and certainly in London, the slow concentration of political power in the mayor and court of aldermen had by the early seventeenth century managed to restrict the filling of most importance offices to a process of selection among themselves on the basis of seniority.[2] In elections for parliament, county aristocrats and gentry (often joined by courtiers, even the monarch) manoeuvred among themselves in the pre-election process to ensure that only two candidates for the two posts would be offered to the electorate. In this way, no more than simple acclamation (favourable shouts and cheers, 'voices') was required from the voters, and no candidate need pursue the distasteful and demeaning task of canvassing for votes. In a highly status-conscious society which valued public tranquillity and unanimous acquiescence in the *status quo*, 'election' was based not on political positions or promises of future service; rather, it constituted the community's confirmation of a candidate's personal worth and social standing; rejection brought deep dishonour to the individual as well as to those who had nominated him.[3] Any actual contest was likely to produce embittered

[1] Hirst, *The Representative of the People?*, p. 12 and ch. 3; see also Peter Clark and Paul Slack (eds.), introduction to *Crisis and Order in English Towns, 1500–1700*, 1972, pp. 21–2.
[2] Hirst, *The Representative of the People?*, pp. 47–9; Robert Ashton, *The City and the Court, 1603–1643*, 1979, p. 10. For a more general survey of borough practices, see Mark A. Kishlansky, *Parliamentary Selection: Social and Political Choice in Early Modern England*, 1986, pp. 31–7.
[3] Kishlansky sees this traditionalist view of the selection for parliamentary office as more like the bestowal of knighthood, a ratification of what one is and has done, than a modern election (*Parliamentary Selection*, pp. 16, 22–5). On the consequent bitterness over rejection, see *ibid.*, pp. 79–80.

rival camps that could, and often did, cause the whole community problems for years to come.[1]

In this respect, each step in a contested election proved more dangerous because it stripped anonymity and forced neighbours visibly to take sides: if election by voice did not indicate which candidate had the majority, the next resort was by view (either show of hands or separating into partisan groups), and the last was individual polling.[2] Contested elections challenged the local authorities and exposed the failure of the patriarchal system adequately to sift possible candidates and mediate among potential rivals before election day. To be forced to the stage of polling was not merely inconvenient in the time spent determining who among those present was actually a qualified freeholder; it could provoke social antagonism. The principle of one man, one vote violated the status norms which governed other community relations, and gentlemen might refuse to be counted 'where fellows without shirts challenge a voice as good as mine'.[3] With personal honour at stake and vilification of opponents common, tempers could flare, and scuffles or even drawn swords were not unknown. The 1601 Denbighshire election was dissolved when violence broke out between the candidates' supporters, and Sir John Salusbury, one of the candidates, observed that 'the preparations made for the election were more befitting a civil war'.[4]

In such a context the consular selection process in Acts 2 and 3 of *Coriolanus*, and the attitudes displayed there, would have made a good deal of sense to a Jacobean audience, and Shakespeare nudges Plutarch's account of the workings of the Roman oligarchy in a contemporary direction.[5] Eliminating Plutarch's platform of several candidates, Shakespeare makes Coriolanus the senate's unanimous nominee, presented to the commonalty for its ratification, and the play underlines the parallels by shifting from classical to contemporary status designations: the only offer of the consulship that counts for Coriolanus is 'the suit of the gentry to him / And the desire of the nobles' (2.1.212–13). Plutarch's description of the market-place ceremony in the gown of humility offers an analogue to canvassing for votes, but Shakespeare replaces the candidate's acquiescence in Plutarch with disdain for the plebeian voices, 'needless vouches' of an honour 'which first we do deserve' (2.3.99–103). Coriolanus raises to a principle the senate's practical assumption that political office is theirs to bestow; one need only go through the customary rituals with the citizens to ensure election: 'The senate, Coriolanus, are well pleased / To make thee consul'; now 'go fit you to

[1] *Ibid.*, pp. 83–4 and, for an extended example from 1614, pp. 85–101.
[2] On the selection sequence, see *ibid.*, pp. 5–7, 62, and Hirst, *The Representative of the People?*, p. 238 n. 21.
[3] Sir Henry Maynard, quoted in Kishlansky, *Parliamentary Selection*, p. 61. On the residual gentry belief that status rather than numbers was what really counted, see also Hirst, *The Representative of the People?*, p. 14.
[4] Quoted in Kishlansky, *Parliamentary Selection*, p. 58 n. 14; for other examples of election violence or its threat, see *ibid.*, pp. 49–55, 59, and for 'the acerbic tinge of personal invective' that helped generate such dangerous passions, pp. 80–3.
[5] Using *Coriolanus* to introduce his own analysis of electoral procedures in early modern England, Kishlansky discusses some of Shakespeare's alterations in *Parliamentary Selection*, pp. 4–8; see also Parker, pp. 41–3. In *Will Power*, ch. 4, Wilson sees the play's handling of its political struggle as solidly grounded in Shakespeare's Stratford viewpoint on the troubled 1601 election of Sir Fulke Greville as MP for Warwickshire.

the custom and / Take to you . . . Your honour with your form' (2.2.127–8, 137–9). The traditional 'form' breaks down when the commoners finally refuse to endorse the senate's nominee; an apparently straightforward selection procedure takes on all the dangerous animus of a contested election. With the tribunes' call for Coriolanus's arrest and punishment for treason the play departs from English electoral practices, but the wounded pride and desire for revenge following electoral defeat evident in contemporary examples would have given added urgency to the sight of Coriolanus's and the tribunes' supporters squaring off for violent confrontation. The kind of internecine gentry feuding that local authorities feared would result from contested elections here threatens a civil war between classes.[1]

In raising to prominence and altering Plutarch's account of the electoral process and popular trial for treason, in which Coriolanus is sentenced by unanimous shouts, Shakespeare explores a political model with a wide franchise, one in which electoral choice is now made on ideological as well as personal and social grounds. In so doing he was touching on confusions and undercurrents that would later become sharper features of the political landscape of pre-revolutionary England. The whole question of the franchise in the late sixteenth and early seventeenth century was in practice rather ill-defined, and the right to choose candidates might vary with locale. In the countryside the traditional forty-shilling freehold requirement laid down by statute in 1430 no longer offered clear instructions to local sheriffs, for proliferating forms of land tenure had introduced confusion, and inflation had eroded its restrictive force. Town authorities varied in what they considered the equivalent in rent, but the increased power of the town corporations and the exclusiveness of the guilds seem to have effected a narrowing of the franchise in urban areas.[2] In an overview, historians see little political awareness in the modern sense before the 1620s, which were marked by the House of Commons's efforts to widen the franchise in order to break the power of town oligarchies and by more vigorous canvassing among 'the vulgar', often on national issues on which the candidates took positions.[3]

What became more common later was not unknown earlier, however. There were instances in which the people rebelled against their assigned role as acquiescent 'voices', although commoner candidates were almost always unsuccessful before the widening of the franchise.[4] As early as 1614 London voters rejected the proposed candidates for parliament, reportedly because of their close connections to the

---

[1] There were always fears that gentry discontent would spread to the lower orders: when a second election was called for in Buckinghamshire in 1604, the Privy Council warned the local authorities to take care 'respectinge the Mean and inferior sorte of that Cuntrie [county] whom this busines of severall elleccions hath afflicted and troubled' (quoted in Hirst, *The Representative of the People?*, p. 191).

[2] Hirst, *The Representative of the People?*, pp. 29–43, 51.

[3] *Ibid.*, pp. 60–75, 142. In contrast, Kishlansky does not find, except in a few isolated cases, ideology as a factor in the parliamentary process before 1640 (*Parliamentary Selection*, p. 16).

[4] J. H. Plumb, 'The growth of the electorate in England from 1600 to 1715', *P&P* 45 (1969), 94; Plumb notes that in the 1580s the Puritans seemed the first to realise the political value of the electorate in bringing about changes opposed by the crown and corporation oligarchies. J. E. Neale describes the successful campaign of the Puritan Job Throckmorton in Warwick in 1586 (*The Elizabethan House of Commons*, 1949, pp. 250–4).

court.¹ And, as in other towns, London citizens were not always satisfied with the actions of their local political and economic authorities. Within the livery companies there were complaints against guild officials by journeymen and handicraftsmen who were virtually unenfranchised because below the rank of liveryman;² the unrepresented sometimes revolted and attempted to form breakaway associations of their own. Some in *Coriolanus*'s first audience – journeymen, apprentices, small craftsmen – might well have identified on a local, personal level with the 'mutinous citizens', not only as bread rioters but as effectively powerless workers struggling against the wealthy city elite who ruled from on high through their self-selected lord mayor and aldermen. Fluid terminology encouraged such an identification, for contemporary dictionaries defined 'senator' as 'An Alderman, or grave Magistrate of a citie'. 'Senate' sometimes was understood as the Roman equivalent of parliament, sometimes as 'The Counsell house, where the Magistrates of a citie assemble themselves'.³

Local and national applications for the Roman city-state could thus easily overlap and, given the patterned hierarchical organisation of life in Renaissance England, London's Common Council in function and powers roughly paralleled the House of Commons in parliament.⁴ There, questions of the subjects' rights, liberties and the privileges of their representative body came immediately to the fore in explicit, theoretical terms in the early days of James's first parliament (1604–10). The 1604 disputed election in Buckinghamshire provoked immediate confrontation over whether the House of Commons was privileged to be final judge in the election of its own members. James's absolutist insistence that the Commons had no innate, inherited rights of its own but rather 'derived all manner of privilege from him' was met by *The Form of Apology and Satisfaction to be presented to his Majesty*, in which the Commons purported to teach their 'misinformed' new king that 'our privileges and liberties are our right and due inheritance, no less than our very lands and goods', as well as to explain its position on specific economic grievances.⁵ Any infringement of 'the very fundamental privileges of our House' was equally a threat to the 'rights and liberties of the whole Commons of your realm of England'.⁶ It is for 'the whole Commons' that

¹ Hirst, *The Representative of the People?*, p. 143.
² Ashton, *The City and the Court*, pp. 6–8, 56–8. Less than a fifth of those who were companymen and free of the city 'wore the livery', though liverymen dominated the guilds' social, economic and political life (Rappaport, *Worlds within Worlds*, pp. 218–19).
³ Both definitions from John Bullokar, *An English Expositor* (1616). John Higgins, *Huloets Dictionarie* (1572), indicates both the analogous city and national bodies: 'common counsayle house, as the convocation or parliament house'. Compare Shakespeare's use in the prologue-chorus to Act 5 of *Henry V*: 'How London doth pour out her citizens! / The Mayor with all his brethren in best sort, / Like to the senators of th'antique Rome, / With the plebeians swarming at their heels' (5.0.24–7).
⁴ Ashton, *The City and the Court*, pp. 6–8, where he also notes that the functions and power of the Court of Aldermen were probably more analogous to the Privy Council than to the House of Lords.
⁵ The terms of this struggle seem reflected in *Coriolanus* in the senate's assumption, cited above, that the consulship is patrician property, to be bestowed as it chooses, and in the language of Volumnia's delight at the prospect: 'I have lived / To see inherited my very wishes'; she has no doubt that 'Our Rome' will make her son consul (2.1.172–6).
⁶ King James's assertion of the king's prerogative and authority is quoted from J. H. Hexter, 'Power, struggle, parliament, and liberty in early Stuart England', *Journal of Modern History* 50 (1978), 35; the *Apology* from J. R. Tanner, *Constitutional Documents of the Reign of James I*, 1960, p. 221. Although the *Apology* was not formally presented to the king, he knew its contents, and it was repeatedly referred to by MPs in later parliaments.

the House claimed to speak, and for this reason it should be heeded in matters of 'civil estate and government', for 'the voice of the people, in the things of their knowledge, is said to be as the voice of God'.[1] Despite the fact that the House of Commons was composed largely of gentry, lawyers and wealthy merchants, in such statements and at least some of its actions, such as the enactment of the Poor Laws in 1597–8 and its later opposition to purveyance and monopolies, it could be seen as standing for the 'commonalty'.

The appositeness of *Coriolanus* to the political tug-of-war over the locus of authority being staged in James's first parliament has not been lost on students of the play, and it has received more analysis by critics than the municipal applications.[2] Classical precedents for parliamentary procedures had been raised earlier, as when Thomas Cartwright had been questioned in 1591 about whether he had stated the subversive belief that 'in every monarchy there ought to be certain magistrates like to the Spartaine Ephori' (Spartan analogues to the Roman tribunes),[3] or when in Queen Elizabeth's last parliament her spokesman had argued for certain rights for the Speaker of the House on the basis that the Speaker's position in the House was analogous to that of a Roman consul in the senate.[4] King James's difficulty with the independent-minded members of the House of Commons in his first parliamentary session provoked repeated references to them as 'Tribunes of the people' in his opening address to the second session.[5] The Earl of Salisbury's report of his chiding the Commons in the king's name in February 1606 used the phrase,[6] and the term, applied to particular members, seemed to gain wide currency: Sir Edward Hoby, reporting to Sir Thomas Edmondes directly after an inflammatory speech on 14 February 1606 by John Hare which described the Treasury as 'a royal cistern', suggested that 'if your lordship had heard them, you would have said that Hare and [Lawrence] Hyde had represented the tribunes of the people'.[7] For arguing against purveyance in the same year, Henry Yelverton was dubbed 'the old Tribune of the house'.[8] Despite the Commons's failure to gain its proposed legislation, a new spirit was evident, and some appeared sufficiently committed to limiting the royal prerogative that they might provide leadership for a troublesome 'popular

---

[1] Tanner, *Constitutional Documents*, p. 230.

[2] Leah Marcus, however, locates the play's political context in the jurisdictional disputes between the London corporation and the crown which resulted in a new city charter in 1608 that guaranteed the city's 'liberties and franchises' (*Puzzling Shakespeare: Local Reading and its Discontents*, 1988, pp. 208–9).

[3] Quoted from Matthew Sutcliffe's account of the government's inquiry, *Examinations and Confrontations on a Scurrilous Treatise . . . published by M. Kellison* (1606), in Clifford Chalmers Huffman, '*Coriolanus*' *in Context*, 1971, p. 142. The ephors were understood to have the right to 'curbe and bridle' the Spartan kings when they inclined to tyranny (*OED* Ephor *sb* 1); my thanks to F. J. Levy for pointing out the revolutionary nature of such a belief.

[4] W. Gordon Zeeveld, '"Coriolanus" and Jacobean politics', *MLR* 57 (1962), 326.

[5] William Cobbett, *Parliamentary History of England*, 36 vols., 1806–20, I, 1071–2.

[6] In a report to the Lord Treasurer of Scotland; see Hirst, *The Representative of the People?*, p. 168.

[7] Zeeveld, '"Coriolanus" and Jacobean politics', p. 328. Zeeveld relates the image of the 'royal cistern' and James's redefinition of himself as *fidus depositorius* to the belly fable in *Coriolanus* (p. 333).

[8] *The Parliamentary Diary of Robert Bowyer, 1606–1607*, ed. David Harris Willson, 1931, p. 123 n. 1, which quotes Dudley Carleton's letter to John Chamberlain, 17 April 1606. Since purveyance was the crown's right to purchase carts and goods at below market prices, attacking this practice indirectly challenged the royal prerogative.

party'.[1] In 1610, looking back over the first parliament, Lord Chancellor Ellesmere worried that 'the popular state ever since the beginning of his Majesty's gracious and sweet government hath grown big and audacious, and in every session of parliament swelled more and more. And if way be still given unto it (as of late hath been) it is to be doubted what the end will be.'[2]

The extent to which what was happening in James's first parliament would have reverberated with Shakespeare's audience doubtless varied, but London was full of courtiers, lawyers, clients, visiting gentry and influential merchants who all had a stake in what transpired between the king and parliament. Shakespeare's audience, especially at the Blackfriars Theatre, probably included some who were or would be MPs, and many more of sufficient standing to have voted in parliamentary elections and to be directly and financially concerned with how the Commons was succeeding in its campaign against monopolies and other abuses of the royal prerogative, as well as the extent of the subsidy granted to the king. Parliament was debating and resisting, not acquiescing quietly to the crown's dictates, and controversy provokes discussion. Even in the last years of Elizabeth's reign, parliamentary activity was no secret beyond its doors. During the monopoly debates of 1601 Secretary Cecil complained that 'Parliament matters are ordinarily talked of in the streets. I have heard myself, being in my coach, these words spoken aloud: "God prosper those that further the overthrow of these monopolies. God send the prerogative touch not our liberty."'[3] Even allowing for exaggeration by a concerned member of the Privy Council, it is evident that what went on inside parliament enjoyed a fair currency outside and that others, besides a few fractious MPs, could see that particular grievances might involve larger constitutional questions.

Shakespeare makes his version of Plutarch available for consideration in this light by devoting the middle of the play to the political process whose breakdown is the catalyst for the protagonist's personal tragedy. And in 3.1 Coriolanus places the immediate situation – the senate's concession of tribunes to represent the people's interests – in the context of the larger, theoretical, issue of divided authority.[4] The tribunes argue at the same level the opposing case. As Shakespeare had borrowed typical complaints and accusations from contemporary food and enclosure riots, he sharpens linguistic reference to parliamentary debates over the scope of royal authority by colouring the struggle between Coriolanus and the people's representatives with the politically charged words 'liberties' and 'prerogative'. The tribunes three times warn the citizens they are in danger of losing their 'liberties', one of which includes reference to 'the charters that you bear / I'th'body of the weal' (2.3.166–7; see also 2.3.200–3, 3.1.195).

[1] As terms for the government's critics, 'the popular party', as well as 'the patriots' and 'the populars', are cited in D. H. Willson, 'The Earl of Salisbury and the "court" party in parliament 1604–1610', *American Historical Review* 36 (1931), 279.
[2] Quoted in Theodore K. Rabb, 'The role of the Commons', *P & P* 92 (1981), 77.
[3] Quoted in Hirst, *The Representative of the People?* p. 178.
[4] Some see direct, critical parallels between King James and Coriolanus. Shannon Miller argues that the play's subversive 'fusion of James's conflicts with the Common Law' and Coriolanus's growth into a traitor offers 'an image of King James as a traitor' ('Topicality and subversion in William Shakespeare's *Coriolanus*', *SEL* 32 (1992), 288, 295). See also Patterson, *Shakespeare and the Popular Voice*, p. 123.

The form in which the tribunes will sentence Coriolanus – 'It shall be so / I'th'right and strength o'th'commons' – consciously insists 'on the old prerogative' of the people's traditional privilege of judging traitors (3.3.14–18).[1] In the election process and the arguments over the validity of time-honoured 'prerogative' and 'custom', *Coriolanus* presents the political struggles of ancient Rome in terms pertinent to the politics of early-seventeenth-century England.

ESSEX AND RALEGH

Although *Coriolanus* shares thematic interests with *Troilus and Cressida* and *Antony and Cleopatra*, it lacks the glamour and familiarity of their characters or historical periods. Yet two contemporary figures would have made this relatively obscure Roman soldier immediately 'recognisable' even to those in the audience who did not know his story: Sir Walter Ralegh and, especially, Robert Devereux, second Earl of Essex. Despite their significant differences, certain traits of personality and aspects of their careers were bound to cast their shadows behind the Coriolanus being dramatised on stage. Both Ralegh and Essex had distinguished themselves on the battlefield at an early age and achieved their initial prominence as superlative soldiers. Both then became entangled in the world of court intrigue in which they sought to rise, where military prowess was only one asset on a much more complex battlefield; in the end, neither seems fully to have understood the rules of the court game he tried so hard to master. Overbearing pride and a touchy sense of personal honour, and consequent critical outspokenness, created powerful enemies at court for both Essex and Ralegh. Coriolanus's foray into politics is unsought and lasts a matter of days, not years, but it ends in the same charge Essex and Ralegh faced: treason.

Essex won his first honours at nineteen in the Netherlands campaign at Zutphen with Sir Philip Sidney in 1586.[2] Known for reckless bravery on the battlefield and several stunning military successes, as well as for his often equally imprudent and irascible behaviour at court as Queen Elizabeth's on-again, off-again favourite, he early captured the popular imagination; after becoming Earl Marshal in 1597, he seemed England's most important military leader. As the inheritor of Sidney's followers and leader of one of the court's two major political factions, Essex was sought out as sponsor both by aspirants to court office and by writers seeking literary patronage from him or members of his circle. Shakespeare's connection with the Essex circle was the Earl of Southampton, one of Essex's chief friends and supporters; to him were dedicated the two non-dramatic poems through which Shakespeare appears to have sought noble patronage in the 1590s, *Venus and Adonis* and *The Rape of Lucrece*.[3] Shakespearean

---

[1] In North's Plutarch 'libertie' and 'prerogative' each occur once, in less inflammatory contexts; see Bullough, *Sources*, v, 518, 524. Shakespeare makes the threat more pointed by having Coriolanus favour abrogating the 'custom' that grants power to the people's voices in both consular elections and treason trials.

[2] Harrison, *Robert Devereux, Earl of Essex*, p. 21.

[3] Many critics think Southampton the addressee of Shakespeare's sonnets, and Sonnet 107 has been taken as a veiled reference to Southampton's release from prison in 1603; see G. Blakemore Evans's edn of *The Sonnets*, 1996, pp. 112–13, 216–17, and Margot Heinemann, 'Rebel lords, popular playwrights, and political culture: notes on the Jacobean patronage of the Earl of Southampton', *Yearbook of English Studies* 21 (1991), 69.

dramatic portraits that might have been suggestive of Essex, during the time he was in Elizabeth's favour and seemed a bulwark of England's military strength, include the valiant Talbot in *1 Henry VI* and Bullingbrook's courtship of the London crowd, described by King Richard in *Richard II* (1.4.24–36).[1] The Chorus before Act 5 in *Henry V* explicitly anticipates Essex's success in Ireland and triumphant return to London (5.0.29–34).

Literary topicality had its dangers, especially when its reference was to one whose popularity and ambition displeased the queen. In an apparent bid for patronage, John Hayward added a fulsome dedication to Essex to his history of the late-fourteenth-century struggle for power between monarch and noble subject that ended in King Richard II's deposition, *The First Part of the Life and Raigne of King Henrie IIII*; it was published in February 1599, just before Essex's departure for Ireland. The initial controversy was over the dedication, which was ordered to be removed. By the time of Hayward's trial in July 1600, Essex was back in London in disgrace; Hayward was now also accused of manipulating history to stress the Essex–Bullingbrook parallels, and he was imprisoned for three years.[2] At Essex's treason trial in February 1601, Hayward's dedication and choice of historical subject were part of the evidence offered by the prosecution.[3] Well aware of the parallels, Essex's supporters paid for a command performance of *Richard II* (probably Shakespeare's) the day before the abortive rebellion of 8 February 1601, and Shakespeare's company, the Lord Chamberlain's Men, later had to defend themselves for having played it. After the rebellion's failure, Robert Barker, 'Printer to the Queen', issued *A Declaration of the Practices & Treasons attempted and committed by Robert late Earle of Essex and his Complices* (1601), a carefully slanted defence of the government's actions composed by Francis Bacon at the queen's behest and edited by the Privy Council and the queen herself.[4] It was quite clear about the inflammatory potential of staging English history. The queen's situation was compared to that of Edward II and Richard II, and the reader told that Sir Gelly Meyrick was charged with treasonous intentions in having arranged the special performance of *Richard II*: 'So earnest he was to satisfie his eyes with the sight of the tragedie, which hee thought soone after his Lord should bring from the Stage to the State' (K3ʳ). Editions of *Richard II* printed in Elizabeth's lifetime lacked the Deposition scene, and

---

[1] *1 Henry VI* may have been composed too early for Shakespeare to have had Essex specifically in mind; for a discussion of the controversy over dating the play, see Michael Hattaway (ed.), *The First Part of King Henry VI*, 1990, pp. 34–41. If newly written for the 3 March 1592 performance recorded by Henslowe, however, the pertinent Essex expedition would have been the siege of Rouen, October 1591–January 1592, his first military command (p. 37); though the campaign was unsuccessful, Essex had cut a dashing figure in the field.

[2] Margaret Dowling, 'Sir John Hayward's troubles over his *Life of Henry IV*', *The Library*, 4th ser. 11 (1930), 212–24; see also F. J. Levy, 'Hayward, Daniel, and the beginnings of politic history in England', *Huntington Library Quarterly* 50 (1987), 15–20.

[3] Robert Lacey, *Robert, Earl of Essex*, 1971, p. 283; Levy, 'The beginnings of politic history in England', p. 17.

[4] Edward P. Cheyney, *A History of England: From the Defeat of the Armada to the Death of Elizabeth*, 2 vols., 1926 (rpt 1967), II, 547; James Spedding, *The Life and Letters of Francis Bacon*, 7 vols., 1861–90, VII, 240.

the 1600 quarto of *Henry V* omits the Choruses and the Scottish and Irish captains, as well as some other by then potentially offensive matter.[1]

Although he sought court preferment desperately, and for a time successfully, Essex was no natural politician. Sir Henry Wotton commented that he was 'a great resenter and no good pupil to my Lord of Leicester [Essex's step-father and early mentor at court] who was wont to put all passions in his pocket';[2] on the contrary, as Essex's private secretary, Henry Cuff, told William Camden, Essex undiplomatically 'carried alwayes his love and hatred in his forehead, and could not conceale it'. Camden sums up Essex's character: 'No man was more ambitious of glory by vertue, no man more carelesse of all things else.'[3] Another trait that might link Shakespeare's protagonist with the national hero turned traitor lies in their devotion to war. Essex was commonly thought to prefer war and soldiers to peace and courtier-diplomats, and he felt compelled to provide a self-defence in *An Apologie of the Earle of Essex*, written in 1598 and circulated in manuscript; it was published in London in 1603, two years after his execution with the explanatory subtitle 'Against those which jealously, and maliciously, tax him to be the hinderer of the peace and quiet of his country'.

Coriolanus's proud autonomy and self-assertion against those he considers inferiors might also have recalled Essex. The product of an aristocratic 'honour culture', Essex believed in a natural political elite distinguished by lineally inherited status, and he despised Secretary Cecil and his faction not simply because they opposed Essex's own policies but as cowardly social upstarts.[4] Political frustration was an affront to his innate personal and family honour, yet in the centralised nation-state of late-sixteenth-century England, the conferring of honour had been monopolised by the state, to be dispensed by the monarch. Essex felt obedience could not be demanded if it entailed personal dishonour; Elizabeth required complete submission.[5] Essex tried to accommodate himself to the conditions under which honour and influence were to be won at court, but although he courted Elizabeth's favour in the guise of suppliant Petrarchan lover, he could never for long bend his will to her position as ruler or woman;

[1] Censorship probably extended to performance, since by midsummer success in the Irish campaign no longer seemed likely and by late 1599 Essex had failed in Ireland, alienated the queen, and been denounced in Star Chamber; see Janet Clare, *'Art Made Tongue-tied by Authority': Elizabethan and Jacobean Dramatic Censorship*, 1990, pp. 71–3, and for a different explanation of the Deposition scene's absence from the early quartos, Leeds Barroll, 'A new history for Shakespeare and his time', *SQ* 39 (1988), 448–9. For more extended discussions of the quarto and Folio versions of *Henry V* and their relation to the Essex affair, see Patterson, *Shakespeare and the Popular Voice*, ch. 4, and Gary Taylor (ed.), *Henry V*, 1982, pp. 4–7.
[2] Quoted in Edwin A. Abbott, *Francis Bacon: An Account of His Life and Works*, 1885, p. 54.
[3] William Camden, *Annales*, trans. R. N. Gent (3rd edn, 1635), p. 552.
[4] Mervyn James, *Society, Politics and Culture*, 1986, pp. 422–3. The whole chapter, 'At a crossroads of the political culture: the Essex revolt, 1601' (reprinted from *P & P*, Supplement no. 3 [1978]), is instructive on the larger significance of Essex's career and on the shift in the meaning of honour under the Tudor consolidation of power.
[5] F. J. Levy reminds me that Essex's habit of withdrawing from court when he felt slighted and then waiting for Elizabeth to request his return might have been recalled by Coriolanus's tendency to turn his back on the political arena when his will is crossed, necessitating the intervention of the senate (2.1) or his mother (3.2; 5.3); both men felt their personal honour threatened by the peacetime world of duplicitous verbal negotiation. Essex's use of silent withdrawal was, however, a self-conscious political technique; see Lacey, *Robert, Earl of Essex*, pp. 82, 87, 175, 200–4, 212, 215.

he continued to believe, disastrously and against counsel, that he could bully her into acquiescence and that she 'could be brought to nothing, but by a kind of necessitic and authority'.[1]

After his trial and execution, the government's propaganda justifying its actions against this popular figure made an association with Coriolanus more likely, even in one case explicit. The preface of the 1601 *Declaration of the Practices & Treasons . . . by Robert late Earle of Essex*, cited above, makes clear the need for an 'official' version: 'divers most wicked and seditious Libels thrown abroad' show that 'the dregs of these treasons . . . do yet remaine in the hearts and tongues of some misaffected persons' (A4r). Essex was accused of intending 'the altering of the governement' (G4v) and even of plotting to become king (A4v). Shakespeare uses similar charges from his source (3.3.68–70),[2] but Coriolanus is also explicitly charged with 'treason' and labelled 'traitor', words not found in Plutarch. Coriolanus's march on Rome at the head of enemy troops could also recall some of the most serious charges against Essex. According to Sir Christopher Blount's confession on the scaffold, Essex had intended that Lord Mountjoy, Essex's successor as head of the Irish campaign, should send his troops back to England to support the rebellion, thus turning internal, 'loyal' protest by an aggrieved subject into foreign invasion and Essex into an enemy instead of 'a Patron of his Countrey . . . which by this meanes hee should have destroyed' (P3v). In his 'Directions for the Preachers' for their sermons on the Sunday following Essex's execution and later in a speech to the Star Chamber, Robert Cecil promoted the additional accusation that Essex had made a pact with the very Irish rebel he had been sent to subdue, an arrangement by which Tyrone should lend his Irish army of 8,000 to Essex's cause in England.[3]

The aftermath of the Essex affair dragged on into James's reign. Essex's own *Apologie* of 1603 was followed in 1604 by Robert Prickett's elegiac poem *Honour's Fame in Triumph Riding, or the Life and Death of the Late Honourable Earl of Essex*, dedicated to two of Essex's surviving supporters, Southampton and Mountjoy.[4] In response to a threatening popular rehabilitation of Essex and consequent condemnation of his enemies, there appeared two editions, in 1604 and 1605, of *Sir Francis Bacon his Apologie, in Certaine imputations concerning the late Earle of Essex*, in which Bacon denies having betrayed Essex and claims that his good advice was ignored (c2v). Those involved with Essex's trial remained concerned with managing popular attitudes. In 1605 Samuel Daniel was brought before the Privy Council to answer charges that his play *Philotas* contained a sympathetic portrait of Essex by portraying a treason trial in which malicious and self-interested prosecutors corrupt the process of justice; Daniel felt compelled to add disclaimers in the dedication and 'Argument' of the 1605 quarto

---

[1] Francis Bacon, from his *Apologie* (1604), p. 18, quoted in John Channing Briggs, 'Chapman's *Seaven Bookes of the Iliads*: mirror for Essex', *SEL* 21 (1981), 65.

[2] In Plutarch he is accused of wanting 'to chaunge the present state of the common weale' and of 'aspir[ing] . . . to usurpe tyrannicall power over Rome' (Bullough, *Sources*, v, 522, 524).

[3] Cheyney, *A History of England*, II, 535–6; Clare, '*Art Made Tongue-tied by Authority*', p. 64. Although not mentioned at his arraignment, the charge of plotting with Tyrone reappeared in the 'official' *Declaration*.

[4] James, *Society, Politics and Culture*, p. 462. James also cites the appearance of ballads glorifying Essex and lamenting his death; see also Lacey, *Robert, Earl of Essex*, pp. 311, 317.

and later to append an 'Apology' in his 1623 *Whole Workes.*[1] A scene in Chapman's *Conspiracy of Charles Duke of Byron* (acted and printed 1608), a staged interview in which Queen Elizabeth discourses on Essex as a warning to the French traitor-to-be Byron, was for the quarto cut by the censor.[2] Fulke Greville, a member with Daniel of the Countess of Pembroke's circle and a writer of political closet-drama, in his posthumously-published *Life of Sir Philip Sidney* specifically connects the fall of Essex with his own decision in the early years of the century to burn his tragedy on a classical subject, Antony and Cleopatra, as being dangerously apt 'to be construed or strained to a personating of vices in the present Governors and government'.[3]

Not only English history, then, but classical events and personalities could suggest contemporary parallels.[4] As noted, Daniel had been suspected of using the history of one of Alexander the Great's generals to reflect on Essex's fall and trial. Lord Henry Howard brought Ben Jonson before the Privy Council for 'treason' detected in his classical tragedy *Sejanus* (acted, by Shakespeare's company, 1603), although whether the offending allusion was to Essex or to Ralegh remains unclear, since no trial records exist and Jonson took defensive action by altering the text before it reached print in 1605.[5] Before Essex's fall, Chapman had flatteringly seen him in Homer's Achilles. Less favourably, at Essex's trial his conspiracy was likened to Catiline's by Serjeant Yelverton and then by Attorney-General Coke; Francis Bacon compared Essex to the Athenian rebel Pisistratus.[6] In one of the sermons ordered by the Council to 'explain' the trial to the disgruntled populace, William Barlow cites Coriolanus as 'a gallant, young, but discontented Roman, who might make a fit parallel for the late Earl, if you read his life'.[7]

As Jonson's case indicates, the other soldier-hero recently indicted for treason whose career might have been evoked by Coriolanus is Sir Walter Ralegh. Indeed, the

[1] Reprinted in Laurence Michel (ed.), *'The Tragedy of Philotas' by Samuel Daniel,* 1949, p. 79; for the whole history of Daniel's troubles, see *ibid.,* pp. 36–65. Of the Essex affair's effect of dramatic censorship, Clare notes that 'for several years it provoked an increased vigilance towards plays which might revive memories of his popular appeal' (*'Art Made Tongue-tied by Authority'*, p. 66).
[2] John Margeson (ed.), *The Conspiracy and Tragedy of Charles Duke of Byron,* 1988, pp. 9–10; elsewhere in the printed text, however, Essex is several times mentional negatively. Unlike Margeson, Clare thinks the scene was 'most probably suppressed before the play was performed' (*'Art Made Tongue-tied by Authority'*, pp. 143–4).
[3] Sir Fulke Greville, *The Life of the Renowned Sir Philip Sidney,* 1652, pp. 155–6. Bullough speculates that although *Antony and Cleopatra* makes a natural companion piece to *Julius Caesar* by continuing its story, Shakespeare might have seen the potential danger of dramatising, at least until after Elizabeth's death, the story of a queen who caused the decline and death of a great general (*Sources,* v, 216).
[4] On the 'involvement of historical thought with politics', see Levy, 'The beginnings of politic history in England', pp. 7–9, 13–14; Lisa Jardine and Anthony Grafton, '"Studied for action": how Gabriel Harvey read his Livy', *P & P* 128–9 (1990), 30–78; A. B. Worden, 'Literature and political censorship in early modern England', in *Too Mighty to be Free,* ed. A. C. Duke and C. A. Tamse, 1987, pp. 51–2; and A. R. Braunmuller, *'King John* and historiography', *ELH* 55 (1988), 309–32.
[5] Although the contemporary application of this play about the fall and death of a royal favourite has often been assumed to be Essex, Philip Ayres, editor of *Sejanus his Fall,* 1990, makes a persuasive case that the modern parallel for the trial of Caius Silius in Act 3 would have been the treason trials of 1603 and particularly the unjust conviction of Sir Walter Ralegh.
[6] Harrison, *Robert Devereux, Earl of Essex,* pp. 298–9, 305.
[7] *A Sermon Preached at Paules Crosse . . . Martij 1. 1600. With a Short Discourse on the Late Earle,* 1601, c3ᵛ.

notorious arrogance that led to a description of him in 1587 as 'the best hated man of the world in Court, city, and country' brings him closer in one aspect of his personality to Coriolanus than the widely popular Essex.[1] Ralegh, too, had won precocious fame through military service, first as a teenager in France supporting the Huguenot cause and later in Ireland.[2] From 1582 Queen Elizabeth's chief favourite, Ralegh enjoyed the financial rewards and political offices that followed; a commoner by birth, he was also resented as undeserving such wealth and status, and neither his arrogance nor his bitter rivalry with Essex, after the earl had begun to replace him in Elizabeth's favour, improved his popularity. As with many rivals, Ralegh and Essex were also alike in more than their military backgrounds: both were known for volatile tempers and disrupted the court with periodic outbursts of wounded pride. Ralegh's eminence was, like Essex's, reflected in literary allusions and dedications.[3] At the more popular level of epigram and ballad, allusions to Ralegh were usually negative, for among the commons his pride and ostentatious life-style were seen as evidence of vanity and contempt.[4] Ralegh did not soften his behaviour at court: even his political ally Henry Percy, Earl of Northumberland, described him as 'insolent, extremely heated, a man that desired to seem to be able to sway all men's courses'.[5] Like the tribunes in *Coriolanus*, Ralegh's enemies counted on his temper to work against him. Henry Howard judged that to the extent that Ralegh could not by nature or art 'countenance a pride above the greatest Lucifer . . . by so much shall he sooner run himself on ground in rage and make the queen more sensitive in scorning so great sauciness in so great infirmity'.[6]

Although Ralegh had supported Secretary Cecil and the government's prosecution of Essex, he was himself subject to Cecil's manoeuvring to eliminate rivals. Even before King James VI of Scotland became King James I of England, Cecil and Howard had poisoned his mind against Ralegh.[7] With the new king, Cecil and Howard (now Earl of Northampton) all eager to be rid of him, Ralegh's fate was virtually a foregone conclusion when he was implicated in the Bye and Main plots and committed to the Tower in July 1603. Ralegh was accused only of concealing his knowledge of the Bye plot, but he was indicted as a principal contriver (with, among others, Lord Cobham) in planning the Main, or 'Spanish treason', plot.[8] The crown's case seemed strengthened by a letter written by Essex, acquired by Cecil at Essex's death, which claimed Ralegh and Cobham were working to prevent James's succession. The alternative to James

---

[1] Quoted by William Stebbing in *Sir Walter Ralegh: A Biography*, 1841, p. 61; see also Steven May, *Sir Walter Ralegh*, 1989, p. 9.

[2] Stebbing, *Sir Walter Ralegh*, pp. 18–19.

[3] On Ralegh's role as patron, see Stebbing, *Sir Walter Ralegh*, ch. 6, and James P. Bednarz, 'Ralegh in Spenser's historical allegory', *Spenser Studies* 4 (1984), 52–7. Ralegh is the addressee of Edmund Spenser's prefatory letter to *The Faerie Queene* and makes an allegorised appearance in Book III.

[4] May, *Sir Walter Ralegh*, pp. 124–6.

[5] Quoted in Stebbing, *Sir Walter Ralegh*, p. 58.

[6] Quoted in Linda Levy Peck, *Northampton: Patronage and Policy at the Court of James I*, 1982, p. 20.

[7] See *The Secret Correspondence of Sir Robert Cecil with James VI, King of Scotland*, ed. Edmund Goldsmid, *Collectanea Adamantaea* 19, 3 vols., 1887, 1, 23–40.

[8] The unstable Cobham accused Ralegh of inciting him to treason, later rescinded his charges in a letter to Ralegh, then subsequently reiterated them as true; he was the only witness against Ralegh, and the crown refused to produce him at the trial to face Ralegh's questioning (May, *Sir Walter Ralegh*, p. 19).

was to be the Spanish infanta and the means a conjectured treasonous subversion of Ralegh's and Cobham's offices as governor of Jersey and Lord Warden of the Cinque Ports by which they would allow a Spanish army to enter the realm and march on London.[1] However unlikely the charges, given Ralegh's fierce Protestantism and hatred of Spain, after a trial of *ad hominem* attacks and legal shuffling that sought rhetorically to convert Ralegh from loyal courtier into 'something of a revenger, a man seeking redress for piqued pride', he was convicted on 17 November 1603.[2] Sentenced to execution, Ralegh was instead reprieved and remained imprisoned in the Tower until 1616.

Arrogant, contemptuous of the common people, and a vengeful traitor who conspired to arrange a foreign invasion of his own country – the portrait painted at the trial by Attorney-General Coke and Lord Chief Justice Popham would seem tailor-made to forge a memory to be triggered by Shakespeare's Coriolanus. In fact, history determined that the memory evoked would be considerably more complicated, though perhaps in this way even more appropriate. Ralegh's courage and eloquence at his trial, contrasting as they did with Coke's and Popham's malice and manipulation of the law, reversed his popular reputation. Dudley Carleton reported that one of the men bringing the news of sentencing to the king remarked that although when he first saw Ralegh at the trial 'he was so led with the common hatred that he would have gone a hundred miles to have seen him hanged, he would ere he parted, have gone a thousand to have saved his life'.[3] The crown had calculated that a very public trial for this widely despised man would ensure a general acquiescence in the verdict it was determined to procure; instead, a multitude of eye-witnesses spread the story of judicial insult committed against a courageous victim. Anecdotes, probably apocryphal, appeared in which Ralegh's judges and jury themselves admitted culpability.[4] Like the nostalgically rehabilitated Essex, though with more cause, Ralegh was seen as a victim of political manoeuvring by courtiers eager to consolidate their own power. Despite the strength of their differences, their common fate produced a persistent linkage: when Carleton received Chamberlain's report of Ralegh's execution in 1618, he immediately recalled Essex's, and it 'proves a subject of much contemplation'.[5]

All this is not to say that *Coriolanus* is in any literal way 'about' Essex or Ralegh, or that Shakespeare based his protagonist on a contemporary figure. *Coriolanus* is not political allegory, nor did Shakespeare distort his historical source to point up the broad similarities in personality: the 'passion and choller', 'selfe will and opinion', 'wilfulnes', the spitting 'out anger from the most weake and passioned parte of the hearte', and belief that 'to overcome allwayes, and to have the upper hande in all matters, was a token of magnanimitie' are all in Plutarch, though the 'solitarines' and 'spite and malice

[1] Peck, *Northampton*, pp. 21–2; see also May, *Sir Walter Ralegh*, p. 19.
[2] Karen Cunningham, '"A Spanish heart in an English body": the Ralegh treason trial and the poetics of proof', *Journal of Medieval and Renaissance Studies* 22 (1992), 344.
[3] *Dudley Carleton to John Chamberlain, 1603–1624: Jacobean Letters*, ed. Maurice Lee, Jr, 1972, p. 39.
[4] Stebbing, *Sir Walter Ralegh*, pp. 229–31; Edward Thompson, *Sir Walter Ralegh: The Last of the Eliza-bethans*, 1935, pp. 198–9.
[5] *Dudley Carleton to John Chamberlain*, letter of 14 November 1618, p. 20.

against the people' would recall only Ralegh.[1] Even the tribunes' charges (with the notable exception of 'treason' and 'traitor') can be found in Plutarch. That Shakespeare saw the parallels and chose to stress them to enhance a contemporary resonance for his story of early republican Rome might perhaps be inferred from his decision to include these charges even though some no longer pertain to the Coriolanus of his play, who lacks political ambition and refuses to court the people by showing his wounds.[2] The lack of 'fit' in Shakespeare's play darkens the tribunes, who sound like Essex's and Ralegh's prosecutors grasping at any accusation to help convict their personal enemy, and points up the political power struggle at the play's heart. The similarities in a general way call on his audience's personal experience of the ambivalence felt toward such larger-than-life, but also dangerous, military figures whose pride might drive them from the extreme of national heroism to its opposite, betrayal. They also offer Shakespeare a familiar context in which to explore what such a career might mean in terms of personal tragedy.

The play

> For much imaginary work was there,
> Conceit deceitful, so compact, so kind,
> That for Achilles' image stood his spear,
> Gripped in an armèd hand, himself behind
> Was left unseen, save to the eye of mind:
>   A hand, a foot, a face, a leg, a head
>   Stood for the whole to be imaginèd.

The Rape of Lucrece, 1422–8

As Achilles' spear, so Coriolanus's sword. Lucrece gazes at a tapestry of the Trojan War whose art is one of condensation and allusiveness. On stage Shakespeare gives us a whole, three-dimensional man, but to the 'eye of mind' that wants to understand as well as see, Coriolanus is as elusive as Achilles' fragmentary body behind the weapon that defines the warrior's occupation and represents his heroic status. What can we glimpse behind the sword that at one point, when his soldiers hold him aloft before battle, Coriolanus becomes: 'O' me alone? Make you a sword of me?' (1.6.76)?[3] As Shakespeare's least self-reflective tragic hero, Coriolanus himself offers little help. Unlike the protagonists of most of the other major tragedies, he never asks 'Who am I?' or 'What have I become?' His two brief soliloquies comment on external events, and when not absorbed with his sword and its work, he is usually seen waging verbal battle against not only the common people, both as citizens and soldiers, and the tribunes,

---

[1] Bullough, *Sources*, V, 519.

[2] The same motive may lie behind Brutus's and the messenger's narratives of Coriolanus's popularity with the commonalty after his military triumph (2.1.179–92, 235–9), descriptions that recall accounts of the people's response to Bullingbrook in Shakespeare's *Richard II* and Hayward's *Life and Raigne of Henry IIII* that were thought to shadow Essex. There is no such popular adulation of Coriolanus in Plutarch.

[3] This line is one of the play's cruxes (see 1.6.76 n.), but whether it is a question or an exclamation, Coriolanus sounds ecstatic. As Michael Goldman puts it, 'It is his happiest moment in the play' ('Characterizing Coriolanus', *S.Sur.* 34 (1981), 80).

but against senators and patricians as well.[1] On the other hand, elsewhere we are swamped with portraits. Extending a dramatic technique used in *Antony and Cleopatra*, Shakespeare presents the audience with different, often conflicting, perspectives on his protagonist.[2] Everywhere, in Rome and Antium, others evaluate and try to explain the man and what drives him.

It is as much the chosen technique as Coriolanus's own self-righteousness and lack of self-awareness that frustrates our involvement in his fate. And, distrustful of language, taciturn or inarticulate at critical moments, he lacks the glorious hyperbole of Antony or an affirmation of emotional commitment that might counter the external presentation; the positive aspects of his ethic remain largely implicit, buried in his usual verbal mode, the furious diatribes against all who oppose his will. Not surprisingly, Coriolanus is probably Shakespeare's least sympathetic tragic hero. Indeed, some would deny him that title and shift the role of tragic protagonist to Rome itself or, taking into account the play's insistent political focus or Coriolanus's manipulability by others, reclassify its genre as debate, or satire, or even comedy.[3] Given the objectivity with which the dramatist holds not only his protagonist but all the play's competing factions at a distance, it is also not surprising that critical appraisals both of Coriolanus and of what the play reveals about Shakespeare's politics stretch from one end of the conservative–radical spectrum to the other. The two poles of Shakespeare's interest in *Coriolanus* are the political struggle and his tragic protagonist as an individual, with a life and history of his own. In this play, where everyone's self is public, the two are inextricably entwined.[4]

Shakespeare embeds his protagonist in the play's turbulent political and social world from the opening lines. When the company of armed, 'mutinous' citizens bursts onto the stage, Rome seems on the brink of civil war, one whose cleavage is not between aristocratic factions (as in the other Roman plays and the English histories), but between rich and poor, patricians and plebeians. And central to the citizens' concerns is Caius Martius (later surnamed Coriolanus), not only Rome's greatest soldier but also, in a seeming paradox that foreshadows the play's divisions, 'chief enemy to the people' (1.1.5–6). He represents patrician attitudes in their harshest form, hence there is a logic to First Citizen's otherwise surprising suggestion that if they kill Martius, 'we'll have corn at our own price' (1.1.8). Yet what looks to be a violent mob bent on open rebellion dissolves immediately into rational debate among differing individuals, men concerned

---

[1] Of the two soliloquies (2.3.99–110; 4.4.1–6, 12–26), the first may be Coriolanus talking to himself but overheard by others (see 2.3.75 SD. 1 n. and Textual Analysis, pp. 303–4 below). His most self-reflective moments lie in the series of 'asides' as his family approaches, 5.3.20–37.

[2] Lee Bliss, *The World's Perspective*, 1983, p. 72 and ch. 2 *passim*; see also William Rosen, *Shakespeare and the Craft of Tragedy*, 1960, pp. 190, 206–7, R. A. Foakes, *Shakespeare: The Dark Comedies to the Last Plays*, 1971, pp. 85–93, and E. A. J. Honigmann, *Shakespeare: Seven Tragedies*, 1976, pp. viii, 181–2.

[3] For example, D. J. Enright, '*Coriolanus*: tragedy or debate?', *Essays in Criticism* 4 (1954), 1–19; O. J. Campbell, *Shakespeare's Satire*, 1943, pp. 198–217. George Bernard Shaw is alone in calling *Coriolanus* 'the greatest of Shakespeare's comedies' (dedicatory epistle to *Man and Superman*, Penguin edn, 1946, p. 31).

[4] In *Angel with Horns*, 1961, A. P. Rossiter calls *Coriolanus* Shakespeare's 'only great political play . . . and hard to come to terms with, because it is *political tragedy*' (p. 251). For the politics of theatrical production, see the stage history, pp. 67–98 below.

not merely with facts but with the motives that might allow their evaluation and dictate appropriate action. Unlike the unruly artisans who open *Julius Caesar*, the citizens we first meet in *Coriolanus* are not comic figures; nor are they incapable of shrewd analysis of their situation. Second Citizen temperately urges that Martius's pride and contempt for the common people are ingrained character traits, 'What he cannot help in his nature', to be offset by the 'services he has done for his country' (1.1.31, 22–3). First Citizen denies the premise of patriotic motive: whatever its incidental benefit to Rome, Martius's military prowess is exercised in the interest of his own fame and 'to please his mother and to be partly proud' (1.1.29–30). In each case, private concerns take priority over the public good. In appropriately confusing and contradictory terms, the first few lines present us with the major explanations of Martius's character that we will later have to sort out for ourselves.

Class is power in the current political organisation of Rome: 'patricians' and 'authority' are synonyms in First Citizen's indictment of the rich for hoarding (1.1.13). Rebellion is justified because the patricians have placed status interests above their duty as rulers. The 'superfluity' of grain that 'authority' should distribute is instead inhumanely withheld to keep the starving poor in their place as the measure of patrician abundance and superiority.[1] Shakespeare expands the political debate through Menenius's attempts to pacify the rebels, first with arguments and then with political allegory. Although we soon learn that he shares Martius's disdain for the common people, in attempting to avert the threatened rupture he presents himself and his class as idealistically compassionate in their 'charitable care' of the people (1.1.51). His flattering address – 'masters, my good friends, mine honest neighbours' – minimises class distinctions; he reattributes to the gods all responsibility for the dearth and maintains that the 'helms o'th'state . . . care for you like fathers' (1.1.48, 63). In Plutarch only Menenius speaks; in *Coriolanus* his assertions are met with open contradiction. The reality is not paternal solicitude but systematic oppression, for the citizens' concerns go beyond the patrician 'storehouses crammed with grain': the senate 'daily' repeals acts 'established against the rich' and passes more statutes 'to chain up and restrain the poor' (1.1.66–9).

Unsuccessful at making reality palatable by simply redefining it, Menenius turns to the fable of the body's rebellion against the belly as a corporeal analogy for the body politic that should persuade the citizens to abandon their protest. The fable sits oddly enough in its Plutarchan context (where the complaint is against usurers), for it is surrounded by accounts of continuing class struggle. Shifting its context to a corn riot undercuts Menenius's attempt to identify its image of a harmoniously functioning physical body with the Roman *polis* under patrician rule. In the fable the rebellious members learn that the apparently parasitic belly contributes the essential function of distributing life-giving blood to the rest of the body; in Menenius's application, the belly stands for the 'senators of Rome' who are, by analogy, as crucial to the life of the body politic. As political argument, the fable now seems comically ill-chosen,

---

[1] For the contemporary relevance of the citizens' complaints, see pp. 17–27 above.

since the senate is manifestly not distributing its stores or providing 'that natural competency / Whereby they live' to the other corporeal members (1.1.122–3).[1]

In both Plutarch and Livy, Menenius successfully placates the rebellious citizens. Shakespeare's citizens have heard this fable before and see through Menenius's mystification of political and economic realities.[2] Second Citizen impatiently interrupts and even breaks into verse to show that he knows another version, one in which the 'cormorant belly' is the basest member, the 'sink o'th'body' (1.1.104–5). He refuses to draw the traditional moral, that the citizens should return obediently to their proper place in the body politic. The fable's image of an interdependent, mutually sustaining society in which different individuals and classes form an organic unity may offer an ideal, but since the analogy with the *status quo*, which Menenius wishes to preserve, fails, it is also in a sense irrelevant.[3] Moreover, while the fable's ideological content is about unity, in Shakespeare's expansion the rich detail and the individualising of bodily components focus us on fragmentation and set the tone for a play whose imagery oscillates between grotesque bodies and dislocated body parts.[4] Rome is divided between two 'bodies politic' struggling over the power that controls the most basic necessities by which real bodies survive. The depth of the antagonism between these fat and thin bodies is underlined by the first of the play's images of cannibalism, Second Citizen's prediction of the patricians that 'If the wars eat us not up, they will; and there's all the love they bear us' (1.1.69–70). These bodies are tied to each other 'by the cruelty of the market and not by bonds of community'.[5]

Menenius warns the rebels that the course of the Roman state 'will on / The way it takes, cracking ten thousand curbs / Of more strong link asunder than can ever / Appear in your impediment' (1.1.55–8). He is wrong. The rioters do change the course of Roman history: protest yields tribunes and a voice in the way Rome will be governed. The creation of the tribunate challenges the political meaning of 'Rome'. The patricians have always identified it with themselves – 'Our Rome', in Volumnia's phrase (2.1.176) – as does the play: of the eighty-eight uses of 'Rome', only six belong to the tribunes and none to the plebeians.[6] To Volumnia the plebeians are not fellow citizens; they are 'woollen vassals, things created / To buy and sell with groats' (3.2.10–11). To Coriolanus they are less than human, 'scabs' on the body politic, and certainly not Roman, 'Though calved i'th'porch o'th'Capitol' (1.1.149, 3.1.242). By 'mingling' tribunes with 'us, the honoured number', the senate has polluted the aristocratic body politic, introduced a 'measles' that will require 'dangerous physic'

---

[1] In '*Coriolanus* and the body politic', *S.Sur.* 28 (1975), 63–9, Andrew Gurr notes that in Shakespeare's context, Menenius's fable demonstrates his 'contempt for his hearers and his faith in verbal smokescreens' (p. 67). On Menenius's complexity, see Honigmann, *Shakespeare: Seven Tragedies*, pp. 175–8.

[2] Thomas Sorge, 'The failure of orthodoxy in *Coriolanus*', in *Shakespeare Reproduced*, ed. Jean E. Howard and Marion F. O'Connor, 1987, p. 233.

[3] David G. Hale, '*Coriolanus*: the death of a political metaphor', *SQ* 22 (1971), 201.

[4] In *Tragic Alphabet: Shakespeare's Drama of Language*, 1974, Lawrence Danson notes that the fable 'largely determines the nature of the succeeding imagery, and determines it in the direction of metonymy' (p. 145). On the fable's images of 'multiplicity and fragmentation', see Leonard Barkan, *Nature's Work of Art*, 1975, pp. 100–8.

[5] Zvi Jagendorf, '*Coriolanus*: body politic and private parts', *SQ* 41 (1990), 459.

[6] Gail Kern Paster, '"To starve with feeding": the city in *Coriolanus*', *S.St.* 11 (1978), 127.

(3.1.79, 155).[1] Coriolanus would destroy Rome rather than share it, but the senators do not answer his call for armed suppression, and the only body he can oppose to the Hydra populace is his own. Since he alone refuses to accept the people's admission to governance, in his eyes he alone stands for 'Rome'. Sicinius's comic exaggeration springs from a kernel of truth: Coriolanus would 'depopulate the city and / Be every man himself' (3.1.266–7). Later, still a body politic of one, he banishes his banishers.

Coriolanus thinks of himself as whole, heroically complete, and the physician who knows the remedy for Rome's present sickness. But in the play's imagery his body is no more healthy or an exemplary civic model than the plebeian one it opposes. His superhuman prowess is also inhuman, and even before in banishment he turns dragon, descriptions that help establish his heroic stature also assimilate him to uncontrollable natural forces that have nothing to do with, indeed threaten, the civilised, human-scale world of the city. He is likened to an earthquake (1.4.62–5), thunder (1.6.25), the sea, and a planet laying waste whole cities (2.2.93, 107–8); his human body is reduced to 'a thing of blood' and a 'flayed' carcass (2.2.103, 1.6.22) or anatomised into a collection of wounded parts – neck, thigh, shoulder, left arm – that should buy him the consulship (2.1.123–6). Volumnia can even pick through her son's qualities to claim those he received from her in her breast-milk (3.2.130–1). Subject to internal rebellion as well, he is likened to a madman who must be restrained from harming himself (1.9.55–7). Rather than Coriolanus representing the health of the Roman body politic, what was once 'the arm our soldier' has to the tribunes in Act 3 become a gangrened foot that must be 'cut away' before its infection spreads (1.1.99, 3.1.300).

This now unbridgeable division within the body politic has produced a crisis whose acuteness is witnessed in the language of self-mutilation. Menenius's image for the unnaturalness of the tribunes' initial decree of death is one of grotesque feeding, both cannibalism and self-consumption: 'the good gods forbid / That our renownèd Rome . . . like an unnatural dam / Should now eat up her own' (3.1.295–9). In exile, Coriolanus tells Aufidius that 'Coriolanus' now exists only as a meaningless name; the 'cruelty and envy of the people . . . hath devoured the rest' (4.5.71–3). Such representations of Coriolanus's treatment by his native city project in the most shocking form a pattern of imagery that has established Roman civic relations in general as feral and antagonistic rather than harmonious. G. Wilson Knight first noted how the play's animal imagery underscores natural inequalities and antipathies by emphasising extremes – lions and hares, foxes and geese, osprey and fish.[2] The opposition is between strong and weak but also predators and prey. Yet no natural hierarchy prevails among

---

[1] On Coriolanus's relation to the 'grotesque body' of the populace, see Michael D. Bristol, 'Lenten butchery: legitimation crisis in *Coriolanus*', in Howard and O'Connor, *Shakespeare Reproduced*, p. 214. On the disease imagery which figures so strongly in this play, see Maurice Charney, *Shakespeare's Roman Plays: The Function of Imagery in the Drama*, 1961, pp. 157–63.

[2] *The Imperial Theme*, 1931 (rpt 1954), p. 163. Knight's point, however, is that such pairings relate only to the Coriolanus/plebeian opposition and that they elevate him by associating him with 'nature's aristocracy'.

men; which side is which depends on who is speaking. The plebeians fear the patricians will devour them; Coriolanus thinks that without strong senatorial supervision the plebeians would 'feed on one another' (1.1.171). To the tribunes Coriolanus is the wolf threatening the plebeian lamb (2.1.6–7); for Menenius and Cominius the roles are reversed (2.1.8–9, 4.6.114–16).

The reversibility comically points up the problem: predatory opposition is the only form in which each side, each claiming to be 'Rome', can conceive the other. The political results of this conviction are explored in the manoeuvring by both sides over the consular election which Shakespeare puts at the play's centre. Plutarch's tribunes are individualised and made more prominent. Repeatedly we see them alone, plotting their strategy, and Shakespeare adds the scene (2.3) in which they coax the plebeians into rescinding their votes. That the patricians are no more high-minded is made clear in 3.2, where Coriolanus is in turn 'lessoned' in political tactics. The parallel underscores the moral levelling of patricians and tribunes as equally opportunistic scrappers for power, and it is underscored by Coriolanus's insistence that honour and deception are incompatible.[1] His surly inflexibility takes on a more positive aspect as it forces Volumnia to a blunt defence of hypocrisy: 'You are too absolute, / Though therein you can never be too noble, / But when extremities speak' (3.2.40–2). When ends justify means, circumstances dictate an infinitely malleable individual, and 'honour' and 'policy' undergo a semantic collapse in which they no longer convey distinctions. When 'Honour and policy, like unsevered friends . . . grow together' in both war and peace, then it cannot dishonour him to speak to the people in words that are 'bastards and syllables / Of no allowance to your bosom's truth' (3.2.43–4, 57–8). For Volumnia, honour means class loyalty, so that if 'My fortunes and my friends' require dissembling, 'I should do so in honour' (3.2.64–5).

Shakespeare here focuses our attention on honour and truth disappearing into expediency, politics into role-playing. Coriolanus is told what to say and the physical gestures most likely to make his part persuasive. For him, such calculating deception is no casual matter, and his revulsion at the prospect of 'my body's action' teaching 'my mind / A most inherent baseness' (3.2.123–4) overflows into images of harlots, eunuchs, knaves and beggars.[2] His commitment to his own private integrity will ultimately pit him against all Rome; his resistance here completes Shakespeare's anatomy of the Roman political process and highlights its moral cost, not just to the individual but to Rome. As Volumnia's analogy makes clear, politics is war in a different guise, class war of Roman against Roman, with no ploys barred. The state, in

---

[1] Shakespeare alters the ambitious willingness to display his wounds of Plutarch's Coriolanus and suppresses the elaborate stratagem by which Aufidius and Coriolanus later entice the Volscians into desiring to renew their war against Rome.

[2] The reaction against politics as theatre rests ultimately on the philosophic debate over the relation of accidentals to substance, here of words and actions to 'mind'; in 'Name and fame: Shaespeare's *Coriolanus*' (1964; rpt in *The Renaissance Imagination*, ed. Stephen Orgel, 1975), D. J. Gordon notes that in his rejection Coriolanus uses the language of the schools: this is Shakespeare's only use of 'inherent', and Gordon thinks he must have known its 'technical use in connection with substance' (p. 214).

Machiavelli's sense of 'the object of exploitative control by the prince', has replaced the 'commonwealth'.[1]

This failure, on both sides, to act in the spirit of the belly fable's mutually supportive ideal rests not only on the fact of class antagonism, but on the presumed absence of any third, mediating term.[2] Yet although in the play 'citizen' and 'plebeian' are used as synonyms, 'citizen' also bore a more general, non-class significance that, if recognised, would acknowledge a link between patricians and plebeians: all are citizens of the same city.[3] Coriolanus is able only once, in the excitement of battle, to conceive of himself as agent of such an inclusive Rome: when he rallies the common soldiers' courage and accepts his status as their sword, they together become a single-purposed unit. The other patricians may share his resentment of the political changes wrought by the commoners' rebellion, but they accommodate themselves to reality and, more important, understand the overriding necessity of preserving the city.[4] They fulfil their responsibility for good stewardship when they 'give forth / The corn o'th'storehouse gratis' (3.1.114–15), and as tension mounts they urge restraint on both Coriolanus and the tribunes. This is not altruism, but it is a practical acceptance that the fabric of the Roman state is woven of more than patrician thread and that the rift Coriolanus has created in the name of preserving their power must be 'patched / With cloth of any colour' if Rome is to survive (3.1.254–5).

It is a tense truce between the plebeians and the patricians, but rather than the chaos Coriolanus predicted from shared governance, what we see, in a scene of Shakespeare's creation, is a functioning peacetime *polis* with 'Our tradesmen singing in their shops and going / About their functions friendly' (4.6.8–9). Of course, this vision of a harmonious commonwealth creates its own irony, for we have just heard the banished Coriolanus vow revenge; even had he not joined the enemy, we know from 4.3 that the Volscians were about to attack Rome. Insupportable he may be, but Coriolanus is also necessary in a world intermittently, but continually, at war. One reason that the play's ending feels inconclusive is that Shakespeare leaves the focus on politics, which dominates Acts 2 and 3, at a double impasse. The play posits no solution to

---

[1] Patricia Meszaros, '"There is a world elsewhere": tragedy and history in *Coriolanus*', *SEL* 16 (1976), 276, where she also notes that in the modern sense of 'the political organization which is the basis of civil government' (*OED* State *sb* 29), 'state' appears eighteen times in *Coriolanus*, twice the number of instances in any of Shakespeare's other plays (*ibid.*). In 'Changing attitudes towards the state during the Renaissance', Garrett Mattingly sums up the chief concern of Machiavelli's *The Prince* as 'How to keep the government running and how to keep running the government' (in *Facets of the Renaissance*, ed. William H. Werkmeister, 1963, p. 29).

[2] Perhaps for this reason Shakespeare omits one of Plutarch's few details about Menenius, that the commoners found him sympathetic because he had been born a plebeian. Shakespeare's Rome lacks the 'middling' range of people who were becoming increasingly important to the political as well as the economic life of Stuart England; 'Politics and the franchise' (pp. 27–33 above) considers the extent to which Roman plebeians are figured as London citizens. For a contrasting view, see Theodore B. Leinwand, 'Shakespeare and the middling sort', *SQ* 44 (1993), 295–6.

[3] On this point, see Ralph Berry, *Shakespeare and Social Class*, 1988, pp. 157–8. 'City' is a key word and occurs here more frequently (39 times) than in any other Shakespeare play.

[4] David L. Krantz derives a similar conclusion from reading the play in terms of Aristotle's *polis*; see '"Too great a mind": the "mentis integritas" of Shakespeare's Roman heroes', *Classical and Modern Literature* 4 (1984), 154–6.

the problem of accommodating the needs of war (a warrior class eager to risk death to gain glory) with those of peace (an atmosphere conducive to pursuing the humble arts of nurturing the physical bodies of all the state's citizens). By leaving out Plutarch's conclusion to his narrative – where we learn that Coriolanus was not indispensable, since after his assassination the next Volscian attack ended in defeat and Aufidius's death – Shakespeare enhances our sense of continued instability. Coriolanus's decision to spare Rome seems less a crisis resolved, thus providing a sense of closure, than one averted now but destined to recur.

Internally, too, uncertainty marks Rome's future, for neither peace nor threat of destruction can bridge the fundamental antagonisms. The tribunes are undiplomatically smug in victory: 'The commonwealth doth stand, / And so would do were he [Coriolanus] more angry at it' (4.6.15–16). They become craven evaders of responsibility when it appears they miscalculated, and the people, too, deny their contribution to Rome's plight, claiming their votes for banishment were given 'willingly' but also 'against our will' (4.6.148–9). The patricians' response reveals the strength of their class antipathy to be undiminished and, hence, the fragility of the current political compromise. Menenius and Cominius taunt the tribunes with the result of their misused power and revel in the expected punishment of the upstart tribunes and commoners: 'He'll shake your Rome about your ears', and 'Your franchises, whereon you stood' will be annihilated (4.6.103, 90). Although they acquiesced in the new 'Rome', they clearly do not fully accept it or see themselves as partners in a more inclusively constituted polity. We are left with the Roman Republic's system of checks and balances finally fully in place – consuls, senate, tribunes – but it is a political organisation predicated on the assumption of competition among self-interested components of the body politic. *Coriolanus* seems to accept, or at least present, this agonistic and self-divided state, not the organic commonwealth ideal, as the order of things.[1] It is perhaps not surprising that such a bleak vision had no successors. *Coriolanus* is Shakespeare's last serious political play[2] as well as probably his last tragedy.

If the Roman political process (and Coriolanus's mistaken agreement to submit himself to it) is central to his story, it is rather the catalyst than the cause of his tragedy. These causes lie deep, and Shakespeare seizes upon the few bare facts with which Plutarch introduces his life – that orphaned Martius was raised by his mother, that for 'lacke of education' he was 'churlishe, uncivill, and altogether unfit for any mans conversation'[3] – as the basis for one of his most searching explorations of a character's complex psychological composition.[4] We know more about Coriolanus's upbringing than about any other Shakespearean tragic hero's. With the Plutarchan supplication scene (5.3) to work toward, Shakespeare greatly expands Volumnia's part;

---

[1] James Holstun, 'Tragic superfluity in *Coriolanus*', *ELH* 50 (1983), 498. Holstun, however, thinks the play deconstructs the organic body-politic metaphor and that in *Coriolanus* Shakespeare 'is satirizing tragedy' (p. 507 n. 20).

[2] An exception might be the more abstract, theoretical analysis of *The Tempest*.

[3] Bullough, *Sources*, v, 506. Martius's mother, initially not even mentioned by name, does not reappear in Plutarch until her son, at the head of a Volscian army, is at the gates of Rome.

[4] Goldman, 'Characterizing Coriolanus', p. 74.

the solitariness and social alienation as well as the martial fierceness cited by Plutarch become connected to Volumnia and her teaching.

Volumnia is a particular 'type' of mother: Roman, aristocratic, exponent of a culture in which, according to Plutarch, 'valliantnes was honoured . . . above all other vertues'.[1] She is also ambitious. If male patrician honour is won on the battlefield, her son must there prove his excellence; she basks in the reflected glory of his superiority, since she claims him as her creation. War is for him, to borrow the terminology of Othello and Antony, his 'occupation'; and he acknowledges, says Volumnia, that 'My praises made thee first a soldier' (3.2.109). Early in the play she recalls how she shaped both his 'occupation' and his values: 'When yet he was but tender-bodied and the only son of my womb . . . I, considering how honour would become such a person . . . was pleased to let him seek danger where he was like to find fame' (1.3.4–11). The softer maternal feelings – for Martius was of an age when 'a mother should not sell him an hour from her beholding' (1.3.7–8) – have no place in this training programme.[2] Indeed, she stresses her own active agency in creating the adolescent warrior-hero: 'To a cruel war I sent him . . . I sprang not more in joy at first hearing he was a man-child than now in first seeing he had proved himself a man' (1.3.11–14). She vividly pictures her son in the current war, stamping and cursing his reluctant soldiers, and it is as though she has scripted his behaviour in the following scenes at Corioles.[3]

What might to modern audience seem an unnatural maternal obsession with fame might not to a culture whose values derived from this aristocratic ethos and for which Rome was still the standard by which other cultures were judged and found wanting. In his essay on 'The Instruments of a States-man', Sir William Cornwallis uses Roman mothers as well as fathers to condemn his effeminate countrymen's lack of the ancients' proper regard for shame, honour and noble custom: 'You shall hardly finde a father now a daies that will care rather how his sonne is dead, then dead, that prizeth his valour dearer then his life, yet in times past, mothers had that hardines that they hated more that hee should be wounded in the backe then dead.'[4] 'Hardiness' Volumnia surely has, and for much of the play's history this Roman matron has been seen as an ideal: 'Her lofty patriotism, her patrician haughtiness, her maternal pride, her eloquence, and her towering spirit, are exhibited with the utmost power of effect; yet the truth of female nature is beautifully preserved, and the portrait, with all its vigour, is without harshness.'[5]

Yet the 'modern' response is not simply an anachronistic imposition. In 1.3 Virgilia's interjections – 'O Jupiter, no blood!' and 'Heavens bless my lord from fell

---

[1] Bullough, *Sources*, V, 506.

[2] As Brockbank points out, Shakespeare may have developed Volumnia on the model of Spartan as well as Roman mothers (pp. 48–9).

[3] Janet Adelman, *Suffocating Mothers: Fantasies of Maternal Origin in Shakespeare's Plays, 'Hamlet' to 'The Tempest'*, 1992, p. 152.

[4] *A Second part of Essayes*, 1601, I.l 3^r–v. Old Siward in *Macbeth* shares this admired concern with honour: told of his son's death in battle, he immediately asks, 'Had he his hurts before?' (5.9.12).

[5] Anna Jameson, *Shakespeare's Female Characters*, 1840, p. 263. The idealisation of both Volumnia and Coriolanus also dominated stage productions in the eighteenth and nineteenth centuries; see pp. 71–5 below.

Aufidius!' – shock by their very contrast: to only one of these women is Martius a loved individual. Blood and wounds are positively desirable to Volumnia, since they are badges of honour that in sufficient number will secure her final ambition for her son, the consulship. To his mother he is curiously abstract, identical with the one function for which she bred him; hence the man and his reputation are interchangeable. Had he died in the 'cruel war' to which she sent him, 'Then his good report should have been my son' (1.3.16). Equally disturbing is her possessiveness, her voracious need to occupy every position in her son's life. Instructing Virgilia in the proper hierarchy of values, she easily substitutes herself as wife while at the same time denying Virgilia a wife's privileges: 'If my son were my husband, I should freelier rejoice in that absence wherein he won honour than in the embracements of his bed where he would show most love' (1.3.2–4).[1] Her image of her son in battle is oddly unheroic, even debasing – 'forth he goes, / Like to a harvestman that's tasked to mow / Or all or lose his hire' (1.3.30–2) – yet it catches both her sense of Martius as her day-labourer in the field of honour and the steep requirement demanded of his performance. Less than 'all' risks rejection, the loss of her praise which is his 'hire'. She lays personal claim to his pre-eminent virtue: 'Thy valiantness was mine, thou suck'st it from me' (3.2.130). As the awkward syntax of her rebuke to Virgilia's fear of blood reveals, *being* his mother accords her the same stature: 'The breasts of Hecuba, / When she did suckle Hector, looked not lovelier / Than Hector's forehead when it spit forth blood / At Grecian sword, contemning' (1.3.35–8). The negative is metrically unstressed, and the balance of the lines combined with the shocking content of the comparison gives both images equal weight.[2]

In a temporal sense, the lactating breast is replaced by its only *raison d'être*, the honourably wounded warrior. It is not surprising that late-twentieth-century commentators, especially those with feminist and psychoanalytic interests, have reversed the earlier idealisation of Volumnia, or that this speech should be central to their analyses of her responsibility for the distortions in her adult son's psyche. She has taught him that neediness – for food, for love – is a mark of dependency and that the best defence against this weakness lies in aggression, where the wound becomes an instrument of attack that denies its own vulnerability.[3] In 1.3 Shakespeare offers an explanation for Coriolanus's behaviour not only on the battlefield but in the market-place and senate-chamber: not Plutarch's incivility due to lack of education, but the necessity for aggression taught by a particular kind of education given at his mother's knee. He has been thrust into

---

[1] In later requesting him to return to the market-place, she arrogates to herself the right to speak for all: 'I am in this / Your wife, your son, these senators, the nobles' (3.2.65–6).

[2] In 'A disturbance of syntax at the gates of Rome', *Stanford Review* 2 (1985), 185–208, Page du Bois finds that in this image 'the role of the mother is equated with the warrior's violence' (p. 193) and goes on to outline the psychological 'double binds' by which Volumnia controls and destroys her son.

[3] Adelman, *Suffocating Mothers*, p. 149. See also Coppélia Kahn, *Man's Estate: Masculine Identity in Shakespeare*, 1981, pp. 151–72, and Madelon Sprengnether, 'Annihilating intimacy in *Coriolanus*', in *Women in the Middle Ages and the Renaissance*, ed. Mary Beth Rose, 1986, pp. 89–111.

manhood (his childhood as elided as the leap from suckling infant to adult soldier),[1] yet denied his independence.[2] With the plebeians his compulsive, almost hysterical, invective seeks to differentiate him wholly from such hungry mouths, potential representatives of his own dependency.[3] He spends his life trying – futilely since Volumnia cannot let him go[4] – to prove himself unneedy and self-sufficient. The emotionally-starved son is forced to live on anger, displaced from its primal source, his mother. Her words could as aptly be his: 'Anger's my meat. I sup upon myself, / And so shall starve with feeding' (4.2.52–3).[5] His response to banishment is so extreme because Rome, always identified with the mother who taught him how to be 'Roman', has repeated the traumatic childhood rejection. Inadmissible aggressive impulses toward his mother can be acted on when seen as honourable retaliation against an ungrateful city. Destroying Rome, and the mother within it, would allow him to forge a new identity, one finally independent of her.[6]

Yet Coriolanus is not simply an extension of Volumnia and her masculine ambitions, although the fact that neither of them understands this distinction initiates the tragic action. To reduce Coriolanus's fate to the psychodynamics of one private relationship is to ignore Shakespeare's attention to political processes initiated by creating the tribunate and the extent to which he uses Volumnia as patrician spokeswoman in this public realm. As the battle scenes in Act 1 and Cominius's praise of Coriolanus's 'deeds' in Act 2, Scene 2 make clear, Volumnia was merely the instrument of her male-oriented, militaristic society, the conveyor of its ideal of aristocratic manhood.[7] The problem is that this ideal is no longer adequate to Rome's actual situation; it was generated by an earlier, simpler Rome, one whose need for warriors was so acute

---

[1] Such a curtailed childhood results from Volumnia's hostility to the period of dependency before he can become the adult extension of her ambition for fame and political power; see Charles Mitchell, 'Coriolanus: power as honor', *S.St.* 1 (1965), 199, and Derek Traversi, *Shakespeare: The Roman Plays*, 1963, p. 219.

[2] Michael McCanles puts in even stronger terms ('master–slave') the relation that allows Volumnia to prevail in both 3.2 and 5.3; see his 'The dialectic of transcendence in Shakespeare's *Coriolanus*', *PMLA* 82 (1967), 51–3.

[3] See Leonard Tennenhouse, '*Coriolanus*: history and the crisis of semantic order', *Comparative Drama* 10 (1976–7), 328–46. For different readings of why the citizens represent what Coriolanus most fears in himself, see Christopher Given, 'Shakespeare's *Coriolanus*: the premature epitaph and the butterfly', *S.St.* 12 (1979), 143–4, and Robert Watson, *Shakespeare and the Hazards of Ambition*, 1984, pp. 149–50. On Coriolanus's hair-trigger response to single words, and other linguistic traits, see Carol M. Sicherman, '*Coriolanus*: the failure of words', *ELH* 39 (1977), 199–201.

[4] Emmett Wilson, Jr, 'Coriolanus: the anxious bridegroom', in *'Coriolanus': Critical Essays*, ed. David Wheeler, 1995, p. 108.

[5] Stanley Cavell sees both mother and son as starving throughout and finds that 'self-consuming anger is the presiding passion of her life', taught to her son 'under the name of valiantness'; see '*Coriolanus* and interpretations of politics ("Who does the wolf love?")', in Cavell, *Themes Out of School*, 1984, pp. 65–6. See also Marilyn Williamson, 'Violence and gender ideology in *Coriolanus*', in *Shakespeare Left and Right*, ed. Ivo Kamps, 1991, pp. 147–66.

[6] David B. Barron, '*Coriolanus*: portrait of the artist as infant', *American Imago* 19 (1962), 175–6, 180. Adelman notes that virtually all psychoanalytic critics comment on Coriolanus's identification of Rome with his mother (*Suffocating Mothers*, p. 328 n. 65).

[7] On the Roman 'ethnocentrism' that 'appropriates' Martius, see Michael Long, *The Unnatural Scene*, 1976, pp. 68–72, and Parker, p. 61. On the patricians' 'magnification' of him to fit their own fantasies, see Brian Vickers, *Shakespeare: 'Coriolanus'*, 1976, pp. 19–23.

that 'valiantness' became synonymous with 'virtue'.[1] Children were bred to fulfil this demand, as we see not only in Volumnia's description of her son's youth but in the repetition of that 'education' for her grandson, who would 'rather see the swords and hear a drum than look upon his schoolmaster' and who, to her delight, in 'One on's father's moods' tears to pieces the butterfly he had been chasing (1.3.50–1, 59). But the political conditions have altered and, with the tribunes as the people's voice, the kind of actions that constitute public service. The peacetime exercise of a consul's power will now be judged in terms of its responsiveness to the well-being of plebeians as well as patricians. When debate and accommodation become part of the way politics is conducted, words – the flexible art of rhetoric – become as important as heroic deeds.[2] Cominius perhaps senses the change, for he begins his encomium with a qualification not found in Plutarch: 'It is held / That valour is the chiefest virtue and / Most dignifies the haver. If it be, / The man I speak of cannot in the world / Be singly counterpoised' (2.2.77–81). Yet the rest of the speech belies the conditional 'If', and the programme of training for Roman warriors makes no provision for the arts peace might require. It produces, in its extreme form, a warrior unable to accommodate himself to the non-combative role of consul;[3] it also skews important aspects of human relationships necessary to communal life.

Departing from Plutarch, Shakespeare explores the implications of an ideology that privileges the battlefield and displaces to it the satisfaction of both bodily and emotional needs usually associated with peace. Volumnia's equation of wounded warrior and lactating breast lays a foundation for the play's persistent linkage of fighting with both nourishment and love. Cominius worries that wounded Martius is unfit for 'a second course of fight', and the secondary meaning of 'course', associated with banqueting, becomes explicit when he refers to Martius's joining the second battle as coming to 'a morsel of this feast, / Having fully dined before' (1.5.16, 1.9.10–11). The war/food equation holds equally strongly in Antium, where one of Aufidius's servingmen figures the assault on Rome as dessert to the banquet at which Coriolanus commits himself to the Volscian senators, 'to be executed ere they wipe their lips' (4.5.209). War nourishes, vitalises the body; it is 'sprightly walking, audible, and full of vent' (4.5.214). It also provides substitute erotic objects and satisfactions.[4] Both Coriolanus and Aufidius react to victory with nuptial metaphors; indeed, the pleasures of male bonding equal (for Martius as he clasps Cominius, 1.6.29–32) or exceed (for Aufidius embracing Coriolanus, 4.5.111–15) those of the wedding-night. Some modern critics (and directors) have seen in the Coriolanus–Aufidius rivalry not the homosocial

[1] On the problems associated with the historical point in Rome's development that the play dramatises, see Adrian Poole, '*Coriolanus*', 1988, pp. 44–6, Tony Parr (ed.), *Coriolanus*, 1985, pp. 8–9, 22–3 and Brockbank, pp. 40–2.
[2] Tennenhouse, '*Coriolanus*: history and the crisis of semantic order', pp. 333–4.
[3] Coriolanus does not want the consulship and scorns Brutus's assertion that, as tribune, he too has done Rome 'service' (3.3.90–1).
[4] Ralph Berry, 'Sexual imagery in *Coriolanus*', *SEL* 13 (1973), 314. In '*Coriolanus*: Shakespeare's anatomy of *virtus*', *Modern Language Studies* 13 (1983), 68–79, Phyllis Rackin notes that for Martius honour won on the battlefield is 'a kind of secondary sexual characteristic' proving masculinity (p. 73). A relevant general sociological study is Walter J. Ong, *Fighting for Life: Contest, Sexuality, and Consciousness*, 1981.

relationship characteristic of an aristocratic warrior culture but a homoerotic attraction complicating the desire for dominance.[1] Certainly they are obsessed with each other and, at least for Aufidius, that obsession is figured in sexually suggestive imagery. He has dreamed nightly of 'encounters 'twixt thyself and me' where 'We have been down together . . . Unbuckling helms, fisting each other's throat' (4.5.120–2). A servant reports that Aufidius 'makes a mistress' of Coriolanus and 'turns up the white o'th'eye to his discourse' (4.5.189–90).

Marital love, indeed private life in general, is subordinated to the male, public world of valour and fame.[2] In pleading with her husband in 5.3, Virgilia refers to Young Martius not as a pledge of their love or a reminder of the joys of parenthood; rather, she 'brought you forth this boy to keep your name / Living to time' (5.3.126–7). Virgilia has throughout represented the possibility of a different set of priorities, or at least one more receptive to the claims of private life and love.[3] She is not weakly acquiescent – she resists her mother-in-law's bullying in 1.3 and joins in cursing the tribunes in 4.2 – but she cannot change Volumnia's mind or alter the system of values that has shaped her husband and will claim her son. Coriolanus's two salutes to his wife suggest deep attachment and, perhaps, an appreciation of the respite she offers from the demands of Volumnia and the vehement public world of formal encomium and political ritual (2.1.148, 5.3.27–8).[4] Yet given the kinds of scenes Shakespeare had written into the stories of Macbeth and Antony, it is noteworthy that he creates no substantial private life for Coriolanus; husband and wife are never at home or alone together on stage.

Patrician ideology posits 'Romans' as public, socially-constructed beings, and its hierarchy of values exalts the victorious soldier. Initially Coriolanus seems the embodiment of Rome's official self-image, yet he is also curiously alienated from it in ways that have no basis in Plutarch. Paradoxically, he is 'at once an embodiment of a culture and totally unrepresentative of its members'.[5] The Roman hero of Act 1 ends up the dragon at her gate in Act 5 in part because he does not understand how fundamentally removed he is from 'Rome'. Shakespeare indicates this isolation in physical terms by increasing Martius's solitariness from the beginning: the word 'alone' occurs more frequently in *Coriolanus* than in any other play by Shakespeare.[6] He enters the gates

---

[1] Bruce R. Smith, 'Rape, rap, rupture, rapture', *Textual Practice* 9 (1995), 430–2, and Sprengnether, 'Annihilating intimacy', p. 93. See also pp. 85–7 below.

[2] Recent emphasis on the play's homoeroticism obscures the way in which 'Roman' values skew all forms of sexuality, from Volumnia's usurping Virgilia's position as wife to reminders that widows and orphans are proofs of manhood (2.1.151–2, 4.4.2–4, 5.6.154).

[3] Commenting on 1.3, David Margolies notes that while 'Virgilia considers warfare from the standpoint of everyday living, Volumnia views ordinary life from the perspective of war' (*Monsters of the Deep: Social Dissolution in Shakespeare's Tragedies*, 1992, p. 129). See also Matthew N. Proser, *The Heroic Image in Five Shakespearean Tragedies*, 1965, pp. 154–5.

[4] Una Ellis-Fermor, *Shakespeare the Dramatist*, ed. Kenneth Muir, 1961, p. 68; see also Parker, p. 54, and Thomas Clayton, '"So our virtue lie in th'interpretation of the time": Shakespeare's tragic *Coriolanus* and Coriolanus, and some questions of value', *Ben Jonson Journal* 1 (1994), 160.

[5] S. P. Zitner, 'Shakespeare's *Coriolanus* and the Aristotelian modes of pathos', in *Greek Tragedy and Its Legacy*, ed. Martin Cropp, Elaine Fantham and S. E. Scully, 1986, p. 302.

[6] Harry Levin (ed.), *Coriolanus*, 1956, p. 24.

of Corioles alone, and in preparation for the final boast to the Volscians in 5.6, we are reminded of this mark of his valour in his taunt to Aufidius – 'Alone I fought in your Corioles' walls / And made what work I pleased' (1.8.8–9) – and by Cominius's description of Coriolanus's heroism when 'Alone he entered / The mortal gate of th'city' (2.2.104–5). To his comrades such martial singularity isolates him as something different, complete in itself (though also notably unhuman) – 'a carbuncle entire' (1.4.59), a 'planet' (2.2.108).

At a deeper level, Coriolanus's alienation reveals itself in his response to praise. When Cominius awards the honorific 'Coriolanus' on the battlefield (1.9) or proclaims his 'deeds' to the senate (2.2), he is fulfilling Rome's side of a reciprocal relation between individual and state. He expresses the classical world's understanding of honour as extrinsic to the individual, in Cicero's words, 'given to someone by the judgment and enthusiasm of the citizens'.[1] In this view, 'honour', 'fame', 'renown' are synonymous, the good words that others have to say about us, as they are for Volumnia (1.3.8–11).[2] At times Coriolanus seems to share this view and subordinate himself wholly to Rome's needs, as when he demurs at Cominius's praise after the victory (1.9.15–19). But what sounds like modesty is also a kind of arrogance that in refusing praise refuses Rome the right to determine the value of his actions. The fame and booty Cominius offers 'In sign of what you are' Coriolanus rejects as 'A bribe to pay my sword' (1.9.26, 38). The intensity with which he spurns Rome's right to name his deeds suggests that for Coriolanus honour is 'a quality of action, not of action's effects'.[3] It is not just that the common people are unworthy either to praise or blame him but that even Cominius's admiration is irrelevant to something deeply personal and subjective; his wounds 'smart / To hear themselves remembered' in others' mouths (1.9.28–9). He fights to prove his identity, his superiority, but according to his own absolute standards of excellence. Cominius seems to intuit this private relation to honour when in praising Coriolanus's lack of covetousness he adds that Coriolanus 'rewards / His deeds with doing them, and is content / To spend the time to end it' (2.2.121–3).[4]

Coriolanus's sense of honour includes a principle of personal integrity and truthfulness not found in Plutarch or Shakespeare's Rome. It gives him a vantage point from which to resist Volumnia's collapse of honour into policy in 3.2 and to avoid Aufidius's cynical acceptance that 'our virtues / Lie in th'interpretation of the time' (4.7.49–50). But part of the reason for Coriolanus's shocking reversals of allegiance

---

[1] Cicero's definition of honour is quoted, in Gordon's translation, on p. 210 of 'Name and fame: Shakespeare's *Coriolanus*'; Gordon notes that precisely because it was extrinsic, honour could not be 'the good', though it was the goal of the political or public life. See also Norman Council, *When Honour's at the Stake: Ideas of Honour in Shakespeare's Plays*, 1973, ch. 1.

[2] In terms of the plays' debates over whether value and honour are intrinsic or conferred, Bulman traces the parallels between Volumnia counselling Coriolanus and Ulysses advising Achilles in *Tro.* (*Heroic Idiom*, pp. 17–20).

[3] Norman Rabkin, '*Coriolanus*: the tragedy of politics', *SQ* 17 (1966), 203; see also William W. E. Slights, 'Bodies of text and textualized bodies in *Sejanus* and *Coriolanus*', *Medieval and Renaissance Drama in England* 5 (1991), 190.

[4] In 'Voiceless bodies and bodiless voices: the drama of human perception in *Coriolanus*', *SQ* 43 (1992), 170–85, Jarrett Walker argues that Coriolanus's contempt for speech is 'also a contempt for linear time and a desire to live in a single transcendent moment, such as the moment of violence' (p. 171).

lies in the fact that he himself remains unaware of the distinctions Shakespeare has introduced into Plutarch's straightforward 'Roman' idea of honour; rather, they have been unconsciously assimilated to the warrior ideal he has been bred to fulfil, and that ideal is as much a cultural construction as his aristocratic contempt for the commonalty. What he takes as an essential nature that must not be compromised is a performative role requiring others, if not as applauding audience then as the opposition necessary to demonstrate that one has fulfilled the role, that one is superior.[1] The standard of value is inherently comparative. He speaks more profoundly than be realises when he protests against his mother's demand that he act a conciliatory part to appease the people: 'Rather say I play / The man I am' (3.2.16–17). He has been 'playing' the super-masculine patrician warrior since his youth,[2] as Shakespeare subtly suggests in Cominius's description of Martius's first battle: 'When he might act the woman in the scene, / He proved best man i'th'field' (2.2.90–1). Volumnia's request introduces the unsettling possibility that there might be a gap between self and role. The near-hysteria of his response suggests the extent to which his role is his shield, his only identity.

If Rome is not for him the source of honour, it can be of insult. He can deny the people's right to define him, refusing the epithet 'traitor' and reversing the verdict of banishment, but verbal defiance cannot erase the fact that he has had to submit his will to others. For a man who expresses his noble superiority through military prowess, the only way to establish a worthy identity is to forge a new out 'o'th'fire / Of burning Rome' (5.1.14–15). There is no Stoic depth to Coriolanus that would allow him to find consolation in his private sense of himself as honourable.[3] His soliloquy in 4.4 reveals no soul-searching, no awareness of the magnitude of his choice, but only bemusement at the world's 'slippery turns' that have sent him from Rome to Antium. He does not see the irony – the man committed to being true to his private identity in fact dependent on others, unable to live 'titleless' (5.1.13) – just as he had not seen the implications of Aufidius's inability to recognise him without his name in 4.5. Without the public identity given him by Rome, he is not a unique, self-created individual but a blank.[4] He has tried to take into exile his ideal image of himself, divorced from the loyal service of defending Rome which was the *raison d'être* of its construction. The dangers of such self-referentiality, of severing one's sense of meaning and value from the community, are clear: isolation and solipsism. In Acts 4 and 5 the fantasy

---

[1] Katherine Stockholder, 'The other Coriolanus', *PMLA* 85 (1970), 229.

[2] For slightly different formulations of how Coriolanus's 'authentic self is irrepressibly social', see Michael Taylor, 'Playing the man he is: role-playing in Shakespeare's "Coriolanus"', *Ariel* 15 (1984), 26–7, and David L. Kranz, 'Shakespeare's new idea of Rome', in *Rome in the Renaissance: The City and the Myth*, ed. P. A. Ramsey, 1982, pp. 375–6.

[3] In '"Solitariness": Shakespeare and Plutarch', *Journal of English and Germanic Philology* 78 (1979), 325–44, Janette Dillon observes that in Antony, Timon and Coriolanus Shakespeare was drawn to figures who were an anomaly in Plutarch, the biographer of public men: 'solitary public men with no inner capacity for solitude' (p. 335).

[4] In '*Coriolanus*: wordless meanings and meaningless words', *SEL* 6 (1966), 211–24, James L. Calderwood notes that Aufidius has to request the name five times; by withholding it Coriolanus seems to be trying to 'impose his private identity' as though 'the force of his unique nature could make him recognizable' (p. 221). See also Jonathan Dollimore, *Radical Tragedy*, 1984, pp. 218–22.

of self-sufficient superiority is freed to pursue the perversely egocentric form toward which it had always tended.

After Coriolanus leaves Rome, in his own eyes 'like to a lonely dragon', he seems finally to assume the godhead to which Brutus had accused him of aspiring ('You speak o'th'people / As if you were a god to punish, not / A man of their infirmity', 3.1.81–3).[1] A servant reports that the Volscian lords defer to Coriolanus 'as if he were son and heir to Mars' and that Aufidius 'sanctifies himself with's hand' (4.5.186–90). Even the common soldiers 'use him as the grace 'fore meat, / Their talk at table, and their thanks at end' (4.7.3–4). He now refuses not only the title 'Coriolanus' but all his names. He sits 'in gold, his eye / Red as 'twould burn Rome' (5.1.64–5), an enthroned deity whose righteous anger seems fierce enough to kindle the city by force of will alone. At the approach of the suppliant women he reiterates his vow to 'stand / As if a man were author of himself' (5.3.35–6). Yet he is not his own point of origin, as the synecdoche for Volumnia admits: 'the honoured mould / Wherein this trunk was framed (5.3.22–3). The power of godhead is ceded to his mother, whose bow is 'As if Olympus to a molehill should / In supplication nod' (5.3.30–1). He responds immediately to the women's gestures (curtsying, bowing, nodding) and to his son's silent 'aspect of intercession', and this flood of instinctual emotion cracks his resolve. The first to speak, Virgilia reclaims the kinless man with the simple assertion of their bond: 'My lord and husband!' (5.3.37). Feeling that 'Like a dull actor now / I have forgot my part' (5.3.40–1), he for the first time speaks of the soldier's honour as a role that might not be 'an indissoluble property of the self'.[2]

The echoes of 3.2 are unmistakable, and 5.3 both draws together strands of the preceding play and determines the performance possibilities of 5.5 and 5.6.[3] As in 3.2, it falls to Volumnia to make her son perform a role against his will. The circumstances have altered, however, and with them our response. Although in 3.2 he finally gave in, she convinced neither us nor her son that dissembling with his nature for political gain was honourable. In 5.3 her tactics may be as shameless, but the goal is not shameful nor are the arguments now specious. She saves Rome; more important, in Shakespeare's telling of the story she restores her son to himself and his own humanity. With his decision to join the Volscians against Rome, Coriolanus had lost his way, not merely his identity but his defining quality, honour. The vow to Aufidius and the Volscian army that he now feels honour-bound to maintain itself violated the tenets of honour, as Shakespeare makes clear by anticipating Coriolanus's arrival in Antium with the debasing parallel of a Roman traitor whose analogy for Coriolanus trivialises his stature and his cause: 'I have heard it said the fittest time to corrupt a man's wife is when she's fallen out with her husband' (4.3.26–8). As he tries to resist the emotions aroused by

---

[1] As is often noted, Shakespeare seems to be exploring both extremes of Aristotle's assertion that to live alone one must be either a god or a beast (*Politics* 1.2, 1253a 27–9).

[2] Jacques Berthoud, 'Coriolanus's audience', *Hebrew University Studies in Literature and the Arts* 19 (1991), 124.

[3] Brower notes that 5.3's replay of 3.2 is only one example of the way events in the last half of the play have been ironically foreshadowed, giving them an 'almost nightmarish quality' of '*déjà vu*' (*Hero and Saint*, p. 378).

the sight of his family, his own words reveal the danger he is in: to keep a soldier's vow prompted by spite, he must refuse instinct, banish 'affection', and break 'All bond and privilege of nature' (5.3.24–5). He had equated inflexibility with his goal of Stoic constancy, but his wish – 'Let it be virtuous to be obstinate' (5.3.26) – betrays his doubt.[1]

His capitulation is followed by a scene that begins with Rome contemplating its nemesis. Critics usually gather all the imagery of isolation and un- or super-humanness together to illustrate Coriolanus's aspiration to godhead,[2] but it is worth noting that Shakespeare saves some of the most disturbing analogies for this scene, where they no longer apply. Their juxtaposition with the Coriolanus we have just seen, whose eyes 'sweat compassion', emphasises what has been averted (5.3.197). He is likened by Menenius to the unfeeling implacability of stone, 'yond quoin o'th'Capitol', and to an awesome, metallic fighting-machine: 'When he walks, he moves like an engine, and the ground shrinks before his treading. He is able to pierce a corslet with his eye, talks like a knell, and his hum is a battery' (5.4.1, 15–17). Had Coriolanus allowed obstinacy to purge him of the natural vulnerabilities of flesh and blood, he would have been 'as a thing made for Alexander', natural rigidity having ossified the man into a lifeless statue of his self-image (5.4.17–18).[3]

Denying his kin and destroying his native city would have been unnatural because inhuman, not simply inhumane; it would have translated Coriolanus beyond the world of men, beyond the possibility of tragedy. Sicinius's rejoinder to Menenius's assertion that Coriolanus 'wants nothing of a god but eternity and a heaven to throne in' – 'Yes, mercy' – reminds us of the enormous personal significance of his choice (5.4.19–21). To the many arguments borrowed from Plutarch, Shakespeare adds Volumnia's reminder that 'the fine strains of honour' that lead a nobleman 'To imitate the graces of the gods' include mercy as well as terror (5.3.149–50).[4] Sicinius's remark singles out this idea from her other appeals, but whether in 5.3 Coriolanus or Volumnia realises its powerful implications for the whole set of values that promoted valour as the 'chiefest virtue' remains unclear in the text. Shakespeare's reticence thus opens the play's final scenes to radically different interpretations and, hence, stagings. Stage production of necessity must fill the crucial silences in the script – Coriolanus's during his mother's two long pleas and while he *holds her by the hand, silent*; hers after his capitulation – and the choices made about movement, gestures and expression can generate almost diametrically opposite final effects. Here, reference to actual productions can suggest how such different effects might be attained.

If Volumnia in 5.3 'dissembles' with her nature, opportunistically pressing into service any appeal that might achieve her goal, then this scene merely recapitulates 3.2.

---

[1] On the distinction between constancy and obstinacy, see Charles and Michelle Martindale, *Shakespeare and the Uses of Antiquity*, 1990, p. 181.

[2] An exception is Charney, *Shakespeare's Roman Plays*, p. 195.

[3] Compare the difference in Cleopatra's dream of Antony as a colossus, where the defining attributes are generosity and pleasure ('bounty' and 'delights'); in her idealising dream, transcending the human condition paradoxically intensifies Antony's most human, social qualities and makes him an ideal of masculinity (*Ant.* 5.2.79–92).

[4] The added emphasis on mercy relates this pagan mother's plea to more overtly Christian arguments elsewhere in Shakespeare: *MV* 4.1.189–96, *MM* 2.1.116–25, *Temp.* 5.1.20–30.

Forte domi Gracchus geminos ut ceperat angues Gracche, marem, uxori Tusus respondit aruspex Quid non se debere tuis, Cornelia, tandem
Marémque, foeminamque si dimiseris,   Sin faeminam mors ingruet prior tibi   Maritus arbitratus est virtutibus
                          Mabuit ille marem, sefeque proinde, necari, Tantae superstes quam manere coniugi.

3 *Women of the Gracchi*. Engraving by Pieter Furnius, from Jan van der Straet, *Celebrated Roman Women* (1573)

Certainly the rhetorical strategy – moving from public issues of honour to the private demand for filial obedience – is similar, although in 5.3 the final threat would break all familial bonds (5.3.178–80). His capitulation represents another triumph of her will over his, and the fact that her victory entails his death either had not occurred to her or, if we adopt the psychoanalytic interpretation, was always part of the subtext of her relationship to her son, who is not only the agent of her own anger and aggression but also its object.[1] In such a reading, 5.5 is the jewel in Volumnia's crown. In 2.2 she witnessed her son's triumphal entry and basked in a reflected glory; now the triumph is her own, and she herself is hailed as 'the life of Rome' (5.5.1). She says not a word, but her entry could be staged as Sarah Siddons's entry with her son in 2.2: 'with flashing eye and proudest smile . . . [she] rolled, and almost reeled across the stage; her very soul, as it were, dilating and rioting in its exultation'.[2] In 1933 Bridges-Adams directed it in this manner; in fact, he made this six-line scene the most elaborate and populous

[1] Du Bois, 'A disturbance of syntax at the gates of Rome', p. 193; Adelman, *Suffocating Mothers*, p. 157; Sprengnether, 'Annihilating intimacy', p. 98; Robert J. Stoller, 'Shakespearean tragedy: Coriolanus', *Psychoanalytic Quarterly* 35 (1966), 273.
[2] From the actor Charles Young's account, quoted in Julian Charles Young, *Memoirs of Charles Mayne Young*, 1840, p. 41.

of his production. The RSC production of 1977 added a dramatic moment in which, at the climax of the music, Volumnia 'flung off Young Martius' cloak to show him, hands crossed over a sword, black leather armour and defiant chin, the young image of his father'.[1]

Such an interpretation emphasises personal and political stasis. The Volumnia of 5.5 is the Volumnia of 1.3: she has salvaged her son's 'good report' in Rome and willingly substitutes it for him, as she had said she would. Young Martius will receive the same training, be taught the same values, as his father. Rome will lavish praise on its victorious warriors and banish them when they pose a threat (as historically it did, though not all chose Coriolanus's response). An exultant Volumnia and a spectacular homecoming procession increase the irony of Coriolanus's visually parallel entry in 5.6 at the head of a celebrating Volscian crowd. Such an interpretation of Volumnia would also be consonant with a view of Martius himself as fundamentally unchanged: he gives in to his mother in 5.3 in the same way as in 3.2, swayed not by her 'colder reasons' but by the threat of rejection.[2] In 3.2 he had been reduced to a child, pleading that she 'Chide me no more' and comically drawing her attention to his prompt obedience (3.2.133–5). Coriolanus could, in expression or posture, recall that corrected child.[3] At least in Aufidius's later description of the scene, Coriolanus was a 'boy of tears' whose whining submission made pages blush and Volscian soldiers look 'wondering each at others' (5.6.100–3), and in 5.6 Aufidius manipulates him into bringing on his own death as easily as the tribunes had his banishment in 3.3. The opportunistic tribunes held the stage at the end of 3.3; in 5.6 the astute soldier–politician stands on his rival's body. Stressing the parallels and elaborating Volumnia's triumphal procession in 5.5 drains the last scene of its power and makes it almost anticlimactic.[4]

Yet there are other ways of reading, and performing, Volumnia and Coriolanus in these last scenes. Christina Luckyj argues for psychological depth and change in Volumnia: the Roman virago of 1.3 is shocked by Coriolanus's banishment into realising that her scenario for her son and herself suddenly no longer obtains. Her former self-assurance shattered, in 5.3 she argues with passionate conviction, not the cynical manipulation she urged in 3.2; when he finally speaks she learns she has won but also that her victory may prove 'most mortal to him' (5.3.190).[5] R. B. Parker, too,

---

[1] David Daniell, 'Coriolanus' in Europe, 1980, p. 40. Terry Hands's later (1989) RSC production also presented a triumphant Volumnia and a battle-ready Young Martius; see Robert Smallwood's review, *SQ* 41 (1990), 497.

[2] See, for instance, Michael Goldman, *Shakespeare and the Energies of Drama*, 1972, pp. 110–11. Vickers titles one segment of his discussion 'Death of a puppet' (*Shakespeare: 'Coriolanus'*, p. 49).

[3] In the 1977 RSC staging she 'rose and moved forward to face Alan Howard [Coriolanus]. He in an instant movement, *with a military snap*, clasped her hand to his breast and gazed on her' (Daniell, 'Coriolanus' in Europe, p. 39, italics mine). The strength of her command over him was also suggested by Howard's reciting 5.3.22–4 straight to the audience, with his back turned to the entry he is describing (*ibid.*, p. 38).

[4] In 'Beast or god: the *Coriolanus* controversy', *Critical Quarterly* 24 (1982), 35–50, W. Hutchings notes that a 'surprising number of critics, from Bradley on, think that the play really ends at Act V scene iii, rather than Act V scene vi' (p. 43).

[5] Christina Luckyj, 'Volumnia's silence', *SEL* 31 (1991), 327–42. In contrast, Wilbur Sanders believes neither Volumnia nor Virgilia 'has the faintest inkling of the disaster' ahead for Coriolanus (Wilbur Sanders and Howard Jacobson, *Shakespeare's Magnanimity*, 1978, p. 171).

feels that 'the most plausible explanation' for her silence here and in 5.5 is grief, and that 'if she is facing the reality of a sacrifice she glibly exaggerated in 1.3 . . . her fate too is tragic'.[1] Perhaps most effective, in Tim Supple's 1992 production at the Chichester Festival Theatre, Judi Dench struck a powerful balance between the two readings of Volumnia in 5.3. During her last appeal 'nothing else mattered to her but regaining her control over him, exerting her will single-mindedly. And the result was that she had never envisaged the consequence.' Coriolanus's perception of his fate came as a complete shock: 'her face pulled suddenly into a mask of grief', and in 5.5 she entered Rome 'as a mourning statue of horror'.[2]

Unhelpfully, for critics and actors alike, Volumnia's reticence about her motives and emotions is more than matched by her son's. His speech of capitulation is, like his soliloquy, an evasion of self-awareness. Instead, he withdraws from the intensity of the moment to imagine the response of divine spectators who 'look down, and this unnatural scene / They laugh at' (5.3.185–6). The speech tells us that he accepts his humanity – that he is Martius, not Mars – and foresees his imminent danger, but 'unnatural' goes unexplained. Is it his mother's kneeling, or her asking a decision that will be fatal to her son? Or has Martius made the scene unnatural by betraying Mars, the soldier's god? Or does he finally see himself as responsible for the grotesque situation in which she as well as he must choose, but where either choice will be an 'evident calamity' (5.3.112)? And to which appeal does he respond? Does he hold out to the end and give in only to the mother's demand for obedience, repeating the pattern of 3.2? Although the scene's chronology might seem to suggest this conclusion (and does in most psychoanalytic readings and productions stressing the mother–son relationship as paramount), it also seems significant that while some of Coriolanus's speech is taken from Plutarch, there are significant omissions as well as additions: Shakespeare's Coriolanus does *not* say 'I see my self vanquished by you alone.'[3] And why should we take Aufidius's description in 5.6 as implicit instructions on how to stage the moment of surrender in 5.3? He has every reason to falsify his account in a direction that will incite both the Volscian citizens and Coriolanus. Coriolanus may instead be moved by the dual appeal to honour. Volumnia holds out the (novel) possibility that the role of peacemaker might not be 'poisonous' of a soldier's honour and, hence, offers a way out of his dilemma that avoids dishonourable betrayal of one of the sides claiming his loyalty. She also reminds him that it is Rome, its 'chronicle', that will determine his reputation and the 'name' he passes on to his son; the project of self-definition is futile.

Or are both Volumnia's arguments and threats in a sense irrelevant, good theatre but really only a marker of the time it takes him to realise and accept that his 'slippery' world has turned again? For all his mother's volubility, the emphasis of Coriolanus's remarks is on the power of visual and physical effects – the 'dove's eyes / Which

---

[1] Parker, p. 53.

[2] Peter Holland, review in *S.Sur.* 46 (1993), 185. Luckyj (see p. 58 above) illustrates her argument with five earlier productions which also played Volumnia's silence in 5.5 as despair rather than triumph.

[3] Bullough, *Sources*, v, 541. Crucial additions are the reference to the laughing gods, the words of tragic acceptance ('But let it come') and the final address to Aufidius.

can make gods forsworn', 'Great Nature' speaking through his son's countenance, his wife's kiss, his mother's bow and kneeling.[1] He rises and turns away after Volumnia's first appeal because 'Not of a woman's tenderness to be / Requires nor child, nor woman's face to see' (5.3.129–30). While Volumnia has by far the major speaking role, the scene can also be staged to underscore the powerful 'argument' represented by his wife and son. His first words are to Virgilia, and their kiss – 'Long as my exile, sweet as my revenge' (5.3.45) – sets up a different sense of the poles of his choice.[2] In allowing his mother's lengthy supplication Coriolanus lets her, in effect, rationalise a choice he makes instinctively, on the basis of feeling; that is, he concedes not because of what she says but of who she is, 'my mother', a relation he finds he can no more deny than that of 'wife' or 'child'. He submits to 'the ordinary', what Plutarch calls 'natural affection'.[3] The 'bond' he finally recognises and accepts can carry the weight and significance it gains in *Lear*. Depending on how Volumnia is played, she will see this or depart, uncomprehending, to her victory procession.

If the interpretation of Volumnia in 5.3 determines the staging of 5.5, how we understand Coriolanus's submission in 5.3 affects 5.6 and the way in which we respond to his death. If he is psychologically or morally unchanged, no more than the 'boy of tears' who cannot refuse his mother's command, his physical destruction is bound to feel anticlimactic. He has already been destroyed, and his acceptance of the consequences of failing to assert his independence from her – 'But let it come' (5.3.190) – is merely pathetic. Choosing to spare Rome, he knows he bids farewell to his identity as warrior-hero, and his loss is reflected in his words to Aufidius, words unimaginable for the Coriolanus of earlier scenes: 'though I cannot make true wars, / I'll frame convenient peace' (5.3.191–2). If, unable to endure such a loss, he seeks a kind of suicide in Corioles, the scene of his assassination is bleak indeed. Parker reads Coriolanus in 5.6 in a slightly more positive way, though still as essentially unaltered by his experience in 5.3. Rather, the humiliation of yielding his revenge project pushes him deliberately to risk death again; in a compulsive repetition of 1.4 and 4.5, he will again 'brave the Volscians single-handedly, and thus recover his identity'.[4] In 5.6 he enters playing a politician's 'part', the popular hero accepting the commoners' adulation and rationalising having made peace not war.[5] Under Aufidius's provocations this 'bad faith' performance collapses; Coriolanus reasserts his earlier identity and turns his death into 'a last act of aggression, his final humiliation of Aufidius'.[6] Stagings consonant with such a reading include the 1984 Peter Hall production in which, as he urges them to 'cut me to pieces', Coriolanus

---

[1] Joyce Van Dyke, 'Making a scene: language and gesture in *Coriolanus*', *S.Sur.* 30 (1977), 145.

[2] Walker sees Coriolanus's choice as between Aufidius and Virgilia, 'the two characters who occupy all of his erotic attention', now both before him on stage ('Voiceless bodies and bodiless voices', p. 179); on Virgilia's importance see also T. McAlindon, '*Coriolanus*: an essentialist tragedy', *Review of English Studies* 44 (1993), 515–16.

[3] For Zitner, Volumnia's speeches 'are needed to give ceremonial weight to a scene whose course is all too predictable' ('Shakespeare's *Coriolanus* and the Aristotelian modes of pathos', p. 307).

[4] Parker, p. 68; see also Sanders, *Shakespeare's Magnanimity*, pp. 184–5.

[5] In the 1984 Peter Hall production, Coriolanus in 5.6 'acknowledges the whistles, cheers and throwing of gold confetti with an easy satisfaction as he runs a triumphal lap around the circle' (Kristina Bedford, *'Coriolanus' at the National*, 1992, p. 133).

[6] Parker, p. 69; see also Brockbank, p. 65.

'tears off his Volscian uniform in an effort to get back to the primitive warrior of Act 1'.[1]
In Terry Hands's 1977 RSC production, the two rivals stood in duel-like proximity;
when the unarmed Coriolanus flung himself on his abandoned sword, now held by
Aufidius, he was clearly asserting his own victory.[2]

In my own reading, Coriolanus is genuinely affected by his recognition in 5.3 of the
power and worth of the natural affinities that make him humanly vulnerable. He has a
glimpse 'into a new territory of value and of moral experience',[3] though it remains on
the level of feeling, inarticulable to himself and probably incomprehensible to those
who await his response. His silence reflects not humiliation or an inability to argue
with his mother (or not only these) but an attempt to register, to come to terms with,
a profound challenge to his sense of himself and the soldier's code. Self-sufficiency
had been central to his ideal of manhood, yet seeing that some people are needed
and irreplaceable, 'a place is made for lack and, through the mediation of lack, for
others'.[4] The barriers restricting tenderness and human feeling to his private relations
with Virgilia prove permeable. And Shakespeare has provided hints that such feelings
could extend beyond his immediate family: the obvious warmth of his friendship with
Cominius and, in a different way, with Menenius; the Volscian host who used him
'kindly' and whose life he intended to save. In each of these earlier cases, 'wrath
o'erwhelmed my pity' (1.9.85), but that such 'pity' exists to be tapped prepares us for
the reversal of that pattern in 5.3.[5] The man who enters in 5.6 can be seen as acting
a new 'part', but sincerely; he is trying to unite the mercy and honour that Aufidius
can only, with grim satisfaction, see as fatally at odds (5.3.201–3). Aufidius limits his
rival's attempt to one speech, but Coriolanus transcends his idea of himself as a 'lonely
dragon' in accepting not only his familial bond but also a new relation to the community
of others.

He chooses to return with the Volscians,[6] and whereas in Plutarch he is killed before
he can say anything, Shakespeare gives expression to two Coriolanuses in this scene,
one we have seen before but also one struggling to combine in the role of peacemaker
the martial and political virtues which had always for him been as opposed as deeds and
words. It does not come easily, since he has never been a conciliator and has always been
averse to naming his deeds. He cannot get the tone of his entry speech quite right, but
that does not necessarily mean it is hypocritical bombast. Aggressive and surly in his
public role in Rome, he 'seems at last to have accepted the idea that his actions require
explanation to the community at large, and that this can be done only by himself,

---

[1] Bedford, 'Coriolanus' at the National, p. 135.
[2] Daniell, 'Coriolanus' in Europe, p. 41.
[3] Brockbank, p. 59; Brockbank's formulation, in full, is less qualified than mine.
[4] Paul Ricoeur, Oneself as Another, trans. Kathleen Blamey, 1992, pp. 181–2. In this section of his argument
   Ricoeur is analysing how in Aristotle friendship catalyses the transition between self-esteem, a solitary
   virtue, and justice, 'the virtue of human plurality belonging to the political sphere' (p. 182).
[5] Elizabeth Story Donno, 'Coriolanus and a Shakespearean motif', in Shakespeare and Dramatic Tradition,
   ed. W. R. Elton and William B. Long, 1989, p. 66.
[6] The return is a narrative fact in Plutarch, a conscious choice in Shakespeare. Shakespeare could also have
   adopted Livy's report that Coriolanus died in embittered exile, like Timon.

through the medium of language . . . He is using language like a social being.'[1] And this is what Aufidius fears, for he has already given the Volscian lords his version (the 'annals' of the campaign, suitably rewritten). To reactivate the absolutist warrior-rival, he hurls at Coriolanus the public accusation 'traitor' and adds to it the private insult of his demeaning description of 5.3. As Aufidius had earlier astutely seen, Coriolanus has striven all his life 'Not to be other than one thing' (4.7.42); the tentative attempt to recognise complexity and negotiate a peace crumbles before Aufidius's taunts, and he reverts to being that 'one thing' only.[2] He reasserts his lineage, identifying himself with Rome's predatory symbol: it was as an eagle that he 'Fluttered your Volscians' (5.6.118). Again 'alone, / To answer all the city', he dies invoking Corioles and victories in single combat over Aufidius. Wrath again 'o'erwhelms' all other emotions; words again become merely acts of aggression, weapons to provoke violence.

Coriolanus addresses Aufidius the rival warrior; in fact, he faces Aufidius the politician. Shakespeare constructs 5.6 to resemble the earlier banishment, but the darker tone elicits a wider range of sympathies. In 3.3 the tribunes were underhanded plotters and the fickle people as manipulable as Coriolanus. But what the tribunes said about Coriolanus was true, if a selective truth; the trial was held openly and according to traditional form. Securing his banishment ensured their own power, but the plebeians benefited and Rome was spared the civil war Coriolanus threatened to ignite. Our response to the banishment was ambivalent: it was fraudulently obtained but also deserved. Watching him again 'on trial' in another market-place in 5.6, our sympathies are substantially less divided. Aufidius is wholly self-interested, consumed by envious hatred, and intends a ruthless murder. With the conspirators' help he transmits his own barbaric passion – which once vowed to 'Wash my fierce hand in's heart' (1.10.27) – to the Volscian populace. With distortions of fact and outright lies, he turns the cheering crowd into a blood-seeking mob. The cry is not 'Let him away! / He's banished', but 'Tear him to pieces!' (3.3.113–14, 5.6.123).[3]

Coriolanus's retort is more than a simple assertion of martial superiority. He dies demanding the truth. It is a narrow, personal truth, to be sure, but the attractiveness of the idealist's insistence that the Volscian 'annals' be 'writ . . . true' is enhanced by our watching Aufidius in the process of cynically revising them to 'th'interpretation of the time', *his* time. We are reminded of what was admirable in the man who could not say what he did not feel. And there is irony but also pathos in watching the man who tried to be self-defining discover his truth to be at the mercy of those who write Rome's chronicles and the Volscian annals. Despite the faults and lack of self-knowledge that ensured he would bring on his own death – not on the battlefield, where he reigned supreme, but in the market-place of a new political order – when the man who engineered that death stands insultingly on Coriolanus's body, we do not need

---

[1] Anne Barton, '*Julius Caesar* and *Coriolanus*: Shakespeare's Roman world of words', in *Shakespeare's Craft: Eight Lectures*, ed. Philip H. Highfill, Jr, 1982, p. 39.

[2] Kahn, *Man's Estate*, pp. 170–1.

[3] In contrast, in Plutarch the 'mutinous people' quiet themselves to listen and 'the honestest men . . . who most rejoyced in peace, shewed by their countenaunce that they would heare him willingly, and judge also according to their conscience' (Bullough, *Sources*, v, 543).

to be told he has 'done a deed whereat valour' – and honour – 'will weep' (5.6.135).[1]
Coriolanus is eulogised as 'noble' by the man who has turned his back on the values
that define that nobility. On the battlefield Aufidius had invoked the heroic world by
comparing Coriolanus to Hector (1.8.11); the final visual image evokes that earlier
death of chivalry in *Troilus and Cressida*, unarmed Hector slaughtered by Achilles'
Myrmidons. The world will be a more manageable place without Coriolanus, but it
will be smaller and, when 'extremities' of situation and one's own 'best ends' dictate
policy and action in Rome as well as Corioles (3.2.42, 48), one wholly without principles.
The Volscian lord's final comment catches perfectly the tone of this pragmatic new
world: 'Let's make the best of it' (5.6.149).

In *Coriolanus* contemporary literary critics, and directors, are clearly grappling with
unusually challenging material. Though it is true of all plays, it is particularly so of
Coriolanus that its virtues lie 'in th'interpretation of the time'. While modern democratic
audiences seem to have no trouble imaginatively accepting concepts like the divine right
of kings or the nobility of suicide while watching plays set in earlier historical periods,
Coriolanus's frontal assault on the rights of man is more difficult to stage, and to
receive. And our attitude toward militarism has become more complex. While even in
Shakespeare's time there were premonitory grumblings over the impact of gunpowder
on aristocratic martial ideals, the glamour of chivalry and the romance of war as proving
ground of manhood persisted – and still exist, for some people. But just as no modern
audience can come to *The Merchant of Venice* without the hovering presence of the
Holocaust, *Coriolanus* in our time will be shadowed by the disillusionment of two
world wars and a lot of other nasty butchery in the name of patriotism and honour. It
is well to recognise that most of the late-twentieth-century productions cited here and
in the stage history below, however different their emphases, would to a teleported
eighteenth- or nineteenth-century audience seem incomprehensible, offensive, and
certainly not what Shakespeare 'meant'. We may think Shakespeare ahead of his time,
or 'universal' and 'timeless', in the extent to which he scrutinised the values and
practices of his day, but from the Dudley Diggeses in his first audience until well into
the twentieth century, most customers for *Coriolanus* would have missed the bitterly
ironic overtones in the title of Joan Littlewood's 1963 musical satire, *Oh What A Lovely
War*.

Coriolanus on Shakespeare's stage

Costuming was probably eclectic, though more historically accurate than the early-
eighteenth-century propensity for dressing Roman generals in full-bottomed wigs.[2]

---

[1] On the latent sadism in the honour code that leads to this 'insultment' on one's rival's corpse, see Clifford
Ronan, *'Antike Roman': Power Symbology and the Roman Plays in Early Modern England, 1585–1635*, 1995,
pp. 121, 129.

[2] Around mid century David Garrick restored more historically accurate costumes; see Allardyce Nicoll,
The Garrick Stage, ed. Sybil Rosenfeld, 1980, p. 162. The very 'Roman' Coriolanus in the frontispiece
to Rowe's 1709 edition is modelled on Poussin's neo-classical painting and probably does not reflect
contemporary stage practice; see illustration 4 and W. M. Merchant, 'Classical costume in Shakespearian
productions', *S. Sur.* 10 (1957), 72.

The earliest sketch based on a Shakespeare play, dating from about 1595, may draw on memories of a theatrical staging; it is an 'illustration' accompanying some verses from the Roman tragedy *Titus Andronicus*, and it suggests contemporary Elizabethan dress was used for commoners (whether soldiers or artisans) but 'the Roman breastplate, shaped to the figure . . . the military skirt or kilt, the draped scarf and plumed helmet' for patrician warriors.[1] At least versions of classical peacetime clothing for the patricians were available: Henslowe's records mention a senator's gown and senators' capes, and Coriolanus refers to his gown of humility as 'this wolvish toge [toga]' (2.3.101).[2] Changes of clothing for this man who would 'Not . . . be other than one thing' (4.7.42) indicate the actual fluidity of his public identity by emblematically marking the roles through which he passes. After the first scene in Act 1 he is seen in his favoured garb, the soldier's armour and helmet; in Act 2, Scene 1 the helmet has been exchanged for the oaken garland symbolising his martial excellence. His peacetime role as political candidate in Act 2, Scene 3 requires replacing armour with the gown of humility and the garland with a simple bonnet, a bonnet which must, in a further debasement, be removed as a sign of deference to the people whose voices he requests (but which they later note he waved 'in scorn'); his mother urges him to return and submit himself to the people bare-headed, 'with this bonnet in thy hand' (3.2.74). In banishment he is again a petitioner, now in Antium, and his 'mean apparel' recalls the gown of humility; successful, he again dons armour and helmet, but they are Volscian, not Roman.[3] The women's single costume change also visually underlines their altered status: patrician gowns are replaced by a female version of Coriolanus's 'mean apparel' for the supplication scene.[4]

Although in its stage life *Coriolanus* has been played with as few as 12 actors and as many as 240, in 1608–9 it was probably as populous as the company could afford but modest by the standards of eighteenth- and nineteenth-century productions (when supers to swell the crowds were cheap). T. J. King estimates that 11 men can play the 16 principal male roles, with three boys needed for the principal female roles;

[1] Merchant, 'Classical costume in Shakespearian productions', p. 71. The Peacham sketch does not correspond with any specific scene, but its costumes are likely to give a fairly accurate account of a remembered performance; see Eugene M. Waith's introduction to his edn of *Titus*, 1984, pp. 20–7, and R. A. Foakes, *Illustrations of the English Stage 1580–1642*, 1985, pp. 50–1. In 'Some principles of Elizabethan stage costume', *Journal of the Courtauld and Warburg Institutes* 25 (1962), Hal H. Smith notes that the baldrics worn by the soldiers were a conventional way of turning contemporary costumes into classical ones (p. 242). The Romans pictured in the woodcuts of Holinshed's chronicles (1577) wear breastplate armour over Elizabethan doublets, sandals, and hose sometimes gartered below the knee (Charney, *Shakespeare's Roman Plays*, p. 208).

[2] Arthur Humphreys, introduction to his edn of *Julius Caesar*, 1984, pp. 50–1; *Henslowe's Diary*, ed. R. A. Foakes and R. T. Rickert, 1961, p. 317. Some costumes might have been recycled from earlier productions of *Julius Caesar*, *Sejanus* and *Antony and Cleopatra*, despite their belonging to different periods of Roman history.

[3] Frances Teague discusses the symbolic force of these changing costumes and headgear for a Renaissance audience in *Shakespeare's Speaking Properties*, 1991, pp. 128–33; see also Parker, pp. 97–8, who adds another, theatrically effective though not textually specified, costume change: a prematurely-donned consul's robe for Coriolanus's entry in 3.1.

[4] The visual echo of Coriolanus's earlier 'mean apparel' was lost in eighteenth- and nineteenth-century productions, whose directions call for elaborate mourning dress for the women in 5.3.

P. 1905.

4   Frontispiece for *Coriolanus* in Nicholas Rowe, *The Works of Mr. William Shakespear*
(1709). Engraving by Elisha Kirkhall

together these 14 actors speak 93 per cent of the play's lines. He suggests another 14 men for 34 small speaking-parts and mutes, and an additional four boys for two small speaking-parts and mute attendants.[1] Indefinite stage directions (e.g. *seven or eight citizens* at 2.3.0, or *with Captains and Soldiers* at 2.1.134, or Titus's *power* at 1.9.11) suggest that the number of available mutes was understood to be flexible.[2] Consideration of the original cast of *Coriolanus* raises a significant question: the sex of the actor playing the principal female role. It has been generally assumed that before the Restoration all women's parts on the English stage were played by boys,[3] but this assumption has been challenged. M. C. Bradbrook thinks 'it was customary for men to take the parts of older women' and that both Cleopatra and Volumnia are roles 'too demanding for a boy'.[4] Carol Chillington Rutter has found in Henslowe's records an expenditure for a woman's gown for an adult male player and suggests that, once this possibility is recognised, 'it is not difficult to imagine casting men in preference to boys' in such roles as Volumnia, Juliet's Nurse, Cleopatra, Lady Macbeth, Paulina, Mistress Overdone and Mistress Quickly.[5] Yet Rutter's evidence is not conclusive, and boys played some very demanding roles in tragedies written for the children's companies. Since 'boys' might continue in female roles until the age of nineteen, even in one recorded case twenty-one,[6] Volumnia might have been played by a young man, perhaps not yet fully 'masculine' in musculature or voice.

Specified properties are generally simple and easily portable (stools, cushions, weapons, letters, embroidery). Scaling-ladders are mentioned in the dialogue in 1.4, though not specified in the stage directions; Coriolanus may have brought a rostrum to stand on in the vote-canvassing scene (perhaps the one left over from the 'mountebank' scene in *Volpone*). There was probably some kind of central curtained recess at the rear of the stage which could have stood in for the entrance to Aufidius's dining-hall in 4.5 and for Coriolanus's tent in 5.2, although there may have been a free-standing booth for the latter.[7] It could also have represented the gates of Corioles in 1.4, with the balcony above used as the walls of the city on which the senators enter for the parley; for appropriate plays, it may have been fitted with solid wooden property gates.[8] A chair of state was almost certainly revealed, or brought forth from the 'tent', for the

[1] T. J. King, *Casting Shakespeare's Plays: London Actors and Their Roles, 1590–1642*, 1992, pp. 92, 236–8, 255.
[2] On such indefinite directions, see Textual Analysis, p. 302 below.
[3] See G. E. Bentley, *The Profession of Player in Shakespeare's Time, 1590–1642*, 1984, pp. 113–14, 117; see also Andrew Gurr, *The Shakespearean Stage, 1574–1642*, 1980, p. 93, and King, *Casting Shakespeare's Plays*, p. 77.
[4] M. C. Bradbrook, *Shakespeare: The Poet in His World*, 1978, p. 213.
[5] Carol Chillington Rutter, *Documents of the Rose Playhouse*, 1984, pp. 124–5, 224–5.
[6] Gurr, *The Shakespearean Stage*, p. 93, and Jonathan Bate's introduction to Bate and Jackson (eds.), *Shakespeare: An Illustrated Stage History*, p. 6. King's evidence suggests that the usual age for changing from female roles to male ones was eighteen or nineteen (*Casting Shakespeare's Plays*, p. 270 n. 60).
[7] On the free-standing booth, see Gurr, *The Shakespearean Stage*, pp. 137–8.
[8] Chambers, *The Elizabethan Stage*, III, 83, and Irwin Smith, '"Gates" on Shakespeare's stage', *SQ* (1956), 159–76. However, in *Brawl Ridiculous: Swordfighting in Shakespeare's Plays*, 1992, Charles Edelman argues that the actual gates 'are offstage, and in the spectators' imaginations' (p. 142).

supplication scene, since earlier Cominius reports Coriolanus 'does sit in gold' (5.1.64) and in 5.3 Coriolanus says 'I have sat too long' (5.3.131).[1] Such use of the stage would prove suitable for the amphitheatre Globe as well as the indoor Blackfriars Theatre.

Stage history

Coriolanus offered contemporary political applications to its first audiences, and it continued to suggest an immediate relevance in the Restoration and early eighteenth century. In his 'Remarks on the Plays of Shakespear' Charles Gildon, a staunch Whig, takes the play as political and reprimands its author: 'Our Poet seems fond to lay the Blame on the People, and everywhere is representing the Inconstancy of the People: but this is contrary to Truth; for the People have never discover'd that Changeableness, which Princes have done.'[2] In seeing the play's struggle for power as between 'those born to govern and those elected to govern', Gildon reformulates that conflict into the central political struggle of his time, that between monarch and parliament.[3] *Coriolanus*'s actual ambivalence about the politics it stages, its willingness to air each side's case, made it suitable for appropriation and, *via* excision and addition, retooling into propaganda. Of the early adaptations, George C. D. Odell notes that *Coriolanus* 'seemed destined to be launched, with new trimmings, during or after each of England's successive politico-civic upheavals',[4] and this remained true until Sheridan removed most of the controversial political material and increased the amount of visual spectacle and pageantry. While scholarly editions continued to appear after Rowe, with rare exceptions playhouse audiences from the reopening of the theatres to the mid nineteenth century saw adaptations.

Nahum Tate's rewriting, *The Ingratitude of a Common-Wealth* (produced December 1681), was his third Shakespearean adaptation and second attempt at political intervention.[5] It appeared in the wake of the Popish Plot, while parliament was attempting to bar the succession of the exiled James, Duke of York (later James II), with the Exclusion bills.[6] Tate declares his royalist allegiances in the dedicatory epistle: 'Upon a close view of this Story, there appear'd in some Passages, no small Resemblance with the busie *Faction* of our own time. And I confess, I chose rather to set the *Parallel* nearer to Sight,

---

[1] The 'chayre of state' is also mentioned in Plutarch's account, which Shakespeare was following closely in this scene. Brockbank thinks the chair might also have been used earlier: Coriolanus might have sat at 5.2.58 to hear Menenius's plea (p. 73).

[2] Pope, VII, 389; Gildon's 'Remarks' had first appeared in 1710, as vol. VII of Rowe². Gildon goes on to speak of Greek and Roman generals in the same terms, apparently equating them with princes as unelected rulers.

[3] David Wheeler, 'To their own purpose: the treatment of *Coriolanus* in the Restoration and eighteenth century', in Wheeler (ed.), *'Coriolanus': Critical Essays*, p. 275. See pp. 29–33 above for the extent to which Shakespeare's audience might have seen the play in similar terms.

[4] George C. D. Odell, *Shakespeare from Betterton to Irving*, 2 vols., 1921, 1, 59–60.

[5] Although *Lear* was the first written, the adaptation of *Richard II*, under the title *The Sicilian Usurper*, was the first staged, December 1680; despite the change of locale, it was promptly suppressed by government order. See Ruth McGugan, *Nahum Tate and the Coriolanus Tradition in English Drama with a Critical Edition of Tate's 'The Ingratitude of a Common-Wealth'*, 1987, p. xxvi.

[6] *Ibid.*, pp. lxix–lxxi; see also Wheeler, 'To their own purpose', pp. 276–7.

then to throw it off at further Distance.' His targets are 'those *Troublers* of the State, that out of private Interest or Mallice, Seduce the Multitude to *Ingratitude*, against Persons that are not only plac't in Rightful Power above them; but also the heroes and Defenders of their Country'.[1] Tate retains about 60 per cent of Shakespeare's lines (though nearly two-thirds of these are revised),[2] but even before the rewritten last act, he has changed the tone. Restoration comic social banter is injected by means of a trans-formed Valeria, and Martius is made altogether more noble in socially approved ways – generous to those he calls his 'Fellow-Citizens' (until they turn cowardly and greedy), determined to find out the old Coriolan whose name he has forgotten, concerned to honour his slain soldiers with religious rites. The tribunes are 'Faction-Mongers', and a villainous turn-coat Roman, Nigridius, exacerbates Aufidius's envy and uses him to gain his own revenge on Coriolanus. In Act 5, as the play moves on from Coriolanus's banishment (the final parallel with James), its at least nodding acquaintance with contemporary politics evaporates.[3] The death scene is pure melodrama. Coriolanus kills several conspirators and wounds Aufidius before falling to lie a bloody witness to subsequent events. Menenius and Coriolanus's family have come to Corioles, and Aufidius intends to rape Virgilia. Instead he dies on stage, but to prevent dishonour Virgilia has already stabbed herself and enters for a tearful farewell with her husband. Meanwhile, Nigridius brags that he has killed Menenius and tortured Young Martius, whose broken body is brought on by a maddened Volumnia, who then kills Nigridius with a partisan snatched from a Guard and rushes off, leaving Young Martius to die in his dying father's arms. If there is any political moral in this blood-bath, it seems less the specific topical sentiments of the dedicatory epistle than a more diffuse fear that political rivalry threatens chaos and civil war. In Tate's version, while the assassination works out its bloody consequences on stage, we hear the off-stage sounds of skirmishes between Coriolanus's and Aufidius's troops.

When John Dennis's *The Invader of His Country: or, The Fatal Resentment* was produced in November 1719, the situation had sufficiently changed that the same pro-*status quo* moral could now support an opposite political position. Queen Anne had been succeeded by George I and power had passed from the Tories to the Whigs. The parallels between the Old Pretender, who wanted to be James III of England, and Coriolanus were now not to the first of the play's crises, the banishment, but to the second, the threat of invasion. The intrigues of James's supporters led to an abortive attempt to invade England in 1708 and then to James's participation in the Scottish 'Jacobite Rebellion' of 1715.[4] Yet Dennis's motive may have been as much aesthetic and moral as topically political: because it failed to adhere to the concept of poetic justice

---

[1] Dedication 'To the Right Honourable Charl's Lord Herbert', A2^{r-v} (roman for italic). The play is available in a facsimile reprint of the 1682 edition, Cornmarket Press, 1969.

[2] McGugan, *Nahum Tate and the Coriolanus Tradition*, p. xxvii.

[3] McGugan argues, however, that Tate's Aufidius and Nigridius together constitute a 'composite' of the worst qualities attributed to Shaftesbury by his Tory enemies (*Nahum Tate and the Coriolanus Tradition*, pp. lxxii–lxxiv).

[4] *Ibid.*, pp. lxxv–lxxvi; see also Wheeler, 'To their own purpose', pp. 284–5.

that Dennis thought essential to tragedy, Shakespeare's untidily sprawling *Coriolanus* was 'without Moral'.[1] In Act 1 Dennis reduces Shakespeare's ten scenes to one, the battle for Corioles, and Act 5 (largely rewritten) to two, the supplication scene and the assassination. Having pruned the structure, he also revises the ending. Aufidius and three conspirators are killed by Coriolanus, while a fourth brings him down with a stab in the back; the trouble-mongering tribunes are haled off to execution by the people. Since in the political allegory Coriolanus stands in for James and the feared French–Jacobite alliance, foreign threat is emphasised over personal relationships.[2] The supplication scene is more a debate than a mother's plea; when Coriolanus gives up his revenge he is not a 'boy of tears' but a magnanimous hero who has been persuaded by patriotic argument to subordinate his life to the good of his country. Dennis's play ran for only three nights at Drury Lane. In the same 1719–20 season the competition at Lincoln's Inn Fields offered Shakespeare's play twice, mockingly advertised as '*The Invader of His Country*. Written by Shakespear', and presented it under Shakespeare's title for five more performances between 1720 and 1722. James Quin may have played the title role; the extant playbills list only the actors for comic citizen parts which, together with the only surviving picture of Quin as Coriolanus (see illustration 5), suggests these performances were not serious revivals of Shakespeare's text.[3]

James Thomson, best known as the poet of *The Seasons*, wrote his *Coriolanus* around the time the Young Pretender, Charles Stuart, was being defeated in the Scottish uprising of 1745. Thomson did not tinker with Shakespeare, however; he produced a neo-classic, declamatory verse tragedy of his own based not on Plutarch but on Dionysius of Halicarnassus and Livy (where Veturia is the name of Coriolanus's mother, Volumnia that of his wife). Thomson's play begins after the banishment; unity of place is established by confining the locale to the Volscian camp. Such a structure minimises Rome's political crisis and Coriolanus's conflict with the tribunes and the populace; it also gives Tullus (Shakespeare's Aufidius) greater prominence and shifts the emphasis from action to psychological motivation. If motive is narrowed to personal jealousy in the warriors' rivalry, so the supplication scene emphasises filial love over patriotism; at the climax of her appeal, Veturia pulls out a dagger from beneath her robe and threatens suicide. The scene does not end with the ladies' exit; a lengthy quarrel between Coriolanus and Tullus culminates in a swift assassination and ends with the arrest of Tullus and a patriotic assertion that 'Above Ourselves our Country should be dear.'[4] After Thomson's death his play was given ten performances at Covent Garden, in January 1749, as an act of piety by his friend James Quin that

---

[1] John Dennis, *Essay on the Genius and Writings of Shakespear*, 1712, quoted in Wheeler, 'To their own purpose', p. 285.
[2] Wheeler notes a topical religious element in Dennis's foreign threat that reflected early-eighteenth-century fears of any French (Catholic) influence in English affairs ('To their own purpose', p. 288).
[3] C. B. Hogan, *Shakespeare in the Theatre, 1701–1800*, 1952, pp. 100–1. See Parker, p. 117, for further evidence that the Lincoln's Inn Fields performances were almost certainly played as farce.
[4] James Thomson, *Coriolanus. A Tragedy*, 1749, v.iv, p. 62.

in the Character of Coriolanus.

5   James Quin as Coriolanus, *c.* 1722

also helped pay the author's debts.[1] Thomson's *Coriolanus* was not revived, but its influence was assured by Sheridan's adaptation, which became the basis of Kemble's.

Enthusiasm for Shakespeare, not political topicality, motivated the adaptation of Thomas Sheridan, actor-manager of Smock Alley Theatre, Dublin. In the spring of 1749, he decided on Thomson's new *Coriolanus* as the concluding work for his theatre season, but then postponed the announced performance; when *Coriolanus* did appear in Dublin in February 1752, it was not Thomson's play but Sheridan's amalgam of what he thought the best features of Shakespeare and Thomson.[2] His 'Advertisement' to *Coriolanus: or the Roman Matron* explains that he wished to preserve Shakespeare's 'inimitable' characters but found the play itself 'ill calculated for representation'; yet while Thomson's tragedy offered 'great beauties' and a regular plot, it was 'too much of the epic kind, and wanted business'.[3] Sheridan contributed little actual rewriting; cutting and splicing restored some of Shakespeare's characterisation of Coriolanus in Rome and his struggle with the tribunes while avoiding what Sheridan considered dramatic pitfalls or irregularities. Basically, the first two acts are Shakespeare, Acts 3 largely Thomson, but even in the first part a regularising impulse is evident: Shakespeare's busy Act 1 is compressed into Sheridan's first scene, Shakespeare's 1.3 with the addition of a messenger who reports the Roman victory. The remainder of Sheridan's Act 1 provides a shortened version of Shakespeare's Act 2; Sheridan's Act 2 is Shakespeare's Act 3, although with Coriolanus's tirades about the tribunes and the 'mutable, rank-scented meinie' reduced to two brief attacks on the tribunes only. Thereafter Thomson's staging holds sway, with only minor interpolations of Shakespeare, and we get Thomson's supplication scene with, of course, the drawn dagger.

Condensing two long plays into one requires major excisions, but Sheridan's approach to Shakespeare's text also conforms to a later era's idea of tragic heroes: cutting all the Coriolanus scenes in Shakespeare's Act 1 and several of his later harangues makes Sheridan's protagonist less insistently arrogant, irascible and contemptuous. Thomson's closing words of praise – 'This man was once the glory of his age, / Disinterested, just, with every virtue / Of civil life adorn'd' – are not as ludicrous for Sheridan's Coriolanus as they would be for Shakespeare's. Sheridan's major addition also reflects mid-eighteenth-century taste and set a fashion that lasted into the twentieth century. Coriolanus's triumphal entry into Rome is turned into a full Roman ovation in which, according to the 'Advertisement', 'In the military Procession alone, independent of the Civil, there were an hundred and eighteen persons.' The play was a

[1] Odell, *Shakespeare from Betterton to Irving*, 1, 354, and Brockbank, p. 78. The only other recorded performance was at the Southwark Theatre in Philadelphia, 8 June 1767; see John Ripley, 'David Daniell's "*Coriolanus*" in Europe', in *Drama and Symbolism*, ed. James Redmond, 1982, p. 215. Ripley's excellent '*Coriolanus*' *on Stage in England and America, 1609–1994*, 1998, appeared too late to be incorporated here, but it is recommended to anyone interested in the play's stage history.
[2] The play was published anonymously, but since Sheridan produced and played the title role in 1752, tradition has long given him authorship of the adaptation; in addition, Esther K. Sheldon observes that the 'Advertisement' by the author is 'very much like Sheridan's prose style' ('Sheridan's *Coriolanus*: an 18th-century compromise', *SQ* 14 (1963), 154 n. 8).
[3] *Coriolanus: or the Roman Matron, A Tragedy*, 1755, A3ʳ.

success in Dublin in 1752; Sheridan performed it at Covent Garden in 1754–5 to good reviews, reviews whose emphasis on the principal actors (Sheridan and the renowned Peg Woffington as Coriolanus's mother) witnesses another shift in taste: in the era of actor-managers, plays were chosen (and doctored) to provide star vehicles as well as visual spectacle.[1] Jumping the gun on Sheridan in his London season, David Garrick opened Shakespeare's *Coriolanus* at his Drury Lane Theatre in November 1754 with Henry Mossop in the title role, so that for a time the productions played as rivals.[2] Sheridan's *Coriolanus* did as well as Shakespeare's, and it was revived successfully at Covent Garden in 1758, 1759, 1760, 1765 and 1768.[3] A play that he could put on profitably for only nine performances did not, apparently, satisfy Garrick, and *Coriolanus* was not produced again at Drury Lane under his management.[4]

The major eighteenth-century actor-manager who succeeded Garrick was John Philip Kemble who, in physical endowment and temperament, was born to play characters 'of a certain classic nobility and detachment' – Cato, Cardinal Wolsey and (with two-inch lifts in his sandals) his signature role, Coriolanus. The two portraits painted of him as Coriolanus standing majestically on Aufidius's hearth (see illustration 6) give some credence to the report that 'when Nature made Kemble she built not a man but a hero. His outline was monumental. The impression he made in private life was that he was too big for a room.'[5] Kemble's idealisation of Coriolanus and reduction of the plebeians to fickle clowns rested on his belief that tragedy should offer 'a perception of something superior to common life . . . and furthermore, that in exhibiting the heroes of the Roman world, it was not amiss to invest them with the additional dignity they had received from the length of their renown and the enthusiasm of scholarship'.[6] His patrician hauteur, 'his determined look, his dignified delivery, placed, as it were, in a vision before us, the most splendid glories of the classic page'.[7] His setting was Imperial Rome, and his version of the triumphal entry in 2.1 outdid Sheridan's, with a pageant of four divisions – including one of choristers singing 'See the Conquering Hero Comes' – followed by 28 senators, 27 ladies, 4 Roman matrons,

[1] McGugan, *Nahum Tate and the Coriolanus Tradition*, p. xcv; Sheridan's subtitle suggests a new prominence for Volumnia. Wheeler points out that by mid century the political situation had stabilised, and a change in poetics meant that 'poetry and drama were far less likely to be employed as partisan weapons' ('To their own purpose', p. 295).

[2] Shakespeare's text was of course heavily cut and, in a bow to the taste of the time, beginning with the second performance a Roman triumph was introduced in Act 2 (Dougald MacMillan, *Drury Lane Calender 1747–1776*, 1938, p. 227).

[3] *The London Stage 1660–1800*, Part 4 (1747–76), ed. George Winchester Stone, Jr, 3 vols., 1962, vol. II, pp. 654, 664, 692, 709, 787, 1099.

[4] Sheldon, 'Sheridan's *Coriolanus*', p. 161.

[5] *These Were Actors: Extracts from a Newspaper Cutting Book, 1811–1833*, ed. James Agate, 1943, p. 54. See also William Winter, *Shakespeare on the Stage*, third series, 1916, p. 207.

[6] *The Tatler*, 25 July 1831, rpt in Leigh Hunt, *Dramatic Essays*, ed. William Archer and Robert W. Lowe, 1894, pp. 222–3.

[7] *Morning Herald*, 26 April 1817, quoted in Agate (ed.), *These Were Actors*, p. 65. His acting was 'meant to be seen at a distance', and it was said in approbation that his performances were 'animated paintings' (quoted in Richard Findlater, *Six Great Actors*, 1957, p. 69). On the influence of neo-classical painting on Kemble's staging, see David George, 'Poussin's *Coriolanus* and Kemble's *Roman Matron*', *Theatre Notebook* 48 (1994), 2–10.

6 John Philip Kemble as Coriolanus: *Coriolanus at the Hearth of Aufidius* (4.5). Oil painting by
Sir Thomas Lawrence

Coriolanus's family and friends, and finally the hero himself followed by the standard-bearer of the Chief Eagle.[1] The effect was enhanced when Kemble was joined by the legendary Sarah Siddons (his sister, only two years his senior) as Volumnia: of her silent entry Charles Young reports, 'her dumb-show drew plaudits that shook the building'.[2] Kemble followed Sheridan in adapting Thomson, so Act 5 was reduced to the amalgamated supplication and assassination scenes; since the promptbook calls 'Everybody for last Act', presumably all 240 people on stage for the ovation were again there to swell the exit procession after the body.[3]

Kemble restored more of Shakespeare's original for his *Coriolanus: or the Roman Matron*, as well as Plutarch's and Shakespeare's names for the women. He did not, however, present Shakespeare's play with merely the addition of Sheridan's ovation and ending; his cuts eliminated many of the play's distinguishing features. Gone is the battle for Corioles and the duel with Aufidius; Menenius's part is diminished, as is that of Aufidius. Political conflict in Rome is reduced almost to a plot device, since Coriolanus's inflammatory diatribes to the senators are cut to a few lines, Volumnia no longer voices her scorn for the plebs, and the people's case is further weakened by suppressing the near-riot initiated by Coriolanus in 3.1. Shakespeare's varied commentary on his protagonist has virtually disappeared: Kemble cut the officers at the beginning of 2.2, the servingmen's discussion ending 4.5, 4.7's extended analysis by Aufidius, and Coriolanus's own soliloquy in 4.4. In this form, it received high praise from George Daniel: while perhaps 'yielding in some higher qualities' to 'Macbeth, Lear, and Hamlet, Coriolanus, as an *acting* drama, stands in the foremost rank'.[4] Kemble's version held the stage in his own productions from 1789 to 1817 and for many years after in his disciples' work; it was the only acting text available in the British provinces and the United States for most of the nineteenth century.[5]

Kemble mounted his first *Coriolanus* on 7 February 1789. In July Parisian citizens stormed the Bastille, and political events in both France and England determined the gaps in the record of performances of this, one of his most successful productions.[6] He established his heroic, anti-republican interpretation not merely out of an ideal

---

[1] The military divisions, numbering around a hundred, were, according to Thomas Goodwin (*Sketches and Impressions*, ed. R. Osgood, 1887, p. 34) composed of members of the Life Guards, each over six feet tall (cited in John Ripley, '*Coriolanus*'s stage imagery on stage, 1754–1901', *SQ* 38 (1987), 342).

[2] Quoted in Joseph Knight's stage history of *Coriolanus* in *The Works of William Shakespeare*, ed. Henry Irving and Frank A. Marshall, 8 vols., 1889, VI, 224.

[3] Kemble appears to have consulted Thomson's *Coriolanus* independently, since the lines he borrows are not always those adopted by Sheridan. The 1789 and 1806 acting editions are available in Cornmarket Press facsimiles (1970), his 1811 promptbook in *John Philip Kemble's Promptbooks*, ed. Charles H. Shattuck, 11 vols., 1974, II.

[4] 'Remarks', appended to the Kemble version reprinted in *Lacy's Acting Edition of Plays, Dramas, Farces, Extravaganzas*, 1843–73, vol. 95, p. 5.

[5] David George, 'Restoring Shakespeare's *Coriolanus*: Kean versus Macready', *Theatre Notebook* 44 (1990), 101. Since Kemble had a keen eye for the temper of his time, even those acting editions that shed Thomson's influence adopted most of Kemble's cuts.

[6] David Rostron, 'Contemporary political comment in four of J. P. Kemble's Shakespearean productions', *Theatre Research* 12 (1972), 114; Jonathan Bate, 'The Romantic stage', in Bate and Jackson (eds.), *Shakespeare: An Illustrated Stage History*, pp. 98–9.

of tragic elevation but in reaction to the French Revolution, and the popularity of Kemble's *Coriolanus* and the availability of his text effectively determined the play's ideological tone for the rest of the century. It was a Kemble production that prompted William Hazlitt's general remarks on the play's politics ('Shakespeare himself seems to have had a leaning to the arbitrary side of the question') and his sense that the poetic imagination is 'an aristocratical . . . faculty' naturally excited by the single man who braves the mob. 'There is nothing heroical in a multitude of miserable rogues not wishing to be starved', but 'the assumption of a right to insult or oppress others . . . carries an imposing air of superiority with it. We had rather be the oppressor than the oppressed.'[1] Himself a liberal who offered a substantial argument for why we should not admire the protagonist, Hazlitt yet concluded that 'The whole dramatic moral of *Coriolanus* is, that those who have little shall have less, and that those who have much shall take all that others have left.'[2]

William Charles Macready played Kemble's text of *Coriolanus* in 1819 at Covent Garden, where Kemble had given his farewell performance in 1817, and found enough success to revive it fifteen times over the next twenty years. In 1838 and 1839, when he had become playhouse manager, he tried breaking with the Kemble tradition by restoring more Shakespeare to the script and returning the sets to the period of the early Republic.[3] Perhaps because it was now six years after the passage of the Reform Bill, his citizens were no longer a fickle, ill-dressed, comic mob. To at least one reviewer, when the citizens enter in 1.1 'we become sensible that it is not merely a coward crowd before us, but the onward and increasing wave . . . of men who have spied their way to equal franchises, and are determined to fight their way to the goal'.[4] A less liberal reporter described them as 'a proper, massy crowd of dangerous, violent fellows' who were 'for the first time shown . . . as agents of the tragic catastrophe'.[5] Yet Macready's emphasis was still on Coriolanus's nobility, and a sentimental dumbshow prevailed over Shakespeare's ending: Volumnia and Virgilia return after the assassination to appal the consciences of the murderers; Volumnia leaves, 'erect and defiant', followed by Aufidius, 'bareheaded and repentant'.[6] Despite Macready's success in other Shakespearean plays, *Coriolanus* was not one of his great roles. Unlike Kemble, he was best at characters who 'were domestic rather than ideal'; as a consequence, he 'was

---

[1] *Examiner*, 15 December 1816, rpt in William Hazlitt, *Dramatic Essays*, ed. William Archer and Robert W. Lowe, 1895, pp. 124–6. Only in the last paragraph do we learn that he is reviewing a specific Kemble production.

[2] *Ibid.*, pp. 127–8. Hazlitt's response to *Coriolanus* is far richer than these quotations suggest; see Jonathan Bate, *Shakespearean Constitutions: Politics, Theatre, Criticism 1730–1830*, 1989, pp. 164–72.

[3] Only a few speeches from Thomson remain, connecting 5.3 and 5.6: Macready was determined not to give up the impressive 'armed array' of Volscian soldiers for the death scene (contemporary review, quoted in Odell, *Shakespeare from Betterton to Irving*, II, 198).

[4] *John Bull*, 19 March 1838, quoted in Odell, *Shakespeare from Betterton to Irving*, II, 212–13.

[5] John Forster, quoted in Findlater, *Six Great Actors*, p. 119. Forster was equally impressed by 'the Volscian army on the Appian way, with battering-rams and moving-towers, [that] seemed to spread over the stage in their thousands' (*ibid.*, p. 120).

[6] John Coleman's account of a 12 March 1838 performance (*Players and Playwrights I Have Known*, 2 vols., 1888–9, I, 19–20; extracted in Abraham J. Bassett, 'Macready's *Coriolanus*: an early contribution to modern theatre', *Ohio State University Theatre Bulletin*, 13 (1966), 23–4).

irritable where he should have been passionate, querulous where he should have been terrible'.[1]

Kemble's Coriolanus gave way, briefly, to Edmund Kean's, offered at Drury Lane in 1820 but failing after only four performances. Kean used Shakespeare's text (though heavily cut), but he could not escape the shadow of Kemble's grand style and opulent spectacle.[2] A small and unimposing man, Kean unwisely restored the battle for Corioles and proved unconvincing as military hero. And while Leigh Hunt thought Kean's passionate and more naturalistic acting far preferable to Kemble's 'dry, tearless, systematical' depiction of 'not the man, but his mask',[3] the public was used to Kemble's noble pride and sonorous delivery. Hazlitt, still a Kemble admirer, did not appreciate the psychological complexity Kean had introduced: instead of '"keeping his state" . . . on his pedestal of pride', Kean too often descended 'into the common arena of men . . . to prove the hollowness of his supposed indifference to the opinion of others'; his 'I banish you' speech expressed the 'rage of impotent despair . . . instead of being delivered with calm, majestic self-possession'.[4] Nor was the restored text applauded: one reviewer maintained that 'The alterations in *Coriolanus*, which were made by John Kemble with the aid of Thomson's Play, seem to us singularly felicitous.'[5]

With the exception of Kean in 1820 and, to a lesser extent, Macready's 1838–9 productions, Kemble's text prevailed. It was used in Britain by John Vandenhoff in numerous performances in the 1820s and 1830s and by William Conway in England and America from 1819 to 1827; initially imported by British actors (Thomas Cooper, James Wallack, and later Thomas S. Hamblin as well as Conway and Vandenhoff), it proved popular for American actors as well.[6] Edwin Forrest played the Kemble text in the Kemble manner between 1831 and 1866, actually increasing the degree of spectacle. Coriolanus made his triumphal entry in a chariot drawn by citizens and at the end, after the usual grand exit procession, Forrest's promptbook outlines an added scene: the curtain rose on a night-time grove in which Coriolanus was cremated, accompanied by a dirge and watched by his kneeling kinsfolk as well as soldiers and senators; the climactic image was a bird ascending heavenward from the flaming pyre. Forrest was succeeded by John McCullough, another imposing, athletic actor, who elaborated the fights and processions and made the plebeians 'dirty swine'.[7] In 1883 New York saw a German production starring Ludwig Barnay, a former member of the Meiningen Company which in Germany had made *Coriolanus* the most popular of the

[1] G. H. Lewes, quoted in Agate (ed.), *These Were Actors*, p. 17.

[2] The text provided by Kean and the Drury Lane manager, Robert Elliston, retained the ovation procession in Rome (adding a new 'Ode to Triumph') and Kemble's named, small-part characters; the cuts, with some exceptions, follow Kemble's 1789 text (George, 'Restoring Shakespeare's *Coriolanus*', p. 104).

[3] Hunt, *Dramatic Essays*, p. 224.

[4] *London Magazine*, February 1820, rpt in Hazlitt, *Dramatic Essays*, p. 203.

[5] *The Champion*, 29 January 1820, quoted in Ripley, 'David Daniell's *"Coriolanus" in Europe*', pp. 215–16.

[6] George, 'Restoring Shakespeare's *Coriolanus*', pp. 102, 106.

[7] *New York Daily Tribune*, 19 December 1878. Professional performances are usually the only ones whose texts reach print, but the Folger Shakespeare Library has the instructor's copy of the text ('printed by an amateur', a pencil note tells us) for a 10 November 1899 performance by the 'A and B Classes' at the New York State Reformatory for Boys. There are very few deletions and, of course, no added spectacle.

Roman plays. Two years later, on his fourth American tour, Tommaso Salvini received acclaim for his production, although the effect of Salvini speaking Italian and the rest of the cast English must have required getting used to for those who had missed his earlier *Othello* or *Macbeth*. Unlike Forrest and other Kemble followers, Salvini played Coriolanus as 'restless and impetuous rather than statuesque, natural and human in his reactions rather than classical and conventional'.[1]

Shakespeare finally reclaimed the London stage with Samuel Phelps, who opened the 1848–9 Sadler's Wells season with *Coriolanus* and was still offering it in 1860, its last London appearance for forty years. Yet nineteenth-century scenic demands meant that Phelps, too, had to trim the play severely; as a result, what the public saw was not so very different from Kemble's version. It was about half the length of Shakespeare's text, and Phelps followed most of Kemble's excisions.[2] Both sides of the political contest were muted: the citizens' most bitter accusations in 1.1 and later claim that the 'people are the city' disappeared, as did Coriolanus's diatribes against the people and the craven senate. Nor had the interpretation changed. In Phelps's last scene, at Aufidius's taunt 'the loftiness of [Coriolanus's] disdain carries all sympathies with it'.[3] The first Stratford-upon-Avon production of *Coriolanus*, produced by F. R. Benson in 1893, also used Shakespeare's text, but Kemble's influence could still be seen in the elaborate ovation (which included a religious procession with votive lamb as well as prisoners and spoils of war),[4] and the amalgamated 5.3 and 5.6, set in the Volscian camp. One reviewer's favourable comparison with Kemble suggests Benson's interpretation: 'Given the stateliness of "John Philip," the graceful limbs, the studied poses, the sonorous utterance, and *Coriolanus* is already three parts played. Now Mr Benson has all this and something more. There is a natural note of aristocratic exclusiveness in him.'[5] On 13 February 1901 he played the role at the Comedy Theatre, London, now with the illustrious Geneviève Ward as Volumnia. Fourteen years later he was still playing in the slow, deliberate manner of 1893, though by 1915 the mob scenes seemed particularly incongruous because presented 'in a much more modern style, with much ingenuity, and quite reminiscent of Galsworthy'.[6]

Two months after Benson opened in London in 1901, Henry Irving mounted a lavish production at the Lyceum with himself in the title role and Ellen Terry as Volumnia. Although Terry was at least visually imposing (see illustration 7), both were miscast, and it was particularly unfortunate in Irving's case. He was by now sixty-three and in ill health; though he cut all the fight scenes, he still lacked 'robustness and power of declamation'.[7] Adding four white horses to pull Coriolanus's gilded triumphal

---

[1] Marvin Carlson, *The Italian Shakespearians*, 1985, pp. 122–7; between 1856 and 1870 Ernesto Rossi and Salvini, acting in the new verse translations of Giulio Carcano, had established Shakespeare on the Italian stage (*ibid.*, p. 22). See also Winter, *Shakespeare on the Stage*, pp. 227–31 ('Barnay and Salvini').

[2] The Phelps and Kemble promptbooks are in the Folger Shakespeare Library collection, Washington, D.C.; on Kemble's texts, see also p. 74 n. 3 above.

[3] Henry Morley, *The Journal of a London Playgoer*, 1866, pp. 261–3.

[4] *Birmingham Daily Gazette*, 18 August 1893.

[5] *The Theatre*, 1 October 1893.

[6] 'The Gordon Crosse Theatrical Diary, 1890–1953', Shakespeare Library, Birmingham, vol. VI, p. 24.

[7] *Ibid.*, VIII, p. 66. Irving reduced 27 scenes to 17, omitting many and splicing others.

7   Ellen Terry as Volumnia in Sir Henry Irving's 1901 production, Lyceum Theatre, London

8 *The House of Aufidius*. Sir Lawrence Alma-Tadema's design for Sir Henry Irving's 1901 production, Lyceum Theatre

chariot was not enough to win his audience. The only real successes of the production were the Etruscan-period scenery and costumes of Sir Lawrence Alma-Tadema.[1] Irving had wanted simulated marble, but his designer insisted on the historical accuracy of mud bricks and wood. One reviewer promised that 'A visit to *Coriolanus* . . . is a liberal education in the attire, the furniture, the weapons, and the architecture of Rome five hundred years before Christ.'[2] Alma-Tadema was also an innovator in the use of electric light, and his 'Sunrise in Corioli' in Act 1 and the moonlight of Antium 'left audiences gasping with delight' (see illustration 8).[3]

Irving's and Benson's Coriolanuses were tradition-bound, but not Benson's citizen crowds. Not since Macready's 1838–9 productions had they been presented as a substantive political force. As early as Benson's first *Coriolanus* in 1893 they were

[1] Alma-Tadema's scrupulous research and ability to draw architecture were admired by archaeologists and architects alike. Irving had planned to produce *Coriolanus* as early as July 1879; the publication of eight of Alma-Tadema's designs in 1880 was instrumental in his election to the Royal Institute of British Architects (Vern G. Swanson, *The Biography and Catalogue Raisonné of the Paintings of Sir Lawrence Alma-Tadema*, 1990, p. 56).

[2] *The Era*, 20 April 1901, quoted in Sybil Rosenfeld, 'Alma-Tadema's designs for Henry Irving's *Coriolanus*', *Deutsche Shakespeare-Gesellschaft West Jahrbuch*, 1974, p. 95.

[3] Mario Amaya, 'The Roman world of Alma-Tadema', *Apollo*, December 1962, p. 77.

described as 'frowning, sullen, malignantly threatening', and in 1910, in a production that moved from Beerbohm Tree's His Majesty's Theatre in London back to Stratford, the tribunes were mauled and strangled on stage at the end of Act 4.[1] Reviews no longer focused almost exclusively on the principal actors and the spectacle. The reviewer for the *Stratford-upon-Avon Herald* (6 May 1910) opined that 'There is a peculiar appositeness in [this play's] present-day appearance, when a social upheaval or struggle is taking place between the aristocracy and democracy – British peers and people are engaged in mental and parliamentary conflict.'[2] A rather schizophrenic review in the *Birmingham Post* (3 May 1910) first asserted that 'one may safely conclude that the drama was not intended as a piece of political propagandism, and that it had no political significance' but went on to a most untraditional interpretation of the protagonist who, in Shakespeare's hands, 'becomes in language and manners a man of the people, proud, vigorous, lion-hearted, but certainly with no blue blood in his veins'.

On the continent, political events had a more immediate and decisive impact on the play's fortunes. Germany's tradition of plays based on the Coriolanus story dates back to Hermann Kirchner's tragicomedy of 1599, though it did not take tragic form until two translations of Thomson's version appeared in 1756 and 1760;[3] it was on this neo-classical model that Heinrich Josef von Collin wrote his *Coriolan* in 1804, for which Beethoven composed his overture.[4] While there were various German translations and adaptations of Shakespeare, the play became popular only in the twentieth century, when its clash of military and democratic values became acutely apposite. Between 1911 and 1920 there were 103 performances in Germany, more than half of them in 1919, and up to 108 in each of the next two decades.[5] Foreign-language productions tend to be – or to seem, in times of instability – more politically radical, in part from the director's intentions but also because translation into contemporary diction inevitably updates the historical setting. Hans Rothe's 1932 modern translation premiered on 3 March 1933 in Dessau, but he was forced into exile by the emergent Nazi government in 1934 and his works banned in 1936. Other editions, prepared for school children, were used to provide an example of 'bravery and heroism' that will make 'our children . . . enthusiastic for great men'. H. Hüsges is specific about its meaning for 'the new Germany': 'The poet . . . shows a misled people, a false democracy . . . Above these weaklings towers the figure of the true hero and *Führer*, Coriolanus, who desires to lead the misguided *Volk* to restoration, just as Adolf Hitler does in our day for our

---

[1] *Stratford-upon-Avon Herald*, 25 August 1893; *The Stage*, 21 April 1910. According to David Rostron, 'F. R. Benson's early productions of Shakespeare's Roman plays at Stratford', *Theatre Notebook* 25 (1970–1), Benson was influenced by the well-drilled crowds in the Saxe-Meiningen production of *Julius Caesar* that had visited London in 1881 (p. 49).

[2] In Russia Alexander Lenski was breaking even more sharply with the theatrical emphasis on romantic character study. In his 1902 *Coriolanus* for the Maly Theatre, Moscow, the portrayal of Rome and its people was central to understanding the hero, and the prominence given the Roman crowd seems to have impressed the young Stanislavski, for there were echoes of Lenski's production in the Moscow Art Theatre's 1903 *Julius Caesar* (Joyce Vining Morgan, *Stanislavski's Encounter with Shakespeare*, 1984, p. 16).

[3] Martin Brunkhorst, *Shakespeares 'Coriolanus' in Deutscher Bearbeitung*, Berlin, 1973, p. 17.

[4] Wilhelm Münch, 'Collin und Shakespeare', *Shakespeare Jahrbuch* 41 (1906), 23.

[5] Brunkhorst, *Shakespeares 'Coriolanus' in Deutscher Bearbeitung*, p. 157.

beloved fatherland.'[1] In the early years of occupation after the Second World War the play was black-listed and not produced again in Germany until 1953.

France has its own independent history of Coriolanus plays dating back to Alexandre Hardy's *Coriolan* (published 1625),[2] which may have been the inspiration for a long list of continental dramatic and operatic versions in the seventeenth and eighteenth centuries.[3] Shakespeare's play was readily available in the several translations of the complete works produced in the nineteenth century. Yet a new translation by René-Louis Piachaud, mounted by Émile Fabre at the Comédie Française on 9 December 1933 with an enormous cast (231 in all; 92 citizens on stage for 1.1), proved incendiary. In January 1934 the government's radical socialist leader fell in the wake of the Stavisky financial scandal, and the production was now taken as right-wing polemic against democratic institutions in general and the current socialist Daladier government in particular. It provoked partisan shouts and later riots between applauding royalists and Fascists and hissing defenders of the government. Daladier unwisely replaced the popular Fabre with the head of the Sûreté Nationale; after more rioting during a 4 February 1934 performance, the theatre was closed. Fabre was reinstated the next day, Daladier soon resigned over the continuing Stavisky scandal, and the production reopened in March without incident. That its reception in early 1934 depended on very specific political conditions is confirmed by later peaceful revivals of the same translation.[4]

When Benson revived *Coriolanus* at Stratford in 1919, just after the war, he ended the play with 5.3 and the agreement for 'convenient peace'.[5] Perhaps owing to the rise of Fascism in England, too, between 1919 and 1924 there was only one brief London production, running for six performances at the Old Vic. By February 1926 England seemed to many to be on the verge of class warfare; indeed, the General Strike called in May provoked fears of a Bolshevik revolution. In this atmosphere *Coriolanus* was staged at the Stratford Festival in April, directed by W. Bridges-Adams.[6] There were no riots, perhaps because, although he was 'using scenographic techniques derived from German political theatre',[7] Bridges-Adams offered a cut and rearranged text emphasising the protagonist's pride rather than politics. Three months after Hitler was appointed chancellor in 1933, Bridges-Adams restaged *Coriolanus* in a production

---

[1] Quoted in *ibid.*, p. 157 (translation, David Van Dyke). On Rothe's translation running afoul of Goebbels, see *The Play Out of Context: Transferring Plays from Culture to Culture*, ed. Hanna Scolnicov and Peter Holland, 1989, pp. 113–14.

[2] In his edition of *Coriolan*, 1978, Terence Allott argues that Hardy's play was written between 1600 and 1615, perhaps around 1607 (p. viii).

[3] There were seven French contributions on the Coriolanus tradition, three Spanish verse dramas and six continental operas before 1820 (McGugan, *Nahum Tate and the Coriolanus Tradition*, p. xlvii).

[4] Events of 1933–4 taken from Daniell, '*Coriolanus' in Europe*, pp. 61–4; see also Robert Speaight, *Shakespeare on the Stage*, 1973, pp. 199–200. Ruby Cohn, however, argues that Piachaud's translation, though not 'Fascist-inspired', does vulgarise the plebeians and ennoble Coriolanus (*Modern Shakespeare Offshoots*, 1976, pp. 11–16).

[5] The curtailed ending was noted in the *Birmingham Mail*, 24 April 1919.

[6] On the politics surrounding this event, see Terence Hawkes, *Meaning by Shakespeare*, 1992, pp. 45–51.

[7] Dennis Kennedy, *Looking at Shakespeare: A Visual History of Twentieth-Century Performance*, 1993, p. 126.

that was chiefly remembered for the 'epic excitement' of the battle scenes.[1] Indeed, a studied avoidance of contemporary relevance marked all Stratford productions of the 1930s, though this is particularly clear in Iden Payne's 1939 *Coriolanus*.[2] Promotional information released to the *Stratford-upon-Avon Herald* (5 May 1939) promised costumes true to its original performance and maintained that 'Shakespeare, like all Elizabethans, regarded a play as a contemporary happening, with the result that the feeling and tone of *Coriolanus* are essentially of the Renaissance and should be so expressed' (see illustration 9). The set turned out to be a series of graceful Palladian arches, and the Volscians' costumes made them look like Turkish harem guards. Some reviewers made political connections the production avoided. The *Daily Sketch* (10 May 1939) was aware that in America Coriolanus had recently been presented as a Fascist and the Volscians dressed as contemporary Italian soldiers;[3] it was the current context that prompted this reviewer's description of Sicinius as stirring 'on his followers as cunningly as any modern Communist agitator'.

In London, William Poel's curious 1931 production at the Chelsea Palace in London attempted, at least in part, to point contemporary themes. Poel chose costumes of the French Directoire period to emphasise what the programme stated as the play's aim, 'to show the ageless spirit of militarism', though he also 'tried to suppress every word, tone, or gesture which could give offence' to the Conservative government and did nothing to sentimentalise the plebs.[4] Perhaps because he believed much of the dialogue was not by Shakespeare, Poel savagely cut and rearranged the play, and he omitted 5.4–5.6 entirely, ending with the protagonist re-entering Corioles and the sounds of his off-stage murder.[5] In Lewis Casson's 1938 production at the Old Vic, with Laurence Olivier as Coriolanus, a single 'marquee' set faintly evocative of Stonehenge suggested a more primitive, brutal era. Olivier established a contemporary reference through his performance, since to one observer his noble Roman shaded into the 'embryo Fascist dictator', but primarily he was the consummate patrician warrior, 'a pillar of fire on a plinth of marble',[6] and the production emphasised his relationship with his mother. The crises of the 1930s were more directly reflected in the Manchester Repertory Company production during election week in November 1935. The effects of the Depression and the rise of Mussolini in Italy seemed to be its targets: Coriolanus wore a white drill cavalry uniform (in exile, a blue pinstripe suit and black homburg),

---

[1] On both Bridges-Adams productions, see Sally Beauman, *The Royal Shakespeare Company: A History of Ten Decades*, 1982, p. 91. He also reintroduced Benson's on-stage murder of the tribunes by their constituents.

[2] *Ibid.*, p. 160.

[3] The reviewer may have been referring to the Federal Theatre Project production, directed by Charles Hopkins in February 1938 in New York, mentioned in William Babula, *Shakespeare in Production, 1935–1978*, 1981, p. 44.

[4] According to Robert Speaight, *William Poel and the Elizabethan Revival*, 1954, pp. 255–61. Despite the programme note, Poel insisted to Speaight that the play was about pride, not politics, and that 'all his other conflicts, political or military, were incidental' to his 'surrender to his mother' (p. 258).

[5] The programme's 'Producer's Note' states Poel's view that 'the greatest lines in "Coriolanus" were written by Chapman'. The production lasted only ninety minutes.

[6] The first quotation is from Laurence Kitchin, *Mid-Century Drama*, 1960, p. 51, the second from J. C. Trewin, *Shakespeare on the English Stage 1900–1964*, 1964, p. 175.

9 Alec Clunes (Coriolanus), Dorothy Green (Volumnia) and R. Lesley Brook (Virgilia) costumed for the 1939 Iden Payne production, Stratford Memorial Theatre. Photograph by Ernest Daniels

gave the Fascist salute, and was in the last scene shot in the back; the tribunes wore tweed suits and red ties, and Sicinius was made up to resemble Lenin.[1] Records suggest a few other stagings that favoured the plebeians and portrayed an unsympathetically authoritarian Coriolanus, notably in Russia (at the Maly Theatre in Moscow, 1934) and Poland (the Grand Theatre in Leopol, 1935).[2] Such proto-Brechtian productions were unusual in the years between the wars; more common was the heroic interpretation dating back to the eighteenth century, supported by a similar strategic cutting of the text.

By and large this remained true of the post-war period in Canada and America as well as England until the 1980s.[3] Following a tradition harking back to Kemble, the Old Vic company's 1948 staging at the New Theatre presented the plebeians as 'gaping village idiots, a bedraggled band of zanies';[4] the production's major interest lay in Alec Guinness's delicately nuanced Menenius. In 1952 in Glen Byam Shaw's *Coriolanus* at Stratford, Anthony Quayle gained sympathy for Coriolanus by playing him as a tough, virile soldier, disengaged from patricians and plebeians alike and humanised by occasional touches of boyishness.[5] That sympathy was also achieved through the old-fashioned method of cutting some of the more objectionable patrician sentiments and making the tribunes comic and the mob more picturesque than a credible political force. In the United States the play received less severely cut but still traditional productions in 1953 by the Provincetown Repertory company in Greenwich Village and at the Oregon Shakespeare Festival at Ashland.[6]

In 1959 Olivier returned to the role that had made his name as a Shakespearean actor, now in Peter Hall's acclaimed Memorial Theatre production at Stratford-upon-Avon. The contempt for the plebeians was still played to withering effect, but Hall cut nearly a quarter of the text and, although in general they were 'practical rather than interpretative',[7] the loss of all of 2.2 helped tip the emphasis toward personal relationships. The titanism of Coriolanus's harangues was undercut by the extent to which this 'spoilt son' was emotionally dependent, even comically so, on his mother.[8]

---

[1] Unidentified newspaper cutting, '"Coriolanus" in Modern Dress / THE REPERTORY', quoted by David George in his typescript stage history for the New Variorum *Coriolanus*, p. 46; see also the *Manchester Evening News*, 12 November 1935.

[2] Speaight, *Shakespeare on the Stage*, p. 200.

[3] Ralph Berry, *Changing Styles in Shakespeare*, 1981, p. 27; see also Samuel L. Leiter (comp.), *Shakespeare Around the Globe*, 1986, pp. 83–6.

[4] T. C. Worsley, *New Statesman and Nation* 35 (1948), 292; reported in Babula, *Shakespeare in Production*, p. 44.

[5] *The Times*, 14 March 1952. Berry notes that in 1952 soldiering would have been 'a shared bond between actor and audience' (*Changing Styles in Shakespeare*, p. 27).

[6] John Houseman also directed it at the Phoenix Theatre in New York City in 1954 with exciting crowd scenes but a weak centre in screen actor Robert Ryan. Brooks Atkinson, *New York Times*, 24 January 1954, noted that outside of six performances by the Federal Theatre Project in 1938, *Coriolanus* had not appeared in New York City since 1885.

[7] Stanley Wells, *Royal Shakespeare: Four Major Productions at Stratford-upon-Avon*, 1977, p. 9. Hall later urged using full texts, 'but this was not his policy, nor that of the Stratford theatre in general, in 1959' (p. 8).

[8] Kitchin, *Mid-Century Drama*, p. 137. The danger such emotional dependence boded would have been emphasised by Olivier's maturity: he was 52 when he played in Hall's production.

On the other hand, Olivier gained sympathy by playing Coriolanus as a plain-speaking military man 'sickened equally by flattery and by the need to flatter'.[1] Stressing this aspect gave greater prominence to Aufidius and the conflict between 'flawed chivalry and ruthless expediency'; for some the production revolved finally on their relationship, and its climax was the 'extraordinary handshake' with which Olivier sealed his pact with his rival.[2] The assassination was violent and shockingly underscored the fact that Coriolanus's ideals of martial and personal honour are out-of-date. Olivier dashed up a steep flight of stairs to 'vent his rage' but then threw away his sword and, after issuing his challenge, 'allow[ed] a dozen spears to impale him'. He toppled forward 'to be caught by the ankles so that he dangle[d], inverted, like the slaughtered Mussolini'[3] (see illustration 10). While ignominiously hanging head down, he was stabbed in the belly by Aufidius.[4]

One reason for the increased prominence of Aufidius in post-war productions lies in the adoption of an Elizabethan acting-space – if not a bare stage, then an all-purpose set that obviates the time-consuming scenery changes of most pre-First World War productions. When all of the text can be staged (or all of the scenes, with only minor internal cuts), Aufidius's importance to Shakespeare's conception becomes clear. (In most earlier acting texts he does not appear until the scene in Antium, 4.5.) Another can be traced to a post-Freudian interest in the psychodynamics of the bond between the lover-rivals as well as mother and son. Tyrone Guthrie's 1963 Nottingham Playhouse production, staged in French Empire costume, emphasised the Coriolanus–Aufidius relationship and gave it an 'hysterical and homosexual element'.[5] The staging of the duel in 1.8 and Aufidius's welcome of Coriolanus in 4.5 prepared for the explosion of rivalrous hatred and love in 5.6. After killing Coriolanus, Aufidius stamped on his groin; then, realising what he had done, he flung himself on the body with a long moan, a kind of crooning 'wordless elegy'.[6] In more muted form the homoerotic element has figured in several subsequent productions, indicated in the staging and, sometimes, costumes. In the RSC productions of 1967 (directed by John Barton) and 1977 (Terry Hands) the rivals wore identical armour, and in 1967 even matching blond hair. The 1977 duel resembled 'some elaborate mating-dance';[7] in 1981 at Stratford, Ontario, Brian Bedford ritualised the battle scenes and transformed the single combat

[1] Kenneth Tynan, *Curtains*, 1961, p. 240. Emphasising the professional soldier aspect to detach Coriolanus from any simple identification with the patricians may have been inspired by Anthony Quayle's 1952 performance (compare Tynan's description of Quayle, p. 34).
[2] Kitchin, *Mid-Century Drama*, p. 136.
[3] Tynan, *Curtains*, p. 241.
[4] Wells, *Royal Shakespeare*, p. 21. In his 1984 National Theatre production, which mixed Roman and modern costumes, Hall found another way to make Coriolanus's death 'undercut any representation of romantic heroism': the planned knife-ambush was jettisoned in favour of a blocking in which, sword drawn, Coriolanus lunged toward Aufidius but was brutally gunned down by the conspirators (Bedford, '*Coriolanus' at the National*, pp. 135–6).
[5] Guthrie's programme note explains that this element 'seems so usual and powerful an ingredient in the composition of intensely vigorous men of action'.
[6] Berry, *Changing Styles in Shakespeare*, p. 29; see also Geoffrey Reeves, 'Guthrie's *Coriolanus* in Nottingham's new Playhouse', *Encore* 11 (1964), 43–9.
[7] Francis King, quoted in the 1978 Aldwych Theatre programme.

10 Laurence Olivier's death-fall in the 1959 Peter Hall production, Stratford Memorial Theatre. Photograph: Angus McBean

in 1.8 into two 'bodies glistening in the half-light, twisting in an eerie, sexualized dance-wrestle'.[1]

In contrast, a Marxist-oriented *Coriolanus* was performed at the Army Theatre in Prague in 1959 in much the same way it had been staged in Eastern Europe in the 1930s, with 'wise, honest, sincere' tribunes, an 'extremely derisive' and 'rather nasty' Menenius, and a Coriolanus who had betrayed the people.[2] The most significant European post-war *Coriolanus* was the adaptation by Bertolt Brecht, who had been interested in the play as early as 1925.[3] His productions sought to break with the German Shakespearean tradition that produced a 'lumpy, monumental' drama celebrating a single heroic individual.[4] When he turned to *Coriolanus* in 1951–2 he was adamant that the play must not become the tragedy of an irreplaceable individual and that events must be shown as alterable, not a fate to be accepted passively. The citizens are individualised and their plight emphasised; hope for a better world is represented by the added 'Man with the Child' who had intended to emigrate but finally decides to stay in the new, more democratic Rome. The tribunes are more honourable than in Shakespeare and become true leaders when they encourage resistance to the invading army; the people are less fickle and learn to unite as an independent force, and Cominius and some other patricians decide to join them in defending Rome. Coriolanus's relation to his mother is subordinated, and Aufidius is simply another military 'specialist' who, like Coriolanus, glories in war. In the supplication scene Coriolanus learns from Volumnia's rewritten speech that 'The Rome you will be marching on / Is very different from the Rome you left. / You are no longer indispensable / Merely a deadly threat to all.'[5] In a new final scene, perhaps inspired by Plutarch, Coriolanus's family's request to be allowed to wear mourning for ten months is, in the play's last word, 'Rejected', and the stage direction indicates *The senate resumes its deliberations.*[6]

This strongly partisan work reflects what Brecht felt to be the exigencies of the early 1950s: many in his audience would have been brought up in the Hitler Youth and would still have been under the influence of the Nazi glorification of the military hero.[7] The adaptation was still in draft form at Brecht's death in 1956; when his collaborators in the Berliner Ensemble, Manfred Wekwerth and Joachim Tenschert, revised it for performance in 1964 they restored a good deal of Shakespeare, including the importance

[1] Anthony B. Dawson, *Watching Shakespeare*, 1988, p. 210. The 1983 BBC television production, directed by Elijah Moshinsky, also emphasised Coriolanus's special love–hate relation with Aufidius.
[2] Bretislav Hodek, review in *S.Sur.* 14 (1961), 118.
[3] Brecht and his designer for the adaptation of Marlowe's *Edward II*, Caspar Neher, both worked on Erich Engel's 1925 Berlin production of *Coriolanus* (Kennedy, *Looking at Shakespeare*, p. 204).
[4] Daniell, '*Coriolanus' in Europe*, pp. 117–18.
[5] *Coriolan*, trans. Ralph Manheim, in *Bertolt Brecht: Collected Plays*, ed. Ralph Manheim and John Willett, 9 vols., 1970–2, IX, 142.
[6] *Ibid.*, p. 146. According to Inga-Stina Ewbank in 'Shakespeare translation as cultural exchange', *S.Sur.* 48 (1995), Brecht used Livy and Plutarch for additional historical material; his base text was a revised version of Dorothea Tieck's nineteenth-century translation, but he also consulted two editions in English and the promptbook from Erich Engel's 1936 staging at the Deutsches Theater (p. 8).
[7] Margot Heinemann, 'How Brecht read Shakespeare', in *Political Shakespeare*, ed. Jonathan Dollimore and Alan Sinfield, 1985, p. 221.

of Volumnia and Aufidius. Brecht would probably have approved, since, especially after working on *Coriolanus*, he became increasingly impressed that many of his 'alienation effects' were already there in Shakespeare. The last entry in his working diary refers to *Coriolanus*: 'wonder if it would be possible to stage it without additions . . . or with very few, just by skilful production'.[1] In Wekwerth's and Tenschert's conception Coriolanus was indeed valuable, though the price to Rome was finally too high, and they felt the battle scenes that showed him doing what he was good at would be at 'the center of our production'.[2] A version of Brecht's *Coriolan* was produced by Heinrich Koch at the Frankfurt Schauspielhaus in September 1962, and the 'official' Wekwerth–Tenschert revision in Berlin in September 1964; it toured Europe and was brought by the Berliner Ensemble to London in 1965, and its rhythmic, pounding clashes, stylised in the manner of Chinese opera, have reappeared in many English stagings of Shakespearean battle scenes.[3] In 1971, Wekwerth and Tenschert were invited to direct a 'Brechtian' production of Shakespeare's *Coriolanus* for the National Theatre at the Old Vic, with Anthony Hopkins in his first Shakespearean leading part. In the textual cuts and interpretation Brecht was superimposed on Shakespeare, with not entirely successful results.

In Italy, Giorgio Strehler had been producing Shakespeare at the Piccolo Teatro in Milan since 1947. By the time he staged *Coriolanus* in 1957 he had met Brecht and was convinced the play was about the dialectic of history as well as the protagonist's conscience. He borrowed some 'epic theatre' techniques, dividing the play into 22 scenes (each introduced by an interpretative caption) and using a simple set with constant bright lighting. Unlike Brecht, Strehler also stressed the private conflicts within the protagonist and between him and his mother, and in Tino Carraro he had an actor who could substantiate the political moral without making Coriolanus either a monster or merely a hero who had outlived his era: 'Portrayed with every antiheroic trait, found guilty on all counts by director, audiences, and critics alike, he still won sympathy.'[4] In Germany, Hans Hollmann staged a less even-handed adaptation in 1971 in Munich and then in 1977 in Hamburg. Modern battle scenes demonstrated Second World War atrocities; everything tending to make Coriolanus sympathetic was eliminated, and he became a model of the danger of *Spezialismus*, particularly of being a specialist in war.[5] In a new translation by Jean-Michel Déprats, Bernard Sobel in 1983 directed *La Tragédie de Coriolan* for the Théâtre de Gennevilliers, located

---

[1] Quoted from John Willett (ed. and trans.), *Brecht on Theatre*, 1964, p. 265.

[2] Quoted in Cohn, *Modern Shakespeare Offshoots*, p. 19. On the 1964 changes, see also Lawrence Guntner, 'Brecht and beyond: Shakespeare and the East German stage', in *Foreign Shakespeare*, ed. Dennis Kennedy, 1993, pp. 112–14.

[3] A critique of Brecht's politicised adaptation by the West German writer Günter Grass, *The Plebeians Rehearse the Uprising: A German Tragedy*, appeared in Berlin in 1966 (trans. into English by Ralph Manheim, 1966). John Osborne contributed his own politically conservative adaptation of Shakespeare, *A Place Calling Itself Rome*, in 1973.

[4] Icilio Ripamonti's analysis, quoted from Leiter, *Shakespeare Around the Globe*, pp. 91–2. See also Speaight, *Shakespeare on the Stage*, p. 264, Kennedy, *Looking at Shakespeare*, pp. 216–17, and Parker, pp. 129–30.

[5] Daniell, *'Coriolanus' in Europe*, pp. 92–3. The production also played at an annual workers' drama festival in the Ruhr and toured to Warsaw, Poland.

in a working-class community outside Paris. While the translation stayed close to the Folio text, word choices sharpened the antagonism between Coriolanus and the plebeians and strengthened the justice of the citizens' grievance.[1] Littered with wheelbarrows, scaffolding pipes and rubble, the set suggested social breakdown; battles conducted with toy wooden swords were, in the Berliner Ensemble tradition, balletic and silent.[2]

The appeal of *Coriolanus* to a theatrical tradition accustomed to using Shakespeare for political purposes is clear, and in these years there were also a remarkable number of productions in the Soviet Union and its satellite countries. In 1978 at the Teatrul Nottara in Bucharest, Dinu Cernescu's staging showed the influence of both Brecht and Antonin Artaud, the former in its lucid exposition of the mechanism of social relations and elimination of psychological complexity, the latter in a haunting musical score, a set 'consisting of black vertical lines with dark red spots that suggested both blood stains and the map of a ruined country', and costumes that symbolised the characters' nature and behaviour in the manner of Asian theatre.[3] Another three followed in 1979 alone: the Georgian production at the Kutaissi 'Lado Meskvishile' Theatre in Tbilisi also visited Moscow in 1981; an Armenian staging by Ratschya Kaplanyan at the Gabriel Sundukyan Theatre in Yerevan later toured Berlin and Weimar in 1980 and Moscow in 1981;[4] Oto Sevcik's Czech production at the Tyl Theatre, Pilsen, was said in 1979 to be the tenth *Coriolanus* in that country.[5] There were other Czech productions in 1981 (Checheno-Ingustian 'Nuradilov' Theatre) and 1984 (Workers' Theatre, Most); in 1982 there was a Polish production in Warsaw, and in 1985 the Hungarian National Theatre staged the play at Komarno.[6]

Outside of the stylised battle scenes, Brecht's and his collaborators' versions did not immediately influence productions of *Coriolanus* at Stratford or London.[7] Although John Barton's 1967 RSC programme mentions the recent visit of the Berliner Ensemble and offers 'Brechtian' historical material and political quotations indicating relevance to both Shakespeare's time and the present, the production itself did not seem geared to fulfil such expectations. The major British and North American productions of the 1960s and 1970s tended to emphasise the personal over the political. In 1961 Michael Langham directed Paul Scofield at Stratford, Ontario, in a production that, despite being set in the period of the French Directoire, concentrated on the human

---

[1] Leanore Lieblein, 'Translation and mise en scène: the example of contemporary French Shakespeare', in Kennedy, *Foreign Shakespeare*, pp. 82–6. This translation was again used by the Théâtre National de Belgique in 1984.

[2] Leanore Lieblein, review in *Cahiers Élisabéthains* 24 (1983), 96–7.

[3] Ileana Berlogea, review in *SQ* 31 (1980), 407.

[4] Armin-Gerd Kuckhoff, review in *Shakespeare Jahrbuch* 117 (1981), 168, 170.

[5] Otto Roubiack, review in *Ceske divadlo* 8 (1983), 169 ff., cited in Parker, p. 128.

[6] Parker, p. 128; George, typescript stage history for the New Variorum *Coriolanus*, p. 59.

[7] However, in Glasgow in 1974 the Citizens Theatre Company played *Coriolanus* in repertory with Brecht's *Saint Joan of the Stockyards*, and in 1975 the Everyman Theatre in Liverpool offered Brecht's *Coriolan* in English with Pete Postlethwaite in the title role. At the Liverpool Repertory Theatre in 1970 Antony Tuckey directed *Coriolanus*, starring Michael Gambon, set in Germany at the time of the Kaiser and sympathetic to its working-class citizens.

11   Fight sequence (Act 1, Scene 4) in the 1972 Trevor Nunn production, Royal Shakespeare Theatre, Stratford-upon-Avon, with Volscians costumed as primitive, vaguely Aztec warriors. Photograph: Joe Cocks Studio

dimension.[1] In 1972 a nearly uncut *Coriolanus* directed by Trevor Nunn and Buzz Goodbody opened a Stratford-upon-Avon season of the four Roman plays. Staging was epic in scale, with exciting battles and balletic, slow-motion close combats under strobe lights (see illustration 11). Although the tribunes were neither villains nor clowns, the Roman crowd was unimpressive; class conflict within Rome faded before an anthropological emphasis that made the primary contest one between civilisations. Romans and Volscians were not different tribes; they were different races, with the darker, more primitive Volscians costumed as ancient Aztecs with 'a strong belief in the purifying effect of fire'.[2] In this context, Coriolanus's primary relationship was again with Aufidius, but it suffered from a Coriolanus (Ian Hogg) who seemed unable to find the 'nobility, passion, or magnetism of the role'.[3]

---

[1] This emphasis was also clear in the 1965 productions at the American Shakespeare Festival in Stratford, Connecticut, and the San Diego National Shakespeare Festival. More experimental was the casting of an African American and a Puerto Rican as the tribunes 'to lend a local as well as general timeliness' and staging the mob scenes 'with an almost frightening realism' in Gladys Vaughan's 1965 production at the Delacorte Theater in New York's Central Park (Alice Griffin, 'The New York Shakespeare Festival 1965', *SQ* 16 (1965), 339).

[2] Leiter, *Shakespeare Around the Globe*, p. 97; see also Berry, *Changing Styles in Shakespeare*, p. 32. In 1977 the Utah Shakespeare Festival at Cedar City presented a variant of this kind of differentiation, with the Volscians presented as Asiatic, vaguely Assyrian, barbarians (John A. Mills, *SQ* 29 (1978), 254–5).

[3] *Birmingham Post*, 12 April 1972. Revived with greater success at the Aldwych in London in 1973, with Nicol Williamson replacing Hogg, the production's emphasis had changed to the personal tragedy of the hero; the interpretation 'was altered from a Sixties approach to a Fifties one' (Beauman, *The Royal Shakespeare Company*, p. 317).

The most successful *Coriolanus* of the 1970s was directed by Terry Hands, with Alan Howard in the title role; it opened at Stratford in October 1977, toured Europe, and reopened at the Aldwych in May 1978. A black stage with raked wings that doubled as walls and gates offered an ahistorical, monochrome setting; costumes were studded black leather for Aufidius and Coriolanus (until the last act, when he entered in blood-red) and black for most of the rest of the cast, but individual actors gained a heightened prominence from directional, brilliant-white lighting (see illustration 12). The effect was a reduction to theatrical essentials, abstract and apolitical, which supported Howard's portrayal of Coriolanus as a man 'marooned in the heroic myths', trying, and finally failing, to be the superman 'Coriolanus'.[1] To help separate the hero from even his patrician supporters, Cominius's setpiece on 'the deeds of Coriolanus' was not given as the usual straight panegyric but rather in the tones of one 'appalled at the man's recklessness and extravagance'.[2] Playing Coriolanus as 'a strong man, full stop', rather than also suggesting his weaknesses, was most effective in the first half of the play. Since he was not a 'mother's boy', there was 'no great emotional crack-up to Volumnia's supplications': 'He simply chooses to spare Rome', just as he later chooses to impale himself on Aufidius's sword.[3]

More theatrically experimental and politically self-conscious productions began to appear on mainstream stages in the 1980s. The Nottingham Playhouse in 1983 set the play on the eve of the English Civil War, with Royalist patricians, Roman tribunes dressed in Puritan black with high-crowned hats, and Volscians clad as highland Scots. In this setting, Coriolanus's 'uncompromising stance increasingly resembled that of Charles I'.[4] Peter Hall's striking 1984 National Theatre production used a 'timeless' set (a circular sandpit backed by a vaguely classical gateway), eclectic costuming (mixed modern and Roman, knotted jock-straps for the duel), and cued participation by audience members seated on stage, to make his point about parallels with the political divisions and military jingoism of Thatcherite Britain. In practice, the political conflicts were less effectively presented than the personal ones, especially the tense struggles between Coriolanus (Ian McKellen) and his mother (Irene Worth). The crowd scenes lost their sense of danger and committed opposition when angry Roman plebeians were represented by embarrassed, obviously middle-class, theatre patrons. When left to the actors, that tension could be effectively established: 'the Aediles's attempt to arrest Coriolanus has all the ugliness of real violence with McKellen grabbing two of the people round the neck and using them as a batteringram'.[5] Projecting both charismatic physical strength and psychological fragility, McKellen was perfectly matched by Worth's surprisingly unmartial, dangerously cosy Volumnia, 'so sure of her rightmindedness, so complacent in her power and emotionally mesmeric' that in

---

[1] Benedict Nightingale, *New Statesman*, 28 October 1977; see also Peter Ansorge, *Plays and Players* 25 (December 1977), pp. 22–3, and Berry, *Changing Styles in Shakespeare*, p. 33. On the production's concern with the power of dramatic illusion and its place in society, see Daniell, '*Coriolanus' in Europe*, pp. 160–2.

[2] J. R. Mulryne, '*Coriolanus* at Stratford-upon-Avon: three actors' remarks', *SQ* 29 (1978), 331.

[3] Irving Wardle, *The Times*, 22 October 1977; see also Ripley's review, 'David Daniell's "*Coriolanus*" in Europe', p. 222.

[4] Roger Warren, review in *SQ* 35 (1984), 335.

[5] Michael Billington, *The Guardian*, 17 December 1984; see also Stephen Wall, *TLS*, 28 December 1984.

12 Alan Howard, raised on his soldiers' spears (1.6.76, 'Make you a sword of me?'), in Terry Hands's 1977 production, Royal Shakespeare Theatre, Stratford-upon-Avon. Photograph: Joe Cocks Studio

3.2 she needed only turn her back on her son to ensure his reversion to a 'gauche, guilty adolescent'.¹ In 1989, Jane Howell directed the play for the Young Vic, updated in costume to the Victorian period but rather confusingly set in an arena encircled by steel mesh on which a gridiron of bars descended for the battle scenes (fought to loud rock music, with red confetti representing blood) and for Coriolanus's assassination.²

In these years North America also offered some inventive, politically-engaged stagings. In 1980, at the Villanova University Summer Shakespeare, Eric Forsythe directed a simplified, Brechtian production set in the 1930s, with the patricians costumed as Fascist brownshirts, plebeians as left-wing workers, and (a distinctly odd choice) Coriolanus as a young boxer. 'Class conflict and militarist imperialism' dominated the production, and the personal dimension was 'intentionally deemphasized'.³ William Gaskill's 1991 staging at the Folger Shakespeare Library, Washington, D.C., offered a Coriolanus in US military-issue desert camouflage facing a Volscian army in Palestinian guerrilla gear, but this topical allusion to the recent Operation Desert Storm went nowhere and was further muddled by costuming elsewhere that mixed Indian Nehru jackets and turbans with Roman togas and by incongruously staging the battle scenes with swords.⁴ Obviously, contemporary directors' interest in the play's often-neglected political argument runs the danger of imposing a topical but ultimately superficial 'concept' that distorts more than it illuminates, but this is not an inevitable fate. More successful, in part because more consistent, was John Hirsch's 1988 production at the Old Globe Theatre in San Diego, set in Washington and Nicaragua and with Coriolanus dressed as a decorated Marine officer who resembled Oliver North. Catching the play's concern with political image-making and manipulation, banks of video monitors on either side of the proscenium arch showed the audience bits of the war that was being 'filmed' by news crews on stage, interspersed with patriotic music and commercials promoting Coriolanus's victories. A white-suited Menenius nearly stole the show as 'a kind of wily Huey Long with a Southern drawl'.⁵

Without updating the play historically, Brian Bedford at Stratford, Ontario, in 1981 presented a *Coriolanus* fundamentally concerned with Rome as a political entity. He foregrounded the people (cutting some of the class-conflict references

¹ The first phrase is from Benedict Nightingale's review, *New Statesman*, 20 December 1984, the second from Irving Wardle, *The Times*, 17 December 1984.
² Peter J. Smith, review in *Cahiers Élisabéthains* 36 (1989), 97–8. Terry Hands's RSC production in the same year was, given the events in Eastern Europe and Tiananmen Square, surprisingly old-fashioned and apolitical, but it offered a commanding Volumnia in Barbara Jefford, who 'alternated the steely and the voluptuous' in her hold over her son, in 3.2 first stroking his hair and then 'administering a huge slap across his face at his recalcitrance' (John Porter, *The Times*, 10 December 1989).
³ Cary M. Mazer, 'Shakespeare in Philadelphia', *SQ* 32 (1981), 202.
⁴ Margaret M. Tocci, review in *Shakespeare Bulletin* 10 (1992), 37–8. Earlier, a 1982 production at the Champlain Shakespeare Festival (Burlington, Vermont) was set between the Second World War and Vietnam and included such contemporary touches as joggers, TV crews and secret service agents wearing sunglasses.
⁵ Charles Marowitz, *Recycling Shakespeare*, 1991, pp. 122–6. In the play's second half the modern parallels broke down, so that Coriolanus joining the Nicaraguan Sandinistas made very odd sense of Shakespeare's revenge motif.

to forestall a crude Marxist or Brechtian message[1]), and his Roman crowd of 24 was substantial. The play opened to rhythmic panting sounds from a darkened stage, then 'light disclosed a frieze of citizens on the upper stage'. Their continued presence, especially in the play's later stages, 'enforced a sense of the body to which Coriolanus was ultimately answerable, and to which he answered'. In the last scene the Roman crowd metamorphosed into the Volscian mob which rent the hero's dead body; it parted to reveal a crumpled form, then faced the audience 'with looks of candid, open-eyed complicity. They had devoured the hero, and we became a part of that eating.'[2] Coriolanus had been sacrificed to preserve the community.[3] The production also made use of the crowd for effective tableaux and fight scenes, and it underscored dramatic points with imaginative lighting and eerie 'soundscapes'.

The National Youth Theatre, which had staged *Coriolanus* in 1964 and 1975, offered a new production under the direction of Matthew Warchus in 1990 at the Tramway Theatre, Glasgow (revived in 1991 at the Bloomsbury Theatre, London). Impressively choreographed crowd scenes with individualised citizens established the class war within Rome, and popular modern tunes allusively underscored applications that shifted between eras and countries.[4] A huge white-paved performance space containing crowd-control barriers vaguely suggested Eastern Europe or Sergei Eisenstein's cinematic crowd scenes, while later 'women planting poppies during the battle scenes bring back to mind notions of Flanders', and Coriolanus returned in triumph to Rome to the strains of 'Land of Hope and Glory', connecting the play's themes also to the Falklands invasion.[5] Personal relationships were not subordinated, though they were strongly related to the public world: 1.3 was broken up so that domestic life was interrupted by the battle scenes at Corioles and, in a striking visual touch, Virgilia spent 1.3 sewing an arm back on a doll. In 1990 Michael Bogdanov directed a Brechtian modern-dress production for the English Shakespeare Company that included Solidarity banners and was set, in more general terms, in the context of the crumbling Eastern bloc. Bogdanov had been drawn to the play (in 1989) 'from a gut feeling that things were on the move in Europe', and by the time

[1] Rather than Brecht, the inspiration seems to have been the Polish existentialist critic Jan Kott, whose *Shakespeare Our Contemporary* (1962; English trans. 1964) has been influential in theatrical as well as literary circles.

[2] Quotations from Ralph Berry, review in *SQ* 33 (1982), 201–2; see also Leiter, *Shakespeare Around the Globe*, pp. 98–9. Berry develops his discussion of Bedford's use of the crowd in *Shakespeare in Performance*, 1993, pp. 50–1.

[3] Staging the final moments to suggest Coriolanus as sacrificial victim also marked Michael Benthall's 1954 Old Vic production, starring Richard Burton, and Terry Hands's return to *Coriolanus* for the RSC in 1989, with Charles Dance in the title role. For critical readings of *Coriolanus* emphasising this interpretation, see Kenneth Burke, '*Coriolanus* – and the delights of faction', *Hudson Review* 19 (1966), 185–202, and Cavell, '*Coriolanus* and interpretations of politics', pp. 75–87.

[4] Although Warchus cut the text by about an hour's playing time, Simon Reade thought all the important inter-relationships had been retained and that it was 'one of the most spectacular *Coriolanus*es in recent years' (*City Limits*, undated newspaper cutting at the National Youth Theatre, London).

[5] *The Scotsman* (Edinburgh), 25 August 1990. *Scotland on Sunday*, 29 July 1990, noted a deliberately androgynous style and cross-casting that produced perhaps the first female Aufidius.

rehearsals were under way the Berlin Wall had fallen and Eastern Europe was in turmoil.[1]

Strongly influenced by European theatrecraft, with its emphasis on expressionistic visual effects, actor-director Steven Berkoff staged *Coriolanus* three times in as many countries. Invited by Joseph Papp to direct it for the 1988 New York Shakespeare Festival, he mounted a fast-paced production that mixed contemporary characterisation with individual and ensemble stylisation. Christopher Walken's Coriolanus dressed in fashionable 1980s black and 'strutted in rhythm with the percussive score, which combined martial music with a new-wave urban sound'; he suggested both the elegant, snobbish aristocrat and a gang leader intent on 'maintaining his turf in a bleak world of brute force'.[2] Berkoff's nine extras doubled as citizens, Roman and Volscian soldiers, and senators; they formed an ominously synchronised choric mob. Battle scenes, too, were given highly stylised choreography and carried out as mime (including the Romans 'riding' toward the Volscians using Agnes deMille's 'dressage' movements). This was a world of 'overwhelming masculine brutalism' in which Coriolanus, facing the rebellious plebeians alone in 3.1, punched them out with his fists and was himself later impaled on the conspirators' spears, then given the *coup de grâce* by Aufidius's sword. The final image in this dark production was the rejected envelope containing the Roman–Volscian peace treaty returned to its briefcase, which snapped shut to a drumbeat and the lights went black.[3] This conception was the basis for Berkoff's 1991 production at the Prince Regent Theatre in Munich, with German actors using the Dorothea Tieck translation (heavily cut and reordered, as in New York).[4] In the 1996 London production at the Mermaid Theatre, Berkoff himself played Coriolanus, catching the character's 'charismatic aggression' and vanity but missing his insecurity and the complexity of his relationship with his mother, just as the stylised, filmic, visually rewarding production flattened the play's political subtlety.[5]

The influence of film and popular culture was even more markedly evident in the post-modernist adaptation of Robert Lepage's Quebecois Théâtre Répère troupe which played Paris, Montreal, the Edinburgh Festival and the Nottingham Playhouse in 1992–3.[6] This ten-actor *Coriolan* was seen, as on a small CinemaScope screen, through a 4 foot × 16 foot rectangular frame which cut off the actors' legs or, when they stood on tables, their heads, so 'they look like ruined figures in a Roman frieze'. Action took

---

[1] Michael Bogdanov, '*Coriolanus*': *Director's Notes for Teachers & Students*, 1992, pp. 12–13; the production toured Britain before opening at the Aldwych in London in 1991. In Europe, 1990 also saw Shakespeare's play (in J. M. R. Lenz's translation) produced at the Stadttheater, Basel, and Brecht's adaptation at the Rheinisches Landestheater in Neuss, Germany ('Bibliography of stage productions', *SQ* 42 (1991), 683–4).

[2] William Over, review in *SQ* 41 (1990), 365.

[3] Gary Wills, *The New York Review of Books*, 19 January 1989; Robert Brustein, *The New Republic*, 2 January 1989.

[4] Some alterations to the New York staging were made; see Berkoff's diary of mounting the Munich production in '*Coriolanus*' *in Deutschland*, 1992.

[5] Benedict Nightingale, *The Times*, 13 June 1996.

[6] Translation and adaptation were by the Quebecois playwright Michel Garneau, and playing time was cut to just over two hours.

place in bars, restaurants and, for the public speeches, a broadcasting studio, and was punctuated by 'the modern alarums of a city caught in a traffic jam'; battle scenes were represented by visibly manipulated puppets except for the duel, in which Coriolanus and Aufidius wrestled naked on the ground, seen by the audience in a slanting mirror which made them appear to tussle in mid air.[1] This funny, Fellini-esque rendition of a decadent Rome and an unheroic hero dealt 'a death blow to all that banner-waving, smoke-infested triumphalism' characteristic of major British productions;[2] at the end Coriolanus was stabbed in the neck by Aufidius's loyal catamite.

While the Berkoff and Lepage productions represent the extreme of high concept, 'director's' Shakespeare, others have tried to present in a more balanced way the play's complex blend of political argumentation and private tragedy, heroism and self-delusion – often now to the dissatisfaction of critics who think the play requires a political stance on the director's part. But to give due weight to each argument, and to each evasion or self-interested manoeuvre, is not to regress to the pre- and post-war apolitical approach; it is to take the play seriously as, among other things, Shakespeare's most searching exploration of the political life of a community.[3] To this end, in 1992 Tim Supple experimented with the effect of a large, non-professional crowd at the Chichester Festival Theatre in a co-production with the Renaissance Theatre Company. Because 'the tragedy of Rome . . . is as central to the play as Coriolanus is – and in modern political circumstances you have to address this', he felt a small chorus would require stylisation inappropriate to this play.[4] Permitted by Equity to recruit local residents, his crowd of over fifty (ranging in age from twelve to eighty) in the first scene enlisted the audience's sympathy by their very 'unactorish normality' and put Martius's tirades in a new light. They helped by their physical presence, as well as the thunder of their 'The people are the city!' in 3.1, to establish and hold the play's balanced structure of oppositions, so that the private relation of mother and son did not usurp the audience's sense of public issues at stake.[5]

Balance was also the goal of both of Deborah Warner's productions, although in other respects they could not have been more different. In 1986 her Kick Theatre Company staged a minimalist, virtually uncut, *Coriolanus* at the Almeida Theatre in London with a cast of twelve who, when not 'on stage', knelt beside orange-crates arranged in a circle. Costumes were timeless, vaguely Asian, baggy pyjamas, and both battles and assassination were mimed; sound effects for the 'crowd' were provided by

---

[1] Robert Tanitch, *Financial Times*, 26 June 1993.

[2] Michael Coveney, review of the Montreal production, *The Observer*, 6 June 1993; see also his later review, preparatory to the production's Nottingham opening, which includes an interview with Lepage, *The Observer*, 14 November 1993. For a less favourable account see Michael Billington, *The Guardian*, 26 November 1993.

[3] Despite an overall subordination of politics to Ian McKellen's flamboyant Coriolanus, Peter Hall's 1984 production did attempt to present a serious and fairly straightforward 'centrist' political debate that displayed the flaws of both extremes (Michael Billington, *The Guardian*, 17 December 1984).

[4] Interview with Georgina Brown, *The Independent*, 6 May 1992.

[5] Peter Holland, *S.Sur.* 46 (1993), 184–5. The complex mother–son relationship suffered from a Coriolanus (Kenneth Branagh) who was more spoiled child than arrogant warrior and no match for Judi Dench's fierce Volumnia.

'syncopated shouts, the drumming of boxes and rapid percussive slapping of thighs'.[1]
At the opposite extreme in terms of spectacle, for the 1993 Salzburg Festival in Austria
she mounted extensive battle scenes on the enormous stage of the Felsenreitschule, a
converted seventeenth-century riding school, with a cast of 38 and 200 extras, 'entire
armies scaling walls and hacking away at each other'.[2] Unlike the manic-depressive
hero portrayed by Douglas Hodge in the 1986 Almeida production, Bruno Ganz's
Coriolanus was 'a man obsessed with the purity of his own vision' whose contempt
for the crowd derived less from arrogance than 'a rigid sense of his own integrity'.[3]
In neither case, however, was the production visibly slanted. Some German critics
bewailed the lack of directorial 'concept', but audiences (and the Austrian critics) were
enthusiastic, perhaps relieved, in Warner's words, that 'the play's not being limited by
having lines painted through it'.[4]

In 1994 David Thacker staged *Coriolanus* for the RSC in the small, thrust-stage
Swan Theatre at Stratford, then transferred it to the larger, proscenium-arch Barbican Theatre in London the following summer. Thacker revived the French setting
of Poel and Langham, here with a bare stage dominated by a huge unfinished sketch
of Delacroix's *Liberty Leading the People* framed in a smashed back-wall and on the
balconies tattered, bloodied banners proclaiming the ideals of 1789 that suggested a
'post-revolutionary state where liberty, fraternity, and equality had proved elusive'.[5]
A stunning opening visual image neatly motivated the plebeians' discontent: a cas-
cade of golden grain poured from above into an open trap that closed before the
starving commoners could get their hands on it. A very young, faintly Napoleonic-
looking Coriolanus (twenty-four-year-old Toby Stephens) had the physical presence
and magnetism of a martial hero, and the battles were great thwacking affairs from
which he returned so bloodied as to appear truly 'flayed'. His age was appropriate to
the interpretation – a brash, petulant, swaggering public-schoolboy soldier who easily
persuaded himself that uninterrupted battlefield success made him a demigod – and it
made credible both his political naïveté and the real threat of Aufidius's taunting 'Boy!'
His raging pride and obstinate commitment to honesty isolated him the more by being
played against the steely calm of Aufidius's 'warrior as politician, a man who, from our
first encounter with him, was in total control of events in Volscian power politics',[6]
and Philip Voss's brilliant Menenius, a 'constantly inviting and dangerously deceptive
guide to the political maze' whose doting affection for the wayward 'son' he had helped

[1] Michael Coveney, *Financial Times*, 19 September 1986. See also Michael Billington, *The Guardian*, 20
September 1986, and Thomas Clayton, '"Balancing at work": (r)evoking the script in performance and
criticism', in *Shakespeare and the Sense of Performance*, ed. Marvin and Ruth Thompson, 1989, pp. 248–9.
[2] John Rockwell, *The New York Times*, 5 August 1993.
[3] Denis Staunton, *The Observer*, 1 August 1993. Staunton also praised Hans-Michael Rehberg's Menenius,
'a magnificent, cajoling dervish', and 83-year-old Maria Wimmer, 'monumental as Volumnia, like a female
goddess of war'.
[4] Quoted in Rockwell's review (n. 2 above).
[5] Russell Jackson, *SQ* 46 (1995), 345. Costumes suggested the later Directoire period (1795–9), while
Delacroix's painting was a response to the July 1830 revolution. 'Thacker's aim was a general evocation
of revolutionary times' rather than historical specificity, and he replaced the painting's French tricolour
with a plain red banner.
[6] Peter Holland, review in *S.Sur.* 48 (1995), 216–17.

to spoil made his rejection one of the production's most moving scenes.[1] The rant of Coriolanus's biting contempt and the excitement of the battle scenes were matched by the energy and earnestness of the arguments. The political debates of Act 3, so often truncated to make Coriolanus more attractive or just to get more quickly to the banishment and revenge, were given full weight.

Thacker ended his production on another striking visual image. At Aufidius's last lines calling for assistance, both citizens and conspirators backed off furtively, leaving Aufidius with the body. Unable to lift Coriolanus alone, he fell back in such a way that the final tableau, with Aufidius cradling Coriolanus's body, resembled a pietà as the lights went black.[2] It was an effective, even haunting, visual climax that caught up and focused two aspects of the play. By isolating Aufidius as well as Coriolanus, it emphasised the private nature of their rivalry; the departure of the Volscians suggested that Aufidius's patriotic claims had been seen through. He was left literally bearing the weight of his treachery, forced to recognise what it meant to have destroyed the heroic figure against whom he had measured and defined himself, and to have destroyed him in a way that branded Aufidius in his own eyes for ever. Since Volumnia was played as devastated in 5.5, the staging of 5.6 paralleled Aufidius with the other agent of Coriolanus's death: what is either of them without Coriolanus? The emotional force of this 'private' ending also visually demonstrated the irrelevance, to ordinary citizens, of either aristocratic political manoeuvring or the patrician obsession with honour that had led to such tragic waste.[3]

Recent stage and critical interpretations by Bridget Escolme[4]

Recent *Coriolanus* criticism has developed the themes of political history and gender identity which preoccupied much late twentieth-century work on the play. Theories of the play's relationship to its sources have continued to flourish beyond further exploration of the adaptation from Plutarch.[5] Performance criticism has been a significant critical movement, exploring not only particular productions, but the inherent theatricality of gender, identity and *romanitas* in the play, and the effect of dramaturgy and stage space on a live audience. This turn to theatricality is an interesting one, given

---

[1] John Stokes, '. . . Rome as Paris', *TLS*, 3 June 1994.

[2] I saw the restaged 1995 Barbican production, which may have altered aspects of the original Swan staging. I am grateful to A. R. Braunmuller for some details of the Swan production.

[3] There have been no commercial films of *Coriolanus*, though several 'educational' ventures: in 1951 Worthington Miner directed a one-hour modern-dress version for the American 'Studio One' television programme; in 1963 the BBC also reduced it to one hour as part of a series titled 'The Spread of the Eagle'; Irish Television offered a 1972 production with Frank Barry as Coriolanus. As part of the BBC complete series of Shakespeare's plays, available on video, Elijah Moshinsky directed it in 1983 with Alan Howard in the lead role and Irene Worth as Volumnia.

[4] Bridget Escolme is Senior Lecturer in Drama at Queen Mary, University of London.

[5] See, for example, Barbara L. Parker's exploration of the play in terms of Platonic notions of oligarchy in *Plato's Republic and Shakesepeare's Rome*, 2004, pp. 54–73, and the links Chikako D. Kumamoto makes between the anger of Achilles in Homer, and that of Martius and his suggested convergence of Hecuba, Hera and Priam in Volumnia: 'Shakespeare's Achillean Coriolanus and Heraean Volumnia: textual contamination and crossing of Homer's *Iliad* in *Coriolanus*', *Journal of the Wooden O Symposium* 7 (2007), 51–64.

the anti-theatrical bent of the play's hero. Martius's recalcitrant refusal to perform and display himself in return for the 'needless voices' of the Roman citizens has long been seen as intrinsic to his character. However, recent performance criticism has reflected less upon the drama as a series of encounters and tensions between psychological characters, or even as the staging of political positions and debates, than on 'the rift opened by the *performance* of politics',[1] in Cynthia Marshall's phrase, and has found psychological and political meaning in the live encounter between performers and audiences. As Martius stands before the on-stage citizens, reluctant to beg their vote, he stands, also, before his paying audience, with their myriad physical, perceptual, historical and political perspectives.

THE PEOPLE AND THE CITY: THE POLITICS OF *CORIOLANUS*
In her survey 'What hath a quarter-century of *Coriolanus* criticism wrought?', Lee Bliss traces a shift, during the late twentieth century, away from a 'Tillyardesque' view of the play as essentially conservative – a view that left literary critics 'to concentrate on character, theme and how . . . Coriolanus could be considered a tragic hero'.[2] Bliss argues that, in the latter part of the twentieth century, though '[p]olitical and economic analyses have not supplanted character criticism', diverse but essentially more liberal readings of *Coriolanus* as the staging of a clash of political cultures replaced an earlier understanding of the play as monolithically pro-patrician. Oliver Arnold has gone further and characterised late twentieth-century *Coriolanus* criticism as figuring 'Coriolanus as the work of a prescient liberal who championed "the people" and "belie[ved] that Jacobean England desperately needed to borrow from the strengths, as well as learn from the difficulties, of republican political theory"'.[3] Rita Banerjee's intertextual reading of *Henry V* and *Coriolanus* argues that republican values emerge even in the earlier play, and that both plays suggest that war, when not undertaken for defence, is not conducive to the common good and demonstrates the need for popular participation in the general weal.[4] There is still recent work that comes down clearly in favour of *Coriolanus* as a play with absolutist tendencies. In 2000, Jerald W. Spotswood could still assert that 'Shakespeare rewrites individuality as a characteristic of the elite and denigrates collective action by associating it with a rabble which by definition holds no interest in the social order.'[5] However, Bliss's characterisation of politicised, historicist criticism of *Coriolanus* as concerned with political debate and with cracks and fissures in dominant political culture still holds good at the end of the first decade of the twenty-first century.

[1] Cynthia Marshall, '*Coriolanus* and the politics of theatrical pleasure', in *A Companion to Shakespeare's Works*, Vol. I: *The Tragedies*, ed. Richard Dutton and Jean E. Howard, 2005, p. 454.
[2] Lee Bliss, 'What hath a quarter-century of Coriolanus criticism wrought?' in *The Shakespearean International Yearbook 2*, ed. W. R. Elton and John M. Mucciolo, 2002, p. 63.
[3] Oliver Arnold, 'Worshipful mutineers: from *Demos* to electorate in *Coriolanus*', in *The Third Citizen: Shakespeare's Theater and the Early Modern House of Commons*, 2007, pp. 179–214 (p. 192), citing Annabel Patterson, *Shakespeare and the Popular Voice* (Madison: University of Wisconsin Press: 1984), p. 122.
[4] Rita Banerjee, 'The common good and the necessity of war: emergent republican ideals in Shakespeare's *Henry V* and *Coriolanus*', *Comparative Drama* 40 (2006), 29–49.
[5] Jerald W. Spotswood, '"We are undone already": disarming the multitude in *Julius Caesar* and *Coriolanus*', *Texas Studies in Literature and Language* 42.1 (2000), 62.

Cathy Shrank's reading of Martius as a 'complex portrait of incivility' points to an early modern England concerned with the problematic relationship between the civil and the civic. 'Through Martius's indecorous speech', argues Shrank, 'Shakespeare signals his protagonist's inability to live within the urban community and, beyond that, his ultimately detrimental effect on civic society.'[1] In D. J. Hopkins's study of early modern London's civic and stage spaces, Martius's notorious reluctance to perform is similarly framed as detrimental to civic life. Hopkins uses Robert Weimann's categorisations of stage *locus* and *platea*—*locus* being the stage space in which the dramatic fiction is played out, *platea* the shared space of player and audience in which the Renaissance player brings the world of the play into dialogue with the world of the theatre:[2] 'Unlike Antony who asserts his facility with performance by moving into the *platea* to win over the plebeians of Caesar's Rome, Coriolanus remains always in his own private *locus*, and even when alone he will address a city in the abstract, rather than speak to the city's people or to the people in the audience of the theatre.'[3] In this 'refusal to contribute to the public performance practices that unify the city and the citizens', argues Hopkins, 'Martius threatens the integrity of city life itself'.[4]

Recent historicist criticism has tackled again the question of *Coriolanus*'s topicality and developed or shifted this debate away from links between the Roman citizens' uprising and the Midland Revolt (see Lee Bliss, above, pp. 17–25). David George uses the harvest failure of 1608 to date the play in his account of the ways in which contemporary events enliven Shakespeare's dramaturgy.[5] Nate Eastman suggests that it is London disturbances and discontents that are played out in Menenius's fable of the belly: the 'changing political realities (as Tudor and Stuart autocracy gave way to increasingly bureaucratic systems of local government, at least in London)',[6] which would have directly affected theatre audiences. Alex Garganigo discusses the importance of body metaphors to James I's government and links the play's 'obsession with bodies natural and politic within the controversy over James's plans to combine England and Scotland into a larger Great Britain'.[7] He points out that a belly fable like Menenius's is used in 1604 in a pro-Union tract addressed to James.[8] Garganigo argues not that Martius represents one Elizabethan or Jacobean political figure, but that the play posits relationships between the body of the state and the bodies of several characters and that, ultimately, the play protests against 'the need to disguise disagreement with the king in fables of the body'.[9] Barbara L. Parker, on the other

---

[1] Cathy Shrank, 'Civility and the city in Coriolanus', *SQ* 54 (2003), 409.

[2] See Robert Weimann, '*Platea* and *locus*: flexible dramaturgy', in *Shakespeare and the Popular Tradition in the Theatre*, 1978, pp. 73–85.

[3] D. J. Hopkins, *City/Stage/Globe: A Genealogy of Space in Shakespeare's London*, 2007, p. 178.

[4] *Ibid.*, p. 175.

[5] David George, 'Plutarch, insurrection and death', *S.Sur. 53* (2000), 70.

[6] Nate Eastman, 'The rumbling belly politic: metaphorical location and metaphorical government in *Coriolanus*', *Early Modern Literary Studies* 13.1 (2007), http://purl.oclc.org/emls/13-1/eastcori.htm, accessed 13 August 2008.

[7] Alex Garganigo, '*Coriolanus*, the Union controversy and access to the royal person', *SEL*, 42 (2002), 335.

[8] John Russell's 1604 'Treatise of the Happie and Blissed Union Betuixt the Tua Ancienne Realmes of Scotland and Ingland', in Garganigo, p. 337.

[9] Garganigo, p. 351.

hand, relates Martius's behaviour directly to the absolutism of James I, arguing that patrician rule 'hews closely to the Platonic paradigm' of an exploitative oligarchy[1] and that Martius's banishment prefigures 'both verbally and contextually Charles' trial "in the name of the people of England"'.[2]

GENDER, SEXUALITY, IDENTITY

Late twentieth-century explorations of the inflexible masculinity produced by Roman warrior culture and, more specifically, Volumnia's raising of Martius have recently been refigured in terms of the ways in which gender can be said to be performed. In Coppélia Kahn's significant feminist reading of Shakespeare's Roman plays, Martius's sense of self lies in an essential masculinity, a nature that, he wants to believe, is beyond the playing of roles but which is undone by his relationship with his mother. Volumnia does not merely emasculate him, then, when she suggests he takes on 'some harlot's spirit' (3.3.113) by bending his knee and doffing his cap to the citizens. She undoes his very self with her 'theatrical metaphor' of calculated abasement to the people's will, suggesting that every aspect of his identity is mere performance, taught by a woman: '[B]oth the warrior's ferocity and the politician's "insinuating nods" are the man's part, and he learns them both from a woman who thereby serves as his cultural father.'[3] Similarly, Euan Fernie, in his study of Shakespeare and shame, suggests that Martius faces death at the end of the play 'not so much because his mother's victory makes him traitor . . . and thus endangers his physical safety, as because it jeopardises his conception of himself to the point of extinction'.[4]

By contrast, Shakespeare's one stage direction that directly suggests a silent stage picture, the celebrated '*holds her by the hand, silent*' (5.3.183 SD), continues to be read by some as the moment in which Martius discovers his humanity, despite the fact that capitulation to his mother, as he predicts, leads to a shameful death. For Eve Rachelle Sanders, the anti-theatrical hero learns the value of theatricality in this scene and Sanders equates this with emotional growth.[5] Andrew Mousley's *Re-Humanising Shakespeare* is similarly optimistic: in this moment, Martius has learned ordinariness and humanity.[6] In Wes Folkerth's work on sound in the early modern theatre, the theatrical sound of capitulation after this silence supports Mousley's and Sanders's optimistic humanist readings:

the sound of [o:] forms the refrain of the entire speech, from its groans of agonized resignation, to the long vowel sounds in [words]. The repetition of [o:] marks Coriolanus' entry back into the shared world of human speech, into an acoustic community in which he is merely a player, and not the sole figure. It is the sound of him opening up, becoming receptive to the claims of the Other.[7]

[1] Barbara L. Parker, *Plato's Republic and Shakesepeare's Rome*, 2004, p. 54.
[2] *Ibid.*, p. 55.
[3] Coppélia Khan, *Roman Shakespeare: Warriors, Wounds and Women*, 1997, p. 155.
[4] Euan Fernie, *Shame in Shakespeare*, 2002, p. 219.
[5] Eve Rachelle Sanders, 'The body of the actor in *Coriolanus*', *SQ* 57 (2006), 387–412.
[6] Andrew Mousley, *Re-Humanising Shakespeare: Literary Humanism, Wisdom, and Modernity*, 2007, pp. 92–5.
[7] Wes Folkerth, *The Sound of Shakespeare*, 2002, p. 210.

Explorations of sexuality in the play have been extended beyond a literal exploration of Martius's relationship with Aufidius, though Robin Headlam Wells takes pains to argue against an explicitly homoerotic element here, suggesting instead that the comradeship between the warriors recalls chivalric tradition. Aufidius, argues Headlam Wells, is shrewd in his desire to let 'his old adversary . . . know that he recognises in him a kindred spirit who will be Trystram to his own Lancelot'.[1] For Claudia Corti, on the other hand, the relationship is distinctly and subversively homoerotic and must therefore be put to death by the dominant political culture: 'The object of any socially illegitimate and psychologically uncanny strain needs to be ideologically suppressed. With the killing of Coriolanus, and with Aufidius's foot symbolically trampling upon his corpse, a previous sexual and political order takes the lead again, condemning the unorthodox upsurge of passions to practical silence and political absence.'[2]

Mark Kuzner approaches this theme more theoretically, drawing on queer theory to posit a politically transgressive and culturally disruptive Martius. For Kuzner, far from seeking a bounded and socially proscribed patrician or masculine selfhood, Martius seeks to undo the very ideas about the self whereby the Roman state – or any state – controls its citizens: 'He speaks in order to be undone; he wants words to make him into a sword, not a respected Roman citizen; he hopes that opening his mouth will relieve him of the supposedly safe borders and acknowledged agency of which the people seem so covetous.'[3] Caius Martius Coriolanus as a radical disrupter of social norms might seem far-fetched in the light of his views of citizens as cannon-fodder. But Kuzner's argument is about Martius's presence in the world of the theatre as well as in the world of the play; whilst the Roman general is a patrician snob, he also defies society's notions of who gets to look and be looked at, within both the fiction and the theatre, particularly where the citizens of Rome are described as disregarding social hierarchy and decorum to get a look at him (2.1.200–5). Martius's determination not to become the monumental body Rome wants to make of him becomes central to his paradoxical theatrical attraction and disrupts the sexual and social hierarchies of the Roman state.

A THEATRE OF SHAME

As is clear from Corti's work, psychoanalytic readings of the play, pioneered by work such as Janet Adelman's[4] and Stanley Cavell's,[5] are still a significant critical strand. Maurice Hunt suggests that Martius, in his insults to the citizens, offers 'the extreme invectives against humankind that constitute the "backward voice", an anal voice that utters curses always concerned with disease, putrefaction, waste and stench'. According to Hunt, the backward voice reduces an audience's sympathy for a character;

[1] Robin Headlam Wells, *Shakespeare on Masculinity*, 2000, p. 166.
[2] Claudia Corti, '"As if a man were author of himself": the (re-)fashioning of the Oedipal hero from Plutarch's Martius to Shakespeare's Coriolanus' in *Italian Culture in the Drama of Shakespeare and his Contemporaries*, ed. Michele Marrapodi, 2007, p. 195.
[3] Mark Kuzner, 'Unbuilding the city: *Coriolanus* and the birth of republican Rome', *SQ* 58 (2007), 192.
[4] In Aldelman, *Suffocating Mothers*.
[5] Stanley Cavell, '*Coriolanus* and interpretations of politics ('Who does the wolf love?')', in *Themes out of School*, 1984, pp. 60–96.

it is primitive and fails to acknowledge human complexity. Theatrically, then, it is powerful but ultimately shaming: 'this Roman warrior seems to lack an inner censor, the primitive equivalent of the Freudian superego, that represses and regulates the expression of id-like passions and urgings. That such an incomplete character might be the victim of infantile rages and speak with an anal voice is thus not surprising.'[1]

The ultimate shame for Martius, before Aufidius stands on his dead body, is Aufidius's insult of 'boy'. Name and reputation are, of course, central to Roman heroism, and as David Lucking points out, 'Not only does [Aufidius] despoil [Martius] of his name, but he even denies his right to name, adjuring him to "Name not the god, thou boy of tears!" when Martius apostrophizes Mars (5.6.101).'[2] Lucy Munro puts the emasculation and infantilisation of Martius in the context of historical habits of theatre going, arguing that 'the play's problematization of heroic masculinity lies in the ironic gap between actor and role – a separation common in the children's company plays', and one with which Blackfriars' audiences would have been familiar. Like Lee Bliss (see above, p. 67), Munro supports the notion that *Coriolanus* could have been written with the Blackfriars in mind. 'Like the Queen's Revels' boy actors', Munro continues, 'Martius is "in drag", playing out the role of the hypermasculine military hero'.[3] Alexander Welsh, too, notes the ways in which the play attends to childhood, this time in terms of the tensions around identity held by Roman honour culture, in which membership of the group of free, adult males is paramount for social acceptability.[4]

Critical interest in the infantilisation of Coriolanus has coincided with a number of recent productions. Jonathan Cake, in the Shakespeare's Globe production of 2006 – in Jacobean dress on the Globe's bare stage, with wooden gates across the tiring house to slide open for exits such as the entrance to Corioles – gives just the impression evoked by Lucy Munro of a drag performance of hyper-masculinity, in a characterisation which drew a number of references to the British public school system from reviewers.[5]

THE PLAY IN PERFORMANCE AND PERFORMANCE CRITICISM:
ANTI-THEATRICALITY, STAGE PRESENCE AND CHARISMA

In '*Coriolanus*, antitheatricalism, and audience response', Robert Ormsby returns to a well-explored theme, the anti-theatrical controversies of the period, and discusses how early modern English anti-theatricalism can help to 're-invigorate a sense of theatre's "corporeality" by focusing on anti-theatrical constructions of the [on stage] audience'. The play's attention to the bodily presence of the actor on stage and the body of Martius in the fiction has been of significant interest to performance critics. Ormsby argues that *Coriolanus* 'places the protagonist's body at the centre of the phenomenal, lived

---

[1] Maurice Hunt, 'The backward voice of Coriol-anus', *S.St.* 32 (2004), 237.
[2] David Lucking, '"The price of one faire word": negotiating names in *Coriolanus*', *Early Modern Literary Studies* 2.1 (1996), http://purl.oclc.org/emls/02-1/luckshak.html, accessed 17 August 2008.
[3] Lucy Munro, 'Coriolanus and the little Eyases: the boyhood of Shakespeare's hero', in *Shakespeare and Childhood*, ed. Kate Chedgzoy, Susanne Greenhalgh and Robert Shaughnessy, 2007, p. 84.
[4] Alexander Welsh, 'Shakespeare's Coriolanus and Roman honour', *The Shakespearean International Yearbook 5*, ed. W. R. Elton and John M. Mucciolo, 2005, pp. 196–200.
[5] See *Guardian* 12 May 2006, *The Stage* 12 May 2006, *New York Times* 20 May 2006.

13 *Coriolanus* dir. Dominic Dromgoole, 2006, Shakespeare's Globe. Martius – Jonathan Cake; Aufidius – Mo Sesay

experience of performative exchange, an exchange it depicts as profoundly unstable'.[1] His work develops Keir Elam's challenge to New Historicist criticism,[2] the primarily textual focus of which neglects, it could be argued, the affective aspect of the theatre experience. The 'non-rational, "infectious," . . . empathic response'[3] of citizens and soldiery and the power of such a response to make Martius's body *mean* is foregrounded in this play and chimes with early modern anti-theatrical anxieties concerning theatre's dangerous power to transform actor and audience alike.

For Eve Rachelle Sanders, *Coriolanus* offers a rebuff to anti-theatrical sentiment; she argues that Martius learns the value of performative flexibility through the play. When he capitulates to his mother in her request to spare Rome, 'it is as if the experience of acting the role of a beggar [in Antium] has indeed changed him, as if it had made him more susceptible to emotion and more aware of the social basis of his identity'.[4]

An awareness of Martius as an anti-theatrical figure produced in the theatre has been a significant way in to reconsidering his seeming lack of depth and self-awareness as a protagonist. As Sanders suggests, Martius is horrified by the emotional flexibility required by the actor. How does the audience experience a dramatic hero who lacks

---

[1] Robert Ormsby, '*Coriolanus*, antitheatricalism and audience response', *Shakespeare Bulletin* 26 (2008) 45.
[2] In Keir Elam, 'In what chapter his bosom?: Reading Shakespeare's Bodies', in *Alternative Shakespeares 2*, ed. Terrence Hawkes, 1996, pp. 140–63.
[3] Ormsby, p. 51.
[4] Sanders, 'The body of the actor in *Coriolanus*', p. 405.

the empathetic quality of vulnerability in soliloquy and who refuses to stand still and be looked at? In production, Martius can appear startlingly aware of his own theatrical impact, of the ability to draw all eyes his way that Sicinius speaks of so despairingly in 2.1. 'It is the power of the charismatic leader to inspire devotion that is his most dangerous quality', remarks Robin Headlam Wells in his study *Shakespeare on Masculinity*, 'and it is this phenomenon that the theatre is uniquely capable of reproducing'.[1]

Martius's charisma, when embodied by the actor on stage, can render him compelling in ways that might serve to rebuff interpretations of the play as potentially pro-republican. Wendy Ribeyrol has called Martius an 'urban warrior of Rome'. She compares him to the action heroes of recent cinema: 'loners, uncommunicative and unsociable . . . what they share is a tendency to resort to unrestrained violence in the righting of wrongs',[2] suggesting that today's Western audience will equate Martius with a violent, exciting but ultimately conservative popular heroism. A number of recent production decisions have found mythic and historical equivalents for Martius, and critics have pointed to the conservative tone such decisions have given the play.

Rod Carley set his Toronto production (1997) in the Wild West of the 1880s and compared Martius directly to Wyatt Earp, asserting that 'all of the great shootists of this time shared a tough pride, even arrogance, and a certain disregard for human life'. Mythologising the action thus led, quite intentionally, to an empathetic Martius: 'Coriolanus, like Wyatt Earp, for all his faults and weaknesses was an honourable man.'[3] David Farr's *Coriolanus* at the Swan, Stratford (2003), and Yukio Ninagawa's production, first performed at the Théâtre des Bouffes du Nord, Paris, and later presented at the Barbican's BITE festival, London, in 2007, both imbued the world of the play with the warrior values of the ancient Far East. These were very different theatrical experiences: displays of physical virtuosity in the Ninagawa production, as warriors leaped down designer Nakagoshi's steep steps; stillness, intimacy and an attempt at encompassing the audience within the action in Farr's at Stratford, with the citizens' voices emerging from behind the audience. Setting the play within a warrior culture produced a similar politics of heroism, however. Michael Billington remarked of Farr's production that his 'oriental approach makes Coriolanus . . . an effortlessly dominant, disturbingly sympathetic samurai hero. Even as Shakespeare's starving citizens are protesting that "what authority surfeits on would relieve us", we are arrested by the upstage presence of Hicks' Caius Martius. . . . The impression is of a samurai superman whose very stillness and authority diminish his political opponents.'[4]

In Farr's production, after a compelling centre-stage opening from Lindsey Fawcett's First Citizen, Greg Hicks was repeatedly placed centrally whilst those

[1] Headlam Wells, *Shakespeare on Masculinity*, 2000, p. 146.
[2] Wendy Ribeyrol, 'Coriolanus: a natural born warrior', in *Lectures de Coriolan de William Shakespeare*, ed. Delphire Lemonnier-Texier and Guillaume Winter, 2006, p. 50.
[3] Programme note to *Coriolanus*, dir. Rod Carley, Walking Shadow Theatre in association with Theatre Brockville, 1997.
[4] Michael Billington, review of *Coriolanus*, dir. Farr, *Guardian*, 28 November 2002.

who spoke of him were visually sidelined. Martius was the central myth around which the drama revolved and the tribunes' and citizens' opinions of him could not deflate it. Martius's eroticised embrace by Aufidius when he arrives at Antium – the Volscian general cradles his head like a lover, as Katherine Wilkinson remarks[1] – and the ripping-out of his heart by Aufidius in the last scene were engaging moments but did not serve to interrogate the myth.

Scenography and direction conspired to mythologise Toshiaki Karasawa's Martius, too, as the invulnerable and irreproachable warrior hero, always to be gazed upon with awe even where he least desires the gaze of audience or Roman citizen; the citizens, tumbling down the precipitous stairway in fear at his very presence, are not only treated with contempt by Martius but are physically diminished by the choreography.

Ninagawa pushed warrior charisma to its tragic limit at Martius's death, offering a last virtuoso fight scene to replace the more familiar ignominious back-stabbing, with Martius finally displayed on the grand steps, still waving his sword in his death throes.

If, as Charles Spencer argued, Hicks's Martius 'also superbly captures . . . the little boy lost who lurks somewhere inside Shakespeare's killing machine',[2] Karasawa's remained a violent automaton until the last. There was little potential for critique of this automaton figure and the society that had made him, however, when he appeared as irreproachable warrior archetype.

Even where a performance of Martius is centred on a comical boyishness, as in Dominic Dromgoole's first production at Shakespeare's Globe in 2006, with Jonathan Cake as Martius, audience sympathy for Martius over citizens and tribunes can be difficult to undermine. There can be no doubt that there was humorous intent behind Cake's boyish snootiness: his victims were as much the Globe's groundlings as the on-stage crowd of citizens. At one point he entered through the yard, waving an imagined, unpleasant smell from his nose in disgust at having to approach so near to mere theatre punters. As Shakespeare was clearly aware when he insulted both the groundlings and the English in *Hamlet*, audiences enjoy a little abuse, and Cake's inclusion of this audience as part of the unwashed did not seem to diminish their affection for him. Audience members in at least two performances emitted a sentimental 'aaah!' when Aufidius first twined his arms about Martius's body (4.5.103–4), and the tribunes were booed on their first entrance after Martius's banishment.

Several recent productions have succeeded in offering more of an interrogation of Martius's charisma by placing it in theatrical quotation marks. Richard Hudson's set design for Greg Doran's 2007 production pushed the action forward before a city of glimpsed walks and colonnades in which citizens might gather to gossip, so that Will Houston's Martius often appeared to be posing as monumental Roman hero against a backdrop of the political machinations he so despised, creating an effect of a macho pose by a hero who purports to despise posturing.

---

[1] Katherine Wilkinson, review of *Coriolanus*, dir. Farr, performance at The Dukeries, Ollerton, *Early Modern Literary Studies* 9.1 (2003), http://purl.oclc.org/emls/09-1/coriorev.html, accessed 23 August 2008.

[2] Charles Spencer, review of *Coriolanus*, dir. Farr, *Telegraph*, 28 November 2002.

14 *Coriolanus* dir. Greg Doran, RSC 2007. Volumnia (Janet Suzman) tries to persuade Martius (Will Houston) to humble himself before the citizens

Saxon Palmer's contempt for the citizens in John Dillon's production at the Georgia Shakespeare Festival 2004 was presented as overtly theatrical. Kirk Melnikoff remarked upon his theatrical tendency to parody the citizenry: 'after repeating his request for "your voices" in a speech that was more a vaudeville routine than anything else, he kneeled and at the word "consul" doffed his cap, to which the Citizens clapped appreciatively'.[1]

A stage presence produced by theatrical self-consciousness is not limited to the figure of Martius himself. Whilst Martius, according to Ann C. Christensen's nuanced account of the 'domestic' in *Coriolanus*, 'appears always uncomfortable on the public street, Volumnia walks tall among the people of Rome, eventually becoming their patroness'.[2] In Dromgoole's Globe production, Margo Leicester's Volumnia was highly aware of the need to control the performance of appeal and capitulation in 5.1. She turned aside to the other women to announce that 'this is the last' (5.3.173) before her ultimate attempt to move her son to pity Rome. She thus comically acknowledged the scene as a theatrical and rhetorical game without reducing the dramatic and emotional stakes. Indeed, if there is a dominant aesthetic in late twentieth-century Shakespeare production, it could be said to centre upon a renewed awareness of the plays' metatheatrical qualities – perhaps, in Britain at least, under the influence of the work of the Globe, where direct address to the day-lit audience and an acknowledgement of the theatrical is a physical inevitability. What this potentially does to *Coriolanus*

[1] Kirk Melnikoff, review of *Coriolanus*, dir. John Dillon, *Shakespeare Bulletin* 23 (2005), p. 175.
[2] Ann C. Christensen, 'The return of the domestic in *Coriolanus*', *SEL* 37.2, 1997, 295–316, p. 297.

is to produce an uncomfortable metatheatrical paradox for the hero, who hates to be looked at but makes the most of it when he is, and who is continually obliged to play political parts he despises.

Two productions have demanded that the audience consider the fate of Martius's son in inheriting his status as monument to *romanitas*. Flaneur Productions' 2006 promenade production in and around the Bedlam Theatre, Minneapolis, leaves the boy (Aidan Haarman) alone on stage as his father's body is paraded from the performance space accompanied by the rest of the cast; the boy hestitates as if uncertain whether to follow, but finally does so. Director Henry Woronicz, preparing for his Utah Shakespearean Festival production (2007), reveals an anxiety that Martius simply won't be likeable enough to engage audiences, and emphasises his casting choice of James Newcomb as someone who will 'give a trememdous stage presence and charm and charisma which will go a long way to making this guy likeable'.[1] However, he finally asks the audience to question Martius's legacy to his son, in an added sequence at the end of his production, in which Virgilia watches her son race across the stage wearing armour. Blackout follows.[2]

Two directors of recent French productions have been particularly interested in the play's figurings of the city and have clearly been convinced of the play's multiplicity of voices. Jean Boillot reveals the city as central to his thinking for his production at the Théâtre Gerard Philipe, Saint-Denis, France: 'Monter *Coriolan* aujourd'hui c'est, selon Jean Boillot, donner au théâtre, "non la mission de guider ou délivrer un message, mais de faire entendre une polyphonie, historique, sociale, intime" permettant à chacun de s'interroger sur sa place dans la cité.'[3] Christian Schiaretti, interviewed about his production for Théâtre Nanterre-Amandiers at the 2008 Festival D'Automne, emphasises his own concerns with questions of the civic and the democratic through his large cast of citizens, without which, he argues, one fails to pose to the audience questions of 'les fondements réflexifs dont on a besoin pour vivre en commun. Ainsi, monter *Coriolan*, oui, l'acte est citoyen, c'est le moins qu'on puisse dire!'[4]

The portrayal of the civic politics in recent production has perhaps, however, emphasised political corruption rather than civic debate, and a sense that 'all politics is rotten, and nothing is going to save us'.[5] For Billington, in Doran's production at the RSC in 2007, 'Fred Ridgeway's Sicinius Velutus is an unkempt demagogue and Darren Tunstall's Junius Brutus a grubby opportunist given to bribing officials. The effect

---

[1] Publicity interview with Henry Woronicz, www.bard.org/news/audio/commentscoriolanus.html, accessed 1 September 2008.

[2] For a full account of this moment and the transpositions at the end of this production see Amy M. Green, '*Coriolanus*', *Shakespeare Bulletin* 25.4 (2007), pp. 107–13.

[3] 'To put on *Coriolanus* today is not, for Jean Boillot, to suggest that "the theatre's mission is to offer guidance or deliver a message, but to let us hear a polyphony of historical, social and personal voices" letting each question his or her place in the city.' Publicity for *Coriolan*, dir. Boillot, www.theatreonline.com/guide/detail_piece.asp?i_Programmation=10781, accessed 3 September 2008.

[4] '. . . the reflexive foundations one needs in order to live together. So, to put on *Coriolanus*, yes, it's the act of a citizen, to say the least!' Schiaretti, interviewed in *La Terrasse* 162 (2008) www.journal-laterrasse.com/coriolan-1-3371.html, accessed 3 September 2008.

[5] Bill Varble, review of *Coriolanus*, dir. Williamson, Oregon Shakespeare Festival, *Mail Tribune* (Medford, Oregon), 31 March 2008.

is to undercut what Coleridge called Shakespeare's "philosophic impartiality" and to diminish the legitimate grievances of the starving people.'[1] In Laird's Stratford Festival production (2007), the tribunes 'are business-clad opportunists, more interested in the latest news feed or email coming through their handhelds or laptops than they are the consequences and rightness of their actions'.[2]

SPATIAL AND SARTORIAL POLITICS IN THE EARLY AND
POST-MODERN THEATRE

In another analysis of the meanings made by the actor's bodily presence, Jennifer Low's '"Bodied forth": spectator, stage, and actor in the early modern theater' points to the ways in which the self or subject is constructed through its experience of physical sensation in space. Low analyses the dramatic character's fictional experience in the drama alongside the spectator's bodily experience in the early modern, indoor playhouse. She describes the audience's experience of the citizens' first entry 'as violence, as attack; the audience would have felt the shock of reverberating boards, of crowdedness very different from that of the spectators crammed together'; and when the stage empties through the gates of Corioles – that is to say through the central exit in the *frons scaenae* of the Jacobean theatre – fictional action collides with physical experience and the audience 'feel the stage's detumescence as a sudden emptying out, an absence of tension in the immediate vicinity and a sense of closure to the scene that is suggested by the outflow, which, on a primitive level, would carry a sense of the Romans' attack as almost inevitably successful'.[3] Low's evocation of the 'primitive' suggests that the exits and entrances of citizens and soldiery in the play might provoke a universal, phenomenological response. How have visual and spatial elements of *mise en scène* combined to produce audience experience in recent production?

In the Doran and Ninagawa productions, the hero takes centre-stage with an ease that makes patrician power appear inevitable. A number of recent productions have set the play in current political milieus and conflict zones and these *mises en scène* have had a range of effects on *Coriolanus*'s politics. Flaneur Productions' promenade version explored what political charisma might mean in an analogous modern state, in which Coriolanus's 'gown of humility' is the lumberjack shirt that signifies a US leader's willingness to pose as an earthy man of the people, working on his ranch. In her account of the process of working with Flaneur on an initial workshop for this production, Bridget Escolme suggests that it is through spatial configurations of performer and audience that an interrogation of a society's use of the mythologised hero can take place: Martius is monumentalised, displayed on a plinth to receive his new name, to beg the citizens' votes and, finally, is heaved back aloft as a frozen image, in death. The audience, in this production, surrounded him like the viewers of a Roman monument; the tribunes, on the other hand, were stuck behind the unglamorous table of

---

[1] Michael Billington, review of *Coriolanus*, dir. Doran, RSC, *Guardian*, 7 March 2007.
[2] Denise Battista, www.playshakespeare.com/coriolanius-reviews/313-theatre-reviews/3631, 26 June 2008, accessed 23 August 2008.
[3] Jennifer Low, '"Bodied forth": spectator, stage, and actor in the early modern theater', *Comparative Drama* 39 (2005), 4.

quotidian democracy, inspired, explains Escolme, by Paul Shambroom's photographs of small-town council meetings.[1] Audience members found themselves gazing up at a live monument to *romanitas*, or staring confrontationally across a table at the long-suffering politicians. Tina Packer's production at the Stables Theatre (2000), Lenox, Massachusetts, remounted as the opening production at the Founders Theatre (2001), made yet fuller use of the pedestal as a commentary on the monumentalising tendency of Roman culture, with characters making speeches from a number of small plinths and standing statue-like upon them when being spoken of.

When Packer staged *Coriolanus* six years later, with an all-male cast at Colchester's Mercury Theatre, modern military fatigues were worn beneath togas. The décor, on the other hand, maintained the sense of a decaying ancient world complete with the pedestals for orators. Other recent productions have made explicit connections to modern politics, the most excitingly excessive, perhaps, being Ivo van Hove's version for the Dutch company Toneelgroep, shown in Amersterdam in 2007, then at the 2008 Avignon Festival as part of a trilogy of Roman tragedies, performed as one event. Here the audience could choose to view the play from the auditorium or from on-stage, where they became part the action as it was played out as a huge media event, with coffee and refreshments available to take back to their seats throughout. This is probably the most self-consciously audience-inclusive recent production of *Coriolanus*, aiming to implicate the audience in the political action of the play not simply via visual analogy to current political concerns but through physical involvement. Other radical performer/audience configurations have been Flaneur's promenade versions, James Symons's production for the Colorado Shakespeare Festival (1995) – where the audience-space was extended by actors watching the action throughout, from a gallery around the stage – and Laird Williamson's 2008 Stratford, Ontario, version, whose audience entered a space of modern warfare, lit from below through gaps and gratings, to be enclosed within police scene-of-crime tape.

Eclectically costumed productions have sought to make political points, from dressing particular sectors of Roman society in recognisable street or business dress, a choice criticised by the *Journal of Canadian Studies* in response to Richard Rose's production at Stratford, Onatario, 'which sought to be modern with a vengeance. His citizens were clumsy, lumpish oafs with metal poles for staffs and uniforms deliberately evocative of punk subculture. His senators were well-dressed businessmen, though Menenius inexplicably wore a gas-mask for the first scene, making his opening speech unintelligible.'[2] Ivan Rajmont's production for the National Theatre of Prague (2004) had, perhaps, a more readily comprehensible system of eclectic costuming, with Coriolanus dressed as a seventeenth-century French aristocrat and the tribunes as modern businessmen – an old political system visually overtaken by a new.

Stage space has sometimes suggested audience involvement in the politics of *Coriolanus* but still proved essentially pictorial, to wit the impressive Gainsborough Studios

---

[1] Bridget Escolme, 'Living monuments: the spatial politics of Shakespeare's Rome', *S.Sur.* 60 (2007), 170–83; Shambroom's images can be viewed at www.paulshambroomart.com/art/ meetings%20revA/index.html, accessed 14 August 2008.

[2] Keith Garebian, *Journal of Canadian Studies*, Spring 1998, 158.

setting of Jonathan Kent's production for the Almeida in 2000. This was the building's last artistic use before it was turned into luxury apartments; Ralph Fiennes starred in a double bill of *Richard II* and *Coriolanus* there. The audience were arranged in a pit-and-galleries configuration; the impressive back wall of the building soared up into dry-iced oblivion and sported a huge, powerfully symbolic crack from the roof to the floor, where it became the actors' central entrance. There was little by way of a thrust-stage, however, and a dark band of shadow separated actors from audience; this and the facts that the central crack was not considered wide enough to represent the entrance to Corioles, and that Fiennes exited through a great oven-like door that opened and closed him in stage right, meant that the overall effect of the piece was one of a detached stage picture. Lisa Hopkins remarks that Fiennes's more frequent turning to address the audience than one often sees in productions of the play may have been an attempt to bridge the gap.[1] Dominic Dromgoole's Globe production, on the other hand, broke with historical performance convention by closing the gap between performer and audience entirely and having Martius voice his contempt for the Roman people whilst standing in the yard amongst the London ones.

This account of recent criticism and production of *Coriolanus* ends with Martius's reluctant appeal to the citizens for their votes in his gown of humility – for Martius, a potentially shameful display of wounded, vulnerable selfhood in which he is reluctant to play a full part. For the greater part of the play, Martius can be seen as in active control of where he positions himself in theatrical space, and who gets to look at him, whereas here he becomes the vulnerable, the shameful, object of the citizens' controlling gaze. In playing an ironic wit at the ghastliness of his situation, however, the RSC 2003 Farr/Hicks production gave Martius the theatrical control of the successful stand-up artist fending off his hecklers: shame and exposure are averted. Even William Houston, in Greg Doran's RSC production of 2006 which, according to the *Guardian*, emphasised 'Coriolanus' unchecked animal arrogance',[2] raised a laugh, as Houston looks to the audience in grim recognition at just how humiliating the gown of humility really is. Perhaps what recent productions have discovered here are theatrical alternatives to the supposed problem of Martius's subjective emptiness, his lack of empathy as a tragic hero. Moments of self-acknowledgement may be few in this play, but they are powerful and highly theatrical, in that they acknowledge the presence of the performer on stage and the subject performing in the world who, like a dull actor, can forget his part (5.3.40–1) and become vulnerable, shamed, exposed.

[1] Lisa Hopkins, 'Review of *Coriolanus*' dir. Dromgoole, *Early Modern Literary Studies* 6.2 (2000), http://purl.oclc.org/emls/06-2/hopkrev.htm, accessed 24 August 2008.
[2] Billington, review of *Coriolanus*, dir. Doran, RSC, *Guardian*, 7 March 2007.

NOTE ON THE TEXT

The copy-text for this edition is the First Folio of 1623 (F), which is probably based on a transcript of Shakespeare's manuscript that had been annotated to serve as playbook for production; for a more detailed discussion of this and other matters mentioned only briefly here, see the Textual Analysis, pp. 289–307 below. Spellings have been silently modernised in accordance with New Cambridge Shakespeare practice, but the collation will record distinctive F spellings that might affect pronunciation or sense, or where a pun has been lost in choosing a modern spelling. Where there is no modern form of an F reading, the now-obsolete word will be explained in the Commentary and suggestions offered for substitutions roughly equivalent in meaning and metre that could be used in a modern production.

The punctuation in F is relatively heavy and manifestly inaccurate in places. The present edition lightens the F punctuation considerably, while also trying to clarify the meaning for a contemporary reader. Uncontroversial normalisation and modernisation of punctuation (of possessives, plurals and vocatives, for instance) have not been collated unless noteworthy, nor has this edition's provision of the terminal periods sometimes absent in F. Where the present edition departs significantly from F, or where F is ambiguous in syntax or mood, the F punctuation is recorded in the collation.

Contractions (*o'th'*, *i'th'*, *'tis*, *it's*, etc.) have been retained as being a distinctive component of Shakespeare's late style, but pseudo-grammatical apostrophes (*ha's*, *do's*, *doe's*), probably scribal in origin, have been silently removed and syncopations, with or without apostrophes in F (*encountring*, *utt'rance*), expanded (*encountering*, *utterance*). In accordance with NCS practice, elided *-ed* endings of past participles, indicated in F by an apostrophe (*controll'd*), have been silently expanded; where metrical considerations require such an ending to be pronounced as a separate syllable, it is marked with a grave accent (*controllèd*). Abbreviations (such as tildes, ampersands, etc.) have been silently expanded, and characters' names regularised and spelled out in full in speech headings and stage directions.

In the collation format, the authority for this edition's reading follows immediately after the square bracket enclosing the quotation from the text; other readings, if any, follow in chronological order. When one of the later seventeenth-century folios of Shakespeare's plays appears, it will be distinguished as F2 (1632), F3 (1663) or F4 (1685). The previous editor or commentator responsible for adopting or suggesting the emendation is given in abbreviated form, such as *Theobald* or *conj. Tyrwhitt*, keyed to the List of Abbreviations and Conventions, pp. viii–xiii above; readings new to this edition will be so noted, *This edn*.

Act divisions follow F; scene divisions, added by later editors, have been collated. Stage directions lacking in F but obvious from the context have been added, as have some clarifying details to existing directions. All such editorial intrusions are enclosed in square brackets; the collation records both the edition in which they first appeared and where other editions differ in placing or content. In more problematic cases, rather than close off options for reader or director, I have retained F and discussed the possibilities in a Commentary note. According to the conventions of this series, emended speech headings are not marked as such by brackets; the F reading will be given in the collation, however, and the reasons for thinking it erroneous outlined in the Commentary. In addition, the Commentary offers some account of the ironies in language and staging created by the play's developing action, as well as of the complexities of grammar and syntax so common in Shakespeare's late style. This late style is also marked by frequent straining of the basic iambic pentameter verse line. In F, evidence of this refusal to be bound by the constraints of regular, end-stopped verse has been in some cases suppressed, in others exacerbated, by compositorial setting of verse as prose and prose as verse, and by the unusually high degree of other mislineation in setting verse. Mislineation is so extensive in *Coriolanus* that in order to avoid overburdening the collation that accompanies the text, this edition provides a separate collation in the Appendix, pp. 308–13 below.

Except in the provision of additional stage directions, this edition presents a generally conservative text. Indeed, it often returns to F readings long abandoned by previous editors, such as the retention of Second Citizen in 1.1 and of undesignated senators and soldiers in scenes where F leaves to the playhouse the decision as to which actor will speak the lines assigned to *Sena.* or *Sould.* As the Commentary will testify, I am frequently less than confident not only about F's correctness or readings new to this edition, but also about particular emendations accepted from previous editors. There are often good defences of choices here, in the end, rejected, and I will try to indicate this evidence fairly while recording the rationale for my own final decision.

The Tragedy of Coriolanus

LIST OF CHARACTERS

CAIUS MARTIUS, *later Caius Martius* CORIOLANUS
MENENIUS AGRIPPA, *friend to Coriolanus*
TITUS LARTIUS, *a general*
COMINIUS, *consul and commander-in-chief of the army*
VOLUMNIA, *Coriolanus's mother*
VIRGILIA, *his wife* — *Roman Patricians*
YOUNG MARTIUS, *his son*
VALERIA, *a virtuous lady and friend to his family*
GENTLEWOMAN, *attendant on Volumnia and Virgilia*
SENATORS
NOBLES
SICINIUS VELUTUS
JUNIUS BRUTUS — *Tribunes of the people* — *Roman Plebeians*
CITIZENS
SOLDIERS
TULLUS AUFIDIUS, *general of the Volscian army*
LIEUTENANT *to Aufidius*
Three SERVINGMEN *to Aufidius*
CONSPIRATORS *with Aufidius*
Two Volscian SENATORS
Volscian LORDS — *Volscians*
SOLDIERS *in the Volscian army and as the Volscian* WATCH
Volscian CITIZENS
ADRIAN, *a Volscian spy*
NICANOR, *a Roman traitor*
Roman AEDILES
Two OFFICERS *in the Roman Capitol*
Roman HERALD
Roman LIEUTENANT *to Titus Lartius*
MESSENGERS
Usher, Roman Drummer, Trumpeter, Scout, and Captains, Lictors, Attendants on the Roman women and on Aufidius

Notes

No list of characters appears in F.

CAIUS MARTIUS Shakespeare followed North's spelling *Martius*, and probably favoured 'Martius' over 'Caius' because of its appropriate Latin meaning, 'pertaining to Mars'. Despite some exceptions demanded by the metre, the honorific 'Coriolanus', bestowed for singular bravery in the battle for Corioles, is in general pronounced Coriolánus and usually compressed to four syllables (the *rio* sounding like that in *chariot*). The dates for this semi-legendary hero are *c.* 525–493 BC.

MENENIUS AGRIPPA In Plutarch simply one of the 'pleasauntest olde men' sent by the senate to conciliate the people; after winning them over with his rendition of the belly fable, he disappears from the narrative.

TITUS LARTIUS For some irregularities in the spelling of his name and of confusion about his movements, see Textual Analysis, pp. 292, 303 below.

VALERIA Important in Plutarch because inspired in a temple with the idea of the Roman ladies' expedition to seek mercy from Coriolanus, after the embassies of his friends and the Roman priests and soothsayers have failed.

SICINIUS VELUTUS Shakespeare follows North's (and Amyot's) error for Plutarch's *Bellutas*.

TULLUS AUFIDIUS Standardised to North's spelling; F has *Auffidius* and *Auffidious*.

ADRIAN *and* NICANOR Named in the dialogue in 4.3 but in the entry direction and SHS generic: 'Roman', 'Volsce'. For possible sources for the names, which are not found in the 'Life of Coriolanus', see pp. 11, 15 n. 3 above.

THE TRAGEDY OF CORIOLANUS

1.[1] *Enter a company of mutinous* CITIZENS *with staves, clubs, and other weapons*

FIRST CITIZEN Before we proceed any further, hear me speak.
ALL Speak, speak.
FIRST CITIZEN You are all resolved rather to die than to famish?
ALL Resolved, resolved.
FIRST CITIZEN First, you know Caius Martius is chief enemy to the   5
people.
ALL We know't, we know't.
FIRST CITIZEN Let us kill him, and we'll have corn at our own price. Is't
a verdict?
ALL No more talking on't. Let it be done. Away, away!   10
SECOND CITIZEN One word, good citizens.
FIRST CITIZEN We are accounted poor citizens, the patricians good.

Title] The Tragedy of Coriolanus: F   Act 1, Scene 1   1.1 *Actus Primus. Scœna Prima.* F   5 First, you know] F4;
First you know, F

Act 1, Scene 1
A street in Rome. The vigorous, bustling entrance of the angry citizens establishes both the real threat of violence (mutinous attitudes leading to full rebellion) and the underlying cause of the central conflict. The current dearth has exposed the class enmity, which now becomes political opposition as well, felt by both sides.

0 SD.1 *company* On permissive SDs, calling for an unspecified or a loosely specified number of actors, see Textual Analysis, p. 302 below.

2 SH F's *All* here, and frequently elsewhere, cues not speech in unison but lines or phrases divided among several members of the on-stage group; see Textual Analysis, pp. 294–5 below.

3 You . . . famish See pp. 17–18 above for similar expressions recorded by the protesters involved in the Midland Revolt of 1607. The sentiment is ultimately biblical and appears in sermons preached in time of dearth. In the first of the Zurich minister Lodovike Lavatere's *Three Christian Sermons . . . Of Famine and Dearth of Victuals*, translated from Latin and published by William Barlow in 1596 as appropriate to the current conditions in England, it is noted that King

David thought famine worse than pestilence or war and that 'Verie true is that speech of Jeremy [= Jeremiah], It was better with them that they were slaine with the sword, then with them that died for hunger' (D6ᵛ).

8 corn . . . price 'Corn' is a general term for grain, here probably referring to wheat or barley necessary for bread. Shakespeare combines Plutarch's two plebeian protests, first over usury, then over corn, into one.

9 verdict agreed judgement. The grounds for this formal conclusion are laid in the legal terminology of the preceding lines ('proceed', 'resolved') and picked up in one of the meanings of 'proceed' (20). Such allusions to rational, judicial deliberation create a taut counter-current to the rebellious violence proposed by First Citizen as its consequence.

10 on't of it.

12 patricians aristocrats, the noble class.

12 good wealthy, good for credit; in contrast to 'poor citizens' (both 'impoverished' and 'undesirable'), with a scornful verbal play on the use of 'good' (= 'worthy') in Second Citizen's address to his fellows as 'good citizens' (11).

What authority surfeits on would relieve us. If they would yield us
but the superfluity while it were wholesome, we might guess they
relieved us humanely. But they think we are too dear. The leanness   15
that afflicts us, the object of our misery, is as an inventory to
particularise their abundance; our sufferance is a gain to them. Let
us revenge this with our pikes, ere we become rakes; for the gods
know, I speak this in hunger for bread, not in thirst for revenge.
SECOND CITIZEN Would you proceed especially against Caius Martius?   20
ALL Against him first. He's a very dog to the commonalty.
SECOND CITIZEN Consider you what services he has done for his
    country?
FIRST CITIZEN Very well, and could be content to give him good report
    for't, but that he pays himself with being proud.   25
SECOND CITIZEN Nay, but speak not maliciously.
FIRST CITIZEN I say unto you, what he hath done famously, he did it to
    that end. Though soft-conscienced men can be content to say it was

---

21 SH] F; 1. *Cit.* / *Hudson²*, conj. Malone; Oxford *redistributes:* / *Third Citizen* Against . . . first. *Fourth Citizen*
He's . . . commonalty.   26 SH] *Malone* (2. *Cit.*); *All.* F; *Fifth Citizen* / Oxford   28–30 end. Though . . . it . . .
country, he . . . proud,] F *subst.* (end: though . . . it . . . Countrey, he . . . proud,) end – though . . . 'it . . . country',
'he . . . proud' – *Oxford*   28 soft-conscienced] F (soft conscienc'd)

13 **authority** those in authority, the patricians.
14 **superfluity** excess (what remains after the
patricians' needs have been satisfied and which
now goes to waste).
14 **guess** deduce, conclude.
15 **humanely** out of compassion for us as fellow human beings. This sentiment is not from
Plutarch's account but rather echoes *Lear* 3.4.33–
6 and 4.1.61–5 (Parker).
15 **too dear** too costly, not worth the expense
of maintaining us. Secondary meanings of 'dear'
now obsolete – 'of high estimation; precious, valuable' (*OED* Dear *a* 4a) – give the citizen's remark
its bitter irony; as the succeeding lines indicate,
they feel that to the patricians they are only 'valuable as we are'.
16 **object** spectacle.
16–17 **inventory . . . abundance** The citizens'
poverty acts as an itemised account ('inventory')
of the patricians' wealth.
17 **sufferance** suffering, distress.
18 **pikes . . . rakes** Combines the proverbial
expression 'lean as a rake' (Dent R22) with a pun
on two meanings for 'pike'. First Citizen urges
that they turn the agrarian 'pitchforks' by which
they earn a peacetime living into the 'spears'

(*OED* Pike *sb⁵* 1) they carry when mustered for
military service as infantrymen; now the weapons
would be turned against their own oppressive
rulers. Menenius later mocks the commoners'
rustic language (see 109 n.), and Martius contemptuously parodies their addiction to proverbs
(188–91).
21 **a very dog** i.e. pitiless, ruthless. As early
as *TGV* 2.3.10–11, Shakespeare forges the association of dogs and cruelty, and in *JC* when Mark
Antony unleashes 'the dogs of war' (3.1.273), civil
war is the result. See also 'curs' at 3.3.128.
21 **commonalty** common people.
25 **pays himself** Since Martius rewards himself for 'services' nominally done for Rome, First
Citizen does not feel the people owe him further accolades. The issue of what Rome owes its
military hero and what he should, or will, accept
becomes crucial both on the battlefield (1.9) and
in the market-place where he stands for consul
(2.3).
26 **SH** This objection seems unlikely to be made
by *All* (F), and it is Second Citizen who defends
Martius (31–2).
27–8 **to that end** i.e. to become famous.
28 **soft-conscienced** easy-going, lenient; with
a possible suggestion of partiality to Martius.

for his country, he did it to please his mother and to be partly
proud, which he is, even to the altitude of his virtue.   30

SECOND CITIZEN What he cannot help in his nature you account a vice
in him. You must in no way say he is covetous.

FIRST CITIZEN If I must not, I need not be barren of accusations. He
hath faults, with surplus, to tire in repetition.

Shouts within

What shouts are these? The other side o'th'city is risen. Why stay   35
we prating here? To th'Capitol!

ALL Come, come!

FIRST CITIZEN Soft, who comes here?

Enter MENENIUS AGRIPPA

SECOND CITIZEN Worthy Menenius Agrippa, one that hath always
loved the people.   40

FIRST CITIZEN He's one honest enough. Would all the rest were so!

29–30 it to please . . . to be partly proud] F; it to please . . . partly to be proud *Hanmer;* it partly to please . . . to be proud *Capell*   29 partly] F; portly *conj. Staunton*   35 these] F; those F2

29 **to please his mother** First Citizen is here
given part of Plutarch's description of Martius's
motivation: 'the only thing that made him to love
honour, was the joye he sawe his mother did
take of him' (Bullough, *Sources*, V, 508); although
Shakespeare omits other Plutarchan examples of
Martius's subordination of himself to Volumnia,
these words help prepare for his response to her
appeals in 3.2 and 5.3.

29–30 **to be partly proud** The construction is
ambiguous. It may mean 'partly to be proud' or 'in
order that he might be proud' (see Abbott 420),
but it may also mean 'partly out of pride' (Abbott
20). The dialogue here between First and Second
Citizen foreshadows the difficulties of others who,
periodically, try to interpret Martius's character.

30 **to . . . virtue** to the height of his valour.
First Citizen means that Martius's pride and bravery are equally excessive, but in so doing he grants
a 'Roman' respect for martial courage. North's
Plutarch recounts that 'in those dayes, valliantnes
was honoured in Rome above all other vertues:
which they called *Virtus*, by the name of vertue
self' (Bullough, *Sources*, V, 506); this equation
is picked up by Cominius in praising Martius,
2.2.77–9.

32 **covetous** inordinately desirous, here of
material goods (*OED* Covetous *a* 2). Both

Plutarch and Shakespeare stress Martius's contempt for the spoils of victory.

34 **tire in repetition** exhaust anyone reciting
them.

34 SD *within* off stage, within the tiring-house.

36 **prating** chattering idly.

36 **Capitol** Strictly speaking, the Temple of
Jupiter on the Capitoline Hill; here used more
loosely as the location of the Roman senate
house. Historically, there was no special building
devoted to senate meetings, and they took place in
some building in the Forum. Shakespeare chooses
to make a spatial contrast between the locus of
patrician political power (the Capitol) and that of
the plebeians (the market-place).

38 **Soft** Wait a moment.

39–40 **one . . . people** North lays the ground-
work for this characterisation of Menenius: 'The
Senate . . . dyd send unto them certaine of
the pleasauntest olde men, and the most acceptable to the people . . . Of these, Menenius
Agrippa . . . was sent for chief man of the message from the Senate' (Bullough, *Sources*, V, 510).
In Plutarch Menenius succeeds, while in Shakespeare he is still attempting to persuade the citizens when interrupted by Martius and the news
of the new tribunes' appointment.

MENENIUS What work's, my countrymen, in hand? Where go you
            With bats and clubs? The matter, speak, I pray you.
SECOND CITIZEN Our business is not unknown to th'senate. They have
            had inkling this fortnight what we intend to do, which now we'll   45
            show 'em in deeds. They say poor suitors have strong breaths; they
            shall know we have strong arms too.
MENENIUS Why, masters, my good friends, mine honest neighbours,
            Will you undo yourselves?
SECOND CITIZEN We cannot, sir; we are undone already.   50
MENENIUS I tell you, friends, most charitable care
            Have the patricians of you. For your wants,
            Your suffering in this dearth, you may as well
            Strike at the heaven with your staves as lift them
            Against the Roman state, whose course will on   55
            The way it takes, cracking ten thousand curbs
            Of more strong link asunder than can ever
            Appear in your impediment. For the dearth,
            The gods, not the patricians, make it, and
            Your knees to them, not arms, must help. Alack,   60

43 With] F; with your F2   43 matter,] F *subst.* (matter); matter – *Rowe;* matter? *Johnson;* matter. *Oxford*   44 SH] F
(2 *Cit.*); 1. *Cit.* / *Capell (and to end of scene)*   52 you. For . . . wants,] *Johnson;* you for . . . wants. F; you, for . . .
wants, F4

42–3 **What . . . you** Menenius speaks in verse, as befits his patrician standing, but his manner is conciliatory and his address familiar. That he does not in fact consider the citizens 'my good friends, mine honest neighbours' (48) is clear in his angry name-calling when they do not immediately capitulate to his 'application' of his fable (140–6).

42 **work's** Printed here as a contraction of 'work is', followed by a vocative. F lacks commas, however, and 'work's' may represent 'work has', a singular verb followed by a plural subject ('countrymen'); Shakespeare often uses singular verbs with plural nouns.

43 **bats** cudgels or thick pieces of wood. Bats and clubs were the common weapons of an Elizabethan or Jacobean crowd and 'Clubs! Clubs!' was the rallying cry of riotous apprentices.

44 SH Capell's emendation, here and to the end of the scene, has been adopted by most subsequent editors; for discussion of the issue and this editor's decision to follow F, see Textual Analysis, pp. 293–4 below.

46 **suitors** petitioners.

46 **strong breaths** Slighting reference to the populace's bad breath (caused by drinking, tobacco or, more usually, garlic) is common in the period; see 4.6.102. The imputed insult is

countered with the threat implied in 'strong arms'.

49 **undo yourselves** make things worse. Possibly Menenius asks if they will disarm themselves (*OED* Undo *v* 3a: 'to unfasten'), and the citizen's reply plays on what is to him a more pertinent meaning.

50 **undone** ruined (*OED* Undone *ppl a²* 1). Second Citizen suggests that they have nothing to lose.

52 **For** As for (as also in 58).

55 **on** continue on.

56 **curbs** Literally, 'curbs' are the chains attached to the bit of a horse's bridle; figuratively, the Roman state is a horse whose course cannot be altered even by stronger links than those represented by the rebellious commoners.

58 **your impediment** the obstruction you create.

60 **knees** i.e. in prayer; contrasted with 'arms', the bodily limbs and, in this case, 'arms' in the military sense of weapons raised against the state. The argument would have been familiar to Shakespeare's audience: sermons in time of dearth – even those quite sharp about the evils of engrossers, usurers, monopolists and hoarders – emphasised that famine required the people's prayer and submission.

You are transported by calamity
Thither where more attends you, and you slander
The helms o'th'state, who care for you like fathers,
When you curse them as enemies.
SECOND CITIZEN Care for us? True indeed, they ne'er cared for us yet.   65
Suffer us to famish, and their storehouses crammed with grain;
make edicts for usury, to support usurers; repeal daily any whole-
some act established against the rich, and provide more piercing
statutes daily to chain up and restrain the poor. If the wars eat us not
up, they will; and there's all the love they bear us.   70
MENENIUS Either you must
Confess yourselves wondrous malicious,
Or be accused of folly. I shall tell you
A pretty tale. It may be you have heard it,
But since it serves my purpose, I will venture   75
To scale't a little more.

---

65 True indeed, they] F; True, indeed! – they *Theobald*   76 scale't] F; stale't *Theobald*

61 transported carried away (referring both to the citizens' physical movement through the streets and to the volatile anger that motivates them).
61 calamity disaster. Menenius suggests that their actions will only compound the misery and famine they suffer, conditions that Menenius identifies as 'natural forces' of the gods and, hence, amendable only through prayer.
62 attends awaits.
63 helms helmsmen (of the ship of state); perhaps with a play on the piece of armour that covers and protects the head (*OED* Helm *sb*¹ 1a).
63 fathers paternal figures, but also a literal translation of *Patres*, the title of the senators in ancient Rome.
65 indeed, they Although most editors follow Theobald, F's punctuation is not manifestly incorrect; it may indicate sarcasm directed at these supposedly paternal senators.
67 edicts . . . usurers A reference to legal codes that allow the lending of money at high interest, thus favouring those (the patricians) who lend the money. In Plutarch the first citizen rebellion is over usury, the second over dearth of corn.
68–9 piercing statutes severe laws.
69–70 wars . . . will Imagery of cannibalism will recur, in accusations by both sides, throughout *Coriolanus* (see 1.1.169–71, 2.1.8–9, 3.1.298–9, 4.5.71–3, 183–4, 4.7.3–4 n.). Here, it appears in a familiar context: rich men generally, and espe-

cially usurers and landlords seeking to enclose traditionally common lands, were often referred to as 'cormorants' to the poor (see 104); sermons during famine years traced the horrors of cannibalism back from modern to biblical times (see p. 20 above).
74 pretty pleasing; but also with the now obsolete meaning of 'artful' or 'ingeniously made'.
76 scale't a little more produce a valuable application in retelling it (as golden flakes or scales are struck from a coin). Theobald's emendation has been generally adopted, but in defending F, W. F. Bolton notes a pertinent, though now obsolete, meaning of 'scale': 'to split off scales or flakes from (coin) for the purpose of fraud' (*OED* Scale *v*² 2b, which quotes a 1576 statute against illegally scaling coins of the realm). Bolton points out that the Second Citizen's reply indicates he understands the submerged metaphor of language as coin and also that the 'act of scaling is fraudulent, only an apparent extension of the value of the coin or the story' (*ELN* 10 (1972), 111). A different meaning is suggested by the note in Steevens's 1793 edition: 'In the North they say "scale" the corn, i.e. scatter it: "scale" the muck well, i.e. spread the dung well.' Theobald's emendation is, however, plausible, since *c* could easily be misread as *t* in Secretary hand; given that these 'scale' meanings are now obsolete, 'stale't' would be a sensible modern substitution for the stage.

SECOND CITIZEN Well, I'll hear it, sir; yet you must not think to fob off
    our disgrace with a tale. But, and't please you, deliver.
MENENIUS There was a time when all the body's members
        Rebelled against the belly, thus accused it: 80
        That only like a gulf it did remain
        I'th'midst o'th'body, idle and unactive,
        Still cupboarding the viand, never bearing
        Like labour with the rest, where th'other instruments
        Did see and hear, devise, instruct, walk, feel,   85
        And, mutually participate, did minister
        Unto the appetite and affection common
        Of the whole body. The belly answered –
SECOND CITIZEN Well, sir, what answer made the belly?
MENENIUS Sir, I shall tell you. With a kind of smile,   90
        Which ne'er came from the lungs, but even thus –
        For look you, I may make the belly smile

---

86 And, mutually participate,] *Malone;* And mutually participate, F; And mutually participate; *Knight;* And, mutually participant, *Hudson²*   87 appetite] F4 *subst.* (Appetite,); appetite; F   88 body. The . . . answered –] *Rowe;* body, the . . . answer'd. F   90 you. With] *Theobald;* you with F   91–3 thus – . . . speak –] F (thus: . . . speak,)

77 Well, I'll Brockbank suggests this may represent the compositor's misreading and false correction of his manuscript's 'We'll' or 'Wele'.

77 fob off evade, 'set aside by a trick' (*OED* Fob v¹ 3b); a 'fob' is a cheat. Second Citizen expresses a justifiable suspicion of Menenius's motives that is lacking in Plutarch.

78 disgrace Both 'hardship' and 'degrading misfortune' (*OED* Disgrace *sb* 5), since the people's destitution is a source of shame and reproach.

78 and't if it.

79 There was a time Sidney's version in his *Apologie for Poetrie* (1595) begins with the same words; like a fairy tale's 'Once upon a time', the formulaic opening foregrounds the artificiality as well as the timelessness of what follows. For sources of the belly fable, see pp. 11–12 above, and Commentary notes to 81, 83, 84, 86, 90, 99, 104, 105, 118–23, 120.

81 gulf whirlpool; often figuratively applied to a 'voracious appetite' (*OED* Gulf *sb* 3b). The version in Camden's *Remaines* uses the phrase 'swallowing gulfe' (Camden, p. 199) and in Averell's *Mervailous Combat* appears 'bottomlesse whirlpoole of all gluttonie' (Averell, c1ʳ).

82 unactive habitually or naturally inactive; indisposed or unable to act, hence sluggish, slothful (*OED* Unactive *a* 1). The only instance of this word in Shakespeare.

83 Still Always.

83 cupboarding stowing away, hoarding. Averell describes a 'gluttonous Pantry' (A3ᵛ).

83 viand food; usually plural in Shakespeare, but the singular appears in Averell (A3ᵛ).

84 Like Similar, equal.

84 where whereas.

84 instruments organs. In specifying various functions performed by the body's other 'instruments', Shakespeare seems to be guided by Camden's translation of John of Salisbury: 'for whereon the eies beheld, the eares heard, the hands labored, the feete traveled, the tongue spake, and all partes performed their functions' (Camden, p. 199); neither Livy nor North offers such detail.

85 devise think, deliberate, plan.

86 participate 'participant or participating' (Malone). This unusual form also appears in Averell (D1ʳ), although verbal adjectives ending in –*ate* are common in Shakespeare. Shakespeare coins 'mutually participate' for Camden's last phrase (see 84 n.).

86 minister impart, contribute (in Averell on c3ʳ).

87 affection desire, inclination. North's phrase is 'carefull to satisfie the appetites and desiers of the bodie' (Bullough, *Sources*, v, 510).

90 With . . . smile Shakespeare goes on to elaborate North's 'the bellie . . . laughed at their follie' (Bullough, *Sources*, v, 510).

91 lungs i.e. vehicle of laughter; see *Temp.* 2.1.174: 'lungs that they always use to laugh'.

91–3 thus . . . speak Menenius here acts out the contemptuous smile, perhaps with his lips but perhaps, more insultingly, by belching. In the

As well as speak – it tauntingly replied
To th'discontented members, the mutinous parts
That envied his receipt; even so most fitly   95
As you malign our senators for that
They are not such as you.
SECOND CITIZEN   Your belly's answer – What?
The kingly crownèd head, the vigilant eye,
The counsellor heart, the arm our soldier,
Our steed the leg, the tongue our trumpeter,   100
With other muniments and petty helps
In this our fabric, if that they –
MENENIUS   What then?
'Fore me, this fellow speaks! What then? What then?
SECOND CITIZEN Should by the cormorant belly be restrained,
Who is the sink o'th'body –
MENENIUS   Well, what then?   105

---

93 tauntingly] F4; taintingly F; tantingly F2   95 receipt] F (receite)   97 answer – What?] *Hanmer;* answer: What
F; answer? What! *Collier*   98 kingly crownèd] F (Kingly crown'd); kingly-crowned *Theobald;* kingly, crownèd
Parker   103 'Fore me] *Theobald;* Foreme F   105 body –] *Rowe;* body. F

1994 RSC Swan production, the actor playing
Menenius wryly manipulated the folds of his
sash.
  93 tauntingly F's 'taintingly' is more likely to
be a minim error than a form of 'taint' (Schmidt)
or 'attaint' (Herford).
  95 his receipt what it received.
  95 fitly fittingly, justly. Menenius may use the
word ironically, or he may mean that as the rebellious citizens resemble the 'mutinous parts', so
the belly's answer applies to or 'fits' both.
  96 for that because.
  98–102 The . . . they Impatient with Menenius's long-winded loquacity, Second Citizen
takes over the tale, in verse, and demonstrates that
he knows all the well-worn political clichés. The
role-reversal also skilfully breaks 'up a narrative
to give it dramatic life' (Hibbard).
  98 kingly crownèd i.e. having a crown like a
king. The king was commonly referred to as holding the place of head in the state. Other adjectives
formed by adding -*ed* to nouns appear in 'fielded'
('encamped in the field', 1.4.13) and 'servanted'
('made subservient', 5.2.77).
  99 counsellor heart In Averell the heart is
'the place of understanding, and onlie seate of
wisdome' (D2ʳ); in Camden's version, the body's
members 'desired the advise of the Heart' and are
answered by 'Reason' (p. 199).
  101 muniments fortifications, defences (con-

tinuing the military terminology); furnishings.
  101 petty helps insignificant contributors.
  102 fabric body. Although the first recorded
instance of this meaning (*OED* Fabric *sb* 3) is
1695, Menenius's tale employs architectural references, and a metaphoric use of *OED* Fabric *sb* 1
('an edifice, a building') would be natural. In *Of
the Fabrique of the Church*, 1604, William Tooker
also moves beyond literal usage when his discussion proceeds from physical church buildings to
a plea for 'the maintenance of the fabrique of this
faire order and economy . . . of Church policie
and discipline' (p. 131).
  103 'Fore me 'Upon my soul'; a form of mild
oath, probably used instead of the more common
''Fore God' to avoid the penalties attached, in
1606, to the use of profanity on the stage.
  103 fellow speaks Menenius acknowledges,
condescendingly ('fellow'), the citizen's eloquent
verse.
  104 cormorant 'insatiably greedy' (*OED* Cormorant 2a *fig.*); a cormorant is a voracious long-
necked seabird. The word was frequently used of
those who oppressed the poor (see 69–70 n.), and
it appears twice in Averell (A3ᵛ, C1ʳ); compare also
Tro. 2.2.6, 'cormorant war'.
  104 restrained kept in check, repressed.
  105 sink Organs of digestion and excretion
(*OED* Sink *sb*¹ 3b). This pejorative description
occurs in Averell (A3ʳ).

SECOND CITIZEN The former agents, if they did complain,
     What could the belly answer?
MENENIUS   I will tell you.
     If you'll bestow a small – of what you have little –
     Patience awhile, you'st hear the belly's answer.
SECOND CITIZEN You're long about it.
MENENIUS   Note me this, good friend: 110
     Your most grave belly was deliberate,
     Not rash like his accusers, and thus answered:
     'True is it, my incorporate friends', quoth he,
     'That I receive the general food at first
     Which you do live upon; and fit it is,   115
     Because I am the storehouse and the shop
     Of the whole body. But, if you do remember,
     I send it through the rivers of your blood
     Even to the court, the heart, to th'seat o'th'brain;
     And, through the cranks and offices of man,   120
     The strongest nerves and small inferior veins
     From me receive that natural competency

108–9 small – of . . . little – / Patience] F (small (of . . . little) / Patience); small of . . . little – / Patience – *Oxford*   109
you'st] F; you'll *Rowe*³   110 You're] F (Y'are)   113 'True . . . friends'] *Capell;* True . . . Friends F   114–23 'That
. . . once'] *Capell subst.;* That . . . once F   119–20 brain; . . . man,] *Theobald;* Braine, . . . man, F; brain, . . . man; *Pope*

---

106 agents The word refers to the previously
enumerated parts of the body but is chosen for
its connotation of 'those who do the actual work'
(*OED* Agent *sb* 4a).

108 small small quantity or amount (*OED*
Small *sb²* 5).

109 you'st Possibly a provincial contraction of
'you shalt' (Clarendon); Helge Kökeritz (*Shakespeare's Pronunciation*, 1953, pp. 279–80) lists this
ending as a weak form of 'shall' (which also
appears as an *se* in 'thou'se' in *Rom.* 1.3.9), but
agrees that it is a dialect form. Here Menenius
perhaps uses it mockingly to remind the citizens
of their status.

110 long about it slow in reaching your point,
long-winded.

111 Your The impersonal use, i.e. 'this most
dignified, respected belly we're discussing'.

111 deliberate careful, slow in deciding.

113 incorporate belonging to one body.
Menenius's joke lies in his use of the word in
its strictly literal sense.

114 general food food for all of us.

118–23 I . . . live Shakespeare expands with
vivid particularity the source passage in Holland's
Livy: 'it digesteth and distributeth by the veines

into all parts, that fresh and perfect blood whereby
we live, we like, and have our full strength' (p. 65).

119 to the court . . . brain i.e. to the heart, the
'court' or crucible where the blood is purified to
'vital spirits', and to the brain, the 'seat' or throne.
J. C. Maxwell takes *o'* (= of) as the genitive of
definition and 'seat' to mean 'throne' (*N & Q* 198
(1953), 329). Although in humours physiology
brain and heart are distinct, the heart needing to
purify the blood before it can be distributed to the
brain and other organs, Menenius's syntax blurs
that distinction, perhaps because both brain and
heart were associated with the understanding (see
99 n.).

120 cranks winding, crooked paths or channels (*OED* Crank *sb²* 1a).

120 offices organs, bodily functions (*OED*
Office *sb* 3ᵇ). Shakespeare also plays on 'offices'
as those 'parts of a house, or buildings attached
to a house, especially devoted to household work
or service' (*OED* Office *sb* 9). NS cites a passage in Holland's Livy to which Shakespeare may
have been indebted, though the word also appears
twice in Averell (c3ᵛ, c4ʳ).

121 nerves sinews.

122 competency sufficiency.

Whereby they live. And though that all at once' –
You, my good friends, this says the belly, mark me –
SECOND CITIZEN Ay, sir, well, well.
MENENIUS   'Though all at once cannot   125
See what I do deliver out to each,
Yet I can make my audit up that all
From me do back receive the flour of all
And leave me but the bran.' What say you to't?
SECOND CITIZEN It was an answer. How apply you this?   130
MENENIUS The senators of Rome are this good belly
And you the mutinous members. For examine
Their counsels and their cares, digest things rightly
Touching the weal o'th'common, you shall find
No public benefit which you receive   135
But it proceeds or comes from them to you
And no way from yourselves. What do you think?
You, the great toe of this assembly?
SECOND CITIZEN I the great toe? Why the great toe?
MENENIUS For that being one o'th'lowest, basest, poorest   140
Of this most wise rebellion, thou goest foremost.
Thou rascal, that art worst in blood to run,

123–4 once' – / You, . . . friends, . . . belly, . . . me –] *Clarendon;* once / (You . . . Friends, . . . Belly) . . . me. F; once, / You, . . . friends, (. . . belly) . . . me – *Rowe;* once, / You, . . . friends' – . . . belly, . . . me, – *Capell* 125–9 'Though . . . bran.'] *Capell;* Though . . . Bran. F   128 flour] F (Flowre); flower *Capell* 133 cares, digest] *Cam.;* Cares; disgest F   137 think?] F; think, *Collier²;* think, – *Dyce*   142 worst in blood to run,] F; worst, in blood, to ruin, *Steevens, conj. Johnson;* worst in blood, to run Steevens²

127 audit itemised balance sheet. The belly had earlier referred to itself as the body's 'shop' (1.1.116).

128 flour i.e. the good part, which can be made into bread; also a pun on 'flower' as 'finest' (as late as Johnson's *Dictionary*, 1755, both senses are spelled 'flower'); see 1.6.33, 'Flower of warriors!'

129 bran The portion of grain typically discarded; technically, it is the husk of wheat, barley or other grain separated from the flour after grinding. To the tribunes, Menenius later tries to excuse Martius's harsh language as unbolted, mixing 'meal and bran together' (3.1.327).

130 It . . . answer To Menenius's annoyance, Second Citizen refuses to see in the belly's answer any application to the state of affairs in Rome.

133 digest things rightly understand things correctly (with a play on the gastronomic sense of 'digest' that continues the alimentary imagery).

134 weal o'th'common public welfare.

137 What . . . think? Although most editors replace F's '?' with a comma, F's punctuation

better captures Menenius's increasing frustration that his audience has not capitulated; he turns to name-calling and then to outright confrontation.

142–3 rascal . . . vantage A 'rascal' is the inferior deer of a herd, which occasions the hunting metaphor; 'worst in blood to run' refers to the citizens' low social status, but 'in blood' is also a technical hunting term meaning 'in full vigour'. Applied to people, 'rascal' signifies an unprincipled fellow or rogue as well as a man of low birth or station (*OED* Rascal *sb* 2a and 3). 'Rascal' might also refer to a mongrel dog (*OED* Rascal *sb* 4c), as seen in the fifth section of Dr John Caius's *Of Englishe Dogges* (trans. Abraham Fleming, 1576): 'Containing Curres of the mungrell and rascall sort'. Johnson may thus be right in seeing here the image of a ferocious dog-pack and paraphrasing, 'Thou that art a hound, or running dog of the lowest breed, lead'st the pack, when anything is to be gotten.' In compressed but vivid insults, Menenius accuses Second Citizen of eager self-interest despite being morally, socially

Lead'st first to win some vantage.
But make you ready your stiff bats and clubs.
Rome and her rats are at the point of battle;   145
The one side must have bale.

          Enter CAIUS MARTIUS

             Hail, noble Martius!
MARTIUS Thanks. What's the matter, you dissentious rogues,
   That, rubbing the poor itch of your opinion,
   Make yourselves scabs?
SECOND CITIZEN   We have ever your good word.
MARTIUS He that will give good words to thee will flatter   150
   Beneath abhorring. What would you have, you curs,
   That like nor peace nor war? The one affrights you,
   The other makes you proud. He that trusts to you,
   Where he should find you lions finds you hares,
   Where foxes, geese you are – no surer, no,   155
   Than is the coal of fire upon the ice,
   Or hailstone in the sun. Your virtue is

---

146 bale] F (baile)   150 thee] F; ye *Dyce*   155 geese you are – no] F (are: No); geese. You are no *Theobald*

and physically unfit to lead even a pack of rebels. The mongrel dog image for the citizens most forcefully returns when Coriolanus banishes the 'common cry of curs' who have just banished him (3.3.128), but see also 1.1.151 and 189, 1.6.44–5, 3.1.241–2, 5.6.109 (insulting Aufidius). Coriolanus is himself seen as a 'dog to the commonalty' (1.1.21).

  146 bale dire injury, woe. Mason takes F's 'baile' to mean 'bane' (rat-poison); while appropriate to the context, this meaning would suggest a Menenius confident that if it comes to open, physical confrontation, the citizens will lose and get what they deserve. 'Bale' leaves the outcome more in doubt.

  147 Thanks Capell, Granville-Barker and others note the curtness of Martius's reply; he almost brushes aside Menenius's salute in order to turn immediately on the citizens.

  147 dissentious rebellious.

  148–9 rubbing . . . scabs Martius's dismissal of the citizens' political opinions reveals the physical revulsion so deeply a part of his own.

  149 scabs (1) scabs on yourselves (by picking at your grievances), (2) low, 'scurvy' fellows or scoundrels (*OED* Scab *sb* 4).

  151 curs worthless dogs; here used figuratively

of the commoners as surly, ill-bred and cowardly (*OED* Cur *sb* 1b), echoing Menenius's accusation at 142.

  152 like . . . war are satisfied with neither peace nor war (explained in the subsequent sentence: because they are rebellious in one and frightened in the other).

  153 proud arrogant, presumptuous. The citizens have already accused Martius of the same failing (30).

  155 foxes The insult is twofold, since 'fox' was also the name of a kind of sword (*OED* Fox *sb* 6).

  155 geese you are – F's punctuation makes sense and expresses Martius's unstoppable, sometimes nearly incoherent rage. Theobald's emendation imposes more control over what is the first of many syntactically contorted or compressed tirades.

  155 no surer no more dependable.

  156 coal . . . ice The image may have been suggested by the freezing of the Thames during the winter of 1607–8, when braziers stood upon the frozen river; see p. 2 above and illustration 1, p. 3. At 5.3.28 Martius speaks of his own implacable determination as melting before the warmth of family affection.

  157–9 Your virtue . . . it Your distinguishing

To make him worthy whose offence subdues him
And curse that justice did it. Who deserves greatness
Deserves your hate, and your affections are   160
A sick man's appetite, who desires most that
Which would increase his evil. He that depends
Upon your favours swims with fins of lead
And hews down oaks with rushes. Hang ye! Trust ye?
With every minute you do change a mind   165
And call him noble that was now your hate,
Him vile that was your garland. What's the matter,
That in these several places of the city
You cry against the noble senate, who,
Under the gods, keep you in awe, which else   170
Would feed on one another? [*To Menenius*] What's their
    seeking?
MENENIUS For corn at their own rates, whereof they say
    The city is well stored.
MARTIUS   Hang 'em! 'They say'?

---

164 Hang ye! Trust ye?] *Cam.;* Hang ye: trust ye? F; Trust ye? Hang ye! *Hudson², conj. Coleridge*   171 SD] *Bevington subst.; not in* F   175 'They say'] *This edn;* They say F

quality is to honour a man who deserves his punishment and revile the justice that convicted him.
(The relative 'that' may be omitted after 'justice'
or, possibly, 'that' may be used for 'because'; see
Abbott 244, 284.) Martius puns by using 'virtue'
in both its neutral sense of a characteristic or trait
and, sarcastically, as referring to an admirable
moral quality. Such a belief in the citizens' inability to judge worth leads to Martius's assumption
that true greatness will always earn the commoners' hatred.

159 Who He who.

160 affections desires, inclinations. Bevington suggests that the object of scorn here is any
great man who prizes popular approval and that
'your affections are' should be read as meaning
'being loved by you is', but it seems more likely
that 'and' functions as 'because': i.e. since the citizens lack the judgement to choose what is good
for them over what is injurious, the truly great
man will incur their hatred; indeed, it is his right
and a mark of his worth.

162 evil disease, malady (*OED* Evil *sb* 7).

164 Hang ye! Trust ye? Coleridge's suggestion that these phrases have been mistakenly
transposed, while not wholly implausible, would
also impose an apparently logical order where it
may not have been intended; see 155 n.

167 garland i.e. ideal, hero. The garland was
a special wreath given in Roman times for bravery
in battle; see 1.3.11–12 n.

168 several places Plutarch does not mention
riots in different locations.

171 Would . . . another The same idea occurs
in Hand D of *STM* (though the wording there is
'on on' and so could be read as 'one on') and in
Lear 4.2.46–50. It is not original with Shakespeare
(F. P. Wilson, 'Shakespeare's reading', *S.Sur.* 3
(1950), 19–20), but does accord well with the
imagery of cannibalism that pervades this play
(see 69–70 n).

171 What's their seeking Martius's turning
to Menenius for information establishes a characteristic aversion to interaction (even the recognition implied by dialogue) with the citizens.

172–3 corn . . . stored North's marginal gloss
to the episode is 'Great store of corne brought to
Rome' (Bullough, *Sources*, V, 519). Shakespeare's
wording suggests hoarding by avaricious Romans
(compare First Citizen, 13–14); it also brings
the situation closer to that of the 1607 English
enclosure riots, when similar accusations were
made in both sermons and official reports on the
underlying grievances (see pp. 18, 25–6 above).

They'll sit by th'fire and presume to know
What's done i'th'Capitol, who's like to rise,   175
Who thrives and who declines; side factions and give out
Conjectural marriages, making parties strong
And feebling such as stand not in their liking
Below their cobbled shoes. They say there's grain enough!
Would the nobility lay aside their ruth   180
And let me use my sword, I'd make a quarry
With thousands of these quartered slaves as high
As I could pitch my lance.

MENENIUS Nay, these are almost thoroughly persuaded,
For though abundantly they lack discretion,   185
Yet are they passing cowardly. But I beseech you,
What says the other troop?

MARTIUS   They are dissolved. Hang 'em!
They said they were an-hungry, sighed forth proverbs –
That hunger broke stone walls, that dogs must eat,
That meat was made for mouths, that the gods sent not   190
Corn for the rich men only. With these shreds
They vented their complainings, which being answered

---

179 enough!] enough? F   183 pitch] picke F   184 almost] F; all most *Collier²*   188 proverbs –] *Rowe subst.;*
Prouerbes F   189 hunger broke] F3; Hunger-broke F   191 rich men] F (Richmen)

174 They'll . . . fire NS compares North's 'the
home-tarriers and housedoves that kept Rome
still' (i.e. refused to join Martius in a foray against
the Antiates).

176 side take sides with; possibly looking
ahead to 'making parties strong' and so meaning 'create factions in their gossiping about their
betters'.

177 Conjectural marriages i.e. the commoners gossip about marriages within the patrician class; 'marriages' in this context probably
means political alliances, and the accusation is
that the citizens presume to discuss matters of
state altogether beyond (and above) them.

178 feebling (1) enfeebling, (2) declaring
weak.

179 cobbled roughly mended.

180 ruth compassion.

181 quarry heap of dead men (*OED* Quarry
sb¹ 2b *transf.*). The primary meaning is a heap
made of the deer killed at a hunting (*OED* Quarry
sb¹ 2), so 'quarry' picks up Menenius's imagery at
142–3 and looks forward to Martius's at 219–20.

182 quartered cut into quarters, like criminals
in Shakespeare's day (who were 'drawn and quartered'); figuratively, slaughtered or cut to pieces.

183 pitch F's 'picke' is a collateral form of
'pitch' (*OED* Pick *v²* 2).

186 passing exceedingly.

187 other troop i.e. the citizens on the other
side of the city (whose cries were heard at 34).

188 an-hungry hungry. Using the prefix 'an',
an archaic intensifier, Martius mocks as provincial
the citizens he claims to be quoting.

188–91 proverbs . . . only Of the four proverbs
cited, the first is common (Tilley H811). For
the second (Tilley D533 and D487), Furness also
quotes Ray's *Collection of English Proverbs*, 'It's an
ill dog that deserves not a crust', and Case cites
Matt. 15.27. For the third (Tilley M828), compare
Thomas Dekker's 'A Prayer in time of Famine',
in *Foure Birds of Noahs Arke* (1609): 'As thou
hast made mouthes, so make meate to fill those
mouthes; lest otherwise Christians feede upon the
blood of Christians' (F12ʳ). The last seems to be a
nonce creation generated by the first three and the
specific current conditions. That the citizens have
and express political opinions enrages Martius;
that those opinions have cogency is even worse,
and he tries to dismiss them as only 'shreds' or
scraps of wisdom.

192 vented aired, expressed; also a play on the
more vulgar result of flatulence, in keeping with
Martius's usual debasement to the physical when
referring to the commoners.

And a petition granted them – a strange one,
To break the heart of generosity
And make bold power look pale – they threw their caps   195
As they would hang them on the horns o'th'moon,
Shouting their emulation.
MENENIUS   What is granted them?
MARTIUS Five tribunes to defend their vulgar wisdoms,
Of their own choice. One's Junius Brutus,
Sicinius Velutus, and I know not. 'Sdeath,   200
The rabble should have first unroofed the city
Ere so prevailed with me! It will in time
Win upon power and throw forth greater themes
For insurrection's arguing.
MENENIUS This is strange.   205
MARTIUS [*To the Citizens*] Go get you home, you fragments.

Enter a MESSENGER *hastily*

193–5 them – a . . . pale –] F (them, a . . . pale,)   197 Shouting] F (Shooting); Suiting *Rowe*³   199 Brutus,] F;
Brutus, one *NS, conj. Walker*   201 unroofed] *Theobald;* vnroo'st F   207 SD.1] *Oxford; not in* F

194 'To give the final blow to the nobles'
(Johnson). 'Generosity' is primarily a class distinction in this period (rooted in the Latin *generous*, of noble birth), and the first definitions in
Cotgrave (1611) are 'gentilitie, gentrie'. Cotgrave
adds 'generousnesse, noblenesse', which would
include both valour and magnanimity, so a secondary meaning, the modern one, is probably also
operative, suggesting that the senators' generosity
has led them to give away too much, to grant what
will destroy them. Brockbank notes that 'to break
the heart' may mean either 'to break the spirit' or
'to end the life'.

195 power After the period of kings, ending
with the banishment and final military defeat of
the tyrant Tarquin (the battle in which Martius first proved his prowess), political power
had resided with the patricians. Parker notes that
'power' in the political sense is used 38 times in
Cor.; in comparison, the next highest rate is only
18, in *R2*.

197 emulation (1) ambitious rivalry (to shout
the loudest), where 'emulation' = imitation,
desire to exceed another (*OED* Emulation 1),
(2) grudge against those who are superior (*OED*
Emulation 3), the kind of rivalry of which Martius accuses the citizens (174–9). The pejorative meaning of emulation is now obsolete but
lies behind, for instance, the preacher William
Perkins's negative list, citing Gal. 5.20, of 'emu-
lations, wrath, strife, seditions' (Perkins, *Works*,
1605, p. 52).

198 Five tribunes Plutarch gives names to
only two, which is the number Shakespeare subsequently adopts; here, forgetting the other names
indicates Martius's contempt for the whole political compromise. Contemporary dictionaries were
in agreement about the function, if not the number, of Roman tribunes: 'Tribunes of the people,
that is, officers that were alwaies readie to suc-
cour and ayde the commonaltie, and for that cause
hath the gates or doores of their houses standing
alwaies open both night and day' (*The Nomencla-
tor*, 1585, p. 487).

200 'Sdeath By God's death (an oath).

201 unroofed F's 'vnroo'st' suggests scribal or
compositorial misreading of *f* as long *s*. This architectural image of the total destruction of Rome is
repeated by First Senator and Cominius as they
try to stem the breakdown of the political process
at 3.1.199, 206–9.

203 Win . . . power (1) 'gain advantage over
those now in authority' (Clarendon), (2) 'take
advantage of the power already won to win more'
(Chambers).

203–4 themes . . . arguing arguments justifying (arguing for) insurrection. Possibly, however,
this construction should be read as meaning that
the issues to be debated (the 'themes') will be
settled ('argued') by further rebellion, not words.

206 fragments scraps of uneaten food.

MESSENGER Where's Caius Martius?

MARTIUS   Here. What's the matter?

MESSENGER The news is, sir, the Volsces are in arms.

MARTIUS I am glad on't; then we shall ha' means to vent
    Our musty superfluity.

Enter SICINIUS VELUTUS, JUNIUS BRUTUS, COMINIUS, TITUS
    LARTIUS, *with other* SENATORS

                     See, our best elders.   210

FIRST SENATOR Martius, 'tis true that you have lately told us:
    The Volsces are in arms.

MARTIUS   They have a leader,
    Tullus Aufidius, that will put you to't.
    I sin in envying his nobility,
    And were I any thing but what I am,   215
    I would wish me only he.

COMINIUS   You have fought together!

MARTIUS Were half to half the world by th'ears and he

---

207 matter?] matter! F   210 SD.1 JUNIUS BRUTUS, COMINIUS] F4 *subst.; Annius Brutus Cominisn* F (SD *after* elders F,
F2–4)   216 together!] together? F*; together. Capell*

209–10 **vent . . . superfluity** (1) discharge
or cast out our mouldy excess, (2) a secondary meaning of 'vend' or 'sell' is probably
also intended. Shakespeare here seems to recall
Plutarch's account of the senate's solution to
this threat by angry citizens in a time of dearth:
some of the 'mutinous and seditious persones,
being . . . superfluous ill humours', to be levied
to fight the Volscians in foreign wars, some sent
to colonise the plague-decimated city of Velitrea
(Bullough, *Sources*, v, 516).
210 **elders** Shakespeare is giving his Rome
a contemporary flavour. In *A Table Alphabet-
icall* (1613), Robert Cawdry defines *senator* as
'alderman, or counsailer'. The more etymologi-
cally inclined Richard Verstegan, discussing the
Anglo-Saxon *ealdor* in *A Restitution of Decayed
Intelligence* (1605), says it 'is properly an *Elder* or
Senior, yet an *Ealdorman*, which wee now call an
Alderman, was such in effect among our anceters
[*sic*] as was *Tribun Plebis* with the Romans' (SS3ᵛ);
see also p. 30 above. Following Malone, some
editors rearrange the order of entry to give the
senators priority. F's SD has the tribunes enter
first, rather than last; depending on how Shakespeare understood *elder*, in addition to the general
reference to 'wise elder statesmen' Martius sarcastically refers either to Sicinius and Brutus as
now our best senators, in practical terms equal

in power to the noble voting members of that
body, or to the senators having in their generosity
demeaned themselves to the level of the tribunes.
  211 **that** that which, what.
  211 **lately told us** Since Martius has just
learned this 'news' (208), 'told' here may mean
'warned' or predicted' (*OED* Tell *v* 5b). Johnson noted the implication of prior knowledge; the
theme of spying, and more generally the use of
policy in war and peace, is thus introduced early
and extended in Aufidius's remarks in 1.2.
  213 **Tullus Aufidius** Plutarch introduces
Aufidius only late in his narrative, when Coriolanus has deserted Rome to join the Volscians;
Shakespeare from the beginning develops him as
Martius's rival, parallel, contrast and most astute
observer.
  214–16 **I . . . he** Martius's obsession with
the only man he considers a worthy opponent
is matched by Aufidius's with him, although we
learn (1.10.12–16) that Martius's belief in his
opposite's nobility of mind is misplaced.
  217–19 **Were . . . him** On the contrary, Martius's later 'revolt' from his 'party' will include
an alliance with Aufidius. In this scene Martius
expresses a self-image the play will question; compare 223, 'I am constant.'
  217 **by th'ears** at odds, fighting each other like
animals.

> Upon my party, I'd revolt to make
> Only my wars with him. He is a lion
> That I am proud to hunt.

FIRST SENATOR   Then, worthy Martius,   220
> Attend upon Cominius to these wars.

COMINIUS It is your former promise.

MARTIUS   Sir, it is,
> And I am constant. Titus Lartius, thou
> Shalt see me once more strike at Tullus' face.
> What, art thou stiff? Stand'st out?

LARTIUS   No, Caius Martius.   225
> I'll lean upon one crutch and fight with t'other
> Ere stay behind this business.

MENENIUS   O true bred!

A SENATOR Your company to th'Capitol, where I know
> Our greatest friends attend us.

LARTIUS [*To Cominius*]   Lead you on.
> [*To Martius*] Follow Cominius. We must follow you,   230
> Right worthy you priority.

COMINIUS   Noble Martius!

A SENATOR [*To the Citizens*]
> Hence to your homes, begone.

MARTIUS   Nay, let them follow.
> The Volsces have much corn; take these rats thither
> To gnaw their garners. Worshipful mutineers,

---

223 Lartius] *Rowe; Lucius* F   225 SH] F (*Tit. / and to end of scene*)   228 SH, 232 SH A SENATOR] F (*Sen.*); 1. *Sen. /
Rowe*   229 SD *To Cominius*] *Globe, conj. Malone; not in* F   230 SD *To Martius*] *Globe, conj. Malone; not in* F   230
Follow Cominius.] Follow Cominius, F; Follow, Cominius; *Theobald*   231 you] F; your F4   231 Martius] F; Lartius
Theobald   232 SD] *Rowe; not in* F   234 garners.] F; garners. *Citizens steal away / NS*

221 **Attend upon** (1) Accompany, (2) Serve
under (the military command of Cominius).
223 **Lartius** On the F spelling 'Lucius' here
and 'Latius' elsewhere, see Textual Analysis,
p. 292 below.
225 **stiff** With age or wounds, or both. Lartius
may actually be on crutches here, or his reference
could be a joking expansion on the idea of stiffness
keeping him out of the war; he is at any rate soon
seen to be an active soldier in the war against the
Volscians.
225 **Stand'st out?** Staying out of this war?
227 **true bred** bred to the wars. Lartius's
eagerness to fight shows him to be Martius's ideal
patrician.
229 **attend** expect, await.
231 **Right . . . priority** You well deserve to

precede me. Out of respect and admiration, Lartius yields priority to Martius in the processional
exit of the patricians, and Cominius's exclamation
suggests that he shares Lartius's feelings.
234 **garners** granaries.
234 **Worshipful mutineers** Esteemed rebels.
The mocking use of an honorific title of address
aptly introduces Martius's comment on their
bravery; they have presumably done something to
attract his attention, perhaps shuffling nervously.
Globe, followed by some editors, moves part of F's
SD at 235 (*Citizens steal away*) to follow 'garners',
so that Martius's scornful remark on the citizens'
valour is addressed to their retreating backs. 'Pray
follow' in this case would be addressed to the
senators only. The emendation is attractive, yet
it would also make Martius violate decorum by

       Your valour puts well forth. Pray follow.   235
             Citizens steal away. [*Exeunt all but*] *Sicinius and Brutus*
SICINIUS Was ever man so proud as is this Martius?
BRUTUS He has no equal.
SICINIUS When we were chosen tribunes for the people –
BRUTUS Marked you his lip and eyes?
SICINIUS   Nay, but his taunts.
BRUTUS Being moved, he will not spare to gird the gods.   240
SICINIUS Bemock the modest moon.
BRUTUS The present wars devour him! He is grown
       Too proud to be so valiant.
SICINIUS   Such a nature,
       Tickled with good success, disdains the shadow
       Which he treads on at noon. But I do wonder   245
       His insolence can brook to be commanded
       Under Cominius.
BRUTUS   Fame, at the which he aims,
       In whom already he's well graced, cannot
       Better be held nor more attained than by
       A place below the first; for what miscarries   250
       Shall be the general's fault, though he perform
       To th'utmost of a man, and giddy censure

---

235 SD *Exeunt . . . Brutus*] *Globe subst.; Exeunt. / Citizens steale away. Manet Sicin. & Brutus.* F (*Manent* F2)   238
people –] F3; people. F   242 him!] *Hanmer;* him, F   247 Cominius.] *Cominius?* F

ordering the senators to follow him. Martius's comment that the citizens' 'valour puts well forth', addressed to their faces, would sarcastically comment on their late rebellion against the patricians, and 'Pray follow' would invite them to prove truly valiant by joining the senators and chief soldiers at the Capitol to learn more about the coming war. There is ambiguity of stage action and address here, but F seems likely to be correct, and the citizens quietly disperse as Martius and the patricians turn away to exit.

235 puts well forth begins to bud (*OED* Put v^1 43g), promises well.

240 moved angered.

240 gird sneer or scoff at (*OED* Gird v^2 4b).

241 modest chaste, because associated with Diana, virgin goddess of the hunt and worshipped as a moon-deity; compare Coriolanus's salute to Valeria, 5.3.65–7.

242–3 The . . . valiant Hanmer's punctuation, adopted here, yields the likeliest sense: 'May the present wars destroy him! He has become too proud of being so valiant' ('too' means, in any

case, 'excessively' but its political implications for the tribunes extend to 'dangerously', since such bravery coupled with such pride is likely to prove unmanageable). F's punctuation (him,) can yield a different meaning: 'He is consumed with thoughts of the present wars, for he is too proud of his reputation for valiancy.' The tribunes' ill-will toward Martius is already clear, however; a wish that the war should take care of their problem for them seems appropriate, and elsewhere in F a comma represents what in modern punctuation would be an exclamation point.

244 disdains scorns, considers less worthy.

246 brook put up with, tolerate.

246–7 commanded . . . Cominius under the command of Cominius.

248 In whom 'Fame' is personified as a figure in whose good graces Martius already stands.

252 giddy censure inconstant opinion; used of persons, 'giddy' suggests mental intoxication or an incapacity for serious thought or steady attention (*OED* Giddy *a* 3).

Will then cry out of Martius, 'O, if he
Had borne the business!'
SICINIUS   Besides, if things go well,
Opinion, that so sticks on Martius, shall   255
Of his demerits rob Cominius.
BRUTUS   Come,
Half all Cominius' honours are to Martius,
Though Martius earned them not; and all his faults
To Martius shall be honours, though indeed
In aught he merit not.
SICINIUS   Let's hence, and hear   260
How the dispatch is made and in what fashion,
More than his singularity, he goes
Upon this present action.
BRUTUS   Let's along.

                                                        Exeunt

1.[2] *Enter* TULLUS AUFIDIUS *with* SENATORS *of Corioles*

FIRST SENATOR So, your opinion is, Aufidius,
That they of Rome are entered in our counsels
And know how we proceed.
AUFIDIUS   Is it not yours?
What ever have been thought on in this state
That could be brought to bodily act ere Rome   5

253–4 'O . . . business!'] *Capell;* Oh . . . businesse. F   **Act 1, Scene 2**   1.2] *Rome; not in* F   4 have] F; hath F2   4
on] F (one), F3

255 **Opinion** Honour, fine reputation, and
also the public opinion that confers ('sticks') it
on him.
256 **demerits** merits.
260 **aught** anything.
261 **dispatch** management of this business.
262 **singularity** (1) usual distinctive
behaviour (*OED* Singularity 8a), (2) 'desire
to be odde from other men' (Henry Cockeram,
The English Dictionarie, 1626). Perhaps, however,
'singularity' here means 'single self', as in
Johnson's paraphrase: 'We will learn what he is
to do, besides going himself; what are his powers,
and what is his appointment.'

Act 1, Scene 2
Corioles. Although 'Corioli' is the correct form,
this is North's spelling and the usual form in F.
The scene has no basis in North, but it introduces Aufidius early, establishes his own emulous rivalry with Martius (compare 1.1.214–16),
and prepares for their meeting on the battlefield
in 1.8 (see also 1.1.213 n.).
2 **entered in** acquainted with.
4 **What ever have** 'What' is plural here (=
what things); NS assumes a compositor's error
and adopts F2, 'hath'.

    Had circumvention? 'Tis not four days gone
    Since I heard thence. These are the words – I think
    I have the letter here; yes, here it is:
    [*Reads*] 'They have pressed a power, but it is not known
    Whether for east or west. The dearth is great,   10
    The people mutinous. And it is rumoured
    Cominius, Martius your old enemy,
    Who is of Rome worse hated than of you,
    And Titus Lartius, a most valiant Roman,
    These three lead on this preparation   15
    Whither 'tis bent. Most likely 'tis for you.
    Consider of it.'
FIRST SENATOR   Our army's in the field.
    We never yet made doubt but Rome was ready
    To answer us.
AUFIDIUS   Nor did you think it folly
    To keep your great pretences veiled till when   20
    They needs must show themselves, which in the hatching,
    It seemed, appeared to Rome. By the discovery
    We shall be shortened in our aim, which was
    To take in many towns ere, almost, Rome
    Should know we were afoot.
SECOND SENATOR   Noble Aufidius,   25
    Take your commission; hie you to your bands.
    Let us alone to guard Corioles.
    If they set down before's, for the remove
    Bring up your army; but, I think, you'll find
    They've not prepared for us.
AUFIDIUS   O, doubt not that;   30

---

6 circumvention?] F (circumuention:)   9 SD] *Theobald subst.; not in* F   9–17 'They . . . it.'] *Theobald;* They . . . it. F   16 Whither] F (Whether)   27–8 Corioles./If . . . before's,] F4 *subst.; Corioles* / If . . . before's: F   30 They've] F (Th'haue)

6 circumvention warning, foreknowledge for prevention.

6 gone ago.

9 pressed a power conscripted an army.

16 bent headed.

20 pretences designs, plans.

21 needs must must of necessity.

21 in the hatching as soon as announced.

23 shortened . . . aim frustrated of our goal and have to be satisfied with less.

24 take in capture.

24 ere, almost even before (Onions). Perhaps Percy Simpson is correct, however, in taking 'almost', because in brackets in F, as 'a qualifying expression or afterthought' rather than an intensifier (*Shakespearean Punctuation*, 1911, p. 89).

26 hie hasten.

26 bands troops, organised companies of soldiers.

27 Let us alone Either 'Leave it to us', or 'Leave us alone' (Brockbank).

27–8 Corioles . . . before's F's punctuation makes sense grammatically but not in terms of military strategy.

28 set down encamp (in order to lay siege).

28 remove lifting of the siege.

I speak from certainties. Nay, more,
Some parcels of their power are forth already,
And only hitherward. I leave your honours.
If we and Caius Martius chance to meet,
'Tis sworn between us we shall ever strike   35
Till one can do no more.
ALL SENATORS The gods assist you!
AUFIDIUS And keep your honours safe.
FIRST SENATOR Farewell.
SECOND SENATOR Farewell.   40
ALL Farewell.

Exeunt [Aufidius at one door, Senators at another door]

1.[3] *Enter* VOLUMNIA *and* VIRGILIA, *mother and wife to Martius. They
set them down on two low stools and sew*

VOLUMNIA I pray you daughter, sing, or express yourself in a more
comfortable sort. If my son were my husband, I should freelier
rejoice in that absence wherein he won honour than in the
embracements of his bed where he would show most love. When yet
he was but tender-bodied and the only son of my womb, when   5
youth with comeliness plucked all gaze his way, when for a day
of kings' entreaties a mother should not sell him an hour from
her beholding, I, considering how honour would become such a
person – that it was no better than picture-like to hang by th'wall,
if renown made it not stir – was pleased to let him seek danger   10
where he was like to find fame. To a cruel war I sent him, from

---

37 SH] F (*All.*)   41 SD] *Oxford; Exeunt omnes* F   Act 1, Scene 3   1.3] *Rome; not in* F   7 kings'] *Theobald;* Kings
F; King's *Johnson*   7 sell] F (sel); let *conj. Anon. (in Cam.)*

32 parcels portions (i.e. of their army).
35 ever continue to.

Act 1, Scene 3
Rome, a room in the house of Caius Martius.
Plutarch reports that Martius married at his
mother's wish and continued to live with his
wife and two children at his mother's house;
Shakespeare makes no use of this motive for the
marriage or the number of children assigned it
by Plutarch, but does suggest that they all live
together (see 2.1.169).
0 SD.1–2 They . . . sew Props and occupation
establish a domestic atmosphere; see illustration
3 (p. 57 above) for a possible visual source.

2 comfortable sort cheerful manner (*OED*
Comfortable *a* 9).
5 son . . . womb A familiar biblical locution
(Prov. 31.2).
7 should would. On this use of the conditional,
see Abbott 322.
7 sell give him up, let him out of her sight.
9–10 it was . . . stir i.e. if not animated by
desire for renown, such a handsome youth would
be merely decorative.
11–12 cruel . . . oak According to Plutarch,
as a 'stripling' Martius fought against Tarquin
the Proud and was crowned with a garland of
oaken boughs for saving a Roman soldier's life
(Bullough, *Sources*, V, 507); see also 2.1.125 n.

whence he returned, his brows bound with oak. I tell thee, daughter, I sprang not more in joy at first hearing he was a man-child than
now in first seeing he had proved himself a man.

VIRGILIA But had he died in the business, madam, how then?   15

VOLUMNIA Then his good report should have been my son. I therein
would have found issue. Hear me profess sincerely: had I a dozen
sons each in my love alike, and none less dear than thine and my
good Martius, I had rather had eleven die nobly for their country
than one voluptuously surfeit out of action.   20

Enter a GENTLEWOMAN

GENTLEWOMAN Madam, the Lady Valeria is come to visit you.

VIRGILIA Beseech you, give me leave to retire myself.

VOLUMNIA Indeed you shall not.
       Methinks I hear hither your husband's drum;
       See him pluck Aufidius down by th'hair;   25
       As children from a bear, the Volsces shunning him.
       Methinks I see him stamp thus, and call thus:
       'Come on, you cowards! You were got in fear,
       Though you were born in Rome.' His bloody brow
       With his mailed hand then wiping, forth he goes,   30
       Like to a harvestman that's tasked to mow
       Or all or lose his hire.

VIRGILIA His bloody brow? O Jupiter, no blood!

---

19 Martius] F; Martius' *Oxford*   28–9 'Come . . . Rome.'] *Hanmer;* Come . . . Rome; F   31 that's] F2 (thats); that F

Shakespeare, however, seems to take the oaken
garland as acknowledging the bravest soldier of
the battle (see Cominius's account, 2.2.81–92).
The phrase 'cruell warre' appears in Plutarch's
comparison of Coriolanus and Alcibiades (Bullough, *Sources*, v, 546), where it refers to Martius's
later declaration of war against his own country.
Although 'cruel' modifies 'war', its connotation
of unnatural severity also colours our response to
Volumnia as the mother who 'sent' him there.

14 now then (at Martius's triumphant return
from his first battle).

17 issue offspring, progeny (with an overtone
of legal succession; *OED* Issue *sb* 6).

20 voluptuously surfeit overindulge in sen-
sual pleasure, dissipate.

20 SD GENTLEWOMAN NS notes that having an
attendant 'Gentlewoman' rather than a servant is
a mark of Volumnia's high social status.

22 retire myself retire, go in by myself. For

the reflexive use of the verb, see Abbott 296.

24 hither coming this way (the verb of motion
is implied; see Abbott 322).

26 shunning fleeing in fright.

27 thus . . . thus Cues for Volumnia to act
out what she is describing. The imprecations she
imagines for her son are close to those he hurls
at the retreating Roman soldiers (1.4.35–9) and
indicate the source of his contempt for the commonalty.

28 got begotten, conceived (Martius echoes
Volumnia's phrasing at 3.1.240–2).

30 mailed i.e. covered in armour ('mail').

31–2 Like . . . hire The image of the agricultural labourer as grim reaper also appears in *Tro.*
5.5.25–9; used to describe Martius on the battlefield, it recurs in even more grotesquely mechanical form at 2.2.101–4, 112–14.

32 Or . . . or Either . . . or.

32 hire wages.

VOLUMNIA Away, you fool! It more becomes a man
        Than gilt his trophy. The breasts of Hecuba,   35
        When she did suckle Hector, looked not lovelier
        Than Hector's forehead when it spit forth blood
        At Grecian sword, contemning. [*To the Gentlewoman*] Tell
        Valeria
        We are fit to bid her welcome.

                                                  Exit Gent[lewoman]

VIRGILIA Heavens bless my lord from fell Aufidius!   40
VOLUMNIA He'll beat Aufidius' head below his knee
        And tread upon his neck.

        Enter VALERIA *with an Usher, and a Gentlewoman*

VALERIA My ladies both, good day to you.
VOLUMNIA Sweet madam.
VIRGILIA I am glad to see your ladyship.   45
VALERIA How do you both? You are manifest housekeepers. What are
    you sewing here? A fine spot, in good faith. How does your little
    son?
VIRGILIA I thank your ladyship; well, good madam.
VOLUMNIA He had rather see the swords and hear a drum than look   50
    upon his schoolmaster.
VALERIA O'my word, the father's son! I'll swear 'tis a very pretty boy.
    O'my troth, I looked upon him o'Wednesday half an hour together.

---

38 sword, contemning.] *Keightley, conj. Seymour;* sword. *Contenning,* F; *swordes Contending:* F2; *swords' contending.*
Capell; sword contemning. *Leo;* sword, contemning 't *conj. Cam.²;* sword-contending. *Schmidt*   38 SD] *Oxford; not
in* F   39 SD] F *(Exit Gent.)*   53 o'Wednesday] F (a Wensday)

34–5 It . . . trophy Blood is more suitable for
a man than gilding is fitting for his monument.
The Elizabethans, as well as the Romans, gilded
their monuments (see *MV* 2.7.67); elsewhere in
Shakespear 'gold' is thought of as 'red' (see *LLL*
5.2.44, *John* 3.1.11–12, *Mac.* 2.3.112).
   35–8 breasts . . . contemning See pp. 49–50
above.
   35 Hecuba The Queen of Troy.
   36 Hector Hecuba's son, the bravest of the
Trojans defending Troy against the Greeks.
   38 At . . . contemning Hector's blood scorned
(spat upon) the Grecian sword that wounded it.
A minim error (*nn* for *mn*) and lack of punctuation may have led the compositor to read a Roman

name, as though Volumnia were calling the Waiting Gentlewoman, and to set it in italics; see
Textual Analysis, p. 305 below.
   40 bless protect, guard.
   42 tread . . . neck A prediction reversed at
5.6.132 SD.2.
   43 SD *Usher* The male attendant of a lady who
walked before her to announce her presence.
   46 manifest housekeepers Parker notes
Valeria's pun on (1) good housewives, and (2)
stay-at-homes (compare 1.3.62–3).
   47 spot embroidered pattern.
   50 swords Case notes that by metonymy this
could mean 'soldiers'.

'Has such a confirmed countenance! I saw him run after a gilded
butterfly, and when he caught it, he let it go again, and after it again,   55
and over and over he comes, and up again, catched it again. Or
whether his fall enraged him, or how 'twas, he did so set his teeth
and tear it. O, I warrant how he mammocked it!

VOLUMNIA One on's father's moods.

VALERIA Indeed, la, 'tis a noble child.   60

VIRGILIA A crack, madam.

VALERIA Come, lay aside your stitchery. I must have you play the idle
huswife with me this afternoon.

VIRGILIA No, good madam, I will not out of doors.

VALERIA Not out of doors?   65

VOLUMNIA She shall, she shall.

VIRGILIA Indeed, no, by your patience. I'll not over the threshold till
my lord return from the wars.

VALERIA Fie, you confine yourself most unreasonably. Come, you must
go visit the good lady that lies in.   70

VIRGILIA I will wish her speedy strength and visit her with my prayers,
but I cannot go thither.

VOLUMNIA Why, I pray you?

VIRGILIA 'Tis not to save labour, not that I want love.

VALERIA You would be another Penelope. Yet they say all the yarn she   75

---

54 'Has] F4 *subst.* (h'as); ha's F; He's *Oxford*   74 SH] F3 (*Vir.*); *Vlug.* F   75 yarn] F (yearne)

54 **'Has** He has.
54 **confirmed countenance** determined appearance.
54 **gilded** Perhaps gold-coloured, but perhaps only appearing golden in a certain light.
56 **over and over** head over heels.
58 **mammocked it** tore it into fragments or shreds.
59 **on's** of his.
59 **moods** furies, rages. Shakespeare alters Plutarch's two small children to one older son whose behaviour mirrors his father's response to opposition. Volumnia and Valeria's remarks suggest the values with which Martius was raised, and some productions have included Young Martius in this scene, playing soldiers.
60 **la** An exclamation that calls attention to an emphatic statement (*OED* La *int*). Brockbank remarks that its frequent use in *Wiv.* may suggest it was a modish affectation.
60 **noble** Ironic in its implications, although apparently intended only as praise by Valeria.

61 **crack** lively lad (*OED* Crack *sb* 11); Virgilia's hesitation to participate in the women's conversation suggests that 'crack' could also mean 'boast, exaggeration' (*OED* Crack *sb* 4).
63 **huswife** housewife. The mocking addition of 'idle' may suggest a playful reference to making Virgilia an 'unproductive hussy' by luring her away from her proper housework.
67 **by your patience** by your leave.
70 **lady that lies in** expectant mother.
71 **speedy strength** a quick recovery.
74 **want** lack.
75–6 **Penelope . . . moths** Penelope was the faithful wife of Ulysses who put off her suitors by claiming she had to finish her weaving but who then unravelled it every night. The 'moths' are both the fabric-eating insects and, figuratively, the idle suitors who wasted away Ulysses' wealth. F's 'yearne' allows a pun on Penelope's 'yearning' for her absent husband. F's 'Athica' may be a misreading, though it might also be 'a corruption of Ithaca by Attica' (King).

spun in Ulysses' absence did but fill Ithaca full of moths. Come, I
would your cambric were sensible as your finger, that you might
leave pricking it for pity. Come, you shall go with us.

VIRGILIA No, good madam, pardon me; indeed I will not forth.

VALERIA In truth, la, go with me, and I'll tell you excellent news of your   80
husband.

VIRGILIA O, good madam, there can be none yet.

VALERIA Verily, I do not jest with you. There came news from him last
night.

VIRGILIA Indeed, madam?   85

VALERIA In earnest, it's true. I heard a senator speak it. Thus it is: the
Volsces have an army forth, against whom Cominius the general is
gone with one part of our Roman power. Your lord and Titus
Lartius are set down before their city Corioles. They nothing doubt
prevailing and to make it brief wars. This is true, on mine honour,   90
and so, I pray, go with us.

VIRGILIA Give me excuse, good madam. I will obey you in everything
hereafter.

VOLUMNIA Let her alone, lady. As she is now, she will but disease our
better mirth.   95

VALERIA In troth, I think she would. Fare you well, then. Come, good
sweet lady. Prithee, Virgilia, turn thy solemness out o'door and go
along with us.

VIRGILIA No, at a word, madam. Indeed, I must not. I wish you much
mirth.   100

VALERIA Well then, farewell.

Exeunt

76 Ithaca] F3; *Athica* F   85 madam?] F4; madam. F   94 lady. As . . . now,] *Pope subst.*; Ladie, as . . . now: F; Lady,
as . . . now, F4   101 SD] F (*Exeunt Ladies*); *Exeunt Valeria, Volumnia, and usher at one door, Virgilia and Gentlewoman
at another door* / Oxford

77 **cambric** A fine linen, named after Cam-
bray in Flanders where it was first made, on which
Virgilia embroiders her 'spots'.

77 **sensible** sensitive.

78 **leave** leave off.

90 **brief wars** a brief war. The plural was often
used in the same sense as the singular (*OED* War
sb[1] 1c), as it is at 4.5.217, 222.

94–5 **disease . . . mirth** trouble or disturb

our good cheer (*OED* Disease *v* 1). In a play so
concerned with the body's well-being, both physical and political, overtones of 'infect' are surely
present and foreshadow the imagery used by Martius at 3.1.78–81 and 154–6, and about him at
3.1.300–2.

99 **at a word** in a word, in short.

1.[4] *Enter* MARTIUS, TITUS LARTIUS, *with Drum[mer, Trumpeter,] and Colours, with Captains and* SOLDIERS, *as before the city Corioles. To them a* MESSENGER

MARTIUS Yonder comes news. A wager they have met.
LARTIUS My horse to yours, no.
MARTIUS   'Tis done.
LARTIUS   Agreed.
MARTIUS Say, has our general met the enemy?
MESSENGER They lie in view, but have not spoke as yet.
LARTIUS So, the good horse is mine.
MARTIUS   I'll buy him of you.   5
LARTIUS No, I'll nor sell nor give him. Lend you him I will
           For half a hundred years. [*To the Trumpeter*] Summon the
           town.
MARTIUS How far off lie these armies?
MESSENGER Within this mile and half.
MARTIUS Then shall we hear their 'larum, and they ours.   10
           Now, Mars, I prithee make us quick in work,
           That we with smoking swords may march from hence
           To help our fielded friends! [*To the Trumpeter*] Come, blow
           thy blast.

           They sound a parley. Enter two SENATORS *with others on the walls*
                                    of Corioles

           Tullus Aufidius, is he within your walls?
FIRST SENATOR No, nor a man that fears you less than he: 15

Act 1, Scene 4   1.4] *Rowe; not in* F   0 SD.1 *Trumpeter*] NS *subst.; not in* F   0 SD.2 SOLDIERS, *as*] F; *Soldiers carrying scaling ladders, as* / Oxford   0 SD.2 *Corioles. To*] F (*Corialus: to*)   7 SD] NS; *not in* F   13 SD.1] *Oxford; not in* F   15 nor] F; *but* Keightley   15 that] F; *but conj.* Johnson   15 less] F; *more* Hudson², *conj.* Johnson

Act 1, Scene 4
Before the city of Corioles. Historically, Martius earned his honorific surname capturing this city in 493 B.C. The 'walls' on which the senators enter were presumably represented by the stage-gallery. The Roman soldiers may enter carrying the scaling-ladders called for by Lartius (23), or he may shout to off-stage soldiers; the need for ladders is forestalled by the immediate entry of the Volscian army on ground level. Capell has 'Trenches before Corioli', although it is not clear whether 'trenches' were simulated (see 30 SD.1 n.).
   1 met met in battle.
   4 spoke fought.
   7 Summon Summon to parley (see 13 SD.2).

Martius seems to be asserting his own authority when he suspends Lartius's order while he questions the messenger, and again when he orders Lartius to advance (26), although in Plutarch Lartius is clearly Cominius's second-in-command.
   9 mile and half The distance is 'not a mile' at 1.6.16. Cominius's tactical retreat may have brought the forces closer together, but Shakespeare tended to be casual about such details, as he is with Menenius's arithmetic in 2.1.
   10 'larum alarum, a call to arms with drums or trumpet.
   13 fielded friends fellow soldiers already on the battlefield with Cominius.
   15 less The sting in the senator's reply depends on the taunting series 'less', 'lesser',

That's lesser than a little.

Drum afar off

Hark, our drums
Are bringing forth our youth. We'll break our walls
Rather than they shall pound us up. Our gates,
Which yet seem shut, we have but pinned with rushes;
They'll open of themselves.

Alarum far off

Hark you, far off!   20
There is Aufidius. List what work he makes
Amongst your cloven army.

MARTIUS   O, they are at it!
LARTIUS Their noise be our instruction. Ladders, ho!

Enter the army of the Volsces [from the gates]

MARTIUS They fear us not, but issue forth their city.
Now put your shields before your hearts and fight   25
With hearts more proof than shields. Advance, brave Titus.
They do disdain us much beyond our thoughts,
Which makes me sweat with wrath. Come on, my fellows!
He that retires, I'll take him for a Volsce,

18 up. Our] F4 *subst.;* vp our F   20 SD] *Globe; after* far off! F   22 army.] F; army. *Exeunt Volscians from the walls /
Oxford*   23 SD *Volsces . . . gates] Bevington subst.; Volsces.* F   28 fellows!] *Bevington;* fellows F

'little', though the first rather confuses the sense
and has generated various emendations. The senators claim that both citizens and soldiers of Corioles are as fearless of Martius as Aufidius, their
greatest warrior.

16 SD Brockbank notes that 'Theatrically, the
topography of the battle is established by distant
trumpets and drums, much as is that of the rioting
city by distant shouts.'

17 break our walls break out of our walls; the
ordinary meaning ('break down') would also fit
their eagerness to engage the Romans.

18 pound us up confine us (like impounded
animals).

19 rushes flimsy, hollow-stemmed reeds.

22 cloven split, divided. NS suggests 'being
hacked to pieces', but it seems more likely that
the senator refers to the fact that the Roman army

has divided itself so as to fight on two separate
fronts.

23 Their . . . instruction Let the sound of
their fighting be a lesson to us to begin our own.
Although there is no SD for them, the Volscians
presumably exit from the walls at this point.

24 issue forth come or flow out of.

26 proof impenetrable (because of tested or
'proved' strength).

26 Advance . . . Titus Lartius must leave the
stage at some point, since he re-enters at 50 SD.
He could plausibly exit here, in search of 'ladders' (23), or in the first skirmish with the Volscian army (30 SD.1); on other ambiguities about
Lartius's movements, see 1.9.74–5 n.

27 thoughts our own opinion of our abilities,
our expectations about the result of the battle.

And he shall feel mine edge.   30

Alarum. The Romans are beat back to their trenches

Enter MARTIUS, *cursing*

MARTIUS All the contagion of the south light on you,
You shames of Rome! You herd of – boils and plagues
Plaster you o'er, that you may be abhorred
Farther than seen, and one infect another
Against the wind a mile! You souls of geese   35
That bear the shapes of men, how have you run
From slaves that apes would beat! Pluto and hell!
All hurt behind: backs red, and faces pale
With flight and agued fear! Mend and charge home,
Or by the fires of heaven, I'll leave the foe   40
And make my wars on you! Look to't. Come on!

---

30 SD.1 *back to . . . trenches*] F; *back to . . . trenches and thus exeunt / Bevington, after Collier; back and exeunt to . . . trenches, the Volsces following / Oxford*   30 SD.2 *Enter . . . cursing*] F; *Enter . . . cursing, with soldiers / Bevington; Enter Roman Soldiers in retreat, followed by . . . cursing / Oxford, marking new scene*   32 *you herd of – boils*] *Johnson;* you Heard of Byles F; *you! herds of boils Pope²,* conj. *Theobald, 'SR';* Unheard-of boils *Collier²*   37 hell!] F (Hell,)   38 behind:] F (behinde,)   39 fear!] F (feare,)

30 **mine edge** sharp edge of my sword.

30 SD.1 The phrasing is lifted directly from North's Plutarch, but the stage action it cues remains unclear. Some editors clear the stage here, on the assumption that all exit fighting, and then have Martius re-enter with some Roman soldiers, whom he curses for cowardice; Oxford starts a new scene with Martius's entrance. The 'trenches', however, may have been represented by the extreme edge of the stage, or even part of the yard; see Textual Analysis, p. 304 below.

30 SD.2 *cursing* In Plutarch Martius merely called them 'againe to fight with a lowde voyce' (Bullough, *Sources*, V, 512); on a possible significance of such over-explicit, 'literary', SDs, see p. 6 above, n. 3. Shakespeare gives Martius a string of invective in which animal metaphors and images of disease tumble together, expressing his physical revulsion as well as his anger at the common soldiers. Martius throughout demonstrates the temperament of the 'choleric' man, and Brutus later sees how this trait can be turned to the tribunes' advantage (3.3.28–31).

31 **contagion of the south** Contagious disease carried on the warm, damp winds from the south.

31 **light** descend.

32 **herd of – boils** 'Byle' and 'bile' are the Shakespearean spellings of modern 'boil'. John-

son's indication of a pause, while Martius's racing mind shifts the terms of his curse, has been accepted by most subsequent editors. Broken syntax and headlong bursts of imagery are elsewhere characteristic of Martius in moments of intense anger.

33–5 **abhorred . . . mile** despised for your smell even before 'seen' (which implies proximity) and your disease carry a mile, even against the wind, and so infect your own troops.

38 **hurt behind** wounded in the back (during cowardly flight from battle).

39 **agued** trembling, as with an ague (a violent fever).

39 **Mend** (1) Correct this situation, (2) Cure yourselves of this fever of cowardice (continuing the medical metaphor).

39 **home** into battle with the enemy ('home' = mark aimed at).

40 **fires of heaven** stars, but perhaps also lightning.

40–1 **I'll . . . you** The threat here seems exaggerated, a negative incentive balanced by the positive promise of victory if they 'stand fast' (42–3). Later, of course, the commoners' refusal to 'follow' Martius, to ratify his consulship, will lead to exactly this outcome; then, his revenge will be associated with the fires that will destroy Rome.

If you'll stand fast, we'll beat them to their wives,
As they us to our trenches. Follow!
Another alarum. [The Volsces fly,] and Martius follows them
to [the] gates
So, now the gates are ope. Now prove good seconds!
'Tis for the followers fortune widens them,   45
Not for the fliers. Mark me, and do the like.
                         Enters the gates
FIRST SOLDIER Foolhardiness! Not I.
SECOND SOLDIER Nor I.
              [Martius] is shut in. Alarum continues
FIRST SOLDIER See, they have shut him in.
ALL To th'pot, I warrant him.   50

                Enter TITUS LARTIUS

LARTIUS What is become of Martius?
ALL SOLDIERS Slain, sir, doubtless.
FIRST SOLDIER Following the fliers at the very heels,
     With them he enters, who upon the sudden
     Clapped to their gates. He is himself alone,   55
     To answer all the city.
LARTIUS   O noble fellow!

43 trenches. Follow!] *Collier²*; Trenches followes. F; trenches followed. F2; trenches: follow me. *Dyce²*, conj. Lettsom
(*in Walker*); trenches. Follow's. *Sisson, conj. Collier³*; trenches. *Clarendon*   43 SD.1–2 alarum. *The Volsces fly, and*
Martius followes them to the gates] Globe; *Alarum, and Martius followes them to gates, and is shut in.* F; *The Romans*
come forward towards the walls. Another alarum, and enter the army of the Volsces. Martius beats them back through the
gates / Oxford   45 followers fortune] followers, Fortune F2; followers Fortune, F   46 SD] F2 *subst. (Enter); Enter the*
Gati. F   48 SD] *Johnson; part of* SD *at 43* F   49 SH] F (1. *Sol.*); 3. *Sol.* / Johnson   50 SH] F; *Third Soldier* / Oxford
51 SH] F (*Tit.*)   52 SH] F (*All.*); *Fourth Soldier* / Oxford; *Third Soldier* / Parker

43 Follow F's 'followes' could be retained, as a plural form with 'they' as its subject. More probably, it was picked up by eye-skip from the SD in the subsequent line. Some final exhortation seems appropriate (as at 46); this edition follows Collier rather than Sisson's 'Follow's', which seems less apt for a man who tends to think of himself as separate and above the common herd. Presuming 'followes' to have been inadvertently lifted from the SD, Globe and NS omit it entirely but, as Brockbank notes, 'that would be more probable if something resembling it stood in the copy'.

43 SD.1–2 Shakespeare's omnibus SD appears to have been left to the book-keeper to distribute, which he proceeded to do without cancelling the now superfluous end of the original. The Volscian soldiers are probably upstage, regrouping and catching their breath while Martius rallies

his troops; the Volsces then advance for another pitched battle signalled by the alarum, but are beaten back into the city gates and followed in by Martius.

44 seconds supporters.

45 followers pursuers.

46 fliers those who flee, i.e. the Volscian soldiers.

50 To th'pot To his destruction. The metaphor is compressed: the soldiers expect Martius to be cut in pieces like meat for the cooking-pot.

50 SD See 26 n.

54 upon the sudden suddenly.

55 himself alone quite alone. In Plutarch Martius is followed into Corioles by a few hardy soldiers; Shakespeare emphasises Martius's isolation and extraordinary (and reckless) bravery.

Who sensibly outdares his senseless sword
And, when it bows, stand'st up. Thou art lost, Martius.
A carbuncle entire, as big as thou art,
Were not so rich a jewel. Thou wast a soldier   60
Even to Cato's wish, not fierce and terrible
Only in strokes, but with thy grim looks and
The thunder-like percussion of thy sounds
Thou mad'st thine enemies shake, as if the world
Were feverous and did tremble.   65

Enter MARTIUS, *bleeding, assaulted by the enemy*

FIRST SOLDIER Look, sir.
LARTIUS O, 'tis Martius!
       Let's fetch him off, or make remain alike.
                            They fight, and all enter the city

1.[5] *Enter certain* ROMANS, *with spoils*

FIRST ROMAN This will I carry to Rome.

57 sensibly outdares] F; sensible, out-does *Theobald* (*Thirlby*); sensible, out-dares *Johnson*   58 stand'st] F; stands *Rowe*   58 lost] *Singer*², *conj. Collier*; left F; reft *conj. Nicholson* (*in Cam.*)   59 entire,] F3; intire: F   60 Were] F (Weare)   61 Cato's] *Theobald; Calues* F; Calvus *Rowe*   **Act 1, Scene 5**   1.5] *Capell; not in* F; 1.6 *Oxford*

57–8 Who . . . up Who, although sensible to pain and danger, outdoes his merely material sword; it may bend, but he will not. Steevens noted a possible adaptation from Sir Philip Sidney's *Arcadia* (1633 edn, p. 293): 'Their very armour by piece-meale fell away from them: and yet their flesh abode the wounds constantly, as though it were lesse sensible of smart than the senselesse armour.'

58 lost Singer's conjecture seems likely; in Secretary hand *e* and *o* and long *s* and *f* could easily be confused, and 'lost' suits the subsequent use of the past tense, which assumes Martius already dead. If 'left' is correct, Lartius would seem to suggest that Martius, left alone to answer 'all the city', is also 'left alone among men, without a rival' (Brockbank). F's punctuation of this sentence suggests that Compositor B did not understand the sense of what he was setting.

59 carbuncle A precious stone of red or fiery colour, anciently thought to shine in the dark.

59 entire flawless.

61 Cato's wish Theobald based his emendation on North: 'For he was even such another, as Cato would have a souldier and a captaine to be' (Bullough, *Sources*, V, 512). While appropri-

ate to Plutarch, the reference to Marcus Porcius Cato (234–149 B.C.), known as 'the Censor', is a gross anachronism in Lartius's mouth: Cato's celebrated censorship in 184 B.C. occurred more than 300 years after Martius's banishment.

62 Only in strokes Only in individual blows. Martius's fierceness extends to all aspects, 'looks' and 'sounds' as well as 'strokes'.

64–5 as . . . tremble Martius's superhuman but also disturbingly non-human stature is felt strongly in the evocative images surrounding the specific praise borrowed from North: the richly and mysteriously glowing jewel the size of a man, the earth trembling in the presence of something threatening and unnatural (see also p. 44 above). In *Mac.*, of the night King Duncan was murdered Lennox observes, 'Some say, the earth / Was feverous, and did shake' (2.3.60–1).

68 fetch him off rescue him.

68 make remain alike stay to share his fate. For 'remain' as a noun meaning 'stay', see *OED* Remain *sb*².

Act 1, Scene 5
Although many editors follow Capell's 'Within the Town, A Street', no change of location is

SECOND ROMAN And I this.

THIRD ROMAN A murrain on't! I took this for silver.

Alarum continues still afar off

Enter MARTIUS, *and* TITUS [LARTIUS] *with a Trumpet*[*er*]

Exeunt [*looters*]

MARTIUS See here these movers that do prize their hours
    At a cracked drachma! Cushions, leaden spoons,   5
    Irons of a doit, doublets that hangmen would
    Bury with those that wore them, these base slaves,
    Ere yet the fight be done, pack up. Down with them!
    [*Alarum continues*]
    And hark, what noise the general makes! To him!
    There is the man of my soul's hate, Aufidius,   10
    Piercing our Romans. Then, valiant Titus, take
    Convenient numbers to make good the city,

---

3 SD.2 *Enter . . .* TITUS LARTIUS *. . . Trumpeter*] *Enter . . . Titus . . . Trumpet.* F   3 SD.2 MARTIUS] F; *Martius, bleeding,* / Oxford   3 SD.3 *Exeunt looters*] *This edn; exeunt.* F (*at 3, after* silver); *at 8, after* them! *Kittredge*   4 hours] F; honours *Rowe³*   5 drachma] F (Drachme)   7 them,] F3; them. F   8 SD] *This edn; not in* F   9 him!] *Pope subst.;* him F; him, F3

necessary. The soldiers may be carrying their spoils out from the town gates (represented by the façade doors or curtains).

3 murrain plague (strictly, 'cattle plague').

3 SD.3 *Exeunt looters* Martius's first words indicate that he and Lartius see the retreating soldiers and that F's *exeunt* is misplaced. F's space-saving *exeunt*, which even with its lower-case *e* fills the remaining space in the third soldier's last line, may be a compositorial compression of a longer SD (such as *Souldiers steale away*, similar to the SD at 1.1.235 for the citizens).

4 movers active persons (used with contemptuous irony, since they should be occupied with the war); Brockbank suggests a possible play on 'removers' as 'scavengers'.

4 hours F's 'hours' comports with Martius's concern with wasting time and with North, which Shakespeare follows closely in this battle sequence: 'Martius was marvelous angry with them, and cried out on them, that it was no time now to looke after spoyle . . . whilest the other Consul and their fellowe cittizens peradventure were fighting their enemies' (Bullough, *Sources*, v, 512–13). Rowe's 'honours' would also make sense, but is unnecessary.

5 drachma Greek silver coin whose weight and value varied in different places but never amounted to much. Shakespeare may have thought it a Roman coin, since he found the word

in North's report of Caesar's will (see *JC* 3.2.244). F's *Drachme* suggests a monosyllabic pronunciation.

6 Irons . . . doit Swords (perhaps more generally, given the context of non-military items, 'tools or utensils made of iron') worth a Dutch coin ('doit') valued at only half an English farthing.

6–7 doublets . . . them The hangman had the right to the deceased's clothing, but not even a man of such low status as a hangman would want these doublets. A doublet was a close-fitting coat, sometimes without sleeves, worn over ('doubling') another garment. It was an Elizabethan, not a Roman, item of clothing, although as NS points out, both North's Caesar and Shakespeare's Caesar wear doublets.

8 pack up F's punctuation suggests a pun on 'pack up' as 'quit', although Shakespeare does not elsewhere use the phrase in that sense.

8 SD The 'alarum' is called for by the dialogue and reminds the audience that the Romans have not yet won the day. It may have been omitted by Compositor B because the long verse lines left no appreciable free space in the right margin; nowhere else does a 'hark' fail to have its immediately corresponding sound cue.

9 the general Cominius, fighting Aufidius's army nearby.

12 make good hold, secure.

Whilst I with those that have the spirit will haste
To help Cominius.
LARTIUS   Worthy sir, thou bleed'st.
Thy exercise hath been too violent   15
For a second course of fight.
MARTIUS   Sir, praise me not.
My work hath yet not warmed me. Fare you well.
The blood I drop is rather physical
Than dangerous to me. To Aufidius thus
I will appear and fight.
LARTIUS   Now the fair goddess Fortune   20
Fall deep in love with thee, and her great charms
Misguide thy opposers' swords! Bold gentleman,
Prosperity be thy page!
MARTIUS   Thy friend no less
Than those she placeth highest. So, farewell.
LARTIUS Thou worthiest Martius!   25

         [Exit Martius]

Go sound thy trumpet in the market-place.
Call thither all the officers o'th'town,
Where they shall know our mind. Away!

          Exeunt

1.[6] *Enter* COMINIUS, *as it were in retire, with Soldiers*

COMINIUS Breathe you, my friends. Well fought! We are come off

---

22 swords! Bold gentleman,] *Johnson;* swords, Bold Gentleman: F; swords: bold gentleman! *Rowe*   25 SD] *Capell; not in* F   28 SD *Exeunt*] F; *Exeunt severally / Oxford*   Act 1, Scene 6   1.6] *Capell; not in* F; 1.7 *Oxford*

16 course passage at arms, bout. There may be a play on 'course of a banquet'; see the feasting metaphors at 1.9.10–11, 4.5.208–9.

18 physical curative, good for the health (*OED* Physical *a* 5b), picking up the connotations of 'exercise' (15) and 'warmed me' (17). Bloodletting was a common medical treatment.

23 Prosperity . . . page May success attend you.

23–4 Thy . . . highest May she be no less thy friend than those she most favours.

Act 1, Scene 6
Somewhere on the battlefield, less than a mile (16) from the 'trenches' of scene 4.

0 SD *in retire* in retreat (as in 3).
1 Breathe you Take pause, rest.
1 are come off disengaged from battle. As Cominius's next words make clear, he sees this as a strategic regrouping, not a full retreat. He is a calmer, more mature military tactician than Martius and understands that in some circumstances continuing to press on in battle can be 'foolish' (2). Martius's assault on Corioles with apparently inadequate forces was termed 'Foolhardiness' by one of the soldiers who refused to follow him (1.4.47).

Like Romans, neither foolish in our stands,
Nor cowardly in retire. Believe me, sirs,
We shall be charged again. Whiles we have struck,
By interims and conveying gusts we have heard   5
The charges of our friends. The Roman gods
Lead their successes as we wish our own,
That both our powers, with smiling fronts encountering,
May give you thankful sacrifice!

Enter a MESSENGER

                                   Thy news?
MESSENGER The citizens of Corioles have issued   10
          And given to Lartius and to Martius battle.
          I saw our party to their trenches driven,
          And then I came away.
COMINIUS   Though thou speak'st truth,
          Methinks thou speak'st not well. How long is't since?
MESSENGER Above an hour, my lord.   15
COMINIUS 'Tis not a mile; briefly we heard their drums.
          How couldst thou in a mile confound an hour
          And bring thy news so late?
MESSENGER   Spies of the Volsces
          Held me in chase, that I was forced to wheel
          Three or four miles about; else had I, sir,   20
          Half an hour since brought my report.

Enter MARTIUS[, *bloody*]

COMINIUS   Who's yonder,

---

6 The Roman gods] F (Gods,); Ye Roman Gods, *Hanmer*   9 SD] *Collier; after* news? F   13 speak'st] *Rowe³; speakest
F   16 briefly] F; briefly, *Theobald*   21 report.] F; report. *Exit / Oxford*   21 SD MARTIUS, *bloody*] *Oxford; Martius.* F
21 Who's] F (Whose)

---

4 struck fought, been striking blows.

5 By interims . . . gusts At intervals and carried on the wind.

6 The Hanmer's emendation is unnecessary,
for Shakespeare elsewhere uses 'The' with the
vocative; see 2.3.48, 4.1.37.

7 Guide their fortunes, as we wish our own, to
a prosperous outcome. 'Success' was frequently
used in the neutral sense of 'outcome of events'.

8 fronts faces; with a possible secondary
meaning of the 'front ranks' of the two armies.

9 SD *Enter* There is no exit direction for the
messenger, and Martius's 'Call him hither' (41)
suggests that he may have left after imparting his

news. He may, however, have merely joined the
other soldiers on stage.

10 issued This incident is reported by North
as a Coriolan 'salye out upon' the besieging
Romans (Bullough, *Sources*, V, 511) and dramatised by Shakespeare in 1.4.

14 speak'st Metrically, both this and the next
line require 'speak'st', and F's 'speakest' may be a
copyist's or compositor's error. F's extrametrical
syllable has been defended by Gomme, however,
as a deliberate retardation in tempo.

16 briefly a short while ago.

17 confound waste, consume.

19 that so that.

That does appear as he were flayed? O gods!
He has the stamp of Martius, and I have
Before-time seen him thus.

MARTIUS   Come I too late?

COMINIUS The shepherd knows not thunder from a tabor   25
More than I know the sound of Martius' tongue
From every meaner man.

MARTIUS   Come I too late?

COMINIUS Ay, if you come not in the blood of others
But mantled in your own.

MARTIUS   O! Let me clip ye
In arms as sound as when I wooed, in heart   30
As merry as when our nuptial day was done
And tapers burned to bedward.

                 [*They embrace*]

COMINIUS Flower of warriors! How is't with Titus Lartius?

MARTIUS As with a man busied about decrees:
Condemning some to death and some to exile,   35
Ransoming him or pitying, threatening th'other;
Holding Corioles in the name of Rome
Even like a fawning greyhound in the leash,

---

22 flayed] F (Flead)   24 Before-time] *Hanmer;* Before time F   30 wooed, in heart] *Theobald subst. (Thirlby);* woo'd in heart; F   32 SD] *NS; not in* F

22 **flayed** Martius has received so many wounds that his bloody body appears to have had its skin stripped off. Rodney Poisson (*SQ* 15 (1964), 450) suggests that this striking image may have been inspired by Golding's translation of Ovid's *Metamorphoses* (VI, 494), where the satyr Marsyas is described as 'Nought else he was than one whole wounde.'

23 **stamp** form or impress (as a coin from the mint), hence 'distinguishing characteristics'.

24 **Before-time** Formerly.

24 **Come . . . late** Assuming Cominius's lines indicate that Martius has not yet appeared and F's SD to be premature, Dyce and a number of subsequent editors add a SD *within*. Martius's approach has been noted, however (21); the extent of his wounds makes him at first unrecognisable.

25 **tabor** A small drum, used chiefly as an accompaniment to the pipe or fife.

27 **meaner** inferior, less noble.

29–32 **Let . . . bedward** Cominius kisses and embraces Martius at this point in Plutarch, a not uncommon expression of the extraordinary bond-

ing established between men in a patriarchal military culture. Shakespeare's addition of Martius's wedding-night comparison suggests a homoerotic dimension; Aufidius tips the balance when he effusively declares that Martius's appearance in Antium surpasses his wedding-day joy (4.5.110–15); see pp. 51–2 above. Parker notes that the war-love connection is reversed with Virgilia: Martius cannot embrace his wife without thinking of war (see 5.3.44–5), although there it is more precisely 'revenge'.

29 **clip** clasp, embrace.

30 **wooed, in heart** Theobald's repunctuation, followed in a modified form here, is persuasive although, as Brockbank observes, 'F's "woo'd in heart" may chime rhetorically with "clip ye in arms".'

32 **tapers . . . bedward** Either candles burned low, indicating it was time for bed, or candles carried to show the way to the marital bedroom.

36 **Ransoming . . . pitying** Releasing a man for money, or for pity (i.e. releasing him without requiring a ransom).

        To let him slip at will.

COMINIUS   Where is that slave
        Which told me they had beat you to your trenches?   40
        Where is he? Call him hither.

MARTIUS   Let him alone;
        He did inform the truth. But for our gentlemen,
        The common file – a plague! Tribunes for them! –
        The mouse ne'er shunned the cat as they did budge
        From rascals worse than they.

COMINIUS   But how prevailed you?   45

MARTIUS Will the time serve to tell? I do not think.
        Where is the enemy? Are you lords o'th'field?
        If not, why cease you till you are so?

COMINIUS Martius, we have at disadvantage fought
        And did retire to win our purpose.   50

MARTIUS How lies their battle? Know you on which side
        They have placed their men of trust?

COMINIUS   As I guess, Martius,
        Their bands i'th'vaward are the Antiates
        Of their best trust; o'er them Aufidius,
        Their very heart of hope.

MARTIUS   I do beseech you,   55
        By all the battles wherein we have fought,
        By th'blood we have shed together, by th'vows we have made
        To endure friends, that you directly set me
        Against Aufidius and his Antiates,

---

42 truth. But . . . gentlemen,] F (truth: but . . . Gentlemen,); truth – but . . . gentlemen. *Hibbard, conj. Anon.*   43 file – a plague! . . . them! –] file, (a plague- Tribunes for them) F; file – a plague – . . . them? – *Oxford*   46 tell? . . . think.] F3 *subst.;* tell, . . . thinke: F; tell? . . . think – *Rowe*   51 which] F ($\frac{c}{w}$); what F2   53 vaward] F; vanguard *Oxford*   53 Antiates] *Pope;* Antients F; Ancients F3

39 let him slip unleash him (continuing the canine metaphor initiated by 'fawning greyhound').

42 inform report.

42 But for As for.

42 gentlemen Martius's sarcasm is clear from the succeeding lines.

43 common file common rank of soldiers. 'File' refers to the depth of formation in an infantry line.

44 budge flinch; perhaps 'fly', referring to the soldiers who were driven to their trenches in 1.4.

46 think think so. On omission of 'so' after 'think', see Abbott 64.

51 battle army, battle-formation.

53 vaward vanguard. Shakespeare uses only this form, which was a common seventeenth-century spelling.

53 Antiates Soldiers of Antium (the Volsces' chief city and Aufidius's native town). Compositor B's 'Antients' makes sense (taking 'ancients' as a corruption of 'ensigns'), but 59 (F 'Antiats') confirms Pope's correction.

54 o'er overseeing (as their general).

58–9 set . . . Antiates Martius's plea is picked up from North: 'Then prayed Martius to be set directly against them [Aufidius and the 'vaward' Antiates]' (Bullough, *Sources*, v, 513).

And that you not delay the present, but,   60
Filling the air with swords advanced and darts,
We prove this very hour.
COMINIUS   Though I could wish
You were conducted to a gentle bath
And balms applied to you, yet dare I never
Deny your asking. Take your choice of those   65
That best can aid your action.
MARTIUS   Those are they
That most are willing. If any such be here,
As it were sin to doubt, that love this painting
Wherein you see me smeared; if any fear
Lesser his person than an ill report;   70
If any think brave death outweighs bad life,
And that his country's dearer than himself,
Let him alone, or so many so minded,
Wave thus [*Waving his sword*] to express his disposition,
And follow Martius.   75

They all shout and wave their swords, take him up in their arms,
and cast up their caps

O'me alone? Make you a sword of me?
If these shows be not outward, which of you
But is four Volsces? None of you but is

60–1 but, . . . advanced] *Rowe subst.*; (but . . . aduanc'd) F   70 Lesser] F3; Lessen F; Less for *Rowe*   72–3 himself, . . . alone, or] himselfe, . . . alone: Or F   74 SD] *Singer²*, *after Johnson; not in* F   75 SD.1–2 *They . . . swords, take . . . caps*] F; *They . . . swords. / Brockbank* (*They take . . . caps. / after 76*)   76 O'me] F (Oh me); *Soldiers.* O, me *Brooke, conj. Style* (*in Cam.²*)   76 O'me alone? . . . sword of me?] *Sisson, after Collier²*; Oh me alone, . . . sword of me: F; O, me alone! . . . sword of me? *Capell*; O, me alone! . . . sword of me! *Steevens*; Come! along! . . . sword of me, *Singer²*; O me! alone! . . . sword of me? *Keightley*; Of me alone . . . sword? of me? *Deighton*; O'me alone, . . . sword of me. *Hibbard*
77 If] F; *Mar.* If *Brooke, conj. Style*

60 delay the present let slip this moment, make any delay now (see Abbott 305).
61 advanced raised; also 2.1.134.
61 darts lances.
62 prove put ourselves to the test, try our fortune.
68 painting i.e. blood (with which he is covered).
69–70 fear . . . report fear less for his physical safety than for a bad reputation. F's 'Lessen' is probably a minim error.
74 thus A cue for a gesture to stir his listeners to assenting action.
75 SD.1 *take . . . arms* Martius's eagerness to get to the battle with Aufidius and Antium's best warriors has made him a genuinely charismatic leader, and he here accepts physical contact with the commoners that he elsewhere shuns.
76 Make you a sword of me alone? The line is problematic both in tone and meaning (where F's 'Oh' and punctuation are ambiguous) and, to some, in speaker. Brockbank follows Style and Brooke in assigning this line to the soldiers, making them eagerly volunteer to be Martius's 'swords' (i.e. swordsmen). F's assignment to Martius makes sense, however, and Sisson's 'O'', adopted here, suggests surprise and even exultation; see p. 40 n. 3 above.
77 shows demonstrations.
77 outward external, deceptive appearances.
78 But is Is not equal to.

Able to bear against the great Aufidius
A shield as hard as his. A certain number,   80
Though thanks to all, must I select from all.
The rest shall bear the business in some other fight
As cause will be obeyed. Please you to march,
And I shall quickly draw out my command
Which men are best inclined.
COMINIUS   March on, my fellows.   85
Make good this ostentation, and you shall
Divide in all with us.

                                                   Exeunt

1.[7] TITUS LARTIUS, *having set a guard upon Corioles, going with*
Drum[mer] and *Trumpet[er]* toward Cominius and Caius Martius, enters
with a LIEUTENANT, *other Soldiers, and a Scout*

LARTIUS   So, let the ports be guarded. Keep your duties
As I have set them down. If I do send, dispatch
Those centuries to our aid; the rest will serve
For a short holding. If we lose the field,
We cannot keep the town.
LIEUTENANT   Fear not our care, sir.   5

82–3 The rest . . . fight / As . . . obeyed.] F ((As . . . obey'd:)); The rest (as . . . obey'd) shall bear / The . . . fight:
conj. Rossiter (in Brockbank)   83–4 march, / And I] *Hudson²*, *conj. Capell;* March, / And foure F; March before; /
And I *Collier²*; march; / And some *Singer²*; march; / And forth *Keightley, conj. Tollet (in Steevens²*)   Act 1, Scene 7
1.7] *Capell; not in* F; 1.8 *Oxford*   0 SD.2 *Drummer and Trumpeter*] *Drum and Trumpet* F

81–3 **Though . . . march** F can stand as it
is, though Rossiter's transposed clause and relineation become plausible if one assumes that 'As
cause will be obeyed', which in F is oddly in brackets, was a marginal or interlinear correction in the
manuscript that Compositor B misplaced when
setting up the line.
83 **As . . . obeyed** As circumstances may
demand.
84 I NS notes that F's 'foure' is a likely misreading of Shakespeare's manuscript *I* as the numeral
4; the 'foure' above (78) may also have originally
been represented by a numeral. Martius has just
said (81) that he intends to do the selecting himself.
84 **draw . . . command** choose for my forces.

86 **ostentation** demonstration (of support).
87 **Divide in all** Share in the honour – and
perhaps also, as NS suggests, in the captured
spoils of war.

Act 1, Scene 7
Before the gates of Corioles.
0 SD.1–3 The SD summarises what the tiny
scene reveals in dialogue. Parker notes that the
scene prepares us for Lartius's entry at 1.9.11 and
gives Martius time to reach the battlefield to fight
Aufidius in 1.8.
1 **ports** gates.
3 **centuries** Companies consisting each of a
hundred men (Latin *centuria*).

LARTIUS Hence, and shut your gates upon's.
    [*To the Scout*] Our guider, come; to th'Roman camp conduct
      us.

                    [*Exeunt*]

1.[8] *Alarum, as in battle. Enter* MARTIUS *and* AUFIDIUS *at several doors*

MARTIUS I'll fight with none but thee, for I do hate thee
    Worse than a promise-breaker.
AUFIDIUS   We hate alike.
    Not Afric owns a serpent I abhor
    More than thy fame and envy. Fix thy foot.
MARTIUS Let the first budger die the other's slave,   5
    And the gods doom him after!
AUFIDIUS   If I fly, Martius,
    Hollo me like a hare.
MARTIUS   Within these three hours, Tullus,
    Alone I fought in your Corioles' walls
    And made what work I pleased. 'Tis not my blood
    Wherein thou seest me masked. For thy revenge   10

---

6 upon's.] F; upon's. *Exit Lieutenant / Oxford*   7 SD.1 *To . . . Scout*] *Oxford; not in* F   7 SD.2 *Exeunt*] *Pope; Exit / Alarum, as in Battaile* F   **Act 1, Scene 8**   1.8] *Capell; not in* F; 1.9 *Oxford*   0 SD.1 *Alarum, as in battle. Enter*] NS; *Enter* F   4 fame and envy] F; fame I envy *Collier²*; fame, and envy't *conj. Kinnear (in Cam.²)*   7 Hollo] F (hollow)

Act 1, Scene 8
On the field of battle; in Plutarch, Aufidius does not figure in the Romans' war against the Coriolans.

  0 SD *Alarum . . . battle* F places this SD at the end of 1.7. It is clearly a 'bridging' sound-cue preparing for the action of 1.8 and may have been a book-keeper's marginal annotation later misread as to location by the compositor.

  0 SD *several* separate; see headnote, 1.9.

  1–2 hate . . . alike Although this scene of single combat is not in Plutarch, the dialogue was probably inspired by North's assertion that they had fought many times, 'In so muche, as besides the common quarrell betweene them, there was bred a marvelous private hate one against another' (Bullough, *Sources*, v, 526–7).

  2 Worse . . . promise-breaker See 1.1.217–19, 223 for other instances of dramatic irony in referring to Aufidius.

  3 Afric . . . serpent For Africa as the country

of serpents, Globe cites Thomas Heywood's *The Silver Age* (*Works*, ed. Pearson, 1874, III, 125–6) and Case Golding's translation of Ovid's story of the Gorgon's head breeding serpents in Libya (*Metamorphoses*, IV, 756–63).

  4 fame and envy (1) by hendiadys, 'envied fame', (2) fame and the envy it occasions, (3) 'envy' may be a verb (i.e. 'I abhor and envy thy fame'). Malone glosses 'envy' as 'malice', which has some warrant in North: 'Tullus dyd more malice and envie him [Martius], then he dyd all the Romaines besides' (Bullough, *Sources*, v, 526).

  4 Fix . . . foot Stand and fight (as for a formal duel).

  5 budger See 1.6.44 n.

  7 Hollo . . . hare Chase me with shouts as you would a hare (a timid, fearful animal). The metaphor is from hunting.

  10 masked Compare Martius's blood-'mantled' body (1.6.28–9).

Wrench up thy power to th'highest.

AUFIDIUS   Wert thou the Hector
That was the whip of your bragged progeny,
Thou shouldst not 'scape me here.
Here they fight, and certain Volsces come in the aid of Aufidius
Officious and not valiant, you have shamed me
In your condemnèd seconds.   15
          Martius fights till they be driven in breathless. [*Exeunt*]

1.[9]   *Alarum. A retreat is sounded.* [*Flourish.*] *Enter at one door* COMINIUS
with the ROMANS; *at another door* MARTIUS, *with his* [*left*] *arm in a scarf*

COMINIUS   If I should tell thee o'er this thy day's work,
Thou't not believe thy deeds. But I'll report it
Where senators shall mingle tears with smiles;
Where great patricians shall attend and shrug,
I'th'end admire; where ladies shall be frighted   5
And, gladly quaked, hear more; where the dull tribunes,

---

13 SD *Aufidius*] Capell subst.; *Auff. Martius fights til they be driuen in breathles.* F; *Aufidius. Martius fights till they be driven breathless, Martius following* / Oxford   15 condemnèd] F; contemned *conj. Johnson*   15 SD *Martius . . . breathless*] NS; *at 13* F   15 SD *Exeunt*] Hanmer; *not in* F; *Exeunt fighting, driven in by Marcius. Alarum. Retreat.* / Capell; *Exit* / Oxford   Act 1, Scene 9   1.9] Capell; *not in* F; 1.10 Oxford   0 SD.1 *Alarum . . . sounded. Flourish. Enter*] Malone; *Flourish. Alarum . . . sounded. Enter* F; *Flourish. Enter* / Capell   0 SD.2 *left arm*] Parker; *arm* F   2 Thou't] F; Thou'lt F4; Thou'ldst *White*

---

11 **Wrench** Strain, wrest; NS compares *Mac.* 1.2.60: 'screw your courage to the sticking place'. Martius also plays on the hare metaphor: 'of a hare: to veer or come round at less than a right angle' (*OED* Wrench *v* 2).

11 **Hector** See 1.3.36 n.

12 **whip of** whip belonging to. Hector is seen as the whip with which the Trojans scourged the Greeks.

12 **your bragged progeny** the race (ancestors) you brag of; possibly the sense 'your boastful race' is also intended. After Troy fell, one of its defenders, Aeneas, was thought to have founded Rome.

13 SD, 15 SD In F both SDs appear together after 13, and the scene lacks a final exit SD. NS argues persuasively that Aufidius's address to the Volscians would precede their being 'driven in breathless'. Moreover, there is reason to believe that to save space Compositor B amalgamated at 13 what were originally two separate SDs; see Textual Analysis, pp. 304–5 below.

14 **Officious** Interfering, meddlesome.

15 By seconding me in such a damnable fashion; see 1.4.44 n.

Act 1, Scene 9
The Roman camp. Brockbank notes that the Romans' entry from both sides of the stage visually expresses their total command of the field.

0 SD.1 *Flourish* Malone's suggestion that F's *Flourish* is misplaced is surely correct; Capell may be right to move *Alarum. Retreat* to the end of 1.8. This is another 'bridging' SD that aurally represents the Volscians' defeat and introduces the victorious Romans.

0 SD.2 *scarf* sling; that it is his left arm we learn at 2.1.123.

2 **Thou't** Thou wouldst; an abbreviation of the colloquial 'thou woot' (Parker).

4 **attend** listen.

5 **admire** marvel at.

6 **quaked** disturbed, made to tremble.

6 **dull** sullen, spiritless.

That with the fusty plebeians hate thine honours,
Shall say against their hearts, 'We thank the gods
Our Rome hath such a soldier.'
Yet cam'st thou to a morsel of this feast,   10
Having fully dined before.

Enter TITUS [LARTIUS] *with his power, from the pursuit*

LARTIUS   O general,
Here is the steed, we the caparison.
Hadst thou beheld –
MARTIUS   Pray now, no more. My mother,
Who has a charter to extol her blood,
When she does praise me grieves me. I have done   15
As you have done, that's what I can; induced
As you have been, that's for my country.
He that has but effected his good will
Hath overta'en mine act.
COMINIUS   You shall not be
The grave of your deserving. Rome must know   20
The value of her own. 'Twere a concealment
Worse than a theft, no less than a traducement,
To hide your doings and to silence that

8–9 'We . . . soldier.'] *Hanmer;* We . . . Souldier. F   11 SD TITUS LARTIUS] *Titus* F   11 SH] F (*Titus Lartius.*)

7 fusty ill-smelling. 'Fusty' is most often applied to food, wine or air that has lost its freshness and become rotten or stale.

7 plebeians Accented here on the first syllable (see Abbott 492).

10–11 Yet . . . before Martius came late, to a 'morsel' of the feast of battle against Aufidius, yet he had already had a full feast of his own at Corioles. For other instances of the gruesome battle–banquet analogy, see 1.5.16, 4.5.208–9; in a related metaphor, wars devour those who fight in them at 1.1.69–70, 242.

12 'This man performed the action, and we only filled up the show' (Johnson). A 'caparison' is the ornamental cloth covering of a horse; here it comes from North, where Cominius's gift (60–1) is described as 'a goodly horse with a capparison, and all furniture to him' (Bullough, *Sources*, V, 514). Cominius and Martius had earlier wagered a horse on whether the Volscian and Roman armies had yet engaged in battle (1.4.1–2).

13–15 Pray . . . me Martius's aversion to public praise, here and in 2.2, is lacking in Plutarch

but central to Shakespeare's characterisation; see pp. 52–3 above.

14 charter right, prerogative.

18–19 He . . . act He who has simply carried out his good intentions has accomplished more than I. In implying that his own potential has not as yet been fulfilled, Martius reveals a sense of his own superiority even as he apparently disclaims it.

19–27 You . . . me The occasion is taken from North: 'the Consul Cominius going up to his chayre of state, in the presence of the whole armie, gave thankes to the goddes for so great, glorious, and prosperous a victorie: then he spake to Martius, whose valliantnes he commended beyond the moone' (Bullough, *Sources*, V, 514). Shakespeare, however, uses the occasion to stress the social function of praise and to point out that it is mutually necessary, to Rome and to her valiant soldier.

22 traducement defamation, slander (paralleling 'concealment'). Shakespeare's only use of the word.

Which, to the spire and top of praises vouched,
Would seem but modest. Therefore, I beseech you –   25
In sign of what you are, not to reward
What you have done – before our army hear me.

MARTIUS I have some wounds upon me, and they smart
To hear themselves remembered.

COMINIUS   Should they not,
Well might they fester 'gainst ingratitude   30
And tent themselves with death. Of all the horses –
Whereof we have ta'en good, and good store – of all
The treasure in this field achieved and city,
We render you the tenth, to be ta'en forth
Before the common distribution, at   35
Your only choice.

MARTIUS   I thank you, general,
But cannot make my heart consent to take
A bribe to pay my sword. I do refuse it,
And stand upon my common part with those
That have beheld the doing.   40

A long flourish. They all cry, 'Martius! Martius!', cast up their caps and
lances. Cominius and Lartius stand bare
May these same instruments which you profane
Never sound more! When drums and trumpets shall
I'th'field prove flatterers, let courts and cities be
Made all of false-faced soothing. When steel grows

25–7 you – . . . done –] F (you, . . . done,)   31–2 horses – . . . store – of all] *Rowe subst.;* Horses, . . . store of
all, F   40 beheld] F; upheld *Capell*   40 SD.1 '*Martius! Martius!*',] *Cam.; Martius, Martius,* F   41 May] *Capell; Mar.*
May F   43 courts and] F; camps, as *Theobald (Warburton)*

24 to . . . vouched attested to in the highest
terms of praise.
25 but modest only moderate, inadequate (to
what you have done).
26 In sign As a token of our recognition.
30 'gainst in the face of (i.e. 'fester' because
infected by 'ingratitude').
31 tent . . . death make death their remedy or
cure. To 'tent' a wound meant to probe it or to
treat it by applying a 'tent', a roll of linen used to
probe wounds and keep them clean and open so
they would heal (*OED* Tent *v*⁴ a, b).
32 good, and good store good ones and
plenty of them.
35 common distribution apportionment to
the rest of the soldiers.
35–6 at . . . choice entirely at your choice.

39 stand . . . part insist on having only the
same share as others.
40 beheld the doing Capell may be correct in
thinking F's 'beheld' an error for 'upheld', but it is
an unnecessary emendation and loses the possible
implication that, despite the assertion of equality,
some at least of those soldiers passively watched
while Martius did the fighting, as at Corioles.
40 SD.2 *stand bare* stand bare-headed (as a sign
of respect).
44 Made . . . soothing Given over entirely to
hypocritical flattery.
44–6 When . . . wars A major crux, occasioned
by Martius's tendency toward incoherence when
angry (see 1.4.32 n.) and the strong possibility
that F's 'Ouerture' is a misreading of some other,
probably partly illegible, word in the original MS.

Soft as the parasite's silk, let him be made   45
An ovator for th'wars. No more, I say!
For that I have not washed my nose that bled,
Or foiled some debile wretch, which without note
Here's many else have done, you shout me forth
In acclamations hyperbolical,   50
As if I loved my little should be dieted
In praises sauced with lies.
COMINIUS   Too modest are you,
More cruel to your good report than grateful
To us that give you truly. By your patience,
If 'gainst yourself you be incensed, we'll put you,   55
Like one that means his proper harm, in manacles,
Then reason safely with you. Therefore be it known,
As to us, to all the world, that Caius Martius
Wears this war's garland, in token of the which
My noble steed, known to the camp, I give him   60

45–6 him . . . An ovator] *Brockbank, conj. Hulme;* him . . . an Ouerture F; Hymns . . . An overture *Theobald* (*Warburton*); this . . . a coverture *conj. Tyrwhitt;* him . . . a coverture *Steevens;* them . . . an overture *Knight;* him . . . an ovation *conj. Staunton;* him . . . an armature *Deighton;* him . . . An ovante *conj. this edn*   **49** shout] F (shoot)   **52** praises sauced] *Hanmer;* prayses, sawc'st F

'Ovator', proposed by Hilda M. Hume (*Explorations in Shakespeare's Language*, 1962, pp. 155–6, 205–6), offers a plausible reading; her argument is strengthened by David George, who finds 'ovator' glossed as 'He that reioyceth' in Thomas Thomas's 1594 *Dictionarium* ('Ovator and parasite: *Coriolanus*, 1.ix.41–6', *N&Q* 242 (Dec. 1997), 510). An 'ovator' is one who receives an ovation; with 'him' referring to 'parasite' (a sycophant who earned his meals by flattery), the sense would be, 'When the soldier's steel ['armour', but also 'resoluteness, bravery'] grows soft as the courtly parasite's silk, let the flatterer receive an ovation for his part in the wars.' Possibly 'Ovante' (i.e. 'Ouante' in F) was the word misread. Although not in John Florio's 1598 *A World of Words*, it appears in his 1611 *Queen Anne's New World of Words*, glossed as 'one that did triumph in the second degree'. Or Shakespeare might have coined it from the Latin *ovant* (from the present participle of *ovare*, to have an ovation). The *OED* (Ovant *a*) cites, among other earlier uses, one of Shakespeare's sources, Holland's Livy, IV.43.166: 'A Generall was said to enter Ovant into the citie, when ordinarily without his armie following him, he went on foot, or rode on horseback only, and the people in their Acclamation of joy, redoubled Ohe.' A remoter

possibility is 'Armourer' (pronounced, and often spelled, 'armer'); but while it fits metrically and makes perfect sense by literally substituting 'silk' for 'steel', it is graphically less likely to have been misread as F's 'Ouerture'.
47 For that Because.
48 foiled overthrown, defeated.
48 debile feeble.
48 note notice taken.
49 shout me forth acclaim me. The phrasing recalls Martius's distaste for the plebeians' emulous shouts at being granted tribunes (1.1.195–7).
51 little minor achievements.
51–2 dieted . . . lies fed with praises spiced with exaggeration. Another of Martius's ungraciously phrased protestations of modesty and a significant metaphorical linking of praise with food.
54 give report (*OED* Give *v* 25, where it is the earliest example).
54 By . . . patience By your leave. Cominius's phrase also tactfully reminds Martius to exercise more restraint.
56 means . . . harm intends to injure himself. Cominius sees Martius's irate refusal to accept Rome's praise as suicidal, not as commendable modesty.
59 Wears . . . garland See 1.3.11–12 n.

>   With all his trim belonging; and from this time,
>   For what he did before Corioles call him,
>   With all th'applause and clamour of the host,
>   Martius Caius Coriolanus.
>   Bear th'addition nobly ever!   65

Flourish. Trumpets sound, and drums

ALL SOLDIERS Martius Caius Coriolanus!

CORIOLANUS I will go wash,
>   And when my face is fair you shall perceive
>   Whether I blush or no. Howbeit, I thank you.
>   I mean to stride your steed, and at all times   70
>   To undercrest your good addition
>   To th'fairness of my power.

COMINIUS   So, to our tent,
>   Where, ere we do repose us, we will write
>   To Rome of our success. You, Titus Lartius,
>   Must to Corioles back. Send us to Rome   75
>   The best, with whom we may articulate
>   For their own good and ours.

LARTIUS   I shall, my lord.

CORIOLANUS The gods begin to mock me. I, that now
>   Refused most princely gifts, am bound to beg
>   Of my lord general.

COMINIUS   Take't, 'tis yours. What is't?   80

64, 66 Martius Caius] F *subst.* (*Marcus*); Caius Martius *Rowe*   66 SH] *Capell; Omnes.* F   67 SH] *Steevens; Martius.* F (*and to end of scene*)   67 I] F; [*To Cominius*] I *Oxford*   70 I] F; [*To Cominius*] I *Parker*

61 trim belonging trappings that go with him; see 12 n.

64 Martius Caius The sequence of names here is unlikely to be a compositor's error, for it is repeated at 2.1.137 and 2.2.40, although the correct form, 'Caius Martius', appears thirteen times in the play. See Textual Analysis, pp. 291–2 below.

65 addition title.

67 SH Although F retains 'Martius' to the end of this scene, most editors change to 'Coriolanus' with the conferring of the new title.

70 stride bestride.

71 undercrest . . . addition i.e. bear the title you have given me as a crest and support it. The new title or 'addition' is seen as something added to a heraldic coat of arms. 'Undercrest' is apparently a Shakespearean coinage; *OED* gives no other instance.

72 To . . . power (1) As fittingly as I can, (2) To the best of my power.

74–5 You . . . back Lartius's movements have not been fully clarified in the play; see 1.4.26 n. Here he is directed back to Corioles, yet he appears in 2.1 for the ovation in Rome even though the senate is said to have just voted to send for him at 2.2.32. At the beginning of 3.1 he brings news of Aufidius but then seems forgotten, since he is given no lines in the riot and no exit cue; see Textual Analysis, p. 303 below.

76 best chief men; compare 'our best elders' (1.1.210).

76 articulate negotiate terms (the articles of a treaty).

79 bound to Either 'obliged to', conveying a sense of duty, or 'about to', anticipating his plea (85–6).

CORIOLANUS I sometime lay here in Corioles
    At a poor man's house. He used me kindly.
    He cried to me; I saw him prisoner,
    But then Aufidius was within my view,
    And wrath o'erwhelmed my pity. I request you   85
    To give my poor host freedom.
COMINIUS   O, well begged!
    Were he the butcher of my son, he should
    Be free as is the wind. Deliver him, Titus.
LARTIUS Martius, his name.
CORIOLANUS   By Jupiter, forgot!
    I am weary; yea, my memory is tired.   90
    Have we no wine here?
COMINIUS   Go we to our tent.
    The blood upon your visage dries; 'tis time
    It should be looked to. Come.
                [*A flourish. Cornets.*] *Exeunt*

1.[10] *Enter* TULLUS AUFIDIUS, *bloody, with two or three* SOLDIERS

AUFIDIUS The town is ta'en.
A SOLDIER 'Twill be delivered back on good condition.

---

82 kindly.] F3; kindly, F   93 SD *A . . . Cornets*] Oxford subst., conj. Granville-Barker; at 1.10.0 SD F   Act 1, Scene 10
1.10] Capell; not in F; 1.11 Oxford   0 SD Enter] Oxford, conj. Granville-Barker; A flourish. Cornets. Enter F   2 SH, 16
SH, 29 SH, 33 SH] F (*Sould. / Sol. / Soul.*); 1. S. / Capell

81 **sometime** lay once lodged.
82 **poor man's** In Plutarch the former host
was a 'wealthie man' whom Coriolanus wishes to
spare 'from being solde as a slave', and his name
is omitted, not forgotten (Bullough, *Sources*, v,
515). Shakespeare has made Coriolanus respon-
sive to kindness from an individual commoner,
but shows him unable to do so in political terms
when the Roman plebeians ask that he use them
'kindly' (2.3.67).
82 **used** treated.
83 **cried** cried out (during the capture of the
city).
85 **wrath . . . pity** This characteristic response
is finally reversed by his mother's pleas in 5.3.
89 **By Jupiter, forgot** Coriolanus's forget-
fulness is Shakespeare's addition, turning the
request into a failed gesture of magnanimity. It
is caused by battle fatigue, but also subtly comments on how personal commitments suffer from
the exigencies of war.
93 SD *A . . . Cornets* The flourish of cornets

more properly accompanies the victorious
Romans' exit than F's position at the beginning
of 1.10. It is a 'bridging' direction, however,
and would have the same effect in continuous
performance between scenes; see 1.9.0 SD.1 n.
Unlike its modern counterpart, the Renaissance
cornet was a kind of horn made of an animal tusk
or wood covered in leather.

Act 1, Scene 10
Outside Corioles. The scene has no precedent in
Plutarch, but Shakespeare uses it to set up at an
early stage Aufidius's turn from valour to calculation; the scene also serves as a transition from the
military exploits of war to the less straightforward
strategies of peacetime politics that occupy Acts
2 and 3.
2, 6 good condition Shakespeare plays on
two meanings of 'condition': the soldier means
'favourable terms', but Aufidius puns on the sense
of 'state of well-being'.

AUFIDIUS Condition!
        I would I were a Roman, for I cannot,
        Being a Volsce, be that I am. Condition?   5
        What good condition can a treaty find
        I'th'part that is at mercy? Five times, Martius,
        I have fought with thee; so often hast thou beat me,
        And wouldst do so, I think, should we encounter
        As often as we eat. By th'elements,   10
        If e'er again I meet him beard to beard,
        He's mine or I am his. Mine emulation
        Hath not that honour in't it had, for where
        I thought to crush him in an equal force,
        True sword to sword, I'll potch at him some way.   15
        Or wrath or craft may get him.
A SOLDIER   He's the devil.
AUFIDIUS Bolder, though not so subtle. My valour's poisoned
        With only suffering stain by him, for him
        Shall fly out of itself. Nor sleep nor sanctuary,
        Being naked, sick, nor fane nor Capitol,   20
        The prayers of priests, nor times of sacrifice –
        Embargements all of fury – shall lift up
        Their rotten privilege and custom 'gainst
        My hate to Martius. Where I find him, were it
        At home, upon my brother's guard, even there   25

---

3 Condition!] F (Condition?)   15 sword, . . . way.] *Pope subst.;* Sword: . . . way, F; sword, . . . way *Globe, conj. Malone,*
'Supp.'   15 potch] F; poach *White, conj. Heath*   17–18 valour's poisoned . . . by him,] F *subst.* (valors poison'd, . . .
by him:); valour (poison'd . . . by him) *Pope, conj. Tyrwhitt*   21–2 sacrifice – . . . fury –] F (Sacrifice: . . . Fury,)   22
Embargements] F (Embarquements); Embarkments *Rowe;* Embankments *Hanmer;* Embarrments *Warburton*

4–5 I would . . . am This recalls Coriolanus's
willingness to contemplate switching sides at
1.1.217–19.
    7 part . . . mercy defeated side (at the 'mercy'
of the victors).
    12 emulation rivalry, desire to equal or bet-
ter; see 1.1.197 n.
    13 where whereas.
    14 in . . . force on equal terms.
    15 potch stab, poke. The vulgar word befits
Aufidius's desertion of honourable combat.
    16 Or . . . or Either . . . or.
    16 craft craftiness, cunning; compare the
'cautelous baits and practice' to which Coriolanus
later refers (4.1.33).
    18 stain disgrace; possibly 'eclipse' (*OED*
Stain *sb* 3c).

    19 fly . . . itself deviate from its own nature,
desert the bounds of true valour; possibly, 'fly out
of its proper orbit' (because eclipsed), if 'stain' is
taken in an astronomical sense (18 n.).
    20 naked unarmed, defenceless.
    20 fane temple.
    22 Embargements Impediments (because
laying an embargo on 'fury').
    23 rotten . . . custom Aufidius's disdain for
civilised customs and pieties when they stand in
the way of his personal desire prefigures Coriolanus's protest against the 'custom' of patricians
asking for plebeian votes for consul (2.2.130–3,
2.3.103–9) and later willingness to destroy his
country to gain his revenge.
    25 upon . . . guard under my brother's ward
or protection.

> Against the hospitable canon, would I
> Wash my fierce hand in's heart. Go you to th'city.
> Learn how 'tis held, and what they are that must
> Be hostages for Rome.

A SOLDIER   Will not you go?

AUFIDIUS I am attended at the cypress grove. I pray you –   30
> 'Tis south the city mills – bring me word thither
> How the world goes, that to the pace of it
> I may spur on my journey.

A SOLDIER   I shall, sir.

> [*Exeunt separately, Aufidius at one door, Soldiers at another*]

2.[1] *Enter* MENENIUS *with the two Tribunes of the people,* SICINIUS *and*
BRUTUS

MENENIUS The augurer tells me we shall have news tonight.

BRUTUS Good or bad?

MENENIUS Not according to the prayer of the people, for they love not
> Martius.

SICINIUS Nature teaches beasts to know their friends.   5

MENENIUS Pray you, who does the wolf love?

---

30 cypress] F (Cyprus)   31 mills] F (Mils); a mile *conj. Tyrwhitt*   33 SD] *Oxford subst.; not in* F; *Exeunt / Rowe*
Act 2, Scene 1   2.1] *Rowe; Actus Secundus* F   1 augurer] F (Agurer); augur *Pope*

26 **hospitable canon** law of hospitality. Aufidius does violate this central 'canon' of aristocratic honour by welcoming Coriolanus to Antium and then betraying him.

27 **Wash . . . heart** The image suggests both barbaric ritual sacrifice and the hunter's treatment of his finally slaughtered prey.

28 **what** who.

30 **attended** expected, awaited.

31 **south . . . mills** A London, not a Roman, reference. Clarendon cites a 1588 petition to build four corn mills on the south bank of the Thames; when the Globe theatre was built, they would have stood nearby.

32 **that** so that.

33 SD F lacks any exit direction, though it is clear from the context. Since their destinations are different, Aufidius and his soldiers would presumably exit at different doors.

Act 2, Scene 1

A public place in Rome. This scene of Cori-

olanus's return to Rome in an ovation is a Shakespearean addition to Plutarch, where the honorific title is conferred only once, after the battle against the Volscians has been won (already staged in 1.9). In Rome, both the ovation and the more elaborate triumph began outside the city itself and proceeded to the Capitol. Shakespeare uses this, the first of the play's several processions, to enhance our sense of Coriolanus as publicly celebrated hero, at the crest of that popularity which his mother hopes will carry him to the peacetime honour of the consulship. Beginning in the eighteenth century, his return was made the occasion for an elaborate, if historically inaccurate, show-stopping spectacle (see pp. 71–2 above).

1 **augurer** soothsayer, Roman priest who studied the behaviour of birds and the entrails of sacrificial animals in order to foretell the future.

5–8 **Nature . . . him** Compare Ecclus. 13.16, 18: 'Everie beast loveth his like . . . How can the wolfe agre with the lambe?' Brockbank (following Noble) cites Isa. 1.3.

SICINIUS The lamb.

MENENIUS Ay, to devour him, as the hungry plebeians would the noble
    Martius.

BRUTUS He's a lamb indeed, that baas like a bear.   10

MENENIUS He's a bear indeed, that lives like a lamb. You two are old
    men. Tell me one thing that I shall ask you.

BOTH TRIBUNES Well, sir.

MENENIUS In what enormity is Martius poor in that you two have not
    in abundance?   15

BRUTUS He's poor in no one fault, but stored with all.

SICINIUS Especially in pride.

BRUTUS And topping all others in boasting.

MENENIUS This is strange now. Do you two know how you are cen-
    sured here in the city, I mean of us o'th'right-hand file? Do you?   20

BOTH TRIBUNES Why? How are we censured?

MENENIUS Because you talk of pride now – will you not be angry?

BOTH TRIBUNES Well, well, sir, well.

MENENIUS Why, 'tis no great matter. For a very little thief of occasion
    will rob you of a great deal of patience. Give your dispositions the   25
    reins and be angry at your pleasures – at the least, if you take it as
    a pleasure to you in being so. You blame Martius for being proud.

BRUTUS We do it not alone, sir.

MENENIUS I know you can do very little alone, for your helps are many,
    or else your actions would grow wondrous single. Your abilities are   30
    too infant-like for doing much alone. You talk of pride. O that you

---

10 baas] F (baes)   13 SH, 23 SH] F (*Both.*)   16 with all] F3; withall F   20 file? Do you?] F (File, do you?)   21 SH] F
(*Both.*); *Bru.* F3   21 How are] F (ho ware)   22 Because you . . . now –] F (Because you . . . now,); Because – you . . .
now – *Oxford*   26 pleasures – at the least,] F (pleasures (at the least))   27 proud.] F; proud? *Capell*

8–9 hungry . . . Martius Menenius's apparently grotesque inversion of the expected sides
of his analogy foreshadows the situation in 3.3,
where the tribunes threaten Coriolanus with a
traitor's death before commuting it to banishment. The class conflict undermining the Roman
body politic is here put in terms – cannibalism –
that join it to one of the play's most shocking
patterns of imagery; see 1.1.69–70 n.

10 baas . . . bear Brutus imitates the lamb's
baa and turns it into the bear's growl.

11–12 old men The implication is that because
they are 'old', they should therefore also be wise.

13 SH, 21 SH, 23 SH, 34 SH F's *Both* does not necessarily mean that the tribunes speak in unison;
in some cases the line might be divided between
them, as with *All* (see 1.2.2 n.).

14 enormity Literally, divergence from a
norm or standard; here, vice or 'fault' (16). The
sense of the question is, 'What vice mars Coriolanus's nature that you two do not excel in
yourselves?'

19–20 censured judged, estimated.

20 th'right-hand file i.e. the conservative
patricians, with an implication of the superiority of this 'file' or faction, since the right hand
is generally the stronger and 'the place of honour to military men has always been the right
of the line' (J. W. Fortescue, in S. Lee and
C. T. Onions (eds.), *Shakespeare's England*, 2
vols., 1916, I, 114).

24 a very . . . occasion the slightest pretext.

30 single solitary (contrasted with 'many'),
with a play on 'feeble'.

could turn your eyes toward the napes of your necks and make but
an interior survey of your good selves! O that you could!

BOTH TRIBUNES What then, sir?

MENENIUS Why, then you should discover a brace of unmeriting,   35
proud, violent, testy magistrates, alias fools, as any in Rome.

SICINIUS Menenius, you are known well enough too.

MENENIUS I am known to be a humorous patrician, and one that loves
a cup of hot wine with not a drop of allaying Tiber in't; said to be
something imperfect in favouring the first complaint, hasty and   40
tinder-like upon too trivial motion; one that converses more with
the buttock of the night than with the forehead of the morning.
What I think, I utter, and spend my malice in my breath. Meeting
two such wealsmen as you are – I cannot call you Lycurguses – if
the drink you give me touch my palate adversely, I make a crooked   45
face at it. I cannot say your worships have delivered the matter well,
when I find the ass in compound with the major part of your
syllables. And though I must be content to bear with those that say
you are reverend grave men, yet they lie deadly that tell you have

34 SH] F (*Both.*); *Men.* F4; *Bru.* / *Rowe*   41 upon too] *Rowe*³; vppon, to F   44 are – . . . Lycurguses – if] are (. . .
Licurgusses,) if F; are, . . . Lycurguses. If *Parker*   46 cannot . . . have] *Capell;* can . . . haue F; can't . . . have *Theobald;*
can . . . have not *Collier*   49 you have] F; you, you have *Pope*

32 toward . . . necks inward (to examine yourselves).

35 brace pair.

36 testy irritable; possibly in the root sense
'headstrong'.

37 known well enough notorious.

38 humorous whimsical, governed by
humours.

39 hot mulled (heated with spices), but perhaps merely 'strong'.

39 allaying Tiber The River Tiber runs
through Rome; Menenius means that he likes his
wine undiluted (unalloyed) with water.

40 something . . . complaint somewhat at
fault for favouring the plaintiff before hearing the
other side of the case.

41 tinder-like quick-tempered.

41 motion legal proposal; perhaps, more generally, 'cause'.

41–2 converses . . . morning more often
keeps company with the late hours ('buttock') of
the night than the early hours ('forehead') of the
morning. Menenius's reduction of all considerations to the body and its needs and pleasures is
characteristic; here he also intimates the patrician
leisure and self-indulgence that separate him from
the plebeian labourers.

43 spend . . . breath exhaust my malice in
words.

44 wealsmen statesmen. Menenius ironically
compliments the tribunes on being devoted to the
public good and may also pun on 'wellsmen', since
'well' is one of their favourite ejaculations. This is
the only instance of the word in Shakespeare and
the only citation in the *OED*.

44 Lycurguses wise lawmakers. The allusion
is to Lycurgus, the famous Spartan lawgiver; NS
notes that the reference may have been suggested
by Plutarch's 'Life of Lycurgus' ('Lycurgus . . .
beganne to devise howe to alter the whole government of the common weale') and may imply that
the tribunes, while not wise, are, like Lycurgus,
political innovators.

44–6 if . . . it i.e. if I don't like what you say,
you'll see it in my face.

46 cannot Brockbank retains F's 'can', arguing
that it is said sarcastically, but it seems more likely
that an error erased a parallel with 'cannot' above
(44).

47–8 ass . . . syllables stupidity in most of
what you say.

49 deadly excessively (*OED* Deadly *adv* 4),
punning on 'grave'.

49 tell say, report that.

good faces. If you see this in the map of my microcosm, follows 50
it that I am known well enough too? What harm can your bisson
conspectuities glean out of this character, if I be known well enough
too?

BRUTUS Come, sir, come. We know you well enough.

MENENIUS You know neither me, yourselves, nor anything. You are 55
ambitious for poor knaves' caps and legs. You wear out a good
wholesome forenoon in hearing a cause between an orange-wife and
a faucet-seller, and then rejourn the controversy of threepence to
a second day of audience. When you are hearing a matter between
party and party, if you chance to be pinched with the colic, you 60
make faces like mummers, set up the bloody flag against all patience, and, in roaring for a chamber-pot, dismiss the controversy
bleeding, the more entangled by your hearing. All the peace you
make in their cause is calling both the parties knaves. You are a pair
of strange ones. 65

BRUTUS Come, come, you are well understood to be a perfecter giber
for the table than a necessary bencher in the Capitol.

MENENIUS Our very priests must become mockers if they shall encoun-

---

51 bisson] F (beesome)   58 faucet] F (Forset)

50 **good** A word-play on 'honest' and 'hand-some' seems intended.

50 **this** i.e. depiction of myself, 'character' (52). 'Character' also refers specifically to a literary genre of witty delineations of personality types popular in the early seventeenth century.

50 **map . . . microcosm** my face, which charts what goes on in the little world ('microcosm') of myself.

51–2 **bisson conspectuities** blind or blear-eyed understanding. 'Bisson' meant blind or pur-blind, and 'conspectuities' refers to the faculty of sight (Latin *conspectus*). Menenius is prone to coining words; see 'empiricutic' (95) and 'fid-iussed' (108).

55 **You . . . anything** A possible echo of John 8.19: 'Ye nether knowe me, nor my Father' (Shaheen).

56 **caps and legs** doffing of caps and making of legs (the male equivalent of a curtsy), both marks of respect.

56–60 **You . . . and party** In Plutarch the tribunes have no such judicial function; Shakespeare again seems to think of them as equivalent to English 'magistrates' (36).

57 **orange-wife** A woman who sells oranges.

'Wife' was still used in Shakespeare's time to mean 'woman'.

58 **faucet-seller** A seller of spigots or vent-pegs for wine casks.

58 **rejourn** adjourn, postpone.

59 **audience** hearing.

60 **party** litigant.

61 **mummers** Grimacing actors in a dumb-show or country mumming.

61 **set . . . flag** declare war (the red flag signals battle).

63 **bleeding** (1) unresolved, like an unhealed wound, (2) 'bleeding' also applies to the colic-stricken tribunes, who need a chamber-pot for their bloody urine. As Parker notes, Menenius here conflates the play's legal, military and dis-ease imagery.

66–7 **perfecter . . . Capitol** more accom-plished as a scoffing wit ('giber') for the dinner table or tavern than as an indispensable official (on a senate bench) concerned with national affairs. In contemporary terms, a 'bencher' was one of the senior members of the London Inns of Court who formed for each Inn a self-elective body that managed its affairs (*OED* Bencher *sb* 3).

ter such ridiculous subjects as you are. When you speak best unto
the purpose, it is not worth the wagging of your beards, and your   70
beards deserve not so honourable a grave as to stuff a botcher's
cushion or to be entombed in an ass's pack-saddle. Yet you must be
saying Martius is proud, who, in a cheap estimation, is worth all
your predecessors since Deucalion, though peradventure some of
the best of 'em were hereditary hangmen. Good e'en to your wor-   75
ships. More of your conversation would infect my brain, being the
herdsmen of the beastly plebeians. I will be bold to take my leave of
you.

Brutus and Sicinius [stand] aside

Enter VOLUMNIA, VIRGILIA, *and* VALERIA

How now, my as fair as noble ladies – and the moon, were she
earthly, no nobler – whither do you follow your eyes so fast?   80

VOLUMNIA Honourable Menenius, my boy Martius approaches. For
the love of Juno, let's go.

MENENIUS Ha? Martius coming home?

VOLUMNIA Ay, worthy Menenius, and with most prosperous approbation.   85

MENENIUS [*Tosses up his cap*] Take my cap, Jupiter, and I thank thee.
Hoo! Martius coming home?

69–70 are. When . . . purpose, it] F4 *subst.;* are, when . . . purpose. It F   73 saying . . . proud,] saying, . . . proud:
F   75 Good e'en] F (Godden)   78 SD.1] *Theobald; Bru. and Scic. Aside.* F   79–80 now, my . . . noble ladies – . . .
nobler –] *Johnson;* now (my . . . Noble) Ladyes, . . . Nobler; F   86 SD] *Collier² subst.; not in* F

69 **subjects** citizens (emphasising their politically subordinate status), with a play on 'subjects
for conversation'.
69–70 **are. When** . . . **purpose,** F's punctuation is possible but yields a sense less vigorous
than F4's.
71 **botcher's** A botcher was a mender or
patcher of old clothes or shoes. Presumably the
'cushion' (72) was for him to sit on while he
worked, but perhaps 'pincushion' is meant.
73 **cheap estimation** conservative evaluation.
74 **since Deucalion** since the Flood. Deucalion, the classical counterpart of the biblical
Noah, with his wife Pyrrha survived a great flood
by which Zeus destroyed the rest of the human
race.
74 **peradventure** perhaps.
75 **hereditary hangmen** executioners, generation after generation. The occupation was considered ignoble.
75 **Good e'en** Good evening (said to bid them

farewell). F's 'Godden' indicates more clearly that
it is an abbreviated form of 'God give you good
even'; 'e'en' could be used for any time after noon.
76 **conversation** (1) society (*OED* Conversation *sb* 5), (2) talk.
76 **being** you being.
79 **moon** i.e. Diana, goddess of chastity; see
1.1.241 n. Menenius's language switches abruptly
to courtly compliment when addressing ladies of
his own class, and he here anticipates Coriolanus's
greeting of Valeria at 5.3.65–7.
80 **whither** . . . **fast** where are you hurrying
in hopes of some sight.
82 **Juno** Chief Roman goddess and consort of
Jupiter; Volumnia compares her wrath to Juno's
at 4.2.55.
84–5 **approbation** either 'success and praise',
or 'with proof of success'.
86 **Take** . . . **Jupiter** Menenius expresses his
excitement with the same gesture as the plebeians
(see 1.1.195–7, 2.1.240–1, 3.3.143 SD.2).

VIRGILIA *and* VALERIA Nay, 'tis true.

VOLUMNIA Look, here's a letter from him. The state hath another, his
wife another, and I think there's one at home for you.   90

MENENIUS I will make my very house reel tonight. A letter for me?

VIRGILIA Yes, certain, there's a letter for you. I saw't.

MENENIUS A letter for me! It gives me an estate of seven years' health,
in which time I will make a lip at the physician. The most sovereign
prescription in Galen is but empiricutic and, to this preservative, of   95
no better report than a horse-drench. Is he not wounded? He was
wont to come home wounded.

VIRGILIA O no, no, no!

VOLUMNIA O, he is wounded; I thank the gods for't.

MENENIUS So do I too, if it be not too much. Brings 'a victory in his   100
pocket? The wounds become him.

VOLUMNIA On's brows. Menenius, he comes the third time home with
the oaken garland.

MENENIUS Has he disciplined Aufidius soundly?

VOLUMNIA Titus Lartius writes they fought together, but Aufidius got   105
off.

MENENIUS And 'twas time for him too, I'll warrant him that. And he
had stayed by him, I would not have been so fidiussed for all the
chests in Corioles and the gold that's in them. Is the senate possessed of this?   110

---

88 SH] Capell (*Vir. Val.*); 2. *Ladies.* F; *Both.* / *Rowe; Vol. Vir.* / *Dyce*   90 I think] (I thinke) F   93 me!] F (me?)
95 empiricutic] F (Emperickqutique); *emperic Pope;* empiric physic *Collier²*   97 home wounded.] *Pope;* home
wounded? F   100 'a] *Theobald² subst.;* a F; he a *Pope;* he *Malone*   101 pocket? The] F; pocket, the *Hanmer*   102
brows. Menenius,] F (Browes: *Menenius,*); brows, Menenius; *Theobald*   108 fidiussed] F (fiddious'd)

93 gives ... estate of endows me with (a legal,
property image appropriate to a patrician).
94 make a lip curl the lip, express scorn.
94 sovereign efficacious.
95 Galen Galen was a renowned physician of
the second century A.D. whose work was still cited
as a medical authority in Shakespeare's time; as
with Cato (1.4.61), the allusion, though loosely
'classical', is anachronistic.
95 empiricutic quackery. A nonce word
(combining 'empiric' and 'pharmaceutic') meaning 'based only on experience', as opposed to
Galen's scientific principles; 'empiric' doctors
were scorned by educated physicians.
95 to this preservative compared to this letter which preserves my health.
96 horse-drench dose of horse medicine.
100 'a he. F's 'a' stands for 'ha' (= he), a frequent Renaissance form, though the F compositors usually standardised to 'he'. Editors who

follow Hanmer's repunctuation (101 n.) read 'a',
where 'Brings a' = If he brings a.
101 pocket? ... him F's punctuation seems
correct, since Volumnia (102) appears immediately to answer this question: Coriolanus's victory
is brought home 'On's brows' in the form of 'the
oaken garland' (see 1.3.11–12 n.). Defenders of
Hanmer think Menenius qualifies his enthusiasm
for Coriolanus's wounds by suggesting that only
victory will justify them.
104 disciplined beaten, thrashed. The word
suggests a parent– or teacher–child relationship
which Aufidius tries to reverse when he taunts
Coriolanus in 5.6.103.
107 And he If he.
108 fidiussed Menenius ridicules Aufidius by
using his name to coin a word to mean 'beaten as
Aufidius deserves'.
109–10 possessed fully informed.

VOLUMNIA Good ladies, let's go. – Yes, yes, yes. The senate has letters
from the general, wherein he gives my son the whole name of the
war. He hath in this action outdone his former deeds doubly.

VALERIA In troth, there's wondrous things spoke of him.

MENENIUS Wondrous? Ay, I warrant you, and not without his true   115
purchasing.

VIRGILIA The gods grant them true.

VOLUMNIA True? Pow waw.

MENENIUS True? I'll be sworn they are true. Where is he wounded? [*To
the Tribunes*] God save your good worships! Martius is coming   120
home. He has more cause to be proud. [*To Volumnia*] Where is he
wounded?

VOLUMNIA I'th'shoulder and i'th'left arm. There will be large cicatrices to show the people when he shall stand for his place. He
received in the repulse of Tarquin seven hurts i'th'body.   125

MENENIUS One i'th'neck and two i'th'thigh – there's nine that I know.

VOLUMNIA He had, before this last expedition, twenty-five wounds
upon him.

MENENIUS Now it's twenty-seven. Every gash was an enemy's grave.

A shout and flourish

Hark, the trumpets.   130

VOLUMNIA These are the ushers of Martius. Before him
He carries noise, and behind him he leaves tears.

115 Wondrous?] Wondrous: F; Wondrous, *Oxford*   119–20 wounded? . . . worships!] *Theobald;* wounded, . . .
Worships? F   119–20 SD] *Theobald; not in* F   121 SD] *Craig; not in* F   129 SD] *Capell; after* trumpets F

112 name credit, honour. He has also, of
course, literally been given the 'name' of the war
in the honorific 'Coriolanus'.

116 purchasing deserving, earning.

118 Pow waw Pish (expressing amused scorn);
compare Thomas Dekker, *Worke for Armourers*,
G2ʳ, 'baw waw'.

123–4 cicatrices scars.

124 when . . . place Volumnia's 'when' reveals
her mistaken certainty that her son's intentions
are identical with her own, and she assumes he
will seek the consulship ('his place'); see 174–6.

125 Tarquin Tarquinius Superbus, the last
king of Rome, was expelled from the city and
finally defeated at the battle of Lake Regillus,
c. 509 B.C. It was in this battle that Martius, at
the age of sixteen, first distinguished himself; see
Cominius's account, 2.2.81–92.

126 nine The apparently faulty arithmetic
could result from Menenius's having begun softly
totting up the number of wounds to himself and

then, after a pause, concluding aloud that he can
think of nine; it may also be carelessness on the
part of the author. There is grim humour in this
competitive 'body-count' of wounds that seems
to exclude concern for the son and friend who
suffered them.

131–2 F's three, short, end-stopped verse lines
probably result from there being too little room
for 'Before him' on the first line of Volumnia's
speech and the fact that Compositor A seems to
have disliked enjambment (see Textual Analysis,
p. 306 below). Some editions print these lines as
prose. It has been suggested (White) that the succeeding couplet (133–4) is spurious; its aptness
could be argued from its position, as conclusion
to the prose opening of 2.1: after the surprise of
the trumpet flourish, it focuses all attention on
the entrance through which the procession will
arrive. It also picks up Menenius's last equation
of 'gashes' and 'graves' and reworks it into another
description of Coriolanus as a dehumanised,

> Death, that dark spirit, in's nervy arm doth lie,
> Which being advanced, declines, and then men die.

A sennet. Enter [in state] COMINIUS the general and TITUS LARTIUS;
between them CORIOLANUS, crowned with an oaken garland; with
Captains and Soldiers and a HERALD. Trumpets sound

HERALD Know, Rome, that all alone Martius did fight   135
   Within Corioles' gates, where he hath won,
   With fame, a name to Martius Caius; these
   In honour follows 'Coriolanus'.
   Welcome to Rome, renownèd Coriolanus!
                Flourish
ALL Welcome to Rome, renownèd Coriolanus!   140
CORIOLANUS No more of this, it does offend my heart.
   Pray now, no more.
COMINIUS   Look, sir, your mother.
CORIOLANUS   O!
   You have, I know, petitioned all the gods
   For my prosperity.   *Kneels*
VOLUMNIA   Nay, my good soldier, up,
              [Coriolanus rises]
   My gentle Martius, worthy Caius, and   145
   By deed-achieving honour newly named –

---

134 SD.1–3 *A sennet. Enter in state . . . Herald. Trumpets sound*] This edn, *after Parker; A sennet. Trumpets sound. Enter . . . Herauld.* F; *Trumpets sound a sennet. Enter in state . . . Herald* / Oxford   134 SD.1 LARTIUS] F (*Latius*)   137 Martius Caius] F; Caius Martius *Rowe*   138 follows 'Coriolanus'] *Steevens;* followes *Martius Caius Coriolanus* F   139 SD *Flourish*] *Sound. Flourish.* F; *Shout. Flourish.* / *Capell*   144 SD.2] *Collier² subst.* (*at 148* hail!); *not in* F; *after 145*, Oxford; *after 147*, Parker

godlike yet strangely mechanical, warrior. Here, he is reduced to his arm, and the arm to death's instrument, as it rises and falls again and again (compare 2.2.101–2). As Parker notes, the final four heavy stresses 'give an effect of inevitability'.

133 nervy sinewy.

134 SD.1 *A sennet* F joins this SD with *Trumpets sound* (134 SD.3), placing both at the beginning of the SD. Parker, however, argues persuasively that the first is a ceremonial flourish accompanying the soldiers' entrance and that the second would introduce the Herald's speech which follows.

134 SD.1 COMINIUS *the general* The descriptive label of office may indicate full military uniform, which would be appropriate for this occasion. At 2.2.30 SD.2, where he is COMINIUS *the consul*, he has presumably changed back to the consular robes of

his peacetime office; but see next note.

134 SD.1 TITUS LARTIUS According to 1.9.74–5 and 2.2.31–2, Lartius should still be in Corioles. It has been argued that the F spelling, *Latius*, indicates that 2.1 and 2.2 were not written in consecutive order; see Textual Analysis, p. 292 below, n. 4.

137 With Along with.

137 to in addition to.

137 Martius Caius See 1.9.64 n.

137–8 these . . . 'Coriolanus' the honorific 'Coriolanus' follows these ('Martius Caius'). Steevens's emendation is generally adopted on the assumption that F's hypermetrical line results from unconscious repetition.

140 SH F's SH does not, of course, include Coriolanus.

146 deed-achieving achieved through deeds.

What is it? 'Coriolanus' must I call thee? –
But, O, thy wife!
CORIOLANUS   My gracious silence, hail!
Wouldst thou have laughed had I come coffined home,
That weep'st to see me triumph? Ah, my dear,   150
Such eyes the widows in Corioles wear,
And mothers that lack sons.
MENENIUS   Now the gods crown thee!
CORIOLANUS And live you yet? [*To Valeria*] O my sweet lady,
      pardon.
VOLUMNIA I know not where to turn. O welcome home!
And welcome, general, and you're welcome all.   155
MENENIUS A hundred thousand welcomes! I could weep
And I could laugh; I am light and heavy. Welcome.
A curse begin at very root on's heart
That is not glad to see thee! You are three
That Rome should dote on; yet, by the faith of men,   160
We have some old crabtrees here at home that will not
Be grafted to your relish. Yet welcome, warriors!
We call a nettle but a nettle, and
The faults of fools but folly.
COMINIUS Ever right.   165
CORIOLANUS Menenius, ever, ever.
HERALD Give way there, and go on.

---

147 it?] *Johnson;* it F   147 'Coriolanus'] *Oxford; (Coriolanus)* F   151 wear] F (were)   153 SH] *Theobald; Com.* F
153 SD] *Theobald; not in* F; *before* And . . . yet? *Oxford*   155 you're] F (y'are)   158 begin at] F; begnaw at *Craig;*
begnaw the *NS*   159 You] F2; Yon F   162 relish] F (Rallish)

148 **gracious** lovely, but also possessing spiri-
tual grace.
148 **silence** Virgilia's reticence again contrasts
sharply with her mother-in-law's voluble offi-
ciousness. Case quotes North's Plutarch, 'Life of
Numa' (in the edn of 1595, p. 72): 'He much frequented the Muses in the woddes. For he would
say he had the most part of his revelations of the
Muses and he taught the Romans to reverence one
of them above all the rest, who was called *Tacita*,
as ye would say *Lady Silence*'.
153 SH F's *Com.* is an easy misreading of *Cor.*
in Secretary hand; see Textual Analysis, p. 301
below.
153 SD Given Menenius's age and the impo-
liteness of ignoring his greeting, Theobald's SD
seems judicious in location.

158 **begin** F's 'begin' suggests a spreading
infection; Craig's 'begnaw', though followed by
some editors, is unnecessary.
159 **You** F's 'Yon' is probably the result of misreading or a turned *u*; F2's 'You' is more forceful
with 'your' (162).
161 **crabtrees** Literally, wild apple trees, usually with crooked, knotted branches; here, 'sour-
natured men', in reference to Sicinius and Brutus,
who refuse to be altered ('grafted') to a more positive attitude.
162 **to your relish** (1) to a liking for you, (2)
to your way of thinking (Parker).
163–4 **We . . . folly** i.e. some nuisances cannot
be changed and must be accepted for what they
are. Compare Prov. 14.24: 'The folie of fooles is
foolishnes.'

CORIOLANUS [*To Volumnia and Virgilia*] Your hand, and yours.
    Ere in our own house I do shade my head
    The good patricians must be visited,   170
    From whom I have received not only greetings,
    But with them change of honours.
VOLUMNIA   I have lived
    To see inherited my very wishes
    And the buildings of my fancy. Only
    There's one thing wanting, which I doubt not but   175
    Our Rome will cast upon thee.
CORIOLANUS   Know, good mother,
    I had rather be their servant in my way
    Than sway with them in theirs.
COMINIUS   On, to the Capitol.
              Flourish [*of*] *cornets. Exeunt in state, as before*
                  Brutus and Sicinius [*come forward*]
BRUTUS All tongues speak of him, and the blearèd sights
    Are spectacled to see him. Your prattling nurse   180
    Into a rapture lets her baby cry
    While she chats him. The kitchen malkin pins
    Her richest lockram 'bout her reechy neck,

---

168 SD] *Capell subst.; not in* F   168 yours.] yours? F   172 change] F; charge *Theobald*   178 SD.1 *Flourish of*] F (*Flourish, Cornets.*)   178 SD.2 *Brutus . . . come forward*] *Theobald; Enter Brutus and Sicinius.* F   182 chats] F; cheers *Collier²*; claps *conj. Singer, 'SV'*; chats of *Keightley*   182 malkin] F (*Malkin*); Maukin *Rowe*

172 change of honours fresh honours, perhaps looking forward to Cominius's public account of 'the deeds of Coriolanus' (2.2.76–116).

173–4 inherited . . . fancy In Coriolanus Volumnia's desires and dreams ('buildings of my fancy') have been realised and given form. The patrician property image ('inherited') echoes Menenius (93); the phrasing ('my . . . my') emphasises that the ambition was hers.

178 sway (1) bear sway, go along, (2) govern.

178 SD.1 *Flourish of cornets* On the possibility that 'cornets' was a book-keeper's annotation, see Textual Analysis, p. 303 below. Nineteenth-century productions ended the first of their three acts here, with a spectacular exit procession.

178 SD.2 *come forward* The tribunes have stood aside during the formalities of Coriolanus's triumphant return, and they now step forward to analyse its political implications; on F's *Enter* elsewhere directing characters who have not in fact left the stage, see Textual Analysis, p. 303 below.

179–80 blearèd . . . spectacled those with bleary eyesight put on spectacles. 'Spectacled' is another anachronism, but the whole description is of an early-seventeenth-century crowd; see 184–7 n.

180 Your The impersonal use, i.e. 'this nurse I am telling you about'; see 1.1.111 n., 5.4.9.

181 rapture fit, paroxysm (*OED* Rapture *sb* 5c).

182 chats him gossips about him. The only instance of the transitive form in *OED* (Chat *v¹* 4).

182 malkin An untidy female servant, wench; diminutive of Maud or Matilda, and F's italics treat it as a proper name.

183 lockram Coarse linen fabric.

183 reechy grimy, greasy; the sound-play on 'richest' emphasises Brutus's distaste for such members of his constituency.

Clambering the walls to eye him. Stalls, bulks, windows
Are smothered up, leads filled, and ridges horsed   185
With variable complexions, all agreeing
In earnestness to see him. Seld-shown flamens
Do press among the popular throngs and puff
To win a vulgar station. Our veiled dames
Commit the war of white and damask in   190
Their nicely guarded cheeks to th'wanton spoil
Of Phoebus' burning kisses. Such a pother
As if that whatsoever god who leads him
Were slily crept into his human powers
And gave him graceful posture.

SICINIUS   On the sudden,   195
I warrant him consul.

BRUTUS   Then our office may,
During his power, go sleep.

SICINIUS He cannot temperately transport his honours
From where he should begin and end, but will

---

191 guarded] *N.S, conj.* Lettsom (*in Dyce²*); gawded F; gauded *Kittredge*   192 pother] F (poother)   195 SH] *Scicin.* F (*and to end of scene*)   199 and end] F; t'an end *conj.* Johnson; to th'end *Hudson, conj.* Seymour

184–7 Clambering . . . flamens Parker notes the similarity to Thomas Dekker's description of King James's coronation procession through London in *The Magnificent Entertainment*, 1604, B3–3ᵛ: 'the streets seemed to be paved with men; stalls instead of rich wares were set out for the children, open casements filled up with women'; David George (*N & Q* 241 (June 1996), 164) adds that 'rapture' and 'throngs' also echo Dekker's description, and that the 'Seld-shown flamens' may have been suggested by *Ben Jonson His Part of King James his Royall and Magnificent Entertainement through his Honorable Cittie of London*, 1604, C4ᵛ.

184 Stalls Benches set in front of shops to display wares (*OED* Stall *sb*¹ 6).

184 bulks Frameworks projecting from the front of shops (*OED* Bulk *sb*²).

185 smothered up crowded with people.

185 leads roofs covered with lead.

185–6 ridges . . . complexions people of all sorts astride the ridges of the housetops; 'complexions' refers to the character-types (phlegmatic, melancholy, choleric, sanguine) thought to derive from the mixture of the four basic 'humours'. *OED* gives this as the only instance of 'horse' meaning 'bestride' (Horse *v* 7).

187 Seld-shown flamens Priests who rarely appear in public; Brutus's disdain is apparent in 'puff' and 'vulgar station'.

189 vulgar station vantage-point in the crowd of common people (with a contemptuous play on 'station' as social status).

189 veiled usually veiled (1) out of modesty, (2) to protect the delicate balance of white and pink ('damask', 190) in their cheeks against sunburn from 'Phoebus' burning kisses' (192).

191 nicely guarded carefully protected. F's 'gawded' would yield the sense of 'carefully made-up' (with cosmetics), but it would be an easy misreading of 'garded' in Secretary hand, and 'guarded' better agrees with 'veiled'.

191 spoil (1) ruin (i.e. the resulting unfashionable suntan), (2) defeat in which the cheeks become Phoebus's spoils of war. The 'war of white and damask' (190) is a Petrarchan commonplace but particularly apt here in that it carries the military metaphor into the description of the peacetime crowd.

192 pother commotion, fuss.

193 'As if that god who leads him, whatsoever god that be' (Johnson).

194–5 human powers . . . graceful posture i.e. the god he follows has transformed his merely human body into one of divine impressiveness.

195 On the sudden Suddenly, at once.

196 warrant guarantee, predict.

198–9 He . . . end He will not be able to maintain with restraint his honours from their beginning to their proper end. The tribunes are

Lose those he hath won.

BRUTUS   In that there's comfort.

SICINIUS   Doubt not   200
The commoners, for whom we stand, but they
Upon their ancient malice will forget
With the least cause these his new honours, which
That he will give them make I as little question
As he is proud to do't.

BRUTUS   I heard him swear,   205
Were he to stand for consul, never would he
Appear i'th'market-place nor on him put
The napless vesture of humility,
Nor showing, as the manner is, his wounds
To th'people, beg their stinking breaths.

SICINIUS   'Tis right.   210

BRUTUS It was his word. O, he would miss it rather
Than carry it but by the suit of the gentry to him
And the desire of the nobles.

SICINIUS   I wish no better
Than have him hold that purpose and to put it
In execution.

BRUTUS   'Tis most like he will.   215

SICINIUS It shall be to him then as our good wills,
A sure destruction.

BRUTUS   So it must fall out
To him, or our authority's for an end.

---

200 not] *Knight;* not, F   208 napless] F (Naples)   216 wills] F; will is *conj. Theobald;* will's *conj. Tyrwhitt* (*in Steevens³*)   218 authority's for an end.] *Hibbard, conj. Thirlby;* Authorities, for an end. F; authorities. For an end, *Pope;* authority's at an end. *conj. Thirlby* (*in Furness*)

not always astute in their assessments of Coriolanus, but here they predict accurately; see Aufidius's later observation, 'he could not / Carry his honours even' (4.7.36–7).

200–1 Doubt . . . but Doubt not but that the commoners, whom we represent.

202 Upon . . . malice Owing to their long-standing animosity.

203 which the which (referring to 'least cause').

204 make . . . question I have as little doubt.

205 As As that.

208 napless vesture threadbare garment. North's 'poore gowne' and 'meane apparell' misunderstands a passage in Amyot's translation of Plutarch, referring to a toga with no tunic beneath,

as a sign of humility and convenient for showing scars on the body.

210 stinking breaths An insulting reference to the voices (i.e. votes) of the commoners.

211–12 miss . . . but by forgo the office rather than attain it otherwise than by. The terminology ('gentry', 'nobles') refers to English, not Roman, class distinctions.

216 as . . . wills as we wish, as our interests require.

218 authority's . . . end authority is bound to end. Thirlby's conjectured 'authority's' is strong and plausible, since F's text of this play five times omits the apostrophe from 's = is (e.g. 1.10.17, 'my valours poison'd'), and Brutus at 3.1.210 speaks of 'our authority' in the singular.

We must suggest the people in what hatred
He still hath held them; that to's power he would   220
Have made them mules, silenced their pleaders, and
Dispropertied their freedoms, holding them
In human action and capacity
Of no more soul nor fitness for the world
Than camels in their war, who have their provand   225
Only for bearing burdens and sore blows
For sinking under them.
SICINIUS   This, as you say, suggested
At some time when his soaring insolence
Shall teach the people – which time shall not want
If he be put upon't, and that's as easy   230
As to set dogs on sheep – will be his fire
To kindle their dry stubble, and their blaze
Shall darken him for ever.

Enter a MESSENGER

BRUTUS   What's the matter?
MESSENGER You are sent for to the Capitol. 'Tis thought
That Martius shall be consul. I have seen   235

---

225 their war] F; the war *Hanmer*   227–31 This, as you say, . . . people – . . . sheep –] F *subst.* (This (as you say) . . .
People, . . . Sheepe,); This – as you say, . . . people, . . . sheep – *Bevington*   229 teach] F; reach *Pope²*, *conj. Theobald*,
'*SR*'; touch *Hanmer*   231 his] F; the *Pope*; as *Capell*

---

219 **suggest** insinuate to, instruct.
220 **still** always.
220 **to's power** to the extent of his power.
222 **Dispropertied** Dispossessed (them) of.
225 **their war** i.e. the patricians' war, in which the plebeians are considered of no more value than beasts of burden ('camels'). Hanmer's 'the' is possible, if one assumes 'their' here anticipates 'their' later in the line, but unnecessary.
225 **provand** food, provisions (especially for an army).
229 **teach** (1) teach the people his true nature (and thus inflame them to rebel), (2) arrogantly lecture the people on their duty to their rulers and their own unworthiness (as he had at 1.1.150–83). A misreading of manuscript 'touch' as 'teach' (perhaps 'tuch' as 'teich') is possible, and many editors follow Hanmer; 'touch' would yield a play on 'touch to the quick' and 'inflame, kindle' (anticipating the metaphor in 231–3).
230 **put upon't** provoked, incited to it.
231–2 **his . . . stubble** i.e. his insolence will be the spark that will kindle the people like dry

stubble. The tribunes see both Coriolanus and the people as flammable elements of a situation the tribunes believe they can control. The probable biblical allusion is to Isa. 5.24, 'As the flame of fyre devoureth the stubble, and as the chaffe is consumed of the flame [of the Lord's wrath]', and 47.14, 'They shalbe as stubble: the fyre shal burne them'; in immediate terms, Shakespeare may have been led to the image by Averell, who urges Englishmen to unite against the enemy by means of 'divine love, being a fire to burne up the stubble of dissention' (D4ʳ).
233 **darken** obscure, eclipse.
235–41 **I . . . shouts** Shakespeare is again merging Rome with contemporary England: gloves, scarves and handkerchiefs were common favours given by ladies to knights entering a tournament (Malone). Suggestions of deification come from the reference to 'Jove's statue' (240) and the echo (236–7) of Christ at Galilee, Matt. 15.30: 'And great multitudes came unto him, having with them, halt, blinde, domme . . . and cast them downe at Jesus fete.'

The dumb men throng to see him and the blind
To hear him speak. Matrons flung gloves,
Ladies and maids their scarves and handkerchiefs,
Upon him as he passed. The nobles bended
As to Jove's statue, and the commons made   240
A shower and thunder with their caps and shouts.
I never saw the like.
BRUTUS   Let's to the Capitol,
And carry with us ears and eyes for th'time,
But hearts for the event.
SICINIUS   Have with you.

Exeunt

2.[2] *Enter two* OFFICERS, *to lay cushions, as it were in the Capitol*

FIRST OFFICER Come, come, they are almost here. How many stand for
  consulships?
SECOND OFFICER Three, they say, but 'tis thought of everyone
  Coriolanus will carry it.
FIRST OFFICER That's a brave fellow, but he's vengeance proud and   5
  loves not the common people.
SECOND OFFICER Faith, there hath been many great men that have
  flattered the people who ne'er loved them, and there be many that

---

Act 2, Scene 2   2.2] *Capell; not in* F   7 hath] F; have F4

243 **th'time** the present situation. The tribunes intend to be alert for any opportunities that
present themselves; compare Aufidius's similarly
pragmatic attitude, 1.10.31–3.
  244 **event** outcome (the political revolt they
have been discussing).
  244 **Have with you** Both 'I'm with you' and
'Let's go.'

Act 2, Scene 2
In the Capitol. The scene is Shakespeare's,
though a few lines, noted below, have been borrowed from North.
  0 SD *two* OFFICERS As prologue to the formal encomium by Cominius before the senators,
Shakespeare provides another in the series of discussions of Coriolanus that try to define his character and motives. The objectivity of these civil
servants, who have no part in the play's action and
do not reappear, lends their remarks a choric quality absent from the self-interested observations

of the tribunes. The officers' comments derive
in part from the 'Comparison of Alcibiades with
Martius Coriolanus', where Plutarch judiciously
weighs both men's vices and virtues.
  0 SD *cushions* See 3.1.102 and 4.7.43, where the
cushion symbolises administrative office. Brockbank suggests that the cushions would be large,
serving as seats, like the wool-sacks for the judges
to sit on in the House of Lords in Shakespeare's
day.
  1 **stand for** present themselves as candidates
for selection by the senate as its nominee; for the
contemporary resonance of this procedure, see
pp. 27–9 above.
  5 **vengeance** exceedingly, intensely; perhaps
also with the sense that he is over-confident owing
to his recent vengeance against Aufidius (and
ironic in light of his future revenge against Rome).
  8–9 **who ... them ... they** 'who' appears
to refer to 'great men', 'them' and 'they' to 'the
people'. The pronoun shifts remain ambiguous,

they have loved they know not wherefore; so that if they love they
know not why, they hate upon no better a ground. Therefore, for   10
Coriolanus neither to care whether they love or hate him manifests
the true knowledge he has in their disposition, and out of his noble
carelessness lets them plainly see't.

FIRST OFFICER If he did not care whether he had their love or no, he
waved indifferently 'twixt doing them neither good nor harm; but   15
he seeks their hate with greater devotion than they can render it him
and leaves nothing undone that may fully discover him their opposite. Now to seem to affect the malice and displeasure of the people
is as bad as that which he dislikes, to flatter them for their love.

SECOND OFFICER He hath deserved worthily of his country, and his   20
ascent is not by such easy degrees as those who, having been supple
and courteous to the people, bonneted, without any further deed to
have them at all into their estimation and report. But he hath so
planted his honours in their eyes and his actions in their hearts that
for their tongues to be silent and not confess so much were a kind of 25
ingrateful injury. To report otherwise were a malice that, giving
itself the lie, would pluck reproof and rebuke from every ear that
heard it.

---

21 ascent] F (assent)   22 people, bonneted,] F; people bonneted, *Hanmer;* people, unbonnetted, *conj. Johnson*   22–3
bonneted, . . . report.] F; bonneted into their estimation and report, without any further deed at all: *Hudson*   23 have]
F; heave *Pope*

however, and Brockbank thinks 'who' refers to
'the people' and 'them' to 'great men'.
  9 wherefore why.
  12 in of.
  12–13 noble carelessness patrician indifference to what the people think of him.
The ambiguous phrase suggests highmindedness
becoming to one of the nobility but also contempt
for the commoners whose opinion he rejects.
  15 waved would waver (*OED* Wave *v* 2); on
use of the indicative for the subjunctive see Abbott
361.
  15 indifferently impartially, without bias.
  15 'twixt . . . harm Two constructions are
confused: 'he waved indifferently 'twixt good and
harm' and 'doing them neither good nor harm'
(Cam.).
  17 discover reveal, disclose.
  17–18 opposite opponent, adversary; also with
the sense of Coriolanus's being diametrically
'opposite' in nature.

  18 seem to affect seem to desire, seek out.
The passage in Plutarch's comparison of Alcibiades and Coriolanus is more judgemental: 'he
is lesse to be blamed, that seeketh to please and
gratifie his common people: then he that despiseth
and disdaineth them, and therefore offereth them
wrong and injurie, bicause he would not seeme
to flatter them, to winne the more authoritie'
(Bullough, *Sources*, V, 545).
  21 degrees steps (used of the rungs of a
ladder).
  21 supple yielding, compliant.
  22 bonneted took off their bonnets as a sign
of respect for the people. Second Officer's comment prepares for Coriolanus's behaviour in the
market-place, 2.3.85–91, and Volumnia's advice,
3.2.74–9.
  23 estimation and report esteem and good
opinion.
  26–7 giving . . . lie showing itself false.

FIRST OFFICER No more of him; he's a worthy man. Make way, they are
    coming.   30

A sennet. Enter the PATRICIANS *and the Tribunes of the people, lictors*
    before them; CORIOLANUS, MENENIUS, COMINIUS *the consul.*
    [*The Senators take their places and sit.*] SICINIUS *and* BRUTUS *take*
    their places by themselves. CORIOLANUS *stands*

MENENIUS Having determined of the Volsces and
         To send for Titus Lartius, it remains
         As the main point of this our after-meeting
         To gratify his noble service that
         Hath thus stood for his country. Therefore please you,   35
         Most reverend and grave elders, to desire
         The present consul and last general
         In our well-found successes to report
         A little of that worthy work performed
         By Martius Caius Coriolanus, whom   40
         We met here both to thank and to remember
         With honours like himself.
                      [*Coriolanus sits*]
FIRST SENATOR   Speak, good Cominius.
         Leave nothing out for length, and make us think
         Rather our state's defective for requital
         Than we to stretch it out. [*To the Tribunes*] Masters o'th'people,   45
         We do request your kindest ears and, after,

---

30 SD.3 *The Senators . . . sit.*] *Singer²; not in* F   37–8 last . . . well-found] F; late . . . well-fought *conj. Capell,*
'Notes'   40 Martius Caius] F (*Martius Caius*); Caius Martius *Rowe*   41 met] F; meet *Hanmer;* are met *Capell*   42
SD] *White²; not in* F   44 state's] F4; states F   45 SD] *Globe; not in* F   46 ears and, after,] F3 *subst.;* eares: and after F

30 SD.1 **lictors** Attendants upon Roman magistrates who carried the *fasces* before them and executed their sentences. The *fasces* were rods bound
with an axe in the middle which symbolised that
Rome's strength lay in unity.
  30 SD.4 CORIOLANUS *stands* At some point Coriolanus must sit, since F directs him to 'rise' at 60,
but it would be natural that he at least initially
stand, since he is a soldier, not a senator; he would
perhaps sit at 42, as his sponsor Menenius cedes
the floor to First Senator, who asks for Cominius's
account of Coriolanus's 'deeds'.
  31 **determined of** reached a decision concerning.

33 **after-meeting** follow-up meeting.
34 **gratify** show gratitude for, requite.
35 **stood for** stood up for, defended.
37 **last** most recent.
38 **well-found** Both 'found to be good, confirmed' and 'fortunate'.
41 **met** are convened.
42 **like himself** befitting him (i.e. the honours
he deserves).
43 **for length** for fear of going on too long.
44–5 **Rather . . . out** Rather that Rome lacks
means to reward than that we are unwilling to
strain its resources to reward him appropriately.
46 **after** afterward.

Your loving motion toward the common body
To yield what passes here.

SICINIUS   We are convented
Upon a pleasing treaty, and have hearts
Inclinable to honour and advance   50
The theme of our assembly.

BRUTUS   Which the rather
We shall be blessed to do if he remember
A kinder value of the people than
He hath hereto prized them at.

MENENIUS   That's off, that's off.
I would you rather had been silent. Please you   55
To hear Cominius speak?

BRUTUS   Most willingly;
But yet my caution was more pertinent
Than the rebuke you give it.

MENENIUS   He loves your people,
But tie him not to be their bedfellow.
Worthy Cominius, speak.

Coriolanus rises and offers to go away
                                Nay, keep your place.   60

A SENATOR Sit, Coriolanus. Never shame to hear
What you have nobly done.

CORIOLANUS   Your honours' pardon.
I had rather have my wounds to heal again
Than hear say how I got them.

BRUTUS   Sir, I hope

---

48 SH] *Scicin.* F (*and to end of scene*)   51 our] F; your *conj. Warburton*   52 blessed] F; prest *Collier²*   61 SH, 117 SH]
F (*Senat.*); 1 *Sen. / Rowe*   62 honours'] *Theobald;* Honors F; Honour's *Rowe*

47 loving . . . body well-disposed influence
with the common people.

48 yield assent to.

48 convented convened, summoned.

49 treaty matter to be treated of (*OED* Treaty
sb 2), proposal (in nominating Coriolanus to the
consulship). Sicinius does not expressly agree to
'yield' (48); his phrasing suggests good-will but
also keeps open the possibility of negotiation.

50 Inclinable Favourably disposed.

52 blessed happy, glad.

53 kinder value more generous estimation.

54 off off the subject, impertinent; see
Brutus's retort at 57–8.

58 your people Menenius may here use the
impersonal form (i.e. 'these people we are talking about') or be differentiating himself from the
commoners whom the tribunes represent. In the
latter case, as Brockbank notes, he could mean
'the people you care about' or, more negatively,
'those people of yours'.

59 tie oblige.

60 SD *offers* starts, prepares to.

61 SH This may be First Senator, who spoke
at 42, but in F he is an unnumbered *Senat.*; see
Textual Analysis, pp. 292–3 below.

My words disbenched you not?

CORIOLANUS   No, sir. Yet oft   65
When blows have made me stay I fled from words.
You soothed not, therefore hurt not. But your people,
I love them as they weigh –
MENENIUS   Pray now, sit down.
CORIOLANUS I had rather have one scratch my head i'th'sun
When the alarum were struck than idly sit   70
To hear my nothings monstered.   *Exit*
MENENIUS   Masters of the people,
Your multiplying spawn how can he flatter –
That's thousand to one good one – when you now see
He had rather venture all his limbs for honour
Than one on's ears to hear it? Proceed, Cominius.   75
COMINIUS I shall lack voice; the deeds of Coriolanus
Should not be uttered feebly. It is held
That valour is the chiefest virtue and
Most dignifies the haver. If it be,
The man I speak of cannot in the world   80
Be singly counterpoised. At sixteen years,
When Tarquin made a head for Rome, he fought
Beyond the mark of others. Our then dictator,
Whom with all praise I point at, saw him fight
When with his Amazonian chin he drove   85

71 SD] F (*Exit Coriolanus*)   72–5 flatter – . . . one – . . . it?] *Capell*; flatter? . . . one, . . . it. F; flatter, . . . one? . . . it.
Rome   75 one on's] F3; on ones F   85 chin] F3; Shinne F

65 **disbenched you not** did not cause you to
leave your seat.
67 **soothed** flattered.
68 **as . . . weigh** according to their deserts;
Brockbank suggests the comment is more
derisory, 'as lightly as they weigh'. F's final dash
implies that Coriolanus intended to enlarge on
this theme, but Menenius forestalls him.
70 **alarum** battle summons; see 1.4.10 n.
71 **monstered** exhibited as marvels; the verb
also implies 'monstrously exaggerated'. *OED*
gives this as the only example of the sense 'exhibit
as a monster'.
72 **multiplying spawn** 'The lower classes of
Romans were known as *proletarii*, good only to
breed children (*proles*)' (Chambers); the only use
of 'spawn' in Shakespeare.
73 **thousand** i.e. a thousand plebeians.
75 **on's** of his.
76 **voice** adequate expression, eloquence.
77–9 **It . . . haver** This scene and Cominius's

laus, or formal speech of praise (76–116, 118–
23), are not in Plutarch, but elsewhere North's
wording is close to this passage (see 1.1.30 n.).
Shakespeare introduces the crucial conditional in
the next sentence; see pp. 50–1 above.
81 **singly counterpoised** equalled (in power,
quality, honour) by any other single man.
81–2 **At . . . Rome** On this battle, see
2.1.125 n.
82 **made . . . for** advanced an army against.
83 **mark** reach, capacity. In archery the 'mark'
is the target.
83 **dictator** The term is not pejorative: a
Roman 'dictator' was a leader constitutionally
given authority to deal with a specific emergency,
such as a war.
84 **Whom . . . at** Chambers notes a reminis-
cence of the common phrase in Latin speeches
quem honoris causa nomino (whom I mention with
respect).
85 **Amazonian** i.e. beardless. The Amazons

The bristled lips before him. He bestrid
An o'erpressed Roman and i'th'consul's view
Slew three opposers. Tarquin's self he met
And struck him on his knee. In that day's feats,
When he might act the woman in the scene,   90
He proved best man i'th'field, and for his meed
Was brow-bound with the oak. His pupil age
Man-entered thus, he waxèd like a sea,
And in the brunt of seventeen battles since
He lurched all swords of the garland. For this last,   95
Before and in Corioles, let me say
I cannot speak him home. He stopped the fliers
And by his rare example made the coward
Turn terror into sport. As weeds before
A vessel under sail, so men obeyed   100

---

86 bristled] F (brizled)   95 of the] F; o'th F2   99 weeds] F; Waves F2

were women warriors in classical mythology;
young Martius is likened to them because he had
not yet reached full manhood.
    86 bristled bearded (i.e. more mature oppo-
nents).
    86 bestrid past tense of 'bestride'. In North,
'a Romaine souldier being throwen to the ground
even hard by him, Martius straight bestrid him,
and slue the enemie with his owne handes
that had before overthrowen the Romaine' (Bullough, *Sources*, v, 507). Brockbank notes that
North mistranslates Plutarch's 'standing before'
as 'straight bestrid' but, as A. R. Braunmuller
reminds me, North's wording updates Plutarch
to medieval–early modern practice. Falstaff asks
Hal to 'bestride' him if he is wounded in battle (*1H4* 5.1.121–2), and Macduff applies the
idea metaphorically when he urges Malcolm that,
rather than weep for Scotland's plight under Macbeth, they should 'like good men / Bestride our
downfall [downfallen] birthdom' (*Mac.* 4.3.3–4).
    87 o'erpressed overwhelmed.
    89 struck . . . knee fought him to his knee(s).
The episode with the tyrant Tarquin is not in
Plutarch; it undercuts the tribunes' accusations
at 3.3.1–2, 68–70 and 4.6.34–5.
    90 might . . . scene (1) was young enough to
be excused for behaving like a woman, either by
retreating or crying, (2) was of an age to play a
woman's role on stage (since boys acted women's
parts until their voices broke). The latter would

be an anachronism, since theatres for exhibiting
plays did not exist in Rome until 250 years after
the death of Coriolanus (Malone).
    91 meed reward.
    92 brow-bound . . . oak See 1.3.11–12 n.,
2.1.102–3.
    92–3 His . . . thus (1) 'Having entered like
a man the age when he might fittingly have
been a pupil' (Brockbank), (2) 'Having started
his apprenticeship in the style of one who had
already completed it' (Hibbard).
    94 brunt assault, violent attack.
    94 seventeen The number of 'battles' was
probably suggested by the number of *years*
Plutarch says Martius had been a soldier (which
would have made him about thirty-two at the time
of the play's events).
    95 lurched . . . garland (1) easily won the
victory garland over all the other soldiers (where
'lurch' means the 'concluding state of the score
in which one player is enormously ahead of the
others' in various games (*OED* Lurch *sb*[1] 2)), (2)
robbed all other soldiers of the victory garland
(where 'lurch' means 'to get the start of (a person)
so as to prevent him from obtaining a fair share
of food, profit, etc.' (*OED* Lurch *v*[1] 2)). For Ben
Jonson's parody of this line in *Epicoene*, see p. 1
above.
    97 speak him home adequately describe his
deeds, bring the events home to you.
    100 obeyed yielded.

And fell below his stem. His sword, death's stamp,
Where it did mark, it took; from face to foot
He was a thing of blood, whose every motion
Was timed with dying cries. Alone he entered
The mortal gate of th'city, which he painted   105
With shunless destiny; aidless came off,
And with a sudden reinforcement struck
Corioles like a planet. Now all's his,
When by and by the din of war 'gan pierce
His ready sense; then straight his doubled spirit   110
Requickened what in flesh was fatigate,
And to the battle came he, where he did
Run reeking o'er the lives of men as if
'Twere a perpetual spoil; and till we called
Both field and city ours, he never stood   115
To ease his breast with panting.
MENENIUS   Worthy man!

101 stem] F; stern *Pope*   102 took; . . . foot] *Steevens²*, conj. *Tyrwhitt;* tooke . . . foot: F   104 timed] F; trim'd F2;
tun'd *Collier²*   105–6 he painted . . . destiny;] F (he painted . . . destinie:); he painted . . . defamy F2; he parted . . .
destiny, *Keightley;* he, painted . . . destiny, *Oxford*   108 Now all's his] F; now all's this F2; Nor all's this *Rowe;* Nor's
this all *Hanmer*

101 stem prow (literally, the main timber of a ship's prow).

101 stamp A tool used for imprinting a design on softer material; compare 2.1.133–4.

102 took (1) made its mark, (2) took possession of, killed.

102 took; . . . foot F's punctuation may be correct, but the 'death's stamp' metaphor (101) becomes diluted when the 'stamp' is imagined as tearing a body from head to foot, and an absolute pause after 'took' vividly suggests the finality of death. Tyrwhitt's punctuation also allows a sharper recollection of Cominius's description of Martius as 'flayed' (1.6.22).

104 Was timed Was accompanied, kept time. Collier's 'tun'd' is appropriate in its own way with 'dying cries', but less forceful; compare *Mac.* 4.3.235, where either 'This tune' (Rowe²) or 'This time' (F) 'goes manly'.

105 mortal gate fatal gate, both because it threatened Coriolanus with death and because through it he brought defeat and death into the city.

105–6 painted . . . destiny stained with the blood of those who could not avoid their death. Oxford's punctuation provides a meaning that agrees with Coriolanus's being covered in blood

but, as Parker notes, is grammatically awkward in requiring 'which' to mean 'from which'.

107 reinforcement (1) fresh assault, (2) troops led by Titus Lartius that eventually came to his aid. If only (1), Cominius's account suggests that Coriolanus took the city by himself and suppresses Lartius's crucial aid.

108 like . . . planet (1) with the force of a planet, (2) with the malign influence of a planet (striking the earth with plague).

110 ready sense alert or acute hearing.

110 straight immediately.

110 doubled increased twofold, made double.

111 Requickened Revivified, reinvigorated.

111 fatigate fatigued, weary.

113 reeking steaming with his enemies' blood; see 'smoking swords', 1.4.12.

114 spoil slaughter, destruction; with a secondary allusion to hunting, where 'spoil' refers to the massacre of the quarry, especially deer (see 1.1.181 and n.), that accords with 'run reeking' and 'ease his breast with panting'. Coriolanus finds physical satisfaction in fighting and killing, and his 'spoil' is the life of his enemy; 'spoils' means 'material booty' when Cominius resumes at 118.

115 stood stood still.

A SENATOR He cannot but with measure fit the honours
      Which we devise him.
COMINIUS   Our spoils he kicked at
      And looked upon things precious as they were
      The common muck of the world. He covets less   120
      Than misery itself would give, rewards
      His deeds with doing them, and is content
      To spend the time to end it.
MENENIUS   He's right noble.
      Let him be called for.
A SENATOR Call Coriolanus.   125
OFFICER He doth appear.

           Enter CORIOLANUS

MENENIUS The senate, Coriolanus, are well pleased
      To make thee consul.
CORIOLANUS   I do owe them still
      My life and services.
MENENIUS   It then remains
      That you do speak to the people.
CORIOLANUS   I do beseech you,   130
      Let me o'erleap that custom, for I cannot
      Put on the gown, stand naked, and entreat them
      For my wounds' sake to give their suffrage. Please you
      That I may pass this doing.
SICINIUS   Sir, the people
      Must have their voices, neither will they bate   135
      One jot of ceremony.
MENENIUS   Put them not to't.

---

118 kicked] F (kickt); keck'd *conj. Badham, 'Crit.'*   123 the time to end it. / MENENIUS He's] F; his time – / *Men.* To end it, he's *conj. Warburton;* his time to spend it. / *Men.* He's *conj. Johnson*   125 SH] F (*Senat.*); 1. S. / *Capell*   133 suffrage] F (sufferage); suffrages *Rowe*

117 **He . . . fit** He cannot fail to measure up to.

121 **misery** privation, utter poverty.

122–3 **content . . . it** satisfied that spending his time thus is its own reward. The sentiment is close to that of George Chapman in his prefatory remarks to *Achilles Shield* (1598): 'I had the reward of my labours in their consummation, and the chief pleasure of them in mine owne profit' (B2ʳ).

126 SH Presumably one of the two officers who opened the scene.

128 **still** always.

131 **o'erleap** pass over, skip.

132 **naked** (1) exposed, (2) naked beneath the outer gown (see 2.1.208 n.).

134 **pass** let pass, omit.

135 **voices** votes. For contemporary applications, see pp. 27–9 above.

135 **bate** abate, curtail.

136 **Put . . . to't** (1) Do not ask them to forgo this (referring to Sicinius's last words), (2) Do not press them too hard (to Coriolanus).

Pray you, go fit you to the custom and
Take to you, as your predecessors have,
Your honour with your form.
CORIOLANUS   It is a part
That I shall blush in acting, and might well   140
Be taken from the people.
BRUTUS [*To Sicinius*]   Mark you that.
CORIOLANUS To brag unto them 'Thus I did, and thus',
Show them th'unaching scars, which I should hide,
As if I had received them for the hire
Of their breath only!
MENENIUS   Do not stand upon't. –   145
We recommend to you, tribunes of the people,
Our purpose to them, and to our noble consul
Wish we all joy and honour.
SENATORS To Coriolanus come all joy and honour!
   Flourish [*of*] *cornets. Exeunt* [*all but*] *Sicinius and Brutus*
BRUTUS You see how he intends to use the people.   150
SICINIUS May they perceive's intent! He will require them
As if he did contemn what he requested
Should be in them to give.
BRUTUS   Come, we'll inform them
Of our proceedings here. On th'market-place
I know they do attend us.   155
                                                           [*Exeunt*]

---

141 SD] *Cornwall; not in* F   141 that.] F; that? *Rowe*³   142 them 'Thus . . . thus',] F3 *subst.;* them, thus . . . thus F
145 only!] onely. F   147 purpose to them, and] F; purpose; – to them, and *Collier, conj. Mason*   149 SH] *Dyce; Senat.*
F; *Sic. / Rowe*²   149 SD *Flourish of . . . Exeunt all but . . . Brutus*] *Globe; Flourish Cornets. / Then Exeunt. Manet . . .*
Brutus. F (*Manent* F4)   154 here . . . market-place] *Theobald;* heere . . . Market place, F   155 SD] *Rowe; not in* F

139 your form the formalities decreed by custom.
139–40 part . . . acting On politics as theatre, see pp. 45–6 above.
140–1 might . . . people An inflammatory opinion that fulfils the tribunes' observations (2.1.205–13), as Brutus notes (141), and prepares for Coriolanus's arguments to the senators in 3.1. Coriolanus disapproves of the rebellious citizens and the innovation of the tribunate, but here he himself expresses revolutionary sentiments (compare 2.3.101–7); Sicinius tries to arrest him as a 'traitorous innovator' at 3.1.176 (see also 3.3.68–71).
145 breath voice, vote; compare the revulsion at 2.1.210.
145 stand upon't insist on it, make an issue of it. As usual, Menenius tries to moderate Coriolanus's absoluteness.

146 recommend commit, entrust.
147 purpose to them proposal to the people.
150–5 The tribunes accurately predict the manner in which Coriolanus will canvass for votes. In theatrical terms, their conversation also allows time for the officers to clear the stage of cushions; if it were staged in this way, the officers would be busy in the background and would exit either during the tribunes' conversation or at 155 through a different door.
151 require ask, solicit (their votes).
152 what that what.
154 here. F's punctuation needs correcting, since the events of 2.2 take place in the Capitol, not the market-place.

2.[3] *Enter seven or eight* CITIZENS

FIRST CITIZEN Once if he do require our voices, we ought not to deny
him.
SECOND CITIZEN We may, sir, if we will.
THIRD CITIZEN We have power in ourselves to do it, but it is a power
that we have no power to do. For if he show us his wounds and tell   5
us his deeds, we are to put our tongues into those wounds and speak
for them; so if he tell us his noble deeds, we must also tell him our
noble acceptance of them. Ingratitude is monstrous, and for the
multitude to be ingrateful were to make a monster of the multitude,
of the which we, being members, should bring ourselves to be   10
monstrous members.
FIRST CITIZEN And to make us no better thought of, a little help will
serve; for once we stood up about the corn, he himself stuck not to
call us the many-headed multitude.
THIRD CITIZEN We have been called so of many, not that our heads are   15
some brown, some black, some abram, some bald, but that our wits

---

Act 2, Scene 3 2.3] *Capell; not in* F   1 Once] F; Once, *Theobald*   13 once] F; once when *Rome*   16 abram] F;
auburn F4

Act 2, Scene 3
Rome, the market-place. This scene initiates the
political confrontation between the people and
Coriolanus; it is based on Plutarch but altered to
Shakespeare's purposes (see p. 45 above).
  0 SD *seven or eight* On permissive entry directions, see Textual Analysis, p. 302 below. Here the
citizens are numbered independently of those in
1.1, and in this scene Shakespeare begins renum-
bering with the second and third groups of citizens who approach Coriolanus.
  1 Once if When once, as soon as (*OED* Once
conjunctive adv C); see also Proudfoot, p. 204. F's
punctuation emphasises First Citizen's good-will.
  1 voices Parker notes that of the play's 48 uses
of this word, 34 occur in Act 2, of which 30 are in
this scene.
  4–5 power . . . no power Third Citizen's punning distinction is important; it contrasts 'power'
in the sense of legal ability or capacity with 'power'
as the moral right to exercise that ability.
  6 tongues . . . wounds A characteristic Shakespearean image (see *JC* 3.1.263–4, 3.2.223–4, *R3*
1.2.55–6, *1H4* 1.3.96), but particularly apt in a
play that sees politics in terms of the body and
so often presents the body as wounded, dismem-
bered or diseased.

  8 noble acceptance Third Citizen's appropriation of the patrician word 'noble' suggests
an understanding of the reciprocity involved: the
citizens demonstrate their capacity for noble generosity in recognising Coriolanus's noble achievements.
  8 Ingratitude is monstrous This has a
proverbial ring appropriate to the plebeians' discourse, although there is no record of such a
proverb; it also echoes Cominius's insistence that
Martius allow Rome to acknowledge his value, lest
Rome fail its own high standards and his wounds
'fester 'gainst ingratitude' (see 1.9.19–31).
  12–13 And . . . serve It will not require much
effort on our part to make the patricians think us
no better than monsters.
  13 once once when. On the missing relative,
see Abbott 244.
  13 stuck hesitated, scrupled.
  14 many-headed multitude A proverbial
expression (Tilley M1308) of classical origin
denoting the instability of human nature and, by
extension, democracy; compare 'Hydra', 3.1.92–
6, and 'The beast / With many heads', 4.1.1–2.
  15 of by.
  16 abram A colloquial variant of 'auburn',
which then meant light yellow (*OED*).

are so diversely coloured. And truly I think if all our wits were to
issue out of one skull, they would fly east, west, north, south, and
their consent of one direct way should be at once to all the points
o'th'compass.   20

SECOND CITIZEN Think you so? Which way do you judge my wit would
fly?

THIRD CITIZEN Nay, your wit will not so soon out as another man's
will; 'tis strongly wedged up in a blockhead. But if it were at liberty,
'twould sure southward.   25

SECOND CITIZEN Why that way?

THIRD CITIZEN To lose itself in a fog where, being three parts melted
away with rotten dews, the fourth would return for conscience' sake
to help to get thee a wife.

SECOND CITIZEN You are never without your tricks. You may, you   30
may.

THIRD CITIZEN Are you all resolved to give your voices? But that's no
matter, the greater part carries it. I say, if he would incline to the
people, there was never a worthier man.

Enter CORIOLANUS *in a gown of humility* [*and a hat*], *with* MENENIUS

Here he comes, and in the gown of humility. Mark his behaviour.   35
We are not to stay all together, but to come by him where he stands,
by ones, by twos, and by threes. He's to make his requests by
particulars, wherein every one of us has a single honour in giving
him our own voices with our own tongues. Therefore follow me,
and I'll direct you how you shall go by him.   40

ALL CITIZENS Content, content.   [*Exeunt Citizens*]

MENENIUS O sir, you are not right. Have you not known

---

24 wedged] F (wadg'd)   33 it. I say,] *Theobald;* it, I say. F   34 SD *humility . . . with*] *Oxford;* Humility, with F   36
all together] F3; altogether F   41 SH, 122 SH, 151 SH, 240 SH] F (*All.*)   41 SD] *Capell; not in* F

19 consent . . . way agreement to go in one
direction.

23 out come out, 'issue out' (18).

25–8 southward . . . dews See 1.4.31 n. on
disease-bearing winds from the south.

28 rotten corrupting, unwholesome; compare
3.3.129.

28–9 for . . . wife out of conscience to help the
poor 'blockhead' (24) woo a wife.

30–1 You . . . may As a verb of complete pred-
ication 'may' means to prevail over (*OED* May *v*¹
1), hence, 'You win, have your little joke.'

33 greater part majority vote.

33 it. I say, F's punctuation is possible, though
Theobald's makes better sense.

33 incline to sympathise with.

34 SD *gown of humility* See 2.1.208 n.,
2.3.101 n.

34 SD *and a hat* A prop required by 2.3.87–9,
153, 3.2.74–5.

37–8 by particulars to individuals, one by
one.

38 single individual, separate.

42 you . . . right you are not handling this in
the right spirit. Coriolanus's discomfiture should
be obvious even before he speaks; modern productions often choose a gown and hat design that
verges on the silly and so emphasises his sense of
humiliation.

The worthiest men have done't?

CORIOLANUS   What must I say?
'I pray, sir'? Plague upon't, I cannot bring
My tongue to such a pace. 'Look, sir, my wounds.   45
I got them in my country's service, when
Some certain of your brethren roared and ran
From th'noise of our own drums.'

MENENIUS   O me, the gods!
You must not speak of that. You must desire them
To think upon you.

CORIOLANUS   Think upon me? Hang 'em!   50
I would they would forget me, like the virtues
Which our divines lose by 'em.

MENENIUS   You'll mar all.
I'll leave you. Pray you speak to 'em, I pray you,
In wholesome manner.   *Exit*

                Enter three of the CITIZENS

CORIOLANUS   Bid them wash their faces
And keep their teeth clean. So, here comes a brace. –   55
You know the cause, sir, of my standing here.

THIRD CITIZEN We do, sir. Tell us what hath brought you to't.

CORIOLANUS Mine own desert.

SECOND CITIZEN Your own desert?

CORIOLANUS Ay, but not mine own desire.   60

43–4 say? / 'I . . . sir'?] *Cam.;* say, / I . . . Sir? F   45–8 'Look . . . drums.'] *Cam.;* Looke . . . Drummes. F   54 SD.1
Exit] F; *Exit Menenius / Staunton (after 55* clean)   54 SD.2 *Enter three . . .* CITIZENS] F; *Enter two . . . Citizens / Rowe;*
Re-enter two . . . Citizens / after 55 clean *and / Re-enter a third Citizen / after 55* brace *Globe*   57 SH, 61 SH, 64 SH, 74
SH] F (3 *Cit.*); 1 *Cit. / Rowe*   59 desert?] *Rowe;* desert. F; desert! *Globe*   60 but not] *Globe;* but F; not F3

45 **pace** manner of proceeding; the metaphor comes from training horses to a measured pace.
50 **think upon** think kindly of. There may be an echo of Jonah 1.6, 'Call upon thy God, if so be that God will thinke upon us.' Hibbard notes that this phrase was part of the Elizabethan beggar's patter to those they solicited; hence Coriolanus's furious repudiation, since he already feels like one 'begging' (63) for 'alms' (73).
51–2 **like . . . 'em** as they do the virtuous sermons our priests waste on them.
54 **wholesome** Menenius means the figurative sense, 'beneficial' or possibly 'decent'; Coriolanus sarcastically takes it more literally, as referring to physical cleanliness. On the possible relation of clean teeth to famine conditions, see p. 25 above.

Some editions, following Staunton, move Menenius's exit down two lines, so that Coriolanus's reply is directed to him, but Coriolanus could as well be muttering resentfully to himself.
55 **brace** pair, couple (usually used of animals or things, hence mildly contemptuous). On the apparent contradiction with 54 SD.2, *three*, see Textual Analysis, pp. 303–4 below.
59 **desert?** Rowe's punctuation fits the context of this terse interchange, where Second Citizen expresses eagerness to talk to the great warrior but also, as Parker notes, a certain surprise at Coriolanus's proud abruptness.
60 **but not mine** Third Citizen's question in the next line indicates that Compositor B dropped a 'not' from Coriolanus's assertion.

THIRD CITIZEN How not your own desire?

CORIOLANUS No, sir, 'twas never my desire yet to trouble the poor
with begging.

THIRD CITIZEN You must think, if we give you anything, we hope to
gain by you.   65

CORIOLANUS Well then, I pray, your price o'th'consulship?

FIRST CITIZEN The price is to ask it kindly.

CORIOLANUS Kindly, sir, I pray let me ha't. I have wounds to show
you, which shall be yours in private. [*To Second Citizen*] Your good
voice, sir. What say you?   70

SECOND CITIZEN You shall ha't, worthy sir.

CORIOLANUS A match, sir. There's in all two worthy voices begged. I
have your alms. Adieu.

THIRD CITIZEN But this is something odd.

SECOND CITIZEN And 'twere to give again – but 'tis no matter.   75

Exeunt [Citizens]

Enter two other CITIZENS

CORIOLANUS Pray you now, if it may stand with the tune of your voices
that I may be consul, I have here the customary gown.

FOURTH CITIZEN You have deserved nobly of your country, and you
have not deserved nobly.

CORIOLANUS Your enigma?   80

FOURTH CITIZEN You have been a scourge to her enemies; you have

---

68 Kindly, sir,] F (Kindly sir,); Kindly, Sir? *Johnson;* Kindly! Sir, *Steevens*[3]   69 SD] *Hibbard; not in* F   71 SH] F (2
Cit.); *Both Cit.* / *Johnson*   75 SD.1] *Cornwall; Exeunt.* F   76 voices] voices, F   78 SH, 81 SH, 94 SH] *Globe;* 1. F; 3
Cit. / *Steevens*[4]   80 enigma?] Aenigma. F

67 kindly (1) courteously, (2) with natural
affection, in the spirit of kinship that recognises
we are all fellow human beings (*OED* Kindly *adv*
2). First Citizen offers a delicate rebuke to Coriolanus's mercantile metaphor ('price'), but Coriolanus echoes him mockingly in the next line,
reducing 'Kindly' to the equivalent of 'Please'.

69 yours available for you to see. In Plutarch,
Coriolanus freely shows his wounds because he
seeks the consulship for himself, unprompted by
his mother; in Shakespeare, a viewing is vaguely
promised the first group of citizens, then denied
the second group (95) and, as the citizens later
attest (148–51), never produced for any.

72 A match Agreed! It's a deal! ('match' =
bargain or contract).

75 And 'twere If it were.

75 SD.1 Possibly one of the citizens merely

withdraws to observe what follows; see Textual
Analysis, pp. 303–4 below.

76 stand agree, accord.

76 tune disposition (to say 'yes').

77 have here A curious expression that dis-
tances Coriolanus from the gown he is wearing;
his discomfort is also clear in the tonal swings,
from terse arrogance with the first group of citizens to more garrulous levity with the second.

78–83 You . . . people Fourth Citizen is the
only one who attempts to challenge Coriolanus in
the way the tribunes later say they instructed the
people (162–3).

80 enigma riddle.

81–2 scourge . . . rod There may be biblical
echoes of 1 Kings 12.11, 'My father hathe chastised you with rods, but I wil correct you with
scourges'; see also Ps. 89.32.

been a rod to her friends. You have not indeed loved the common
people.

CORIOLANUS You should account me the more virtuous that I have not
been common in my love. I will, sir, flatter my sworn brother, the   85
people, to earn a dearer estimation of them; 'tis a condition they
account gentle. And since the wisdom of their choice is rather to
have my hat than my heart, I will practise the insinuating nod and
be off to them most counterfitly. That is, sir, I will counterfeit the
bewitchment of some popular man and give it bountiful to the   90
desirers. Therefore, beseech you I may be consul.

FIFTH CITIZEN We hope to find you our friend, and therefore give you
our voices heartily.

FOURTH CITIZEN You have received many wounds for your country.

CORIOLANUS I will not seal your knowledge with showing them. I will   95
make much of your voices and so trouble you no farther.

BOTH CITIZENS The gods give you joy, sir, heartily! [*Exeunt Citizens*]

CORIOLANUS Most sweet voices!
Better it is to die, better to starve,
Than crave the hire which first we do deserve.   100
Why in this wolvish toge should I stand here

85–6 brother, the people,] F (Brother the people)   92 SH] *Globe; 2.* F; *4 Cit. / Steevens*⁴   97 SH] F (*Both.*)   97
SD] *Rowe subst.; not in* F   99 starve] F (sterue)   100 hire] F2; higher F   101 wolvish toge] *Malone, conj. Steevens*
(wolvish); Wooluish tongue F; Woolvish gowne F2; woolish toge *conj. Becket;* woolless togue *Collier²* ; wolfish throng
conj. Staunton; foolish toge *Leo, conj. Mason;* womanish toge *Oxford*

85 common indiscriminate and vulgar (punning on 'common' in 'common people'). Coriolanus's elaborate reply ironically agrees with
the citizen's accusation: because he has not been
indiscriminate in his love, he has withheld it from
the unworthy commoners.

85 sworn brother Brockbank notes that the
phrase may derive from the *fratres jurati* of
medieval chivalry, knights bound by oath to share
each other's fortunes. Coriolanus's use here is sar-
castic, since the flattery he proffers would be an
offence against such a noble bond; the citizens
seem to take his offer as genuine.

86 dearer . . . them higher place in their
regard (with a pun on 'dearer' as 'costlier'; see
66, 'price').

86–7 'tis . . . gentle Either 'they believe flattery an attribute of the nobility', or 'they account
the condition of the flatterer a noble one' (Brockbank).

88 hat i.e. courtesy ('hat in hand'). Most
eighteenth-century editors adopted Pope's 'cap'
to blunt the anachronism, losing thereby the allit-
erative dichotomy of 'hat . . . heart'.

88 heart Coriolanus presumably means 'hon-

est opinion', but the word betrays his deliberate
misunderstanding of the citizens; it is precisely
his 'heart', or good-will, that they are requesting.

88 insinuating ingratiating.

89 be . . . counterfeitly hypocritically doff my
hat to them.

89–90 counterfeit . . . man imitate the crowd-
pleasing charms of the demogogue.

90 bountiful bountifully. (See Abbott 1 on the
use of adjectives as adverbs.)

95 seal confirm, authenticate (from the practice of affixing official seals to legal documents;
see 5.3.206).

99–110 The first of Coriolanus's two soliloquies
(the other is 4.4.1–6, 12–26) reveals how unbear-
able he finds this public importuning of those he
despises. The rhyming couplets further distance
him from the market-place, in which he is
forced to beg in vulgar prose.

100 hire . . . deserve reward already merited.

101 wolvish toge Coriolanus sees himself
wearing the 'napless vesture of humility' (2.1.208)
as the proverbial wolf in sheep's clothing (punning on 'wool'). NS suggests that F's 'Wooluish'
might be a misreading of 'Woolish' (i.e. woolyish),

To beg of Hob and Dick that does appear
Their needless vouches? Custom calls me to't.
What custom wills, in all things should we do't,
The dust on antique time would lie unswept   105
And mountainous error be too highly heaped
For truth to o'erpeer. Rather than fool it so,
Let the high office and the honour go
To one that would do thus. I am half through;
The one part suffered, the other will I do.   110

Enter three CITIZENS *more*

Here come more voices.
Your voices! For your voices I have fought,
Watched for your voices; for your voices bear
Of wounds two dozen odd. Battles thrice six
I have seen and heard of; for your voices have   115
Done many things, some less, some more. Your voices!
Indeed, I would be consul.

SIXTH CITIZEN He has done nobly, and cannot go without any honest
man's voice.

SEVENTH CITIZEN Therefore let him be consul. The gods give him joy   120
and make him good friend to the people!

ALL CITIZENS Amen, amen. God save thee, noble consul!

[Exeunt Citizens]

CORIOLANUS Worthy voices.

---

102 does] F; do F4   104 wills, . . . things] *Capell;* wills . . . things, F   104 do't,] *Theobald;* doo't? F   111 more] F
(moe)   112, 116 voices!] F (Voyces?)   115 of; . . . . voices] F *subst.* (of: . . . Voyces,); of . . . voices, *Oxford*   118 SH]
Globe; 1. *Cit.* F; 5 *Cit. / Steevens*⁴   120 SH] *Globe;* 2. *Cit.* F; 6 *Cit. / Steevens*⁴   122 SD] *Rowe subst.; not in* F

referring to the fact that the gown of humility is a coarse woollen coat like that of the 'woollen vassals' he despises (3.2.10). F's 'tongue' is presumably a misreading of manuscript 'toge' (a common English form of the Latin *toga*); *Oth.*, 1.1.24, offers an instance of the same mistake, where F has 'Tongued Consuls' for 'toged consuls'.

102 **Hob . . . Dick** Typical names for English rustics, hence an Elizabethan version of 'any Tom, Dick or Harry' ('Hob' being the familiar form of Rob, a diminutive for Robin or Robert).

103 **needless vouches** unnecessary confirmation (because the senate's appointment is sufficient; compare 2.1.211–13).

105 **antique time** ancient traditions (with the implication that these traditions are now old-fashioned and obsolete).

107 **o'erpeer** see over.

107 **fool it so** make such a fool of myself.

109–10 **I . . . do** Angry refusal to debase himself further gives way to weary acceptance that he must complete the task, an emotional pattern that is repeated with his mother in 3.2.

112–17 Coriolanus's huckster manner openly mocks those whose votes he seeks, and they sense the derision (147–59), though here they generously overlook it to reward his achievements.

113 **Watched** Kept watch, done guard duty.

114 **thrice six** See 2.2.94 n. on 'seventeen'.

115 **and heard of** Probably part of the rhetorical teasing continued in the next line's vague 'many things, some less, some more', but possibly meant more seriously and 'heard of' means 'heard, was present at'.

Enter MENENIUS, *with* BRUTUS *and* SICINIUS

MENENIUS You have stood your limitation, and the tribunes
            Endue you with the people's voice. Remains   125
            That, in th'official marks invested, you
            Anon do meet the senate.
CORIOLANUS   Is this done?
SICINIUS The custom of request you have discharged.
            The people do admit you, and are summoned
            To meet anon upon your approbation.   130
CORIOLANUS Where? At the senate-house?
SICINIUS   There, Coriolanus.
CORIOLANUS May I change these garments?
SICINIUS   You may, sir.
CORIOLANUS That I'll straight do and, knowing myself again,
            Repair to th'senate-house.
MENENIUS I'll keep you company. [*To the Tribunes*] Will you along?   135
BRUTUS We stay here for the people.
SICINIUS   Fare you well.
                          Exeunt Coriolanus and Menenius
            He has it now, and by his looks methinks
            'Tis warm at's heart.
BRUTUS   With a proud heart he wore
            His humble weeds. Will you dismiss the people?

Enter the PLEBEIANS

SICINIUS How now, my masters, have you chose this man?   140
FIRST CITIZEN He has our voices, sir.
BRUTUS We pray the gods he may deserve your loves.
SECOND CITIZEN Amen, sir. To my poor unworthy notice,
            He mocked us when he begged our voices.
THIRD CITIZEN Certainly, he flouted us downright.   145
FIRST CITIZEN No, 'tis his kind of speech. He did not mock us.

---

123 SD SICINIUS] *Scicinius* F (*and to end of scene as* SH *Scinin.*)   135 SD] *Hibbard; not in* F   136 SD] F (*Exeunt Coriol. and Mene.*)

124 **limitation** allotted time.
125 **Endue** Endow, invest.
125 **Remains** It remains; for the common omission of 'it', see Abbott 404.
126 **official marks** insignia of office.
127 **Anon** Straight away, immediately.
130 **upon . . . approbation** to confirm your election.

138 **'Tis . . . heart** He is pleased to have got what he wanted. Parker suggests a possible play on 'heartburn' resulting from the discomfort of canvassing for votes.
139 **weeds** clothes.

SECOND CITIZEN Not one amongst us, save yourself, but says
                He used us scornfully. He should have showed us
                His marks of merit, wounds received for's country.
SICINIUS Why, so he did, I am sure.   150
ALL CITIZENS No, no. No man saw 'em.
THIRD CITIZEN He said he had wounds which he could show in private,
                And with his hat, thus waving it in scorn,
                'I would be consul', says he. 'Agèd custom,
                But by your voices, will not so permit me.   155
                Your voices therefore.' When we granted that,
                Here was 'I thank you for your voices. Thank you,
                Your most sweet voices. Now you have left your voices,
                I have no further with you.' Was not this mockery?
SICINIUS Why either were you ignorant to see't,   160
                Or, seeing it, of such childish friendliness
                To yield your voices?
BRUTUS   Could you not have told him
                As you were lessoned? When he had no power,
                But was a petty servant to the state,
                He was your enemy, ever spake against   165
                Your liberties and the charters that you bear
                I'th'body of the weal; and now, arriving
                A place of potency and sway o'th'state,
                If he should still malignantly remain
                Fast foe to th'plebeii, your voices might   170
                Be curses to yourselves. You should have said
                That as his worthy deeds did claim no less
                Than what he stood for, so his gracious nature
                Would think upon you for your voices and

154–9 'I . . . consul', . . . 'Agèd . . . therefore.' . . . 'I . . . you.'] *Hanmer;* I . . . Consull, . . . aged . . . therefore: . . . I . . . you. F   163 lessoned?] *Hanmer;* lesson'd: F   171 yourselves.] F (your selues.); yourselves? *Collier*[3]

152–9 He . . . you Third Citizen's indignant mimicry of Coriolanus's words and actions summarises the whole three-part canvassing scene, though whether he was present at all these recollected moments is not clear; see 75 SD.1 n. In Kemble's productions, and in those of his many followers, this speech was elaborated as a comic turn for a notably diminutive actor.
159 further with further use for.
160 ignorant too dull-witted, blind.
163 lessoned schooled, instructed; see 78–83 n. and 177.
166–7 Your . . . weal Your rights and privileges within the commonwealth; for an earlier

insistence on their traditional rights, see 2.2.134–6.
167 arriving arriving at, attaining; for the omission of prepositions with verbs of motion, see Abbott 198.
168 sway o' authority in.
170 Fast Steadfast, unyielding.
170 plebeii Elsewhere 'plebeians' is the plural form, but they are 'here thought of as an estate of the realm' (NS), which emphasises their status as a distinct class with recognised political rights.
174 Would Should, ought to.
174 think upon think kindly of; see 50 n.

| | Translate his malice towards you into love, | 175 |
| | Standing your friendly lord. | |

SICINIUS   Thus to have said,
As you were fore-advised, had touched his spirit
And tried his inclination: from him plucked
Either his gracious promise, which you might,
As cause had called you up, have held him to;   180
Or else it would have galled his surly nature,
Which easily endures not article
Tying him to aught. So putting him to rage,
You should have ta'en th'advantage of his choler
And passed him unelected.

BRUTUS   Did you perceive   185
He did solicit you in free contempt
When he did need your loves, and do you think
That his contempt shall not be bruising to you
When he hath power to crush? Why, had your bodies
No heart among you? Or had you tongues to cry   190
Against the rectorship of judgement?

SICINIUS   Have you
Ere now denied the asker, and now again,
Of him that did not ask but mock, bestow
Your sued-for tongues?

THIRD CITIZEN He's not confirmed. We may deny him yet.   195
SECOND CITIZEN And will deny him.
      I'll have five hundred voices of that sound.
FIRST CITIZEN I, twice five hundred, and their friends to piece 'em.
BRUTUS Get you hence instantly, and tell those friends
      They have chose a consul that will from them take   200

---

183 aught.] *Rowe subst.;* ought, F   193 Of] F; On *Theobald*   198 I, twice] F4; I twice F; Ay, twice *Rowe*

176 Standing . . . lord Acting on your behalf, as your patron (a common idiom).

177 had touched would have tested (as gold was tested with a touchstone).

180 As . . . up If occasion aroused you.

182 article stipulated condition.

184 choler anger, 'rage' (183).

186 free open, undisguised.

190 heart spirit, implying both courage and wisdom; see 1.1.99, 119 nn.

190–1 cry . . . judgement rebel against the rule or guidance of reason; 'rectorship', another legal term, is not used elsewhere by Shakespeare, and this use is the earliest cited for 'government, rule' (*OED* Rectorship 1).

191–2 Have . . . asker An ambiguous clause that obscures the plebeians' past voting record: either 'Haven't you on previous occasions denied one asking for your support?', or 'Have you ever denied your vote to one who asked in the proper manner?'

193 Of On, upon; on 'of' used for 'on', see Abbott 175.

198 I Rowe's 'Ay,' is possibly correct, but emendation is unnecessary; First Citizen could be competitively trying to best Second Citizen's claim.

198 piece supplement, add to.

Their liberties, make them of no more voice
Than dogs that are as often beat for barking
As therefor kept to do so.

SICINIUS   Let them assemble,
And on a safer judgement all revoke
Your ignorant election. Enforce his pride   205
And his old hate unto you. Besides, forget not
With what contempt he wore the humble weed,
How in his suit he scorned you; but your loves,
Thinking upon his services, took from you
Th'apprehension of his present portance,   210
Which most gibingly, ungravely, he did fashion
After the inveterate hate he bears you.

BRUTUS   Lay
A fault on us your tribunes, that we laboured,
No impediment between, but that you must
Cast your election on him.

SICINIUS   Say you chose him   215
More after our commandment than as guided
By your own true affections, and that your minds,
Preoccupied with what you rather must do
Than what you should, made you against the grain
To voice him consul. Lay the fault on us.   220

BRUTUS   Ay, spare us not. Say we read lectures to you,
How youngly he began to serve his country,
How long continued, and what stock he springs of,
The noble house o'th'Martians, from whence came

---

203 therefor] F (therefore)   211 most gibingly, ungravely] F; gibingly, ungravely *Pope*; gibing most ungravely *Hudson²*, *conj. Lettsom (in Dyce²)*; most ungravely gibing *conj. Kellner*   221 Ay,] *Rowe*; I, F

203 **therefor** This spelling means 'for that reason, on that account' (*OED* Therefor *adv* 1b); the image is degrading and also suggests the plebeians' shifting status, expected to 'bark' as soldiers in the wars but punished for showing any of the same initiative as citizens.

204 **safer** sounder; also 'safer' for us in the long run.

205 **Enforce** Lay stress upon, emphasise.

210 **apprehension . . . portance** comprehension of the significance of his bearing and demeanour at the time.

211 **gibingly** jeeringly, insultingly.

211 **ungravely** not seriously (as befitted the occasion).

213–15 **laboured . . . on him** urged that nothing should prevent you from voting for him.

217 **affections** inclinations.

224–31 **The noble . . . ancestor** Brockbank notes that by putting the genealogical opening of Plutarch's 'Life' into the tribune's mouth, Shakespeare 'allows us to recognize the element of patrician propaganda' in the 'lecture' on inherited nobility. Coriolanus's illustrious family lineage, his descent from a line of kings, is thus ironically made part of the tribunes' scheme to destroy him by fanning the people's fear of his ambition.

That Ancus Martius, Numa's daughter's son,   225
Who after great Hostilius here was king;
Of the same house Publius and Quintus were,
That our best water brought by conduits hither,
[And Censorinus that was so surnamed,]
And nobly naméd so, twice being censor,   230
Was his great ancestor.

SICINIUS   One thus descended,
That hath beside well in his person wrought
To be set high in place, we did commend
To your remembrances; but you have found,
Scaling his present bearing with his past,   235
That he's your fixéd enemy, and revoke
Your sudden approbation.

BRUTUS   Say you ne'er had done't –
Harp on that still – but by our putting on.
And presently, when you have drawn your number,
Repair to th'Capitol.

ALL CITIZENS   We will so. Almost all   240
Repent in their election.   *Exeunt Plebeians*

BRUTUS   Let them go on.
This mutiny were better put in hazard
Than stay, past doubt, for greater.

---

225 Numa's] F (*Numaes*)   229–31 And Censorinus . . . Was . . . ancestor.] *Delius;* And Nobly nam'd, so twice being
Censor, / Was . . . . Ancestor. F; And Censorinus, darling of the people / (And nobly nam'd so for twice being censor)
/ Was . . . ancestor. *Pope;* And Censorinus, nam'd so by the people, / And nobly named so, twice being censor, /
Was . . . ancestor. *Leo;* And Censorinus, nobly named so, / Twice being by the people chosen censor, / Was . . .
ancestor. *Globe;* And Censorinus nobly named so, / Twice being censor, was . . . ancestor. *Sisson*   240–1 ALL CITIZENS
We . . . election.] F; *Oxford redistributes: / A Citizen* We will so. / *Another Citizen* Almost . . . election.

225–7 Ancus Martius . . . Numa . . . Hostilius . . . Quintus Following Plutarch has again led Shakespeare into some historical inaccuracy. Traditionally, Ancus Martius was the fourth king of Rome (642–617 B.C.), Numa Pompilius the second (715–673 B.C.) and Tullus Hostilius the third (673–642 B.C.). Coriolanus's own dates are *c.* 525–493 B.C., so Quintus Martius Rex, who ordered the building of the Aqua Marcia in 144 B.C., is an anachronism. Plutarch's Publius has not been identified.

229 Censorinus Another anachronism: Caius Marcius Rutilius received the title Censorinus in 265 B.C., when he was for the second time made censor. The missing line in F was probably the result of eye-skip between two lines that both began with 'And'. The name Censorinus must have been part of the missing line, and North

reads, 'Censorinus also came of that familie, that was so surnamed, bicause the people had chosen him Censor twise' (Bullough, *Sources*, V, 505).

230 censor Roman magistrate who kept the official list of citizens and supervised public morals.

232 beside . . . wrought in addition has deserved well by his own achievements.

235 Scaling Weighing (in the scales).

237 sudden hasty, rash.

238 putting on urging, putting you up to it.

239 presently immediately.

239 drawn . . . number assembled your supporters.

241 in of (see Abbott 162).

242 put in hazard risked, ventured.

243 Than wait for a greater one that undoubtedly would come later.

If, as his nature is, he fall in rage
With their refusal, both observe and answer   245
The vantage of his anger.
SICINIUS   To th'Capitol, come.
We will be there before the stream o'th'people;
And this shall seem, as partly 'tis, their own,
Which we have goaded onward.

Exeunt

3.[1] *Cornets. Enter* CORIOLANUS, MENENIUS, *all the gentry,*
COMINIUS, TITUS LARTIUS, *and other* SENATORS

CORIOLANUS Tullus Aufidius then had made new head?
LARTIUS He had, my lord, and that it was which caused
Our swifter composition.
CORIOLANUS So then the Volsces stand but as at first,
Ready when time shall prompt them to make raid   5
Upon's again.
COMINIUS   They are worn, lord consul, so,
That we shall hardly in our ages see
Their banners wave again.
CORIOLANUS   Saw you Aufidius?
LARTIUS On safeguard he came to me and did curse
Against the Volsces for they had so vilely   10

Act 3, Scene 1   3.1] *Rome; Actus Tertius.* F   0 SD.2 LARTIUS] *Latius* F (*and to end of scene as* SH)   1 head?] *Rome;*
head. F   5 raid] F (roade); inroad *Pope*

245–6 answer . . . anger take advantage of
the opportunity his anger will provide.

Act 3, Scene 1
Rome, a street leading to the market-place, from
which the tribunes are returning.
   0 SD North reports that Coriolanus's coming
'to the market place with great pomp, accompanied with all the Senate, and the whole Nobilitie' prompted the people's hostility and fear 'to
put this office of soveraine authoritie into his
hands, being . . . one they might doubt would
take away alltogether the libertie from the people' (Bullough, *Sources*, v, 518). In Shakespeare,
the tribunes have already instigated the decision
to refuse Coriolanus the consulship, thus creating
an ironic, un-Plutarchan, context for the patricians' confident entry procession.
   1 made new head raised a fresh army.

3 swifter composition coming to terms
sooner than expected (with the defeated city of
Corioles).
   5 raid attack, incursion; 'raid' was the Scottish,
and subsequently became the modern, form of F's
'roade' (*OED* Raid *sb*).
   6 worn enfeebled, exhausted.
   6 lord consul Cominius's use of the title is
premature; it suggests the patricians' confidence
that the election process is over, an irony that
would be enhanced if, as Parker suggests, Coriolanus were already wearing his consular regalia.
Cominius is also overly complacent about the
Volscian danger.
   7 ages lifetimes.
   9 On safeguard On a guarantee of safe passage.
   10 for because.
   10 vilely basely, deplorably.

Yielded the town. He is retired to Antium.
CORIOLANUS Spoke he of me?
LARTIUS   He did, my lord.
CORIOLANUS   How? what?
LARTIUS How often he had met you sword to sword;
That of all things upon the earth he hated
Your person most; that he would pawn his fortunes   15
To hopeless restitution, so he might
Be called your vanquisher.
CORIOLANUS   At Antium lives he?
LARTIUS At Antium.
CORIOLANUS I wish I had a cause to seek him there,
To oppose his hatred fully. Welcome home.   20

Enter SICINIUS *and* BRUTUS

Behold, these are the tribunes of the people,
The tongues o'th'common mouth. I do despise them,
For they do prank them in authority
Against all noble sufferance.
SICINIUS Pass no further.   25
CORIOLANUS Ha? What is that?
BRUTUS It will be dangerous to go on. No further.
CORIOLANUS What makes this change?
MENENIUS The matter?
COMINIUS Hath he not passed the noble and the common?   30
BRUTUS Cominius, no.
CORIOLANUS   Have I had children's voices?
FIRST SENATOR Tribunes, give way. He shall to th'market-place.
BRUTUS The people are incensed against him.
SICINIUS   Stop,
Or all will fall in broil.
CORIOLANUS   Are these your herd?

20 home.] F; home. *Exit Lartius / Parker*   20 SD SICINIUS] *Scicinius* F   25 SH, 33 SH, 53 SH SICINIUS] *Scicin.* F   32 SH, 64 SH, 76 SH FIRST SENATOR] *Capell* (1. S.); *Senat.* F   34 herd] F (Heard)

16 To . . . restitution Beyond hope of recovery.
19–20 I . . . fully An ironic foreshadowing of their actual meeting in 4.5 as allies; here, the tribunes, who will arrange that he have such 'cause', enter pat upon his words.
23 prank them dress themselves up.
24 Beyond the endurance of the nobility. Cori-
olanus assumes his class stands with him in finding the tribunes intolerable.
30 passed . . . common been approved by both the nobility and the common people.
34 broil tumult, riot.
34 herd Coriolanus's term for the plebeians at 1.4.32 (and Menenius's at 2.1.77); Parker notes a possible word-play on 'herd'/'heard'.

Must these have voices, that can yield them now   35
And straight disclaim their tongues? What are your offices?
You being their mouths, why rule you not their teeth?
Have you not set them on?

MENENIUS   Be calm, be calm.

CORIOLANUS It is a purposed thing and grows by plot
To curb the will of the nobility.   40
Suffer't, and live with such as cannot rule
Nor ever will be ruled.

BRUTUS   Call't not a plot.
The people cry you mocked them; and of late,
When corn was given them gratis, you repined,
Scandalled the suppliants for the people, called them   45
Time-pleasers, flatterers, foes to nobleness.

CORIOLANUS Why this was known before.

BRUTUS   Not to them all.

CORIOLANUS Have you informed them sithence?

BRUTUS   How? I inform them?

CORIOLANUS You are like to do such business.

BRUTUS Not unlike each way to better yours.   50

CORIOLANUS Why then should I be consul? By yond clouds,
Let me deserve so ill as you, and make me
Your fellow tribune.

SICINIUS   You show too much of that

---

36 tongues] F (toungs)   45 suppliants] F4; Suppliants: F   48 How? . . . them?] F; How! . . . them! *Rowe;* How? . . .
them! *Hibbard;* How, . . . them? *Oxford;* How! . . . them? *Parker*   49 SH] *Theobald;* Com. F

35 **yield them** give their votes.
36 **straight** immediately.
36 **offices** duties.
37–8 **You . . . on** Coriolanus transposes the
body-politic metaphor (in which the tribunes
speak for the people) into one of bear-baiting (in
which the people become the biting dogs).
39 **purposed** prearranged, conspired.
41 **live** you will have to live.
43 **of late** lately.
44 **gratis** free. In Plutarch, Coriolanus's objection to the free distribution of corn occurs later,
some time after he has been refused for the
consulship; Shakespeare makes it a running theme
(see 114–26 and, earlier, 1.1.179–83), part of Coriolanus's principled opposition to making any concessions to the people.
44 **repined** expressed regret, complained.
45 **Scandalled** Slandered.
46 Compare North: 'Martius . . . dyd some-

what sharpely take up those, who went about to
gratifie the people therein: and called them people
pleasers, and traitours to the nobilitie' (Bullough,
Sources, v, 520).
48 **sithence** since.
48 **inform** Brutus reacts to the word as well
as the question: 'inform' could imply furnish-
ing accusatory information against a person (*OED*
Inform *v* 5b).
49 SH F attributes this speech to Cominius and
is not certainly wrong, but Brutus's reply clearly
seems addressed to Coriolanus, and, in abbreviated forms, SHs for Cominius and Coriolanus
could easily be confused (see Textual Analysis,
pp. 301–2 below).
50 Not unlikely, in any case, to do better than
you in any business (regarding the welfare of the
state).
53 **that** i.e. that quality.

For which the people stir. If you will pass
To where you are bound, you must enquire your way,   55
Which you are out of, with a gentler spirit,
Or never be so noble as a consul,
Nor yoke with him for tribune.
MENENIUS   Let's be calm.
COMINIUS The people are abused, set on. This paltering
Becomes not Rome, nor has Coriolanus   60
Deserved this so dishonoured rub, laid falsely
I'th'plain way of his merit.
CORIOLANUS   Tell me of corn!
This was my speech, and I will speak't again –
MENENIUS Not now, not now.
FIRST SENATOR   Not in this heat, sir, now.
CORIOLANUS Now as I live, I will.   65
My nobler friends, I crave their pardons. For
The mutable, rank-scented meinie, let them
Regard me, as I do not flatter, and
Therein behold themselves. I say again,
In soothing them, we nourish 'gainst our senate   70
The cockle of rebellion, insolence, sedition,
Which we ourselves have ploughed for, sowed, and scattered

---

59 abused, set on.] *Rowe subst.;* abus'd: set on, F; abus'd. – Set on; – *Theobald*   63 again –] *Rowe;* againe. F   67
meinie] F (Meynie); Many F4

54 **stir** are aroused.
55 **To . . . bound** (1) To the market-place, (2)
To the consulship.
56 **are out of** have strayed from.
56–7 **gentler . . . noble** Sicinius appropriates
the status terms to play them off against the qualities of character they ought to represent, reminding Coriolanus that birth alone is insufficient qualification for high office.
59 **abused** deceived, misled.
59 **set on** incited; see 37–8 n. F's punctuation
might also be read, with Theobald, as Cominius's
urging that they drop this topic and move on.
59 **paltering** equivocation, trickery.
61 **dishonoured rub** dishonourable impediment or obstacle; on 'dishonoured' = 'dishonourable' see Abbott 375. The metaphor is from
lawn bowling: the tribunes are accused of treach-
erously obstructing the lie of the green (the 'plain
way' (62) of Coriolanus's progress).

66 **For** As for.
67 **mutable** changeable, fickle.
67 **meinie** multitude; usually used of servants and other dependants, hence a disparaging reference to 'the common herd' (*OED* Meinie
5a, b).
67–9 **let . . . themselves** let them heed what
I say, since I do not flatter, and they can see
('regard') themselves as in a mirror.
70 **soothing** placating, flattering.
71 **cockle** weed, tares. North reports that
'he sayed they nourrished against them selves,
the naughty seed and cockle, of insolencie
and sedition, which had bene sowed and scattered abroade emongest the people' (Bullough,
Sources, v, 520). NS thinks Shakespeare was led
by association to the parable of the wheat and
the tares (Matt. 13.24–30), which he uses in 72–3.

By mingling them with us, the honoured number,
Who lack not virtue, no, nor power, but that
Which they have given to beggars.
MENENIUS   Well, no more.   75
FIRST SENATOR No more words, we beseech you.
CORIOLANUS   How? no more?
As for my country I have shed my blood,
Not fearing outward force, so shall my lungs
Coin words till their decay against those measles
Which we disdain should tetter us, yet sought   80
The very way to catch them.
BRUTUS   You speak o'th'people
As if you were a god to punish, not
A man of their infirmity.
SICINIUS   'Twere well
We let the people know't.
MENENIUS   What, what? His choler?
CORIOLANUS Choler!   85
Were I as patient as the midnight sleep,
By Jove, 'twould be my mind.
SICINIUS   It is a mind
That shall remain a poison where it is,
Not poison any further.
CORIOLANUS   'Shall remain'?
Hear you this Triton of the minnows? Mark you   90

---

76 How? . . . more?] F; How! . . . more! *Rowe;* How, . . . more? *Oxford*   85 Choler!] F (Choller?)   89 'Shall remain']
Oxford; Shall remaine F

73 **honoured** honourable (see 61 n.), i.e. patrician.
74 **virtue** Not here the diametric opposite of 'power'; see 2.2.77–9 and n.
79 **measles** disease spots on the body politic (compare 'scabs', 1.1.149). Brockbank notes an additional reference to lepers (Old French *mesels*), which was often extended to include the victims and carriers as well as the disease.
80 **tetter** infect us with tetters or pustular skin eruptions; see *Ham.* 1.5.71–3 for an earlier connection with leprosy.
80 **sought** have sought (by making concessions to the people, establishing the tribunate, and allowing them to confer with us now).
83 **man . . . infirmity** man sharing their

human imperfection; see 2.3.67 and n. Editors have cited various biblical passages as analogues: Heb. 4.15, Acts 14.15, Rom. 6.19.
84 **His choler** What he said merely in anger. Menenius tries to minimise in Coriolanus what in North's Plutarch is a grave failing: 'he was so chollericke and impacient, that he would yeld to no living creature: which made him churlishe, uncivill, and altogether unfit for any mans conversation' (Bullough, *Sources*, v, 506).
86 **patient** calm and unperturbed. Coriolanus maintains that his words were spoken out of political conviction, not transitory emotion.
90 **Triton . . . minnows** Captain of the small fry. Triton was a sea-god who trumpeted Neptune's approach.

      His absolute 'shall'?
COMINIUS   'Twas from the canon.
CORIOLANUS   'Shall'?
      O good but most unwise patricians! Why,
      You grave but reckless senators, have you thus
      Given Hydra here to choose an officer
      That with his peremptory 'shall', being but   95
      The horn and noise o'th'monster's, wants not spirit
      To say he'll turn your current in a ditch
      And make your channel his? If he have power,
      Then vail your ignorance; if none, awake
      Your dangerous lenity. If you are learned,   100
      Be not as common fools; if you are not,
      Let them have cushions by you. You are plebeians,
      If they be senators; and they are no less
      When, both your voices blended, the great'st taste
      Most palates theirs. They choose their magistrate,   105

---

91 'shall' . . . 'Shall'] *Pope;* Shall . . . Shall F   91 canon] F (Cannon)   92 good] *Theobald subst.;* God! F; Gods! *Steevens, conj. Heath*   93 reckless] F (wreaklesse)   94 here] F; leave *Collier²;* heart *Dyce², conj. Leo*   95 'shall'] *Pope;* Shall F   96 noise] F; voice *conj. Kellner*   96 monster's] Monsters F; monster *Capell*   98–102 If he . . . power, / Then . . . ignorance; if none . . . not, / Let . . . by you.] F; If they . . . power, / Let . . . by you: if none . . . not, / Then . . . ignorance. *Hanmer*   99 vail] F (vale); rate *conj. Kellner*   99 ignorance] F; impotence *Collier², conj. Badham, 'Crit.'*   99 awake] F; revoke *Collier²;* abate *conj. Jervis*

---

91 **absolute 'shall'** dogmatic or commanding 'shall'. The grammatical distinction between 'will' (mere futurity) and 'shall' (implying necessity imposed on Coriolanus), so important here, Shakespeare elsewhere usually ignores (see Abbott 316, 317).

91 **from the canon** out of order, exceeding the tribune's authority and hence 'a form of speech to which he has no right' (Johnson). Roman tribunes had no right to make decisions or promulgate laws; they did have the power of veto, which led Mason to believe Cominius's comment a concession to the tribunes' constitutional rights (i.e. 'according to the rule'), but this seems a less persuasive reading.

92 **good** Theobald's emendation is supported by the antitheses 'good'/'unwise' and 'grave'/'reckless'; the exclamatory 'O' might have encouraged a misreading of 'good' as 'god'.

94 **Hydra** Permitted, given leave to.

94 **Hydra** The nine-headed monster, slain by Hercules, which could grow two heads for every one cut off; here, the common people (see 2.3.14, 4.1.1–2).

96 **horn and noise** Hendiadys for 'noisy horn'; see 90 n.

96 **o'th'monster's** of the monster (conflating 'Hydra' (94) with 'Triton' (90)). Double genitives are not uncommon in Shakespeare.

97–8 **turn . . . his** divert your power and seize for himself your channel of authority (shifting the metaphor from Triton's power over water to irrigation on land). On a possible contemporary reference, see pp. 3–4 above.

99 **vail your ignorance** in your folly submit yourselves to him. The senators have yielded power in foolish ignorance of the consequences; Collier's 'impotence' is a possible but not probable manuscript original behind F's 'ignorance'.

99–100 **awake . . . lenity** rouse yourselves from this dangerous mildness and toleration. Compare North's report of Martius's argument against conceding to the people in the first rebellion, over usury: 'the lenity that was favored, was a beginning of disobedience' (Bullough, *Sources*, v, 510).

100 **learned** wise (in the art of government).

102 **cushions** seats with you in the senate.

104–5 **great'st . . . theirs** (1) the plebeians' taste most relishes the popular ingredient of the blend, (2) the blend of voices will always taste more strongly of the people. Elsewhere in Shakespeare 'palate' = 'relish', but not 'savours of'.

And such a one as he, who puts his 'shall',
His popular 'shall', against a graver bench
Than ever frowned in Greece. By Jove himself,
It makes the consuls base, and my soul aches
To know, when two authorities are up,   110
Neither supreme, how soon confusion
May enter 'twixt the gap of both and take
The one by th'other.

COMINIUS   Well, on to th'market-place.

CORIOLANUS Whoever gave that counsel to give forth
The corn o'th'storehouse gratis, as 'twas used   115
Sometime in Greece –

MENENIUS   Well, well, no more of that.

CORIOLANUS Though there the people had more absolute power –
I say they nourished disobedience, fed
The ruin of the state.

BRUTUS   Why shall the people give
One that speaks thus their voice?

CORIOLANUS   I'll give my reasons,   120
More worthier than their voices. They know the corn
Was not our recompense, resting well assured
They ne'er did service for't. Being pressed to th'war,
Even when the navel of the state was touched,
They would not thread the gates. This kind of service   125

106–7 'shall' . . . 'shall'] *Pope;* Shall . . . Shall F   116 Greece–] F3; Greece. F   117 power–] *Hudson;* powre F   119 Why] F; Why, *Capell*   122 our] F; their *Hanmer*

107 popular on behalf of the people.
107–8 graver . . . Greece See 114–19 n.
107 bench deliberative body.
110–13 when . . . th'other A more pointed expansion of North: 'the state whereof as it standeth, is not now as it was wont to be, but becommeth dismembred in two factions, which mainteins allwayes civill dissention and discorde betwene us' (Bullough, *Sources*, v, 520).
110 authorities are up are roused as rivals in authority.
111 confusion chaos.
112–13 take . . . th'other by means of one authority overthrow the other.
114–19 Whoever . . . state The passage is close to North, where Coriolanus complains that 'they that gave counsell, and persuaded that the corne should be geven out to the common people *gratis*, as they used to doe in citties of Græce, where the people had more absolute power: dyd but

only nourishe their disobedience, which would breake out in the ende, to the utter ruine and overthrowe of the whole state' (Bullough, *Sources*, v, 520). In Plutarch it is clear that the corn had been imported, however, while in Shakespeare its source is unclear, leaving us to suppose that it may be the hoarded corn of 1.1.13–17.
115 used practised, customary.
122 recompense reward for services rendered.
123 pressed conscripted, pressed into military service.
124 navel . . . touched vital centre of the state was menaced (bringing back the body-politic imagery).
125 thread pass through. Although the passage in Plutarch is general and condemns the conscripted commoners for often refusing to go to the wars (i.e. 'thread' the gates of Rome), the phrasing here evokes memories of the soldiers who refused to follow Martius through the gates of Corioles.

Did not deserve corn gratis. Being i'th'war,
Their mutinies and revolts, wherein they showed
Most valour, spoke not for them. Th'accusation
Which they have often made against the senate,
All cause unborn, could never be the native   130
Of our so frank donation. Well, what then?
How shall this bosom multiplied digest
The senate's courtesy? Let deeds express
What's like to be their words: 'We did request it;
We are the greater poll, and in true fear   135
They gave us our demands.' Thus we debase
The nature of our seats and make the rabble
Call our cares fears, which will in time
Break ope the locks o'th'senate and bring in
The crows to peck the eagles.

MENENIUS   Come, enough.   140
BRUTUS Enough, with over-measure.
CORIOLANUS   No, take more!
What may be sworn by, both divine and human,
Seal what I end withal! This double worship,
Where one part does disdain with cause, the other
Insult without all reason; where gentry, title, wisdom   145
Cannot conclude but by the yea and no

130 native] F; motive *Collier², conj. Heath*   132 bosom multiplied] F (Bosome-multiplied); bisson multitude *Collier²*
134–6 'We . . . demands.'] *Pope subst.;* We . . . demands. F   135 poll] F (pole)   141 over-measure] F (ouer measure)
144 Where one] *Rowe;* Whereon F

128 **spoke not** did not speak well.
130 **All cause unborn** Without any cause, unjustifiably.
130 **native** origin (*OED* Native *a* 3b, 'original, parent'). Heath's (and Johnson's) conjecture 'motive' is graphically plausible, but although there is no recorded use of 'native' to mean 'origin', it may have been prompted by 'unborn', and Brockbank notes an instance of 'native' meaning 'native land' in Chapman's *Odyssey*, IX, 66.
131 **frank** unsolicited, generous.
132 **bosom multiplied** The many-headed Hydra of 94 also contains multiple bosoms, where 'bosom' is used figuratively as the seat of thoughts and feelings (*OED* Bosom *sb* 6); the verb then, characteristically for Coriolanus, translates this downward into multiple stomachs.
132 **digest** assimilate, understand (with a play on the sense in which the people literally consumed the 'donation' of corn).

133 **deeds** i.e. those actions described in 138–40.
135 **greater poll** majority, greater head-count.
138 **cares** concern, benevolent measures.
140 **crows** Coriolanus puns on (1) carrion birds (see 4.5.40), and (2) crow-bars (to break the 'locks' of 139).
140 **eagles** For crows to peck the primate of birds would be unnatural; the eagle was also the symbol of Roman power and appeared on her battle standard.
141 **over-measure** excess, surplus.
143 **Seal** Confirm.
143 **double worship** divided authority (the 'two authorities' of 110).
145 **Insult** Behave insolently.
145 **without all** beyond any.
146 **conclude** make decisions.

Of general ignorance – it must omit
Real necessities, and give way the while
To unstable slightness. Purpose so barred, it follows
Nothing is done to purpose. Therefore beseech you –   150
You that will be less fearful than discreet,
That love the fundamental part of state
More than you doubt the change on't, that prefer
A noble life before a long, and wish
To jump a body with a dangerous physic   155
That's sure of death without it – at once pluck out
The multitudinous tongue; let them not lick
The sweet which is their poison. Your dishonour
Mangles true judgement and bereaves the state
Of that integrity which should become't,   160
Not having the power to do the good it would
For th'ill which doth control't.
BRUTUS   He's said enough.
SICINIUS He's spoken like a traitor and shall answer
    As traitors do.
CORIOLANUS   Thou wretch, despite o'erwhelm thee!
    What should the people do with these bald tribunes,   165

---

147 ignorance–] *Capell subst.;* Ignorance, F   150 you–] you, F   155 iumpe] F (jumpe); vamp *Pope;* imp *Singer²;* purge *conj. Staunton*   156 it–] F (it:)   162 He's] F (Has); H'as F4   163 He's] F (Ha's); H'as F4   165 tribunes,] Tribunes? F

147 **general** common, popular.
147 **it** i.e. 'This double worship' (143).
147 **omit** neglect.
148 **the while** in the meantime.
149 **unstable slightness** vacillating or irresolute trifling.
149–50 **Purpose . . . purpose** Sound policy being thus thwarted, nothing effective is accomplished.
151 **will . . . discreet** wish to be less cowardly than prudent.
153 **doubt . . . on't** fear the results of any change (to the recent law giving power to the tribunes). The wording is ambiguous, however, and the 'change' referred to may be that law itself, which divided authority instead of keeping it vested solely in the patrician class; Johnson's paraphrase captures this sense: 'you who do not so much fear the danger of violent measures, as wish the good to which they are necessary, the preservation of the original constitution of our government'. Coriolanus is trying to rally the patricians as he did his troops at 1.6.67–75.
155 **To . . . physic** To risk ('jump') treating a body with dangerous medicine.

157 **multitudinous tongue** the tongue of the multitude, i.e. the tribunes (continuing the body-politic allusions); see 'Hydra' and his 'officer' at 94.
157–8 **lick . . . poison** taste the power that will be their undoing (either by corrupting them, or by bringing Rome to ruin because they are unfit to govern).
158 **dishonour** (1) dishonourable concession, (2) present dishonourable state.
160 **integrity** unity, wholeness (with a probable play on the idea of moral soundness).
162 **control** overpower, overmaster.
163 **answer** answer for it, pay the penalty.
164 **despite** contempt, disdain.
165 **bald** Both literally (they are old; see 2.1.11–12) and figuratively; Cotgrave defines *Chauve d'esprit* as 'Bauld spirited: that hath as little wit in as he hath haire on his head'. Possibly, however, it is the early and northern form of *bold* (*OED* Bald); in the glossary added in 1710 to Gavin Douglas's 1553 translation of the *Aeneid*, 'bald' is glossed as 'bold'.

On whom depending, their obedience fails
To th'greater bench? In a rebellion,
When what's not meet but what must be was law,
Then were they chosen. In a better hour
Let what is meet be said it must be meet,   170
And throw their power i'th'dust.

BRUTUS Manifest treason!

SICINIUS This a consul? No.

BRUTUS The aediles, ho!

Enter an AEDILE

Let him be apprehended.

SICINIUS Go call the people,

                                                [Exit Aedile]

[*To Coriolanus*]   in whose name myself   175
Attach thee as a traitorous innovator,
A foe to th'public weal. Obey, I charge thee,
And follow to thine answer.

                    [*Lays hold on Coriolanus*]

CORIOLANUS   Hence, old goat!

ALL PATRICIANS We'll surety him.

COMINIUS   Aged sir, hands off.

CORIOLANUS Hence, rotten thing, or I shall shake thy bones   180
Out of thy garments.

SICINIUS   Help, ye citizens!

Enter a rabble of PLEBEIANS *with the* AEDILES

---

167 bench? . . . rebellion,] *Pope subst.;* Bench, . . . Rebellion: F   174 SD] *Globe; after 173* F   175 SD.1 *Exit Aedile*]
Collier; not in F; *Exit Brutus / Capell*   175 SD.2 *To Coriolanus*] *Oxford; not in* F   178 SD] *Rowe subst.; not in* F   179
SH ALL PATRICIANS] F (*All.*)

167 **greater bench** i.e. the senate; see 107 n.

168 **not meet . . . be** not right but what force and circumstance demanded.

168 **was law** (1) ruled events, (2) was made into law (i.e. the creation of the tribunate).

170 **Let . . . be meet** Let us declare that what is right is what must be done.

174 **aediles** The *Aediles Plebeii* were appointed to assist the tribunes. Here they are acting as the equivalent of Elizabethan constables, and North's phrasing reflects this: the tribunes 'sent their sergeants forthwith to arrest him' (Bullough, *Sources*, V, 521).

176 **Attach** Arrest.

176 **innovator** revolutionary. The only use of this noun in Shakespeare, though elsewhere 'innovation' has negative connotations (e.g. *1H4*

5.1.76–8: 'poor discontents / Which gape and rub the elbow at the news / Of hurlyburly innovation').

177 **weal** welfare and prosperity.

178 **answer** trial (where he will answer charges).

178 **goat** Sicinius may be bearded (Furness cites 2.1.70–2), or he may smell like a goat (Case compares 180).

179 **surety** stand bail for.

181 SD *rabble* disorderly mob. The SD cues the manner of their entrance and suggests that in this scene of confrontation Shakespeare thinks of the people as an undifferentiated political faction manipulated by the tribunes, not the reasonable individuals of earlier scenes.

MENENIUS On both sides more respect.

SICINIUS Here's he that would take from you all your power.

BRUTUS Seize him, aediles!

ALL PLEBEIANS Down with him! Down with him!   185

SECOND SENATOR Weapons, weapons, weapons!

They all bustle about Coriolanus

ALL Tribunes! Patricians! Citizens! What ho!

Sicinius! Brutus! Coriolanus! Citizens!

AEDILES Peace, peace, peace! Stay, hold, peace!

MENENIUS What is about to be? I am out of breath.   190

Confusion's near; I cannot speak. You, tribunes

To th'people! – Coriolanus, patience! –

Speak, good Sicinius.

SICINIUS   Hear me, people. Peace!

ALL PLEBEIANS Let's hear our tribune. Peace! Speak, speak, speak.

SICINIUS You are at point to lose your liberties.   195

Martius would have all from you, Martius,

Whom late you have named for consul.

MENENIUS   Fie, fie, fie!

This is the way to kindle, not to quench.

FIRST SENATOR To unbuild the city and to lay all flat.

SICINIUS What is the city but the people?   200

ALL PLEBEIANS True. The people are the city.

BRUTUS By the consent of all we were established

The people's magistrates.

ALL PLEBEIANS You so remain.

185 SH, 194 SH, 201 SH, 204 SH, 231 SH, 275 SH, 286 SH] F (*All.*)   186 SH] F (2 *Sen.*); *Senators, & c. / Globe; A Senator / Sisson*   186 SD *Coriolanus*] F; *Coriolanus, crying / Globe*   187 SH] *Hibbard; at 189 F; 1. S. / Capell; Senators, & c. / Globe (at 186);* CITIZENS *and* PATRICIANS *Oxford (at 187)*   189 AEDILES Peace] *This edn, conj. 'Textual Companion'; All. Peace* F; CIT. Peace *Malone;* Peace *Globe;* PATRICIANS. Peace *Kittredge;* MENENIUS. Peace *Hibbard;* SOME CITIZENS *and* PATRICIANS Peace *Oxford*   191–2 near; I cannot speak. You, tribunes . . . people!] F *subst.* (neere, . . . people:)*; near – I cannot. – Speak you, tribunes, . . . people. Rann, conj. Mason;* near; I cannot speak. – You, tribunes, Speak . . . people: *Dyce², conj. Tyrwhitt;* near; I cannot speak. You tribunes . . . people, *Oxford*   193 SH, 195 SH, 200 SH, 209 SH, 214 SH] F (*Scici.*)   193 people. Peace!] *Rowe³ subst.;* People peace. F   199 SH, 235 SH FIRST SENATOR] *Capell; Sena.* F

187–9 On F's problematic SHS, see Textual Analysis, p. 301 below. This edition not only moves *All* from 189 to 187, it also adopts Oxford's conjecture that 189 should be assigned to the Aediles, who add to the din even as they try to quiet it.

191 **Confusion** Chaos of civil disorder, anarchy.

191–2 **You . . . people** Rann's comma after 'tribunes' is a not implausible addition; if 'go' or 'speak' is understood, Menenius would be asking the tribunes to try to calm the people.

195 **at point to lose** on the point of losing.

195 **liberties** political rights.

196 **Martius . . . Martius** Sicinius deliberately and insultingly omits the honorific 'Coriolanus' which commemorates the deeds that merited the consulship.

200 In one sense, Sicinius corrects the senator by asserting that the city is its inhabitants, not its buildings; in another, more inflammatory, sense he says that only the plebeians are the people and the city, a claim to which their next line responds.

MENENIUS And so are like to do.   205

COMINIUS That is the way to lay the city flat,
        To bring the roof to the foundation
        And bury all, which yet distinctly ranges,
        In heaps and piles of ruin.

SICINIUS   This deserves death.

BRUTUS Or let us stand to our authority   210
        Or let us lose it. We do here pronounce,
        Upon the part o'th'people, in whose power
        We were elected theirs, Martius is worthy
        Of present death.

SICINIUS   Therefore lay hold of him.
        Bear him to th'rock Tarpeian, and from thence   215
        Into destruction cast him.

BRUTUS   Aediles, seize him.

ALL PLEBEIANS Yield, Martius, yield!

MENENIUS   Hear me one word.
        Beseech you, tribunes, hear me but a word.

AEDILES Peace, peace!

MENENIUS Be that you seem, truly your country's friend,   220
        And temperately proceed to what you would
        Thus violently redress.

BRUTUS   Sir, those cold ways,
        That seem like prudent helps, are very poisonous

---

206 SH] F; *Cor. / Pope*   217 SH ALL PLEBEIANS] F (*All Ple.*)   223 poisonous] F; poisons *Rann, conj. Johnson*

205 **like** likely.
206 SH F's ascription is supported by Cominius's position as consul, concerned with the city's fate, and his role in trying to moderate Coriolanus's rage later (247–52) with the same imagery he here uses to urge restraint on the tribunes; in this role it is natural that he echo and elaborate on Menenius's and First Senator's responses (198–9).
208 **distinctly ranges** stretches out in visible order. Cominius refers literally to Rome's architecture and metaphorically to its hierarchical social order. If Shakespeare read more widely in Livy than the Coriolanus story, he might have come on this phrasing from the story of Furius Camillus, a commonly cited contrast to Coriolanus's response to banishment: the rebuilding of Rome 'seemeth as if it were built at random . . . rather than distinctly ranged, and set in good order' (p. 215).

209 **This** i.e. Coriolanus's proposal to abolish the tribunate.
210 **Or** Either.
210 **stand to** stand up for, uphold; see 4.6.10, 'stood to't'.
214 **present** immediate.
215 **rock Tarpeian** A cliff on the Capitoline Hill over which people convicted of treason were thrown.
220 **that** that which.
223–4 **are . . . violent** Coriolanus's proposal of drastic remedies for the diseased body politic (155–7) is turned against him here. The healthy, well-nourished ideal of the belly fable has become, in the eyes of the tribunes as well as Coriolanus, in need of dangerous medicine, even amputation (300). Johnson's conjecture that F's 'poysonous' is a misreading, probably of manuscript 'poysones' (= poisons), could be correct.

Where the disease is violent. – Lay hands upon him
And bear him to the rock.

Coriolanus draws his sword

CORIOLANUS   No, I'll die here.   225
There's some among you have beheld me fighting;
Come, try upon yourselves what you have seen me.

MENENIUS Down with that sword! Tribunes, withdraw awhile.

BRUTUS Lay hands upon him.

MENENIUS   Help Martius, help!
You that be noble, help him, young and old!   230

ALL PLEBEIANS Down with him! Down with him!

In this mutiny, the Tribunes, the Aediles, and the People are beat in

MENENIUS [*To Coriolanus*] Go, get you to your house. Begone, away!
All will be naught else.

SECOND SENATOR   Get you gone.

CORIOLANUS   Stand fast!
We have as many friends as enemies.

MENENIUS Shall it be put to that?

FIRST SENATOR   The gods forbid!   235
I prithee, noble friend, home to thy house;
Leave us to cure this cause.

MENENIUS   For 'tis a sore upon us
You cannot tent yourself. Begone, beseech you.

COMINIUS Come, sir, along with us.

CORIOLANUS I would they were barbarians, as they are,   240
Though in Rome littered, not Romans, as they are not,
Though calved i'th'porch o'th'Capitol.

MENENIUS   Begone!

---

225 SD] F (*Corio.*)   227 seen me] F; seen me do *Keightley;* seen *conj. Hinman (in 'Textual Companion')*   229 SH MENENIUS] F; *Com.* / *Globe*   231 SD *In . . . in*] F (*Exeunt.* / *at end of 231 and* / *In . . . in.* / *after 231*)   232 SD] *Neilson; not in* F   232 your] *Rowe;* our F   233 SH CORIOLANUS] *Warburton; Com.* F   239 SH] F2; *Corio.* F   240 SH] *Steevens³, conj. Tyrwhitt; Mene.* F   242 SH MENENIUS] *Steevens³, conj. Tyrwhitt; not in* F

227 **seen me** seen me do in battle.

231 SD **beat in** i.e. 'exeunt' off stage to the tiring-house.

232 **your** Rowe's emendation is plausible: confusion of 'our' and 'your' is common in F, and there is no suggestion elsewhere that Menenius and Coriolanus share a house.

233 **naught** ruined, brought to nothing.

233 SH CORIOLANUS Warburton's emendation of F's *Com.* accords with Cominius's generally placatory role in this scene (see 239, 247–52), and there is a good deal of confusion in the *Cor.* /

Com. SHS in the first column of F bb2ᵛ; see Textual Analysis, p. 302 below.

237 **cause** disease.

238 **tent** treat, cure; see 1.9.31 n.

239 SH, 240 SH, 242 SH F's assignment of 239 to *Corio.* is obviously an error, and it probably led to the conflation of 240–4 and their assignment to Menenius; see Textual Analysis, p. 302 below.

241–2 **littered . . . Capitol** Coriolanus characteristically thinks of the people in terms of animals; here, the thought that they might have been 'calved' in the precincts of the Temple of

Put not your worthy rage into your tongue.
One time will owe another.
CORIOLANUS   On fair ground
    I could beat forty of them.
MENENIUS   I could myself   245
    Take up a brace o'th'best of them, yea, the two tribunes.
COMINIUS But now 'tis odds beyond arithmetic,
    And manhood is called foolery when it stands
    Against a falling fabric. Will you hence
    Before the tag return, whose rage doth rend   250
    Like interrupted waters and o'erbear
    What they are used to bear?
MENENIUS   Pray you, begone.
    I'll try whether my old wit be in request
    With those that have but little. This must be patched
    With cloth of any colour.
COMINIUS   Nay, come away.   255
                Exeunt Coriolanus and Cominius [and others]
A PATRICIAN This man has marred his fortune.
MENENIUS His nature is too noble for the world.
    He would not flatter Neptune for his trident
    Or Jove for's power to thunder. His heart's his mouth.

---

246 best of them] F; best *Capell*   255 SD *Cominius and others*] *Capell; Cominius.* F   256 SH] F *(Patri.); 1. P / Capell*

Jupiter (see 1.1.36 n.) introduces a hint of sacrilege. Coriolanus denies any kinship with the plebeians: even if technically they were born in Rome, they are more like foreigner barbarians.

243 worthy Both 'justifiable' and 'noble'.

244 One . . . another Another time will compensate for this setback.

245 forty An indefinite but large number.

246 Take . . . brace Take on a couple. Trying to defuse Coriolanus's desire for immediate retaliation, Menenius humorously reduces the number of opponents he could cope with and also prompts Cominius's remark on the tactical folly of violent confrontation now.

247 arithmetic calculation.

248 manhood manliness, courage.

248 foolery folly, foolhardiness; compare 1.4.47.

248–9 stands . . . fabric stands its ground in the face of a falling building.

250 tag rabble, rag-tag. The image is picked up in Menenius's 'patched / With cloth of any colour', since a 'tag' was literally a hanging, ragged or torn piece of cloth (*OED* Tag *sb* 1).

250–2 rend . . . bear break and overwhelm, like turbulent waters, the banks that usually contain them.

253 whether Colloquially contracted to 'wh'er' (Abbott 466).

253 in request welcome, in demand.

255 SD *and others* Capell's addition indicates the presumed exit here of Titus Lartius, the senators and most of the 'gentry' (although Parker takes Lartius off at 20); see 1.9.74–5 n. and Textual Analysis, p. 303 below.

257 too . . . world An ambivalent assessment indicating both admiration and exasperation that Coriolanus refuses to recognise the political reality that power is gained by conciliation and flattery.

259 His . . . mouth What he feels is exactly what he says. Menenius may allude in his appeal to proverbs familiar to the people, such as 'What the heart thinks the tongue speaks' (Tilley H334; see also Whiting H274, H288); compare Ecclus. 21.26, 'The heart of fooles is in their mouth: but the mouth of the wise is in their heart.'

What his breast forges, that his tongue must vent,   260
And, being angry, does forget that ever
He heard the name of death.
                    A noise within
Here's goodly work.
A PATRICIAN   I would they were abed.
MENENIUS I would they were in Tiber! What the vengeance,
        Could he not speak 'em fair?

                    Enter BRUTUS *and* SICINIUS *with the* RABBLE *again*

SICINIUS   Where is this viper   265
        That would depopulate the city and
        Be every man himself?
MENENIUS   You worthy tribunes –
SICINIUS He shall be thrown down the Tarpeian rock
        With rigorous hands. He hath resisted law,
        And therefore law shall scorn him further trial   270
        Than the severity of the public power
        Which he so sets at naught.
FIRST CITIZEN   He shall well know
        The noble tribunes are the people's mouths,
        And we their hands.
ALL PLEBEIANS He shall, sure on't.   275
MENENIUS Sir, sir –
SICINIUS Peace!
MENENIUS Do not cry havoc where you should but hunt

---

263 SH] F (*Patri.*); 1. P. / *Capell*; 2. *Pat. / Malone*   267 himself?] *Rowe*; himself F   267 tribunes –] *Rowe*; Tribunes.
F   275 sure on't] F (ont); sure out F2; be sure on't *Theobald*   276 sir –] *Pope*; sir. F

260 **vent** utter.
264 **What the vengeance** A phrase used to
strengthen interrogations (*OED* Vengeance *sb* 3),
comparable to the modern 'What the hell!'
265 **speak 'em fair** talk courteously to them.
265 **viper** Vipers were believed to eat their way
at birth through their mother's bowels (Pliny,
Nat. Hist., x, 82), hence they became a symbol of treachery; compare 292 and Volumnia's
accusation that in attacking Rome Coriolanus will
'tread . . . on thy mother's womb' (5.3.123–4).
Given the context, Shakespeare may have had
in mind the less common association of 'viper'
with misanthropy (*OED* Viper *sb* 2 *fig.*), perhaps
remembered from Plutarch's use of it in connection with Timon of Athens.

266–7 **depopulate . . . himself** An extreme
assessment of Coriolanus's proud self-sufficiency
and refusal to accept the plebeians as fellow citizens of Rome; on the contemporary urgency of
'depopulate', see pp. 17–18 above.
269 **rigorous** harsh and severe.
273 **noble tribunes** Brockbank notes how the
phrase reverses the earlier class-appropriation of
'noble' (24), and Parker observes that First Senator later uses the same phrase (331).
275 **sure on't** be sure of it, make no mistake.
278 **cry havoc** An army leader's signal for
the seizure of spoil, and so of general slaughter
and plunder. Hibbard notes the ironic inversion
of 1.1.181–3, where Martius saw himself as the
hunter and the plebeians as his 'quarry'.

With modest warrant.
SICINIUS   Sir, how comes't that you
   Have holp to make this rescue?
MENENIUS   Hear me speak.   280
   As I do know the consul's worthiness,
   So can I name his faults.
SICINIUS Consul? What consul?
MENENIUS The consul Coriolanus.
BRUTUS He consul!   285
ALL PLEBEIANS No, no, no, no, no!
MENENIUS If, by the tribunes' leave and yours, good people,
   I may be heard, I would crave a word or two,
   The which shall turn you to no further harm
   Than so much loss of time.
SICINIUS   Speak briefly, then,   290
   For we are peremptory to dispatch
   This viperous traitor. To eject him hence
   Were but one danger, and to keep him here
   Our certain death. Therefore it is decreed
   He dies tonight.
MENENIUS   Now the good gods forbid   295
   That our renownèd Rome, whose gratitude
   Towards her deservèd children is enrolled
   In Jove's own book, like an unnatural dam
   Should now eat up her own!

---

279 comes't] F (com'st)   280 speak.] *Hibbard*; speake? F   293 one] F; our *Theobald*

279 **modest warrant** limited or restricted licence (to kill).
280 **holp** helped (abbreviated from 'holpen'; see Abbott 343).
280 **rescue** Sicinius means the technical sense: the forcible taking of a person or goods out of legal custody (*OED* Rescue *sb* 2); his question suggests that he still thinks Menenius a friend to the people.
289 **turn you to** bring about for you (*OED* Turn *v* 43b).
291 **peremptory** resolved. A Roman legal term meaning 'finally decided' (*OED* Peremptory 1); see 294, 'it is decreed'.
292–4 **To . . . death** To banish him would create only one danger (i.e. alienating his friends and the patricians generally), while allowing him to stay would be fatal to us. F's 'one' restricts the danger attendant on banishment and makes it

the logical choice; orthographically, a misreading is possible, but while Theobald's 'our' provides a parallelism between 'our danger' and 'our . . . death', it weakens the force of the contrast.
297 **deservèd** deserving.
298 **Jove's . . . book** Gordon suggests 'the rolls and registers of the Capitol, which was Jove's temple', citing *JC* 3.2.37–8 ('The question of his death is enrolled in the Capitol'). Less likely, but possible, are suggestions that it is a Roman counterpart to biblical statements that the names of the faithful are written in the book of life (Phil. 4.3, Rev. 21.27, Mal. 3.16, Exod. 32.32).
298–9 **unnatural . . . own** A striking contribution to the play's cannibalism imagery (see 1.1.69–70 n.) which also reverses the positive story of the nurturing she-wolf who, in Roman mythology, suckled the founders of the city; see also 5.3.184–6.

SICINIUS He's a disease that must be cut away.   300
MENENIUS O, he's a limb that has but a disease –
    Mortal to cut it off, to cure it easy.
    What has he done to Rome that's worthy death?
    Killing our enemies, the blood he hath lost –
    Which I dare vouch is more than that he hath   305
    By many an ounce – he dropped it for his country;
    And what is left, to lose it by his country
    Were to us all that do't and suffer it
    A brand to th'end o'th'world.
SICINIUS   This is clean kam.
BRUTUS Merely awry. When he did love his country,   310
    It honoured him.
SICINIUS   The service of the foot,
    Being once gangrened, is not then respected
    For what before it was.
BRUTUS   We'll hear no more.
    Pursue him to his house and pluck him thence,
    Lest his infection, being of catching nature,   315
    Spread further.
MENENIUS   One word more, one word!
    This tiger-footed rage, when it shall find
    The harm of unscanned swiftness, will, too late,
    Tie leaden pounds to's heels. Proceed by process,

---

301 disease –] F3 (disease,); Disease F   304 enemies,] F; enemies? *Hanmer*   304–6 lost – . . . ounce –] F (lost (. . . Ounce))   311 SH] *Hanmer* (*Warburton*); *Menen.* F; *continues* BRUTUS *conj. Lettsom* (*in Dyce²*)   312–13 is . . . was.] F; is't . . . was? *Steevens², conj. Theobald* (*retaining* F SH MENENIUS)   313 SH] F; *Sic.* / *conj. Lettsom* (*in Dyce²*)

300 The tribunes here powerfully combine imagery of the body politic and of disease to argue for Coriolanus's exile.

302 Mortal Fatal.

307 by at the hands of.

309 brand mark of dishonour.

309 clean kam absolutely beside the point, twisted. 'Kam' or 'cam' is a borrowing from Welsh meaning 'crooked, awry' (*OED* Cam *adj*).

310 Merely Completely.

311 SH H. Eardley-Wilmot persuasively defends Warburton's suggested reassignment to Sicinius on the grounds that the metaphor is out of character for Menenius (*TLS*, 13 October 1950, p. 645); NS elaborates on the appropriateness to Sicinius of specifiying the disease as gangrene, whereas this would be a tactical error for Menenius. Editors who follow F usually alter the final punctuation to '?' or '–' to make it more plausible for Menenius.

315 of . . . nature Gangrene is not an infectious disease, but it does spread within the affected body; the tribunes are still talking in terms of the body politic.

317 tiger-footed Case cites instances of the tiger's renowned swiftness, including Holland's Pliny, VIII, 18, and thinks Shakespeare here may be recollecting Pliny's 'for very anger she rageth on the shore and sands'.

318 unscanned unconsidered.

319 to's to its (i.e. the headlong rage will hobble itself, too late, when it realises the damage it has done).

319 process due process of law; see 330, 'lawful form'.

Lest parties – as he is beloved – break out   320
And sack great Rome with Romans.
BRUTUS   If it were so –
SICINIUS What do ye talk?
Have we not had a taste of his obedience?
Our aediles smote, ourselves resisted? Come.
MENENIUS Consider this: he has been bred i'th'wars   325
Since 'a could draw a sword, and is ill-schooled
In bolted language; meal and bran together
He throws without distinction. Give me leave,
I'll go to him and undertake to bring him
Where he shall answer by a lawful form,   330
In peace, to his utmost peril.
FIRST SENATOR   Noble tribunes,
It is the humane way. The other course
Will prove too bloody, and the end of it
Unknown to the beginning.
SICINIUS   Noble Menenius,
Be you then as the people's officer.   335
[*To the Plebeians*]
Masters, lay down your weapons.
BRUTUS   Go not home.
SICINIUS Meet on the market-place. [*To Menenius*] We'll attend you
        there,
Where, if you bring not Martius, we'll proceed
In our first way.
MENENIUS   I'll bring him to you.
[*To the Senators*] Let me desire your company. He must
        come,   340

---

320 parties – . . . beloved –] F (parties (. . . belou'd))   321 so –] F3; so? F   326 'a] F (a)   329–31 go . . . bring
him . . . form, / In peace] *Pope;* go . . . bring him in peace . . . Forme / (In peace) F; go . . . bring him / In peace . . .
Form *Keightley;* go . . . bring him in . . . Forme / (In peace) *Gomme*   335 SD] *This edn, after Oxford; not in* F   337
SD] *Oxford; not in* F   340 SD] *Hanmer; not in* F

320 **parties** factions.
322 **What** Why (*OED* What *adv* 19).
327 **bolted** sifted, refined (anticipating 'meal'
and 'bran'); see 1.1.129 n.
327 **meal and bran** flour and husks.
329 **bring him** F's 'bring him in peace' may
be the compositor's anticipation of 331, but the
duplication could be Shakespeare's, with 331 (in
parentheses in F) intended for emphasis. Proudfoot suggests retaining 'in peace' in 329 but omitting 'go'.

330–1 **answer . . . peril** meet the charges
against him and calmly accept his sentence, no
matter how severe.
332 **humane** properly human (not distinguished from 'human' in spelling or pronunciation in Shakespeare's time); compare 1.1.15,
'humanely'.
337 **attend** await.

> Or what is worst will follow.

FIRST SENATOR   Pray you, let's to him.

> *Exeunt* [*Tribunes and Plebeians at one door, Patricians at another*]

3.[2] *Enter* CORIOLANUS *with* NOBLES

CORIOLANUS Let them pull all about mine ears, present me
    Death on the wheel or at wild horses' heels,
    Or pile ten hills on the Tarpeian rock,
    That the precipitation might down stretch
    Below the beam of sight, yet will I still   5
    Be thus to them.

Enter VOLUMNIA

A NOBLE You do the nobler.

CORIOLANUS I muse my mother
    Does not approve me further, who was wont
    To call them woollen vassals, things created   10
    To buy and sell with groats, to show bare heads
    In congregations, to yawn, be still, and wonder
    When one but of my ordinance stood up
    To speak of peace or war. [*To Volumnia*] I talk of you.
    Why did you wish me milder? Would you have me   15

---

341 SH] *Rowe* (1 *S.*)*; Sena.* F   341 SD] *This edn, after Oxford; Exeunt Omnes* F   Act 3, Scene 2   3.2] *Capell; not in* F   6 SD] F*; after 14* war. *Collier²*   7 SH A NOBLE] F (*Noble*)*.; Pat.* / *Capell;* 1 *Pat.* / *Malone*   11–12 heads . . . congregations,] F*;* heads, . . . congregations *Schmidt*   14 SD] *Johnson, after Hanmer; not in* F

Act 3, Scene 2
The house of Coriolanus. This scene, so crucial in understanding Shakespeare's *Coriolanus* as well as his relation with Volumnia, has no basis in Plutarch.

  0 SD NOBLES While he generally uses the term interchangeably with 'Patricians', Shakespeare may here have had in mind the 'young nobility' who Plutarch says favoured Coriolanus's hard line with the plebeians (see 7), as opposed to the older, more moderate, senators who enter with Menenius at 25.

  1 pull . . . ears As at 1.1.201–2, Coriolanus declares the physical collapse of Rome to be insufficient motive to alter his manner or convictions.

  2 Death . . . heels Death as the result of being tied to a wheel and having one's bones systematically broken by the executioner or being tied by the limbs to wild horses, who were then released to run in different directions. Malone notes that

both were Renaissance, not Roman, forms of execution.

  4 precipitation steepness of descent, precipitousness (*OED* Precipitation *sb* 1b, where this is the only early example).

  5 Below . . . sight Farther than the eye can see.

  6 SD Some editors move Volumnia's entrance to 14, where Coriolanus addresses her directly, but F is more theatrically effective.

  8 muse wonder.

  9 further to a greater degree.

  10 woollen vassals slaves wearing coarse woollen clothing; see 2.3.101 n.

  11 groats English fourpenny coins (i.e. the people are born to be nothing more than petty traders).

  11 show bare heads demonstrate their subservience by removing their caps.

  12 congregations assemblies.

  13 ordinance rank.

False to my nature? Rather say I play
The man I am.
VOLUMNIA   O, sir, sir, sir,
I would have had you put your power well on
Before you had worn it out.
CORIOLANUS   Let go.
VOLUMNIA You might have been enough the man you are   20
With striving less to be so. Lesser had been
The checkings of your dispositions, if
You had not showed them how ye were disposed
Ere they lacked power to cross you.
CORIOLANUS   Let them hang!
VOLUMNIA Ay, and burn too.   25

Enter MENENIUS *with the* SENATORS

MENENIUS Come, come, you have been too rough, something too rough.
You must return and mend it.
A SENATOR   There's no remedy,
Unless, by not so doing, our good city
Cleave in the midst and perish.
VOLUMNIA   Pray be counselled.
I have a heart as little apt as yours,   30
But yet a brain that leads my use of anger

19 Let] F; Lets F3; Let it *Theobald;* Let 't *Parker, conj. NS*   22 checkings] *This edn;* things F; things that thwart *Rowe;* thwartings *Theobald;* things that cross *conj. Clarendon;* taxings *Sisson;* crossings *Hibbard;* tryings *Parker*   25 SH VOLUMNIA] F; *A Patrician / Globe*   25 Ay,] F (I,); [*Aside.*] Ay, *conj. Clarendon*   27 SH] F (*Sen.*); 1. S. / *Capell*   30 as little apt] F; as little soft *conj. Singer, 'SV';* of mettle apt *conj. Staunton;* as tickle-apt *Hudson², conj. Daniel*

16–17 play . . . am With this ambiguous claim, Coriolanus initiates the acting imagery that dominates this scene; see pp. 45–6 above.

19 Let go Have done. Parker (on NS's conjecture) reads 'Let 't go' (i.e. 'Never mind!'), which does accord with Coriolanus's attitude toward the 'power' she urges him to seek.

22 checkings i.e. by the people's will. F's almost certainly erroneous 'things' has been variously emended. 'Checkings' (where manuscript 'chekings' or 'chekyng(e)s' has been misread as 'things') is plausible graphically and, as a coinage from 'check', fits in both the sense of 'check-mating' and the more general sense of 'arrest given to an onward course by some obstruction or opposition; rebuff' (*OED* Check *sb* 5a); it also aurally anticipates 24, 'cross' (compare 'check . . . courage', 3.3.99). In *Foure Paradoxes, or politique Discourses*, 1604, Dudley Digges uses

'check' and 'cheques' for the reprimand due to bad military officers (A4ʳ); Shakespeare may have read this book (see p. 13 above), although the word is not unusual in his own work: 'check' (26 times), 'checked' (9), 'checking' (1), 'checks' (7). Quite possibly it should be 'checking', since one of the commonest printing mistakes is the addition or omission of final *s*.

24 Ere . . . you Before they had lost the ability to prevent you from becoming consul.

25 Volumnia shares her son's contempt for the plebeians but also strategically establishes a common ground to which she can appeal (30–2); her words ironically anticipate her son's later threat literally to burn Rome.

30 apt yielding, willing.

31–2 leads . . . vantage leads me to make more productive use of my anger.

         To better vantage.
MENENIUS   Well said, noble woman!
         Before he should thus stoop to th'herd, but that
         The violent fit o'th'time craves it as physic
         For the whole state, I would put mine armour on,   35
         Which I can scarcely bear.
CORIOLANUS   What must I do?
MENENIUS Return to th'tribunes.
CORIOLANUS   Well, what then? What then?
MENENIUS Repent what you have spoke.
CORIOLANUS For them? I cannot do it to the gods;
         Must I then do't to them?
VOLUMNIA   You are too absolute,   40
         Though therein you can never be too noble,
         But when extremities speak. I have heard you say
         Honour and policy, like unsevered friends,
         I'th'war do grow together. Grant that, and tell me
         In peace what each of them by th'other lose   45
         That they combine not there?
CORIOLANUS   Tush, tush!
MENENIUS   A good demand.
VOLUMNIA If it be honour in your wars to seem
         The same you are not, which for your best ends
         You adopt your policy, how is it less or worse
         That it shall hold companionship in peace   50
         With honour as in war, since that to both
         It stands in like request?
CORIOLANUS   Why force you this?

---

33 herd] *Theobald;* heart F   39 them?] F3; them, F   41–2 noble, . . . speak.] F; noble . . . speak, *Hibbard, after Keightley*

33 herd F's 'heart' is probably a misreading of 'heard' (F's usual spelling of 'herd') influenced by the compositor's having just set 'heart' at 30.

33 but were it not, except.

34 fit (1) fever (see *JC* 1.3.119–20); possibly (2) frenzy (see *Tit.* 4.1.17).

40 absolute inflexible, uncompromising.

41–2 Though . . . speak Given her prior teachings, Volumnia finds herself in an awkward argumentative position, reflected in the fact that the 'Though' and 'But' clauses cancel each other out. Hibbard tries to minimise the contradiction by substituting a full stop after 'noble' and a comma after 'speak'.

42 extremities speak crisis conditions demand.

43 policy stratagems.

43 unsevered inseparable. We have not, however, heard Coriolanus claim (or seen him practise) the union of honour and policy in war.

46 there i.e. in peacetime.

51–2 since . . . request since in both peace and war policy is equally needed.

52 force urge, enforce; possibly also implying that she is straining and distorting the opinion she attributes to him.

VOLUMNIA Because that now it lies you on to speak
         To th'people, not by your own instruction,
         Nor by th'matter which your heart prompts you,   55
         But with such words that are but roted in
         Your tongue, though bastards and syllables
         Of no allowance to your bosom's truth.
         Now, this no more dishonours you at all
         Than to take in a town with gentle words,   60
         Which else would put you to your fortune and
         The hazard of much blood.
         I would dissemble with my nature where
         My fortunes and my friends at stake required
         I should do so in honour. I am in this   65
         Your wife, your son, these senators, the nobles;
         And you will rather show our general louts
         How you can frown, than spend a fawn upon 'em
         For the inheritance of their loves and safeguard
         Of what that want might ruin.
MENENIUS   Noble lady!   70
         [*To Coriolanus*] Come, go with us; speak fair. You may salve
            so,
         Not what is dangerous present, but the loss

---

53 Because that now . . . you on] F; Because . . . on you *Pope*   55 you] F; you to F2   56 roted] F (roated); rooted *Johnson*   57 tongue, though bastards and syllables] *Johnson;* Tongue; Though but Bastards and Syllables F; tongue; bastards and syllables *Pope;* tongue, but bastards, *Capell;* tongue, but bastards and syllables *Steevens;* tongue, thought's bastards, and but syllables *conj. Badham, 'Text'*   58 allowance] F; alliance *Capell, conj. Thirlby*   66 son, these . . . nobles;] *Theobald (Warburton);* Sonne: These . . . Nobles, F   70 lady!] *Rowe;* Lady, F   71 SD] *Oxford; not in* F

53–8 F's lineation is more than usually irregular in this passage, in part because Compositor B was spreading verse lines to fill out the bottom of the second column of bb3, but none of the proposed relinings is fully satisfactory.
   53 lies you on is incumbent on you.
   54 instruction convictions, beliefs.
   56–7 roted . . . tongue i.e. memorised and repeated mechanically ('roted' coined from 'by rote', an idiom found elsewhere in Shakespeare).
   57–8 bastards . . . truth illegitimate words that do not correspond to what you feel. Johnson persuasively argued that F's extrametrical 'but' was mistakenly picked up from the two instances in the preceding line.
   60 take in capture.
   61 put . . . fortune force you to take your chance (in battle).

63–5 where . . . honour if my fortunes and my friends were at risk and I therefore felt honour required it.
   65 I am . . . this In this I speak for, represent. Johnson's comma after 'this', which lays the stress on 'I', invites the meaning 'I am involved in this, and so is your wife . . .', but F's punctuation effectively emphasises Volumnia's dominance in this confrontation and her role as spokeswoman for the patricians.
   67 general louts common, vulgar bumpkins.
   69 inheritance acquisition, obtaining.
   69–70 safeguard . . . ruin protection of what might be lost for lack of their loves.
   71 salve heal, remedy.
   72 Not . . . but Not only . . . but also.

Of what is past.

VOLUMNIA   I prithee now, my son,
Go to them, with this bonnet in thy hand,
And thus far having stretched it – here be with them –   75
Thy knee bussing the stones – for in such business
Action is eloquence, and the eyes of th'ignorant
More learnèd than the ears – waving thy head,
With often thus correcting thy stout heart,
Now humble as the ripest mulberry   80
That will not hold the handling; or say to them
Thou art their soldier and, being bred in broils,
Hast not the soft way which, thou dost confess,
Were fit for thee to use, as they to claim,
In asking their good loves; but thou wilt frame   85
Thyself, forsooth, hereafter theirs so far

---

75 it – . . . them –] F (it (. . . them))   76–8 stones – . . . ears –] F (stones: . . . eares,)   79 With] *Steevens, conj.*
Johnson; Which F; And *Capell;* While *conj. Staunton*   79 often] F; soften *Hanmer, conj. Warburton;* offer *Parker, conj.*
'Textual Companion'   80 Now] F; Now's *Collier²;* Bow *Hudson, conj. Mason*   81 or say] F; say *Hanmer;* so say *conj.*
Kinnear (in Cam.)

73 what is past i.e. the consulship.

74 bonnet cap or hat. Volumnia presumably takes her son's hat from him to demonstrate the elaborate stage business she goes on to describe; there may be a theatrical pun in 'business' (76), though the earliest example in the *OED* for its meaning stage activity as opposed to dialogue is 1671. A 'bonnet' was not an item of Roman clothing, but Shakespeare's Roman conspirators pluck their hats about their ears in *JC* 2.1.73.

75 stretched it extended it in a gesture of obeisance.

75 here . . . them go along with them in this way, do what they expect.

76 bussing kissing; with perhaps in 'business' an 'ironic overtone of a nonce abstract formed from "buss"' (King). In *Tro.*, 4.5.220, 'buss' is associated with vulgar wantonness.

77–8 Action . . . ears Case cites Francis Bacon's 'Of Boldnesse' on the importance of gesture to oratory: 'Question was asked of Demosthenes, What was the Chiefe Part of an Oratour? He answered, Action; what next again? Action . . . the reason is plaine. There is in Humane Nature, generally, more of the Foole then of the Wise' (*Essays*, 1625, no. 12).

78 waving bowing up and down; perhaps 'bowing on all sides'.

79 With often thus Johnson's 'With' posits a plausible misreading of manuscript abbrevia-

tion 'W^th' as 'W^ch' to produce F's 'Which'; 'thus' refers either to the remorseful waving of the head or to another action, perhaps with the hands, that she demonstrates at this point. *Textual Companion* suggests that 'often' is a misreading of manuscript 'offer'.

79 stout proud; compare North's marginal note: 'Coriolanus stowtnes in defence of him selfe' (Bullough, *Sources*, V, 522).

80 humble yielding. For the ripe mulberry as an emblem of a disposition to yield, Case cites Erasmus's *Adagia*, Chil. IV, Cent. VII, Prov. 11 (indexed under 'Proclivitas'), 'Maturior Moro' ('Riper than the mulberry'). Possibly, 'humble' should be read as a verb, i.e. 'make yourself as humble as' (*OED* Humble *v¹* 3b).

81 hold withstand, bear (the very ripe mulberry is so soft it is crushed when picked).

81 or or again. Volumnia is not setting up an alternative mode of appealing to the people; she goes on to suggest apologetic words to accompany and reinforce the gestures.

82–5 Thou . . . loves Compare 3.1.325–8 and 3.3.58–61, where Menenius uses this argument with the tribunes.

82 broils battles, tumults.

86 theirs to suit their wishes; perhaps with the sense of 'their agent' (in peacetime, as 'their soldier' (82) in war).

As thou hast power and person.

MENENIUS   This but done,
Even as she speaks, why, their hearts were yours,
For they have pardons, being asked, as free
As words to little purpose.

VOLUMNIA   Prithee now,   90
Go, and be ruled, although I know thou hadst rather
Follow thine enemy in a fiery gulf
Than flatter him in a bower.

                        Enter COMINIUS

                             Here is Cominius.
COMINIUS I have been i'th'market-place; and, sir, 'tis fit
You make strong party, or defend yourself   95
By calmness or by absence. All's in anger.
MENENIUS Only fair speech.
COMINIUS   I think 'twill serve, if he
Can thereto frame his spirit.
VOLUMNIA   He must, and will.
Prithee now, say you will, and go about it.
CORIOLANUS Must I go show them my unbarbed sconce? Must I   100
With my base tongue give to my noble heart
A lie that it must bear? Well, I will do't.
Yet were there but this single plot to lose,

100–1 Must I / With my . . . give to . . . heart] F; Must my . . . give to . . . heart *Pope;* Must I with . . . give . . . heart
Globe, conj. Keightley, 'SE'; With my . . . give to . . . heart *NS*   101 noble heart] F; heart *Hudson²*   102 bear? Well,]
Pope; beare well? F   103 plot to lose,] *Theobald;* Plot, to loose F

87 **power and person** ability and personal
authority.

89 **free** (1) generous, readily given (modifying 'pardons'), (2) overfree, gratuitous (modifying
'words').

90–1 **Prithee . . . ruled** Parker notes how the
contradiction between plea and command here is
comically reversed at 98–9.

92 **fiery gulf** abyss full of flame (*OED* Gulf *sb*
4, citing this passage); possibly, however, 'gulf'
has its usual meaning in Shakespeare, 'whirlpool'
(see 1.1.81 n.).

93 **bower** (1) arbour, (2) lady's private chamber. Either would offer the desired sharp contrast
with 'fiery gulf', though (2) would be particularly
apt for Coriolanus.

95 **make strong party** go with a strong party
of supporters.

98 **frame** adjust, accommodate.

100 **unbarbed sconce** (1) uncovered head
(demonstrating respect), (2) unhelmeted,
unarmed (elsewhere in Shakespeare 'barbed'
refers to the armour of warhorses). The military
overtones convey his sense of debasement.

101 **noble** patrician and honourable. For
Coriolanus the social and moral evaluations still
coincide.

102 **Well . . . do't** The abrupt switch from
resistance to obedience here recalls his soliloquy
when canvassing for votes (2.3.107–10).

103 **plot** piece of earth or property, i.e. his body
(fashioned from 'dust', 104).

This mould of Martius, they to dust should grind it
And throw't against the wind. To th'market-place!   105
You have put me now to such a part which never
I shall discharge to th'life.
COMINIUS   Come, come, we'll prompt you.
VOLUMNIA I prithee now, sweet son, as thou hast said
My praises made thee first a soldier, so,
To have my praise for this, perform a part   110
Thou hast not done before.
CORIOLANUS   Well, I must do't.
Away, my disposition, and possess me
Some harlot's spirit! My throat of war be turned,
Which choired with my drum, into a pipe
Small as an eunuch or the virgin voice   115
That babies lull asleep! The smiles of knaves
Tent in my cheeks, and schoolboys' tears take up
The glasses of my sight! A beggar's tongue
Make motion through my lips, and my armed knees,
Who bowed but in my stirrup, bend like his   120
That hath received an alms! I will not do't,
Lest I surcease to honour mine own truth
And by my body's action teach my mind
A most inherent baseness.
VOLUMNIA   At thy choice, then.
To beg of thee, it is my more dishonour   125
Than thou of them. Come all to ruin. Let
Thy mother rather feel thy pride than fear

---

113 turned] F (turn'd); tun'd *conj. 'Textual Companion'*   114 choired] F (quier'd)   114 drum, . . . pipe] *Pope;*
Drumme . . . Pipe, F   115 eunuch] F; eunuch's *Hanmer*   116 lull] F; lulls *Rowe*

104 mould (1) earth regarded as the material of the human body (*OED* Mould *sb¹* 4), (2) form.
107 discharge . . . life perform convincingly.
113 harlot's (1) beggar's, (2) prostitute's, (3) actor's (compare 'harlotry players', *1H4* 2.4.395–6).
113 turned Oxford's 'tuned' is possible but unnecessary and loses the sense of forced conversion of one thing into its opposite.
114 choired sang in harmony.
115 Small High in pitch and soft.
116 lull The plural object, 'babies', here governs the verb.
117 Two metaphors drawn from siege warfare: 'encamp' ('Tent') and 'capture, occupy' ('take up').

118 glasses . . . sight eyeballs.
121 alms charity (with a probable play on 'armed', 119).
122 surcease cease.
124 inherent permanently indwelling (*OED* Inherent *a* 2, citing this instance); a word with particular philosophic applications (see p. 45 above, n. 2), not used elsewhere by Shakespeare.
127–8 feel . . . stoutness experience the consequences of your pride rather than fear to confront your dangerous obstinacy. The implication that his failure to yield will result in her death reappears in her threat of suicide at 5.3.118–25.

Thy dangerous stoutness, for I mock at death
With as big heart as thou. Do as thou list.
Thy valiantness was mine, thou suck'st it from me,   130
But owe thy pride thyself.

CORIOLANUS   Pray be content.
Mother, I am going to the market-place.
Chide me no more. I'll mountebank their loves,
Cog their hearts from them, and come home beloved
Of all the trades in Rome. Look, I am going.   135
Commend me to my wife. I'll return consul,
Or never trust to what my tongue can do
I'th'way of flattery further.

VOLUMNIA   Do your will.   *Exit*

COMINIUS Away! The tribunes do attend you. Arm yourself
To answer mildly, for they are prepared   140
With accusations, as I hear, more strong
Than are upon you yet.

CORIOLANUS The word is 'mildly'. Pray you, let us go.
Let them accuse me by invention, I
Will answer in mine honour.

MENENIUS   Ay, but mildly.   145

CORIOLANUS Well, mildly be it then, 'mildly'.

                                        Exeunt

3.[3] *Enter* SICINIUS *and* BRUTUS

BRUTUS In this point charge him home, that he affects
Tyrannical power. If he evade us there,

130 suck'st] F; suck'dst *Rowe³*   138 SD] F (*Exit Volumnia*)   143 'mildly'] *Hanmer;* Mildely F   146 'mildly'] *This edn;* Mildely F   **Act 3, Scene 3**   3.3] *Capell; not in* F

129 big heart noble courage.
129 list please.
131 owe (1) own, (2) be indebted for. Volumnia separates out her son's qualities, claiming his heroism as her legacy and disowning his obstinate pride.
133 mountebank win over with a performance (like that of a quack medicine salesman); earliest instance of the verb in *OED*.
134 Cog Wheedle, swindle.
143 word password.
144 accuse . . . invention bring trumped-up charges against me.

Act 3, Scene 3
The market-place. In Plutarch, the proceedings against Coriolanus are spread over several days, and some take place in the senate house; Shakespeare compresses the sequence of events and places them all in the public sphere.
1 In On.
1 charge . . . home press your accusations against him to the limit.
1 affects aims at.

Enforce him with his envy to the people,
And that the spoil got on the Antiates
Was ne'er distributed.

Enter an AEDILE

What, will he come?   5
AEDILE He's coming.
BRUTUS How accompanied?
AEDILE With old Menenius and those senators
That always favoured him.
SICINIUS   Have you a catalogue
Of all the voices that we have procured,   10
Set down by th'poll?
AEDILE   I have; 'tis ready.
SICINIUS Have you collected them by tribes?
AEDILE   I have.
SICINIUS Assemble presently the people hither,
And when they hear me say 'It shall be so
I'th'right and strength o'th'commons', be it either   15
For death, for fine, or banishment, then let them,
If I say 'Fine', cry 'Fine!', if 'Death', cry 'Death!',
Insisting on the old prerogative
And power i'th'truth o'th'cause.
AEDILE   I shall inform them.

---

5 SD AEDILE] *Edile* F (*and to end of scene in* SH *and* SD); SD *placed as Capell; after* come? F   11 poll] F (Pole)   14–15
'It . . . commons'] *Hanmer;* it . . . Commons F   17 'Fine', . . . 'Fine!', . . . 'Death', . . . 'Death!',] *NS;* Fine, . . . Fine;
. . . Death, . . . Death, F; fine . . . 'Fine!' . . . death . . . 'Death!' *Hanmer*

3 **Enforce him with** Urge against him.
3 **envy** ill-will, malice.
4–5 **spoil . . . distributed** A charge taken from Plutarch which refers to an episode Shakespeare omitted; hence in the play it seems spurious, an 'invention' (3.2.144).
4 **got on** taken from.
10–12 **voices . . . tribes** According to Plutarch, the tribunes strategically arranged for the vote to be taken by 'tribes' (Roman territorial districts), which each had a single block vote determined by a majority within that tribe and where the people's votes thus predominated, rather than by 'centuries' (subdivisions of classes, discriminated by wealth), where the patrician vote predominated. Brockbank notes that Shakespeare follows North who, translating Amyot's French, adds a parenthetical detail which does not appear in Plutarch's

Greek: 'for by this meanes the multitude of the poore needy people . . . came to be of greater force (bicause their voyces were numbred by the polle) then the noble honest citizens' (Bullough, *Sources*, V, 524–5). This made the Roman method of voting appear to resemble that of English parliamentary elections; see pp. 27–9 above.
13 **presently** immediately.
18 **old prerogative** traditional rights and privileges (of the plebeians).
19 **power . . . cause** A demagogic flourish: 'the power that the truth of their cause gives them' (Brockbank). Hibbard argues that the words 'i'th'truth o'th'cause' would probably have had a distinctly Puritan ring to Shakespeare's audience, making the close of Sicinius's speech sound like a rallying cry of King James's Puritan opponents in the House of Commons.

BRUTUS And when such time they have begun to cry,   20
        Let them not cease, but with a din confused
        Enforce the present execution
        Of what we chance to sentence.
AEDILE   Very well.
SICINIUS Make them be strong, and ready for this hint
        When we shall hap to give't them.
BRUTUS   Go about it.   25

                                            [*Exit Aedile*]

        Put him to choler straight. He hath been used
        Ever to conquer and to have his worth
        Of contradiction. Being once chafed, he cannot
        Be reined again to temperance; then he speaks
        What's in his heart, and that is there which looks   30
        With us to break his neck.

        Enter CORIOLANUS, MENENIUS, *and* COMINIUS,
             with [SENATORS *and Patricians*]

SICINIUS Well, here he comes.
MENENIUS [*To Coriolanus*] Calmly, I do beseech you.
CORIOLANUS Ay, as an hostler, that for th'poorest piece
        Will bear the knave by th'volume. [*Aloud*] Th'honoured
              gods   35
        Keep Rome in safety and the chairs of justice
        Supplied with worthy men! Plant love among's!
        Throng our large temples with the shows of peace,

---

20 time] F; tune *conj. Kellner*   25 SD] *Pope; not in* F   27 worth] F; word *Rowe;* wroth *conj. Becket;* mouth *Collier²*
31 SD.2 SENATORS *and Patricians*] *Capell; others* F; *entire* SD *after 32 comes. Parker*   33 SD] *Oxford; not in* F   34 for
th'] F2; fourth F   35 SD] *Parker; not in* F   37 among's!] *Dyce;* amongs F; amongst you, F2   38 Throng] *Theobald.
conj. Thirlby;* Through F

22 **Enforce . . . execution** Demand the immediate carrying-out.
25 **hap** happen.
26 **choler** anger; possibly with a pun on 'collar':
King sees 'choler', 'chafed' (28), 'reined' (29) and
'break his neck' (31) as suggesting the image of a
horse that will not stand a collar.
27–8 **have . . . contradiction** (1) 'have his
pennyworth of answering back (that is, give as
good as he gets)' (Hibbard), (2) earn fame or
glory ('worth' = worthiness) through opposition (Schmidt), in support of which NS cites
North's description of Martius as 'one thincking
that to overcome allwayes, and to have the upper

hande in all matters, was a token of magnanimitie' (Bullough, *Sources*, V, 519). Shakespeare may
have remembered a passage in Holland's Livy in
which the people fear that Coriolanus will 'have
his penniworths of the backe and shoulders of the
commons of Rome' (p. 67).
30 **looks** looks likely, promises.
31 **With us** With our assistance; possibly 'To
help us'.
34 **hostler** A stableman at an inn.
34 **piece** coin, piece of money.
35 **Will . . . volume** Will put up with being
called knave enough times to fill a volume.
38 **shows** ceremonies, pageants.

       And not our streets with war!
FIRST SENATOR Amen, Amen.   40
MENENIUS A noble wish.

Enter the AEDILE *with the* PLEBEIANS

SICINIUS Draw near, ye people.
AEDILE List to your tribunes. Audience! Peace, I say!
CORIOLANUS First, hear me speak.
BOTH TRIBUNES Well, say. – Peace, ho!   45
CORIOLANUS Shall I be charged no further than this present?
       Must all determine here?
SICINIUS   I do demand
       If you submit you to the people's voices,
       Allow their officers, and are content
       To suffer lawful censure for such faults   50
       As shall be proved upon you.
CORIOLANUS   I am content.
MENENIUS Lo, citizens, he says he is content.
       The warlike service he has done, consider. Think
       Upon the wounds his body bears, which show
       Like graves i'th'holy churchyard.
CORIOLANUS   Scratches with briers,   55
       Scars to move laughter only.
MENENIUS   Consider further,
       That when he speaks not like a citizen,
       You find him like a soldier. Do not take
       His rougher accents for malicious sounds,
       But, as I say, such as become a soldier   60
       Rather than envy you.
COMINIUS   Well, well, no more.
CORIOLANUS What is the matter

---

45 SH] F (*Both Tri.*)   51 you.] F4; You? F   59 accents] *Pope²*, *conj. Theobald*, '*SR*'; Actions F   60–1 soldier . . . envy you.] F (Soldier,); soldier . . . envy, you – *Pope*

43 Audience Attention.
46 this present this present accusation.
47 determine be decided, conclude.
49 Allow Acknowledge (the authority of).
55 graves . . . churchyard The comparison is anachronistic and perhaps overly compressed: 'We are left at liberty to think of the size, or the number of the wounds, or of the sanctity of

the hero's person' (Case); compare 'Every gash was an enemy's grave' (2.1.129), also spoken by Menenius.
   59 accents Supporting Theobald, Sisson argues that F represents a misreading of manuscript 'accēts' (= 'accents') as 'accōns' (= 'actions').
   61 envy you show malice toward you.

        That, being passed for consul with full voice,
        I am so dishonoured that the very hour
        You take it off again?   65

SICINIUS Answer to us.

CORIOLANUS Say, then. 'Tis true, I ought so.

SICINIUS We charge you that you have contrived to take
        From Rome all seasoned office and to wind
        Yourself into a power tyrannical,   70
        For which you are a traitor to the people.

CORIOLANUS How? 'Traitor'?

MENENIUS   Nay, temperately! Your promise.

CORIOLANUS The fires i'th'lowest hell fold in the people!
        Call me their 'traitor', thou injurious tribune?
        Within thine eyes sat twenty thousand deaths,   75
        In thy hands clutched as many millions, in
        Thy lying tongue both numbers, I would say
        'Thou liest' unto thee with a voice as free
        As I do pray the gods.

SICINIUS Mark you this, people?   80

ALL PLEBEIANS To th'rock, to th'rock with him!

SICINIUS Peace!
        We need not put new matter to his charge.
        What you have seen him do and heard him speak –
        Beating your officers, cursing yourselves,   85
        Opposing laws with strokes, and here defying

---

67 Say, then.] F (Say then:); Say then! – *Parker*   72–4 'Traitor' . . . 'traitor'] *This edn;* Traytor . . . Traitor F   73
hell fold] F2; hell. Fould F   75–7 deaths, . . . clutched . . . millions, . . . tongue . . . numbers,] F3 *subst.* (tongue,);
deaths . . . clutcht: . . . Millions . . . tongue, . . . numbers. F   78 'Thou liest'] *Hanmer;* Thou lyest F   80 this,] F4;
this F   81 SH, 113 SH, 127 SH, 145 SH, 150 SH] F (*All.*)   84–7 speak – . . . him –] F (speake: . . . him.)

66 **Answer to us** Answer the charges (i.e. We'll
ask the questions, not you).

69 **seasoned** (1) 'established and settled
by time' (Johnson), (2) 'qualified, tempered'
(Schmidt), the antithesis of 'power tyrannical'
(70).

69 **wind** insinuate.

70 **power tyrannical** In North's Plutarch the
tribunes say they will show 'howe he dyd aspire
to be King, and . . . that all his actions tended to
usurpe tyrannicall power over Rome' (Bullough,
Sources, V, 524).

71 **traitor** The word that incenses Coriolanus
is not from Plutarch, where he is most provoked
by the charge that he refused to distribute the spoil
taken from the Antiates (mentioned by Brutus to

Sicinius, 4–5, but not a charge made publicly in
Shakespeare); see also pp. 36–7 above.

73 **hell fold** F's punctuation is probably a careless error, not the mark of an emphatic pause.

73 **fold in** enfold, envelop. In his angry curse,
Coriolanus names the course that his revenge will
later take.

74 **their 'traitor'** a traitor to them.

74 **injurious** insulting.

75 **Within** If within (introducing a series of
subjunctive clauses preparing for 77, 'I would
say').

78 **free** candid, open.

86 **Opposing . . . strokes** 'Taking arms against
legal authority' (Gomme).

Those whose great power must try him – even this,
So criminal and in such capital kind,
Deserves th'extremest death.
BRUTUS   But since he hath
Served well for Rome –
CORIOLANUS   What do you prate of service?   90
BRUTUS I talk of that that know it.
CORIOLANUS You?
MENENIUS Is this the promise that you made your mother?
COMINIUS Know, I pray you –
CORIOLANUS   I'll know no further.
Let them pronounce the steep Tarpeian death,   95
Vagabond exile, flaying, pent to linger
But with a grain a day, I would not buy
Their mercy at the price of one fair word,
Nor check my courage for what they can give,
To have't with saying 'Good morrow'.
SICINIUS   For that he has,   100
As much as in him lies, from time to time
Inveighed against the people, seeking means
To pluck away their power, as now at last
Given hostile strokes, and that not in the presence
Of dreaded justice, but on the ministers   105
That doth distribute it – in the name o'th'people
And in the power of us the tribunes, we,
Ev'n from this instant, banish him our city,
In peril of precipitation
From off the rock Tarpeian, never more   110
To enter our Rome gates. I'th'people's name,

90 Rome –] F3; Rome. F   94 you –] *Rowe;* you. F   96 flaying, pent] F (Fleaing); fleaing. Pent *Johnson*   100 'Good morrow'] *Hanmer;* Good morrow F   102 Inveighed] F (Enui'd); Envy'd *Rowe*   103 as] F; has *Hanmer;* and *conj. Hudson*   106 doth] F; doe F2   106 it –] it. F

88 **capital** punishable by death.
91–2 **I . . . You?** Brutus maintains that he has served Rome, in a civic capacity, even if to Coriolanus the only 'service' that counts is military.
96 **pent** i.e. let me be confined, pent up.
99 **courage** spirit, mettle (Dyce).
102 **Inveighed** While most editors modernise F ('Enui'd') as 'Envied', *Textual Companion* argues that 'envy against' is a combination not found elsewhere in Shakespeare and one not sanctioned by the *OED*; it proposes a misreading of medial *uei* as *uie*. Misreading is not a necessary assumption, however: 'envy' was then also a variant

form of 'inveigh'; *OED* gives a 1611 example in which modern 'inveighs against' appears as 'envies . . . against'. That Shakespeare had this meaning in mind is suggested by the marginal note in Holland's Livy, next to Coriolanus's arguments against giving the people free corn: 'Coriolanus enveieth against the Tribunes' (p. 66).
104 **not** not only.
106 **doth** The singular form may have been influenced by the object, 'it'.
111 **Rome gates** Shakespeare often uses proper names ('Rome') as adjectives (see Abbott 22).

I say it shall be so.
ALL PLEBEIANS It shall be so, it shall be so! Let him away!
    He's banished, and it shall be so!
COMINIUS Hear me, my masters and my common friends –   115
SICINIUS He's sentenced. No more hearing.
COMINIUS   Let me speak.
    I have been consul, and can show for Rome
    Her enemies' marks upon me. I do love
    My country's good with a respect more tender,
    More holy and profound, than mine own life,   120
    My dear wife's estimate, her womb's increase
    And treasure of my loins. Then if I would
    Speak that –
SICINIUS   We know your drift. Speak what?
BRUTUS There's no more to be said, but he is banished
    As enemy to the people and his country.   125
    It shall be so.
ALL PLEBEIANS It shall be so, it shall be so!
CORIOLANUS You common cry of curs, whose breath I hate
    As reek o'th'rotten fens, whose loves I prize
    As the dead carcasses of unburied men   130
    That do corrupt my air, I banish you.
    And here remain with your uncertainty!
    Let every feeble rumour shake your hearts;
    Your enemies, with nodding of their plumes,
    Fan you into despair! Have the power still   135
    To banish your defenders, till at length
    Your ignorance – which finds not till it feels,
    Making but reservation of yourselves,

---

115 friends –] *Rowe;* friends. F   117 for] *Theobald;* from F   123 that –] F3; that. F   131 you.] *Pope;* you, F   137–9 ignorance – . . . foes –] F (ignorance (. . . Foes))   137–8 feels, . . . yourselves,] F; feels – . . . yourselves – *Oxford*   138 but] F; not *Capell*

115 **common** commoner, plebeian.
121 **estimate** honour, reputation.
121–2 **her . . . loins** our children. Parker notes that Cominius's words here show that when Volumnia gave primacy to country over her children in 1.3 she was voicing the patrician code, not merely a personal sentiment.
128 **cry** pack.
129 **reek** stinking vapour.
129 **fens** marshes. Brockbank compares *Temp.* 2.1.48–9: 'As if it had lungs, and rotten ones . . . Or, as 'twere perfum'd by a fen'.
131 **I banish you** Characteristically, Coriolanus seizes on one of his opponent's words and

builds his tirade around it. The speech is entirely Shakespeare's; in Plutarch, Coriolanus 'dyd outwardly shewe no manner of passion, nor care at all of him selfe' (Bullough, *Sources*, V, 525–6).

135–9 **Have . . . foes** The passage may be corrupt, but more likely its ellipses are meant to show the force of Coriolanus's passion, which leads him to cram in two parenthetical elaborations ('which . . . feels' and 'Still . . . foes') before completing his sentence.
137 **which . . . feels** which learns only from experience.
138 (1) Seeking only to preserve yourselves, (2) Leaving no one unbanished but yourselves.

Still your own foes – deliver you
As most abated captives to some nation   140
That won you without blows! Despising
For you the city, thus I turn my back.
There is a world elsewhere.
Exeunt Coriolanus, Cominius[, Menenius, Senators, and Patricians]
They all shout, and throw up their caps

AEDILE The people's enemy is gone, is gone!

ALL PLEBEIANS Our enemy is banished! He is gone! Hoo–oo!   145

SICINIUS Go see him out at gates and follow him
As he hath followed you, with all despite.
Give him deserved vexation. Let a guard
Attend us through the city.

ALL PLEBEIANS Come, come, let's see him out at gates! Come.   150
The gods preserve our noble tribunes! Come.

Exeunt

4.[1] *Enter* CORIOLANUS, VOLUMNIA, VIRGILIA, MENENIUS,
COMINIUS, *with the young nobility of Rome*

CORIOLANUS Come, leave your tears; a brief farewell. The beast

141–2 blows! . . . city,] *Capell, after Pope;* blowes, . . . City. F   143 SD.1 *Menenius . . . Patricians] Capell subst.; with
Cumalijs.* F   143 SD.2 *They . . . caps]* F; *after 145* Hoo–oo! *Malone, after Capell*   145 Hoo–oo!] F (Hoo, oo.); Hoo,
hoo. F3   147 despite.] *Capell, after* F3 (despight,); despight F   Act 4, Scene 1   4.1] *Rowe; Actus Quartus.* F

139 Still . . . foes Always your own worst
enemies.
140 abated beaten, subdued.
141–2 blows! . . . city, Capell's punctuation,
which attaches 'Despising . . . city' to what follows and makes Coriolanus the one 'Despising',
seems more appropriate to Coriolanus's attitude
than F's. Gomme notes Coriolanus's reversal here:
having tried to deny plebeian participation in his
ideal of Rome, he now despises Rome because
they claim to represent it, an attitude that will
allow him to contemplate its total destruction.
142 For you On your account.
143 SD.1 *Menenius . . . Patricians* See Textual
Analysis, pp. 299–300 below, on F's *with Cumalijs.*
147 despite contempt.
148 vexation torment, affliction.

Act 4, Scene 1
Before the gates of Rome. Coriolanus's leave-
taking combines and develops two incidents
briefly mentioned in Plutarch where, after at his
house he 'had taken leave of his mother and
wife, finding them weeping and shrieking out for

sorrowe, and had also comforted and persuaded
them to be content with his chaunce: he went
immediately to the gate of the cittie, accompanied with a great number of Patricians'. Shakespeare leaves the cause of Coriolanus's apparent stoicism ambiguous; in Plutarch Coriolanus
evinces no outward emotion 'bicause he was so
caried awaye with the vehemencie of anger, and
desire of revenge, that he had no sence nor feeling of the hard state he was in', and he departs
not alone but with 'three or foure of his friends'
(Bullough, *Sources*, v, 526).
    o SD The group enters on its way to the 'gate'
(47), but staging remains unclear. They may enter
through the 'gates' of the tiring-house façade,
through which the *young nobility* would return
to Rome while Coriolanus, his family and inti-
mate companions *Exeunt* (58 SD) through the left-
or right-stage door, with three returning from the
same direction at 4.2.8. More effective theatrically
might be an initial entry from a side door, with
Coriolanus finally departing with a few through
the façade door while the others exit to the side.
    1–2 beast . . . heads See 2.3.14 n. and Horace,

With many heads butts me away. Nay, mother,
Where is your ancient courage? You were used
To say extremities was the trier of spirits;
That common chances common men could bear;   5
That when the sea was calm, all boats alike
Showed mastership in floating; fortune's blows
When most struck home, being gentle wounded craves
A noble cunning. You were used to load me
With precepts that would make invincible   10
The heart that conned them.

VIRGILIA O heavens! O heavens!

CORIOLANUS   Nay, I prithee, woman –

VOLUMNIA Now the red pestilence strike all trades in Rome,
        And occupations perish!

CORIOLANUS   What, what, what!
I shall be loved when I am lacked. Nay, mother,   15
Resume that spirit when you were wont to say,
If you had been the wife of Hercules,
Six of his labours you'd have done and saved
Your husband so much sweat. Cominius,
Droop not. Adieu. Farewell, my wife, my mother.   20
I'll do well yet. Thou old and true Menenius,
Thy tears are salter than a younger man's
And venomous to thine eyes. My sometime general,

---

4 extremities] F; Extreamity F2   5 chances common] F4; chances. Common F   8 gentle wounded craves] gentle
wounded, craues F; gently warded, craves *Pope*; greatly warded, crave *Hanmer*; gentle minded craues *Collier²*   12
woman –] *Rowe*; woman. F   23 sometime] *Theobald*; (sometime) F

Epistles, 1.i.76, 'Bellua multorum es capitum' (you
are a monster of many heads).

3 ancient former.

3 were used used, were accustomed; for the
construction see Abbott 295.

4–9 To . . . cunning These sentiments echo
Agamemnon and Nestor in *Tro.* 1.3.20–30, 31–
52; there they are exposed by Ulysses as hollow
commonplaces.

4 extremities utmost adversity or suffering.

7–9 fortune's . . . cunning when fortune
strikes her hardest blows, bearing her wounds
like a gentleman requires a nobleman's wisdom
and ability (*OED* Cunning *sb* 1, 3a); given the preceding nautical imagery, 'cunning' may also pun
on 'conning' (steering).

11 conned studied, memorised.

13 red pestilence Probably typhus, which
causes red skin-eruptions. Volumnia echoes her
son's wishing that disease would plague his faint-
hearted soldiers (1.4.32–5).

14 occupations crafts, trades.

15 lacked missed. *OED* (Lack *v*¹ 2c) gives only
Shakespearean examples of 'lack' meaning 'to perceive the absence of, to miss'.

17 wife of Hercules Volumnia again imagines
herself as the hero's wife, not mother (see 1.3.2–
4). Hercules was the demigod in Greek mythology
who was assigned twelve tasks or 'labours' (18).

22 salter saltier (hence inflaming the eyes);
there may be a precedent for the idea that tears
grow saltier with age in *Lear* 4.7.45–6.

23 sometime former.

I have seen thee stern, and thou hast oft beheld
Heart-hardening spectacles. Tell these sad women   25
'Tis fond to wail inevitable strokes
As 'tis to laugh at 'em. My mother, you wot well
My hazards still have been your solace, and
Believe't not lightly – though I go alone,
Like to a lonely dragon that his fen   30
Makes feared and talked of more than seen – your son
Will or exceed the common or be caught
With cautelous baits and practice.

VOLUMNIA   My first son,
Whither will thou go? Take good Cominius
With thee a while. Determine on some course   35
More than a wild exposure to each chance
That starts i'th'way before thee.

VIRGILIA   O the gods!

COMINIUS I'll follow thee a month, devise with thee
Where thou shalt rest, that thou mayst hear of us
And we of thee. So if the time thrust forth   40
A cause for thy repeal, we shall not send

---

24 thee] F (the)   29–31 lightly – . . . seen –] F (lightly, . . . seene:)   33 My first] F; First, my *Hanmer;* My fierce *conj. Heath;* My fairest *Keightley;* My fair *Hudson²*   35 a while] F2; awhile F   36 exposure] F (expoſture)   37 SH] *Keightley (Vir.);* Corio. F

26 A commonplace; see Tilley C921, C923, F83.
26 **fond** foolish.
27 **wot** know.
28 **My . . . solace** Coriolanus understands at least this aspect of his mother; compare 1.3.4–20.
28 **still** always.
29 **Believe't not lightly** Do not take this promise lightly.
30 To evoke the pathos of isolation, Shakespeare alludes to Job 30.29: 'I am a brother to the dragons, and a companion to the ostriches' (see also Isa. 13.20–2, 34.11–13). The dragon comparison suggests menace (compare Spenser's 'monstrous beasty bred in filthy fen' that is likened to the Hydra of the Lernaean marsh, *Faerie Queene* 1.7.26) and appropriates to Coriolanus the idea of monstrousness he had earlier applied to the plebeians (see 3.1.94 n.).
32 **or . . . or** either . . . or. Ironically, as NS notes, 'both futures await him'.
32 **exceed the common** surpass the ordinary deeds of men.
33 **cautelous** crafty, deceitful; compare Aufidius's vow, 1.10.12–16.

33 **practice** plot, stratagem.
33 **first** Since Volumnia has apparently no other children (see 1.3.5, 5.3.162), she probably means both 'first-born' and 'noblest, most eminent' (Warburton).
36 **exposure** *OED* gives only this instance of F's 'exposure' and also cites Shakespeare for the first examples of 'exposure' (*Tro.* 1.3.195, *Mac.* 2.3.127). He may not yet have decided on the form of his neologism, or 'exposure' may have been the compositor's misreading of the, to him, equally unfamiliar 'exposure'.
37 **starts** springs up suddenly.
37 SH F's *Corio.* is possible, but Keightley's reassignment is persuasive. In each of his other speeches in 4.1 Coriolanus argues for stoic endurance and patience. Virgilia's only F line in this scene (12) would make this ejaculation seem in character for her and a natural wifely outcry at Volumnia's reminder of how desperate her son's circumstances really are.
41 **cause . . . repeal** occasion for recalling you from banishment.

O'er the vast world to seek a single man
And lose advantage, which doth ever cool
I'th'absence of the needer.

CORIOLANUS   Fare ye well.
Thou hast years upon thee, and thou art too full   45
Of the wars' surfeits to go rove with one
That's yet unbruised. Bring me but out at gate.
Come, my sweet wife, my dearest mother, and
My friends of noble touch; when I am forth,
Bid me farewell and smile. I pray you, come.   50
While I remain above the ground you shall
Hear from me still, and never of me aught
But what is like me formerly.

MENENIUS   That's worthily
As any ear can hear. Come, let's not weep.
If I could shake off but one seven years   55
From these old arms and legs, by the good gods,
I'd with thee every foot.

CORIOLANUS Give me thy hand. Come.

                                                Exeunt

4.[2] *Enter the two Tribunes,* SICINIUS *and* BRUTUS, *with the* AEDILE

SICINIUS [*To the Aedile*] Bid them all home. He's gone, and we'll no
        further.

---

46 wars'] F (warres); war's *Rowe*   Act 4, Scene 2   4.2] *Pope; not in* F   0 SD AEDILE] F (*Edile*)   1 SD, 5 SD] *Oxford;*
not in F

43 **advantage** the opportune moment.
46 **wars' surfeits** wearing effects of the wars in which he has fought.
47 **at gate** at the gate. For the omission of the article, see Abbott 143.
49 **noble touch** proven nobility; for the touch-stone metaphor, see 2.3.177 n. A less generous account of the patricians is given to Aufidius at 4.5.72–5.
51–2 **you . . . still** Menenius, however, at 4.6.19–20 says they have received no communication from Coriolanus.
52–3 **aught . . . formerly** anything that does not correspond to what you have known of me.
58 SD The off-stage sound of the plebeian crowd hooting might begin here and continue through the first speeches of 4.2.

Act 4, Scene 2
A street leading to the gate of Rome, which may be represented by the façade centre doors (see 4.1.0 n.). Hibbard notes the symmetry by which this scene, which closes the play's central action, mirrors 2.1, which initiated it. At the end of 2.1 the tribunes, fearing Coriolanus's opposition, were conspiring his overthrow; at the beginning of 4.2 their plans have been successful. At the beginning of 2.1 Menenius was baiting the tribunes; at the end of 4.2 Volumnia is cursing them. Both scenes have no precedent in Plutarch.

    The nobility are vexed, whom we see have sided
    In his behalf.
BRUTUS   Now we have shown our power,
    Let us seem humbler after it is done
    Than when it was a-doing.
SICINIUS [*To the Aedile*]   Bid them home.   5
    Say their great enemy is gone, and they
    Stand in their ancient strength.
BRUTUS   Dismiss them home.
                          [*Exit Aedile*]
    Here comes his mother.

        Enter VOLUMNIA, VIRGILIA, *and* MENENIUS

SICINIUS Let's not meet her.
BRUTUS Why?   10
SICINIUS They say she's mad.
BRUTUS They have ta'en note of us. Keep on your way.
VOLUMNIA O, you're well met. Th'hoarded plague o'th'gods
    Requite your love!
MENENIUS   Peace, peace; be not so loud.
VOLUMNIA If that I could for weeping, you should hear –   15
    Nay, and you shall hear some. Will you be gone?
VIRGILIA You shall stay too. I would I had the power
    To say so to my husband.
SICINIUS [*To Volumnia*]   Are you mankind?
VOLUMNIA Ay, fool, is that a shame? Note but this, fool:
    Was not a man my father? Hadst thou foxship   20

---

7 SD] *Capell; not in* F   13 you're] F (y'are)   14 Requite] F (requit)   15 hear –] F (heare,)   16 Will] F; *To Virgilia Will Hanmer; To Brutus Will Johnson; To the tribunes Will Oxford; To Sicinius Will Parker*   17–18 VIRGILIA You . . . too. I . . . my husband] F; *You . . . too. I . . . thy husband Hanmer (continuing Volumnia's speech); You . . . too.* VIR. I . . . my husband *Warburton*   17 You] F; *To Sicinius You Johnson; To the tribunes You Oxford; To Brutus You Parker*   18 SD] *Oxford; not in* F   19 this, fool:] F (this Foole,); this fool. *Pope*

---

11 **mad** (1) furious (see *1H4* 1.3.53–4), (2) out of her mind.

13 **hoarded** stored up for punishment.

14 **Requite** Repay.

17 SH Following Warburton, editors have often reassigned Virgilia's first sentence to Volumnia, but despite Virgilia's general reticence there is no reason to assume she lacks the spirit to block the other tribune's attempt to leave or that 'I . . . husband' is spoken as an aside.

18 **mankind** Sicinius intends either 'furious, mad' (*OED* Mankind *a²*) or, more probably, 'masculine, virago-like' (*OED* Mankind *a¹* 3); compare

'mankind witch', *WT* 2.3.68. Volumnia, however, takes it in its more usual sense, 'of humankind'.

19 **this, fool** Pope's punctuation suggests that the clause sets up Sicinius for general mockery and is addressed to Virgilia and Menenius, but the rest of the speech is addressed to Sicinius, and the lack of a comma before a vocative is common in F.

20 **foxship** 'craftiness, cunning' but also 'ingratitude' (compare *Lear* 3.7.27), both traditional attributes of the fox; Volumnia also retorts to 'mankind'.

To banish him that struck more blows for Rome
Than thou hast spoken words?
SICINIUS   O blessèd heavens!
VOLUMNIA More noble blows than ever thou wise words,
And for Rome's good. I'll tell thee what – yet go.
Nay, but thou shalt stay too. I would my son   25
Were in Arabia and thy tribe before him,
His good sword in his hand.
SICINIUS   What then?
VIRGILIA   What then!
He'd make an end of thy posterity.
VOLUMNIA Bastards and all.
Good man, the wounds that he does bear for Rome!   30
MENENIUS Come, come, peace.
SICINIUS I would he had continued to his country
As he began and not unknit himself
The noble knot he made.
BRUTUS   I would he had.
VOLUMNIA 'I would he had'! 'Twas you incensed the rabble –   35
Cats that can judge as fitly of his worth
As I can of those mysteries which heaven
Will not have earth to know.
BRUTUS [To Sicinius] Pray, let's go.
VOLUMNIA   Now pray, sir, get you gone.
You have done a brave deed. Ere you go, hear this: 40
As far as doth the Capitol exceed
The meanest house in Rome, so far my son –

22 words?] Hanmer; words. F   23 words,] Rowe; words. F   27–30 VIRGILIA . . . then! . . . posterity. VOLUMNIA . . . all. . . . Rome!] F (then?); VOL. . . . then? . . . posterity. . . . all. . . . Rome! Hanmer; VOL. . . . then? . . . posterity. . . . all. VIR. . . . Rome! White², conj. Clarendon; VIR. . . . then? VOL. . . . posterity, . . . all. . . . Rome! Brockbank   35 'I . . . had'!] Staunton; I . . . had? F   39 SD] Oxford; not in F   42–3 son– . . . do you see? –] Keightley; Sonne . . . (do you see) F

25 too after all ('too' is used to intensify her imperative).
26 in Arabia i.e. in the desert, where no civil constraints would prevent him from dealing single-handedly with the tribunes.
28 There is no real justification for reassigning this line to Volumnia, although for editors who have earlier deprived Virgilia of a spirited retort (see 17 n.), the temptation is obvious.
34 noble knot the bond of noble service by which he bound Rome to him in gratitude. The knot is 'noble' because based on reciprocity, the

virtues that hold society together, not because Coriolanus is a patrician.
36 Cats A general term of contempt, like her son's 'curs' (3.3.128).
37–8 mysteries . . . know Volumnia exalts Coriolanus in cosmic and religious terms, further distancing him from the sub-human beings who dared to judge and banish him; in 41–4 she extends the comparison through the more characteristic patrician analogy of architecture and hierarchy (compare 3.1.199, 206–9; 4.6.86–91, 103).

This lady's husband here, this, do you see? –
Whom you have banished, does exceed you all.

BRUTUS   Well, well, we'll leave you.

SICINIUS   Why stay we to be baited   45
With one that wants her wits?

Exeunt Tribunes

VOLUMNIA   Take my prayers with you.
I would the gods had nothing else to do
But to confirm my curses. Could I meet 'em
But once a day, it would unclog my heart
Of what lies heavy to't.

MENENIUS   You have told them home,   50
And, by my troth, you have cause. You'll sup with me?

VOLUMNIA   Anger's my meat. I sup upon myself,
And so shall starve with feeding.
[*To Virgilia*]   Come, let's go.
Leave this faint puling and lament as I do,
In anger, Juno-like. Come, come, come.   55

Exeunt [*Volumnia and Virgilia*]

MENENIUS   Fie, fie, fie.   *Exit*

4.[3]   *Enter a* ROMAN *and a* VOLSCE

ROMAN   I know you well, sir, and you know me. Your name, I think, is
Adrian?

---

46 SD *Exeunt*] F4; *Exit* F   51 me?] F3; me. F   53 SD] *Hanmer* (*after* let's go); *not in* F   54 faint puling] F (faint-puling)   55–6 Come, . . . come. MENENIUS Fie, . . . fie.] F; Come, . . . come. Fie, . . . fie. *Rowe;* Come, come, fie, fie. *Pope*   55 SD *Exeunt . . . Virgilia*] *Globe; Exeunt* F   56 SD *Exit*] F; *Exeunt / Rowe*   **Act 4, Scene 3**   4.3] *Pope; not in* F   0 SD *a* ROMAN *and a* VOLSCE] F (*Volce*); NICANOR *and* ADRIAN *Staunton*   1 SH] F (*Rom.*); NIC. *Staunton* (*and to end of scene*)

45–6 baited / With harassed by.

49 unclog relieve, unburden. The metaphor derives from the practice of fettering men or animals with blocks of wood called 'clogs' (*OED* Clog *v* 1).

50 told . . . home berated them thoroughly, told them 'home truths'.

53 starve . . . feeding die by consuming my own resources. John Fletcher, who is likely to have known *Coriolanus*, includes in *The Captain* (1609–12) the line 'He dyes in chaines, eating himselfe with anger' (1.1.39).

54 Leave Cease (as at 4.1.1.).

54 faint puling faint-hearted whining.

55 Juno-like Juno was the chief goddess of the Romans and wife of Jupiter; Virgil mentions her unforgiving anger in *Aeneid*, 1, 4.

Act 4, Scene 3

A highway between Rome and Antium, 'a day's journey' (11) from Rome. This encounter between a Volscian spy and a Roman betraying Rome, who is at first unrecognised, is Shakespeare's invention; it anticipates Coriolanus's arrival in Antium. Parker notes that the 1977 RSC staging emphasised this anticipation in the way Nicanor lowered his hood at 5, a gesture and question echoed by Coriolanus at 4.5.60; in modern productions, Nicanor and Adrian often reappear as two of Aufidius's conspirators in 5.6. In theatrical terms the scene changes the mood and marks the time of Coriolanus's journey; like 2.2.1–28, it offers detached commentary by minor characters.

0 SD ROMAN . . . VOLSCE Although both are named in the dialogue, Shakespeare apparently

VOLSCE It is so, sir. Truly, I have forgot you.

ROMAN I am a Roman, and my services are, as you are, against 'em.
   Know you me yet?   5

VOLSCE Nicanor, no?

ROMAN The same, sir.

VOLSCE You had more beard when I last saw you, but your favour is
   well appeared by your tongue. What's the news in Rome? I have a
   note from the Volscian state to find you out there. You have well   10
   saved me a day's journey.

ROMAN There hath been in Rome strange insurrections: the people
   against the senators, patricians, and nobles.

VOLSCE Hath been? Is it ended then? Our state thinks not so. They are
   in a most warlike preparation and hope to come upon them in the   15
   heat of their division.

ROMAN The main blaze of it is past, but a small thing would make it
   flame again, for the nobles receive so to heart the banishment of that
   worthy Coriolanus that they are in a ripe aptness to take all power
   from the people and to pluck from them their tribunes forever. This   20
   lies glowing, I can tell you, and is almost mature for the violent
   breaking out.

VOLSCE Coriolanus banished?

ROMAN Banished, sir.

VOLSCE You will be welcome with this intelligence, Nicanor.   25

ROMAN The day serves well for them now. I have heard it said the fittest
   time to corrupt a man's wife is when she's fallen out with her
   husband. Your noble Tullus Aufidius will appear well in these

---

3 SH] F (*Volce*); ADR. *Staunton* (*and to end of scene*)   4 and] F; but *Pope*   6 Nicanor, no?] *Nicanor: no.* F; Nicanor?
No. F3   9 appeared] F (appear'd); affeer'd *Hanmer;* appayed *Singer;* approved *Collier²,* conj. *Steevens*   18 again,
for] againe. For F   28 will] F2; well F

thought of them as representative figures; on the
origin of the names Nicanor and Adrian, see p. 11
above.

4 **'em** i.e. the Romans.

8–9 **favour ... tongue** identity is made apparent by your speech. On the reflexive construction 'is appeared' see Abbott 296; compare *Tro.*
3.3.3, 'appear it your mind'. Steevens's conjecture
is the most plausible of the alternatives, where
'appeared' is taken as a misreading of 'approved'
(= confirmed).

10 **note** note of instruction.

15 **preparation** A reference to the Volscian
army ready for battle 'at an hour's warning' (38–
9).

19–20 **ripe ... pluck** An example of image
drift in which the fruit image in the nobles'
'ripe' readiness is transferred to the tribunes in
'pluck' (King); 'pluck' also echoes Coriolanus's
urging that the tribunate be abolished (3.1.156–7,
3.3.103).

21–2 **glowing ... out** The analogy between
glowing coals and imminent civil war was a commonplace, but particularly apt in view of Coriolanus's threat to set Rome aflame.

26 **them** i.e. the Volscians.

26–8 **fittest ... husband** A striking metaphor
that domesticates and trivialises Coriolanus's rage
and places him in the role of unconstant, corrupt-
ible woman.

wars, his great opposer Coriolanus being now in no request of his
country. 30
VOLSCE He cannot choose. I am most fortunate thus accidentally to
encounter you. You have ended my business, and I will merrily
accompany you home.
ROMAN I shall, between this and supper, tell you most strange things
from Rome, all tending to the good of their adversaries. Have you 35
an army ready, say you?
VOLSCE A most royal one: the centurions and their charges distinctly
billeted, already in th'entertainment, and to be on foot at an hour's
warning.
ROMAN I am joyful to hear of their readiness and am the man, I think, 40
that shall set them in present action. So, sir, heartily well met, and
most glad of your company.
VOLSCE You take my part from me, sir. I have the most cause to be glad
of yours.
ROMAN Well, let us go together. 45

Exeunt

4.[4] *Enter* CORIOLANUS *in mean apparel, disguised, and muffled*

CORIOLANUS A goodly city is this Antium. City,
        'Tis I that made thy widows. Many an heir
        Of these fair edifices 'fore my wars
        Have I heard groan and drop. Then know me not,
        Lest that thy wives with spits and boys with stones 5

Act 4, Scene 4   4.4] *Capell; not in* F

29 of by, from.
31 cannot choose is bound to.
37 their charges i.e. the troops in their charge
(originally, a hundred men).
37–8   distinctly   billeted   individually
enrolled.
38 in th'entertainment mobilised, on the
payroll.
41 present immediate.

Act 4, Scene 4
Antium, before Aufidius's house (11), represented by the façade of the tiring-house. The
scene serves as a prelude to 4.5 and is virtually
continuous with it; Coriolanus would probably
exit to the house through one of the side doors and
reappear through the other, at 4.5.4, as though
entering its interior.

0 SD *mean . . . muffled* Coriolanus's entry as
suppliant, *in mean apparel*, visually parallels his
entry in 2.3 in the gown of humility; it is the last
of his costume changes before he can re-don the
armour in which he is at home, and he seems
as uncomfortable here as in his other peacetime
roles. Here, his disguise extends to concealing his
face (*muffled*).
3 'fore my wars in the face of my assaults
(*OED* War *sb*¹ 4b).
5 wives Probably 'women' (see 2.1.57 n.),
though perhaps a more specific reference to the
'widows' (2) he has created.
5 spits skewers (on which meat was roasted
over a fire).

In puny battle slay me.

Enter a CITIZEN

Save you, sir.

CITIZEN And you.

CORIOLANUS   Direct me, if it be your will,
Where great Aufidius lies. Is he in Antium?

CITIZEN He is, and feasts the nobles of the state
At his house this night.

CORIOLANUS   Which is his house, beseech you?   10

CITIZEN This here before you.

CORIOLANUS   Thank you, sir. Farewell.

Exit Citizen

O world, thy slippery turns! Friends now fast sworn,
Whose double bosoms seems to wear one heart,
Whose hours, whose bed, whose meal and exercise
Are still together, who twin, as 'twere, in love   15
Unseparable, shall within this hour,
On a dissension of a doit, break out
To bitterest enmity. So fellest foes,
Whose passions and whose plots have broke their sleep
To take the one the other, by some chance,   20
Some trick not worth an egg, shall grow dear friends

---

6 SD] *Placed as Dyce; after* sir F   13 seems . . . one] F; seene . . . on F2; seem . . . one F4   14 hours] F (Houres); house
Colher²

---

6 **Save you** God save you.

8 **lies** dwells.

12–26 O . . . service This soliloquy replaces North's description of the origin of Coriolanus's decision to seek Volscian support, made while he brooded for a few days at his country house, 'turmoyled with sundry sortes and kynde of thoughtes, suche as the fyer of his choller dyd sturre up. In the ende, seeing he could resolve no waye, to take a profitable or honorable course, but only was pricked forward still to be revenged of the Romaines: he thought to raise up some great warres against them . . . Whereupon, he thought it his best waye, first to stirre up the Volsces against them' (Bullough, *Sources*, v, 526). The soliloquy, however, dwells not on the revenge itself but on the instability of even the closest human bonds, an instability he uses to rationalise his change of allegiance (22).

12 slippery turns fickle, treacherous changes. 'Slipper' or 'slippery' was commonly used to con-

vey the unreliable nature of Fortune's wheel, as in Sir Thomas Wyatt's Epigram XLIV, 'the slipper top / Of court's estates' (*The Complete Poems*, ed. R. A. Rebholtz, 1978, p. 94).

13 double 'separate', but with a play on 'deceitful'.

15 still ever.

17 dissension of a doit quarrel over a trifle. See 1.5.6 n.

18 fellest fiercest.

19–20 plots . . . other stratagems to destroy (literally, 'seize') one another awaken them from sleep; compare Aufidius's confession at 4.5.119–23.

21 trick . . . egg worthless trifle. As Parker notes, this phrase and 'dissension of a doit' reveal how little Coriolanus understands the reason for what has happened to him; the whole passage shows him refusing to recognise the magnitude of his choice or, indeed, that he has in a moral sense chosen at all.

And interjoin their issues. So with me.
My birthplace hate I, and my love's upon
This enemy town. I'll enter. If he slay me,
He does fair justice; if he give me way,   25
I'll do his country service.   *Exit*

4.[5] *Music plays. Enter a* SERVINGMAN

FIRST SERVINGMAN Wine, wine, wine! What service is here? I think
    our fellows are asleep.   [*Exit*]

                  Enter [SECOND] SERVINGMAN

SECOND SERVINGMAN Where's Cotus? My master calls for him.
    Cotus!   *Exit*

                      Enter CORIOLANUS

CORIOLANUS A goodly house. The feast smells well, but I   5
    Appear not like a guest.

                  Enter the FIRST SERVINGMAN

FIRST SERVINGMAN What would you have, friend? Whence are you?
    Here's no place for you. Pray go to the door.   *Exit*
CORIOLANUS I have deserved no better entertainment
    In being Coriolanus.   10

---

23 hate] *Capell;* haue F; leave *conj. Proudfoot*   24 enemy] F; Enemy's F4   Act 4, Scene 5   4.5] *Capell; not in* F   2
SD.1 *Exit*] *Rowe; not in* F   2 SD.2 SECOND] *another* F   3 master] F (M.)   8 door.] F3; doore? F   10 SD SERVINGMAN] F
(*Seruant.*)

22 interjoin . . . issues (1) couple their fortunes, (2) permit their children to intermarry.

23 hate Capell's emendation is persuasive in its
contrast with 'love's'; Proudfoot, however, conjectures that the misread word may have been
'leaue' (p. 205).

25 give me way (1) grant my request, (2)
allow me my free course (see 5.6.31–2).

Act 4, Scene 5
A hall in Aufidius's house. The occasion is from
North, although there Coriolanus is a silent,
majestic figure who so cows the servants that
they immediately go and fetch Aufidius; Shakespeare frames the tense encounter between the
erstwhile rivals with low comedy and adds the
irreverent servingmen's commentary on both
warriors.

0 SD *Music plays* The music would probably
be played in the gallery, as in actual dining halls,
and the calls for 'wine' and 'service' and scurrying
servants further establish the context of Aufidius's
feast.

1 What service King notes the ironic echo of
Coriolanus's last word in 4.4, 'service'.

2 fellows fellow servants.

2 SD.1 *Exit* Exits and other stage movement in
this scene have not been fully specified in F (see
18 SD, 46 SD.2, 49 SD), though they can be worked
out from the context; see Textual Analysis, p. 303
below.

8 go . . . door get out of the house; appalled
at the violation of decorum, the servant may also
mean that at the 'door' this poor man might legit-
imately beg scraps.

9 entertainment reception.

Enter SECOND [SERVINGMAN]

SECOND SERVINGMAN Whence are you, sir? Has the porter his eyes in
    his head that he gives entrance to such companions? Pray get you
    out.
CORIOLANUS Away!
SECOND SERVINGMAN Away? Get you away.   15
CORIOLANUS Now th'art troublesome.
SECOND SERVINGMAN Are you so brave? I'll have you talked with
    anon.

Enter THIRD SERVINGMAN, *the* FIRST[, *entering,*] *meets him*

THIRD SERVINGMAN What fellow's this?
FIRST SERVINGMAN A strange one as ever I looked on. I cannot get him   20
    out o'th'house. Prithee, call my master to him.
THIRD SERVINGMAN What have you to do here, fellow? Pray you avoid
    the house.
CORIOLANUS Let me but stand. I will not hurt your hearth.
THIRD SERVINGMAN What are you?   25
CORIOLANUS A gentleman.
THIRD SERVINGMAN A marvellous poor one.
CORIOLANUS True, so I am.
THIRD SERVINGMAN Pray you, poor gentleman, take up some other
    station. Here's no place for you. Pray you avoid. Come.   30
CORIOLANUS Follow your function, go, and batten on cold bits.
                          Pushes him away from him
THIRD SERVINGMAN What, you will not? Prithee, tell my master what
    a strange guest he has here.
SECOND SERVINGMAN And I shall.   *Exit*
THIRD SERVINGMAN Where dwell'st thou?   35
CORIOLANUS Under the canopy.

---

18 SD THIRD . . . FIRST, *entering, meets*] Sisson subst.; 3 . . . 1 *meets* F; *a third . . . second meets* / Keightley, *after*
Capell   20 SH] F (I); 2 S. / Capell   21 him.] F; him. *Retires* / Globe   34 SD *Exit*] F (*Exit second Seruingman.*)

12 **companions** fellows (often, as here, a term   30 **station** 'standing-place', with a pun on 'sta-
of contempt).   tus' (King); see 2.1.189.
  17 **brave** insolent.   31 **Follow your function** Attend to your ser-
  18 **anon** immediately.   vant role.
  22 **avoid** quit, leave.   31 **batten . . . bits** fatten on left-over scraps.
  24 **hearth** In North, 'he got him up straight   36 **canopy** sky; there is perhaps further play
to the chimney harthe' (Bullough, *Sources*, v,   on 'covering for a throne' and the playhouse
527). When Kemble played Coriolanus he radi-   'heavens' under which they stand.
ated noble hauteur, standing by the hearth under
a statue of Mars (see illustration 6, p. 73 above).

THIRD SERVINGMAN Under the canopy?

CORIOLANUS Ay.

THIRD SERVINGMAN Where's that?

CORIOLANUS I'th'city of kites and crows.   40

THIRD SERVINGMAN I'th'city of kites and crows? What an ass it is!
    Then thou dwell'st with daws too?

CORIOLANUS No, I serve not thy master.

THIRD SERVINGMAN How, sir? Do you meddle with my master?

CORIOLANUS Ay, 'tis an honester service than to meddle with thy   45
    mistress. Thou prat'st and prat'st. Serve with thy trencher. Hence!

                        Beats him away

                                    [*Exit Third Servingman*]

        Enter AUFIDIUS *with the* [SECOND] SERVINGMAN

AUFIDIUS Where is this fellow?

SECOND SERVINGMAN Here, sir. I'd have beaten him like a dog but for
    disturbing the lords within.

                [*First and Second Servingmen stand aside*]

AUFIDIUS Whence com'st thou? What wouldst thou? Thy name?   50
    Why speak's not? Speak man. What's thy name?

CORIOLANUS [*Unmuffling*]   If, Tullus,
    Not yet thou know'st me, and, seeing me, dost not
    Think me for the man I am, necessity
    Commands me name myself.

AUFIDIUS   What is thy name?

CORIOLANUS A name unmusical to the Volscians' ears   55
    And harsh in sound to thine.

AUFIDIUS   Say, what's thy name?

---

41 is!] *Theobald;* is, F   46 SD.2 *Exit . . . Servingman*] *Globe; not in* F   46 SD.3 SECOND SERVINGMAN] *Capell subst.;*
Seruingman. F   49 SD] *Riverside, after Capell (at 54); not in* F   51 SD] *Capell; not in* F

40 **kites and crows** i.e. scavenger birds. Coriolanus may be referring to his time spent since
banishment in a hostile natural environment, or
he may be covertly alluding to the Roman plebeians and the city they now dominate (compare
Menenius's reference to Rome as the unnatural
dam eating her own, 3.1.296–9).

42 **daws** jackdaws (proverbially foolish birds;
see Tilley D50).

43 Coriolanus calls the servants fools, though
Third Servingman mistakes it as a reference to
Aufidius (44).

44, 45 **meddle** The servant means 'concern
yourself with, interfere', but Coriolanus picks
up the secondary (slang) meaning of 'have inter-
course with'.

46 **trencher** wooden platter.

50 **name** The word initiates a series of
repetitions that reaches 'an almost incantatory
intensity' (Brockbank); on the importance
of 'name' and Aufidius's failure to recognise
Coriolanus without it, see pp. 54–5 above.

Thou hast a grim appearance, and thy face
Bears a command in't. Though thy tackle's torn,
Thou show'st a noble vessel. What's thy name?
CORIOLANUS Prepare thy brow to frown. Know'st thou me yet?   60
AUFIDIUS I know thee not. Thy name?
CORIOLANUS My name is Caius Martius, who hath done
            To thee particularly and to all the Volsces
            Great hurt and mischief; thereto witness may
            My surname, Coriolanus. The painful service,   65
            The extreme dangers, and the drops of blood
            Shed for my thankless country are requited
            But with that surname – a good memory
            And witness of the malice and displeasure
            Which thou shouldst bear me. Only that name remains.   70
            The cruelty and envy of the people,
            Permitted by our dastard nobles, who
            Have all forsook me, hath devoured the rest
            And suffered me by th'voice of slaves to be
            Whooped out of Rome. Now this extremity   75
            Hath brought me to thy hearth; not out of hope –
            Mistake me not – to save my life, for if
            I had feared death, of all the men i'th'world
            I would have 'voided thee, but in mere spite,
            To be full quit of those my banishers,   80
            Stand I before thee here. Then if thou hast
            A heart of wreak in thee, that wilt revenge

---

61 not. . . . name?] F3; not? . . . Name? F   67–8 requited . . . surname –] *Rowe subst.*; requitted: . . . Surname,
F   75 Whooped] F (Hoop'd)   79 'voided] F (voided); avoided *Pope*   82 that wilt] F; that will *Hanmer;* and wilt
conj. Capell, 'Notes'

58 **a command** authority.
58 **tackle** ship's rigging (i.e. Coriolanus's 'mean apparel').
59 **vessel** (1) ship, (2) 'the body as receptacle of the soul' (NS, citing *AWW* 2.3.205, *Cym.* 4.2.319).
62–98 This speech closely follows North's Plutarch, what the margin calls 'Coriolanus oration to Tullus Aufidius' (Bullough, *Sources*, v, 527–8); Aufidius's effusive reply and the rest of the scene are Shakespeare's invention.
65 **painful** arduous.
66 **extreme** Accented on the first syllable.
68 **memory** memorial; in North, 'a good memorie and witnes' (Bullough, *Sources*, v, 528).
71 **envy** malice, ill-will felt by inferiors.

72 **dastard** cowardly; North has 'dastardly nobilitie'.
75 **Whooped out** A recollection of the 'deserved vexation' suffered at the end of Act 3. In Plutarch Coriolanus is simply banished; the additional humiliation of a jeering crowd is Shakespeare's, made worse by the hunting term 'Whooped'.
79 **'voided** avoided.
79 **in mere spite** out of pure spite.
80 **full quit of** fully even with.
82 **wreak** revenge; compare North: 'if thou hast any harte to be wrecked of the injuries thy enemies have done thee' (Bullough, *Sources*, v, 528).

Thine own particular wrongs and stop those maims
Of shame seen through thy country, speed thee straight
And make my misery serve thy turn. So use it   85
That my revengeful services may prove
As benefits to thee, for I will fight
Against my cankered country with the spleen
Of all the under-fiends. But if so be
Thou dar'st not this, and that to prove more fortunes   90
Thou'rt tired, then, in a word, I also am
Longer to live most weary and present
My throat to thee and to thy ancient malice,
Which not to cut would show thee but a fool,
Since I have ever followed thee with hate,   95
Drawn tuns of blood out of thy country's breast,
And cannot live but to thy shame, unless
It be to do thee service.
AUFIDIUS   O Martius, Martius!
Each word thou hast spoke hath weeded from my heart
A root of ancient envy. If Jupiter   100
Should from yond cloud speak divine things
And say ''Tis true', I'd not believe them more
Than thee, all-noble Martius. Let me twine
Mine arms about that body whereagainst
My grainèd ash an hundred times hath broke   105

---

91 Thou'rt] F (Th'art)   102 ''Tis true'] *Hanmer;* 'tis true F   104 whereagainst] F (where against)

83–4 maims / Of shame dishonouring injuries. Coriolanus refers to the literal destruction caused by siege and pillage and the loss of Volscian territory, but also, more abstractly, to wounds to the body politic.
84 through throughout.
88 cankered corrupted; more specifically, ulcerated, gangrened (*OED* Cankered *ppl a* 1), thus condemning Rome in the same terms the tribunes had used of him at 3.1.300, 311–13. There is no equivalent word in North.
88 spleen ferocity.
89 under-fiends devils from the underworld.
90 prove more fortunes try your fortunes further, take more chances.
93 ancient long-standing.
96 tuns large casks.

97–8 cannot . . . service Introducing the idea of Aufidius's 'shame', Shakespeare underscores Coriolanus's pride even at the moment he places his fate in Aufidius's hands. In North the appeal is pragmatic: 'it were no wisdome in thee, to save the life of him, who hath bene heretofore thy mortall enemie' (Bullough, *Sources*, v, 528).
100–2 If . . . true Aufidius refers to the 'classical conception of thunder as an omen of assent from Jupiter "the thunderer" (*Tonans* or *Tonitrualis*)' (Verity); here and in 'Why, thou Mars' (115) Aufidius contributes to the deification of Coriolanus.
104 whereagainst against which.
105 grainèd ash (1) ashen lance with a long-grained shaft; possibly (2) ashen lance with a pronged head (*OED* Grained *ppl a* 3).

And scarred the moon with splinters.
                    [*He embraces Coriolanus*]
                              Here I clip
The anvil of my sword, and do contest
As hotly and as nobly with thy love
As ever in ambitious strength I did
Contend against thy valour. Know thou first,   110
I loved the maid I married; never man
Sighed truer breath. But that I see thee here,
Thou noble thing, more dances my rapt heart
Than when I first my wedded mistress saw
Bestride my threshold. Why, thou Mars, I tell thee,   115
We have a power on foot, and I had purpose
Once more to hew thy target from thy brawn
Or lose mine arm for't. Thou hast beat me out
Twelve several times, and I have nightly since
Dreamt of encounters 'twixt thyself and me –   120
We have been down together in my sleep,
Unbuckling helms, fisting each other's throat –
And waked half dead with nothing. Worthy Martius,
Had we no other quarrel else to Rome but that
Thou art thence banished, we would muster all   125
From twelve to seventy and, pouring war
Into the bowels of ungrateful Rome,

---

106 scarred] F (scarr'd); scar'd *Rowe²*   106 SD] *Oxford; not in* F   106 clip] F (cleep)   120–2 me– . . . throat –] F (me: . . . Throat,)

106 **scarred** This reading offers a hyperbole appropriate to the context, though as Brockbank notes, Rowe's emendation is made plausible by F spellings of 'scarr'd' for 'scared' (*WT* 3.3.65) and 'scarre' for 'scare' (*Tro.* 5.10.21), and Malone cites *R3* 5.3.341: 'Amaze the welkin with your broken staves.'
106 **clip** embrace.
107 **anvil** i.e. Coriolanus, whose armour Aufidius has struck with his sword as an anvil is hit with a hammer.
107 **contest** compete.
110 **first** Probably 'in the first place', but possibly 'first, or noblest of men' (see 4.1.33 n.).
113–15 **more . . . threshold** Compare Martius's welcome of Cominius, 1.6.29–32 and n.
113 **rapt** enraptured.
115 **Bestride** Step across. Had Shakespeare

consulted Plutarch's *Romane Questions* (in *Moralia*, trans. Philemon Holland, 1603, p. 852) he would have found that Roman tradition required that brides be carried across the threshold.
116 **power** army.
117 **target** A light shield or buckler worn on the arm (hence 'brawn').
118 **out** outright.
119 **several** separate.
121 **down together** fighting hand-to-hand on the ground.
127 **bowels** Aufidius's image suggests a violent purgation of the Roman body politic that recalls Coriolanus's wish 'To jump a body with a dangerous physic' (3.1.155) and anticipates Volumnia's vision of him 'tearing / His country's bowels out' (5.3.102–3).

Like a bold flood o'erbeat. O, come, go in,
And take our friendly senators by th'hands,
Who now are here taking their leaves of me,   130
Who am prepared against your territories,
Though not for Rome itself.
CORIOLANUS   You bless me, gods!
AUFIDIUS Therefore, most absolute sir, if thou wilt have
The leading of thine own revenges, take
Th'one half of my commission and set down   135
As best thou art experienced, since thou know'st
Thy country's strength and weakness, thine own ways,
Whether to knock against the gates of Rome
Or rudely visit them in parts remote
To fright them ere destroy. But come in,   140
Let me commend thee first to those that shall
Say yea to thy desires. A thousand welcomes!
And more a friend than e'er an enemy;
Yet, Martius, that was much. Your hand. Most welcome!
                            Exeunt [Coriolanus and Aufidius]
                    [*The two* SERVINGMEN *come forward*]
FIRST SERVINGMAN Here's a strange alteration!   145
SECOND SERVINGMAN By my hand, I had thought to have strucken
    him with a cudgel, and yet my mind gave me his clothes made a
    false report of him.
FIRST SERVINGMAN What an arm he has! He turned me about with his
    finger and his thumb as one would set up a top.   150
SECOND SERVINGMAN Nay, I knew by his face that there was some-
    thing in him. He had, sir, a kind of face, methought – I cannot tell
    how to term it.

---

128 o'erbeat] F (o're-beate); o'er-bear *Rowe*; o'er-bear't *White, conj. Becket*   135–7 down . . . weakness,] F; down – . . . weakness – *Capell*   144 SD.1 *Exeunt Coriolanus . . . Aufidius*] *Capell; Exeunt* F   144 SD.2 *The . . . forward*] *Globe; Enter two of the Seruingmen.* F   145 SH] F (I); 3. S. / *Capell (and to end of scene)*   145 alteration!] F (alteration?)   152 methought –] *Rowe;* me thought, F

128 **o'erbeat** overpower, beat down. White's 'o'erbear't' is grammatically attractive but unnecessary.
133 **absolute** perfect, incomparable.
135 **my commission** Both 'my warrant from the state to lead this war' and 'the forces under my command'.
135 **set down** determine, decide (*OED* Set v 143g).

146 **By my hand** An oath (see *AWW* 3.6.72); Parker notes that it is also, comically, a dative ('By my hand I had thought to have strucken him with a cudgel') standing in antithesis to 'my mind'.
147 **gave me** misgave me, made me suspect.
150 **set up** set spinning.

FIRST SERVINGMAN He had so, looking as it were – would I were
  hanged but I thought there was more in him than I could think.   155
SECOND SERVINGMAN So did I, I'll be sworn. He is simply the rarest
  man i'th'world.
FIRST SERVINGMAN I think he is. But a greater soldier than he, you wot
  one.
SECOND SERVINGMAN Who, my master?   160
FIRST SERVINGMAN Nay, it's no matter for that.
SECOND SERVINGMAN Worth six on him.
FIRST SERVINGMAN Nay, not so neither. But I take him to be the
  greater soldier.
SECOND SERVINGMAN Faith, look you, one cannot tell how to say that.   165
  For the defence of a town, our general is excellent.
FIRST SERVINGMAN Ay, and for an assault too.

Enter the THIRD SERVINGMAN

THIRD SERVINGMAN O slaves, I can tell you news – news, you rascals!
FIRST *and* SECOND SERVINGMEN What, what, what? Let's partake.
THIRD SERVINGMAN I would not be a Roman, of all nations. I had as   170
  lief be a condemned man.
FIRST *and* SECOND SERVINGMEN Wherefore? Wherefore?
THIRD SERVINGMAN Why, here's he that was wont to thwack our
  general, Caius Martius.
FIRST SERVINGMAN Why do you say 'thwack our general'?   175
THIRD SERVINGMAN I do not say 'thwack our general', but he was
  always good enough for him.
SECOND SERVINGMAN Come, we are fellows and friends. He was ever
  too hard for him; I have heard him say so himself.

---

154 were –] *Rowe;* were, F   158–9 is. But . . . he, . . . one] F; is: but . . . he . . . on *Dyce;* is; but . . . he, . . . on *Brockbank;* is yet . . . he . . . on *Oxford*   167 SD] F; *Re-enter first* SERVANT *Capell*   168 SH] F (3); I.S. / *Capell (and to end of scene)*   169 SH, 172 SH] F *(Both.); 2.3. Capell*   171 lief] F (liue)   175, 176 'thwack . . . general'] *Craig;* thwacke . . . Generall F

158–67 But . . . too The lack of clear referents for the third-person pronouns in this exchange comically underscores the caution with which the servants try to sound out each other's response to the new situation.
  158–9 But . . . one The first servant appears to venture a claim for Aufidius's superiority, only to retreat at 161. Possibly Dyce's reading of 'on' instead of 'one' is correct, since Elizabethan English did not distinguish the two spellings; it would make the assertion more equivocal.

162–3 him . . . him The first 'him' probably refers to Aufidius, the second to Coriolanus, with First Servingman conceding Coriolanus's superiority but rejecting Second Servingman's hyperbole.
  171 lief willingly, gladly.
  173 wont accustomed.
  178 Come . . . friends We're co-workers and friends and can speak openly.

FIRST SERVINGMAN He was too hard for him directly. To say the troth   180
on't, before Corioles he scotched him and notched him like a
carbonado.

SECOND SERVINGMAN And he had been cannibally given, he might
have broiled and eaten him too.

FIRST SERVINGMAN But more of thy news.   185

THIRD SERVINGMAN Why, he is so made on here within as if he were
son and heir to Mars; set at upper end o'th'table; no question asked
him by any of the senators but they stand bald before him. Our
general himself makes a mistress of him, sanctifies himself with's
hand, and turns up the white o'th'eye to his discourse. But the   190
bottom of the news is, our general is cut i'th'middle and but one half
of what he was yesterday, for the other has half by the entreaty and
grant of the whole table. He'll go, he says, and sowl the porter of
Rome gates by th'ears. He will mow all down before him and leave
his passage polled.   195

SECOND SERVINGMAN And he's as like to do't as any man I can
imagine.

THIRD SERVINGMAN Do't? He will do't, for look you, sir, he has as
many friends as enemies; which friends, sir, as it were, durst not –
look you, sir – show themselves, as we term it, his friends whilst   200
he's in directitude.

FIRST SERVINGMAN 'Directitude'? What's that?

180–1 him directly. . . . on't, . . . Corioles] *NS*; him directly, . . . on't . . . *Corioles*, F; him directly, . . . on't: . . .
Corioli *Pope*; him directly, . . . on't. . . . Corioles *Kittredge*; him, directly . . . on't, . . . Corioles; *Riverside*   184
broiled] *Pope*; boyld F   193 sowl] F (sole)   195 polled] F (poul'd)   201 directitude] F; discreditude *conj. Malone*;
dejectitude *Collier²*   202 'Directitude'] *This edn*; Directitude F

180 directly (1) in direct encounter, face to
face (as at 1.6.58); possibly (2) without evasion
(which Brockbank notes is the more usual Shakespearean meaning).
181 scotched scored, gashed.
182 carbonado Meat or fish scored across and
grilled ('broiled', 184) upon hot coals.
183 And If.
184 broiled Pope's emendation better fits 'carbonado' than F's 'boyld', which would be an easy
misreading of 'broyld'.
186 so made on made so much of.
187 at . . . table i.e. next to Aufidius, in the
place of honour.
188 but . . . bald without their removing their
hats (as a sign of respect). Elizabethan gentlemen
wore their hats indoors as well as out.
189–90 sanctifies . . . hand (1) 'touches his

hand as though it were a sacred relic' (Hibbard),
(2) 'clasps it with the same reverence as a lover
would the hand of his mistress' (Malone).
190 turns . . . eye i.e. looks at him admiringly.
191 bottom gist, essential part.
191 cut . . . middle i.e. his authority has been
halved; the image is of half a joint of meat left
over (King) and recalls the 'carbonado' metaphor
at 182.
193 sowl seize roughly by the ears (*OED* Sowl
v³ 1), drag.
195 polled (1) cleared (literally, 'shorn'), (2)
pillaged, despoiled (*OED* Poll *v* 5).
199 friends i.e. among the Roman patricians.
201 directitude Third Servingman seems to
be reaching for an impressive word (such as
'dejectitude' or 'discreditude') to round off his
speech.

THIRD SERVINGMAN But when they shall see, sir, his crest up again and
the man in blood, they will out of their burrows, like conies after
rain, and revel all with him.   205

FIRST SERVINGMAN But when goes this forward?

THIRD SERVINGMAN Tomorrow, today, presently. You shall have the
drum struck up this afternoon. 'Tis as it were a parcel of their feast,
and to be executed ere they wipe their lips.

SECOND SERVINGMAN Why, then we shall have a stirring world again.   210
This peace is nothing but to rust iron, increase tailors, and breed
ballad-makers.

FIRST SERVINGMAN Let me have war, say I. It exceeds peace as far as
day does night. It's sprightly walking, audible, and full of vent.
Peace is a very apoplexy, lethargy; mulled, deaf, sleepy, insensible;   215
a getter of more bastard children than war's a destroyer of men.

SECOND SERVINGMAN 'Tis so. And as wars in some sort may be said to
be a ravisher, so it cannot be denied but peace is a great maker of
cuckolds.

FIRST SERVINGMAN Ay, and it makes men hate one another.   220

THIRD SERVINGMAN Reason: because they then less need one another.
The wars for my money. I hope to see Romans as cheap as
Volscians.

[A sound within]

They are rising, they are rising.

FIRST *and* SECOND SERVINGMEN In, in, in, in!   225

Exeunt

---

211 is nothing] F; is worth nothing F4   214 sprightly walking] F; sprightly, waking *Pope*   214 vent] F; vaunt *Collier²*, *conj. Becket*   215 sleepy] F3; sleepe F   216 war's] *Rowe²*; warres F   217 wars] F (warres); war *Rowe²*   223 SD] *Oxford; not in* F   225 SH] F (*Both.*); *All. / Steevens²*

203 **his crest up** i.e. enraged as a dog with raised hackles, with perhaps an anachronistic play on 'crest' as personal heraldic device (*OED* Crest *sb¹* 3); compare *1H4* 1.1.98–9, *John* 4.3.149.

204 **in blood** in full vigour and cry (a hunting term; see 1.1.142–3 n.).

204 **conies** rabbits.

207 **presently** now, immediately.

208 **parcel** portion, part.

211 **is nothing** is good for nothing.

211 **increase tailors** He may mean that tailors, commonly mocked as cowardly and effeminate, would increase in number without war to thin their ranks, or that in peacetime elaborate clothing replaces armour.

214 **sprightly . . . vent** As Sisson notes, war is here imagined as a hunting hound in full

cry ('audible') as it scents its prey ('vent' = scent given off by a hunted animal); compare *JC* 3.1.273, 'let slip the dogs of war'.

215 **apoplexy, lethargy** Compare *2H4* 1.2.111–13: 'This apoplexy, as I take it, is a kind of lethargy . . . a kind of sleeping in the blood.'

215 **mulled** (1) dull, stupefied (*OED* Mull *v²*), (2) softened, rendered mild as mulled wine (*OED v³*).

216 **getter** begetter, producer.

217 **wars** F's 'warres' may have been contaminated by 'warres' (= war's) in the preceding line (*Textual Companion*), but 'wars' is frequently used in singular constructions in Shakespeare (see 222 and 1.3.90 n.).

4.[6]   *Enter the two Tribunes,* SICINIUS *and* BRUTUS

SICINIUS   We hear not of him, neither need we fear him.
His remedies are tame – the present peace
And quietness of the people, which before
Were in wild hurry. Here do we make his friends
Blush that the world goes well, who rather had,   5
Though they themselves did suffer by't, behold
Dissentious numbers pestering streets than see
Our tradesmen singing in their shops and going
About their functions friendly.

Enter MENENIUS

BRUTUS   We stood to't in good time. Is this Menenius?   10
SICINIUS   'Tis he, 'tis he. O, he is grown most kind of late.
Hail, sir!
MENENIUS   Hail to you both.
SICINIUS   Your Coriolanus is not much missed
But with his friends. The commonwealth doth stand,   15
And so would do were he more angry at it.
MENENIUS   All's well, and might have been much better if
He could have temporised.
SICINIUS   Where is he, hear you?
MENENIUS   Nay, I hear nothing.
His mother and his wife hear nothing from him.   20

Enter three or four CITIZENS

Act 4, Scene 6   4.6] *Pope; not in* F   **2** tame – the] *Sisson (after Rowe);* tame, the F; tame: the *Rowe;* tame i'th'
Theobald; ta'en, the *conj. Johnson;* lame i'the *conj. Mason;* tame. The *White*   **4** hurry. Here do we make] F; hurry
here, do make *Hanmer;* hurry. Here he makes *Warburton;* hurry, here do make *White*   **14** not] F; not now *Parker,
conj. Hinman (in 'Textual Companion')*

Act 4, Scene 6
Rome, the market-place. The sense of harmony
and everyday routine of the scene's opening is
Shakespeare's addition to Plutarch, where the city
is still in 'marvelous uprore, and discord' over
Coriolanus's banishment (Bullough, *Sources*, V,
528), and effectively contrasts with the Volscian
servants' eagerness for war at the end of 4.5; it
also suggests a passage of time before the messengers arrive with news that the Volscian army has
already entered Roman territory.
   2 His . . . tame – The remedies against Coriolanus, or antidotes to him, are to be found in

tameness (i.e. 'the present peace and quiet'); the
tribunes still think of Coriolanus in terms of a
disease that disturbed the body politic. Many editors follow Theobald's emendation ('tame i'th'),
which shifts the meaning to 'His means of redress
are tame' (because by banishing him we have rendered him powerless).
   6 did would.
   7 pestering crowding, blocking.
   9 functions occupations.
   10 stood to't made a stand.
   19–20 Nay . . . him This reflects on Coriolanus's promise at 4.1.51–2.

ALL CITIZENS The gods preserve you both!

SICINIUS   Good e'en, our neighbours.

BRUTUS Good e'en to you all, good e'en to you all.

FIRST CITIZEN Ourselves, our wives, and children, on our knees
        Are bound to pray for you both.

SICINIUS   Live and thrive.

BRUTUS Farewell, kind neighbours.   25
        We wished Coriolanus had loved you as we did.

ALL CITIZENS Now the gods keep you!

BOTH TRIBUNES Farewell, farewell.

                                        Exeunt Citizens

SICINIUS This is a happier and more comely time
        Than when these fellows ran about the streets   30
        Crying confusion.

BRUTUS   Caius Martius was
        A worthy officer i'th'war, but insolent,
        O'ercome with pride, ambitious, past all thinking
        Self-loving.

SICINIUS   And affecting one sole throne
        Without assistance.

MENENIUS   I think not so.   35

SICINIUS We should by this, to all our lamentation,
        If he had gone forth consul found it so.

BRUTUS The gods have well prevented it, and Rome
        Sits safe and still without him.

                    Enter an AEDILE

AEDILE   Worthy tribunes,
        There is a slave, whom we have put in prison,   40
        Reports the Volsces with two several powers
        Are entered in the Roman territories,
        And with the deepest malice of the war

---

21 SH, 27 SH ALL CITIZENS] F (*All.*)   21, 22 Good e'en] F (Gooden)   23 SH] F (1)   33 ambitious, . . . thinking] F;
ambitious . . . thinking, F4   34 Self-loving.] F; self-loving, – *Capell*   35 assistance] F (assistāce); assistants *Hanmer,*
conj. Theobald   36 lamentation] F2; Lamention F

21 **Good e'en** See 2.1.75 n.   37 **found** have found.
29 **comely** decorous, seemly.   41 **several powers** separate armies.
35 **assistance** associates, sharers (in power). 43 **deepest** utmost (implying a greater than
36 **by this** by now.   usual devastation).

Destroy what lies before 'em.

MENENIUS   'Tis Aufidius

Who, hearing of our Martius' banishment,   45

Thrusts forth his horns again into the world,

Which were inshelled when Martius stood for Rome

And durst not once peep out.

SICINIUS Come, what talk you of Martius?

BRUTUS Go see this rumourer whipped. It cannot be   50

The Volsces dare break with us.

MENENIUS   Cannot be?

We have record that very well it can,

And three examples of the like hath been

Within my age. But reason with the fellow

Before you punish him, where he heard this,   55

Lest you shall chance to whip your information

And beat the messenger who bids beware

Of what is to be dreaded.

SICINIUS   Tell not me.

I know this cannot be.

BRUTUS   Not possible.

Enter a MESSENGER

MESSENGER The nobles in great earnestness are going   60

All to the senate-house. Some news is come

That turns their countenances.

SICINIUS   'Tis this slave –

[*To the Aedile*] Go whip him 'fore the people's eyes – his

     raising,

---

53 hath] F; have F4   61 come] *Rowe;* comming F; come in *Malone*   62–3 slave – . . . eyes –] F (Slaue: . . . eyes:);
slave. . . . eyes. – *Oxford*   63 SD] *Oxford; not in* F

---

47 inshelled drawn in (like a snail's horns).
The image of the great Volscian warrior as a snail
would be less comically unthreatening if Shakespeare had in mind the fact that 'snaile' was the
English translation, in manuals of warfare (e.g.
The Foure Bookes of Flavius Vegetius Renatus,
trans. John Sadler, 1572, G7ᵛ), of 'testudo', one
kind of Roman wall-battering machine used in
sieges.
49 what why, for what reason.
51 break break their treaty (made after the
defeat dramatised in Act 1).
52 record Accented on the second syllable.

53 hath 'An example of the surviving plurals in
-*th*, very common in the words 'hath' and 'doth'
especially' (Case).
54 age lifetime.
54 reason discuss, talk.
56 information source of information.
61 come It seems probable that the compositor
picked up -*ing* (in F's 'coming') from 'going' in the
preceding line. If F is correct, it would suggest a
process, news 'coming' in by instalments.
62 turns (1) turns pale, (2) curdles, makes sour
(like milk).
63 raising rumour-raising.

Nothing but his report.
MESSENGER   Yes, worthy sir,
          The slave's report is seconded, and more,   65
          More fearful, is delivered.
SICINIUS   What more fearful?
MESSENGER It is spoke freely out of many mouths –
          How probable I do not know – that Martius,
          Joined with Aufidius, leads a power 'gainst Rome
          And vows revenge as spacious as between   70
          The young'st and oldest thing.
SICINIUS   This is most likely!
BRUTUS Raised only that the weaker sort may wish
          Good Martius home again.
SICINIUS   The very trick on't.
MENENIUS This is unlikely.
          He and Aufidius can no more atone   75
          Than violent'st contrariety.

Enter [a SECOND] MESSENGER

SECOND MESSENGER You are sent for to the senate.
          A fearful army, led by Caius Martius
          Associated with Aufidius, rages
          Upon our territories and have already   80
          O'erborne their way, consumed with fire, and took
          What lay before them.

Enter COMINIUS

COMINIUS O, you have made good work!
MENENIUS What news? What news?
COMINIUS You have holp to ravish your own daughters and   85
          To melt the city leads upon your pates,
          To see your wives dishonoured to your noses –
MENENIUS What's the news? What's the news?

71 likely!] *Theobald;* likely. F   73 Good] F; God *Collier²*   76 contrariety] F; contrarieties *Hanmer;* contraries
Capell   76 SD *Enter a* SECOND] *Globe, after Hanmer (another); Enter* F   77 SH] *Hanmer* (2 *Mes.*); *Mes.* F   87 noses –]
Capell; Noses. F

65 **seconded** supported by a second report.
70 **as . . . between** comprehensive enough to
include.
75 **atone** be reconciled (be 'at one').
76 **violent'st contrariety** most extreme opposites. The singular form is stronger because more

abstract (Brockbank); elsewhere Shakespeare uses
only the plural.
81 **O'erborne their way** Overwhelmed everything in their path.
85 **holp** helped; see 3.1.280 n.
86 **leads** lead-covered roofs.

COMINIUS Your temples burnèd in their cement, and
          Your franchises, whereon you stood, confined   90
          Into an auger's bore.
MENENIUS   Pray now, your news –
          [*To the Tribunes*] You have made fair work, I fear me – Pray,
          your news.
          If Martius should be joined wi'th' Volscians –
COMINIUS   If?
          He is their god. He leads them like a thing
          Made by some other deity than Nature,   95
          That shapes man better, and they follow him
          Against us brats with no less confidence
          Than boys pursuing summer butterflies
          Or butchers killing flies.
MENENIUS [*To the Tribunes*]   You have made good work,
          You and your apron-men, you that stood so much   100
          Upon the voice of occupation and
          The breath of garlic-eaters!
COMINIUS He'll shake your Rome about your ears.
MENENIUS As Hercules did shake down mellow fruit.
          You have made fair work!   105
BRUTUS But is this true, sir?
COMINIUS   Ay, and you'll look pale
          Before you find it other. All the regions
          Do smilingly revolt, and who resists

---

91 auger's bore] F (Augors boare)   92 SD] *Oxford; not in* F   93 wi'th'] *Hudson²; with* F; with the *Rowe*   93 Volscians
–] *Pope;* Volceans. F   99 flies] F (Flyes); sheep *conj. Capell;* pigs *conj. Leo*   99 SD] *Oxford; not in* F   100 apron-men]
F (Apron men)   107 regions] F; legions *Collier², conj. Becket*

89 in their cement to their foundations, into
their mortar; the accent falls on the first syllable
of 'cement'. Plutarch does not report that Coriolanus intended to burn Rome.
  90 Your . . . stood The voting rights on which
you insisted.
  91 auger's bore small hole made by an auger
(a boring tool).
  98 For Coriolanus's son attacking a butterfly,
see 1.3.54–8.
  99 flies References to butchers killing the flies
attracted by their trade are not uncommon in
the period. Although it is possible that 'flies' was
picked up from 'butterflies', emendation is unnecessary.
  100 apron-men artisans and tradesmen (who
wore aprons). Menenius turns into an insult the

complacent vision of a prosperous city of tradesmen with which the tribunes had opened this
scene.
  101 voice of occupation workingmen's vote
(with a play on the literal sense, compare 'breath',
102).
  102 garlic-eaters Garlic was an inexpensive
flavouring, compared to imported spices, and
thought to have medicinal properties; see 1.1.46
n.
  104 The eleventh of Hercules' twelve 'labours'
(see 4.1.17 n.) was to fetch the golden apples from
a tree in the garden of the Hesperides guarded by
a dragon.
  108 smilingly eagerly, cheerfully.
  108 who resists those who resist (see Abbott
251).

Are mocked for valiant ignorance
And perish constant fools. Who is't can blame him?   110
Your enemies and his find something in him.
MENENIUS We are all undone, unless
    The noble man have mercy.
COMINIUS   Who shall ask it?
    The tribunes cannot do't for shame; the people
    Deserve such pity of him as the wolf   115
    Does of the shepherds. For his best friends, if they
    Should say 'Be good to Rome', they charged him even
    As those should do that had deserved his hate
    And therein showed like enemies.
MENENIUS   'Tis true.
    If he were putting to my house the brand   120
    That should consume it, I have not the face
    To say 'Beseech you, cease.' [*To the Tribunes*] You have made
        fair hands,
    You and your crafts! You have crafted fair!
COMINIUS   You have brought
    A trembling upon Rome such as was never
    S'incapable of help.
BOTH TRIBUNES   Say not we brought it.   125
MENENIUS How? Was't we? We loved him, but, like beasts
    And cowardly nobles, gave way unto your clusters,
    Who did hoot him out o'th'city.
COMINIUS   But I fear
    They'll roar him in again. Tullus Aufidius,
    The second name of men, obeys his points   130

---

117 'Be . . . Rome'] *Hanmer;* be . . . Rome F   119 true.] *Rowe;* true, F; true *Bevington*[2]   122 'Beseech . . . cease.']
Hanmer; beseech . . . cease. F   122 SD] *Oxford; not in* F   123 crafts!] *Delius;* Crafts, F   125 SH] *Dyce (Both Tri.);*
Tri. F

110 **constant** loyal.
116 **For** As for.
117–19 **charged . . . showed** would charge . . .
would show. On the subjunctive construction see
Abbott 361. Cominius argues that in pleading
for mercy the patricians would be behaving like
those who are Coriolanus's enemies and deserve
his hate.
118 **those** i.e. the tribunes and plebeians.
122 **made . . . hands** i.e. you have made a real
mess of it (sarcasm inverting the surface meaning); see Tilley H99.
123 **crafts** craftsmen, tradesmen.
123 **crafted** (1) worked like a craftsman, (2)
acted craftily, intrigued.

125 **help** remedy (i.e. the situation is hopeless).
127 **clusters** crowds, mobs.
129 **roar** Either 'roar in pain (or fear) when
he takes Rome' (compare 2.3.47–8), or 'roar for
mercy'. When Aufidius later uses 'roared' against
Coriolanus, it seems to mean 'acted like a bawling
child' (5.6.100).
130 **second . . . men** second (to Coriolanus) in
renown.
130 **points** commands in every point. Brockbank notes that a 'point of war' was a drum or
trumpet signal.

As if he were his officer. Desperation
Is all the policy, strength, and defence
That Rome can make against them.

Enter a troop of CITIZENS

MENENIUS   Here come the clusters.
And is Aufidius with him? You are they
That made the air unwholesome when you cast   135
Your stinking greasy caps in hooting at
Coriolanus' exile. Now he's coming,
And not a hair upon a soldier's head
Which will not prove a whip. As many coxcombs
As you threw caps up will he tumble down   140
And pay you for your voices. 'Tis no matter.
If he could burn us all into one coal,
We have deserved it.
ALL CITIZENS Faith, we hear fearful news.
FIRST CITIZEN   For mine own part,
When I said banish him, I said 'twas pity.   145
SECOND CITIZEN And so did I.
THIRD CITIZEN And so did I, and, to say the truth, so did very many of
   us. That we did, we did for the best, and though we willingly
   consented to his banishment, yet it was against our will.
COMINIUS You're goodly things, you voices.
MENENIUS   You have made good work,   150
You and your cry. Shall's to the Capitol?
COMINIUS O, ay, what else?

Exeunt [Cominius and Menenius]

SICINIUS Go, masters, get you home. Be not dismayed.
These are a side that would be glad to have

---

144 SH ALL CITIZENS] F (*Omnes.*)   150 You're] F (Y'are)   150 made] F; made you F2   152 SD *Cominius and Menenius*]
Capell subst.; both. F

135–6 cast . . . caps See 3.3.143 SD.2.
139 coxcombs fools' heads (referring to the
hood of the professional jester).
142 one coal one cindery mass (on 'coal' =
cinder, see *OED* Coal *sb* 2).
148–9 willingly . . . will This paradox also
appears in George Chapman's translation of the
Iliad, IV, 43; see pp. 6–7 above. But it may also
have been a common coinage: the epistle to the
reader in Richard Stocke's *A Sermon Preached at
Paules Cross*, entered in the Stationers' Register

in 1606 and printed 1609, says that only when
pirated copies had appeared was he persuaded
to publish his sermon, 'willingly against my will'
(*8ʳ).
151 cry pack of hounds; compare 3.3.128, 'cry
of curs'.
151 Shall's Shall we ('go' understood); see
Abbott 215.
154 side faction.

    This true which they so seem to fear. Go home   155
    And show no sign of fear.
FIRST CITIZEN The gods be good to us! Come, masters, let's home. I
    ever said we were i'th'wrong when we banished him.
SECOND CITIZEN So did we all. But come, let's home.
                Exeunt Citizens
BRUTUS I do not like this news.   160
SICINIUS Nor I.
BRUTUS Let's to the Capitol. Would half my wealth
    Would buy this for a lie.
SICINIUS   Pray let's go.
                    Exeunt

4.[7] *Enter* AUFIDIUS *with his* LIEUTENANT

AUFIDIUS Do they still fly to th'Roman?
LIEUTENANT I do not know what witchcraft's in him, but
    Your soldiers use him as the grace 'fore meat,
    Their talk at table, and their thanks at end,
    And you are darkened in this action, sir,   5
    Even by your own.
AUFIDIUS   I cannot help it now,
    Unless by using means I lame the foot
    Of our design. He bears himself more proudlier,
    Even to my person, than I thought he would
    When first I did embrace him. Yet his nature   10
    In that's no changeling, and I must excuse

---

159 SD] F (*Exit Cit.*) 163 SD] F (*Exeunt Tribunes.*) Act 4, Scene 7 4.7] *Capell; not in* F 8 proudlier] F; proudly
F2

Act 4, Scene 7
A military camp near Rome. The scene echoes
1.10, although Aufidius's jealous resentment of
Coriolanus has intensified and the earlier vague
commitment to intrigue rather than honour now
has a focal point, the taking of Rome. In Aufidius's final speech Shakespeare slows the tempo
for a more objective, balanced though also puz-
zled, assessment of Coriolanus's character and
actions that is perhaps out of character for Aufidius but gives his remarks a choric quality, like
those of the nameless officers at the opening
of 2.2.
 3–4 **grace . . . end** See the description of Aufidius's own behaviour, 4.5.188–90; here the submerged suggestion is not merely that Coriolanus

is worshipped by his men but that he becomes
part of the meal they consume.
 5 **darkened** eclipsed; compare 2.1.233.
 5 **action** military action, campaign.
 6 **your own** your own men; possibly with a
pun on 'action' (5), i.e. his making Coriolanus
co-general.
 7–8 **Unless . . . design** Except by using such
means as would hinder our design on Rome.
 8 **more proudlier** A double comparative for
emphasis; see 3.1.121 and Abbott 11.
 11 **changeling** (1) fickle person, (2) renegade,
turncoat (*OED* Changeling *sb* 1, which cites *1H4*
5.1.76).
 11–12 **must . . . amended** Compare Second
Citizen's sentiments at 1.1.31–2.

What cannot be amended.

LIEUTENANT   Yet I wish, sir –
I mean for your particular – you had not
Joined in commission with him, but either
Have borne the action of yourself or else   15
To him had left it solely.

AUFIDIUS   I understand thee well, and be thou sure,
When he shall come to his account, he knows not
What I can urge against him. Although it seems,
And so he thinks, and is no less apparent   20
To th'vulgar eye, that he bears all things fairly
And shows good husbandry for the Volscian state,
Fights dragon-like, and does achieve as soon
As draw his sword, yet he hath left undone
That which shall break his neck or hazard mine   25
Whene'er we come to our account.

LIEUTENANT   Sir, I beseech you, think you he'll carry Rome?

AUFIDIUS   All places yields to him ere he sits down,
And the nobility of Rome are his;
The senators and patricians love him too.   30
The tribunes are no soldiers, and their people
Will be as rash in the repeal as hasty

---

19 him.] *Pope subst.;* him, F   26 Whene'er] F (When ere)   28 yields] F (yeelds); yeeld F2

13 for your particular as far as you personally are concerned.

14 Joined in commission Compare North: 'Thus he was joyned in commission with Tullus as generall of the Volsces' (Bullough, *Sources,* V, 531).

15 Have Could have.

15 borne ... yourself conducted the campaign yourself.

18 account moment of accounting, reckoning (a legal action demanding an accounting from a commercial subordinate; compare *1H4* 3.2.149).

19 What ... him Compare 24–6; what evidence against Coriolanus Aufidius can have at this point we are not told. The obscurity may have been occasioned by Shakespeare's telescoping Plutarch's sequence of events, in which Coriolanus gives his terms to the first group of ambassadors, allows thirty days for Rome to make its decision, and departs to use the interim to conquer more cities allied to Rome. It is this failure to force Rome's immediate surrender that is 'the first matter wherewith the Volsces (that most envied

Martius glorie and authoritie) dyd charge Martius with' (Bullough, *Sources,* V, 534). In Shakespeare there is no departure and return, and the embassies seeking mercy all occur in Act 5.

22 husbandry for management on behalf of.

23 achieve accomplish his aims. This fearsome coincidence of intent and accomplishment is echoed in Menenius's report at 5.4.18–19.

28–57 Shakespeare takes his cue for Aufidius's and the officer's resentment from North (see 19 n.), but Aufidius's semi-soliloquy on Coriolanus is entirely his own.

28 sits down lays siege to them.

29 nobility This may refer to the *young nobility* of 4.1.0 SD.2, who in Plutarch always remained loyal to Coriolanus and backed his demand that no concessions be made to the plebeians. Although technically there is no difference between 'nobility' and 'patricians' (30), the apparent distinction suggested here may have been prompted by the phrase 'Nobilitie and Patricians' in North (Bullough, *Sources,* V, 516).

32 repeal voting to repeal his banishment.

To expel him thence. I think he'll be to Rome
As is the osprey to the fish, who takes it
By sovereignty of nature. First he was   35
A noble servant to them, but he could not
Carry his honours even. Whether 'twas pride,
Which out of daily fortune ever taints
The happy man; whether defect of judgement,
To fail in the disposing of those chances   40
Which he was lord of; or whether nature,
Not to be other than one thing, not moving
From th'casque to th'cushion, but commanding peace
Even with the same austerity and garb
As he controlled the war; but one of these –   45
As he hath spices of them all – not all,
For I dare so far free him – made him feared,
So hated, and so banished. But he has a merit
To choke it in the utterance. So our virtues
Lie in th'interpretation of the time,   50
And power, unto itself most commendable,
Hath not a tomb so evident as a chair

---

34 osprey] F (Aspray)   35 First] *Capell;* First, F   37 'twas] F3; 'was F   39 defect] F2; detect F   43 casque] F (Caske)   45 war; but] *Theobald;* warre. But F   45–7 these – / As . . . them all – . . . free him –] NS; these / (As . . . them all) . . . free him, F; these – / As . . . them all, . . . free him – *Hanmer*   49 virtues] F2; Vertue, F   50 Lie] F; Live *Collier²*   52 tomb] F; tongue *Keightley*   52 evident] F; eloquent *conj. White*   52 chair] F; cheer *Collier²;* claim *conj. Leo;* choir *conj. Bulloch* (*in Cam.*)

34 **osprey** fish-hawk. Lesser fish were supposed to surrender to it by turning belly up.

37 **even** temperately, equably; see 2.1.198–9 and n.

38 **out . . . fortune** as a result of constant success.

39 **happy** fortunate.

40 **the disposing . . . chances** making the most of the opportunities.

41 **whether nature** whether it was his nature.

43 **casque** helmet (representing the military life).

43 **cushion** seat in the senate house (representing the civic life); see 2.2.0 SD n.

44 **austerity and garb** Hendiadys for 'austere demeanour' (for 'garb' = demeanour, see *OED* Garb *sb²* 2).

46–7 **As . . . him** Aufidius seems caught between two qualifications: (1) only one of these flaws, although he has traces of them all, (2) he has traces of all these flaws, but none in full measure.

46 **spices** traces, touches.

47 **free** absolve, free from blame.

48 **merit** i.e. his valour.

49 **To . . . utterance** (1) To stifle any talk of the fatal defect (where 'it' refers back to the fault Aufidius has just tried to specify), (2) Proclaiming his merit discredits it (where 'it' refers to 'merit'). The second reading anticipates the argument developed in 51–3.

49–53 **So . . . done** Compare Ulysses on time and reputation, *Tro.* 3.3.145–80.

50 (1) Are subject to each age's interpretation, (2) Are determined by public opinion.

51–3 **power . . . done** Compressed expression continues to make Aufidius's remarks obscure. He seems to mean that 'power, in itself worthy of commendation, never so certainly entombs itself than when it is proclaimed publicly'. The lines can be read with a greater emphasis on boasting (i.e. 'power, which thinks itself praiseworthy, never so certainly entombs itself than when it proclaims its past achievements'), but this shifts its applicability away from Coriolanus, who is not given to public self-commendation.

52 **chair** public rostrum for formal orations.

T'extol what it hath done.
One fire drives out one fire; one nail, one nail;
Rights by rights foulder, strengths by strengths do fail.   55
Come, let's away. When, Caius, Rome is thine,
Thou art poor'st of all; then shortly art thou mine.

Exeunt

5.[1] *Enter* MENENIUS, COMINIUS, SICINIUS [*and*] BRUTUS, *the two Tribunes, with others*

MENENIUS No, I'll not go. You hear what he hath said
Which was sometime his general, who loved him
In a most dear particular. He called me father,
But what o'that? Go, you that banished him;
A mile before his tent fall down and knee   5
The way into his mercy. Nay, if he coyed
To hear Cominius speak, I'll keep at home.

---

55 Rights by rights foulder] *This edn;* Rights by rights fouler F; Right's by right fouler *Pope;* Right's by right foiled *Hanmer;* Right's by right fouled *Warburton;* Rights by rights founder *Boswell, conj. Johnson;* Rights by rights suffer *Collier²;* Rights by rights falter *Dyce;* Rights by rights fuller *Hibbard, conj. Perring*   57 SD] F (*exeunt*)   Act 5, Scene 1   5.1] *Rowe; Actus Quintus.* F   0 SD SICINIUS *and*] *Cam.; Sicinius,* F   4–5 him; . . . tent] *Pope subst.;* him . . . Tent, F   5 knee] F; kneele F2

54–5 One . . . fail Proverbial statements expressing the idea that a force may be overcome only by a stronger force of the same kind. For the first two, see *TGV* 2.4.188–9 and Tilley F277 and N17; Hibbard finds an analogue for the fourth in Erasmus, *Adagia* (949 c): 'Fortis in alium fortiorem incidit. Dici solitum, ubi quis nimium fretus suis viribus, aliquando nanciscitur, a quo vincatur' ('The strong man meets a stronger. Usually said when a man who relies too much on his own unaided power eventually lights on one who proves too much for him'). The third has not been traced but conveys the same thought.

55 foulder crumble (*OED* Foulder *v²*). F's 'fouler' is almost certainly a misreading or misprinting, probably of this coinage from 'fould', which could also mean 'to give way, collapse, fail' (*OED* Fold *v¹* 5a). NS supports Dyce's 'falter', arguing that the copy read 'faulter' or 'foulter', and Dyce's reading would be a sensible choice for a modern production; Hibbard's 'fuller' is possible but less persuasive.

Act 5, Scene 1
A public place in Rome. Shakespeare splits Plutarch's embassy of nameless 'familiar friends and acquaintance' into two, one reported here and one dramatised (5.2), and personalises them.

0 SD.2 *with others* These could be other patricians, to whom the tribunes have come seeking Menenius's aid, or it could include some plebeians, indicating that the city has united in the face of a common threat. North says that Coriolanus's encamping so near Rome finally 'appeased the sedition and dissention betwixt the Nobilitie and the people' (Bullough, *Sources,* V, 533).

1 he Cominius.

3 In . . . particular With the warmest personal affection (*OED* Particular *sb* 6d).

5–6 knee . . . way make your way on your knees (like pilgrims approaching a shrine). Physical enactments of humility are particularly important in this play.

6 coyed 'condescended unwillingly, with reserve, coldness' (Steevens), rather than 'disdained' (*OED* Coy *v¹* 4b).

COMINIUS He would not seem to know me.

MENENIUS   Do you hear?

COMINIUS Yet one time he did call me by my name.

I urged our old acquaintance and the drops   10
That we have bled together. 'Coriolanus'
He would not answer to; forbade all names.
He was a kind of nothing, titleless,
Till he had forged himself a name o'th'fire
Of burning Rome.

MENENIUS [*To the Tribunes*] Why, so; you have made good work!   15
A pair of tribunes that have wracked for Rome
To make coals cheap – a noble memory!

COMINIUS I minded him how royal 'twas to pardon
When it was less expected. He replied
It was a bare petition of a state   20
To one whom they had punished.

MENENIUS Very well. Could he say less?

COMINIUS I offered to awaken his regard
For's private friends. His answer to me was
He could not stay to pick them in a pile   25
Of noisome musty chaff. He said 'twas folly
For one poor grain or two to leave unburnt
And still to nose th'offence.

---

11 'Coriolanus'] *NS; Coriolanus* F   14 o'th'] F (a'th'); *i'th' Johnson*   15 SD] *Oxford; not in* F   16 wracked for] F; rack'd
for *Pope;* sack'd fair *Hanmer;* reck'd for *Warburton, conj. Theobald;* wreck'd fair *Dyce², conj. Mason;* wrack'd fair *White²*
17 cheap –] F (cheape:)   20 bare] F; base *Cornwall, conj. Mason;* rare *Dyce², conj. Williams*   27 leave] F; leave't
Hudson², conj. Daniel

8 **would not seem to** affected not to.

13–15 He . . . Rome This may be Cominius's
own analysis but, given the preceding lines, it
more likely continues the indirect report of Coriolanus's own words.

14 o'th'fire Johnson's 'i'th'fire' is more pre-
cise with 'forged', but elsewhere 'a'th' ' represents
'o'th' ' and it makes satisfactory sense here.

16 wracked for ruined, brought the downfall
of (*OED* Wrack *v²* 3); with a probable play on
'racked' (= strained, laboured). North says that
as Coriolanus pillaged the Roman territories 'all
went still to wracke at Rome' (Bullough, *Sources,*
v, 532).

17 coals charcoal (which will be 'cheap'
because Rome will be nothing but coals).

17 noble memory fine memorial (with a sar-
castic pun on 'noble' as 'patrician').

19 When . . . less The less it was.

20 bare (1) threadbare (*OED* Bare *a* 6c), (2)
paltry, worthless (*OED* Bare *a* 10b); possibly with
pun on (3) unarmed (*OED* Bare *a* 6b), reminding
Rome of its current helplessness.

22 Very well Very just.

23 offered attempted, ventured.

25–6 He . . . chaff Shakespeare draws on earlier
images of the processing of corn into food and on
Martius's condemnation of the people as Rome's
'musty superfluity' (1.1.210) and combines them
with biblical allusions (the winnowing metaphor
of Matt. 3.12; the destruction of Sodom, in Gen.
18.24–33, because not even a few virtuous citizens
could be found).

26 noisome vile-smelling.

28 nose th'offence smell the offensive matter
(the noisome chaff).

MENENIUS For one poor grain or two!
        I am one of those. His mother, wife, his child,   30
        And this brave fellow too – we are the grains.
        [*To the Tribunes*] You are the musty chaff, and you are smelt
        Above the moon. We must be burnt for you.
SICINIUS Nay, pray be patient. If you refuse your aid
        In this so never-needed help, yet do not   35
        Upbraid's with our distress. But sure, if you
        Would be your country's pleader, your good tongue,
        More than the instant army we can make,
        Might stop our countryman.
MENENIUS   No, I'll not meddle.
SICINIUS Pray you go to him.
MENENIUS   What should I do?   40
BRUTUS Only make trial what your love can do
        For Rome towards Martius.
MENENIUS Well, and say that Martius return me,
        As Cominius is returned, unheard – what then?
        But as a discontented friend, grief-shot   45
        With his unkindness? Say't be so?
SICINIUS   Yet your good will
        Must have that thanks from Rome after the measure
        As you intended well.
MENENIUS   I'll undertake't.
        I think he'll hear me. Yet to bite his lip
        And hum at good Cominius much unhearts me.   50
        He was not taken well; he had not dined.
        The veins unfilled, our blood is cold, and then
        We pout upon the morning, are unapt
        To give or to forgive; but when we have stuffed
        These pipes and these conveyances of our blood   55

29 two!] F (two?)   31 too – . . . grains.] F (too: . . . Graines,)   32 SD] *Oxford; not in* F   46 unkindness?] *Capell;* vnkindness. F

35 In . . . help In this crisis where help was never so sorely needed.
38 instant . . . make kind of army we can raise at this instant.
45 But as What if I return merely as.
45 grief-shot grief-stricken.
47–8 after . . . well commensurate with your good intentions.
49–50 bite . . . hum Conventional signs of anger and impatience. These might be used as

performance cues for the interview with Menenius in 5.2.
50 unhearts disheartens, discourages.
51 taken well approached at the right time.
51–6 not dined . . . souls Characteristically, Menenius thinks of a good meal as the best means to dispose the soul to leniency.
55 conveyances channels (*OED* Conveyance *sb* 12b).

With wine and feeding, we have suppler souls
Than in our priest-like fasts. Therefore I'll watch him
Till he be dieted to my request,
And then I'll set upon him.
BRUTUS You know the very road into his kindness   60
And cannot lose your way.
MENENIUS   Good faith, I'll prove him,
Speed how it will. I shall ere long have knowledge
Of my success.   *Exit*
COMINIUS   He'll never hear him.
SICINIUS   Not?
COMINIUS I tell you, he does sit in gold, his eye
Red as 'twould burn Rome, and his injury   65
The gaoler to his pity. I kneeled before him;
'Twas very faintly he said 'Rise', dismissed me
Thus, with his speechless hand. What he would do
He sent in writing after me, what he would not,
Bound with an oath to hold to his conditions.   70
So that all hope is vain
Unless his noble mother and his wife,
Who, as I hear, mean to solicit him
For mercy to his country. Therefore let's hence,

61–2 him, . . . will.] F; him . . . will, *Staunton subst.*   62 I] F; Ye *conj. Theobald;* You *Hanmer*   63 Not?] F3; Not.
F; No? *Capell*   64 in gold] F; engall'd *conj. Blackstone (in Cam.)*   67 'Rise'] *Hanmer;* Rise F   69 He . . . me, what
. . . not,] F (me:); *What . . . not, he . . . me; conj. Becket;* He . . . me, what . . . not: *Parker*   70 oath to hold to his]
Oxford, conj. Solly (in Leo); Oath to yeeld to his F; oath, not yield to new *Hanmer;* oath to yield no new *conj. Johnson;*
oath, to yield to no *conj. Singer*   71 vain] F (vaine,); vain – *Parker*   72 his noble] F; his *Pope;* from's *Hanmer;* from
his noble *Capell;* in's *White, conj. Heath*   72 wife,] F; wife – *Theobald;* wife; *Malone*   74 country.] F (Countrey:);
country – *Parker*

56 suppler more yielding.
58 dieted to conditioned, by a good meal, to listen to.
61 prove attempt, try.
62 Speed . . . will No matter how it turns out.
63 my success the outcome (good or bad) of my attempt.
64 sit in gold In North, 'he was set in his chayer of state, with a marvelous and unspeakable majestie' (Bullough, *Sources*, v, 534).
65 Red Red eyes elsewhere in Shakespeare express the heart's malice: *2H6* 3.1.154, *John* 4.2.163, *Ham.* 2.2.463. Here, as Brockbank notes, the danger of fire is real.
65 injury grievance, sense of Rome's injustice.
68–70 What . . . conditions A disputed passage in which F's syntax and punctuation, and a probable misreading in 'yeeld', obscure what seems to be meant: Coriolanus 'sent in writing

after' Cominius both what concessions he would make and those he would not, and he 'bound' both lists with an 'oath'. Brooke suggests that 'what he would not' was a marginal addition, mistakenly inserted after 'me' instead of after 'What he would do'. Solly's conjecture is persuasive semantically and graphically, since in Secretary hand 'hold' could easily be misread as 'yeld' and expanded to the compositor's preferred 'yeeld' (NS).
71–4 So . . . country The sense is clear, though not the nature of the ellipsis. NS glosses 'Unless' as 'If it were not for', and Brockbank suggests 'Unless we put hope in his noble mother'. Parker follows Sisson's suggestion that 72–4 is 'a broken construction, significant of Cominius' perturbation' and punctuates accordingly; Parker thinks it also indicates a rebound from the dejection of 71.

> And with our fair entreaties haste them on.   75
>
>   *Exeunt*

5.[2]   *Enter* MENENIUS *to the* WATCH *or Guard*

FIRST WATCH Stay. Whence are you?

SECOND WATCH Stand, and go back.

MENENIUS You guard like men, 'tis well. But, by your leave,
>   I am an officer of state and come
>   To speak with Coriolanus.   5

FIRST WATCH From whence?

MENENIUS From Rome.

FIRST WATCH You may not pass; you must return. Our general
>   Will no more hear from thence.

SECOND WATCH You'll see your Rome embraced with fire before   10
>   You'll 'speak with Coriolanus'.

MENENIUS   Good my friends,
>   If you have heard your general talk of Rome
>   And of his friends there, it is lots to blanks
>   My name hath touched your ears. It is Menenius.

FIRST WATCH Be it so; go back. The virtue of your name   15
>   Is not here passable.

MENENIUS   I tell thee, fellow,

Act 5, Scene 2   5.2] *Rowe; not in* F   I SH] F (1. *Wat. / then* 1 *to end of scene*)   2 SH] F (2. *Wat. / then* 2 *to end of scene*)   11 'speak . . . Coriolanus'] *This edn; speake . . . Coriolanus* F

Act 5, Scene 2
The Volscian camp. It is unclear whether the watch is guarding Coriolanus's tent or the camp more generally. Cominius at 5.1.64 said Coriolanus 'does sit in gold', and Menenius later (5.4.17) speaks of him sitting 'in his state'. The Elizabethan stage may have used some kind of tent-structure, with the chair of state within it; Coriolanus could enter and sit in it while Menenius finishes speaking to the guards (59–64), then come forward to converse with his 'old father' Menenius. The scene blends humour and pathos, and, in Menenius's appeal to his quasi-paternal relation to Coriolanus (66), prepares for the climactic familial embassy in 5.3. It also recalls 4.5, where Volscian servingmen initially barred the suppliant Coriolanus from his goal.

   0 SD WATCH *or* **Guard** Two words for military sentries; possibly 'or' is a misreading of 'on' (Brower).

   13 lots to blanks a certainty, 'a thousand to one' (*OED* Lot *sb* 5). The evidence cited in the *OED* suggests 'lots' sometimes meant the total number of tickets in a lottery (i.e. both prize-winning tickets and 'blanks'), and sometimes only winners. Eric Brown argues for a reference to the most famous lottery of Shakespeare's time, instituted by Queen Elizabeth in 1566 and advertised as 'without any blancks'; the ratio of 'lots to blanks' thus guaranteed winning, though of course most won the minimum two shillings ('A note on the lottery of Queen Elizabeth I and *Coriolanus* V.ii.10', *SQ* 50 (1999), 70–3).

   14–15 touched . . . virtue King suggests that First Watch anachronistically puns on the 'virtue' of the king's 'touch' which healed the sick, as in *Mac.* 4.3.143–5.

   16 passable (1) valid currency, (2) acceptable as a password.

Thy general is my lover. I have been
The book of his good acts, whence men have read
His fame unparalleled, haply amplified;
For I have ever varnishèd my friends,   20
Of whom he's chief, with all the size that verity
Would without lapsing suffer. Nay, sometimes,
Like to a bowl upon a subtle ground,
I have tumbled past the throw and in his praise
Have almost stamped the leasing. Therefore, fellow,   25
I must have leave to pass.

FIRST WATCH Faith, sir, if you had told as many lies in his behalf as you
    have uttered words in your own, you should not pass here, no,
    though it were as virtuous to lie as to live chastely. Therefore go
    back.   30

MENENIUS Prithee, fellow, remember my name is Menenius, always
    factionary on the party of your general.

SECOND WATCH Howsoever you have been his liar, as you say you have,
    I am one that, telling true under him, must say you cannot pass.
    Therefore go back.   35

MENENIUS Has he dined, canst thou tell? For I would not speak with
    him till after dinner.

FIRST WATCH You are a Roman, are you?

MENENIUS I am as thy general is.

---

19 haply] F (happely); happily F3   20 varnishèd] NS, conj. Edwards; verified F; magnified Hanmer; narrified Warburton; notified Singer²; rarefied conj. Staunton; certified conj. Jervis; amplified Hudson², conj. Lettsom (in Dyce²); vivified
conj. Bulloch (in Cam.); glorified Craig, conj. Leo   25 almost] (almost) F   39 am] F; am, F4

17 **lover** dear friend (see 83, 87).
19 **haply** perhaps.
20–2 **For . . . suffer** For I have always embel-
lished the reputation of my friends, of whom he
is chief, to the full extent that truth would allow.
20 **varnishèd** F's 'verified' appears in OED
(Verify v 1c) as 'To support or back up by tes-
timony', but no other instance is offered for this
sense. Adopting Edwards's reading, NS argues
that, under the influence of 'amplified' in the
preceding line and 'verity' in the following,
manuscript 'vernished' could have been misread
as 'verrifyed'; for the usual Shakespearean use of
'varnish' to mean 'embellish, trick out', he cites
Ham., 4.7.131–2: 'And set a double varnish on the
fame / The Frenchman gave you'. 'Varnish' and
'verity' form a natural opposition: e.g. Sylvester's
Du Bartas, I, ii, 1150, 'Though . . . Divinity, For
only varnish, have but verity'.

21 **size** (1) magnitude, also punning on (2)
sticky wash applied to paper or parchment as
ground for gilding or painting (OED Size sb² 1).
22 **lapsing** i.e. lapsing into exaggeration.
22 **suffer** allow.
23–4 **Like . . . throw** Like a bowling ball upon
a tricky green, overshot the mark ('throw' =
distance to be thrown).
25 **stamped the leasing** given the stamp of
truth to falsehood ('leasing' = falsehood, from
Old English léasung).
29 **lie** (1) tell falsehoods, also punning on (2)
fornicate (picked up in 'live chastely').
32 **factionary . . . of** active as a partisan of.
33 **Howsoever** Notwithstanding.
33 **liar** F's 'Lier' suggests Second Watch may
be continuing his fellow soldier's bawdy pun (29).

FIRST WATCH Then you should hate Rome, as he does. Can you, when   40
    you have pushed out your gates the very defender of them and in a
    violent popular ignorance given your enemy your shield, think to
    front his revenges with the easy groans of old women, the virginal
    palms of your daughters, or with the palsied intercession of such a
    decayed dotant as you seem to be? Can you think to blow out the   45
    intended fire your city is ready to flame in with such weak breath as
    this? No, you are deceived. Therefore back to Rome and prepare for
    your execution. You are condemned; our general has sworn you out
    of reprieve and pardon.

MENENIUS Sirrah, if thy captain knew I were here, he would use me   50
    with estimation.

FIRST WATCH Come, my captain knows you not.

MENENIUS I mean thy general.

FIRST WATCH My general cares not for you. Back, I say, go, lest I let
    forth your half-pint of blood. Back, that's the utmost of your hav-   55
    ing. Back!

MENENIUS Nay, but fellow, fellow –

Enter CORIOLANUS *with* AUFIDIUS

CORIOLANUS What's the matter?

MENENIUS Now, you companion, I'll say an errand for you. You shall
    know now that I am in estimation. You shall perceive that a Jack   60
    guardant cannot office me from my son Coriolanus; guess but my
    entertainment with him. If thou stand'st not i'th'state of hanging, or

---

45 dotant] F; dotard F4   57 fellow –] *Theobald;* Fellow. F   59 errand] F (arrant)   61–3 Corioianus; . . . him. . . .
suffering,] F (*Coriolanus,* . . . him: . . . suffering,); Coriolanus. . . . him . . . suffering; *Hanmer subst., conj. Thirlby*   61
but] F; by *Hanmer;* but by *Malone*

43 **front** confront, oppose.
43 **easy** insignificant (*OED* Easy *a* 15).
43–4 **virginal . . . daughters** pleading hands
of your virgin daughters.
44 **palsied** North says that the Romans were so
fearful that 'they properly resembled the bodyes
paralyticke . . . as those which through the palsey
have lost all their sence and feeling' (Bullough,
Sources, v, 535).
45 **dotant** dotard, one in his dotage or second
childhood.
51 **estimation** respect.
55–6 **utmost . . . having** all you are going to
get (in the way of 'estimation'); possibly 'as far as
you can go'. Warburton took it to refer back to
Menenius's 'half-pint of blood'.

59 **companion** fellow; see 4.5.12 n.
59 **say . . . you** deliver the report for you.
60–1 **Jack guardant** Jack-in-office, knave on
guard duty. King notes that 'guardant' is also an
heraldic term (referring to a symbolic beast's posture), which would give more bite to the insult.
61 **office** drive by virtue of your office (*OED*
Office *v* 4), officiously keep.
61–2 **guess . . . him.** F makes sense as a smug
command to those who have been asserting their
power over him. Malone's emendation to 'but
by' and repunctuation have proved attractive to
others on the grounds that it would be easy to
omit one element of a 'by my' combination.

of some death more long in spectatorship and crueller in suffering,
behold now presently and swoon for what's to come upon thee. [*To
Coriolanus*] The glorious gods sit in hourly synod about thy particu-   65
lar prosperity and love thee no worse than thy old father Menenius
does! O my son, my son! Thou art preparing fire for us; look thee,
here's water to quench it. I was hardly moved to come to thee, but
being assured none but myself could move thee, I have been blown
out of your gates with sighs and conjure thee to pardon Rome and   70
thy petitionary countrymen. The good gods assuage thy wrath and
turn the dregs of it upon this varlet here – this, who like a block hath
denied my access to thee.

CORIOLANUS Away!

MENENIUS How? Away?   75

CORIOLANUS Wife, mother, child, I know not. My affairs
       Are servanted to others. Though I owe
       My revenge properly, my remission lies
       In Volscian breasts. That we have been familiar,
       Ingrate forgetfulness shall poison rather   80
       Than pity note how much. Therefore begone.
       Mine ears against your suits are stronger than
       Your gates against my force. Yet, for I loved thee,
           [*Gives him a letter*]
       Take this along; I writ it for thy sake
       And would have sent it. Another word, Menenius,   85
       I will not hear thee speak. This man, Aufidius,
       Was my beloved in Rome; yet thou behold'st.

64, 94 swoon] F (swoond)   64–5 SD] *Pope subst.; not in* F   70 your] F; our F4; yond *conj. Leo*   80 poison] F; prison
Theobald   81 pity note . . . much.] *Theobald (Thirlby); pitty: Note . . . much,* F   83 SD] *Pope subst.; not in* F

63 **spectatorship** watching.
64 **presently** immediately (intensifying 'now').
65 **sit** i.e. may they sit.
65 **synod** council, assembly.
68 **hardly moved** with difficulty persuaded.
70 **your** F is probably correct, in view of 'thy'
(71), although F4's 'our' has been defended as
emphasising Menenius's and Coriolanus's common bond.
71 **petitionary** suppliant, petitioning.
72 **block** (1) obstacle, (2) blockhead.
76 **Wife . . . not** Although Menenius has
stressed his own relation to Coriolanus, and only
vaguely alluded to his countrymen, this reply
shows 'where [Coriolanus's] thoughts are and
what he dreads' (Parker).

77–8 **I owe . . . properly** my revenge is mine
alone (where 'owe' = own).
78 **remission** power to pardon. Brockbank
points out a possible second meaning, taking 'owe'
as 'indebted to' and 'remission' as 'release from
an obligation': although his revenge is a debt he
owes himself, he can only be released from that
debt by the Volscians.
79–81 **That . . . much** Rome's ungrateful for-
getfulness of my services shall poison my memory
of our friendship rather than compassion allow me
to remember how great it was.
83 **for** since.
83, 84, 86 **thee . . . thy . . . thee** Parker notes
the switch to the familiar second-person singular
in an attempt to soften the rejection.

AUFIDIUS You keep a constant temper.

Exeunt [Coriolanus and Aufidius;] the Guard and Menenius [remain]

FIRST WATCH Now, sir, is your name Menenius?

SECOND WATCH 'Tis a spell, you see, of much power. You know the   90
way home again.

FIRST WATCH Do you hear how we are shent for keeping your greatness
back?

SECOND WATCH What cause do you think I have to swoon?

MENENIUS I neither care for th'world nor your general. For such things   95
as you, I can scarce think there's any, you're so slight. He that hath
a will to die by himself fears it not from another. Let your general
do his worst. For you, be that you are, long, and your misery increase with your age! I say to you, as I was said to, 'Away!'   *Exit*

FIRST WATCH A noble fellow, I warrant him.   100

SECOND WATCH The worthy fellow is our general. He's the rock, the
oak not to be wind-shaken.

Exeunt

5.[3] *Enter* CORIOLANUS *and* AUFIDIUS [*with Volscian soldiers*]

CORIOLANUS We will before the walls of Rome tomorrow
Set down our host. My partner in this action,
You must report to th'Volscian lords how plainly

---

88 SD *Exeunt . . . Aufidius*] Capell; *Exeunt* F   88 SD *the . . . Menenius remain*] *Manet the . . . Menenius.* F (*Manent* F2)
96 you're] F (y'are)   99 'Away!'] *Hanmer;* Away. F   102 SD *Exeunt*] F (*Exit Watch.*)   Act 5, Scene 3   5.3] *Pope;
not in* F   0 SD *with Volscian soldiers*] Oxford; *not in* F; *with Others* / *Capell*

92 **shent** reproved, rebuked.
96 **slight** insignificant.
97 **by himself** by his own hand.
98 **long** for a long time.
101–2 **He's . . . wind-shaken** Like Aufidius's
remark on Coriolanus's 'constant temper' (88),
Second Watch's observation helps conclude the
scene on a note of unconscious irony; his 'rock'
also anticipates Coriolanus's prayer that his son
be 'Like a great sea-mark, standing every flaw'
(5.3.74).

Act 5, Scene 3
The Volscian camp, probably continuous with
5.2. If a tent-structure and chair of state are used
in 5.2, they could remain for this scene. 5.3 is
deeply indebted to North, and Shakespeare may
have visualised it in his terms: 'Nowe was Martius
set then in his chayer of state, with all the honours

of a generall, and when he had spied the women
comming a farre of, he marveled what the matter ment: but afterwardes knowing his wife which
came formest, he determined at the first to persist
in his obstinate and inflexible rancker' (Bullough,
Sources, V, 538).

0 SD AUFIDIUS Aufidius's presence is crucial for
Shakespeare's climactic scene; in Plutarch he had
remained at home to protect the Volscian cities
while Coriolanus marched on Rome. The director must decide whether to provide a chair for
'My partner in this action' (2) or, as a visible sign
of the dominance Aufidius so resents, leave him
standing with the other soldiers. Some editions
direct Coriolanus, or both generals, to sit immediately upon entering.

2 **Set . . . host** Encamp our army (to besiege
the city).

3 **plainly** openly, straightforwardly.

I have borne this business.

AUFIDIUS   Only their ends
You have respected, stopped your ears against   5
The general suit of Rome, never admitted
A private whisper, no, not with such friends
That thought them sure of you.

CORIOLANUS   This last old man,
Whom with a cracked heart I have sent to Rome,
Loved me above the measure of a father,   10
Nay, godded me indeed. Their latest refuge
Was to send him, for whose old love I have –
Though I showed sourly to him – once more offered
The first conditions, which they did refuse
And cannot now accept, to grace him only   15
That thought he could do more. A very little
I have yielded to. Fresh embassies and suits,
Nor from the state nor private friends, hereafter
Will I lend ear to.

                        Shout within
                    Ha? What shout is this?
Shall I be tempted to infringe my vow   20
In the same time 'tis made? I will not.

Enter VIRGILIA, VOLUMNIA, VALERIA, YOUNG MARTIUS,
                    with Attendants

15–16 accept, . . . more.] F (accept, . . . more:); accept; . . . more, *Steevens, conj. Heath*   19 SD] *Placed as Capell; after*
this? F   21 SD.2 *Attendants*] F; *Attendants, all in Mourning / Theobald*

---

4 their ends i.e. the Volscians' purposes.
6 general public; contrasted with 'private' or personal (King).
11 godded made a god of. The word does not appear elsewhere in Shakespeare but, as Brockbank notes, is 'aptly coined for this play'.
11 latest refuge last resort.
14 first conditions i.e. those offered Cominius (5.1.68–70).
15–17 accept . . . yielded to If F's colon after 'more' is treated as a full stop (as they frequently must be in F), the 'grace' accorded Menenius is Coriolanus's allowing Rome a second chance to accept his conditions. If it is read as a comma, Menenius appears to have received some extra concession; there is no evidence elsewhere of such an additional concession, however.
18 Nor . . . nor Neither . . . nor.
20–1 These lines begin an extended self-ruminative aside that continues as Coriolanus describes his response to the approaching embassy; he might move downstage and away from the direction of the off-stage shout (whose significance he seems to intuit; see 5.2.76 n.), postponing the necessity for a public reaction to the appeal he fears. The entry of the desperate, raggedly-dressed women could be staged as an inversion of Coriolanus's triumphal entry into Rome in 2.1.
21 SD.2 Many editors follow Theobald's additional direction for mourning habits, but there is no clear evidence for this in the text or in North, whose only descriptive phrase is 'the state of our poore bodies, and present sight of our rayment' (Bullough, *Sources*, V, 539; compare 94–5). More effective might be clothing whose colour and fabric would recall the 'mean apparel' worn by the then-desperate Coriolanus of 4.4.

My wife comes foremost, then the honoured mould
Wherein this trunk was framed, and in her hand
The grandchild to her blood. But out, affection;
All bond and privilege of nature, break!   25
Let it be virtuous to be obstinate.
                              [*Virgilia curtsies*]
What is that curtsy worth? Or those dove's eyes
Which can make gods forsworn? I melt, and am not
Of stronger earth than others.
                              [*Volumnia bows*]
                                        My mother bows,
As if Olympus to a molehill should   30
In supplication nod, and my young boy
Hath an aspect of intercession which
Great Nature cries 'Deny not.' Let the Volsces
Plough Rome and harrow Italy, I'll never
Be such a gosling to obey instinct, but stand   35
As if a man were author of himself
And knew no other kin.
VIRGILIA   My lord and husband!

---

24 out,] *Theobald;* out F; our F3   25 nature,] *Capell;* Nature F   25 break!] *Steevens²;* breake; F   26 SD] *Johnson; not in* F   27 dove's] *Rowe;* Doues F; doves' *Steevens*   29 SD] *Johnson; not in* F   33 'Deny not.'] *Hanmer;* Deny not. F

22 My . . . foremost This follows Plutarch (see headnote), but there Coriolanus is immediately overcome: 'in hast, he went to meete them, and first he kissed his mother, and imbraced her a pretie while, then his wife and litle children' (Bullough, *Sources*, v, 539).

22 mould form, matrix; compare 3.2.104 and *WT* 2.3.103. NS (following J. C. Maxwell) quotes Thomas Nashe (*Works*, ed. R. B. McKerrow, II, 74), where a mother tells her child she is 'The Mould wherein thou wert cast'.

23 trunk body.

24 out, affection let affection be extinguished; 'affection' here means both 'love' and, more generally, 'feeling or passion' (*OED* Affection *sb* 3), since Coriolanus needs to be emotionless to resist.

25 bond . . . nature natural ties and claims of kinship.

26 obstinate hard-hearted, unyielding (a word taken from North).

27 dove's eyes Compare Song of Sol. 1.14, 4.1;

doves were also associated with peace and deliverance from anxiety, as was the dove to Noah (Gen. 8.8–12).

30 Olympus In Greek mythology, the mountain that was the home of the gods. The analogy anticipates his horror at his mother's kneeling to him (56).

32 aspect of intercession pleading look ('aspect' accented on the second syllable).

35 gosling baby goose; compare his disparaging use of 'geese' for the plebeians (1.1.155, 1.4.35).

36 author of himself self-begotten, like a god (*OED* Author *sb* 2a). The conditional 'As if' admits the impossibility and his awarness that he is playing an unnatural role, one that goes against 'instinct'. The situation reverses that of 3.2: there Volumnia had to talk him into the politician's role he felt violated his essential being; now she must convince him to obey his deepest instincts.

CORIOLANUS These eyes are not the same I wore in Rome.
VIRGILIA The sorrow that delivers us thus changed
           Makes you think so.
CORIOLANUS   Like a dull actor now   40
           I have forgot my part and I am out,
           Even to a full disgrace. Best of my flesh,
           Forgive my tyranny, but do not say
           For that, 'Forgive our Romans.'
                              [*They kiss*]
                                O, a kiss
           Long as my exile, sweet as my revenge!   45
           Now, by the jealous queen of heaven, that kiss
           I carried from thee, dear, and my true lip
           Hath virgined it e'er since. You gods! I prate,
           And the most noble mother of the world
           Leave unsaluted. Sink, my knee, i'th'earth;   50
                              Kneels
           Of thy deep duty more impression show
           Than that of common sons.
VOLUMNIA   O, stand up blest!
                       [*Coriolanus rises*]

40 Like] F; *Aside* Like *Hibbard*   44 'Forgive . . . Romans.'] *Hanmer;* forgiue . . . Romanes. F   44 SD] *Bevington (after 45); not in* F; *Virgilia kisses him* / *Oxford*   48 prate] *Pope², conj. Theobald,* 'SR'; pray F   52 SD] *Hibbard subst.; not in* F

38–40 These . . . so Coriolanus tries to deny her claim on him by saying he is now a different man from the one she knew in Rome; Virgilia takes him more literally and says it is their appearance that has changed, altered by grief. In Plutarch Virgilia does not speak to her husband, nor does he kiss her before turning to address his mother.

39 delivers presents.

41 out A theatrical term for forgetting one's lines; compare *LLL* 5.2.152.

43 tyranny harshness, severity (*OED* Tyranny *sb* 3).

44 For that i.e. because I have asked your forgiveness; perhaps alluding to the Lord's Prayer (Gomme).

46 jealous . . . heaven Juno, guardian of marriage.

48 virgined it remained chaste (a Shakespearean coinage).

48 prate Hibbard defends F's 'pray' on the grounds that Coriolanus has just sworn by Juno, but the sense is awkward and the self-rebuke in the next lines makes it more likely to be a compositor's error influenced by 'You gods'.

50 SD In Plutarch, mother, wife and children all kneel at the conclusion of Volumnia's long plea, as they do here at 171, but Shakespeare has added this initial exchange between mother and son; his kneeling is conventional (see 2.1.144), hers shocking.

51 deep profound.

51 more impression show (1) show a clearer sign, (2) make a deeper mark (in the earth). Her reply, that she kneels on 'flint' (53), indicates how much more difficult and unnatural this gesture is for the parent.

52 blest fortunate, lucky. Her whole speech is said ironically, which he recognises at 56–7.

52 SD This seems the appropriate point for Coriolanus to rise, for the maximum visual contrast when she then kneels to him. Collier, however, keeps Coriolanus on his knees until 62, when he rises and raises her; Parker delays his rise to 57 and cites the kneeling of child and parent in *Lear* 4.7.

Whilst with no softer cushion than the flint
I kneel before thee, and unproperly
Show duty as mistaken all this while   55
Between the child and parent.

                                    [*She kneels*]

CORIOLANUS   What's this?
Your knees to me? To your corrected son?

                                    [*He raises her*]

Then let the pebbles on the hungry beach
Fillip the stars. Then let the mutinous winds
Strike the proud cedars 'gainst the fiery sun,   60
Murdering impossibility, to make
What cannot be, slight work.

VOLUMNIA   Thou art my warrior;
I holp to frame thee. Do you know this lady?

CORIOLANUS The noble sister of Publicola,
The moon of Rome, chaste as the icicle   65
That's curdied by the frost from purest snow
And hangs on Dian's temple – dear Valeria!

VOLUMNIA [*Indicating Young Martius*] This is a poor epitome of yours,
Which by th'interpretation of full time

56 SD] *Rowe subst.; not in* F   57 SD] *Kittredge subst.* (*before* What's this?); *not in* F   58 hungry] F; angry *Hudson², conj. Malone*   63 holp] *Pope;* hope F   66 curdied] F; curdled *Rowe³;* curded *Stevens³;* candied *Oxford, conj. Daniel*   68 SH] F; *Val. / Rann, conj. Steevens*   68 SD] *Pope subst.; not in* F

54 unproperly unfittingly, against propriety.

55–6 Show . . . parent Show duty to have been mistaken all this while in thinking itself owed by the child to the parent.

57 corrected chastised.

58 hungry The adjective is transferred from the sea, with which it is usually associated, to the 'beach' from which it drags the pebbles; 'hungry' carries connotations of barrenness and sterility (*OED* Hungry *a* 6b), and it expands the sense of threatening hunger with which the play opened into the natural world.

59 Fillip Strike against. The image is of a nature so disordered that insignificant pebbles threaten the stars instead of submitting to the sea's tides.

61 Murdering impossibility Making nothing seem impossible; compare Macbeth's horror at the apparent loss of stable limits, *Mac.* 1.3.139–42.

62 slight easy, trifling.

64 Publicola Traditionally one of the first consuls of Rome, *c.* 509 B.C.; the relationship comes from Plutarch.

65 moon On the moon's association with chastity and Diana, see 1.1.241 n.

65 chaste . . . icicle Probably inspired by North's praise: 'Valeria . . . did so modestile and wiselie behave her selfe, that she did not shame nor dishonour the house she came of (Bullough, *Sources*, v, 537). In Plutarch it is Valeria, inspired at the altar of Jupiter Capitolinus, who suggests that Volumnia, Virgilia and all the ladies of Rome should go to entreat Coriolanus for mercy; Shakespeare diminishes her role and makes the embassy familial.

66 curdied congealed; a Shakespearean coinage in which the verbal form ('curd') has been influenced by the adjectival ('curdy'), though Rowe may be correct in seeing it as a misprint for 'curdled'.

68–70 epitome . . . yourself an abridgement of yourself that time, like an orator, will develop and expand to its full equivalence; compare Aufidius's different sense of 'th'interpretation of the time' at 4.7.50.

    May show like all yourself.

CORIOLANUS   The god of soldiers,   70
    With the consent of supreme Jove, inform
    Thy thoughts with nobleness, that thou mayst prove
    To shame unvulnerable and stick i'th'wars
    Like a great sea-mark, standing every flaw
    And saving those that eye thee!

VOLUMNIA   Your knee, sirrah.   75

            [*Young Martius kneels*]

CORIOLANUS That's my brave boy!

VOLUMNIA Even he, your wife, this lady, and myself
    Are suitors to you.

CORIOLANUS   I beseech you, peace;
    Or, if you'd ask, remember this before:
    The thing I have forsworn to grant may never   80
    Be held by you denials. Do not bid me
    Dismiss my soldiers or capitulate
    Again with Rome's mechanics. Tell me not
    Wherein I seem unnatural. Desire not
    T'allay my rages and revenges with   85

---

70 soldiers,] F3; Souldiers: F   73 stick] F; strike F2   75 SD] *Bevington; not in* F   80–1 thing . . . denials] F; thing . . . denial F4; things . . . denials *Capell*

70 god of soldiers Mars.

71 inform inspire; with perhaps a play on the root meaning 'give form to' (i.e. noble deeds shape the warrior's thoughts).

73 To shame unvulnerable (1) Incapable of dishonourable deeds, (2) Invulnerable to being dishonoured. Martial courage is what Coriolanus wishes for his son, but his words in another sense apply to his own situation.

73 stick 'stand firm' and 'stand out'.

74 sea-mark A landmark used by mariners to take their bearings and keep on course; compare the 'rock' of 5.2.101. Shakespeare had used the sea-mark image before (Sonnet 116, *Oth.* 5.2.268), but as a metaphor for a great warrior in the midst of battle it might have been inspired by Virgil's *Aeneid*, X, 693–5, verses also quoted and 'Englished' in Florio's 1603 translation of Montaigne's *Essays*, Book III, ch. 10, in a passage considering whether an honourable man ought to seek revenge even for an 'outragious wrong'; see pp. 15–16 above.

74 flaw (1) squall, sudden gust of wind (relating to 'sea-mark'), (2) moral fault, blemish (relating to 'shame'). Given the extensive use of legal terminology in this play, there might be a tertiary reference to the invalidating defect in a legal document (*OED* Flaw *sb*¹ 5c, though the first citation is 1616).

75 those . . . thee those who look to you for guidance.

80–1 The thing . . . denials What I have sworn not to grant must never be taken by you as a denial of your requests. The lack of clarity in phrasing reflects his desperate attempt to define denial as non-denial. Although F's 'thing' could be a compositor's error, the lack of grammatical agreement can also be explained by taking 'thing' as referring to his oath to the Volscians and 'denials' to the fact that there are several pleaders to refuse.

81–6 Do . . . reasons In a series of negative commands, Coriolanus attempts to forestall her arguments and avoid a situation in which he must oppose his mother and then explicitly refuse her petition.

82 capitulate negotiate, come to terms.

83 mechanics workmen (used contemptuously of common labourers).

85 allay abate. Brockbank notes that Shakespeare's use of the word varies, sometimes approximating 'quench', sometimes 'temper', and sometimes 'dilute'.

                          Your colder reasons.
VOLUMNIA   O, no more, no more!
          You have said you will not grant us anything,
          For we have nothing else to ask but that
          Which you deny already. Yet we will ask,
          That if you fail in our request the blame   90
          May hang upon your hardness. Therefore hear us.
CORIOLANUS Aufidius, and you Volsces, mark, for we'll
          Hear nought from Rome in private.
                          [*He sits*]
                                          Your request?
VOLUMNIA Should we be silent and not speak, our raiment
          And state of bodies would bewray what life   95
          We have led since thy exile. Think with thyself
          How more unfortunate than all living women
          Are we come hither, since that thy sight, which should
          Make our eyes flow with joy, hearts dance with comforts,
          Constrains them weep and shake with fear and sorrow,   100
          Making the mother, wife, and child to see
          The son, the husband, and the father tearing
          His country's bowels out. And to poor we
          Thine enmity's most capital. Thou barr'st us
          Our prayers to the gods, which is a comfort   105
          That all but we enjoy. For how can we –
          Alas! How can we for our country pray,
          Whereto we are bound, together with thy victory,
          Whereto we are bound? Alack, or we must lose

---

90 you] F; we *Rowe²*   93 SD] *Capell subst.; not in* F   106 we –] *This edn;* we? F; we, *Rowe³*   107–9 pray, . . . bound?]
F4; pray? . . . bound: F

90 **fail in** fail to grant.
92–3 In North, when it appears Volumnia will
cut short the silent welcome and speak, Coriolanus 'called the chiefest of the counsell of the
Volsces to heare what she would say' (Bullough,
Sources, V, 539); Shakespeare has slightly altered
the circumstances and phrased the request to
indicate Coriolanus's sense of performing before
Aufidius and his soldiers.
94–125, 131–82 Volumnia's great speeches of
supplication are close renderings of North's versions; relevant passages will be quoted from
Bullough, *Sources*, V, 539–40.

94–5 **raiment . . . bodies** i.e. neglected clothing and emaciated bodies; see 21 SD.2 n.
95 **bewray** reveal, expose.
96 **exile** Accented on the second syllable.
96 **Think with thyself** Think to yourself,
consider.
102–3 **tearing . . . out** The body-politic
metaphor is Shakespeare's; North has 'besieging
the walles of his native countrie'.
103 **we** us; 'we' is also used for 'us' in *Ham.*
1.4.33, *JC* 3.1.95 (Clarendon).
104 **capital** deadly, fatal.
109–10 **or . . . or** either . . . or.

The country, our dear nurse, or else thy person,   110
Our comfort in the country. We must find
An evident calamity, though we had
Our wish which side should win. For either thou
Must as a foreign recreant be led
With manacles through our streets, or else   115
Triumphantly tread on thy country's ruin
And bear the palm for having bravely shed
Thy wife and children's blood. For myself, son,
I purpose not to wait on fortune till
These wars determine. If I cannot persuade thee   120
Rather to show a noble grace to both parts
Than seek the end of one, thou shalt no sooner
March to assault thy country than to tread –
Trust to't, thou shalt not – on thy mother's womb
That brought thee to this world.

VIRGILIA   Ay, and mine,   125
That brought you forth this boy to keep your name
Living to time.

BOY   'A shall not tread on me.
I'll run away till I am bigger, but then I'll fight.

CORIOLANUS Not of a woman's tenderness to be
Requires nor child, nor woman's face to see.   130
I have sat too long. [*He rises*]

VOLUMNIA   Nay, go not from us thus.
If it were so that our request did tend
To save the Romans, thereby to destroy

---

115 through] F; thorough *Johnson*   127 'A] F (A)   131 SD] *Capell subst.; not in* F

110 country . . . nurse Shakespeare's phrasing
strengthens Volumnia's equation of Rome with
herself; in different senses both are Coriolanus's
'nurse'. North has 'the nurse of their native
contrie'.

112 evident certain, manifest; compare 4.7.52.

114 foreign recreant i.e. 'foreign' because a
deserter ('recreant') to a foreign power.

117 bear the palm be crowned victor.

119 purpose intend.

120 determine (1) end, are determined, (2)
determine which the outcome will be (of the two
she has just described).

121 grace mercy.

122–4 thou . . . womb North's syntax is
clearer: 'thou shalt no soner marche forward

to assault thy countrie, but thy foote shall
treade upon thy mothers wombe'; Shakespeare's
'Trust . . . not' is an emphatic parenthesis.

125–8 Ay . . . fight Neither Virgilia nor Coriolanus's son speaks in Plutarch; their challenges
break decorum, as had Volumnia's kneeling to her
son. Virgilia's emphasis on 'name' and reputation
is picked up and elaborated by Volumnia in her
next speech (141–8).

127 'A He.

129–30 To avoid becoming as tender as a
woman, one must not look at either a child or a
woman. The rhyme and absence of personal pronouns lend the statement a generalised, gnomic
quality.

The Volsces whom you serve, you might condemn us
As poisonous of your honour. No, our suit   135
Is that you reconcile them, while the Volsces
May say 'This mercy we have showed', the Romans
'This we received', and each in either side
Give the all-hail to thee and cry 'Be blest
For making up this peace!' Thou know'st, great son,   140
The end of war's uncertain, but this certain,
That if thou conquer Rome, the benefit
Which thou shalt thereby reap is such a name
Whose repetition will be dogged with curses,
Whose chronicle thus writ: 'The man was noble,   145
But with his last attempt he wiped it out,
Destroyed his country, and his name remains
To th'ensuing age abhorred.' Speak to me, son.
Thou hast affected the fine strains of honour,
To imitate the graces of the gods,   150
To tear with thunder the wide cheeks o'th'air
And yet to charge thy sulphur with a bolt
That should but rive an oak. Why dost not speak?
Think'st thou it honourable for a noble man
Still to remember wrongs? Daughter, speak you;   155
He cares not for your weeping. Speak thou, boy.
Perhaps thy childishness will move him more
Than can our reasons. There's no man in the world

137–40 'This . . . showed' . . . 'This . . . received' . . . 'Be . . . peace!'] *Hanmer;* this . . . shew'd . . . This . . . receiu'd
. . . be . . . peace. F   141 war's] F3; Warres F   145–8 'The . . . abhorred.'] *Pope;* The . . . abhorr'd. F   149 fine]
Johnson; fiue F; first *Rowe*3   150 gods,] *Hibbard;* Gods. F   152 charge] *Theobald;* change F   154 noble man] F2;
Nobleman F

136 **while** so that at the same time.
139 **all-hail** general acclamation.
144 **Whose** That its.
145 **thus writ** will be thus written.
145–8 **The . . . abhorred** Shakespeare has elaborated and made more vivid Volumnia's assertion in North that, if he conquers Rome, Coriolanus will 'be chronicled the plague and destroyer of thy countrie'.
146 **it** his nobility (and with it his noble reputation).
149–53 **Thou . . . oak** In telling her son what she wishes him to say, Volumnia emphasises that the mercy that threatens yet finally spares humanity is the godlike attribute he should imitate; this sentiment is not from North.

149 **affected** (1) assumed (the 'strains of honour'), (2) aspired to (emulate the gods).
149 **fine strains** niceties, refinements (Johnson), F's 'fiue' probably results from a turned letter *n*, though possibly from a minim error.
150 **graces** i.e. terror and mercy.
151 **cheeks** Map-makers in this period frequently represented the four winds as issuing from the puffed-up cheeks of cherubs.
152 **charge** load, arm.
152 **sulphur** lightning.
152 **bolt** thunderbolt.
153 **but rive** only split.
155 **Still** Always.

More bound to's mother, yet here he lets me prate
Like one i'th'stocks. Thou hast never in thy life   160
Showed thy dear mother any courtesy,
When she, poor hen, fond of no second brood,
Has clucked thee to the wars and safely home,
Loaden with honour. Say my request's unjust,
And spurn me back. But if it be not so,   165
Thou art not honest, and the gods will plague thee
That thou restrain'st from me the duty which
To a mother's part belongs. – He turns away.
Down, ladies. Let us shame him with our knees.
To his surname Coriolanus longs more pride   170
Than pity to our prayers. Down! An end;
                    [*They kneel*]
This is the last. So, we will home to Rome
And die among our neighbours. – Nay, behold's.
This boy, that cannot tell what he would have
But kneels and holds up hands for fellowship,   175
Does reason our petition with more strength
Than thou hast to deny't. – Come, let us go.
                    [*They rise*]

159 lets] F (let's)   163 clucked] F (clock'd)   163 wars . . . home,] F2; Warres: . . . home F   169 him with] F2; him with him with F   171 SD] *Collier² subst. (after 169); not in* F   177 SD] *Collier³; not in* F; *at 190, Oxford*

159 bound (1) indebted; compare North: 'No man living is more bounde to shewe him selfe thankefull in all partes and respects, then thy selfe.' For the audience it may also resonate as (2) tied emotionally.

160 Like . . . stocks Like a prisoner (put in the stocks as public humiliation, whose words go unheeded).

160 never . . . life Shakespeare strengthens North's 'not hitherto' and turns it into an outrageously unjust accusation.

162–3 poor . . . clucked Volumnia's barnyard metaphor is Shakespeare's addition. Her self-characterisation is as comically untrue of the virago of 1.3 as her complaint about her son in the preceding lines, and it implies her own unnaturalness, since the hen is proverbially timid and protective of her young; compare Thomas Dekker's 'A Prayer for the Citie' in *Foure Birds of Noahs Arke* (1609): 'Lord . . . gather they children together as the Hen gathereth her chickens under her wing' (F1ʳ). F's 'clock'd', an authentic dialect form, may indicate a pun on 'clocked' = timed.

162 fond of wishing for.

166 honest (1) truthful, honest with yourself, (2) honourable. Behind this final appeal to filial duty lies North's 'therefore, it is not only honest, but due unto me, that without compulsion I should obtaine my so just and reasonable request of thee'.

167 restrain'st withhold, keep back.

170 surname Coriolanus Volumnia implies that the 'conqueror of Corioli' has become a 'man of Corioli', too proud of being a Volscian to pity their prayers; King notes the anticipation of 178–80.

170 longs belongs; the older form (*OED* Long *v²*) has been superseded by the modern compound.

171 An end Let's make an end.

172 So, we F's comma is grammatically unnecessary and often omitted, but it probably indicates a significant pause.

176 reason argue for.

177 SD In Plutarch, the kneeling petitioners are silent and remain down until Coriolanus has taken his mother's hand. Shakespeare has given Volumnia more dialogue, and 'Come, let us go' would be said most naturally while she rises and the final disavowal more effective if said standing, to his face.

This fellow had a Volscian to his mother;
His wife is in Corioles, and his child
Like him by chance. – Yet give us our dispatch.   180
I am hushed until our city be afire,
And then I'll speak a little.

                      [He] holds her by the hand, silent

CORIOLANUS O mother, mother!
What have you done? Behold, the heavens do ope,
The gods look down, and this unnatural scene   185
They laugh at. O my mother, mother! O!
You have won a happy victory to Rome;
But for your son – believe it, O believe it –
Most dangerously you have with him prevailed,
If not most mortal to him. But let it come. –   190
Aufidius, though I cannot make true wars,
I'll frame convenient peace. Now, good Aufidius,
Were you in my stead, would you have heard
A mother less? Or granted less, Aufidius?

AUFIDIUS I was moved withal.

CORIOLANUS   I dare be sworn you were.   195

---

179 his child] F; this child *Theobald*   181 hushed] F (husht)   182 SD *He holds . . . hand*] F *subst.* (*Holds*); *Holds . . . hands / Pope* (*at 183, after* mother!)   193 stead] F (steed)

178 **to** for.
180 **dispatch** dismissal, leave to go.
181 **hushed** silent.
182 SD Shakespeare creates this powerfully ambivalent gesture of both reconciliation and submission by conflating two passages in North, one from an interval in Volumnia's speech where she expects an answer but 'he held his peace a prety while, and aunswered not a worde', and the other at the end when they are kneeling and he goes immediately to lift her up, 'crying out: Oh mother, what have you done to me? And holding her hard by the right hande, oh mother, sayed he, you have wonne a happy victorie for your countrie.' From Pope through much of the nineteenth century, this SD was moved to follow 183, and in 'Re-enter the stage direction', E. A. J. Honigmann argues that this emendation is correct (*S.Sur. 29* (1976), 119); but F is not clearly in error and is theatrically effective (see Lee Bliss, 'Scribes, compositors, and annotators', *SB 50* (1997), 257–9).
185–6 **The . . . at** In the *Iliad* the gods look down from Olympus to laugh at human folly, and the gods of Erasmus's *Praise of Folly* specifically see the ironies of human situations as comic theatre. A judgemental note is suggested by the

biblical analogue more familiar to Shakespeare's audience, Acts 7.56; 'Behold, I see the heavens open, and the Sonne of man standing at the right hand of God.'
185 **unnatural scene** In immediate terms, the tableau they present to divine as well as Volscian spectators; more generally, the whole 'scene', beginning with Volumnia's 'unnatural' kneeling to her son, that they have just played out (see p. 59 above). The phrase also anticipates his next lines foreseeing that the 'scene' of her triumph seals his own fate. Brockbank notes that Shakespeare uses 'scene' some forty times, 'invariably in a theatrical sense'.
190 **mortal** fatally (adjective used as adverb).
190 **But . . . come** A simple and moving phrase of tragic acceptance not found in North.
191–4 **Aufidius . . . Aufidius** The repetitions suggest how important it is to Coriolanus that his decision be confirmed by his Volscian co-general, who is also the only warrior he considers his equal.
191 **true** i.e. true to my promise to conquer Rome.
192 **convenient** appropriate to both sides, not merely expedient.
195 **withal** by it.

And, sir, it is no little thing to make
Mine eyes to sweat compassion. But, good sir,
What peace you'll make, advise me. For my part,
I'll not to Rome; I'll back with you, and pray you
Stand to me in this cause. – O mother! Wife!   200
AUFIDIUS [*Aside*] I am glad thou hast set thy mercy and thy honour
At difference in thee. Out of that I'll work
Myself a former fortune.
CORIOLANUS [*To the Ladies*]   Ay, by and by.
But we will drink together, and you shall bear
A better witness back than words, which we,   205
On like conditions, will have counter-sealed.
Come, enter with us. Ladies, you deserve
To have a temple built you. All the swords
In Italy, and her confederate arms,
Could not have made this peace.   210
                                              Exeunt

5.[4] *Enter* MENENIUS *and* SICINIUS

MENENIUS See you yond quoin o'th'Capitol, yond cornerstone?

200 Wife!] F; *Wife! He speaks to them apart / Neilson*   201 SD] *Rowe; not in* F   203 a former] F; *my former Hanmer;*
a firmer *Collier*²   203 fortune.] F; *fortune. The Ladies make signs to Coriolanus / Johnson*   203 SD] *Rowe subst. (To*
Vol. Virg. &c.); not in F; *To Vol. / Capell*   207–10 Ladies . . . peace] F; *Auf.* Ladies . . . peace *Hanmer*   Act 5,
Scene 4   5.4] *Pope; not in* F   1 yond . . . yond] F (yon'd . . . yon'd)   1 quoin] F (Coin)

197 **sweat compassion** weep. In North, Coriolanus is moved to tears before Volumnia speaks,
not after.
200 **Stand to** Stand by, support.
200 **O . . . Wife** At this point Coriolanus joins
his family, perhaps even with his back to Aufidius;
in North, 'he spake a litle a parte with his mother
and wife, and then let them returne againe to
Rome'. Some editions, following Johnson, have
the ladies stand apart and then gesture to attract
Coriolanus's attention at 203.
203 **former fortune** fortune like my former
one.
204 **drink together** A traditional mark of
having concluded peace, though objected to as
an offence against female propriety by some
eighteenth-century editors.
205 **better witness** i.e. a formal treaty.
206 **like conditions** i.e. the same conditions
that we have verbally agreed upon.

208 **temple** North reports that after the
ladies' return bearing peace the grateful Roman
senate granted their request to 'build a temple of
Fortune of the women'. Missing the bitter irony
of Coriolanus proposing a memorial to his own
capitulation, Hanmer reassigned the last four
lines ('Ladies . . . peace') to Aufidius.

Act 5, Scene 4
A public place in Rome. The first part of the
scene (1–34) is Shakespeare's addition, the rest
prompted by North's report of Rome's joy when it
sees Coriolanus's army depart. In theatrical terms
it allows the ladies time to return to Rome, and our
knowledge that Coriolanus has spared his native
city makes grimly ironic comedy of Menenius's
dehumanising descriptions of him to Sicinius. It
also shows that adversity has not united Rome; its
political conflicts and instability remain as viru-
lent as in 1.1.
1 **quoin** cornerstone.

SICINIUS Why what of that?

MENENIUS If it be possible for you to displace it with your little finger,
there is some hope the ladies of Rome, especially his mother, may
prevail with him. But I say there is no hope in't; our throats are   5
sentenced and stay upon execution.

SICINIUS Is't possible that so short a time can alter the condition of a
man?

MENENIUS There is differency between a grub and a butterfly, yet your
butterfly was a grub. This Martius is grown from man to dragon.   10
He has wings; he's more than a creeping thing.

SICINIUS He loved his mother dearly.

MENENIUS So did he me; and he no more remembers his mother now
than an eight-year-old horse. The tartness of his face sours ripe
grapes. When he walks, he moves like an engine, and the ground   15
shrinks before his treading. He is able to pierce a corslet with his
eye, talks like a knell, and his hum is a battery. He sits in his state as
a thing made for Alexander. What he bids be done is finished with
his bidding. He wants nothing of a god but eternity and a heaven to
throne in.   20

SICINIUS Yes, mercy, if you report him truly.

MENENIUS I paint him in the character. Mark what mercy his mother
shall bring from him. There is no more mercy in him than there is
milk in a male tiger. That shall our poor city find. And all this is
long of you.   25

9 differency] F; difference F2   25 long] F; 'long *Capell*

6 **stay upon** wait for.
7 **condition** character, disposition (i.e. Coriolanus's attitude toward his family and patrician
friends).
9 **differency** dissimilarity (*OED*'s first
instance).
10 **dragon** See 4.1.30 n., 4.7.23.
14 **than ... horse** than an old horse remembers
his dam.
15 **engine** engine of war (probably a batteringram).
16 **corslet** body-armour.
17 **knell** The sound of the bell rung to
announce a death.
17 **hum** An interjection expressing dissatisfaction or dissent (*OED* Hum *int*); see 5.1.50.
17 **battery** Military assault by means of
artillery, bombardment (here an anachronism).
17 **state** chair of state, throne; see 5.1.64 n.
17–18 **as ... Alexander** like a statue of Alexander the Great.
18–19 **finished ... bidding** i.e. as good as

done once he orders it; compare 4.7.23–4. The
suggested simultaneity of order and accomplishment leads naturally to the next sentence's semi-
deification.
19 **wants** lacks.
19–21 **nothing ... mercy** Richmond Noble,
Shakespeare's Biblical Knowledge, 1935, points
out the Judaeo-Christian analogues for these
attributes of the deity: Isa. 57.15 ('he that inhab-
iteth the eternitie, whose Name is the Holie one');
Isa. 66.1 ('Thus saith the Lord, The heaven is my
throne'). Many scriptural texts speak of mercy as
one of God's primary attributes (e.g. Exod. 34.6,
1 Chron. 16.34, Ps. 106.1, 107.1, 118.1), and it is
frequently mentioned in the Elizabethan homilies
and the Prayer Book; see also p. 56 above, n. 4.
22 **in the character** to the life, as he is; there is
a secondary play on 'character' as a seventeenth-
century literary genre (see 2.1.50 n).
25 **long of** on account of, attributable to (*OED*
Long *a*²).

SICINIUS The gods be good unto us!
MENENIUS No, in such a case the gods will not be good unto us. When
    we banished him, we respected not them; and, he returning to break
    our necks, they respect not us.

Enter a MESSENGER

MESSENGER Sir, if you'd save your life, fly to your house.   30
    The plebeians have got your fellow tribune
    And hale him up and down, all swearing if
    The Roman ladies bring not comfort home
    They'll give him death by inches.

Enter another MESSENGER

SICINIUS What's the news?   35
SECOND MESSENGER Good news, good news! The ladies have
    prevailed,
    The Volscians are dislodged, and Martius gone.
    A merrier day did never yet greet Rome,
    No, not th'expulsion of the Tarquins.
SICINIUS   Friend,
    Art thou certain this is true? Is't most certain?   40
SECOND MESSENGER As certain as I know the sun is fire.
    Where have you lurked that you make doubt of it?
    Ne'er through an arch so hurried the blown tide
    As the recomforted through th'gates.
    Trumpets, hautboys, drums beat, all together
    Why, hark you!
    The trumpets, sackbuts, psalteries and fifes,   45

---

26 The] F; Ye *conj. Hinman* (*in 'Textual Companion'*)   **30** you'd] you'ld F   **36** SH, **41** SH, **56** SH, **58** SH] *Dyce* (*Sec. Mess.*); *Mess., Mes.* F   **44** SD] F (*after* you!)

31 plebeians Here accented on the first syllable.
32 hale drag, haul.
34 death by inches slow, protracted death.
37 are dislodged have withdrawn and broken up their camp (a military term, taken from North).
43 blown (1) swollen, (2) wind-driven; an image appropriate to the River Thames at old London Bridge.
44 SD Shakespeare asks for the loudest possible musical effects to signal Rome's joy. 'Hautboys' were wooden double-reed instruments producing a high, loud sound (from French *hautbois*).

E. W. Naylor, *Shakespeare and Music*, 1896, says their use implies a special occasion 'and is generally connected with a Royal banquet, masque or procession' (p. 175).
45–6 trumpets . . . cymbals The list of instruments may have been suggested by the biblical catalogue, Dan. 3.5, where the people worship the golden image set up by Nebuchadnezzar with 'cornet, trumpet, harpe, sackebut, psalteries, dulcimer, and all instruments of musicke'.
45 sackbuts Bass instruments resembling trombones.
45 psalteries Harp-like stringed instruments.

>   Tabors and cymbals, and the shouting Romans
>   Make the sun dance.

A shout within

>   Hark you!

MENENIUS   This is good news.
>   I will go meet the ladies. This Volumnia
>   Is worth of consuls, senators, patricians,
>   A city full; of tribunes such as you,   50
>   A sea and land full. You have prayed well today.
>   This morning for ten thousand of your throats
>   I'd not have given a doit.

Sound still with the shouts

>   Hark, how they joy!

SICINIUS [*To Second Messenger*] First, the gods bless you for your
>   tidings.
>   Next, accept my thankfulness.   55

SECOND MESSENGER Sir, we have all great cause to give great thanks.

SICINIUS They are near the city?

SECOND MESSENGER Almost at point to enter.

SICINIUS We'll meet them and help the joy.

Exeunt

5.[5] *Enter two* SENATORS, *with Ladies* [VOLUMNIA, VIRGILIA, *and*
VALERIA], *passing over the stage, with other* LORDS

A SENATOR Behold our patroness, the life of Rome!

46 cymbals] F (Symboles)   47 SD] F (*after you!*)   53 SD] F (*after joy!*).; *Music still with shouts / Globe*   54 SD] *Oxford subst.; not in* F   59 SD] F; *going / Capell*   Act 5, Scene 5   5.5] *Dyce; not in* F   0 SD.1–2 *Ladies* . . . VALERIA,] F (*Ladies,*)   0 SD.2 *other* LORDS] F; *Senators, Patricians, and People / Capell*   1 SH] F (*Sena.*); 1. *S. / Capell*

46 Tabors Small drums, often accompanied by pipes.

48 This Volumnia The only time Volumnia's name is mentioned in the play's dialogue; Menenius's 'This' emphatically counterpoises Volumnia's worth against that of everyone else in Rome.

53 doit small, almost worthless, coin; see 1.5.6 n.

58 at point ready, about.

Act 5, Scene 5
Same location. Before Dyce's subdivision, 5.4 and 5.5 were considered one continuous scene, and there is some reason to think they were not distinguished in the manuscript behind F. There is only one *Exeunt* direction, at 5.4.59. After the sen-

ators, ladies and lords enter (here 5.5.0), it is clear that seven lines later a new scene must begin, since the action shifts to Antium/Corioles, but there is no exit direction for the Romans. Possibly the book-keeper, reading through the manuscript fairly quickly to catch specific places that needed annotation, misplaced his *Exeunt* early, an easy mistake to make since neither of the two speeches in 5.5 is by, or obviously addressed to, the characters who were on stage for 5.4. Menenius, Sicinius and the messengers (if they haven't exited after giving their news) might move toward the incoming procession of victorious ladies and help swell the crowd for the *All* shouts of welcome.

0 SD This entry could be staged to recall Coriolanus's triumphal return to Rome in 2.1,

Call all your tribes together, praise the gods,
And make triumphant fires. Strew flowers before them.
Unshout the noise that banished Martius;
Repeal him with the welcome of his mother.   5
Cry 'Welcome, ladies, welcome!'
ALL Welcome, ladies, welcome!
                    A flourish with drums and trumpets

                                                    [*Exeunt*]

5.[6] *Enter* TULLUS AUFIDIUS, *with Attendants*

AUFIDIUS Go, tell the lords o'th'city I am here.
          Deliver them this paper.
                    [*He gives a paper*]
                                Having read it,
          Bid them repair to th'market-place, where I,
          Even in theirs and in the commons' ears,
          Will vouch the truth of it. Him I accuse   5
          The city ports by this hath entered and
          Intends t'appear before the people, hoping

---

4 Unshout] F (Vnshoot)   6 'Welcome . . . welcome!'] *Hanmer*; welcome . . . welcome. F   7 SD.1–2 *A . . . trumpets. Exeunt*] F2 *subst. (Exeunt. A . . . trumpets.); A . . . Trumpets.* F   **Act 5, Scene 6**   5.6] *Dyce; not in* F   2 SD] *Bevington; not in* F   5 accuse] F4; accuse: F

with the mother now substituted for the son, but the scene's effect will depend crucially upon directorial decisions about Volumnia's response to her success (but also to her son's premonition of his fate) and, hence, what emotions she should reveal here; see pp. 56–9 above.

2 Call . . . together There is no entry direction for citizens, and the senator may address his speech to the audience as if it were the Roman populace; most productions, however, crowd the stage with as many citizens as possible.

2 tribes See 3.3.10–12 n.

3 triumphant fires In Plutarch the people wear garlands and sacrifice to the gods, but he says nothing about fires; bonfires were, however, a common Elizabethan expression of thankful celebration, as at the defeat of the Spanish Armada.

5 Repeal Recall.

Act 5, Scene 6

In Plutarch Coriolanus returns with his army to Antium and meets his death there. Initially, Shakespeare seems to follow him, alluding to Aufidius's 'native town' (49), to the city from which he 'parted' (73; see 4.4.1, 8), and to 'the Antiates' (80); when he came to Aufidius's speech of provocation, however, he seized on the dramatic possibilities of 'Coriolanus' in 'Corioles' (90–2) and brought the action full circle, with Coriolanus again 'alone, / To answer all the city' (1.4.55–6).

4 theirs On the use of 'theirs' as a pronominal adjective before the noun, see Abbott 238.

5 Him He whom (see Abbott 208).

6 ports gates.

6 by this by this time.

To purge himself with words. Dispatch.

[Exeunt Attendants]

Enter three or four CONSPIRATORS *of Aufidius' faction*

                                                    Most welcome!
FIRST CONSPIRATOR How is it with our general?
AUFIDIUS   Even so
    As with a man by his own alms empoisoned   10
    And with his charity slain.
SECOND CONSPIRATOR   Most noble sir,
    If you do hold the same intent wherein
    You wished us parties, we'll deliver you
    Of your great danger.
AUFIDIUS   Sir, I cannot tell.
    We must proceed as we do find the people.   15
THIRD CONSPIRATOR The people will remain uncertain whilst
    'Twixt you there's difference, but the fall of either
    Makes the survivor heir of all.
AUFIDIUS   I know it,
    And my pretext to strike at him admits
    A good construction. I raised him, and I pawned   20
    Mine honour for his truth; who being so heightened,
    He watered his new plants with dews of flattery,
    Seducing so my friends; and to this end
    He bowed his nature, never known before
    But to be rough, unswayable, and free.   25
THIRD CONSPIRATOR Sir, his stoutness
    When he did stand for consul, which he lost

---

8 SD.1] *Capell; not in* F   25 free] F; fierce *Hanmer*

10 by . . . empoisoned destroyed by his own generosity.
11 with by (see Abbott 193).
13 parties allies, supporters.
14 Of Out of, from.
15 as . . . find according to the will of. Ever the pragmatist, Aufidius seeks information on the state of public opinion before he decides on action; compare 1.10.31–3.
17 difference disagreement, rivalry.
19 pretext Accented on the second syllable.
19–20 admits . . . construction can be interpreted as honourable.
20 pawned pledged.

21 truth loyalty.
21 heightened raised (to a position of power). The subsequent charges (22–5) have no basis in the play or in Plutarch's 'Life of Caius Martius Coriolanus', though they may have been influenced by Plutarch's later condemnation of Alcibiades as a man 'geven to flatterie' and a shameless courting of 'favour with the common people' (Bullough, *Sources*, v, 545).
22 plants i.e. the Volscians who used to be Aufidius's 'friends' (23).
25 free (1) outspoken, (2) unrestrainable.
26 stoutness obstinacy; compare Volumnia's charge at 3.2.128.

       By lack of stooping –
AUFIDIUS   That I would have spoke of.
       Being banished for't, he came unto my hearth,
       Presented to my knife his throat. I took him,   30
       Made him joint-servant with me, gave him way
       In all his own desires; nay, let him choose
       Out of my files, his projects to accomplish,
       My best and freshest men; served his designments
       In mine own person, holp to reap the fame   35
       Which he did end all his, and took some pride
       To do myself this wrong, till at the last
       I seemed his follower, not partner, and
       He waged me with his countenance as if
       I had been mercenary.
FIRST CONSPIRATOR   So he did, my lord.   40
       The army marvelled at it, and in the last,
       When he had carried Rome and that we looked
       For no less spoil than glory –
AUFIDIUS   There was it,
       For which my sinews shall be stretched upon him.
       At a few drops of women's rheum, which are   45
       As cheap as lies, he sold the blood and labour
       Of our great action. Therefore shall he die,

---

28 stooping –] *Rowe;* stooping. F   33 projects . . . accomplish,] F3; proiects, . . . accomplish F   35 holp] F (holpe); hope F2; hop'd F4   35–6 reap . . . end] F; reap . . . make F4; reap . . . ear *Collier²;* ear . . . reap *Singer², conj. Lettsom,* '*NQ*'; reap . . . bind *conj. Staunton;* reap . . . inn *Keightley*   39 waged] F (wadg'd)   43 glory –] F3; Glory. F   43–6 it, . . . him. . . . lies,] F4 *subst.;* it: . . . him, . . . Lies; F

28 **That . . . of** I would have mentioned that (if you had not interrupted).

31 **joint-servant** equal partner (in service to the Volscian state).

31 **gave him way** gave way to him.

33 **files** 'Files' are lines of soldiers stretching away from the observer; the front of a file is one man, while the depth can be any number.

34 **designments** designs, undertakings.

36 **end all his** gather in as wholly his own ('end' is a harvesting term; *OED* End *v²*).

39–40 **waged . . . mercenary** paid me with his favour ('countenance'), as if I were a hired soldier. This expression of Aufidius's resentment of Coriolanus's condescension is drawn from North's more general description: 'every man

honoured Martius, and thought he only could doe all, and that all other governours and captaines must be content with suche credit and authoritie, as he would please to countenance them with' (Bullough, *Sources*, V, 534).

41 **in the last** at the last.

42 **had carried** (1) was on the point of taking; possibly (2) might have conquered (Abbott 361).

43 **There was it** That was the thing.

44 **my . . . him** I will strain every nerve against him. The image verges on the grotesque: Aufidius's body, his every tendon, stretched to become the net entrapping Coriolanus.

45 **At** At the price of, for.

45 **rheum** Used of secretions from the mucous membranes, here contemptuously for 'tears'.

And I'll renew me in his fall.
Drums and trumpets sound, with great shouts of the people
                              But hark!
FIRST CONSPIRATOR Your native town you entered like a post
      And had no welcomes home, but he returns   50
      Splitting the air with noise.
SECOND CONSPIRATOR   And patient fools,
      Whose children he hath slain, their base throats tear
      With giving him glory.
THIRD CONSPIRATOR   Therefore, at your vantage,
      Ere he express himself or move the people
      With what he would say, let him feel your sword,   55
      Which we will second. When he lies along,
      After your way his tale pronounced shall bury
      His reasons with his body.
AUFIDIUS   Say no more.
      Here come the lords.

                Enter the LORDS *of the city*

ALL LORDS You are most welcome home.   60
AUFIDIUS I have not deserved it.
      But, worthy lords, have you with heed perused
      What I have written to you?
ALL LORDS   We have.
FIRST LORD   And grieve to hear't.
      What faults he made before the last, I think
      Might have found easy fines. But there to end   65
      Where he was to begin, and give away
      The benefit of our levies, answering us

---

48 SD] F (*after* hark!)   48 SD *sound*] F3; *sounds* F   55–7 sword, . . . second . . . way] *Theobald;* Sword: . . . second, . . . way. F   60 SH, 63 SH ALL LORDS] F (*All Lords., All.*)

49 native town Antium. See headnote to this scene.
49 post messenger (i.e. merely a bearer of news of Coriolanus).
53 at your vantage seizing your opportunity, the moment that gives you the advantage. Compare North: 'Tullus . . . sought divers meanes to make him out of the waye, thinking that if he let slippe that present time, he should never recover the like and fit occasion againe' (Bullough, *Sources*, v, 543).
56 along stretched out, prostrate (i.e. dead).
57 After . . . pronounced Telling your version

of his story. The tortuous syntax, in a manuscript lightly or wholly unpointed, may be responsible for F's baffling punctuation.
58 reasons justifications, explanations.
62 with heed carefully.
64 faults . . . last Aufidius earlier referred to unspecified offences; see 4.7.18–26 and 19 n.
64 made committed.
65 easy fines light penalties (*OED* Fine *sb*¹ 8d).
67 benefit . . . levies advantage obtained by our mustering an army.
67–8 answering . . . charge An ambiguous

With our own charge, making a treaty where
There was a yielding – this admits no excuse.
AUFIDIUS He approaches. You shall hear him.   70

Enter CORIOLANUS *marching with drum and colours,*
the COMMONERS *being with him*

CORIOLANUS Hail, lords! I am returned your soldier,
No more infected with my country's love
Than when I parted hence, but still subsisting
Under your great command. You are to know
That prosperously I have attempted and   75
With bloody passage led your wars even to
The gates of Rome. Our spoils we have brought home
Doth more than counterpoise a full third part
The charges of the action. We have made peace
With no less honour to the Antiates   80
Than shame to th'Romans. And we here deliver,
Subscribed by th'consuls and patricians,
Together with the seal o'th'senate, what
We have compounded on.
                    [*He offers a document*]
AUFIDIUS   Read it not, noble lords,
But tell the traitor in the highest degree   85

---

84 SD] *Bevington; not in* F   85 traitor] F; traitor, *Theobald*

phrase which, if it modifies the preceding clause, could mean 'rewarding us with our own expenses; making the cost of war its recompense' (Johnson); in this case, it is contradicted by 77–9. If the phrase is a separate accusation, and if Shakespeare had in mind the passage in North in which 'charge' means 'authority conferred by the Volscian lords', First Lord says Coriolanus defends himself by saying that he acted with the authority the lords themselves had given him (Brockbank).

70 SD An impressive processional entry that could be staged to recall Coriolanus's triumphal return to Rome in 2.1; the reminder would emphasise the precariousness of his current position, where his only supporters seem to be the fickle commoners he so despised in Rome and he returns to be greeted not by his family and friends but by Aufidius and the conspirators.

72 infected influenced by (with a medical secondary sense of 'contaminated').

73 hence i.e. from Antium; see 80 and 5.6 headnote on the shift in location at 92.

73 subsisting continuing.

75 prosperously . . . attempted my efforts have proved prosperous.

78 more . . . part An ambiguous phrase that could mean (1) outweigh more than a third (of the cost of the war to the Volscians), but in context seems more likely to mean (2) outweigh by more than a third. If the latter, Coriolanus reveals the accusation at 67–8 to be part of Aufidius's systematic, self-interested 'revision' of events in his report to the Volscian lords.

82 Subscribed Signed.

84 compounded agreed.

85 in . . . degree of the worst kind; possibly, however, the adverbial sense brought out by Theobald's comma, 'most egregiously'. In North the conspirators 'crie out that he was not to be heard, nor that they would not suffer a traytour

He hath abused your powers.
CORIOLANUS 'Traitor'? How now?
AUFIDIUS Ay, traitor, Martius.
CORIOLANUS 'Martius'?
AUFIDIUS Ay, Martius, Caius Martius. Dost thou think   90
　　　　I'll grace thee with that robbery, thy stol'n name
　　　　Coriolanus, in Corioles? –
　　　　You lords and heads o'th'state, perfidiously
　　　　He has betrayed your business and given up,
　　　　For certain drops of salt, your city Rome –   95
　　　　I say 'your city' – to his wife and mother,
　　　　Breaking his oath and resolution like
　　　　A twist of rotten silk, never admitting
　　　　Counsel o'th'war. But at his nurse's tears
　　　　He whined and roared away your victory,   100
　　　　That pages blushed at him and men of heart
　　　　Looked wondering each at others.
CORIOLANUS   Hear'st thou, Mars?
AUFIDIUS Name not the god, thou boy of tears.
CORIOLANUS   Ha?
AUFIDIUS No more.
CORIOLANUS Measureless liar, thou hast made my heart   105
　　　　Too great for what contains it. 'Boy'? O slave! –
　　　　Pardon me, lords, 'tis the first time that ever
　　　　I was forced to scold. Your judgements, my grave lords,

---

87 'Traitor'] *Riverside;* Traitor F   89 'Martius'] *Riverside; Martius* F   95–6 Rome – . . . 'your city' –] *Cam. subst.;*
Rome: . . . your City F   102 each at others] F; each at other *Rowe;* at each other *Steevens*   104 SH AUFIDIUS] F; *First
Lord / conj. Tyrwhitt (in Cam.)*   106, 115, 119 'Boy'] *Cam.;* Boy F   108 scold] F (scoul'd)

to usurpe tyrannicall power over the tribe of the
Volsces'; they immediately fall on Coriolanus and
kill him, 'none of the people once offering to rescue him' (Bullough, *Sources,* v, 543–4).
95 drops of salt i.e. the tears of Volumnia and
Virgilia; see 45, 99. These references are perhaps
cues for the women's behaviour in 5.3, but since
in the text it is clear only that Virgilia weeps, they
might be another of Aufidius's slanders (see 67–8
n., 78 n.).
97 oath and resolution sworn purpose.
98 twist plaited thread.
98–9 never . . . war never taking counsel of his
other officers.
100 whined and roared An exaggeration of
Coriolanus's capitulation to his mother (5.3.183,
196–7), calculated to challenge Coriolanus's portrait of himself as returning a victorious hero; see
4.6.129 n.

101 heart courage.
102 each at others at one another.
104 No more Tyrwhitt suggested that these
words should be given to the Volscian First Lord
who tries to stop the altercation at 113, but they
are appropriate for Aufidius as a further scornful
provocation (i.e. 'no more than a boy').
105 Measureless Boundless.
106 'Boy'? O slave! As Coriolanus's reply
makes clear, Aufidius's insult is two-pronged:
'boy' also denotes a servant or slave (*OED* Boy
*sb*¹ 3a), thus stripping Coriolanus of his noble
status.
107–8 'tis . . . scold This comically inaccurate
assertion could be read as suggesting a serious
failure in self-knowledge, though Coriolanus is
probably referring more narrowly to his temper-
ate behaviour, till now, before the Volscian lords.

Must give this cur the lie; and his own notion –
Who wears my stripes impressed upon him, that   110
Must bear my beating to his grave – shall join
To thrust the lie unto him.

FIRST LORD Peace, both, and hear me speak.

CORIOLANUS Cut me to pieces, Volsces. Men and lads,
Stain all your edges on me. 'Boy'! False hound,   115
If you have writ your annals true, 'tis there
That, like an eagle in a dovecote, I
Fluttered your Volscians in Corioles.
Alone I did it. 'Boy'!

AUFIDIUS   Why, noble lords,
Will you be put in mind of his blind fortune,   120
Which was your shame, by this unholy braggart,
'Fore your own eyes and ears?

ALL CONSPIRATORS   Let him die for't.

ALL PEOPLE Tear him to pieces! Do it presently! He killed my son! My
daughter! He killed my cousin Marcus! He killed my father!

---

114 Volsces.] F3 *subst.* (Volcies,); Volces F   115 hound,] F (Hound:); hound! *Globe*   118 Fluttered] F3; Flatter'd F
119 it. 'Boy'!] *Rowe subst.;* it, Boy. F; it, Boy! F2   121 braggart,] *Rowe;* Braggart? F

---

109 cur Coriolanus turns on Aufidius his disdainful term for the Roman plebeians when he banished them as 'You common cry of curs' (3.3.128). The 'stripes' and 'beating' assert that he has punished this 'cur' before; compare Menenius's use of 'disciplined', 2.1.104 and n.

109 notion understanding, awareness (of the truth).

110 that who (see Abbott 260).

112 thrust . . . him return the lie against him, make him answer for it.

114 Cut . . . pieces Coriolanus earlier offered his throat to Aufidius (4.5.92–3); absolute validation or death seem the only alternatives he can imagine. In a play so concentrated on the body, its health and its mutilation, the demand for dismemberment is especially shocking, and Shakespeare underscores this effect with the Volscian mob's cry, 'Tear him to pieces!' (123).

115 Stain (1) Colour with blood; possibly also (2) Defile morally, disgrace (compare Aufidius at 1.10.18).

115 edges swords.

116 there recorded there.

117 eagle Coriolanus here identifies himself with Rome as well as the sovereign bird (see

3.1.140 n.); for Aufidius's comparison of Coriolanus to the osprey, see 4.7.34–5.

118 Fluttered F's 'Flatter'd' might be the correct old form, meaning 'to float, flutter' (*OED* Flatter v^2), but it is used intransitively in the only recorded instances and seems to have become obsolete before Shakespeare's time; a misprint or misreading seems more likely.

119 'Boy' Quotation marks indicate that Coriolanus is still mockingly quoting Aufidius; possibly, however, he is turning the taunt back on its speaker.

120 blind fortune mere good luck.

123 SH F's SH refers to the commoners who entered with Coriolanus at 70, perhaps joined for 123 by the conspirators who are trying to incite them.

123–4 Shakespeare makes the Volscian crowd as clamorous for Coriolanus's death as the Roman plebeians were for his banishment; in North, though the people did not try to stop the conspirators (see 85 n.), 'it is a clere case, that this murder was not generally consented unto, of the most parte of the Volsces' (Bullough, *Sources*, V, 544).

123 presently immediately.

SECOND LORD Peace, ho! No outrage. Peace!   125
    The man is noble, and his fame folds in
    This orb o'th'earth. His last offences to us
    Shall have judicious hearing. Stand, Aufidius,
    And trouble not the peace.

CORIOLANUS   O that I had him,
    With six Aufidiuses, or more, his tribe,   130
    To use my lawful sword!

AUFIDIUS   Insolent villain!

ALL CONSPIRATORS Kill, kill, kill, kill, kill him!

    [*The*] *Conspirators draw* [*their swords*] *and kill Martius, who falls;*
                      Aufidius stands on him

LORDS Hold, hold, hold, hold!

AUFIDIUS My noble masters, hear me speak.

FIRST LORD   O Tullus!

SECOND LORD Thou hast done a deed whereat valour will weep.   135

THIRD LORD Tread not upon him. Masters all, be quiet.
    Put up your swords.

AUFIDIUS My lords, when you shall know – as in this rage
    Provoked by him you cannot – the great danger
    Which this man's life did owe you, you'll rejoice   140
    That he is thus cut off. Please it your honours
    To call me to your senate, I'll deliver
    Myself your loyal servant, or endure

---

129 CORIOLANUS] F; CORIOLANUS *(drawing his sword)* / Oxford   130 more,] more: F   132 SD.1 *The Conspirators draw their swords and kill*] Rowe subst. *(all draw, and kill); Draw both the Conspirators, and kils* F *(kill* F4*); Aufidius and the Conspirators draw, and kill* / Capell   132 SD.2 *Aufidius stands*] F; *Aufidius and Conspirators stand* / Oxford   136 him. Masters all,] Rowe subst.; him Masters, all F; him, masters. All *Theobald*

---

126 folds in encompasses, envelops; compare 3.3.73.

128 judicious (1) judicial, according to law, (2) wise, unbiased.

128 Stand Stop, hold off.

129–31 O . . . sword Coriolanus unwittingly almost repeats his mother's words to Sicinius at 4.2.25–7.

130 tribe whole race, everyone related to him by blood.

131 lawful sword (1) justifiable sword (because it will execute justice); but Brockbank suggests (2) 'the sword of lawful war. Coriolanus wishes himself opposed in the battlefield to Aufidius and his kin.' Oxford directs Coriolanus to draw his sword during this speech, but if Brockbank is correct, Coriolanus is wishing for the appropriate

locale to take on his enemy; the ignominy of the assassination would be visually enhanced if Coriolanus were defenceless (see pp. 62–3 above).

132 Case cites Cotgrave: '*A mort, à mort*: Kill, kill; the cry of bloudie souldiors persuing their fearefull enemies unto death'.

132 SD.1 *The . . . draw* F reads *Draw both the Conspirators*, although 8 SD.2 refers to more than two conspirators; see Textual Analysis, p. 300 below.

132 SD.2 *stands on him* An ironic reversal of Volumnia's prediction that her son would 'tread upon' Aufidius's 'neck' (1.3.42) and her later fear that Coriolanus would 'Triumphantly tread on thy country's ruin' (5.3.116); see also 5.3.123–4.

140 did owe you held for you.

142 deliver show, prove.

Your heaviest censure.
FIRST LORD   Bear from hence his body,
And mourn you for him. Let him be regarded   145
As the most noble corpse that ever herald
Did follow to his urn.
SECOND LORD   His own impatience
Takes from Aufidius a great part of blame.
Let's make the best of it.
AUFIDIUS   My rage is gone,
And I am struck with sorrow. Take him up.   150
Help, three o'th'chiefest soldiers; I'll be one.
Beat thou the drum, that it speak mournfully;
Trail your steel pikes. Though in this city he
Hath widowed and unchilded many a one,
Which to this hour bewail the injury,   155
Yet he shall have a noble memory.
Assist.
Exeunt, bearing the body of Martius. A dead march sounded

FINIS

146 corpse] F (Coarse)   FINIS] F (FINIS.)

146–7 herald . . . urn Heralds followed the
general mourning procession, but preceded the
coffin and chief mourner, at funerals of the
English nobility; Case cites the description of Sir
Philip Sidney's funeral (in 1587) in John Nichols,
*Progresses and Public Processions of Queen Eliza-
beth*, 1823, II, 483–94. North reports that 'men
came out of all partes to honour his bodie, and
dyd honorably burie him, setting out his tombe
with great store of armour and spoyles, as the
tombe of a worthie persone and great captaine'
(Bullough, *Sources*, V, 544).
147 urn Probably used loosely for a tomb or
sepulchre (*OED* Urn *sb* 1).
147 impatience rage.
151 one i.e. the fourth bearer.
153 Trail . . . pikes Pikes were trailed by
holding them in reverse, with the pointed head

dragging along the ground; it was a usual sign
of mourning at military funerals in Shakespeare's
time, including Sir Philip Sidney's (see 146–7 n.).
154 widowed and unchilded Coriolanus's
'memory' (156) is linked at the play's close with
his destruction of families, his heroic martial
exploits seen from the loser's point of view. There
may be an echo here of God's judgement on Baby-
lon in Isa. 47.9: 'But these two things shal come
to thee suddenly on one day, the losse of children
and widdowehead, they shal come upon thee in
their perfection.'
156 memory memorial (see the quotation
from North at 146–7 n.); the secondary meaning
of 'posthumous reputation' is also operative.
157 SD *dead march* Funeral music which contrasts sharply with the joyous sounds that celebrated the news of Rome's salvation in 5.4.

TEXTUAL ANALYSIS

General editorial procedures

This edition is based on the First Folio of 1623 (F), the sole authority for the text of *Coriolanus*. The copy from which Compositors A and B set the F text was probably a transcript of Shakespeare's manuscript, the authorial 'fair copy' that may already have been annotated to serve as playbook for theatrical production. With the exception of Act 1, Scene 1 (*Actus Primus. Scæna Prima*), F divides the play by acts only (on the significance of which, see, pp. 4–5 above). The generally adopted scene divisions of modern Shakespearean texts largely derive from the plays' early editors, although those for *Coriolanus* were not complete until Dyce (2857); the collation records the origin of this edition's divisions. Instances of division according to a radically different principle from that adopted here, the cleared stage, do not receive mention; the Oxford *Textual Companion*'s argument for splitting into two scenes what is in this edition 1.4 is included below in the discussion of the nature of the copy.

Spellings have been silently modernised in accordance with NCS practice. Since the F spelling of common words is largely that of the scribe and/or compositors, such modernisations as *a* to *o*, *bin* to *been*, *I* to *Ay*, *on* to *one*, *then* to *than*, *ought* to *aught*, *loose* to *lose* and *least* to *lest* have not been included in the collation unless choosing a modern spelling precludes a possible meaning. The collation does, however, record F spellings that might be distinctively Shakespearean or, when put in their modern form, appear to be another word entirely, like *rallish* for *relish* (2.1.162), *shoot* for *shout* (1.1.197, 1.9.49, 5.5.4) and *roade* for *raid* (3.1.5), or readings where a pun has been lost in choosing a modern spelling, such as *yarn* (1.3.75) for F *yearne*. Where there is no modern form of an F reading, the now-obsolete word is explained in the Commentary and suggestions offered for substitutions roughly equivalent in meaning and metre that could be used in a modern production. Contractions such as *Y'are* and *Th'rt* have been altered to their modern form (*You're* and *Thou'rt*), according to NCS conventions, but here too the change is noted in the collation. Turned letters, like the *us* ligature in *Cominius* in the entry direction at 1.1.210 or *oue* for *one* at 4.6.142, have been silently corrected, but where F is probably wrong but makes sense in context, like F *Yon* where the present edition reads *You* (2.1.159), the F reading appears in the collation. Abbreviations (such as tildes, ampersands, etc.) have been silently expanded, and characters' names regularised and spelled out in full in speech headings (SHs) and stage directions (SDs).

The F punctuation in this play is relatively heavy and manifestly inaccurate in places, much of it having been imposed by the scribe and compositors on a lightly-pointed, probably misleading, original manuscript; the present edition lightens the F punctuation considerably, while also trying to clarify the meaning for a contemporary reader. Uncontroversial normalisation and modernisation (of possessives, plurals and vocatives, for instance) have not been collated, nor has this edition's provision of the terminal full stops sometimes absent in F. Inevitably, modernisation requires interpretation and often imposes a choice between possibilities that early-seventeenth-century punctuation could leave open. For example, because commas in F often stand for what modern grammar represents with a full stop, and because F does not use a comma before the addressee in vocatives, 'Tread not upon him Masters, all be quiet, / Put up your Swords.' (5.6.136–7 / TLN 3812–13)¹ may be modernised as either 'Tread not upon him, masters. All be quiet. [*or* quiet!] / Put up your swords.' or, if the initial comma is thought misplaced because of the lower-case *a* in 'all', as 'Tread not upon him. Masters all, be quiet. / Put up your swords.' Where the present edition departs significantly from F, or where F is ambiguous in syntax or mood, the F punctuation is recorded in the collation. *Coriolanus* is a play rich in excitement and strong language, but only when the substitution of exclamation marks for F's lighter punctuation (',' or '.') might be debatable, or where F's '?' might be read either as a question or as an exclamation, is the text's alteration noted.

While some of F's many contractions may be scribal or compositorial, the high incidence of such forms (*o'th'*, *i'th'*, *to th'*, *'tis*, etc.) seems characteristic of Shakespeare's late style and especially of the rushed, tumultuous language of this play; these have not been expanded in the process of modernisation, although variants (e.g. *a'th'*, *toth'*, *to'th'*) have been normalised to the above forms. Pseudo–grammatical apostrophes (*ha's*, *do's*, etc.), however, are probably scribal in origin and have been silently eliminated. The absence of a pronoun at 1.3.54/422 (*ha's*) has been indicated by '*Has* (= he has), and at 3.1.162/1861 (*Has*) and 3.1.163/1862 (*H'as*) by *He's*. Unlike many editors, I have not retained spellings that mark medial elision for metrical reasons. Of the many instances where the metre seems to require syncopation, or the slurring of a syllable, only a small number are indicated by spelling and sometimes a (probably scribal) apostrophe in F. To normalise so rigorously in other matters but not in this seems inconsistent and potentially misleading, encouraging the reader to think all long lines with uncontracted spellings merely irregular. For the record, however, the elisions expanded in the present edition appear in F as *encountring* (1.6.8/611), *threatning* (1.6.36/647), *suff'ring* (1.10.18/877), *Clambring* (2.1.184/1128), *temp'rately* (2.1.198/1144, 3.1.221/1934), *paltring* (3.1.59/1746), *Heart-hardning* (4.1.25/2463), *marv'llous* (4.5.27/2682, prose), *pestring* (4.6.7/2899), *utt'rance* (4.7.49/3140), *Murd'ring* (5.3.61/3412), *wond'ring* (5.6.102/3768). In accordance with NCS practice, elided *-ed* endings of past participles, indicated in F by an apostrophe (*controll'd*), have been silently expanded; where metrical considerations require such an ending to be pronounced as a separate syllable, it is marked with a grave

---

¹ In quotations from F, *u/v* and long *s* have been modernised, but spelling and punctuation have not otherwise been altered. F's terminal periods for stage directions and unabbreviated speech headings have been omitted; when medial or terminal punctuation, or its absence, is significant, it will be noted in the discussion. When reference to particular features of F is necessary to the argument, this edition's line numbers will, after a slash, be followed by the Through Line Numbers (TLN) keyed to Charlton Hinman's Norton Facsimile of *The First Folio of Shakespeare*, 1968.

accent (*controllèd*). Changes of or additions to punctuation that affect sense or theatrical delivery (e.g. quotation marks and interrupted dialogue or change of addressee marked by a dash) have been collated and the more controversial instances discussed in the Commentary. F's emphasis capitals and use of italic in the dialogue for the names of people and places have not been retained except when F is cited *literatim* in the collation.

Stage directions lacking in F as well as substantive additions to F directions have been enclosed in square brackets; the collation records both the edition in which they first appeared and where other editions differ in placing or content. Uncontroversial modernisation and the dictates of this series's conventions (e.g. no final punctuation in SDs, capitals for speakers' names in entry directions) are not collated. In more problematic cases, rather than close off options for reader or director, I have retained F and discussed the possibilities in a Commentary note. SDs in F are often unusually full and informative. Some, as 1.4's *Another Alarum, and Martius followes them to / gates, and is shut in*, are anticipatory, providing the immediate cues for sound and movement but also detailing the stage action that will subsequently unfold; parts of F's SD have in this edition been redistributed to their appropriate location later in the scene. Such movement is recorded in the collation, as is the bringing forward of directions that in F follow their logical occurrence in the action.

Names and speech headings

In the matter of proper names, this edition, like most modern editions, retains *Martius*, the spelling Shakespeare took from the play's source story in North's Plutarch, rather than 'correcting' to *Marcius* with Theobald and a number of subsequent editors. Departures from it in F, and the various forms of what this edition standardises as *Titus Lartius*, are noted in the collation. A few irregularities in the order as well as the spelling of the protagonist's full name – Caius Martius Coriolanus – appear in F: *Martius Caius* occurs once (2.1.137/1066), *Marcus Caius Coriolanus* twice (1.9.64/821, 66/823), as does *Martius Caius Coriolanus* (2.1.137/1067, 2.2.40/1253; the first is an erroneous, hypermetrical repetition of the first two names from the line above). The two occurrences of *Marcus* in 1.9 may be simple misreadings, the second generated by the one just above it. Although Compositor A had correctly set *Caius Martius* six lines before, aa4 is his first page of work on *Coriolanus*, and he was likely to be particularly careful in copying what he thought he saw rather than assuming an error in a new, foreign name and correcting it. To adapt G. R. Proudfoot's suggestion, the misordering of the names may derive from the original accidental omission of *Martius* and the subsequent interlining of it above *Caius* without any clear indication of whether it should precede or follow;[1] if this were so, the interlined word might also have been less legible and *Martius* misread as *Marcus*. Misplaced or ambiguous interlineation seems a less likely explanation of the instances in 2.1 and 2.2. Brockbank is probably correct in assuming that the cautious Compositor A was reproducing the order that stood in his copy, especially since in

[1] Proudfoot is concerned only with the order, so he argues that either *Caius* or *Martius* could have been the ambiguously interlined name in question (p. 204).

2.1 Volumnia's first speech to her son picks up the names in this order.[1] Since each of these irregular sequences occurs in a public scene celebrating the honour conferred by the new surname, their point seems to be the stress thus laid on the protagonist's connection with the House of the Martians and the god of war.[2] Elsewhere Shakespeare seems to think of his protagonist as Martius (a preference he could have picked up from North's Plutarch): he is consistently *Martius* in the SHs in Act 1 and usually also in the dialogue.

The other character whose names undergo variation, in this case in SHs and SDs as well as the dialogue, is Titus Lartius. Not only does reference to him vary between *Tit.* or abbreviations of Lartius in SHs (*Lart.*, *Lar.*), but he is also once addressed as *Titus Lucius* within a speech (1.1.223/262), becomes *Titus Latius* in the SD at 2.1.134/1060, and later *Titus Latius* in the entry direction and *Latius* as SH throughout 3.1. The first misnaming, at 1.1.223, is by Compositor B, the others by A. In the first case, hasty and therefore slightly illegible script, with an open *a* and a dropped or extremely abbreviated *r*, might have produced *Lucius*, since *t* is easily mistaken for *c* in Secretary hand. Given the other occurrences of *Latius*, however, it is perhaps more likely that this is what the compositor misread as *Lucius*. The edition of North's Plutarch almost certainly used by Shakespeare, that of 1595, mentions this figure, described as 'one of the valliantest men the ROMANES had at that time', only once in the text, as *Titus Latius*; in North's marginal comment the designation is *Titus Lartius, a valliant Romaine*.[3] Both spellings may have stuck in Shakespeare's mind, even though he had provisionally settled on one and used it as the dominant form. While following his source's version of the conquest of Corioles, he expands it in dramatic terms and in Act 1 generally increases the prominence of Titus Lartius. As Shakespeare moved on into scenes of his own creating in 2.1 and 3.1, however, the distinction between 'Latius' and 'Lartius' may have become blurred and one form substituted for the other.[4]

With one exception this edition retains a feature of F changed by nearly all editors since the early eighteenth century: indefinite SHs in which dialogue is assigned to a minor character defined only by function, and where more than one potential speaker is on stage. F offers a mixture of numbered and unnumbered senatorial speakers in 1.1 (where the first two are '1. Sen.' but two more are unnumbered), 2.2 (the first is '1. Sen.', the other four unspecified), and a jumbling of numbered and unnumbered senators in 3.1, as well as the wholly unnumbered soldiers in 1.10 and an occasional unnumbered patrician or noble. Some of the undesignated senators might be the result of scribal

[1] Brockbank, p. 23.

[2] Proudfoot suggests the connection with Mars (p. 204).

[3] *The Lives of the Noble Grecians and Romanes*, trans. Thomas North, 1595, p. 238; the discrepancy does not occur in Bullough, which reproduces the 1579 edn. On Shakespeare's use of the 1595 edn, see p. 10 above.

[4] In *The Stability of Shakespeare's Text*, 1965, E. A. J. Honigmann offers a theory of 'irregular composition' that would explain the *Lartius/Latius* variations differently. In his view, Shakespeare did not begin composition with 1.1 but rather wrote 2.1, 3.1 and perhaps parts of 1.1 'before spotting the misprint in his Plutarch' (p. 147).

or compositorial oversight, but they span both compositors' stints and most probably reflect Shakespeare's thinking in terms of effective crowd scenes, where anonymous voices issue from different parts of the group. Such vagueness about minor characters seems to have been characteristic of Shakespeare's habits during composition: in Hand D's three pages of the manuscript *Booke of Sir Thomas More*, thought by many to be Shakespearean autograph, four speeches are assigned to *other*. In *Coriolanus*, the senators' speeches in 1.1 and the four soldier-speakers in 1.10 may have been intended for a similar effect and not given specific assignment until the play was cast and the number of available 'senators' and 'soldiers' known.[1] Editors have generally assigned these unnumbered speeches to *First Senator* or *First Soldier*, but this procedure gives perhaps unintended prominence to single individuals.[2] The desired degree of verbal involvement in the action by those on stage might have been left open until the actual rehearsals, and this edition has chosen to preserve that option with unspecified SHs (A SENATOR, A SOLDIER). The case of 3.1 is slightly different and, although if I were producing the play I might distribute the senatorial speeches more widely, for the effect suggested above, this edition prints what F (if reliable) suggests was Shakespeare's intention. 3.1 contains seven senatorial speeches, five designated '*Sen.*' or '*Sena.*' and two '2. *Sen.*' The two instances of specification imply that the author was here thinking in terms of two speakers and that the unnumbered speeches should be understood as '1. *Sen.*' and given to the same actor.

In retaining F's assignment of speakers in 1.1, this edition again departs from common editorial practice and, as a result, alters the usual impression given by the 'Company of Mutinous Citizens'. In F the two individualised speakers for the first 41 lines are '1. *Cit.*' and '2. *Cit.*'; thereafter the character who argues so articulately with Menenius is '2. *Cit.*'. Such a distribution suggests not only that this 'Company' includes a hot-head who thinks killing Coriolanus will solve their problems, but also a more reasonable Second Citizen who becomes their natural spokesman, a man who can see the complexity both of their situation and of Coriolanus (as can other commoners later, like the three groups of citizens in 2.3, or the soldiers laying cushions in 2.2). Since Capell, most editors have reassigned all of F's '2. *Cit.*' speeches in response to Menenius's persuasions to '1. *Cit.*', on the grounds that they better fit the personality of '1. *Cit.*' established in the scene's first 41 lines. If F is in error here, the misnumbering probably stood in Shakespeare's original papers, since such a consistent scribal or compositorial misreading of '2' as '1' is highly unlikely. Thomas Clayton suggests that possibly *Cit.* was

---

[1] It should be noted, however, that in some scenes with entry directions of indefinite number, speeches are all assigned: for instance, of the *seven or eight Citizens* who enter at the beginning of 2.3, only '1', '2' and '3' speak, and in 5.6 there are speeches for '1', '2' and '3' of the *3 or 4 Conspirators of Auffidius Faction*.

[2] The Oxford *Complete Works*, followed by Parker, reproduces F's unnumbered soldiers in the last scene of Act 1 (i.e. *A Soldier*), but not the indefinite *Sena.* speech headings in 1.1 and 2.2. See Stanley Wells's argument against the usual editorial assignment of the five *Watch* speeches in *Ado*, 3.3, to '2 *Watch*' ('Editorial treatment of foul-paper texts: *Much Ado About Nothing* as test case', *Review of English Studies*, n.s. 31 (1980), 11).

unnumbered in Shakespeare's manuscript and then misnumbered later.[1] But F may not be in error. Knight's defence of F has been supported by some later editors and critics, and the play can certainly be performed according to F's assignments.[2] This seems to be a case in which F is at least as likely to be correct as not, and this edition chooses to follow it.

No attempt has been made to normalise the various class designations in either SHs or SDs, for they evidently stood in the copy and appear to reflect Shakespeare's thinking at the time of composition. Thus there are SHs for A PATRICIAN (*Patri.* in F), but also for A NOBLE (*Noble*). Classical Rome and seventeenth-century England co-exist comfortably in SDs where the entering *Citizens* of 1.1 are both *Citizens* and *Plebeians* in 2.3, a *rabble of Plebeians* as well as *the People* in 3.1, and back to *Citizens* in 4.6, while their Volscian counterparts in 5.6 are *the Commoners*. The *Patricians* are also *all the Gentry* in 3.1, *Nobles* in 3.2, and some of them *the yong Nobility of Rome* in 4.1. Variant forms of proper names, however, have been silently normalised. The spellings *Volsce* and *Aufidius* used in North's Plutarch have been silently imposed on the various F spellings, just as this edition also silently regularises all four spellings of the captured city to *Corioles* (the dominant F form and that of Plutarch), since the variants (*Carioles, Coriolus, Corialus*) seem insignificant and may be misreadings. Where F SHs seem erroneous, the F reading appears in the collation and the rationale for emendation in the Commentary.

The frequent SH *All* has been left largely untouched. This edition does not go as far as Oxford in aggressively redistributing lines to specific citizens or soldiers, preferring to leave such decisions to the director, but where for clarity *All* has been particularised (e.g. altered to ALL CITIZENS at 4.6.21, 27), the change is noted in the collation. *All* is a common SH in contemporary playbooks (what we now call promptbooks), and it seems to have been conventional to leave what it might mean in individual cases to be worked out in the playhouse.[3] Single words or short lines might be spoken in unison, but distribution among the assembled 'all' is frequently required. At times the words should be distributed as widely as possible, as in the final mêlée when *All People* turn against Coriolanus and should individually cry out what is run together in the text: 'Teare him to peeces, do it presently: / He kill'd my Sonne, my daughter, he kill'd my Cosine / Marcus, he kill'd my Father' (5.6.123–4/3793–5). Other possible rehearsal decisions include distributing parts of an *All* speech to consecutive speakers, as with '*All.* Against him first: He's a very dog to the Commonalty' (1.1.21/29–30),[4] or giving

[1] Thomas Clayton, 'Today we have parting of names: a preliminary inquiry into some speech-(be)headings in *Coriolanus*', in *Shakespeare's Speech-Headings: Speaking the Speech in Shakespeare's Plays*, ed. George Walton Williams, 1997, p. 72.

[2] Sanders mounts a persuasive defence of retaining F in Wilbur Sanders and Howard Jacobson, *Shakespeare's Magnanimity*, 1978, p. 140. See also Michael Warren, 'Textual problems, editorial assertions in editions of Shakespeare', in *Textual Criticism and Literary Interpretation*, ed. Jerome McGann, 1985, pp. 31–2, and Proudfoot, p. 204.

[3] The revising Hand C in *Sir Thomas More*, which seems to have been preparing the manuscript for theatrical production, altered only one of ten *All* SHs in Hand D's three pages. (On the pages of Addition II of *STM*, see *Shakespeare's Hand in 'The Play of Sir Thomas More'*, ed. A. W. Pollard and J. Dover Wilson, 1923.)

[4] In David Thacker's 1994 RSC production at the Swan Theatre in Stratford, for instance, the citizen speeches were passed around the crowd so that no individual became identified with a single point of view.

one player the line while the rest 'howl or clamour or contribute what was known as "confused noise"'.[1]

The printing of *Coriolanus*

Coriolanus was intended to begin F's third and final section, 'Tragedies', and it still initiates the sequential page numbering for that section (i.e. it occupies pages 1–30) and heads the list of tragedies in F's Catalogue. However, at the last minute the difficulties that had held up the printing of *Troilus and Cressida*, originally to have appeared between *Romeo and Juliet* and *Julius Caesar*, were apparently resolved.[2] Although at this point it was too late for inclusion in the Catalogue of F's contents, and *Timon of Athens* had been substituted in its original position, *Troilus and Cressida* was finally printed and inserted before *Coriolanus* when the Folio was bound.

Before turning to the nature of the manuscript copy for F, we must recognise an unusual and determining feature of the printing of *Coriolanus*. Because *Coriolanus* was being set into type by Compositors A and B while Compositor E was simultaneously setting the next play in this section, *Titus Andronicus*, the manuscript pages of *Coriolanus* had to be entirely 'cast off' at the printing-house before work on it could begin.[3] This method estimates the number of printed pages the manuscript will require; to ensure that it takes neither more nor less, each blank F page is assigned a specific portion of the manuscript that the compositor must set into type on that page. Obviously, over- or under-estimation by the man who did the casting off, especially in conjunction with the constant challenge posed by F's narrow double-column format (so inhospitable to long verse lines), could put the compositors' ingenuity to a severe test. This peculiarity in the circumstances under which *Coriolanus* was printed helps explain at least some of the play's high incidence of mislineation, as well as, perhaps, some of the apparent compositorial tampering with SDs.

The nature of the copy

The copy from which Compositors A and B set *Coriolanus* was in manuscript form, but there is less certainty about the provenance of that manuscript or whether it was in Shakespeare's own hand. Many editors have suggested it was Shakespeare's own 'fair copy' of his 'foul' or working papers, perhaps so carefully prepared as to constitute a 'producer's copy'.[4] Some have seen evidence that the manuscript had, in addition, been prepared for theatrical production; others find little or no indication of such playhouse

---

[1] E. A. J. Honigmann, 'Re-enter the stage direction: Shakespeare and some contemporaries', *S.Sur.* 29 (1976), 122. In 'Today we have parting of names', Clayton notes that some *All* speeches, such as 'Speake, speake', call for 'not necessarily only two but for *n* repetitions' (p. 67).
[2] Charlton Hinman, *The Printing and Proof-Reading of the First Folio of Shakespeare*, 2 vols., 1963, II, 526–8.
[3] *Ibid.*, II, 506. In 'Line division in Shakespeare's dramatic verse: an editorial problem', *AEB* 8 (1984), 117 n. 30, Paul Werstine emends Hinman by noting that since four formes of *Cor.* were set before the first of *Titus* was composed, perhaps 'three pages of *Cor.* were *not* set from cast-off copy (aa4, 4^v, 5^v)'.
[4] Riverside, p. 1437a.

annotation.[1] Among the play's most recent editors, disagreement still reigns. The 1987 *Textual Companion* designates the copy as scribal, 'possibly of a prompt-book';[2] in his 1994 Oxford Shakespeare edition, however, R. B. Parker argues that the manuscript beneath F was Shakespearean holograph, though he thinks not a final draft or 'fair copy'.[3] In this section I argue, first, that *Coriolanus* was set from a scribal transcript and, second, that most of the apparent problems created by F's SHs and SDs were introduced either by the scribe or in the printing-house; they should not be taken as certain evidence that the copy manuscript was not yet in a form that could serve as theatrical playbook.[4]

Some features of F certainly seem to reproduce an authorial manuscript – for instance, F's retention of at least one possible 'Shakespearean' spelling and, more generally, its frequent use of full and 'literary' SDs that perhaps reflect either Shakespeare's own 'bridging' thoughts during composition, as he stitched together episodes from North's Plutarch into dramatic form, or a later fleshing out of brief directions with narrative details intended to help his acting company understand the evolving, quite fast-moving and complicated, story.[5] Sweeping claims for Shakespearean spellings surviving into the printed texts have been rightly challenged, but there is more critical agreement about one unusual predilection that does appear in *Coriolanus*.[6] In Hand D's pages of *The Booke of Sir Thomas More*, the noun *silence* is spelled with an *sc*, *scilens*; the preference reappears in scattered early texts of Shakespeare plays thought to have been set from 'foul papers' – *Scilens* for *Justice Silence* in the SHs of quarto *2 Henry IV*, *Sceneca* for *Seneca* in the 1604 quarto of *Hamlet*, *scylence* in quarto *Troilus and Cressida* (altered by the press-corrector to *sylence*) – as well as in the three occurrences of *Scicion* for *Sicyon* in F *Antony and Cleopatra*.[7] In *Coriolanus* one of the tribunes consistently appears as *Scicinius* in SDs and, in abbreviated form, in SHs in Compositor A's stints and, presumably by oversight, twice in Compositor B's. Compositor A is generally thought more trustworthy in following copy (except in matters of lineation), B more prone to alter and regularise, so it is likely that the *Sc* form stood in the manuscript

[1] In 'Textual and critical problems in Shakespeare's *Coriolanus*' (1954 Ph.D. diss., University of Michigan), Albert Gilman concludes that the F text was certainly a promptbook and possibly a transcript (p. 147). Brockbank is cautious on both counts, finding it 'consistent with the evidence to suppose F was set up from autograph copy, at least partly prepared by the playwright for the theatre. It is not possible to be sure that the book-keeper had or did not have a casual, occasional hand in it' (p. 7).

[2] *Cor.* appears in the summary chart of copy-texts on p. 147 of the *Textual Companion*; John Jowett's later discussion of the nature of the copy is more certain of a promptbook original (*ibid.* p. 594).

[3] Although he believes the manuscript was 'a draft that still required revision', Parker finds some evidence for authorial annotation with the Blackfriars Theatre as well as the Globe in mind (pp. 143, 147).

[4] I have offered a fuller, more exhaustively documented, version of this argument in 'Scribes, compositors, and annotators: the nature of the copy for the First Folio text of *Coriolanus*', *SB* 50 (1997), 224–61.

[5] In *Prefaces to Shakespeare*, 2 vols., 1947, Harley Granville-Barker suggested that the elaborate stage directions for this play indicate 'evidence of a retirement to Stratford and . . . a semi-detachment from the theatre' (II, 295); see also NS, p. 131, and Martin R. Holmes, *Shakespeare and Burbage*, 1978, p. 196.

[6] Marvin Spevack (ed.), *Ant.*, 1990, p. 374, questions a number of the characteristic spellings in Wilson's list (NS, pp. 133–4), but he offers support for the unusual use of *Sc* in *Scicinius* for *Sicinius*, unmentioned by Wilson. Brockbank also discusses this example, and he adds several others 'which may indicate Shakespearean idiosyncrasies' – such as *shoot* for *shout*, *strooke* for *struck*, *god* for *good*, *too* for *to*, especially in the form *too't* (pp. 3–4); see also Parker, pp. 138–9.

[7] On the instances of *sc* for *s*, see *Textual Companion*, p. 593, and Spevack (ed.), *Ant.*, p. 374.

from which *Coriolanus* was set.[1] Yet while features of Hand D in *Sir Thomas More* may be significant (and will be referred to elsewhere because of that possibility), there is no incontrovertible evidence that Hand D is Shakespeare's.[2] Nor is it certain, even if Shakespeare could be shown to have preferred *sc* in spelling one word, that he would necessarily transfer that preference to other 'morphologically' similar words.[3] The *Sc* spellings of *Scicinius* in *Coriolanus* thus do not settle the question of F copy, although the other instances of *sc* for *s* in Shakespearean texts of different provenance suggest that it is more likely to be authorial than scribal. And the fact that *Scicinius* is an uncommon Roman name, rather than a common English noun for which a copyist often had his own preferred spelling, might increase its chances of being carefully reproduced by both scribe and Compositor A. Two other *Coriolanus* spellings that have been suggested as distinctively Shakespearean – *shoot* for *shout* and *arrant* for *errand*[4] – are not unusual enough sixteenth- and seventeenth-century spellings to mark them as peculiarly Shakespearean.

Stage directions that exceed the needs of a book-holder include 1.3's informative introduction of the women, specifying their relationship to the protagonist as well as their immediate physical activity: *Enter Volumnia and Virgilia, mother and wife to Martius: They set them downe on two low stooles and sowe.* Titus Lartius's movements are twice tracked with some care: at 1.9.11, *Enter Titus with his Power, from the Pursuit*, and the elaborate entry direction of 1.7 that locates the action in time and space, in its F form nearly half as long as the scene itself: *Titus Lartius, having set a guard upon Carioles, going with Drum and Trumpet toward Cominius and Caius Martius, Enters with a Lieutenant, other Souldiours, and a Scout.* Other stage directions display a literary turn of phrase, as when two officers enter at the beginning of 2.2 *to lay cushions, as it were, in the Capitoll*, or 1.6.0 where Cominius enters *as it were in retire, with soldiers*. Some are 'literary' in the most literal sense, having been lifted almost verbatim from North's Plutarch: at 1.4.30 the *Romans are beat back to their Trenches*, and at 4.4.0 Coriolanus enters *in meane Aparrell, Disguisd, and muffled.*[5]

Some elements of Shakespeare's papers thus survive in the printed text, though this fact does not rule out a scribal transcript faithful to at least some features of the original

---

[1] On the relative trustworthiness of Compositor A and Compositor B, see Paul Werstine, 'Compositor B of the Shakespeare First Folio', *AEB* 2 (1978), 241–63, and 'Line division', cited at p. 295 above, n. 3.

[2] In his editor's preface to the most recent book of essays on the *More* manuscript, *Shakespeare and 'Sir Thomas More': Essays on the Play and Its Shakespearean Interest*, 1989, T. H. Howard-Hill notes that his contributors at the very least agree that the case for Shakespeare as author of Addition II is as strong as any so far made to deny it or identify another playwright as Hand D (p. 2).

[3] T. H. Hill, 'Spelling and the bibliographer', *The Library*, 5th ser. 18 (1963), II; Hill's study of Ralph Crane shows that Crane, at least, was not so predisposed. In *Orthography in Shakespeare and Elizabethan Drama*, 1964, A. C. Partridge cites other examples as a caution against depending on initial *sc* as being spectacularly rare (p. 62).

[4] *Shoot* appears on both Wilson's and Brockbank's lists (see p. 296 above, n. 6); *arrant* is suggested by David Bevington (ed)., *Ant.*, 1990, p. 261.

[5] 'So the Coriolans . . . made a salye out apon them, in the which at the first the Coriolans had the better, and drave the Romaines backe againe into the trenches of their campe' (Bullough, *Sources*, V, 511); later, Coriolanus 'disguised him selfe in suche arraye and attire, as he thought no man could ever have knowen him for the person he was, seeing him in that apparell he had upon his backe . . . his face all muffled over' (p. 527).

manuscript. Although it is impossible to distinguish with complete certainty between scribal and authorial copy, given that both scribe and compositor exercised a free hand in matters of spelling and punctuation, certain aspects of F suggest the compositors' copy was not Shakespearean holograph. The preponderance of *ha's* over *has* and, less decisively, *do's* or *doe's* over *does* is uncharacteristic.[1] The contracted form *a'th* occurs much more frequently in *Coriolanus* than in any other Shakespeare play (twenty-seven times; the next closest play, *All's Well That Ends Well*, is itself unusually high, with nine occurrences); it and its alternative *o'th* are also found in work by both compositors.[2] While *o'th* is not uncommon, especially in Shakespeare's late style, *a'th* is unusual.[3] Finally, the four occurrences of *it's* (three set by Compositor B, one by A) are almost certainly scribal. *'Tis* is the usual form of this contraction, and the only other F play with this number of *it's* is *Henry VIII*, set from scribal transcript.

If Hand D in the *More* manuscript is Shakespeare's, his punctuation was light almost to the point of non-existence: in these three pages there are no colons, round brackets, exclamation or interrogation marks, and 'an average of one comma to every five lines, a lower ratio than in any of the Good Quartos, and about one-sixth of the rate of use in a normally punctuated First Folio text'.[4] Some of the relatively heavy and sophisticated pointing in *Coriolanus* was doubtless added in the printing-house, but compositorial sophistication does not sufficiently explain a number of uncharacteristic features.[5] The high incidence of certain unusual contractions and pseudo-grammatical apostrophes (*ha's, doe's*), noted above, points away from Shakespearean holograph as the manuscript copy for F. In other punctuation too – notably in round brackets and exclamation marks – *Coriolanus* is untypical. Since Compositor B 'heavily interfered with the punctuation of his copy', it is to the more conservative Compositor A that we should look for signs that the copy manuscript was already generously pointed.[6] In Compositor A's stints in F, excluding *The Winter's Tale* (a Ralph Crane transcript that would be rich in brackets), he worked on nine plays and set 112 brackets in 104 pages.[7] At this rate, in *Coriolanus* Compositor A was setting nearly double his usual number per page, and this suggests scribal rather than authorial copy, since he does not seem

---

[1] See *Textual Companion*, introduction to *All Is True*, p. 618, for evidence of Shakespeare's preference for *has* and for the fact that the only other plays in which Compositor B, at least haphazardly following his copy, set a high proportion of *ha's* are *Mac.* and F *Ham.*, both generally agreed to have been set from scribal copy; for *do's* and *does*, see the introduction to F *Lear*, pp. 530–1. Less certain as indication of a scribal intermediary is *Cor.*'s pattern of forty *Oh* against twelve *O*, although *O* 'predominates over *Oh* in nearly all the good quartos of Shakespeare's plays' (MacD. P. Jackson, *Studies in Attribution: Middleton and Shakespeare*, 1979, p. 215); see also Gary Taylor and John Jowett, *Shakespeare Reshaped, 1606–1623*, 1993, Appendix II.

[2] These figures are taken from the *Textual Companion*, p. 593, although I have corrected the number of *a'th* from the *Textual Companion*'s inaccurate twenty-nine.

[3] Contractions and elisions are common in *Ant.* as well, including *o'th*, but *Cor.*'s twenty-seven *a'th* distinguish it from *Ant.*, which has only one instance.

[4] Partridge, *Orthography in Shakespeare and Elizabethan Drama*, p. 58.

[5] On printing-house practice, see *ibid.*, pp. 102–3, and for evidence from Jaggard's 1599 printing of Shakespeare's Sonnet 144 in *The Passionate Pilgrim*, pp. 133–4.

[6] Gary Taylor, 'Folio compositors and Folio copy: *King Lear* and its context', *Papers of the Bibliographical Society of America* 79 (1985), 65.

[7] Taylor and Jowett, *Shakespeare Reshaped*, Appendix I, p. 246.

to add brackets on his own initiative. On the other hand, Compositor A seems to have resisted exclamation marks: there are only nine in 120 pages of his work in F, and he omitted all six in setting from printed copy for F *Richard II*.[1] That there is only one such mark in his seven and a quarter pages of *Coriolanus* is not surprising, though his resistance makes it highly likely that the mark stood in his copy and fairly likely that there were more that he suppressed. In Compositor B's pages there are thirteen, and even though some may be his own additions, it is also probable that he was encouraged by the presence of exclamation marks in his copy. On the basis of his work from printed copy, at least slightly over half the exclamation marks in B's pages of *Coriolanus* came from his copy.[2] One would not expect any in a manuscript in Shakespeare's hand.

Even more unShakespearean are the two instances of the SH *Omnes* (one set by Compositor A at 1.9.66/823 on his first page, one by B at 4.6.144/3065). As a speech heading, *Omnes* is extremely rare in F: its only other occurrences are in *Antony and Cleopatra* (six: two set by Compositor E, four by B). Whether *Omnes* appeared consistently in the manuscript and was almost completely purged in the printing-house, as is possible, we cannot tell; the usual SH in substantive Shakespearean texts (and Hand D's practice in *More*), however, is *All*. *Coriolanus* has an extraordinarily high number of 'crowd' speeches (thirty *All* SHs). It would not be surprising that with so many to set, each compositor should have let one *Omnes* slip through on a page with no other *All* SHs to alert him.[3] Or, a printing-house editor may have gone over the copy first, marking it to bring it into conformity with the general style decided on for F (which seems to have allowed *Omnes* to stand in exit directions but not as SH), and missed these two instances, which both compositors then dutifully reproduced. In any case, *Omnes* is likely to have been the copy's form, and this suggests scribal sophistication rather than Shakespearean autograph.

The latter explanation might seem better to fit the oddity produced by Compositor B in the exit direction at 3.3.143/2424: *Exeunt Coriolanus, Cominius, with Cumalijs*. This (misread) Latin sophistication, too, seems to have been against Jaggard's house style: the only other F instance is the *Cumalijs* in *Hamlet* in the entry direction for 2.2, also set by Compositor B. (What was a *Cum Alijs* in Q2 *Hamlet* at 1.2.0 SD.3, in F has become *Lords Attendant*.) It looks as though the *Coriolanus* manuscript copy had been corrected to house style, though perhaps only cursorily: in the first column of this page, bb4, Compositor B had set *Enter Coriolanus, Menenius, and Cominius, with others* (and elsewhere *with others* twice). At the bottom of the second column, however, he seems to have come upon an undeleted or lightly crossed-out *cum alijs* (possibly with little or no space between words) that had a *with* over it or in the margin;[4] mistaking

[1] *Ibid*.

[2] For tables showing the proportion of exclamation marks taken from printed copy to those added by Compositor B, see Taylor, 'Folio compositors and Folio copy', p. 66.

[3] Facing a similar anomaly with the six *Omnes* (though only eight *All*, all set by B) in *Ant*., Spevack thinks it probable that 'the first instance of *Omnes* . . . set by Compositor E, was the copy's form'. The instances set by B are 'typical of his vacillation between what may be copy and the more economical *All*' (Spevack (ed.), *Ant*., p. 368).

[4] Possibly *with* (or w^{th}) *o*, where the o had been smudged out of existence.

the Latin tag for a one-word proper name, he tacked on both words at the end of the exit direction.

Paul Werstine has argued against the hope of establishing behind Shakespeare's printed texts 'the author's original draft', and he points out that there are 'now thought to be considerably more scribal transcripts than holographs' among the surviving manuscript playbooks.[1] In 1956 Philip Williams suggested that a scribal transcript underlies *Coriolanus*, although he never published his evidence for this conclusion.[2] The Oxford editors in 1987 pointed to features of *Coriolanus*, noted in the preceding discussion, that led them to agree, and I have proposed additional indications that the copy manuscript was not in Shakespeare's hand. Despite Parker's return to a supposition of Shakespearean holograph, to me the weight of evidence points to scribal copy as the manuscript basis for F *Coriolanus*.

My second contention about the copy for *Coriolanus* is that it could have served as playbook. Since variable SHs for the same character, combined with ambiguous or misassigned SHs, have been taken as one sign that a play text has not yet been made fully ready for performance, we should examine *Coriolanus* to see how many difficulties they would actually have presented and at what point these irregularities are likely to have entered the F text. SHs that reflect one or the other of Titus Lartius's names, or variant abbreviations for Coriolanus, Menenius and Aufidius, present no problem. Most indefinite SHs, such as *Both* (four in 2.1, one in 2.3, two in 4.5), are clear from context; the *Exeunt both* at 4.6.152 obviously refers to Menenius and Cominius and may have specified them in the manuscript, since Compositor B is clearly pressed for space here and could not afford a two-line SD.[3] A couple would need to be decided in rehearsal or, more probably, in making up the 'plot' and the individual actors' parts: which two of the three women on stage should speak the words assigned to '2 *Ladies*' at 2.1.88/1004, and does *Tri.* at 4.6.125/3042 mean *Both Tri.* (which appears at 4.6.28/2924) or just one, where either one will do? A *both* that has proved troublesome to some editors appears in the SD *Draw both the Conspirators, and kils Martius* (5.6.132 SD.1/3805), since the entry direction had been for *3 or 4 Conspirators of Auffidius Faction*, but *both* could at this time also refer to more than two.[4] As noted above, such vagueness about minor characters seems characteristic of Shakespeare's habits during composition, and there are F plays whose underlying copy is thought to have been annotated in consultation with a playbook that contain speeches for unspecified (except by function) minor characters, like the gardener's two servants and the queen's two ladies in *Richard II*. Similar ambiguities and even

[1] 'Narratives about printed Shakespeare texts: "foul papers" and "bad quartos"', *SQ* 41 (1990), 69; see also Gary Taylor, 'Post-script', in Taylor and Jowett, *Shakespeare Reshaped*, p. 243.
[2] Philip Williams, 'New approaches to textual problems in Shakespeare', *SB* 8 (1956), 6.
[3] In *Shakespeare's Anonymous Editors*, 1981, Eleanor Prosser notes that in setting the two penultimate pages of F *1H4* from printed copy, Compositor B compressed his copy by shortening SDs to hold them to one line and by omitting one altogether (p. 202 n. 21).
[4] *OED* Both *Adv* 1b ('Extended to more than two objects'). One of the *OED* examples is from *1H6*; 'Margaret shall now be Queene, and rule the King: / But I will rule both her, the King, and Realme' (5.5.107–8).

a mixture of both numbered and unnumbered SHs appear in surviving manuscript playbooks.[1]

Some SHs are either wrong or missing, or have been thought to be so by some editors, but this fact is less a bar than it might seem to the manuscript behind *Coriolanus* having been adequately marked to serve as playbook. Where SHs seem misassigned, some at least of the cruxes facing a modern editor may have been imposed by the scribe or compositors. One ambiguity that requires resolution occurs in the first breakdown of civil order, 3.1.187–9/1894–6, where after the SD *They all bustle about Coriolanus* two lines of what must be 'crowd' noises appear with no SH: 'Tribunes, Patricians, Citizens: what ho: / Sicinius, Brutus, Coriolanus, Citizens'. The previous speaker was '2 *Sen.*', but the words are unlikely to be meant as his. The final line, TLN 1896, reads '*All*. Peace, peace, peace, stay, hold, peace'. The error may be authorial: a SH added after composition two lines below its proper position and not corrected in the playhouse, perhaps because *All* was felt to be implicit in the SD. If the error was introduced later by compositor or scribe, it could be due to the omission of one of two *All* prefixes.[2] It is also possible that two similar-looking SHs stood in the copy and that only one reached print, perhaps because scribe or compositor read them as identical and consciously or subconsciously rejected the repetition. In this hypothesis, TLN 1894–5 were prefixed *All* and 1896 assigned to the Aediles, of which there seem to be at least three on stage. If that were the case, as I think it was, either scribe or compositor was responsible for omitting the *All* at 1894 and misreading *Aed.* as *All*.[3]

Confusion between Cominius and Coriolanus in SHs may have been caused by misreading abbreviations (manuscript *Com* and *Cor*); this would be even more likely if the Shakespearean original contained such severely shortened forms as *Co* and *Cō*.[4] The greeting of Valeria after the triumphal return to Rome at 2.1.153/1087 is by F assigned *Com.*; almost all modern editions adopt Theobald's reassignment to Coriolanus. It is at this point in the text that the SHs for the title character switch, however, and as Brockbank notes, 'it is likely that the transition from *Mar.* to *Cor.* made the slip or misreading *Com.* easier'.[5] Whether the error was scribal or compositorial, the book-keeper and actors did not necessarily make the same mistake. The same misreading of a *Cor* SH as *Com* (or *Co* as *Cō*) is probably responsible for what is in

[1] See Paul Werstine, '"Foul papers" and "prompt books": printer's copy for Shakespeare's *Comedy of Errors*', SB 41 (1988), 232–46, on *The Launching of the Mary* and *The Captives* (p. 242), and also Werstine's 'McKerrow's "Suggestion" and twentieth-century Shakespeare criticism', RenD, n.s. 19 (1988), 152–3.
[2] In 'Today we have parting of names', Clayton notes that in this last case, the two uses of *All* would still need to be distinguished from each other (p. 68); for the possibility of duplicate *All*s as successive SHs, he points to Giorgio Melchiori's persuasive argument that the two instances of *all* in line 38 of *More* mean *some* and *others* ('Hand D in "Sir Thomas More": an essay in misinterpretation', SB 38 (1985), 101).
[3] On such reasoning, I presume, Oxford conjectures AEDILES.
[4] Clayton points out that, on the pattern of Hand D in *STM*, *r* would more likely be mistaken for *m* than vice versa, and both the examples here discussed misread in that direction ('Today we have parting of names', p. 84). In Hand D's pages, SHs become increasingly abbreviated: *other*, *oth*, *o*; *Lincolne*, *Linco*, *Linc*, *Lin*.
[5] Brockbank, pp. 161–2.

F a rebuke of the tribune Brutus by Cominius: 'You are like to doe such businesse' (3.1.49/1734).

A cluster of SH errors in the lower first column on bb2^v suggests a damaged or for some other reason illegible manuscript copy. Here F assigns Cominius as the speaker of 'Stand fast, we have as many friends as enemies' (3.1.233–4/1954) and to *Corio.* 'Come Sir, along with us' (3.1.239/1961). Most editions, including this one, transpose these SHS. Immediately below these two errors, and linked to them in cause, F gives *Mene.* a five-line speech (3.1.240–4/1962–6), the first three lines of which would more properly be spoken by Coriolanus. Brockbank suggests that the misassignment of TLN 1961 'precipitated the careless conflation' of the following lines into one speech 'and its misassignment to Menenius'.[1] Alternatively, the SH at TLN 1962 may have been omitted or eradicated by damage; if the SH *Mene.* was floating ambiguously in the margin, it might have been assumed to apply to all the apparently unassigned lines. If the conflation here results from later damage to the original manuscript, then this error, like the other suspect SH assignments in bb2^v's first column, did not exist in the original playbook.

The evidence of surviving early playbooks suggests that the brevity and precision of SDs in post-eighteenth-century promptbooks had not yet become conventional practice. Analysing the book-keeper's treatment of the author's SDs, W. W. Greg concluded that 'as a rule he left them alone. So long as they were intelligible it mattered little to him the form in which they were couched.'[2] Both the descriptive SDs *They fight, and all enter the City* (at 1.4.68) and *Beats him away* (4.5.46 SD.1, to indicate that Third Servingman is beaten off the stage by Coriolanus) could have been considered sufficient as exit cues. F contains many indefinite entry directions, ranging from the slightly permissive (*seven or eight Citizens* in 2.3) to the wholly unspecified (*a Company of Mutinous Citizens* in 1.1, or *all the Gentry . . . and other Senators* in 3.1). Yet surviving manuscript playbooks indicate that this kind of indefiniteness was not something the book-keeper paid much attention to;[3] his primary concerns were entrances, unusual properties, and music and sound cues. There was almost certainly an understood number of bodies for *with Attendants* or *with others*, and the size of an *army* or *rabble* probably depended on how the doubling of parts had been worked out for this very populous play. If recorded at all, specification of permissive SDs might have appeared only in the actor's part and the 'plot', the important documents for a specific production.[4]

---

[1] Brockbank, p. 210 n. In *New Readings in Shakespeare*, 2 vols., 1956, C. J. Sisson suggested that TLN 1962–4 were a marginal addition, 'prefixed by the compositor in error to the existing speech of Menenius' (II, 127), but Clayton, rightly I think, finds this argument unlikely on grounds of both metre and sense ('Today we have parting of names', p. 77).

[2] W. W. Greg, *Dramatic Documents from the Elizabethan Playhouses*, 2 vols., 1931, I, 213.

[3] Fredson Bowers, '*Beggars Bush*: a reconstructed prompt-book and its copy', *SB* 27 (1974), 132; William B. Long, ' "A bed | for woodstock": a warning for the unwary', *Medieval and Renaissance Drama in England*, II (1985), 93.

[4] In 'Modern textual theories and the editing of plays', *The Library*, 6th ser. 11 (1989), T. H. Howard-Hill notes that, unlike modern promptbooks, Renaissance playbooks 'do not usually record information contained in other necessary playhouse documents', such as actors' parts, casting tables and the 'plot' (p. 111); see also Long, '"A bed | for woodstock"', pp. 106, 110.

As an experienced man of the theatre, Shakespeare himself would be concerned with the sound cues that would help create an effective atmosphere for this most martial of plays, and he might well have contributed at least some of the numerous instances of *Flourish*, of *Musicke playes* (4.5.0) or *Sound still with the Shouts* (5.4.53), and of drum or alarum *a farre off* (1.4.16, 20, and similar cues at 1.4.48 and 1.5.3 SD.1). Yet some SDs point to the likelihood that a practical stage-manager has also gone over the manuscript, clarifying and specifying. Although some *Flourish* directions stand alone, the SDs *A flourish. Cornets* at 1.9.93/857 and *Flourish. Cornets* at 2.1.178 SD.1/1120 suggest two marginal annotations, perhaps in different hands, where the initial cue has been made more specific by indicating the appropriate instruments. Other indications of a practically-minded annotator appear in directions which give redundant information in order to ensure that significant speakers are named on entry. Both in the dialogue and in SHs such as *Both* and *Both Tri.*, Shakespeare appears sometimes to think of the tribunes collectively. It is quite likely that in entry directions Shakespeare went no further than *the two Tribunes* and that the 'doubling' produced by adding both individual names at 2.1.0, 4.2.0, 4.6.0 and 5.1.0 is the playhouse annotator's contribution.[1]

Annotation for performance was not as thorough as in a modern promptbook, but no entries are omitted. Twice *Enter* means 'Come forward' (2.1.178 SD.2/1122; 4.5.144 SD.2/2808), but in the first instance Brutus and Sicinius have been directed to stand *Aside* earlier (2.1.78 SD.1/992), and the second can be worked out from the dialogue.[2] Omitted exits are generally clear from the context; they would have presented no problems to a professional company.[3] A few ambiguities remain. In 1.4 and 3.1 it is unclear when Titus Lartius, a fairly major character in at least Act 1, exits. Incomplete theatrical annotation is not the only explanation for the omissions. The annotator may not have caught the oversight or, in the case of 3.1, may have considered that Lartius's accompanying the exiting Coriolanus and Cominius would be assumed; it is also possible that the two exit directions existed in the manuscript but were accidentally omitted by scribe or compositor. A potential muddle having to do with uncertain exits appears in 2.3, where the citizen who reports to the tribunes on the vote-canvassing alludes to two lines of Coriolanus's soliloquy that he should not, realistically, have heard. Possibly Shakespeare's company adopted a staging like that of some modern productions, where one citizen in the first group enters a bit behind the other two (thus

---

[1] The first doubling at 2.1.0 SD.1–2 may have been authorial (*Enter Menenius with the two Tribunes of the / people, Sicinius & Brutus*), since 'commonly Shakespeare identified a character at his first entrance with a label stating his rank, profession, or relationship to another character' (Honigmann, *The Stability of Shakespeare's Text*, p. 147). Even here, the order suggests that the tribunes' proper names have been tacked onto an existing direction (1.3.0 SD.1, in contrast, begins *Enter Volumnia and Virgilia, mother and wife to Martius*). See also *Textual Companion*, p. 593, on this point.

[2] A SD *Retire* or *Aside* for First and Second Servingman at 4.5.49 would be helpful, but only Capell, followed by Keightley, has been seriously confused by its absence; for another possible example, in 1.4, see the discussion below. *Tro.* 4.5.158 offers another instance where *Enter* applies to characters who have previously only gone 'aside'.

[3] Bowers notes that the 'common failure to mark ordinary and expectable exits wanting in Massinger's papers shows that scrupulous attention to exit directions is no absolute criterion for prompt-copy' ('*Beggars Bush*: a reconstructed prompt-book and its copy', p. 132).

explaining Coriolanus's initial reference to a 'brace' of citizens) and remains behind, hidden, to overhear Coriolanus's words to the second group and then his soliloquy.[1] The *Exeunt* direction for the first group is crowded onto the same line as *Enter two other Citizens*, and it is possible that further information (e.g. *Manet one Citizen*) was omitted by Compositor B for lack of space, just as farther down the same column on aa6ᵛ he omits an *Exeunt* for the second group. I am less convinced that Shakespeare was such a stickler for realism, however. It seems just as likely that he let one citizen sum up the collective experience of all three groups and, since Coriolanus had openly scorned their 'voices' while stressing his compliance with the letter of the ritual ('I have here the customary gown', 2.3.77), happily replicate bits of the phrasing of Coriolanus's soliloquy.

Two other instances of possible confusion over exits, entrances and general stage movement occur in 1.4 (on aa3) and 1.8 (aa3ᵛ). Descriptive, 'literary' SDs in *Coriolanus*, while apparently sometimes annotated, have not here been sufficiently clarified for a modern reading audience, although they are unlikely to have proved insuperably challenging to Shakespeare's own company. At 1.4.30, a two-line SD demands *Alarum, the Romans are beat back to their Trenches / Enter Martius Cursing*. Taken in conjunction with the second line's entry direction and a new SH *Mar.*, even though Martius was also the last speaker before the fighting, the fact that the first line is sufficiently like narrative exit directions at 1.4.68 and 4.5.46 SD.1 led the Oxford editors to assume a cleared stage and a new scene beginning with Martius's (re-)entry. J. W. Saunders, however, suggests a staging in which 'the extreme edge of the stage platform, that is . . . the stage-rails and yard alleys', represents the trenches, and Martius remains visible while driving off the Volscians; the *Enter* SD would then mean, as it does elsewhere in the play, 'Come forward' to berate the soldiers who fled the battle.[2]

Beyond simple omission, space-saving imperatives may have influenced SDs in ways that affect our view of the degree to which the manuscript copy for *Coriolanus* was in its final form. Hard-pressed for space at the very end of the second column of aa3ᵛ, his first page, Compositor B amalgamates 1.8's medial action direction and concluding exit direction in setting TLN 740–1: *Heere they fight, and certaine Volces come in ayde / of Auffi. Martius fights til they be driven in breathles*. The pressure under which Compositor B operated is suggested by the uncharacteristic name abbreviation, lack of spacing between names, and the uncharacteristic spelling *breathles* (instead of *breathlesse*). The scene now lacks any final exit cue, but B managed to include the information about their manner of exiting, for which he had no spare line, by pushing it up to a line on which he could crowd it in. If an *Exeunt* existed in his copy, Compositor B had room for it on the same line as Aufidius's last words of dialogue, but there may well have been no such imperative, if we assume that *driven in breathles* was deemed sufficient

---

[1] Parker, p. 94.

[2] 'Vaulting the rails', *S.Sur.* 7 (1954), 77; in his view, the *Enter* SD is 'similar to those illogically entered in other plays, when a player has not left the stage but has moved between two different visible areas' (*ibid.*).

by both Shakespeare and the theatrical annotator. Here Compositor B's solution has turned a scene that made perfectly good dramatic sense into one in which Aufidius is left awkwardly alone on stage to berate the would-be rescuers who have already exited fighting with Martius.[1]

Some errors of mistaken content may also be compositorial. We have already noted Compositor B's misunderstanding on bb4 of the scribe's or book-keeper's perhaps poorly-spaced Latin tag as a proper name and his appending it to *Exeunt Coriolanus, Cominius, with Cumalijs*. Another possible misreading appears in the dialogue at 1.3.38/405: what most modern editors print as 'At Grecian sword contemning. Tell Valeria' is in F 'At Grecian sword. *Contenning*, tell *Valeria*'. Most likely, the misunderstanding and consequent repunctuation – if Hand D is any indication, caused by a capital *C* and probable lack of all the minims for 'contemning' or a full stop after it – were the scribe's, and were merely reproduced by Compositor B. Even had the error stood in the manuscript playbook, however, the result is an odd name for the Waiting Gentlewoman, but not unintelligible dialogue.

While there are, then, a few ambiguous or misplaced SDs, as well as a number of absent exit directions, these features are common in the surviving manuscript playbooks and also occur in printed quartos thought to have been set from prompt copy or to have been annotated from it. Some were probably created by later misreading of the intended placing for marginal additions; others, by compositorial attempts to solve the problem of lack of space created by cast-off copy. While a few SH errors seem to derive from misunderstanding abbreviations for 'Coriolanus' and 'Cominius', by and large SHs are fairly regular and not misleading. Although modern editors alter a number of them, believing certain speeches to have been misassigned, in many cases there is dispute about which need altering, and the retention of F by one or another editor supports the actability of F as it stands.[2] Where it seems inadequate, the fault can be seen at least plausibly as having been introduced later, by scribe or compositor or both, or, as on bb2[v] for instance, as the result of physical damage to the manuscript suffered sometime in the interval between production and publication. And we must at least entertain the possibility that some ambiguities were straightened out in the actors' parts and the 'plot' but not recorded in the playbook itself.

Lineation

Over three hundred lines of F *Coriolanus* are irregularly divided, and the nature of the mislineation suggests that here, as in other matters, both compositors and scribe contributed errors to what was probably in this respect an already confusing original manuscript. If Hand D in *More* is a reliable guide, Shakespeare was himself misleading:

---

[1] Wilson finds it 'obvious that Auf.'s [*sic*] address to the Volscians precedes their being "driven in breathless"' (NS, p. 167). Many editors, however, retain F and simply add an *Exit* for Aufidius after his final two lines.
[2] That *Cor.* was acted, and in a form that contained at least some of F's lines and stage business, is suggested by contemporary allusions and borrowings; see pp. 1–2 above.

he did not capitalise the initial letter of a verse line, and he tended to crowd the concluding part-line of a speech onto the preceding line to save space. In Hand D's three pages, there are three examples of mislineation.[1] Then, too, by this point in his career Shakespeare's versification was itself becoming less regular and, hence, more likely to present problems when not clearly divided. This late style is full of colloquial 'clipped' forms, syncopation, feminine endings, short-line exchanges that are neither clearly verse nor clearly prose, and mid- or late-line pauses coupled with enjambment which put the integrity of the line's iambic pentameter stress in tension with the grammatical structure of the phrase or sentence running across the line-break.[2] Additionally confusing to a copyist used to more regular verse would be the tendency in Shakespeare's late style for lines to end with a word that we expect to begin a phrase (e.g. *and*, *I*, *but*), or with prepositions or auxiliary verbs whose main verb begins the next line.[3]

Combining a concluding half-line of a speech with its preceding line might produce mislineation in a copyist's rendering of the transition between speakers, and the largest group of lineation errors in *Coriolanus* does occur in such situations. Compositors faced the added technical problem that long verse lines, especially in the first line of a speech that had also to include a SH and indentation, might not all fit in F's narrow double-column format. Dropping a word down to the next line might involve compositorial relining of a whole passage or, for a short speech, two verse lines run together as prose. To complicate a situation already conducive to errors in transmission, inaccurately cast-off copy could push both compositors deliberately to alter what was before them in the manuscript: in some cases cramming one and a half lines onto one line of type, in others needlessly splitting lines to take up space, as well as relining verse as prose and prose as verse. As Werstine points out, Compositor B is in general more faithful to his copy's verse lineation than A, though A is more reliable in lining prose. Compositor A's unreliability with verse frequently stems from his apparent dislike to enjambment and preference for emphasising syntactical structure; as a consequence, he was more than willing to relineate on his own to create end-stopped verse.[4] In such circumstances, Compositor B's pages are more likely to indicate the extent to which the manuscript behind *Coriolanus* was itself ambiguous or erroneous. The same ambiguities in lineation in the Hand D pages of *More* were apparently frequent in the manuscript behind *Coriolanus*, for there Compositor B 'mislined more verse passages containing short lines than he did in all the rest of the plays he shared with A'.[5] Most probably not all instances stood in his copy, since he was also using mislined verse as a way to save and waste space, yet the examples of F *Hamlet* and *Antony and Cleopatra*, where combined verses are spread across the stints of both compositors and which were

---

[1] Werstine, 'Line division', p. 76. On the mislineation in Hand D, see also *Textual Companion*, p. 637.

[2] George T. Wright, 'The play of phrase and line in Shakespeare's iambic pentameter', *SQ* 34 (1983), 155; see also his *Shakespeare's Metrical Art*, 1988, pp. 116–42, and his observation that in this late style, verse diverges from 'regular' metre 'about twenty percent of the time' (p. 105).

[3] Wright, *Shakespeare's Metrical Art*, pp. 121–2.

[4] Werstine, 'Line division', p. 97; see also Brockbank, pp. 12–16, and Parker, pp. 139–42.

[5] Werstine, 'Line division', p. 104.

not set from cast-off copy, 'makes it evident that the source of the combined verses in all three plays probably lies beyond the compositors'.[1] Werstine concludes that the high incidence of mislineation in *Hamlet* is at least in part scribal, since it is generally agreed that a transcript underlies the F version of that play, and speculates that the same may be true for *Coriolanus* and *Antony*.[2]

The relineation of the F text undertaken in this edition, or by previous editors when this edition conservatively follows F, is recorded in the Appendix (pp. 308–13 below). Another lineation problem facing a modern editor is not noted in the apparatus but needs reviewing here. Increasingly, both short lines ending an impressive speech and shared lines (verse lines split between two, or occasionally more, speakers) became an important component of Shakespeare's verse technique.[3] In F, the initial line for each new speaker is printed immediately after the SH, even when that line is less than a full iambic pentameter and might be part of a regular verse line shared with the preceding speaker; typographically, F gives no indication of whether a speech's concluding part-line is the first half of a split verse line or should stand alone, followed by a brief pause. In addition, rapid dialogue often produces a series of incomplete lines in which the second of three consecutive part-lines can be combined 'amphibiously' with either the first or the third. Since the late eighteenth century it has been conventional to indicate a shared line visually by indenting the completion so that it starts immediately below the last word of the preceding speaker's part-line. Where the half-lines are clearly amphibious, or where linking two part-lines creates an irregular pentameter, this edition will follow the caution urged by David Bevington about arbitrarily imposed linkage.[4] Printing such lines without indentation preserves their metrical ambiguity and allows actors alternative ways to handle the dialogue. And, as George T. Wright notes, in the theatre 'we may not be able to tell which ones are best combined; we may actually hear, almost simultaneously, alternative possibilities of combination'.[5]

---

[1] *Ibid.*, p. 96. Werstine notes that only twelve of A's fifteen combined verses and nineteen of A's twenty-nine occur on pages where they were 'demonstrably short of space' (p. 95).

[2] *Ibid.*, p. 97. Of Compositor B, Werstine notes that the example of *Ant.* 'indicates that he reproduced irregularities [in his line division] in his copy when he found them' (p. 101).

[3] Wright, *Shakespeare's Metrical Art*, p. 117; see also Fredson Bowers, 'Establishing Shakespeare's text: notes on short lines and the problem of verse division', *SB* 33 (1980), 74–130.

[4] Bevington (ed.), *Ant.*, pp. 266–70.

[5] Wright, *Shakespeare's Metrical Art*, p. 122; see also p. 103.

APPENDIX: LINEATION

Listed below are the present text's departures from the lineation of F. Also recorded are plausible relineations not adopted in this edition. Since spelling and punctuation are not at issue, the final word in the verse line will be given in modern spelling, and the distraction of variant punctuation has been eliminated.

1.1

42–3 *Theobald; as three lines* hand / . . . matter / . . . you F; *as prose*, Pope
48–9 *Theobald;* honest / . . . yourselves F; *as prose*, Pope
77–8 *Capell; as four lines* Well / . . . think / . . . tale / . . . deliver F
102–3 What . . . then?] *Capell;* speaks / What then? What then? F
229–31 Lead . . . priority] *Pope; as prose* F
243–7 Such . . . Cominius] *Pope; as prose* F
256–7 Come, . . . Martius] *Theobald; as one line* F

1.[3]

64 *Pope;* madam / . . . doors F
94–100 *Pope;* now / . . . mirth / . . . would / . . . lady / . . . o'door / . . . us / No / . . . not / . . . mirth F

1.[4]

1 *Pope; as two lines* news / . . . met F
16 *Pope; as two lines* little / . . . drums F
26 *Pope; as two lines* shields / . . . Titus F

1.[5]

15–16 Thy . . . fight] F; for / . . . fight *Capell*
19–20 Than . . . fight] *Capell; as one line* F

1.[6]

33 F; warriors / . . . Lartius *Pope*
49–50 F; Martius / . . . did / . . . purpose *Capell*
57–9 *Bevington; as four lines* together / . . . made / . . . me / . . . Antiates F; vows / . . . directly / . . . Antiates *Pope*
81–2 select from all. / The rest . . . fight] F; select: the rest / . . . fight *Hanmer;* select from all: the rest / . . . fight *Boswell*

1.[8]

6–7 If . . . hare] *Theobald; as one line* F

1.[9]

13–14 Pray . . . blood] *Pope;* more / . . . blood F
15–17 *Capell, after Hanmer;* grieves me / . . . can / . . . country F; I have done / . . . can / . . . country *Bevington*

308

19–22 You . . . traducement] *Pope;* deserving / . . . own / . . . theft / . . . traducement F
35–6 Before . . . choice] *Theobald;* distribution / . . . choice F
43–4 F; cities / . . . grows *Theobald*
44–50 *Theobald;* soothing / . . . silk / . . . wars / . . . washed / . . . wretch / . . . done / . . .
hyperbolical F; soft / . . . silk / . . . wars / . . . washed / . . . wretch / . . . done / . . . forth
/ . . . hyperbolical *Knight;* soothing / . . . silk / . . . wars / . . . washed / . . . wretch / . . .
done / . . . forth / . . . hyperbolical *Globe*
64–5 *Johnson; as one line* F; Bear / . . . ever *Steevens*[3]; addition / . . . ever *Oxford*
78–80 The . . . general] *Hanmer;* me / . . . gifts / . . . general F

2.[1]

131–2 *Hanmer; as three lines* Martius / . . . noise / . . . tears F; *as prose, Pope*
137–8 *Steevens, after Capell;* Caius / . . . Coriolanus F
141–4 No . . . prosperity] *Pope; as prose* F
145–6 *Theobald;* Caius / . . . named F
154–5 *Pope; as three lines* turn / . . . general / . . . all F
156–64 *Pope; as twelve lines* welcomes! / . . . laugh / . . . Welcome / . . . heart / . . . thee
/ . . . on / . . . have / . . . home / . . . relish / . . . warriors / . . . nettle / . . . folly F
174–6 And . . . thee] *Malone; as four lines* fancy / . . . wanting / . . . Rome / . . . thee F;
wanting / . . . thee *Johnson;* fancy / . . . not / . . . thee *Capell*
184–5 *Pope; as three lines* him / . . . up / . . . horsed F
190–1 *Pope;* damask / . . . spoil F
195–7 On . . . sleep] *Pope; as prose* F
203–4 *Pope;* honours / . . . question F
211–12 *Steevens, after Pope; as three lines* word / . . . carry it / . . . him F
213–15 I . . . execution] *Pope; as prose* F
216–17 It . . . destruction] *Rowe; as prose* F
221–2 *Pope;* pleaders / . . . them F
234–7 *Steevens, after Pope;* Capitol / . . . consul / . . . him / . . . gloves F; thought / . . .
consul / . . . and / . . . gloves *Dyce*

2.[2]

31–2 *Pope;* Volsces / . . . remains F
34–5 *Pope;* hath / . . . you F
48–60 We . . . place] *Pope; as prose* F
64–5 Sir . . . not] *Pope; as one line* F
78–9 F2; virtue / . . . be F
113–14 F2; 'twere / . . . called F
117–18 He . . . him] *Rowe; as prose* F
122 *Pope;* deeds / . . . content F
123–4 He's . . . for] *Pope; as one line* F
127–30 The . . . people] *Rowe*[3]; *as prose* F
133–8 *Capell; as seven lines* suffrage / . . . doing / . . . voices / . . . ceremony / . . . to't / . . .
custom / . . . have F
139–41 It . . . people] *Pope; as two lines* acting / . . . people F

2.[3]

43–4 What . . . bring] *Pope;* sir? / . . . bring F
48–50 O . . . upon you] *Pope; as two lines* that / . . . upon you F

115–17 *Pope;* voices / . . . more / . . . consul F

124–7 You . . . senate] *Pope;* limitation / . . . voice / . . . invested / . . . senate F

138–9 With . . . people] *Pope;* weeds / . . . people F

145 F; Certainly / . . . downright *Capell*

152 *Pope; as two lines* wounds / . . . private F

174–5 F2; voices / . . . love F

191–4 Have . . . tongues] *Pope; as three lines* asker / . . . mock / . . . tongues F; you / . . . and now / . . . mock / . . . tongues *Schmidt*

195–6 F; may / . . . will deny him *conj. Walker;* confirmed / . . . will deny him *Schmidt, after Capell*

203–5 Let . . . pride] *Theobald; as two lines* judgement / . . . pride F

210–11 F; which / . . . fashion *Schmidt*

212–18 Lay . . . do] *Capell; as six lines* tribunes / . . . between / . . . on him / . . . commandment / . . . that / . . . do F

240–1 We . . . election] *Capell, after Hanmer; as one line* F

3.[1]

33–4 Stop . . . broil] *Pope; as one line* F

50 F; unlike / . . . yours *Johnson*

62–3 Tell . . . again] *Pope;* speech / . . . again F

65–9 Now as . . . again] *Hibbard;* will / . . . pardons / . . . meinie / . . . flatter / . . . again F; friends / . . . pardons / . . . them / . . . and / . . . again *Capell;* friends / . . . mutable / . . . them / . . . and / . . . again *Schmidt;* will / . . . pardons / . . . them / . . . and / . . . again *Brower;* live / . . . pardons / . . . meinie / . . . flatter / . . . again *Oxford*

81–6 You . . . sleep] *Capell; as five lines* god / . . . infirmity / . . . know't / . . . His choler / . . . sleep F

87–9 It . . . further] *Pope; as two lines* poison / . . . further F

91–2 'Shall' . . . Why] *Pope; as one line* F

118–19 I . . . state] *Pope; as one line* F

138–40 Call . . . eagles] F; ope / . . . crows / . . . eagles *Pope*

183–6 F; would / . . . aediles / . . . weapons *Johnson;* he / . . . aediles / . . . weapons *Oxford*

192–3 To . . . Sicinius] *Capell; as one line* F

197–8 Fie . . . quench] *Pope; as prose* F

201 F; True / . . . city *Capell*

202–3 By . . . magistrates] *Pope; as prose* F; all / . . . magistrates *Oxford*

217–18 Hear . . . a word] *Johnson; as prose* F; you / . . . a word *Capell*

229–30 Help . . . old] *Malone, after Hanmer; as prose* F

233–4 Stand . . . enemies] *Capell; as one line* F

237–8 For . . . you] F; sore / . . . yourself / . . . you *Parker*

242–3 Begone . . . tongue] *Capell; as one line* F

244–5 On . . . them] *Capell; as one line* F

245–6 I could myself . . . tribunes] *Steevens²*, after *Capell; as prose* F; myself / . . . them / . . . tribunes *Parker*

262–3 He . . . work] F; *as one line, Bevington*

263–7 Here's . . . himself] *Pope;* work / . . . abed / . . . Tiber / . . . fair / . . . viper / . . . . himself F; work / . . . Tiber / . . . fair / . . . viper / . . . and / . . . himself *Oxford*

272–4 He . . . hands] *Johnson; as two lines* are / . . . hands F

276–7 *On one line of type* F

279–82 Sir . . . faults] *Pope;* holp / . . . rescue / . . . know / . . . faults F

287 *Pope; as two lines* leave / . . . people F
310–11 Merely . . . him] *Pope;* awry / . . . him F
329–31 I'll . . . peril] *Pope;* in peace / . . . form / . . . peril F; him / . . . lawful / . . . peril *Keightley*
334–5 Noble . . . officer] *Pope; as one line* F

3.[2]
6–8 Be . . . mother] F; nobler / . . . mother *Steevens²*; *as one line, Oxford;* them / . . . mother *Parker*
26–7 Come . . . it] *Pope; as prose* F
53–7 *Malone; as six lines* that / . . . people / . . . matter / . . . words / . . . tongue / . . . syllables F; Because / . . . people / . . . matter / . . . words / . . . bastards *Capell;* Because / . . . people / . . . by / . . . with / . . . tongue / . . . syllables *Schmidt;* people / . . . matter / . . . words / . . . though but / . . . allowance *Oxford*
58–62 F; To your . . . more / . . . take in / . . . you / . . . blood *Oxford*
93 *Capell; as two lines* bower / . . . Cominius F
97–8 I . . . spirit] *Rowe³; as prose* F
100–1 *Capell;* sconce / . . . heart F

3.[3]
10–11 Of . . . poll] *Pope; as one line* F
35 *Pope; as two lines* volume / . . . gods F
39–41 F; war / . . . wish *Steevens; as one line, Parker*
43 *Johnson; as two lines* Audience / . . . say F
43–5 Peace . . . ho] F; say . . . ho *Steevens; as one line, Oxford*
55–6 Scratches . . . only] *Capell;* move / . . . only F; *as one line, Theobald*
87–8 *Pope;* him / . . . kind F
89–90 But . . . Rome] *Pope; as one line* F
113–14 F; so, / . . . banished / . . . so *Capell*
139–40 F; most / . . . nation *Capell*

4.[1]
58 F; *as two lines* hand / . . . come *Steevens³*

4.[2]
5–7 Bid . . . strength] *Pope; as two lines* gone / . . . strength F
7–8 Dismiss . . . mother] *Pope; as one line* F
13–14 O . . . love] *Capell;* met / . . . love F
27–8 What then! . . . posterity] *Hanmer; as one line* F

4.[4]
7–8 Direct . . . Antium] *Capell; as prose* F; great / . . . Antium *Johnson*
9–10 He . . . night] *Johnson; as prose* F

4.[5]
5–6 *Pope;* house / . . . guest F; *as prose, Johnson;* feast / . . . guest *Oxford*
9–10 *Capell; as prose* F
46 Thou . . . Hence] F; trencher / Hence *Capell*
51–4 If . . . myself] *Steevens²; as prose* F
158–9 *Pope;* he, / . . . one F

4.[6]
11–12 F; kind / . . . sir *Capell*
12–13 Hail, sir! . . . both] *On one line of type* F
14–18 Your . . . temporised] *Steevens, after Capell; as prose* F; Coriolanus / . . . friends / . . .
do / . . . it / . . . if / . . . temporised *Globe;* Coriolanus / . . . commonwealth / . . . it / . . . if
/ . . . temporised *Keightley*
19–20 F; wife / . . . him *Capell*
25–6 F; Coriolanus / . . . did *Hanmer*
34–5 And . . . assistance] *Theobald; as one line* F
49 F; you / . . . Martius *Steevens*³
58–9 Tell . . . be] *Pope; as one line* F
74–6 F; can / . . . contrariety *Capell*
93–4 If? . . . thing] *Capell; as one line* F
103–5 He'll . . . work] F; Hercules / . . . work *Capell;* shake / . . . Hercules / . . . work
*Steevens*³
119–20 'Tis . . . brand] *Pope; as one line* F
126–8 How . . . city] *Pope; as four lines* him / . . . nobles / . . . hoot / . . . city F; How / . . .
cowardly / . . . who / . . . city *Schmidt;* we? / . . . nobles / . . . hoot / . . . city *Oxford*
136–7 *Pope;* hooting / . . . coming F
150–2 F; made / . . . Capitol / . . . else *Malone, after Capell*

4.[7]
14–16 *Malone; as two lines* borne / . . . solely F

5.[1]
22 Very . . . less] F; well / . . . less *Johnson*
43–4 F; Martius / . . . returned / . . . then *Pope*
71–3 *Johnson; as two lines* mother / . . . him F

5.[2]
1–2 F; *as one line, Steevens*
3–5 You . . . Coriolanus] *Pope;* leave / . . . Coriolanus F; well / . . . officer / . . . Coriolanus
Oxford
6–7 FIRST . . . Rome] *On one line of type* F
8–9 *Pope; as prose* F; return / . . . thence *Oxford*
50–1 *Pope;* here / . . . estimation F
90–1 *Pope;* power / . . . again F
101–2 F4; rock / . . . wind-shaken F

5.[3]
4–7 Only . . . friends] *Capell; as three lines* respected / . . . Rome / . . . friends F; stopped
/ . . . Rome / . . . friends *Rowe;* stopped / . . . Rome / . . . no / . . . you *Pope*
36–7 As . . . kin] *Rowe*³; *as one line* F
40–2 Like . . . flesh] *Pope; as two lines* part / . . . flesh F
56–7 What's . . . son] *Pope;* me / . . . son F
62–3 Thou . . . lady] *Pope;* thee / . . . lady F
84–6 Wherein . . . reasons] *Pope; as two lines* t'allay / . . . reasons F
125–8 Ay . . . fight] *Steevens, after Pope;* boy / . . . time / . . . away / . . . fight F
181–2 I . . . little] *Pope; as one line* F
203–4 Ay . . . bear] *Hanmer;* together / . . . bear F

5.[4]
39–40 Friend . . . certain] *Pope;* true / . . . certain F
54–5 F; next / . . . thankfulness *Pope*
56 F; all / . . . thanks *Capell*
57–9 F; city / . . . them / . . . joy *Capell*

5.[5]
6–7 F; ladies / welcome *Steevens*³

5.[6]
9–11 Even . . . slain] *Pope; as prose* F
11–13 Most . . . deliver you] *Pope; as two lines* intent / . . . deliver you F
58–9 Say . . . lords] *Pope; as one line* F
123–4 *Capell;* presently / . . . cousin / . . . father F
129–31 O . . . sword] *Pope; as two lines* more / . . . sword F; Aufidiuses / . . . sword *Oxford*
133–4 Hold . . . speak] F; *as one line, Oxford*
134–5 O . . . weep] *Steevens*³; *as three lines* Tullus / . . . whereat / . . . weep F
136–7 F; masters / . . . swords *Oxford*
138 *Pope; as two lines* lords / . . . rage F
156–7 *Capell; as one line* F

READING LIST

Arnold, Oliver. 'Worshipful mutineers: from *Demos* to electorate in *Coriolanus*', in *The Third Citizen: Shakespeare's Theater and the Early Modern House of Commons*, 2007, pp. 179–214

Banerjee, Rita. 'The common good and the necessity of war: emergent republican ideals in Shakespeare's *Henry V* and *Coriolanus*', *Comparative Drama* 40 (2006), 29–49

Bliss, Lee. 'What hath a quarter-century of Coriolanus criticism wrought?', in *The Shakespearean International Yearbook 2*, ed. W. R. Elton and John M. Mucciolo, 2002, pp. 63–75

Christensen, Ann C. 'The return of the domestic in *Coriolanus*', *SEL* 37 (1997), 295–316

Corti, Claudia. '"As if a man were author of himself": the (re-)fashioning of the Oedipal hero from Plutarch's Martius to Shakespeare's Coriolanus', in *Italian Culture in the Drama of Shakespeare and his Contemporaries*, ed. Michele Marrapodi, 2007, pp. 187–95

Eastman, Nate. 'The rumbling belly politic: metaphorical location and metaphorical government in *Coriolanus*', *Early Modern Literary Studies*, 13.1 (2007), http://purl.oclc.org/emls/13-1/eastcori.htm

Elam, Keir. '"In what chapter his bosom?": reading Shakespeare's bodies', in *Alternative Shakespeares 2*, ed. Terrence Hawkes, 1996, pp. 140–63

Escolme, Bridget. 'Living monuments: the spatial politics of Shakespeare's Rome', *S.Sur.* 60 (2007), 170–83

Fernie, Euan. *Shame in Shakespeare*, 2002

Folkerth, Wes. *The Sound of Shakespeare*, 2002

Garebian, Keith. 'The menopausal and suburban: the 1997 Stratford and Shaw Festivals', *Journal of Canadian Studies* 33 (1998), 154–62

Garganigo, Alex. '*Coriolanus*, the Union controversy and access to the royal person', *SEL* 42 (2002), 335–59

George, David. 'Plutarch, insurrection and death', *S. Sur* 53 (2000), 60–72

Green, Amy M. Review of *Coriolanus*, *Shakespeare Bulletin* 25 (2007), 107–13

Headlam Wells, Robin. *Shakespeare on Masculinity*, 2000

Hopkins, D. J. *City/Stage/Globe: A Genealogy of Space in Shakespeare's London*, 2007

Hopkins, Lisa. Review of *Coriolanus*, *Early Modern Literary Studies* 6.2 (2000), http://purl.oclc.org/emls/06-2/hopkrev.htm

Hunt, Maurice. 'The backward voice of Coriol-anus', *S.St.* 32 (2004), 220–39

Kumamoto, Chikako D. 'Shakespeare's Achillean Coriolanus and Heraean Volumnia: textual contamination and crossing of Homer's *Iliad* in *Coriolanus*', *Journal of the Wooden O Symposium* 7 (2007), 51–64

Kuzner, Mark. 'Unbuilding the city: *Coriolanus* and the birth of republican Rome', *SQ* 58 (2007), 174–99

Low, Jennifer. '"Bodied forth": spectator, stage, and actor in the early modern theater', *Comparative Drama* 39 (2005), 1–29

Marshall, Cynthia. '*Coriolanus* and the politics of theatrical pleasure', in *A Companion to Shakespeare's Works*, Vol. I: *The Tragedies*, ed. Richard Dutton and Jean E. Howard, 2005, pp. 452–72

Melnikoff, Kirk. Review of *Coriolanus*, dir. John Dillon, *Shakespeare Bulletin* 23 (2005), 174–7.

Mousley, Andrew. *Re-Humanising Shakespeare: Literary Humanism, Wisdom, and Modernity*, 2007

Munro, Lucy. 'Coriolanus and the little Eyases: the boyhood of Shakespeare's hero', in *Shakespeare and Childhood*, ed. Kate Chedgzoy, Susanne Greenhalgh and Robert Shaughnessy, 2007, pp. 80–95

Ormsby, Robert. '*Coriolanus*, antitheatricalism and audience response', *Shakespeare Bulletin* 26 (2008), 43–62

Parker, Barbara L. *Plato's Republic and Shakesepeare's Rome*, 2004

Ribeyrol, Wendy. 'Coriolanus: a natural born warrior', in *Lectures de Coriolan de William Shakespeare*, ed. Delphine Lemonnier-Texier and Guillaume Winter, 2006, pp. 49–57

Sanders, Eve Rachelle. 'The body of the actor in *Coriolanus*', *SQ* 57 (2006), 387–412

Shrank, Cathy. 'Civility and the city in Coriolanus', *SQ* 54 (2003), 406–23

Spotswood, Jerald W. '"We are undone already": disarming the multitude in *Julius Caesar* and *Coriolanus*', *Texas Studies in Literature and Language* 42.1 (2000), 61–78.

Weimann, Robert. *Shakespeare and the Popular Tradition in the Theatre*, 1978

Wilkinson, Katherine. Review of *Coriolanus*, *Early Modern Literary Studies* 9.1 (2003), http://purl.oclc.org/emls/09-1/coriorev.html

Welsh, Alexander. 'Shakespeare's Coriolanus and Roman honour', in *The Shakespearean International Yearbook 5*, ed. W. R. Elton and John M. Mucciolo, 2005, 191–210